Asset Price Dynamics, Volatility, and Prediction

Asset Price Dynamics, Volatility, and Prediction

Stephen J. Taylor

Princeton University Press
Princeton and Oxford

Published by Princeton University Press,
41 William Street, Princeton, New Jersey 08540

In the United Kingdom: Princeton University Press,
3 Market Place, Woodstock, Oxfordshire OX20 1SY

Third printing, and first paperback printing, 2007
Paperback ISBN: 978-0-691-13479-6

The Library of Congress has cataloged the cloth edition of this book as follows

Taylor, Stephen (Stephen J.)
Asset price dynamics, volatility, and prediction / Stephen J. Taylor.
p. cm.
Includes bibliographical references and index.
ISBN 0-691-11537-0 (alk. paper)
1. Capital assets pricing model. 2. Finance—Mathematical models. I. Title.

HG4636.T348 2005
332.6'01'51962—dc22   2005048758

British Library Cataloging-in-Publication Data is available

This book has been composed in Times and typeset by T&T Productions Ltd, London

press.princeton.edu

10 9 8 7 6 5 4 3

To Adam, Katherine, and Sarah

Contents

III   Volatility Processes   187

IV High-Frequency Methods   303

V Inferences from Option Prices   351

Contents   xi

Preface

Asset prices are dynamic, changing frequently whenever the financial markets are open. Some of us are curious about how and why these changes occur, while many people aspire to know where prices are likely to be at future times. In this book I describe how prices change and what we can learn about future prices. As financial markets are highly competitive, there are limits to how much guidance I can provide about why particular price changes occur and the precise level of future prices.

Descriptions of past price changes and predictive statements about future prices usually rely on insights from mathematics, economics and behavioral theory. My emphasis in this book is on using statistical analysis and finance theory to learn from prices we have seen about the probabilities of possible prices in the future.

Familiarity with financial, probabilistic, and statistical concepts is advisable before reading this book. A good introductory finance course will provide a satisfactory understanding of financial markets (including derivative securities), efficient market theory and the single-factor, capital asset pricing model. Quantitative courses that cover random variables, probability distributions, data analysis, regression models, and hypothesis testing are the minimum requirement. Mathematical knowledge and expertise are always an advantage, although I assume less prior study than the authors of most graduate texts.

This book is written for students of economics, finance, and mathematics who are familiar with the above topics and who want to learn about asset price dynamics. It is also intended to provide practitioners and researchers with an accessible and comprehensive review of important theoretical and empirical results.

I have taught almost all of the contents of this book, on a variety of undergraduate, postgraduate, doctoral, and executive courses. The topics selected and the mathematical depth of the exposition naturally depend upon the audience.

My final-year, elective, undergraduate course at present includes a review of relevant probability theory (most of Chapter 3), a survey of the established facts about asset price changes (Chapter 4), a popular method for testing if prices changes are random (Chapter 5), an appraisal of trading rules (parts of Chapter 7), an overview of volatility definitions and reasons for volatility changes (Chapter 8), an introduction to the simplest and most often applied volatility models (Chapter 9), a summary of results for prices recorded very frequently (parts of Chapter 12), a description of Black–Scholes option pricing formulae, implied volatilities and risk-neutral pricing theory (Chapter 14, as far as Section 14.4), and a review of volatility forecasting (some of Chapter 15).

My core financial econometrics course for students taking a postgraduate degree in finance also includes additional volatility theory and models (parts of Chapters 10 and 11), option pricing when volatility changes (the remainder of Chapter 14), and methods that produce predictive distributions (parts of Chapter 16). A typical doctoral course covers most of Chapters 8–16.

Any course will be more rewarding if students obtain new skills by analyzing market prices. Students should be encouraged to acquire data, to test random walk theories, to assess the value or otherwise of trading rules, to estimate a variety of volatility models, to study option prices, and to produce probabilities for possible ranges of future prices. I provide several Excel examples to facilitate the appropriate calculations.

Educational resources can be downloaded from my website, as mentioned at the end of Chapter 1. I expect the website to be dynamic, with content that reflects correspondence with my readers.

The topics covered in this book reflect interests that I have acquired and developed during thirty years of research into market prices. My research has been inspired, influenced, and encouraged by very many people and I particularly wish to acknowledge the contributions made by Clive Granger, Robert Engle, Torben Andersen, Richard Baillie, Tim Bollerslev, Francis Diebold, Andrew Lo, Peter Praetz, Neil Shephard, and Richard Stapleton.

My doctoral thesis, completed in 1978, contained analysis of commodity markets. Subsequently, most of my research has focused on stock and foreign exchange markets. Likewise, most of the examples in this book are for equity and currency price series.

My longstanding interest in the predictability of asset prices is reflected in Chapters 5–7, that can be skipped by anyone who considers all nontrivial point forecasts are futile. My thesis contained embryonic volatility models, one of which became the stochastic volatility model I published in 1982. Inspired by Robert Engle's simultaneous and path-breaking work on ARCH models, I also defined and analyzed the GARCH(1, 1) volatility model at about the same time that Tim Bollerslev was working independently on the general GARCH(p, q) model. Volatility models allow us to make informed predictions about future volatility. They are covered in depth in this book, especially in Chapters 8–12, 14, and 15. Much more recently, researchers have used option prices to infer probability distributions for future asset price levels. This is covered in Chapter 16.

Readers will soon notice that I refer to a considerable number of articles by other researchers. These citations reflect both the importance of research into financial market prices and the easy availability nowadays of the price data that are investigated by empirical researchers. A few papers, which I recommend as an introduction to the relevant research literature, are listed at the end of most chapters.

While I have attempted to document empirical regularities and models that will stand "the test of time," I expect important and exciting new results to continue to appear in the years ahead. A good way to keep up to date is to read working papers at www.ssrn.com and papers published in the leading journals. Many of the most important papers for research into asset price dynamics, at the time of writing, appear in the *Journal of Econometrics*, the *Journal of Finance*, the *Journal of Financial Economics*, and the *Review of Financial Studies*.

This book owes much to my wife, Sally, our children, Sarah, Katherine, and Adam, my publisher, Richard Baggaley, and my friends and colleagues at Lancaster University, particularly Mark Shackleton. I thank them all for their encouragement, advice, patience, and support. I also thank my copy-editor, Jon Wainwright, whose friendly collaboration and craftsmanship are much appreciated.

I thank the many reviewers of my original proposal and my draft manuscript for their good advice, especially Neil Shephard and Martin Martens. Many of the results in this book were obtained during my collaborations with my cited co-authors: Xinzhong Xu, Ser-Huang Poon, Bevan Blair, Yuan-Chen Chang, Mark Shackleton, Nelson Areal, Xiaoquan Liu, Martin Martens, and Shiuyan Pong. I thank them all for their contributions to a deeper understanding of asset price dynamics. Finally, I thank Dean Paxson for his positive persistence in enquiring about my progress with this book.

Asset Price Dynamics, Volatility, and Prediction

1

Introduction

1.1 Asset Price Dynamics

Asset prices move as time progresses: they are dynamic. It is certainly very difficult to provide a correct prediction of future price changes. Nevertheless, we can make statements about the probability distributions that govern future prices. Asset price dynamics are statements that contain enough detail to specify the probability distributions of future prices. We seek statements that are empirically credible, that can explain the historical prices that we have already seen.

Investors and fund managers who understand the dynamic behavior of asset prices are more likely to have realistic expectations about future prices and the risks to which they are exposed. Quantitative analysts need to understand asset price dynamics, so that they can calculate competitive prices for derivative securities. Finance researchers who explore hypotheses about capital markets often need to consider the implications of price dynamics; for example, hypothesis tests about price reactions to corporate events should be made robust against changes in price volatility around these events.

Explaining how prices change is a very different task to explaining why they change. We will encounter many insights into how prices change that rely on the empirical analysis of prices. Many general explanations for price changes can be offered: relevant news about the asset and its cash flows, macroeconomic news, divergent beliefs about the interpretation of news, and changes in investor sentiment. It seems, however, to be impossible to provide specific explanations for most price changes.

1.2 Volatility

A striking feature of asset prices is that they move more rapidly during some months than during others. Prices move relatively slowly when conditions are calm, while they move faster when there is more news, uncertainty, and trading. The volatility of prices refers to the rate at which prices change. Commentators and traders define this rate in several ways, primarily by the standard deviation of the return obtained by investing in an asset. Risk managers are particularly

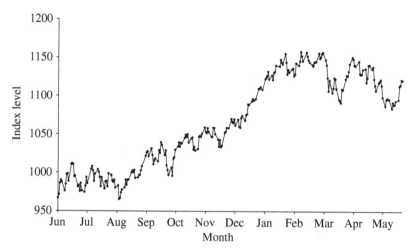

Figure 1.1. A year of S&P 500 index levels.

interested in measuring and predicting volatility, as higher levels imply a higher chance of a large adverse price change.

1.3 Prediction

Predictions concerning future prices are obtained from conditional probability distributions that depend on recent price information. Three prediction problems are addressed in this book. The first forecasting question posed by most people is, Which way will the price go, up or down? However hard we try, and as predicted by efficient market theory, it is very difficult to obtain an interesting and satisfactory answer by considering historical prices. A second question, which can be answered far more constructively, is, How volatile will prices be in the future? The rate at which prices change is itself dynamic, so that we can talk of extreme situations such as turbulent markets (high volatility) and tranquil markets (low volatility). The level of volatility can be measured and predicted, with some success, using either historical asset prices or current option prices. A third and more ambitious question is to ask for the entire probability distribution of a price several time periods into the future. This can be answered either by Monte Carlo simulation of the assumed price dynamics or by examining the prices of several option contracts.

1.4 Information

There are several sources of information that investors can consider when they assess the value of an asset. To value the shares issued by a firm, investors may be interested in expectations and measures of risk for future cash flows, interest rates, accounting information about earnings, and macroeconomic variables that provide information about the state of the economy. These specific sources of

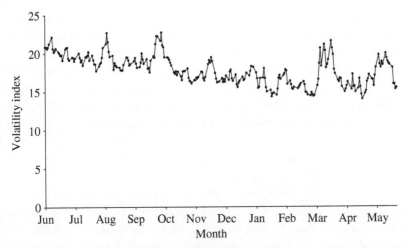

Figure 1.2. A year of VIX observations.

information are generally ignored in this text, because my objective is not to explain how to price assets. Relevant information is not ignored by traders, who competitively attempt to incorporate it into asset prices. Competition between traders is often assumed in finance research to be sufficient to ensure that prices very quickly reflect a fair interpretation of all relevant information.

The prices of financial assets and their derivative securities are the information that we consider when making statements about future asset prices. Our typical information is a historical record of daily asset prices, supplemented in the later chapters by more frequent price observations and by recent option prices. Figure 1.1 shows a year of daily closing levels for the Standard & Poor 500-share index, from June 2003 until May 2004. These numbers could be used at the end of May to answer questions like, What is the chance that the index will be above 1200 at the end of June? Figure 1.2 shows daily observations during the same year for an index of volatility for the S&P 500 index, called VIX, that is calculated from option prices. These numbers are useful when predicting the future volatility of the US stock market.

Studying daily price data and probability models provides a good introduction to asset price dynamics, so we focus on daily data in Chapters 4–11. More can be learnt from more-frequent price observations, as we will later see in Chapters 12 and 15. Option prices are also informative about future asset prices and their study requires models that are specified for a continuous time variable, as in Chapters 13 and 14.

1.5 Contents

The book is divided into five parts, which follow this introductory chapter.

The first part provides a foundation for the empirical modeling of time series of returns from financial assets. Chapter 2 explains how returns from investments are calculated from prices. A set of regularly observed prices can be used to define a time series of returns. Several examples are presented and advice is given about data-collection issues. Chapter 3 commences with a summary of the theoretical properties of random variables. It then continues with the definitions and properties of important probability models for time-ordered sequences of random variables, called stochastic processes. Consideration is given to a variety of stochastic processes that are used throughout the book to develop descriptions of the dynamic behavior of asset prices.

Chapter 4 surveys general statistical properties of time series of daily returns that are known as stylized facts. Any credible stochastic process that represents asset price dynamics must be able to replicate these facts. Three stylized facts are particularly important. First, the distribution of returns is not normal. Second, the correlation between today's return and any subsequent return is almost zero. Third, there are transformations of returns that reveal positive correlation between observations made at nearby times; an example is provided by the absolute values of returns.

The second part presents methods and results for tests of the random walk and efficient market hypotheses. The random walk hypothesis asserts that price changes are in some way unpredictable. Chapter 5 defines and evaluates the popular variance-ratio test of the hypothesis, which relies on a comparison between the variances of single-period and multi-period returns. It is followed in Chapter 6 by several further tests, which use a variety of methods to look for evidence that tomorrow's return is correlated with some function of previous returns. Evidence against the random walk hypothesis is found that is statistically significant but not necessarily of economical importance. Chapter 7 evaluates the performance of trading rules and uses their results to appraise the weak form of the efficient market hypothesis. These rules would have provided valuable information about subsequent prices in past decades, but their usefulness may now have disappeared.

The third part covers the dynamics of discrete-time asset price volatility. Chapter 8 summarizes five interpretations of volatility, all of which refer to the standard deviation of returns. It then reviews a variety of reasons for volatility changes, although these can only provide a partial explanation of this phenomenon. Chapter 9 defines ARCH models and provides examples based upon some of the most popular specifications. These models specify the conditional mean and the conditional variance of the next return as functions of the latest return and previous returns. They have proved to be highly successful explanations of the stylized facts for daily returns. Chapter 10 describes more complicated ARCH models and the likelihood theory required to perform hypothesis tests about ARCH parameters. Guidance concerning model selection is included, based upon tests and diagnostic checks. Chapter 11 is about stochastic volatility models, which are also able to explain the stylized facts. These models represent volatility as a latent and hence unobservable variable. Information about the dynamic properties of volatility can then be inferred by studying the magnitude of returns and by estimating the parameters of specific volatility processes.

The fourth part describes high-frequency prices and models in Chapter 12. The returns considered are now far more frequent than the daily returns of the preceding chapters. Many examples are discussed for returns measured over five-minute intervals. Their stylized facts include significant variations in the average level of volatility throughout the day, some of which can be explained by macroeconomic news announcements. The additional information provided by intraday returns can be used to estimate and forecast volatility more accurately.

The fifth and final part presents methods that use option prices to learn more about future price distributions. Most option pricing models depend on assumptions about the continuous-time dynamics of asset prices. Some important continuous-time stochastic processes are defined in Chapter 13 and these are used to represent the joint dynamics of prices and volatility. Option pricing models are then discussed in Chapter 14 for various assumptions about volatility: constant, stochastic, or generated by an ARCH model. The empirical properties of implied volatilities are discussed, these being obtained from observed asset and option prices by using the Black–Scholes formulae. Chapter 15 compares forecasts of future volatility. Forecasts derived from option-implied volatilities and intraday asset prices are particularly interesting, because they incorporate more volatility information than the historical record of daily prices and often provide superior predictions.

Chapter 16 covers methods for obtaining densities for an asset price at a later date, with a particular emphasis on densities estimated using option prices. Several methods for obtaining risk-neutral densities from options data are described. These densities assume that risk is irrelevant when future cash flows are priced. Consequently, they are transformed to produce asset price densities that incorporate risk aversion.

1.6 Software

Some of the most important calculations are illustrated using Excel spreadsheets in Sections 5.4, 7.6, 9.4, 9.8, 11.4, 11.7, 14.3, and 16.10. Excel is used solely because this software will be available to and understood by far more readers than alternatives, such as Eviews, Gauss, Matlab, Ox, and SAS. Some of these alternatives contain modules that perform many useful calculations, such as the estimation of ARCH models, and it should be a straightforward task to recode any of the examples. The spreadsheets use several Excel functions that are explained by Excel's Help files. More elegant spreadsheets can be obtained by using the Visual Basic for Applications (VBA) programming language.

1.7 Web Resources

Additional information, including price data, end-of-chapter questions, and instructions about sending email to the author, are available online. Some of the questions are empirical, others are mathematical. For all web material, first go to

http://pup.princeton.edu/titles/8055.html

and then follow the link to the author's web pages.

Part I

Foundations

2

Prices and Returns

Methods for creating time series of market prices and returns to investors are described and illustrated in this chapter.

2.1 Introduction

Any empirical investigation of the behavior of asset prices through time requires price data. Some questions to be answered are, Where will we find our data?, How many years of data do we want to analyze?, and How many prices for each year do we wish to obtain? Advice on these topics and other data-collection issues is provided in Section 2.3, after first presenting two representative examples of price series in Section 2.2.

Almost all empirical research analyzes returns to investors rather than prices. Returns are more appropriate for several reasons. The most important is that returns, unlike prices, are only weakly correlated through time. Time series of prices and dividends can be converted into time series of returns using two distinct definitions, which are explained in Section 2.5. Our preferred definition is that returns equal changes in the logarithms of prices, with appropriate adjustments when dividends are distributed. The definitions of returns are preceded by two examples in Section 2.4 and followed by a summary of twenty further time series of returns in Section 2.6.

2.2 Two Examples of Price Series

A *time series* is a set of observations arranged in time order. Figures 2.1 and 2.2 are examples of daily time series, respectively, for a portfolio of large US firms and an exchange rate. Both series contain one number for each trading day from January 1991 to December 2000 inclusive. These series were obtained from Datastream. They can be downloaded from the website mentioned near the end of Chapter 1. They are used to illustrate Excel calculations in Chapters 5, 7, 9, and 11.

The stock picture shows the daily closing level of the Standard & Poor 100-share index. This index does not include dividend payments. There are 2531 index levels in this ten-year series, as there are no observations for Saturdays, Sundays, and holidays. Investors earned high returns from US stock market investments

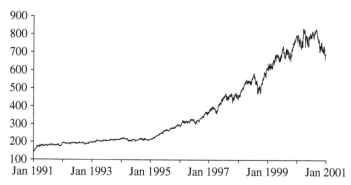

Figure 2.1.   Levels of the Standard & Poor 100-share index.

Figure 2.2.   DM/$ exchange rates.

during this period. The series commences at 153 and ends at 686. The US market commenced a sharp fall in 2000 from the peak level of 833, which continued for a further two years beyond the end of the series. We will refer to index levels as prices whenever this is convenient.

The exchange rate picture shows the number of Deutsche marks (DM) that could be purchased for one dollar at the interbank spot market. This series has 2591 observations, recorded at 12:00 local time in New York, which range from 1.35 to 2.36. The only days excluded are weekend days, 25 December, and 1 January. The DM/$ rate from 1999 onwards is calculated from the Euro/$ rate and the fixed rate for converting German currency into euros.

2.3   Data-Collection Issues

Time series of prices can be obtained from many sources, including websites, commercial vendors, university research centers, and financial markets. Table 2.1 lists web addresses for a variety of data providers.

Table 2.1. Sources of price time series.

Source	Web address	Markets
CRSP	www.crsp.com	US stocks
Commodity Systems Inc	www.csidata.com	Futures
Datastream	www.datastream.com/product/has/	Stocks, bonds, currencies, etc.
IFM	www.theifm.org	Futures, US stocks
Olsen & Associates	www.olsen.ch	Currencies, etc.
Trades and Quotes DB	www.nyse.com/marketinfo	US stocks
US Federal Reserve	www.federalreserve.gov/releases/	Currencies, etc.
Yahoo!	biz.yahoo.com/r/	Stocks, many countries

The majority of sources provide daily data, such as end-of-day prices. Free daily data are available at several websites. For example, at the time of writing, Yahoo! provides long time series of equity returns for many countries. Free data may be less accurate than that provided by vendors such as Datastream and the Center for Research in Security Prices (CRSP). Datastream sells data for all the major asset classes at all important markets, while CRSP sells price records for every stock listed on the major US stock exchanges. Daily futures prices are sold by several organizations, including the Institute for Financial Markets (IFM).

More skill is required to analyze transactions data, such as the time and price of every trade. Vast amounts of transactions data can be bought: for US equities, from the Trades and Quotes database owned by the New York Stock Exchange; for foreign exchange rates and other assets, from Olsen & Associates; and for futures contracts, from IFM.

2.3.1 Frequency

The appropriate frequency of observations in a price series depends on the data available and the questions that interest a researcher. The time interval between prices ought to be sufficient to ensure that trade occurs in most intervals and it is preferable that the volume of trade is substantial. Very often, selecting daily prices will be both appropriate and convenient. Consequently, we focus on the daily frequency in Chapters 2–11. A series of daily prices contains useful information that may be missing in a series of weekly or monthly prices. The additional information increases the power of hypothesis tests, it improves volatility estimates, and it is essential for evaluations of trading rules.

The number of observations in a time series of daily prices should be sufficient to permit powerful tests and accurate estimation of model parameters. Experience shows that at least four years of daily prices (more than 1000 observations) are often required to obtain interesting results; however, eight or more years of prices (more than 2000 observations) should be analyzed whenever possible. The best statistical model and the parameters of any preferred model are, of course, more likely to change as the number of observations increases. Very long price series, spanning several decades, can always be subdivided and then results can be compared across subperiods.

Analysis of prices recorded more frequently than once a day must take account of the uneven flow of transactions during the day, which creates intraday effects. It is also often necessary to consider the consequences of trade prices bouncing between bid and ask quotations. Interesting conclusions can be obtained from high-frequency prices, as will be shown in Chapter 12.

2.3.2 *Price Definitions*

Several choices may be made when daily prices are recorded and it can be important to know how a data vendor defines a representative price for the day. The price is usually some type of closing price. It may be a bid price, an ask price, or an average. It may be either the final transaction price of the day or the final quotation. It may be a settlement price at a futures market in which case it usually equals the average price over the final seconds or transactions of the day's business. Few markets now limit how far prices can move within a trading session, but for such markets it is advisable to identify any prices that are constrained by limit regulations.

Price series should be defined using one price per period, recorded at a constant point within the period such as the market's close. Spurious correlation can occur in "returns" if this convention is ignored. A substantial, positive correlation between consecutive "returns" is created if a weekly average of daily prices is studied (Working 1960), or if the average of the day's high and low prices is used or even simply the day's high (Daniels 1966; Rosenberg 1970).

2.3.3 *Additional Information*

In addition to daily closing prices, it is often possible to obtain daily open, high and low prices, and daily trading volume. This information is routinely recorded by futures markets. High and low prices can be used to improve estimates of price volatility (Parkinson 1980; Garman and Klass 1980). Trading volume can be used to decide if there is a "thin trading" problem. Many instances of zero or low volume imply that published prices may not describe the prices at which transactions could have been agreed. Many occasions of identical prices on consecutive days is also indicative of thin trading.

Some sources provide both bid and ask prices. Large bid–ask spreads can be another indicator of a thin market. Assets that are traded frequently usually have very small spreads and the average of the bid and ask prices can then be used to define the closing price.

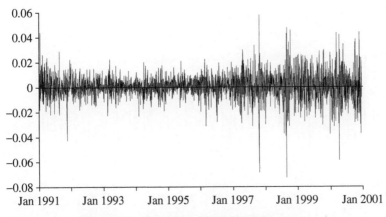

Figure 2.3. Ten years of S&P 100 daily returns.

2.3.4 Futures Prices

Long series of futures prices require several different contracts to be used. This causes few problems providing the derived series of returns contains one return per trading period and each return is calculated using two prices for the same contract. Sellers of futures deliver goods to buyers on one or more days of the delivery month named in the contract. It is advisable to avoid using any of the final prices from a contract that are atypical, perhaps because of delivery options. After excluding such prices, it is conventional to take prices from the contract nearest to delivery to reduce any possibility of thin trading.

2.3.5 Error Checks

Data providers do make mistakes and some providers supply data in a form that includes dates and prices when markets are closed. The correct number of daily prices in one year depends on closures for holidays and weekends. Too few prices indicates that the source has overlooked some days, or that trading has been suspended, while too many prices implies that numbers have been invented for holidays and/or weekends. A substantial error in one price can often be identified by listing all large percentage changes from one day to the next, followed by looking for pairs of consecutive days in the list. Large percentage changes can often be checked against a second source. For futures, a useful second source is often given by the spot market or a contract with a different delivery month.

2.4 Two Returns Series

An investor who owns an asset throughout a trading period obtains a return on investment that depends on the initial price, the final price and any dividend payments. One way to measure the return on investment is $(p_t - p_{t-1})/p_{t-1}$, when p_t is the price for time period t and dividend payouts are ignored.

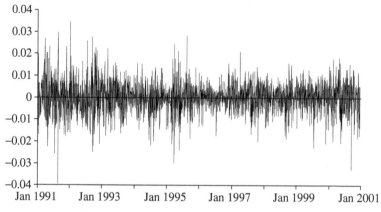

Figure 2.4.   Ten years of DM/$ daily returns.

Figures 2.3 and 2.4 show time series of daily returns calculated from the prices that are plotted in Figures 2.1 and 2.2. These returns vary substantially around their average levels, which are close to zero. The S&P 100 index returns appear to vary more in the second half of the series. Their extreme values are the maximum of 5.8% and the minimum of −7.2%. The corresponding extremes for the DM/$ returns are 3.5% and −3.9%.

Time series plots of returns display an important feature that is usually called *volatility clustering*. This empirical phenomenon was first observed by Mandelbrot (1963), who said of prices that "large changes tend to be followed by large changes—of either sign—and small changes tend to be followed by small changes." Volatility clustering describes the general tendency for markets to have some periods of high volatility and other periods of low volatility. High volatility produces more dispersion in returns than low volatility, so that returns are more spread out when volatility is higher. A high volatility cluster will contain several large positive returns and several large negative returns, but there will be few, if any, large returns in a low volatility cluster.

Clustering effects for the S&P 100 index are more clearly seen in Figure 2.5 for the daily returns from March 1998 to February 1999. This figure shows a high volatility cluster from late August until mid October, with less volatility before August than there is after October. Likewise, Figure 2.6 shows a year of DM/$ returns that have six months of high volatility, which are both preceded and followed by three months of much lower volatility.

2.5   Definitions of Returns

Statistical analysis of market prices is more difficult than analysis of changes in prices. This is because consecutive prices are highly correlated but consecutive

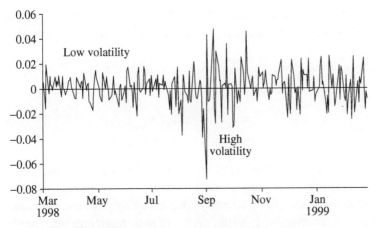

Figure 2.5. One year of S&P 100 daily returns.

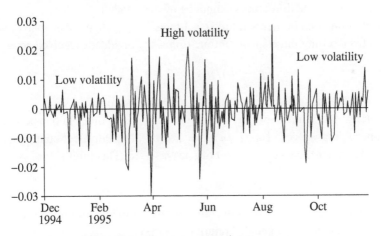

Figure 2.6. One year of DM/$ daily returns.

changes have very little correlation, if any. Consequently, it is more convenient to investigate suitable measures of changes in prices.

Returns to an investor are the preferred way to measure price changes. Returns can be defined by changes in the logarithms of prices, with appropriate adjustments for any dividend payments. We apply this definition to stocks, stock indices, exchange rates, and futures contracts.

2.5.1 *Stock Returns*

Let p_t be a representative price for a stock in period t. Usually this price will be either the final transaction price or the final quotation during the period. Initially, let us assume that the buyer pays the seller immediately for stock bought. Suppose d_t is the present value of dividends, per share, distributed to those people who own stock during period t. On almost all days there are no dividend payments and then $d_t = 0$. Sometimes dividend payments are simply ignored, so then $d_t = 0$ for all days t.

Three price change quantities appear in empirical research:

$$r_t^* = p_t + d_t - p_{t-1},$$
$$r_t' = (p_t + d_t - p_{t-1})/p_{t-1}, \tag{2.1}$$
$$r_t = \log(p_t + d_t) - \log(p_{t-1}). \tag{2.2}$$

The first differences r_t^* are the payoff from buying one share at time $t - 1$ and then selling it at time t, ignoring transaction costs and any differences between buying and selling prices. First differences depend on the price units (e.g. dollars or cents) and thus comparisons across assets are not straightforward. They have the further disadvantage that their variances are proportional to the price level. For these reasons, first differences cannot be recommended.

One dollar invested in shares at time $t - 1$ buys $1/p_{t-1}$ shares. The total dollar proceeds from selling these shares at time t plus any dividends received equals

$$(p_t + d_t)/p_{t-1} = 1 + r_t'.$$

Clearly, r_t' is the one-period return on investment for period t.

The interest rate equivalent to r_t' when interest is paid n times in one period is the number i_n that solves $(1 + (i_n/n))^n = 1 + r_t'$. The equivalent continuously compounded rate is given by the limit of i_n as $n \to \infty$. This limit is

$$\log(1 + r_t') = \log((p_t + d_t)/p_{t-1}) = r_t.$$

Here, and throughout this book, "log" refers to the natural logarithm. We see that r_t is the continuously compounded return for period t.

The return measures r_t and r_t' are very similar numbers, since

$$1 + r_t' = \exp(r_t) = 1 + r_t + \tfrac{1}{2}r_t^2 + \cdots$$

and very rarely are daily returns outside the range from -10% to 10%. Some people prefer to study the continuously compounded return r_t, others prefer the simple return r_t'. It would be surprising if an important conclusion depended on the choice. This book documents several results for continuously compounded returns and generally r_t is called the *return* for period t.

The primary reason for selecting the continuously compounded definition is that multi-period returns are then sums of single-period returns. For example, the proceeds from investing one dollar in stock at time $t - 1$ followed by selling at time $t + 1$ are

$$\exp(r_t + r_{t+1}) = (1 + r_t')(1 + r_{t+1}')$$

and thus two-period returns (ignoring dividends) are

$$r_{t+1,2} = \log(p_{t+1}) - \log(p_{t-1}) = r_t + r_{t+1}$$

and

$$r'_{t+1,2} = (p_{t+1} - p_{t-1})/p_{t-1} = r'_t + r'_{t+1} + r'_t r'_{t+1}.$$

The former equation provides simpler theoretical results than the latter equation for two-period returns, and likewise for general multi-period returns.

The definitions of returns ignore inflation and thus give nominal results. Real returns are nominal returns minus adjustments for inflation but these cannot be estimated satisfactorily for short periods of time. Consequently, it is conventional to study nominal returns, which we do throughout this book.

2.5.2 Delayed Settlement

Stock transactions are often settled a few days after the price is agreed. A stock market price is then, strictly speaking, a forward price for a later date. This fact is usually ignored when calculating returns. Its relevance has diminished in recent years as settlement periods have been reduced. The importance of the settlement issue for older datasets is discussed by Lakonishok and Levi (1982), Condoyanni, O'Hanlon, and Ward (1987), and Solnik (1990).

To quantify the impact of delayed settlement, suppose a transaction at price p_t in period t is settled c_t calendar days later. Also, suppose the relevant continuously compounded daily interest rate is i_t during the settlement period. The spot price s_t for immediate settlement in period t would satisfy

$$p_t = s_t \exp(c_t i_t)$$

if both spot and forward deals were possible, arbitrage profits cannot be made, and there are no dividend payments or transaction costs. Also assuming interest rates are the same at times $t - 1$ and t, it can be deduced that the forward return $r_{t,f} = \log(p_t/p_{t-1})$ equals the spot return $r_{t,s} = \log(s_t/s_{t-1})$ plus a term that only involves interest rates and settlement dates:

$$r_{t,f} = r_{t,s} + (c_t - c_{t-1})i_{t-1}.$$

Thus forward and spot returns are very similar when settlement is after a constant number of business days, but they can differ by more when trades are settled on fixed days during trading accounts (see, for example, Solnik 1990).

2.5.3 Stock Indices

Stock indices are typically weighted averages of the prices of the component stocks. The same formulae as before are used to calculate returns from index levels. Very often dividends are excluded from the index. They are often also excluded from return calculations, perhaps because of the effort required to aggregate the dividends from all the component stocks. The composition of most indices changes occasionally, so that a long time series will not be made up of returns from a homogeneous asset.

2.5.4 Spot Currency Returns

Now suppose p_t is the dollar price in period t for one unit of foreign currency, say euros. A euro investment earns a dividend in the form of euro interest payments. Let i_{t-1}^* be the continuously compounded interest rate for deposits in foreign currency from time $t-1$ until time t. Then one dollar used to buy $1/p_{t-1}$ euros in period $t-1$, which are sold with accumulated interest in period t, gives proceeds equal to $p_t \exp(i_{t-1}^*)/p_{t-1}$ and hence the return is

$$r_t = \log(p_t) - \log(p_{t-1}) + i_{t-1}^*. \tag{2.3}$$

Researchers often ignore the foreign interest rate in this definition, in which case the numbers studied are logarithmic price changes rather than returns. The interest rate term is, however, very small compared with the magnitude of typical daily logarithmic price changes.

2.5.5 Futures Returns

Next suppose $f_{t,T}$ is the futures price in period t for delivery or cash settlement in some later period T. As there are no dividend payouts on futures contracts, it is conventional to define the futures return to be the logarithmic price change:

$$r_t = \log(f_{t,T}) - \log(f_{t-1,T}). \tag{2.4}$$

We will follow this convention. Note that the same futures contract (and hence the same delivery date) should be used to obtain the two prices used in this definition.

Capital is not required to trade futures. Only a margin deposit is required and this could be a security which pays interest to the party making the margin deposit. Consequently, the logarithmic price change can no longer be interpreted as a return on an investment. Nevertheless, to simplify terminology we will use the word "return" when referring to a change in the logarithm of a futures price.

Many goods, such as currencies, have spot and futures prices that are tied to each other by the impossibility of making arbitrage profits. A typical theoretical equation that relates the futures price $f_{t,T}$ to the spot price p_t is then

$$f_{t,T} = p_t \exp((i_t - i_t^*)(T - t))$$

with i_t and i_t^*, respectively, the one-period domestic and foreign interest rates at time t applicable for lending and borrowing until time T (see, for example, Hull 2000, Section 3.8). When interest rates are the same at times $t-1$ and t, it follows that

$$\log(f_{t,T}) - \log(f_{t-1,T}) = \log(p_t) - \log(p_{t-1}) + i_{t-1}^* - i_{t-1}. \tag{2.5}$$

Comparing equations (2.3)–(2.5), it can be seen that what we call the futures return is the spot return minus the one-period domestic interest rate, when our assumptions about arbitrage and interest rates are applicable, i.e.

$$r_t^{(\text{futures})} = r_t^{(\text{spot})} - i_{t-1}.$$

This result simply reflects the fact that a futures trader does not lose interest on capital when financing trades. Similar price equations and conclusions can be obtained for stock index and commodity futures (Hull 2000).

The interpretation of futures returns is more complicated for interest-rate futures. Treasury bond futures, for long-term debt, have delivery options which complicate the relationship between spot and futures prices. If convenient simplifying assumptions are made about delivery options and the shape of the term structure of interest rates, then it is possible to derive an equation of the form

$$r_t^{(\text{futures})} = m_t (r_t^{(\text{spot})} - i_{t-1}).$$

The multiplier m_t is less than 1, reflecting the fact that delivered bonds have a shorter duration than present-day spot bonds. Treasury bill futures, for short-term debt, have market prices defined by equivalent annual interest rates instead of the futures price of a traded bill. The return calculated directly from market prices for 90-day bill futures is then approximately four times the return that would be calculated if prices were quoted for the delivery of 90-day bills.

2.6 Further Examples of Time Series of Returns

A database containing twenty time series of daily returns is used in Chapters 4–7 to illustrate some typical empirical results. Each series covers a decade of trading, concluding on a date in the first half of the 1990s. Nine of the series contain spot returns from equity investments in indices or individual stocks. The other eleven series contain returns calculated from futures prices. Table 2.2 summarizes the dates and assets that define the series.

The price data come from several sources: the Center for Research in Security Prices (CRSP), Datastream, banks, and the London International Financial Futures Exchange (LIFFE). These data cannot be provided to readers, for contractual reasons.

2.6.1 Spot Series

The nine spot equity series are for three indices, three US companies and three UK companies. Returns from the indices provide information about investments in market-wide diversified portfolios, in the US, the UK, and Japan. The US series provides returns on the Standard & Poor 500-share index, with dividends reinvested. The UK and Japanese series are, respectively, for the Financial Times

Table 2.2. Descriptions of twenty time series of daily returns.

| | Spot or | | Inclusive dates | | No. of |
Returns series	Futures	Market	From	To	returns
S&P 500-share	S	New York	01/07/82	30/06/92	2529
S&P 500-share	F	Chicago (CME)	01/07/82	30/06/92	2529
Coca Cola	S	New York	03/01/84	31/12/93	2529
General Electric	S	New York	03/01/84	31/12/93	2529
General Motors	S	New York	03/01/84	31/12/93	2529
FT 100-share	S	London	02/01/85	30/12/94	2529
FT 100-share	F	London	02/01/85	30/12/94	2529
Glaxo	S	London	04/01/82	31/12/91	2528
Marks & Spencer	S	London	04/01/82	31/12/91	2528
Shell	S	London	04/01/82	31/12/91	2528
Nikkei 225-share	S	Tokyo	07/01/85	30/12/94	2464
Treasury bonds	F	Chicago (CBOT)	01/12/81	29/11/91	2528
3-month sterling bills	F	London	05/01/83	31/12/92	2527
DM/$	F	Chicago (CME)	01/12/81	29/11/91	2529
Sterling/$	F	Chicago (CME)	01/12/81	29/11/91	2529
Swiss franc/$	F	Chicago (CME)	01/12/81	29/11/91	2529
Yen/$	F	Chicago (CME)	01/12/81	29/11/91	2529
Gold	F	New York (COMEX)	01/12/80	30/11/90	2522
Corn	F	Chicago (CBOT)	01/12/80	30/11/90	2528
Live cattle	F	Chicago (CME)	01/12/80	30/11/90	2529

Figure 2.7. Relative share index levels.

100-share index and the Nikkei 225-share index. These two series do not incorporate any dividends, so that the numbers we then call returns are simply logarithmic price changes. There was trade on some Saturdays at the Tokyo Stock Exchange until February 1989 but these days are excluded from our time series.

Figure 2.7 is a time series plot of the three indices, from January 1985 to June 1992, with the indices scaled to begin at the same number and denominated in their domestic currencies. All the indices fell sharply in October 1987 and there

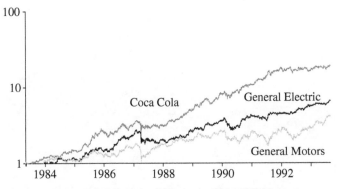

Figure 2.8. Payoffs from US stock investments.

is a global factor that explains the covariation between them. The correlation between US and UK index returns on the same day equals 0.46. It equals 0.36 for the UK and Japan, but only 0.19 for the US and Japan. The US/Japan correlation increases to 0.37 when the American return is correlated with the Japanese return for the previous day.

General Electric, Coca Cola, and General Motors were all among the ten largest firms at the New York Stock Exchange, ranked by market capitalization at the end of 1993. The returns include dividend payments. Figure 2.8 shows the result of investing one dollar in each of the companies at the beginning of 1984, plotted on a logarithmic scale. The correlations between returns on the same day are fairly substantial. They equal 0.60 (CC, GM), 0.51 (GE, GM) and 0.45 (CC, GE).

Glaxo, Shell, and Marks & Spencer have been three of the largest companies whose shares are traded at the London Stock Exchange. The market prices are for settlement on one of twenty-four dates per annum. The returns have been calculated from spot prices implied by market prices, short-term interest rates, and the assumption of no arbitrage profits; they include dividends. The correlations between returns from different stocks on the same day for the three UK pairings are 0.33, 0.35, and 0.37.

2.6.2   *Futures Series*

Each futures series is obtained from a set of forty or more contracts. These contracts have delivery dates in March, June, September, and December, unless stated otherwise. Returns are calculated from the contract nearest to delivery, except in delivery months when the second-nearest contract is used. For example, a March contract provides returns from the first trading day in December until the last trading day in February; the return for the first day in December is calculated from the March contract prices on the last day of November and the first day of December.

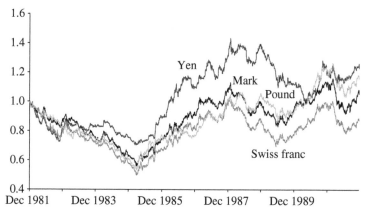

Figure 2.9.   Cumulative returns from currency futures.

Eight of the eleven futures series are for financial futures, reflecting the dominance of this sector of the futures industry. The S&P 500 and the FTSE 100 stock index futures contracts provide returns that can be compared with returns from the underlying spot indices. The impossibility of easy arbitrage profits guarantees that spot and futures returns are similar. The correlation between spot and futures returns for the same day is therefore high. It equals 0.94 for the S&P 500 data. The strong dependence between the returns diminished during the crash of October 1987, when the spot and futures returns for the S&P 500 were $(-0.20, -0.34)$ on Monday, 19 October, $(0.02, 0.07)$ on 20 October, and $(0.08, 0.18)$ on 21 October.

Bill and bond futures contracts provide returns on interest-rate products at opposite ends of the term structure. The short-term sterling contracts are for delivery of three-month UK Treasury bills. The long-term dollar contracts are designed around the delivery of US Treasury bonds with more than fifteen years to maturity.

Currency futures prices are stated as the dollar price of one unit of foreign currency. The currency return series, for Deutsche mark, sterling, Swiss franc, and yen futures, contain returns from an American perspective. Figure 2.9 shows numbers that relate to a one dollar "investment" in long futures positions; after t periods, the number plotted is $\exp(r_1 + r_2 + \cdots + r_t)$. A common factor can be seen that reflects the relative strength or weakness of the dollar. The correlations between returns from different currencies on the same day are substantial. They range from 0.57 for sterling/$ and yen/$ returns to 0.92 for DM/$ and franc/$ returns.

Commodity futures prices provide the returns for the remaining three series. Gold, corn, and live cattle contracts have been some of the most actively traded nonfinancial contracts. The delivery months for gold and cattle are the even months (February, April, ..., December), while the months for corn are March, May, July, September, and December.

3
Stochastic Processes: Definitions and Examples

Prices and returns are modeled throughout this book by time-ordered sequences of random variables, called stochastic processes. This chapter reviews their definitions and properties. A key property is the level of correlation between variables measured at different times. We cover processes that exhibit a variety of correlation patterns, including several processes that possess no correlation across variables.

3.1 Introduction

A time series of returns is a single sample that arises from competitive trading at a market. We are interested in probability models that can explain the data that we see and that can then be used to make predictions. These probability models are called stochastic processes. They are sequences of random variables arranged in time order. This chapter reviews theoretical results. It is followed by data analysis in subsequent chapters that identifies and estimates appropriate models for prices and returns.

Stochastic processes that are important for finance research are often identical or similar to processes that are used to model time series arising in economics and the physical sciences. Some of our definitions need to be more precise than those used elsewhere. In particular, we have to avoid assuming that distributions are normal and we must distinguish between independence and a lack of correlation.

Properties of random variables are reviewed in Section 3.2. Finding a satisfactory model typically requires these properties to remain unchanged as time progresses. This leads us to the concept of a stationary stochastic process, which is covered in Section 3.3. The simplest example of a stationary process is a set of variables that have independent and identical distributions. This type of process and many others have no correlation between different terms from the process. We review a variety of uncorrelated processes in Section 3.4.

More general stochastic processes, whose terms are correlated, are constructed from functions of uncorrelated variables. Autoregressive, moving-average, and mixed processes are introduced in Section 3.5 and their relevance is motivated by theoretical examples for returns in Section 3.6. Integrated processes are defined in Section 3.7 and then fractional integration is described in Section 3.8. Stronger assumptions and their shortcomings for financial models are explained in Section 3.9. Two stochastic processes that are defined for a continuous range of times are mentioned in Section 3.10.

3.2 Random Variables

Anyone reading this book on a Monday will not know the closing level of a stock market index on the following day, assuming the market is open on that Tuesday. Thus, on Monday, we may regard the closing level on Tuesday as a random variable X. A day later we will discover the actual Tuesday closing level, or outcome, which will be some number x. On Monday we will, however, have some relevant information about possible outcomes on Tuesday and so we will be able to talk about a probability distribution for X. We now review standard definitions and results for random variables and probability distributions, focusing on the material that is most used in this book.

3.2.1 *One Variable*

For any random variable X, with possible outcomes that may range across all real numbers, the *cumulative distribution function* (c.d.f.) F is defined as the probability of an outcome at a particular level, or lower, i.e.

$$F(x) = P(X \leqslant x)$$

with $P(\cdot)$ referring to the probability of the bracketed event. Some random variables are *discrete*, such as the number of trades during a period of trading. In contrast, other variables have one or more continuous ranges of possible outcomes. Prices and returns are very often modeled by *continuous* random variables, even though markets prescribe minimum price changes.

Discrete random variables have either a finite or a countable infinite number of possible outcomes. The *probability distribution function* f then states the probabilities of the possible outcomes and we have

$$f(x) = P(X = x), \quad f(x) \geqslant 0, \quad \sum_{x=-\infty}^{\infty} f(x) = 1, \quad F(x) = \sum_{n=-\infty}^{x} f(n).$$

Furthermore, F is not a differentiable function of x. Also, $f(x) = F(x) - F(x-1)$ when the only possible outcomes are integers.

Most of the random variables that we consider are, however, continuous and their cumulative functions are also differentiable. The *density function* (d.f.) f is then

$$f(x) = \frac{\mathrm{d}F}{\mathrm{d}x},$$

with

$$f(x) \geqslant 0, \qquad \int_{-\infty}^{\infty} f(x)\,dx = 1, \qquad F(x) = \int_{-\infty}^{x} f(t)\,dt.$$

The probability of an outcome within a short interval from $x - \frac{1}{2}\delta$ to $x + \frac{1}{2}\delta$ is then approximately $\delta f(x)$, while the exact probability for a general interval from a to b is given by

$$P(a \leqslant X \leqslant b) = F(b) - F(a) = \int_{a}^{b} f(x)\,dx.$$

The *expectation* or *mean* of a continuous random variable X is defined by

$$E[X] = \int_{-\infty}^{\infty} xf(x)\,dx.$$

Here, and in many of the following equations, the equivalent definition for a discrete variable is given by replacing the integral by a sum.

Any function $Y = g(X)$ of a random variable X is also a random variable. The expectation of Y can then be found either from its own density function or, as follows, from the d.f. of X:

$$E[g(X)] = \int_{-\infty}^{\infty} g(x)f(x)\,dx.$$

An important example is the expectation of the squared distance from the mean, now denoted by μ. This defines the *variance* of X, often denoted by σ^2:

$$g(X) = (X - \mu)^2,$$
$$\mathrm{var}(X) = E[g(X)] = \sigma^2 = \int_{-\infty}^{\infty} (x - \mu)^2 f(x)\,dx,$$

which leads to the alternative expression

$$\mathrm{var}(X) = E[X^2] - E[X]^2.$$

For all numbers a and b, the random variable $a + bX$ has expectation $a + bE[X]$ and variance $b^2\,\mathrm{var}(X)$.

The *standard deviation* of X is simply the square root of its variance. The nth *moment* equals $E[X^n]$ and the nth *central moment* is $m_n = E[(X - \mu)^n]$. The second central moment is another name for the variance. As becomes clearer later, of particular importance for us are the *skewness* and *kurtosis* defined by

$$\mathrm{skewness}(X) = m_3/m_2^{1.5} \quad \text{and} \quad \mathrm{kurtosis}(X) = m_4/m_2^2.$$

3.2.2 The Normal Distribution

The normal (or Gaussian) distribution is our most important continuous distribution. It is defined by the density function

$$f(x) = \frac{1}{\sigma\sqrt{2\pi}} \exp\left(-\frac{1}{2}\left(\frac{x-\mu}{\sigma}\right)^2 \right). \tag{3.1}$$

This density has two parameters: the mean μ and the variance σ^2 of the random variable. We use the notation $X \sim N(\mu, \sigma^2)$ when X has the above density.

A linear function of a normal variable is also normal. If $X \sim N(\mu, \sigma^2)$ and $Y = a + bX$, then $Y \sim N(a + b\mu, b^2\sigma^2)$. In particular, with $a = -\mu/\sigma$ and $b = 1/\sigma$,

$$X \sim N(\mu, \sigma^2) \quad \Rightarrow \quad Z = \frac{X - \mu}{\sigma} \sim N(0, 1).$$

We call Z the *standard normal* distribution. Its d.f. is simply

$$f(z) = \frac{1}{\sqrt{2\pi}} \exp(-\tfrac{1}{2}z^2), \tag{3.2}$$

and we may denote its c.d.f. by $\Phi(z)$, which has to be evaluated by numerical methods. The probabilities of outcomes for X within particular ranges can be calculated from

$$P(a \leqslant X \leqslant b) = \Phi\left(\frac{b - \mu}{\sigma}\right) - \Phi\left(\frac{a - \mu}{\sigma}\right).$$

The density of the normal distribution is symmetric about its mean μ. Symmetry ensures that all the odd central moments are zero and therefore the skewness of the distribution is zero. The second and fourth central moments are respectively σ^2 and $3\sigma^4$, so that all normal distributions have a kurtosis equal to three.

Exponential functions of normal variables are often encountered in finance. The general result for their expectations is

$$E[e^{uX}] = \exp(u\mu + \tfrac{1}{2}u^2\sigma^2). \tag{3.3}$$

This applies for all real and complex numbers u.

3.2.3 The Lognormal Distribution

A random variable Y has a lognormal distribution whenever $\log(Y)$ has a normal distribution. When $\log(Y) \sim N(\mu, \sigma^2)$, the density function of Y is

$$f(y) = \begin{cases} \dfrac{1}{y\sigma\sqrt{2\pi}} \exp\left(-\dfrac{1}{2}\left(\dfrac{\log(y) - \mu}{\sigma}\right)^2 \right), & y > 0, \\ 0, & y \leqslant 0. \end{cases} \tag{3.4}$$

From equation (3.3), $E[Y^n] = \exp(n\mu + \frac{1}{2}n^2\sigma^2)$ for all n. Consequently, the mean and the variance of Y are

$$E[Y] = \exp(\mu + \tfrac{1}{2}\sigma^2) \quad \text{and} \quad \text{var}(Y) = \exp(2\mu + \sigma^2)(\exp(\sigma^2) - 1).$$

The mean exceeds the median, namely $\exp(\mu)$, reflecting the positive skewness of this nonsymmetric distribution.

3.2.4 Two Variables

Two random variables X and Y have a *bivariate* c.d.f. that gives the probabilities of both outcomes being less than or equal to levels x and y respectively:

$$F(x, y) = P(X \leqslant x \text{ and } Y \leqslant y).$$

The bivariate d.f. is then defined for continuous variables by

$$f(x, y) = \frac{\partial^2 F}{\partial x \partial y}.$$

We are often only interested in *conditional* densities, such as the density of Y when we know that the outcome for X is a particular number x. Let $f_X(x)$ now denote the density of X. Assuming $f_X(x) > 0$, we adopt the notation $f(y \mid x)$ for the density of Y conditional on the event $X = x$, and its definition is

$$f(y \mid x) = f(x, y)/f_X(x).$$

The *conditional expectation* of Y given x is then

$$E[Y \mid x] = \int_{-\infty}^{\infty} y f(y \mid x) \, \mathrm{d}y.$$

We will also use the notation $E[Y \mid X]$ to refer to the random variable whose outcome is defined by $E[Y \mid x]$ when the outcome of X is x. If we want to emphasize the distinction between $E[Y]$ and $E[Y \mid x]$, then the first term may be called the *unconditional expectation*.

The *covariance* between two variables is one measure of *linear* dependence between them. Using subscripts to indicate the variable,

$$\text{cov}(X, Y) = \text{cov}(Y, X) = E[(X - \mu_X)(Y - \mu_Y)]$$
$$= E[XY] - E[X]E[Y].$$

Note that the special case $X = Y$ shows that $\text{cov}(X, X) = \text{var}(X)$. The *correlation* is another measure of *linear* dependence,

$$\text{cor}(X, Y) = \frac{\text{cov}(X, Y)}{\sigma_X \sigma_Y}.$$

This is often denoted by the symbol ρ and $-1 \leqslant \rho \leqslant 1$. The correlation, unlike the covariance, is essentially unchanged by linear transformations. For all numbers a, b, c, and d,

$$\text{cov}(a + bX, c + dY) = bd\,\text{cov}(X, Y)$$

and, whenever $bd > 0$,

$$\text{cor}(a + bX, c + dY) = \text{cor}(X, Y).$$

The mean and variance of the sum of two random variables are

$$E[X + Y] = E[X] + E[Y]$$

and

$$\text{var}(X + Y) = \text{var}(X) + 2\,\text{cov}(X, Y) + \text{var}(Y).$$

More generally, for any numbers a, b, and c, the first two moments of a linear combination are

$$E[a + bX + cY] = a + bE[X] + cE[Y]$$

and

$$\text{var}(a + bX + cY) = b^2\,\text{var}(X) + 2bc\,\text{cov}(X, Y) + c^2\,\text{var}(Y).$$

3.2.5 Two Independent Variables

Two random variables X and Y are *independent* if and only if the conditional densities of one variable (say Y) all equal that variable's unconditional density:

$$f(y \mid x) = f_Y(y) \quad \text{whenever } f_X(x) > 0.$$

This is equivalent to the factorization of the bivariate d.f. into the product of the two unconditional densities:

$$f(x, y) = f_X(x)f_Y(y) \quad \text{for all } x \text{ and } y .$$

Variables are *dependent* if they are not independent.

Independence has many implications. First, conditional and unconditional expectations are then equal:

$$E[Y \mid x] = E[Y] \quad \text{for all } x \text{ that have } f_X(x) > 0 .$$

Second, the variables $g(X)$ and $h(Y)$ are also independent for all functions g and h. Third,

$$E[XY] = E[X]E[Y]$$

and hence the correlation and covariance between independent variables are both zero.

Although independence implies zero correlation, the converse does not follow. There are many examples in this book of dependent variables that have zero correlation between them. Our first example is provided by the ARCH(1) model described later by equation (3.11).

3.2.6 Several Variables

A general set of n variables $\{Y_1, Y_2, \ldots, Y_n\}$ has the *multivariate* c.d.f. defined by

$$F(y_1, y_2, \ldots, y_n) = P(Y_1 \leqslant y_1, Y_2 \leqslant y_2, \ldots, Y_n \leqslant y_n).$$

The multivariate d.f. for continuous variables is

$$f(y_1, \ldots, y_n) = \frac{\partial^n F}{\partial y_1 \cdots \partial y_n}.$$

It is often stated as the product of the first unconditional density and $n-1$ conditional densities:

$$f(y_1, y_2, \ldots, y_n)$$
$$= f_{Y_1}(y_1) f(y_2 \mid y_1) f(y_3 \mid y_1, y_2) \cdots f(y_n \mid y_1, y_2, \ldots, y_{n-1}).$$

The first two moments of the general linear combination are

$$E\left[a + \sum_{i=1}^{n} b_i Y_i\right] = a + \sum_{i=1}^{n} b_i E[Y_i] \qquad (3.5)$$

and

$$\mathrm{var}\left(a + \sum_{i=1}^{n} b_i Y_i\right) = \sum_{i=1}^{n} b_i^2 \, \mathrm{var}(Y_i) + \sum_{i=1}^{n-1} \sum_{j=i+1}^{n} 2b_i b_j \, \mathrm{cov}(Y_i, Y_j). \qquad (3.6)$$

The combination $a + \sum b_i Y_i$ has a normal distribution when the component variables have a multivariate normal distribution. This distribution has d.f.

$$f(y) = \frac{1}{(2\pi)^{n/2} \sqrt{\det(\Omega)}} \exp(-\tfrac{1}{2}(y - \mu)' \Omega^{-1}(y - \mu)) \qquad (3.7)$$

for vectors $y = (y_1, \ldots, y_n)'$, $\mu = (\mu_1, \ldots, \mu_n)'$, with $\mu_i = E[Y_i]$, and a matrix Ω that has elements given by $\omega_{i,j} = \mathrm{cov}(Y_i, Y_j)$ and a determinant denoted by $\det(\Omega)$.

3.2.7 Several Independent Variables

Random variables are independent if information about the outcomes of some of the variables tells us nothing new about the distributions of the remaining variables. The d.f. then factorizes as

$$f(y_1, y_2, \ldots, y_n) = f_{Y_1}(y_1) f_{Y_2}(y_2) \cdots f_{Y_n}(y_n).$$

An immediate consequence of independence is that all covariances between different variables are zero and hence equation (3.6) simplifies. In particular, the variance of the sum of n variables equals the sum of the n individual variances.

In many probability models, the unconditional distributions of independent variables are assumed to be identical. There is then a common univariate d.f., say $f_Y(y)$, and the multivariate d.f. is simply

$$f(y_1, y_2, \ldots, y_n) = f_Y(y_1) f_Y(y_2) \cdots f_Y(y_n).$$

The n variables $\{Y_1, Y_2, \ldots, Y_n\}$ are then said to be *independent and identically distributed* (i.i.d.). An infinite number of variables are said to be i.i.d. if all finite subsets have the i.i.d. property.

The average $\bar{Y}_n = (Y_1 + \cdots + Y_n)/n$ of a "large" number of i.i.d. variables has an approximate normal distribution for any d.f. $f_Y(y)$ that has finite mean and variance, say μ and σ^2. More precisely, the central limit theorem states that the distribution of $(\bar{Y}_n - \mu)/(\sigma/\sqrt{n})$ converges to the standard normal distribution as n increases.

3.3 Stationary Stochastic Processes

A *stochastic process* is a sequence of random variables in time order. Sometimes it is called the process generating observed data or, more simply, either a process or a *model*. A stochastic process is often denoted by a typical variable in curly brackets, e.g. $\{X_t\}$ with t representing time. Almost all of our examples are for integer times and sometimes an infinite timescale is used. In due course we consider processes for prices, returns, and measures of volatility.

A time-ordered set of observations, $\{x_1, x_2, x_3, \ldots, x_n\}$, is called a *time series*. Much of this book is about methods for inferring and estimating the properties of the stochastic process that generated a time series of returns. It is of particular interest to describe the distribution of X_t conditional upon the historical record until time $t - 1$.

Several categories of stochastic processes are defined in the following pages. A summary of their definitions is provided by Table 3.1.

3.3.1 Stationarity

Stochastic processes are often defined by either multivariate or conditional distributions. These distributions will depend on a set of parameters that may change through time. Parameter estimation from a time series is only feasible when the number of parameters does not exceed the number of observations. Estimation becomes much simpler when all the parameters remain constant as time progresses. This requires that the distributions of random variables remain fixed as time progresses.

Table 3.1. Definitions of ten types of stochastic process.

A process is...	If...
Strictly stationary	The multivariate distribution function for k consecutive variables does not depend on the time subscript attached to the first variable (any k).
Stationary	Means and variances do not depend on time subscripts, covariances depend only on the difference between the two subscripts.
Uncorrelated	The correlation between variables having different time subscripts is always 0.
Autocorrelated	It is not uncorrelated.
White noise	The variables are uncorrelated, stationary and have mean equal to 0.
Strict white noise	The variables are independent and have identical distributions whose mean is equal to 0.
A martingale	The expected value of variable t, conditional on the information provided by all previous values, equals variable $t-1$.
A martingale difference	The expected value of variable t, conditional on the information provided by all previous values, always equals 0.
Gaussian	All multivariate distributions are multivariate normal.
Linear	It is a linear combination of the present and past terms from a strict white noise process.

A stochastic process $\{X_t\}$ is *strictly stationary* if the multivariate, cumulative distribution functions of $(X_i, X_{i+1}, \ldots, X_{i+k-1})$ and $(X_j, X_{j+1}, \ldots, X_{j+k-1})$ are identical, for all integers i, j and for all $k > 0$.

A special example of a strictly stationary process is given by supposing returns have independent and identical normal distributions. All multivariate distributions are then determined by the mean and variance parameters of the identical distributions. An example of a process for daily returns that is not strictly stationary is given by independent normal distributions whose variances depend on the day of the week.

It is only practical to check the stationarity of some of the properties of a stochastic process. Suppose $\{X_t\}$ is strictly stationary. Then X_i and X_j have identical distributions and hence their expectations and variances are all equal to constant values, $\mu = E[X_t]$ and $\sigma^2 = \text{var}(X_t)$. Also, because the pairs $(X_i, X_{i+\tau})$ and $(X_j, X_{j+\tau})$ have identical bivariate distributions, the *autocovariances*

$$\lambda_\tau = \text{cov}(X_t, X_{t+\tau}) = E[(X_t - \mu)(X_{t+\tau} - \mu)] \tag{3.8}$$

only depend on the time interval τ, or *lag*, between the two times t and $t + \tau$. When $\tau = 0$, $\lambda_0 = \sigma^2$.

The first- and second-order moments of a stochastic process are its means, variances, and covariances. If these moments do not change with time, then the stochastic process has various names in the statistical literature: second-order stationary, covariance stationary, and weakly stationary. All these phrases will be abbreviated to the single word, *stationary*. Any process that is not stationary is called *nonstationary*. It is assumed throughout this chapter that stationary processes have finite first- and second-order moments. Processes for which these moments are not defined are discussed in Section 4.8.

Many credible models for returns are stationary. Equity prices and exchange rates, however, are not characterized by stationary processes (Baillie and Bollerslev 1994). Some of the evidence for this general conclusion comes from *unit root* tests (e.g. Baillie and Bollerslev 1989a). The conclusion should not be surprising. Inflation increases the expectations of future prices for many assets. Thus the first moment changes. Deflating prices could provide constant expected values. Even then, however, the variances of prices are likely to increase as time progresses. This is always the case for a random walk process. If P_t represents either the price or its logarithm and if the first difference $Z_t = P_t - P_{t-1}$ has positive variance and is uncorrelated with P_{t-1}, then

$$\text{var}(P_t) = \text{var}(P_{t-1} + Z_t) = \text{var}(P_{t-1}) + \text{var}(Z_t) > \text{var}(P_{t-1}),$$

so that the variances depend on the time t. The real spot prices of commodities might be stationary but the corresponding futures prices are theoretically nonstationary (Samuelson 1965, 1976).

3.3.2 Gaussian Processes

The random variables defining a stationary process have a general probability distribution. A process is called *Gaussian* if the multivariate distribution of the consecutive variables $(X_{t+1}, X_{t+2}, \ldots, X_{t+k})$ is multivariate normal for all integers t and k. A stationary Gaussian process is always strictly stationary, because then the first- and second-order moments completely determine the multivariate distributions.

Although returns are certainly not generated by a Gaussian process, it will be shown in Chapters 9–11 that interesting and useful models for returns can be constructed from one or more stationary Gaussian processes.

3.3.3 Autocorrelation

The correlation between two random variables X_t and $X_{t+\tau}$, whose process is stationary, is called the *autocorrelation* at *lag* τ. The notation ρ_τ is used for this correlation. As the variances of X_t and $X_{t+\tau}$ both equal λ_0,

$$\rho_\tau = \text{cov}(X_t, X_{t+\tau})/\lambda_0 = \lambda_\tau/\lambda_0. \tag{3.9}$$

Then $\rho_0 = 1$ and $\rho_\tau = \rho_{-\tau}$. As ρ_τ is a correlation, $-1 \leqslant \rho_\tau \leqslant 1$.

The notation ρ_τ can also be used for nonstationary processes when the correlation between X_t and $X_{t+\tau}$ depends on τ alone. For example, the variables X_t could have time-dependent autocovariances yet have autocorrelations determined solely by the time lag between variables.

An important property of the autocorrelations of a stationary process is that they determine optimal, *linear forecasts*, where optimal is defined as minimizing the mean square error of a forecast. For example, suppose

$$f_{t,1} = \mu + \delta + \sum_{i=0}^{\infty} \beta_i (X_{t-i} - \mu)$$

is a linear forecast of X_{t+1} made at time t, with $\mu = E[X_t]$, δ, β_0, β_1, ... being constants. It can then be shown that the *mean square error*, $E[(X_{t+1} - f_{t,1})^2]$, equals δ^2 plus λ_0 multiplied by a function of the terms β_i and ρ_τ. Thus the optimal, linear forecast is unbiased ($\delta = 0$) with the best β_i, $i \geqslant 0$, determined by the sequence ρ_τ, $\tau > 0$.

3.3.4 Spectral Density

The autocorrelations ρ_τ and the variance λ_0 conveniently summarize the second-order moments of a stationary process. An equivalent representation of these moments is provided by the *spectral density function*, but it will receive far less attention. It is the function of the frequency ω defined by

$$s(\omega) = \frac{\lambda_0}{2\pi} \left[1 + 2 \sum_{\tau=1}^{\infty} \rho_\tau \cos(\tau\omega) \right]. \tag{3.10}$$

The integral of $s(\omega)$ from 0 to 2π equals λ_0. High values of $s(\omega)$ might indicate cyclical behavior with the period of one cycle equal to $2\pi/\omega$ time units. In financial applications, the frequency-domain function $s(\omega)$ is often more difficult to estimate and interpret than the time-domain sequence λ_τ. Consequently, this text concentrates on time-domain methods.

3.4 Uncorrelated Processes

The simplest possible autocorrelations occur when a process is a collection of uncorrelated random variables, so

$$\rho_0 = 1 \quad \text{and} \quad \rho_\tau = 0 \quad \text{for all } \tau > 0.$$

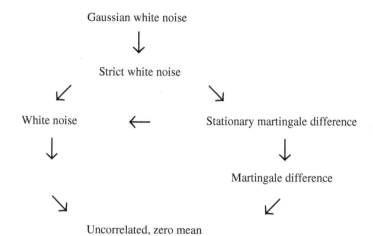

Figure 3.1. Relationships between categories of uncorrelated processes. An arrow pointing from one category to another indicates that all processes in the former category are also in the latter category *and* the converse is false: some processes in the latter category are not members of the former category. It is assumed that all processes have finite means and variances.

Any such process, whether stationary or nonstationary, will be called *uncorrelated*. The optimal linear forecast of X_{t+1} is then simply its unconditional mean. The adjective *autocorrelated* will be used if a process is not uncorrelated.

Uncorrelated processes are often components of models for asset returns, because they are sometimes supported by empirical evidence and, in some circumstances, by the theory of efficient markets. Three categories of uncorrelated processes are of particular importance, namely, white noise processes, strict white noise processes, and martingale differences. These are all *zero-mean* processes, i.e. $\mu = 0$. Figure 3.1 summarizes the relationships between the various categories of zero-mean, uncorrelated processes that are discussed in this section.

A process is *white noise* if it is stationary, uncorrelated, and has zero mean. Its spectral density function is the same constant for all frequencies ω, hence all frequencies contribute equally to the spectrum just as all colors contribute equally to white light.

Our definition of white noise is also used by Hamilton (1994). The definition states less assumptions than are found in some texts (e.g. Tsay 2002). The absence of correlation from a white noise process does not imply independence between variables. The stronger assumptions that the variables are independent and identically distributed (i.i.d.), with zero means, defines *strict white noise* (SWN). Gaussian white noise is strict white noise because uncorrelated variables are independent variables when their multivariate distribution is normal.

The distinction between white noise and strict white noise is important when considering the non-Gaussian processes that are required to model returns. For example, a satisfactory process for exchange rate returns might have zero mean, be stationary, and possess volatility clustering. Then the process is neither i.i.d. nor SWN because information about recent volatility influences the conditional variance of subsequent returns. The process might, nevertheless, be white noise because the volatility information may be irrelevant for predicting the level of returns.

Independent and identically distributed variables are the primary building blocks when constructing stochastic processes. Those white noise processes which are not i.i.d. can often be constructed from a transformation of i.i.d. variables. The ARCH(1) model of Engle (1982), which also has the property of volatility clustering, is a typical example. Let $\{\eta_t\}$ be a zero-mean, unit-variance, i.i.d. process and let

$$X_t = \eta_t (\alpha + \beta X_{t-1}^2)^{1/2}. \tag{3.11}$$

Then $\{X_t\}$ is uncorrelated, because η_t is independent of all variables with earlier time subscripts and hence $E[X_t X_{t-\tau}] = 0$ for all positive lags. The process is stationary for suitable positive choices of α and β and is then white noise. However, the process is not i.i.d. because the conditional expectation $E[X_t^2 \mid X_{t-1}]$ equals $\alpha + \beta X_{t-1}^2$ and thus X_t is not independent of X_{t-1}.

Another category of uncorrelated processes is given by differencing a martingale. A process $\{M_t\}$ is a *martingale*, with respect to the information provided by its own history, if

$$E[M_t \mid M_{t-1}, M_{t-2}, \ldots] = M_{t-1}. \tag{3.12}$$

The differences $X_t = M_t - M_{t-1}$ then define a *martingale difference* process and have the *fair game* property:

$$E[X_t \mid X_{t-1}, X_{t-2}, \ldots] = 0. \tag{3.13}$$

It follows that a martingale difference (MD) is a zero-mean, uncorrelated process. Consequently, a stationary MD is white noise. Other MDs are nonstationary and thus are not white noise.

White noise processes may not be MDs because the conditional expectation of an uncorrelated process can be a nonlinear function. Illustrations of this mathematical result tend to be contrived when discussing models for returns. An example is the following bilinear model mentioned by Granger and Newbold (1986):

$$X_t = \beta X_{t-2} \varepsilon_{t-1} + \varepsilon_t \tag{3.14}$$

with the residuals ε_t a unit-variance SWN process. This bilinear model is white noise when $0 < \beta < 1/\sqrt{2}$. Its conditional expectations (and hence optimal forecasts) are the following nonlinear functions:

$$E[X_t \mid X_{t-1}, X_{t-2}, \ldots] = -\sum_{i=1}^{\infty} (-\beta)^{i+1} X_{t-i} \left(\prod_{j=2}^{i+1} X_{t-j} \right).$$

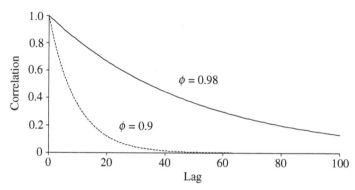

Figure 3.2.   Examples of AR(1) autocorrelations.

The weight attached to X_{t-i} is then a random variable, unlike the constant term that appears in linear forecasts.

3.5   ARMA Processes

A white noise process $\{\varepsilon_t\}$ is often used to construct a general autocorrelated process. Three examples of processes used to model returns and derived series are described. Afterwards, the general autoregressive, moving-average (ARMA) model is presented. The ε_t can have any distribution with finite-variance σ_ε^2. They might be independent variables, but this restriction is not necessary and so it is not assumed. We will often use the following basic properties of white noise:

$$E[\varepsilon_t] = 0, \quad E[\varepsilon_t^2] = \sigma_\varepsilon^2, \quad E[\varepsilon_t \varepsilon_{t+\tau}] = 0 \quad \text{for all } t \text{ and for all } \tau \neq 0.$$

3.5.1   AR(1)

First, consider a process $\{X_t\}$ defined by

$$X_t - \mu = \phi(X_{t-1} - \mu) + \varepsilon_t. \tag{3.15}$$

Then X_t depends linearly on X_{t-1} and the *innovation* (or *residual*) ε_t alone. The process $\{X_t\}$ is called an *autoregressive* process of order one, abbreviated to AR(1). The process is stationary if, as will always be assumed, the autoregressive parameter ϕ satisfies the inequality $|\phi| < 1$. The other two parameters of an AR(1) process are its mean, $\mu = E[X_t]$, and variance, $\lambda_0 = \text{var}(X_t) = \sigma_\varepsilon^2 / (1 - \phi^2)$.

An AR(1) process has autocorrelations

$$\rho_\tau = \phi^\tau, \quad \tau \geq 0. \tag{3.16}$$

These autocorrelations decrease slowly when ϕ is near one. Figure 3.2 illustrates the autocorrelations when ϕ is either 0.9 or 0.98.

An example of a process that has been modeled as AR(1) is the logarithm of price volatility, to be considered in Chapter 11. Figure 3.3 shows a series of

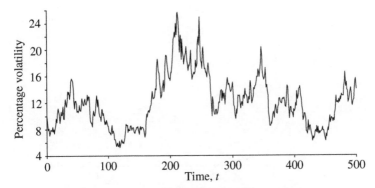

Figure 3.3. Observations from an AR(1) process.

annualized volatility values simulated from this process when $\phi = 0.98$, with Gaussian innovations, for 500 consecutive days. These observations can be far from the median level of 10% for long periods of time.

Equation (3.16) for the autocorrelations, and many others, can be obtained by using the *lag operator* L, defined by $La_t = a_{t-1}$ for any infinite sequence of variables or numbers $\{a_t\}$. Repeated application of the operator L gives $L^k X_t = X_{t-k}$ and $L^k \mu = \mu$ for all integers k. Equation (3.15) can be rewritten as

$$(1 - \phi L)(X_t - \mu) = \varepsilon_t. \tag{3.17}$$

As $|\phi| < 1$, there is the result

$$\frac{1}{1 - \phi L} = \sum_{i=0}^{\infty} (\phi L)^i$$

and therefore

$$X_t - \mu = \frac{1}{1 - \phi L} \varepsilon_t = \sum_{i=0}^{\infty} (\phi L)^i \varepsilon_t = \sum_{i=0}^{\infty} \phi^i \varepsilon_{t-i}. \tag{3.18}$$

Thus X_t is an infinite-order weighted average of the present and past innovations. It follows that ε_t and $X_{t-\tau}$ are uncorrelated whenever τ is positive. The auto-covariances of the AR(1) process are given by multiplying both sides of equation (3.15) by $X_{t-\tau} - \mu$, followed by taking expectations, to give

$$\lambda_\tau = \phi \lambda_{\tau-1} + E[\varepsilon_t(X_{t-\tau} - \mu)] = \phi \lambda_{\tau-1} = \phi^\tau \lambda_0, \quad \tau \geqslant 1,$$

from which the autocorrelations are as stated above in equation (3.16).

The optimal linear forecast of X_{t+N}, made at time t, is given by

$$f_{t,N} = \mu + \phi^N (X_t - \mu). \tag{3.19}$$

This can be deduced from the more general result proved soon for the ARMA(1, 1) process.

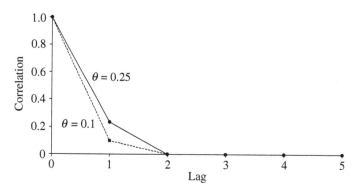

Figure 3.4. Examples of MA(1) autocorrelations.

3.5.2   *MA*(1)

Second, consider a process $\{X_t\}$ defined by

$$X_t = \mu + \varepsilon_t + \theta\varepsilon_{t-1}. \tag{3.20}$$

Now X_t is a linear function of the present and previous innovations. The process $\{X_t\}$ is called a *moving-average* process of order one, summarized by MA(1). The process is always stationary. It will be assumed that the moving-average parameter θ satisfies the invertibility condition $|\theta| < 1$ and then optimal linear forecasts can be calculated. The other two parameters of an MA(1) process are its mean, $\mu = E[X_t]$, and variance, $\lambda_0 = \text{var}(X_t) = (1 + \theta^2)\sigma_\varepsilon^2$.

The autocovariances of an MA(1) process are

$$\lambda_\tau = \text{cov}(X_t, X_{t+\tau}) = E[(\varepsilon_t + \theta\varepsilon_{t-1})(\varepsilon_{t+\tau} + \theta\varepsilon_{t+\tau-1})],$$

which are zero whenever $\tau > 1$, while $\lambda_1 = \theta\sigma_\varepsilon^2$. An MA(1) process thus has autocorrelations

$$\rho_1 = \frac{\theta}{1 + \theta^2}, \quad \rho_\tau = 0 \quad \text{for } \tau \geqslant 2. \tag{3.21}$$

The jump to zero autocorrelation at lags two and higher contrasts with the geometric decay of AR(1) autocorrelations. Figure 3.4 shows the autocorrelations when θ is either 0.1 or 0.25. The optimal linear forecasts are given by

$$f_{t,1} = \mu + \theta(X_t - f_{t-1,1}) \quad \text{and} \quad f_{t,N} = \mu, \quad N \geqslant 2. \tag{3.22}$$

Returns from stock indices are an example of a process that has often been modeled as MA(1) with θ a small positive number. Higher levels of dependence occur for "returns" that are calculated from the monthly average of daily prices. Following Working (1960), a typical model for "returns" is then MA(1) with $\theta = 0.25$. Figure 3.5 shows a series of "returns" simulated from this process, with Gaussian innovations, for 100 consecutive days.

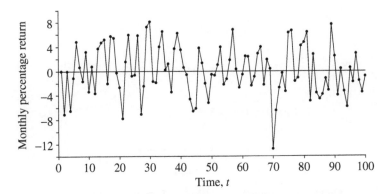

Figure 3.5. Observations from an MA(1) process.

3.5.3 ARMA(1, 1)

Third, consider the combination of the AR(1) and MA(1) models defined by

$$X_t - \mu = \phi(X_{t-1} - \mu) + \varepsilon_t + \theta\varepsilon_{t-1}. \tag{3.23}$$

This mixed model is an autoregressive, moving-average process, which we refer to as ARMA(1, 1). It has often been used to model returns and specific examples are given in Section 3.6. Squared returns have also been modeled by ARMA(1, 1) processes, for example, when returns follow the GARCH(1, 1) model described in Section 9.3.

It is assumed that $0 < |\phi| < 1$, $0 < |\theta| < 1$, and $\phi + \theta \neq 0$, so that $\{X_t\}$ is stationary, invertible and not white noise. Once more the mean is μ. It is shown later in this subsection that the variance and the autocorrelations are given by

$$\lambda_0 = \frac{1 + 2\phi\theta + \theta^2}{1 - \phi^2}\sigma_\varepsilon^2, \tag{3.24}$$

$$\rho_\tau = A(\phi, \theta)\phi^\tau, \quad \tau \geqslant 1, \tag{3.25}$$

with

$$A(\phi, \theta) = \frac{(1 + \phi\theta)(\phi + \theta)}{\phi(1 + 2\phi\theta + \theta^2)}, \tag{3.26}$$

assuming $\phi \neq 0$. Like an AR(1) process, the autocorrelations at positive lags form a geometric progression, with $\rho_{\tau+1} = \phi\rho_\tau$ when $\tau \geqslant 1$. However, unlike AR(1), the ARMA(1, 1) process has $\rho_1 \neq \phi$ when $\theta \neq 0$. When ϕ is positive and θ is negative it is possible for ρ_1 to be very small compared with ϕ.

Figure 3.6 displays two sets of autocorrelations when ϕ is near one and $\phi + \theta$ is near zero, specifically for the parameter pairs $(0.99, -0.95)$ and $(0.9, -0.8)$. The former pair has been used to produce Figure 3.7, which shows a simulation of squared percentage returns obtained from the GARCH(1, 1) process. Volatility clustering effects are clearly visible. The ARMA(1, 1) specification for the

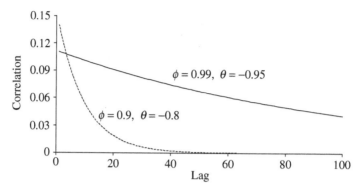

Figure 3.6. Examples of ARMA(1, 1) autocorrelations.

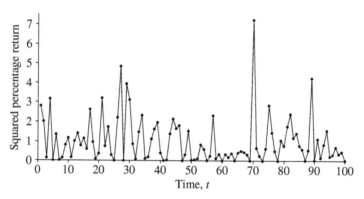

Figure 3.7. Observations from an ARMA(1, 1) process.

squared terms is given later, by equation (9.16); the innovations are white noise, but they are not i.i.d.

Sometimes we wish to recover the moving-average parameter θ when we are told the values of A and ϕ. From (3.26), this requires a solution of the quadratic equation

$$\theta^2 + \left[\frac{1 + (1 - 2A)\phi^2}{(1 - A)\phi}\right]\theta + 1 = 0. \tag{3.27}$$

When $\phi > 0$, there is a unique solution within the interval $[-\phi, 0]$, while for $\phi < 0$ it is within $[0, -\phi]$, in both cases assuming $0 < A < 1$.

The ARMA(1, 1) process can be rewritten using the lag operator as

$$(1 - \phi L)(X_t - \mu) = (1 + \theta L)\varepsilon_t.$$

An infinite-order moving-average model is given by

$$X_t - \mu = \frac{1 + \theta L}{1 - \phi L}\varepsilon_t = \left(\sum_{i=0}^{\infty}\phi^i L^i\right)(1 + \theta L)\varepsilon_t = \varepsilon_t + (\phi + \theta)\sum_{i=1}^{\infty}\phi^{i-1}\varepsilon_{t-i}, \tag{3.28}$$

from which the formula for the variance of X_t follows. Likewise, an infinite-order autoregressive model is given by

$$\varepsilon_t = \frac{1 - \phi L}{1 + \theta L}(X_t - \mu) = (1 - \phi L)\sum_{i=0}^{\infty}(-\theta L)^i(X_t - \mu),$$

which simplifies to

$$X_t - \mu = (\phi + \theta)\sum_{i=1}^{\infty}(-\theta)^{i-1}(X_{t-i} - \mu) + \varepsilon_t. \qquad (3.29)$$

To obtain the autocorrelations, note from (3.28) that any product $(X_{t-\tau} - \mu)\varepsilon_{t-j}$ has zero expectation if time $t - \tau$ is before time $t - j$, i.e. $\tau > j$. Then consider multiplying both sides of (3.23) by $X_{t-\tau} - \mu$ and taking expectations. When $\tau \geqslant 2$, this gives $\lambda_\tau = \phi\lambda_{\tau-1}$, while $\tau = 1$ and $\tau = 0$ respectively give

$$\lambda_1 = \phi\lambda_0 + \theta\sigma_\varepsilon^2 \quad \text{and} \quad \lambda_0 = \phi\lambda_1 + (1 + \phi\theta + \theta^2)\sigma_\varepsilon^2,$$

again making use of (3.28). Eliminating σ_ε^2 from these simultaneous equations gives ρ_1, and then ρ_2, ρ_3, etc., follow from $\rho_2 = \phi\rho_1$, $\rho_3 = \phi\rho_2$, etc.

All forecasts of X_{t+1}, chosen from linear combinations of X_t, $X_{t-1}, \ldots$, must have mean square error at least equal to the variance of the innovation ε_{t+1}. This lower bound is attained by replacing t by $t + 1$ in (3.29) and then substituting zero for ε_{t+1}. The optimal linear forecast of X_{t+1} is thus

$$f_{t,1} = \mu + (\phi + \theta)\sum_{i=1}^{\infty}(-\theta)^{i-1}(X_{t+1-i} - \mu). \qquad (3.30)$$

This forecast is a linear combination of the most recent variable and the forecast made one period earlier:

$$f_{t,1} = \mu + (\phi + \theta)(X_t - \mu) - \theta(f_{t-1,1} - \mu). \qquad (3.31)$$

This formula is a statement about the best linear forecast for a random variable. To forecast observed values we replace the parameters μ, ϕ, and θ by estimates and replace the random variables X_t and $f_{t-1,1}$ respectively by an observed value and the previous observed forecast.

To forecast an ARMA$(1, 1)$ process further ahead, consider the following equation obtained by repeatedly using the definition (3.23):

$$X_{t+N} - \mu = \phi^{N-1}(X_{t+1} - \mu) + \sum_{i=1}^{N}c_i\varepsilon_{t+i}, \quad N > 1,$$

with each constant c_i a function of ϕ, θ, and N. As the optimal linear forecast of ε_{t+i} ($i > 0$) using variables X_{t-j} ($j \geqslant 0$) is zero, it follows that the optimal linear forecast of X_{t+N} made at time t is a linear function of $f_{t,1}$. Denoting this optimal forecast by $f_{t,N}$, it is

$$f_{t,N} = \mu + \phi^{N-1}(f_{t,1} - \mu).$$ (3.32)

The optimal linear forecasts for AR(1) and MA(1) processes can be deduced from (3.31) and (3.32) by respectively substituting $\theta = 0$ and $\phi = 0$.

3.5.4 ARMA(p, q)

General ARMA processes contain p autoregressive and q moving-average parameters. When p and q are both positive, we have the general mixed model,

$$X_t - \mu = \sum_{i=1}^{p} \phi_i(X_{t-i} - \mu) + \sum_{j=0}^{q} \theta_j \varepsilon_{t-j},$$ (3.33)

with $\theta_0 = 1$, $\phi_p \neq 0$, $\theta_q \neq 0$. The AR(p) model is the special case that has $q = 0$. Likewise, the MA(q) model has $p = 0$ and omits the first sum. When $p = q = 0$, the model is merely a constant plus white noise and can then be referred to as MA(0).

The ARMA(p, q) process is stationary if all the solutions of $\phi_1 z + \phi_2 z^2 + \cdots + \phi_p z^p = 1$ are outside the unit circle, $|z| = 1$, z here representing a complex number. The process is said to be *invertible* if optimal linear forecasts can be obtained, which requires all solutions of $1 + \theta_1 z + \theta_2 z^2 + \cdots + \theta_q z^q = 0$ to also be outside the unit circle. Box, Jenkins, and Reinsel (1994) describe the pioneering Box–Jenkins methodology for selecting an appropriate ARMA model. These models have been used to describe many economic and financial time series (see, for example, Granger and Newbold 1986; Mills 1999; Tsay 2002). Most models fitted to data have $p + q \leqslant 2$, as in the three examples we have discussed.

3.5.5 Aggregation of Models

The sum of two independent ARMA processes is also an ARMA process. An example that often occurs in this book is given by the sum of an AR(1) process and an MA(0) process, say

$$Z_t = X_t + Y_t,$$

with

$$(1 - \phi L)(X_t - \mu_X) = \varepsilon_t \quad \text{and} \quad Y_t = \mu_Y + \eta_t.$$

Then

$$(1 - \phi L)(Z_t - (\mu_X + \mu_Y)) = \varepsilon_t + (1 - \phi L)\eta_t,$$

which suggests that $\{Z_t\}$ is an ARMA(1, 1) process, with autoregressive parameter ϕ. By adding the autocovariances of the X- and Y-processes, it can be checked that the autocovariances of the Z-process are indeed those of an ARMA(1, 1) process. The term A in equation (3.26) equals $\text{var}(X_t)/\text{var}(Z_t)$ and hence the moving-average parameter θ can be obtained from (3.27). Further algebra establishes that the terms $\{\xi_t\}$ defined by

$$(1 - \phi L)(Z_t - (\mu_X + \mu_Y)) = (1 + \theta L)\xi_t$$

form a white noise process as expected.

Likewise, it can be shown that the sum of two independent AR(1) processes is an ARMA(2, 1) process when the two autoregressive parameters are different. The most general result is shown in Granger and Newbold (1986) as

$$\text{ARMA}(p_1, q_1) + \text{ARMA}(p_2, q_2) = \text{ARMA}(p, q) \qquad (3.34)$$

with

$$p \leqslant p_1 + p_2 \quad \text{and} \quad q \leqslant \max(p_1 + q_2, p_2 + q_1).$$

Also, the inequalities can be replaced by equalities for most parameter configurations.

3.5.6 *Aggregation through Time*

The autocorrelations of multi-period returns are functions of the autocorrelations of single-period returns. Suppose the j-period sum process is defined by

$$Y_t = X_{j(t-1)+1} + \cdots + X_{jt}.$$

Then the first-lag autocorrelation of $\{Y_t\}$, denoted by $\rho_1^{(j)}$, can be shown to equal the following nonlinear function of the first $2j - 1$ autocorrelations of $\{X_t\}$, denoted by ρ_τ:

$$\rho_1^{(j)} = \frac{\sum_{\tau=1}^{j} \tau\rho_\tau + \sum_{\tau=j+1}^{2j-1} (2j - \tau)\rho_\tau}{j + 2\sum_{\tau=1}^{j-1}(j - \tau)\rho_\tau}. \qquad (3.35)$$

When $\{X_t\}$ is an ARMA(1, 1) process for which $\rho_\tau = A\phi^\tau$, firstly the above expression equals

$$\rho_1^{(j)} = \frac{A\phi(1 - \phi^j)^2}{j(1 - \phi)^2 + 2A\phi[j(1 - \phi) - 1 + \phi^j]} \qquad (3.36)$$

and secondly the higher lag autocorrelations of $\{Y_t\}$ are

$$\rho_\tau^{(j)} = \rho_1^{(j)}\phi^{j(\tau-1)}, \quad \tau > 1.$$

Hence $\{Y_t\}$ is itself an ARMA(1, 1) process, with autoregressive parameter ϕ^j.

3.6   Examples of ARMA(1, 1) Specifications

We may anticipate from the aggregation results that autoregressive and moving-average terms will appear in models defined by the sum of variables that follow simpler models. In particular, ARMA(1, 1) processes for returns have been motivated by supposing the returns process is the sum of two independent processes, one of which is white noise. The autocorrelations of the sum can then be either positive or negative, depending on the assumptions that define the returns process.

3.6.1   A Negative Autocorrelation Example

Negative dependence among returns occurs in the models investigated by Fama and French (1988) and Poterba and Summers (1988). Market prices P_t are supposed to differ from rational (or correct or fundamental) prices P_t^* by temporary pricing errors. The error terms u_t are defined by

$$\log(P_t) = \log(P_t^*) + u_t \tag{3.37}$$

and then

$$R_t = R_t^* + u_t - u_{t-1} \tag{3.38}$$

for terms R_t and R_t^* that respectively represent market and rational returns. The first component of the market return is the rational response to fundamental information given by R_t^*, which is assumed to be white noise from the theory of efficient markets. The second component is $u_t - u_{t-1}$. Assuming pricing errors are only temporary, it is plausible to assume that the process $\{u_t\}$ is AR(1) with a positive autoregressive parameter ϕ. The first differences of an AR(1) process are an ARMA(1, 1) process, with autoregressive and moving-average parameters respectively equal to ϕ and -1. Therefore, the returns process is the sum of an ARMA(1, 1) process and independent white noise, which is also ARMA(1, 1) from the aggregation result stated in equation (3.34).

The autocorrelations of returns depend on the proportion of returns variance that is due to incorrectly interpreted information, namely

$$B = \frac{\text{var}(u_t - u_{t-1})}{\text{var}(R_t)} = \frac{2(1 - \phi)\,\text{var}(u_t)}{\text{var}(R_t)}, \tag{3.39}$$

and on the persistence of the errors, measured by $\phi = \text{cor}(u_t, u_{t+1})$. As

$$\text{cov}(R_t, R_{t+\tau}) = \text{cov}(u_t - u_{t-1}, u_{t+\tau} - u_{t+\tau-1})$$
$$= \phi^{\tau-1}(2\phi - 1 - \phi^2)\,\text{var}(u_t) \quad \text{for all } \tau > 0,$$

these return autocorrelations are

$$\rho_\tau = A\phi^\tau, \quad \tau \geqslant 1, \tag{3.40}$$

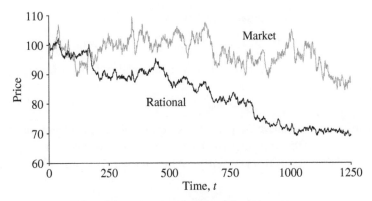

Figure 3.8. Simulated market and rational prices.

with

$$A = -\frac{(1 - \phi)B}{2\phi}. \tag{3.41}$$

As B and ϕ are positive, A must be negative and hence positive persistence of the pricing errors implies negative autocorrelation at all nonzero lags.

An extreme example is given by supposing $B = 0.75$ and $\phi = 0.998$, so that most of the returns variance is due to very slowly corrected pricing errors. With t counting trading days, the first autocorrelation of daily returns is tiny at -0.0008. However, the first autocorrelation is then substantial for long-horizon returns and equals -0.24 for returns measured over three years (using equation (3.36) with $j = 750$), which is near to an empirical estimate in Fama and French (1988). Figure 3.8 shows a series of simulated daily values of P_t and P_t^* for a five-year period. The market prices are far above the rational prices for a long time during this simulation, although the pricing error is certain to change sign at some later time.

3.6.2 A Positive Autocorrelation Example

A simpler model for returns, which possesses positive dependence, is given by separating returns R_t into a "trend" component T_t and an independent white noise component ε_t (Taylor 1982a). The trend term is persistent and it represents either time-varying expectations or the market's response to slowly interpreted information. Then

$$R_t = T_t + \varepsilon_t \tag{3.42}$$

and the proportion of the returns variance that is now explained by the persistent component equals

$$A = \frac{\text{var}(T_t)}{\text{var}(R_t)}. \tag{3.43}$$

The simplest credible model for $\{T_t\}$ is an AR(1) process with a positive autoregressive parameter ϕ. The sum of the AR(1) and white noise components is an

ARMA(1, 1) process, from equation (3.34). As

$$\text{cov}(R_t, R_{t+\tau}) = \text{cov}(T_t, T_{t+\tau}) \quad \text{for all } \tau \neq 0,$$

the autocorrelations of returns have the same mathematical form as for the previous model, namely

$$\rho_\tau = A\phi^\tau, \quad \tau \geqslant 1. \tag{3.44}$$

Now, however, A is positive. A plausible example of the parameter values is $A = 0.02$ and $\phi = 0.95$. The theoretical autocorrelations are then near empirical estimates for daily returns from currency futures in the 1970s and 1980s (Taylor 1994b).

3.7 ARIMA Processes

The acronym ARIMA(p, 1, q) is used for a process $\{X_t\}$ when it is nonstationary but its first differences, $X_t - X_{t-1}$, follow a stationary ARMA(p, q) process, defined by equation (3.33). The additional letter "I" states that the process $\{X_t\}$ is *integrated*, while the numeral "1" indicates that only one application of differencing is required to achieve stationarity.

For example, the pure I(1) process with $p = q = 0$ might be considered for the logarithm of prices, $X_t = \log(P_t)$. Then the first differences are returns, when there are no dividends, and they are simply a constant plus a white noise process:

$$X_t - X_{t-1} = \mu + \varepsilon_t. \tag{3.45}$$

This process for the log-price has a *random walk* property, a concept that is defined more precisely in Section 5.2.

3.8 ARFIMA Processes

For each of our ARMA and ARIMA examples there is a *filter* that transforms the process $\{X_t\}$ into a constant plus a white noise process. For the AR(1), MA(1), and I(1) processes these filters are respectively $1 - \phi L$, $(1 - \theta L)^{-1}$ and $1 - L$ respectively, with L the lag operator that was introduced after equation (3.16).

Fractional integration is a property of stochastic processes that employ a more complicated filter, namely $(1 - L)^d$ for some number d that is not an integer; typically, d is between zero and one. Applications of the fractional filter are difficult. They are referred to in a few sections of this book and are particularly interesting when modeling volatility. Readers who wish to concentrate on simpler models should skip the remainder of this section.

The fractional filter is derived in Granger (1980) as a particular limit of an infinite sum of AR(1) processes that have different AR parameters. This limit is related to volatility dynamics and information flows by Andersen and Bollerslev (1997a). The filter uses only one parameter to efficiently capture some features of empirical data. It is defined by an infinite series expansion that commences with the terms $1 - dL + \frac{1}{2}d(d-1)L^2 - \cdots$.

An ARMA(p, q) process can be described compactly by the equation

$$\phi(L)(X_t - \mu) = \theta(L)\varepsilon_t,$$

where the filters $\phi(L)$ and $\theta(L)$ are polynomials, respectively of orders p and q. The ARFIMA(p, d, q) process of Granger and Joyeux (1980) and Hosking (1981) also contains the fractional filter. When this process is stationary, with mean zero, we can write it as

$$(1 - L)^d \phi(L) X_t = \theta(L)\varepsilon_t, \tag{3.46}$$

while for a general stationary mean μ a precise definition is

$$X_t = \mu + (1 - L)^{-d} \phi(L)^{-1} \theta(L)\varepsilon_t. \tag{3.47}$$

This ARFIMA process is stationary when $d < 0.5$. Assuming d is positive, it is a special case of a *long memory* process. For an excellent review of long memory processes, see Baillie (1996).

There are three essential differences between a stationary ARMA process and a stationary ARFIMA process that has $0 < d < 0.5$. These are stated for the sum of the first n autocorrelations, the n-period variance ratio and the spectral density function, defined by

$$S_n = \sum_{\tau=1}^{n} \rho_\tau, \quad \mathrm{VR}_n = \frac{\mathrm{var}(X_t + \cdots + X_{t+n-1})}{n \, \mathrm{var}(X_t)} = 1 + 2 \sum_{\tau=1}^{n-1} \frac{n - \tau}{n} \rho_\tau, \tag{3.48}$$

and

$$s(\omega) = \frac{\mathrm{var}(X_t)}{2\pi} \left[1 + 2 \sum_{\tau=1}^{\infty} \rho_\tau \cos(\tau\omega) \right].$$

For a stationary ARMA process, the autocorrelations are geometrically bounded (so that $|\rho_\tau| \leqslant C\psi^\tau$ for some $C > 0$ and $1 > \psi > 0$), which ensures the following limiting behavior:

$$S_n \to C_1, \quad \mathrm{VR}_n \to C_2, \quad s(\omega) \to C_3, \quad \text{as } n \to \infty, \ \omega \to 0, \tag{3.49}$$

for constants C_1, C_2, C_3. In contrast, none of these limits exists for a stationary ARFIMA process. Instead, the autocorrelations have a hyperbolic decay rate, the variance ratio increases without limit, and the spectral density is unbounded for low frequencies. Specifically,

$$\frac{\rho_\tau}{\tau^{2d-1}} \to D_1, \quad \frac{\mathrm{VR}_n}{n^{2d}} \to D_2, \quad \frac{s(\omega)}{\omega^{-2d}} \to D_3, \quad \text{as } n \to \infty, \ \omega \to 0, \tag{3.50}$$

for positive constants D_1, D_2, D_3.

3.9   Linear Stochastic Processes

3.9.1   Definition

Any stationary ARMA process equals a constant plus a moving average of white
noise innovations $\{\varepsilon_t\}$, perhaps of infinite order. Equations (3.18) and (3.28) are
examples that show AR(1) and ARMA(1, 1) processes can be represented by
MA(∞) processes. In general, a stationary process always has a representation

$$X_t = \mu + \sum_{j=0}^{\infty} \theta_j \varepsilon_{t-j} \tag{3.51}$$

for some set of constants θ_j and some white noise process $\{\varepsilon_t\}$. The innovations
will be uncorrelated, but they may not be independent variables. There will be a
representation (3.51) for a stationary process if the X_t have identical distributions
and do not contain a deterministic component (Granger and Newbold 1986).

Equation (3.51) is a statement that X_t is a linear function of the uncorrelated
variables $\{\varepsilon_{t-j}, j \geqslant 0\}$. Following statistical convention, this property of the
process $\{X_t\}$ is not sufficient to call the process linear. The reason is that a process
can be *both* a nonlinear function of i.i.d. variables *and* a linear function of white
noise variables; the ARCH(1) model of equation (3.11) defines a simple example.
The convention is to call such a process nonlinear because i.i.d. variables are
the preferred building blocks when constructing models with interdependence
between variables.

A process $\{X_t\}$ is defined to be *linear* if it can be described by (3.51) with
zero-mean innovations $\{\varepsilon_t\}$ that are i.i.d. Any process which is not linear is called
nonlinear. A stationary, Gaussian process is linear. Also, a linear process is strictly
stationary.

The variance of a linear, invertible, ARMA process, conditional upon its past,
is a constant:

$$\mathrm{var}(X_t \mid X_{t-1}, X_{t-2}, \dots) = \mathrm{var}(\varepsilon_t).$$

Constant conditional variance is arguably the fundamental property that is *not*
possessed by the process that generates returns. Periods of high price volatility
and other periods of low price volatility oblige us to discard the idea of constant
conditional variance and so we should expect satisfactory models to be nonlinear.

3.9.2   Autocorrelation Tests

The distinctions between white noise and zero-mean i.i.d. variables, and between
linear and nonlinear processes, are extremely important for finance research. One
important context is when sample autocorrelations are used to test the hypothesis
that returns are uncorrelated through time.

A time series of n returns can be used to estimate the autocorrelations ρ_τ of
the process generating the observations, assuming the process is stationary. These

estimates can be interpreted as the realized values of random variables, denoted by $\hat{\rho}_\tau$. To perform random walk tests it is necessary to apply results about the distributions of the variables $\hat{\rho}_\tau$. Asymptotic results are known for large samples of returns generated by a *linear* process. For the special hypothesis that returns have independent and identical finite-variance distributions, the distribution of $\sqrt{n}\hat{\rho}_\tau$ converges to $N(0, 1)$ as $n \to \infty$ and thus the variance of $\hat{\rho}_\tau$ is approximately $1/n$ (Anderson and Walker 1964). The conclusion about the variance of $\hat{\rho}_\tau$ is generally false for a nonlinear, white noise process (Taylor 1984). Such processes can have a higher variance for $\hat{\rho}_\tau$. This means that if the sample autocorrelations of returns are judged to be significantly different from zero, by supposing their standard errors are $1/\sqrt{n}$, then it is wrong to reject the hypothesis that returns are uncorrelated using the same significance level.

3.10 Continuous-Time Stochastic Processes

Theoretical prices for options and other derivative securities are usually derived from stochastic processes defined for all times t on a continuous scale. Two important examples are introduced here, while more complicated processes are described in Chapters 13 and 14.

A *Wiener* process $\{W(t)\}$ commences at $W(0) = 0$. All of its increments have normal distributions. Whenever time t is after time s, the increment $W(t) - W(s)$ has a normal distribution, with mean zero and variance equal to the time difference $t - s$. Furthermore, increments over nonoverlapping time intervals are independent random variables. Thus, if $t_1 < t_2 \leqslant t_3 < t_4$, then $W(t_2) - W(t_1)$ is independent of $W(t_4) - W(t_3)$. The stochastic differential dW is a quantity which appears in continuous-time analysis. It is defined by the stochastic integral $W(T) = \int dW(s)$, with limits $s = 0$ and $s = T$.

A *geometric Brownian motion* process $\{P(t)\}$ is often represented by the cryptic equation

$$dP/P = \mu\, dt + \sigma\, dW.$$

This equation describes the price process assumed in derivations of the Black–Scholes and related option pricing formulae. Itô's lemma, which is a stochastic calculus theorem, yields an equivalent equation for the process followed by the logarithm of $P(t)$:

$$d(\log P) = (\mu - \tfrac{1}{2}\sigma^2)\, dt + \sigma\, dW.$$

Integrating all terms from time zero until time t gives

$$\log P(t) = \log P(0) + (\mu - \tfrac{1}{2}\sigma^2)t + \sigma W(t).$$

Therefore, the change in the logarithm of the price from time s until a later time t has a normal distribution, with both the mean and the variance proportional to the time difference $t - s$:

$$\log(P(t)) - \log(P(s)) \sim N((\mu - \tfrac{1}{2}\sigma^2)(t - s), \sigma^2(t - s)). \qquad (3.52)$$

The discrete-time process defined by $X_t = \log P(t) - \log P(t - 1)$, for integers t, is i.i.d. and Gaussian. Thus geometric Brownian motion for prices implies that the logarithms of prices follow a random walk, with steps that have independent and identical normal distributions.

3.11   Notation for Random Variables and Observations

The distinction between random variables $X, Y, Z, \ldots$ and possible outcomes or observations $x, y, z, \ldots$ has been emphasized in this chapter by using uppercase letters for the former variables and lowercase letters for the latter variables. It is cumbersome to maintain this distinction and, consequently, it is now discarded. The notation r, for example, may now sometimes refer to an observed return and at other times it will refer to a random variable that models the probability distribution of a return. It should always be possible to infer from the context whether a symbol refers to a random variable or to an observation.

4

Stylized Facts for Financial Returns

Several statistical properties of daily returns are documented and discussed in this chapter, before testing hypotheses and estimating time-series models in later chapters. These properties are presented for the means, variances, distributions, and autocorrelations of returns by referring to empirical evidence obtained from many datasets, including the twenty time series introduced in Chapter 2. This chapter ends by emphasizing that linear stochastic processes cannot explain all the empirical properties of returns.

4.1 Introduction

General properties that are expected to be present in any set of returns are called stylized facts. There are three important properties that are found in almost all sets of daily returns obtained from a few years of prices. First, the distribution of returns is not normal. Second, there is almost no correlation between returns for different days. Third, the correlations between the magnitudes of returns on nearby days are positive and statistically significant. These properties can all be explained by changes through time in volatility, as will be seen in Chapters 8–11. This chapter also covers many other statistical characteristics of daily returns. Those readers who only wish to learn about the stylized facts will find them discussed in Sections 4.7, 4.9, and 4.10.

Incidentally, the three major stylized facts are pervasive across time as well as across markets. They are apparent in daily returns at the Florentine currency market from 1389 to 1432 (Booth and Gurun 2004), the London market for stocks from 1724 to 1740 (Harrison 1998), and the London fixed-income market from 1821 to 1860 (Mitchell, Brown, and Easton 2002).

The first part of this chapter is about features of the distribution of returns. After defining summary statistics in Section 4.2, the empirical means and standard deviations of returns are discussed in Sections 4.3 and 4.4. Average returns have also been estimated for calendar periods, such as all Mondays and all days in January. Calendar anomalies are generally ignored in this book after the detailed review provided in Section 4.5.

Some information about the shape of the distribution of returns is given by the skewness and kurtosis statistics that are discussed in Section 4.6. Comparisons with the normal shape in Section 4.7 show that the distribution of daily returns has more observations near the mean and more in the tails than are expected from a normal distribution. A survey of more appropriate distributions is given in Section 4.8.

The second part of the chapter summarizes the dependence between returns on different days by autocorrelation statistics. The estimates for returns r_t are important because they help to show that it is difficult to predict future returns using a linear combination of previous returns. These correlation estimates are discussed in Section 4.9. More striking results, however, are obtained in Section 4.10 by considering autocorrelations for transformed data, such as absolute returns $|r_t|$. The correlation estimates are then positive and often fairly substantial for absolute returns separated by a few days. Returns are therefore dependent on the returns obtained on previous days, but the form of the dependence is not linear. Any satisfactory model for returns must be a nonlinear stochastic process, as is shown in Section 4.11.

4.2 Summary Statistics

The statistical characteristics of the distribution of a set of returns can be summarized by numbers such as their mean ($\bar{r}$), standard deviation (s), skewness (b), and kurtosis (k). These statistics are defined for a set of n returns $\{r_1, r_2, \ldots, r_n\}$ by

$$\bar{r} = \frac{1}{n}\sum_{t=1}^{n} r_t, \qquad\qquad s^2 = \frac{1}{n-1}\sum_{t=1}^{n}(r_t - \bar{r})^2,$$
$$b = \frac{1}{n-1}\sum_{t=1}^{n}\frac{(r_t - \bar{r})^3}{s^3}, \qquad\qquad k = \frac{1}{n-1}\sum_{t=1}^{n}\frac{(r_t - \bar{r})^4}{s^4}. \tag{4.1}$$

These summary statistics are presented in Table 4.1 for the twenty time series of daily returns introduced in Section 2.6. The table also includes the minimum and maximum returns, three columns that refer to annual returns, and a column that contains the test statistic

$$z = \frac{\bar{r}}{s/\sqrt{n}}.$$

The z-statistic is used to assess the null hypothesis that the expected return is zero.

Several statistics discussed in this chapter are sensitive to extreme outliers in the returns data. The stock return series include such outliers around the crash on 19 October 1987. Consequently, all the returns in the week of the crash are excluded from the calculations of the skewness and kurtosis statistics shown in Table 4.1. The minimum stock returns all occur on either Monday 19th or Tuesday

Table 4.1. Summary statistics for time series of returns.

Series		$10^4\bar{r}$	$10^2 s$	b	k	$G\%$	$A\%$	$A^*\%$	z
S&P 500-share	S	6.42	0.98	−0.67	10.44	17.62	19.23	19.05	3.30
S&P 500-share	F	3.60	1.35	−0.55	10.10	9.53	10.85	12.08	1.34
Coca Cola	S	11.67	1.69	0.08	5.68	34.33	36.89	39.30	3.46
General Electric	S	7.42	1.51	0.03	5.43	20.65	22.35	24.17	2.48
General Motors	S	5.58	1.76	0.13	4.56	15.16	17.45	19.77	1.59
FT 100-share	S	3.60	0.97	−0.19	5.94	9.55	10.47	10.86	1.87
FT 100-share	F	1.44	1.12	−0.23	5.79	3.72	4.52	5.38	0.65
Glaxo	S	14.73	1.79	0.33	6.93	45.15	54.30	51.16	4.14
Marks & Spencer	S	7.25	1.66	0.03	4.40	20.14	23.30	24.39	2.20
Shell	S	7.63	1.30	0.23	5.18	21.29	23.14	23.91	2.95
Nikkei 225-share	S	2.17	1.33	0.35	10.14	5.50	8.75	7.82	0.81
Treasury bonds	F	2.73	0.78	0.09	4.61	7.14	7.65	7.97	1.75
3-month sterling bills	F	−0.52	0.16	2.29	59.84	−1.31	−1.28	−1.28	−1.64
DM/$	F	0.21	0.74	0.27	5.19	0.53	1.61	1.23	0.14
Sterling/$	F	0.60	0.76	0.28	5.71	1.53	3.13	2.27	0.40
Swiss franc/$	F	−0.54	0.82	0.22	4.57	−1.35	0.14	−0.52	−0.33
Yen/$	F	0.85	0.68	0.37	6.66	2.18	3.24	2.78	0.63
Gold	F	−5.35	1.33	−0.06	6.70	−12.63	−10.96	−10.66	−2.02
Corn	F	−3.99	1.20	−0.14	6.36	−9.59	−6.98	−7.92	−1.66
Live cattle	F	2.87	0.99	−0.13	3.37	7.52	8.79	8.87	1.45

S and F respectively indicate spot and futures returns. The sample sizes n are between 2460 and 2560 and are listed in Table 2.2. $\bar{r}$, s, b, and k are the mean, standard deviation, skewness, and kurtosis for a sample of returns, as defined in Section 4.2. The crash week, commencing on Sunday, 18 October 1987, is excluded when the stock skewness and kurtosis figures are calculated. $z = \sqrt{n}\,\bar{r}/s$. The average annual return estimates G, A, and A^* are defined in Section 4.3.

20th of the crash week and a majority of the maximum returns occur on Wednesday 21st.

4.3 Average Returns and Risk Premia

4.3.1 Annual Averages

The average return $\bar{r}$ over one day is, of course, very small and it is often more practical to discuss averages over longer periods, particularly one year. Three annual average measures are listed in Table 4.1 under the headings G, A, and A^*.

To motivate these measures, we represent the wealth of a typical investor by w_t at time t, with $w_t = w_{t-1}\exp(r_t)$. This is appropriate if an investor reinvests dividends and so holds a quantity q_t of the asset defined recursively by $q_t = q_{t-1}(1 + d_t/p_t)$, with d_t the dividend paid out in period t (usually zero) and p_t the price of one unit of the asset. Then $w_t = q_t p_t$. The quantities p_t and w_t will be identical when an asset never pays a dividend and $q_0 = 1$.

Suppose a time series provides returns for T years with $N = n/T$ return observations per year, on average. The constant annual return G that gives the same overall return solves

$$(1 + G)^T = \frac{w_n}{w_0}$$

with w_0 and w_n respectively the initial and final levels of wealth. Note that the average return can be calculated directly from these levels, as

$$\bar{r} = \frac{1}{n}[\log(w_n) - \log(w_0)]$$

and thus

$$G = \exp(N\bar{r}) - 1. \tag{4.2}$$

Investors will also be interested in the annual expected return during a future year, say from time n until time $n + N$. The simple annual return is then

$$R = \frac{w_{n+N} - w_n}{w_n} = \exp\left(\sum_{h=1}^{N} r_{n+h}\right) - 1.$$

One estimate of $E[R]$ is given by averaging simple annual returns, here denoted by $r^{(j)}$. For an integer value of T, the obvious estimate of $E[R]$ is the arithmetic mean

$$A = \frac{1}{T}\sum_{j=1}^{T}\frac{w_{Nj} - w_{N(j-1)}}{w_{N(j-1)}} = \frac{1}{T}\sum_{j=1}^{T} r^{(j)}. \tag{4.3}$$

Note that $1 + G$ is then the geometric mean of the T terms $1 + r^{(j)}$. This implies G is a downwards biased estimate of $E[R]$, because G is less than the arithmetic mean A, which is unbiased.

The sum of a year of N consecutive returns, $\sum r_{n+h}$, is approximately normal from a version of the central limit theorem, when the returns process is stationary and uncorrelated, say with mean μ and variance σ^2. The expected simple annual return is then

$$E[R] \cong \exp(N\mu + \tfrac{1}{2}N\sigma^2) - 1. \tag{4.4}$$

This approximation suggests estimating $E[R]$ by

$$A^* = \exp(N\bar{r} + \tfrac{1}{2}Ns^2) - 1 = (1 + G)\exp(\tfrac{1}{2}Ns^2) - 1. \tag{4.5}$$

This estimate has much less bias than G when the assumptions are valid. The estimate could be useful when $\bar{r}$ and s are known but the annual terms $r^{(j)}$ are not available. However, A^* could be seriously biased if the returns are autocorrelated, because then $\text{var}(\sum r_{n+h}) \neq N\sigma^2$.

Merton (1980) has shown that estimates of annual expected returns must be inaccurate because prices are too volatile to permit accurate estimates. To illustrate the problem, consider the estimate G when ten years of independent daily returns are generated by a normal distribution whose mean and standard deviation are given by the tabulated estimates for the spot S&P 500 index. Then

$\mu = 6.42 \times 10^{-4}$, $\sigma = 0.0098$ and $E[R] = 19\%$ for a year of 250 trading days. With a 95% probability, $250\bar{r}$ is within the interval 0.160 ± 0.096, and thus a 95% probability interval for $G = \exp(250\bar{r}) - 1$ is from 7% to 29%.

Table 4.1 shows the values for G, A, and A^* in percentage units. These figures underestimate average returns for the spot FTSE and Nikkei indices because dividends are excluded from the calculations. The "geometric mean return" G is typically 1–2% per annum less than the "arithmetic mean return" A. The S&P 500 spot returns should exceed the futures returns by a figure similar to the risk-free rate of interest, as capital is only required for spot investments. The actual difference is about 8% per annum. The FTSE 100 spot average should be greater than the futures figure by a risk-free interest rate minus the dividend yield. The actual difference is about 6%.

The z-statistics in the final column of Table 4.1 are for the standard test that returns have a zero population mean. Not surprisingly, several stock series have significant positive values of z, at the 5% level. The stock futures series do not have significant values, although theory states that the expected futures return is positive; it is reasonable to conclude that Type II errors are made. The other futures series have insignificant values of z, except for the gold series, and hence both $\bar{r}$ and G are not significantly different from zero.

4.3.2 Equity Risk Premia

The expected return from an investment in a market portfolio of stocks exceeds the return from riskless investments by an amount known as the equity risk premium. A positive premium is required by finance theory, otherwise there is no incentive to accept undiversifiable risk. The numbers discussed above show that accurate estimates of the equity risk premium require a long historical record and the optimistic assumption that the premium is constant. Estimates of the average premium only require the weaker assumption that the premium follows a stationary process.

Dimson, Marsh, and Staunton (2002) provide information about the equity risk premium for many countries during the twentieth century. A US geometric premium estimate of 6% is given by the difference between the geometric returns G for stocks and bills from 1900 to 2000, while the arithmetic premium estimate A from annual returns is 8%. The standard errors of these estimates are approximately 2%. The premia for many other countries were similar to the US level.

Historic premia estimates between 6% and 8% may well overestimate future expected premia, particularly if the estimates assume the market always survives (Jorion and Goetzmann 1999). Fama and French (2002) use US dividend and earnings growth rates from 1951 to 2000 to obtain premium estimates between 2.5% and 4.5%, compared with the historic estimate of 7% for the same period.

These numbers can be reconciled by saying that US stock returns were much higher than expected. In contrast, Ibbotson and Chen (2003) obtain estimates only 1% less than the historic average by considering several measures of financial and economic performance. Further estimates of rational premia derived from theoretical pricing models are provided by Arnott and Bernstein (2002) and Bansal and Lundblad (2002).

All the above equity premia estimates are only for domestic market portfolios. Other portfolios will have different premia that reflect their exposure to market-wide and other risk factors. The empirical evidence against single-factor capital asset pricing models (CAPMs) finds that firm size and book values relative to market values have either been important factors in the past or proxies for such factors. Cross-sectional asset pricing models are, however, outside the scope of this book. Interesting empirical results can be found in Fama and French (1992, 1995), Daniel and Titman (1997), and Ferguson and Shockley (2003) for the US, and in Fama and French (1998) and Hawawini and Keim (2000) for markets around the world.

4.3.3 Futures Risk Premia

Finance theory states that futures returns equal spot returns minus the risk-free rate when futures prices are determined by spot prices and a no-arbitrage condition (see Section 2.5). When premia are determined by a single-factor CAPM, the futures risk premium is the futures β multiplied by the market risk premium. Black (1976a), following Dusak (1973), developed the idea that β is zero for agricultural futures and hence these futures have zero risk premia and zero expected returns. A similar conclusion holds for currency futures as empirical estimates of β are close to zero (Taylor 1992). It is a mistake to extend Black's conclusion to stock index futures because they have positive β, usually close to one, and hence have expected returns similar to the equity risk premium.

Keynes (1930) and others have argued that producers of agricultural commodities are net sellers of futures, hence speculators are net buyers and can demand to be rewarded by a positive risk premium. Direct tests of this proposition have met with limited success. For example, Bodie and Rosansky (1980) estimate an average premium of 10% per annum (standard error 4%) for portfolios made up of long futures positions. However, their choice of years (1950–1976) may be fortuitous. Later studies have found almost no evidence for a positive premium in commodity futures (Kolb 1992; Bessembinder 1993). The generally small z-statistics in Table 4.1 are evidence against a constant, nonzero premium.

Any risk premium can vary through time. Furthermore, speculators are net buyers of futures at some times and net sellers at other times in the agricultural sector (Chang 1985). The general idea of time-varying risk premia (TVRP), that may average zero in the long run, has been developed for currency futures markets in particular. International asset-pricing models show there can be TVRP in theoretical models (Adler and Dumas 1983; Hodrick 1987). There is an extensive literature on this subject that has found little evidence for TVRP (Hodrick 1987; MacDonald 1988). We return to this subject in Section 7.10 when discussing payoffs from futures trading rules.

4.4 Standard Deviations

The numbers s in Table 4.1 are *unconditional* standard deviations. They provide information about the historical standard deviation of a daily return when nothing is known about the recent past. When recent returns are available we can try to calculate standard deviations conditional on the recent information. These *conditional* standard deviations vary considerably through time as we will see in Chapters 9–11. This phenomenon, known as conditional heteroskedasticity, can be sufficient to cause unconditional estimates to vary considerably from year to year. Estimates of daily standard deviations over periods as long as a decade can also vary from period to period, because of nonstationarity that may be attributed to structural changes in the economic environment.

The daily standard deviations in Table 4.1 are between 0.6% and 1.8%, with the exception of the very low value for bill futures. The column of standard deviations can be ranked to show that returns from currencies and bonds have the least variability, with equity indices more variable and the highest ranks going to the returns from individual stocks. Our figures and others given by Perry (1982), Kon (1984), Brown and Warner (1985), and Blair, Poon, and Taylor (2002) suggest that a large firm may have a standard deviation (s.d.) 50–100% larger than the s.d. for a well-diversified index. Furthermore, the average s.d. for randomly selected firms may be more than three times as large as the s.d. for an index. Hawawini and Keim (1995) show that US portfolios formed by allocating stocks to ten size categories have standard deviations that monotonically increase as the firm size decreases. The s.d. of monthly returns, from 1951 to 1989, was 4.1% for the portfolio of largest stocks, increasing to 6.8% for the portfolio of smallest stocks.

The possibility of a nonstationary variance over long periods of time makes it difficult to produce useful long-run estimates of price volatility. Table 4.2 offers some *approximate* ranges for daily and annual returns. The annual standard deviations are given by multiplying the daily figures by the square root of the number of trading days in one year, here assumed to be 253. This method requires daily returns to be uncorrelated.

These figures can be used to provide some insight into the range of possible payoffs from an annual investment. To do this, suppose daily returns are uncorrelated, that their standard deviation σ is the midpoint of some range above, and that their annual sum has a normal distribution with mean $N\mu$ and variance $N\sigma^2$. Also, suppose the expected simple annual return is known so μ can be deduced

Table 4.2. Typical standard deviations.

| | Percentage standard deviation | |
Asset	Daily returns	Annual returns
Currencies	0.6–0.9%	10–14%
Diversified stock index	0.7–1.3%	11–21%
Stock of a large US firm	1.2–2.0%	19–32%
Commodities	1.0–2.0%	16–32%

from equation (4.4). Then a \$1 investment will produce a payoff \$1 + R after one year that has a lognormal distribution, as $\log(1 + R) \sim N(N\mu, N\sigma^2)$. For spot currency offering an expected annual return of 5%, the payoff will be between \$0.83 and \$1.33 with a 95% probability. Similarly, a \$1 investment in a large firm that returns 12% per annum, on average, will provide a payoff between \$0.70 and \$1.79 with a 95% probability.

4.4.1 Futures

Spot and futures volatility should be very similar when a theoretical no-arbitrage condition ties the futures price to the spot price, as described by the equations in Section 2.5. The two volatility figures are identical, in theory, when price changes are uncorrelated and the real dividend yield is constant (Barone-Adesi and Whaley 1987). This result holds regardless of the final settlement date of the futures contract. It then follows that the standard deviation of futures returns is not a function of the time until delivery. However, Samuelson (1976) shows that when the spot price follows a stationary process (so spot price changes are correlated), then the futures standard deviation ought to increase as the delivery date comes closer. Taylor (1985) found no evidence to support the idea of increasing volatility during the final six trading months of currency and commodity futures contracts. Antoniou and Holmes (1994) report the same conclusion for FTSE 100 futures.

The no-arbitrage prediction of equal volatility is contradicted by the higher standard deviation of stock index futures returns compared with spot measurements for the same index. The numbers in Table 4.1 show the futures standard deviation is 38% higher than the spot figure for the decade of S&P 500 returns considered here, although the estimate falls to 25% if the crash week is excluded. The comparable FTSE 100 figure is an extra 15% for all the data, or 17% when the crash week is ignored. Board and Sutcliffe (1995) survey international evidence and discuss many possible explanations. A strong contender is an understatement of spot volatility due to stale prices being included in the spot index (Stoll and Whaley 1988). This argument is supported by the results in Ahn, Boudoukh, Richardson, and Whitelaw (2002) for 24 indices from 15 countries. The spot standard deviation for daily returns is less than the futures value for 23 of the 24 indices. Some of their estimates are 1.00% (spot) and 1.21% (futures) for the S&P 500, 0.96% and 1.11% for the FTSE 100, and 1.21% and 1.37% for Tokyo's TOPIX index. Additional microstructure explanations, for example, bid–ask bounce in futures prices and noise traders preferring futures transactions, may also be relevant.

4.5 Calendar Effects

Average equity returns have varied significantly depending on the day of the week, the day of the month, the month of the year, and the proximity of holidays. They have even varied with the relative positions of the Sun, Earth, and Moon! These calendar and cyclical anomalies are now discussed in detail. They are, however, ignored in most of this book because their implications for specifying and estimating models for returns are usually unimportant.

Efficient market theory states that anomalies may disappear once they are described by academics to the investment community because any profitable opportunities will be traded out of existence. They will also seem to disappear if they are merely the result of data mining. There is indeed evidence that some anomalies have disappeared in recent years, such as the Monday effect (Rubinstein 2001; Sullivan, Timmermann, and White 2001; Schwert 2003), the turn-of-the-month effect (Maberly and Waggoner 2000), and the size effect (Dimson and Marsh 1999; Schwert 2003).

A more severe criticism of calendar anomalies is that many of them may be merely the result of many researchers testing many hypotheses on the same data. Sullivan et al. (2001) show that the significance of calendar trading rules is much weaker when it is assessed in the context of a universe of rules that could plausibly have been evaluated. They observe that none of the calendar anomalies they investigate were discovered following a theoretical prediction. Instead, almost all the theoretical explanations that now exist are *ex post* rationalizations.

There are two reasons, however, for supposing that calendar effects are not merely curious results uncovered by data mining. First, the anomalous behavior has been found in almost all countries (Hawawini and Keim 1995). Second, effects first discovered in relatively recent US data are also found throughout much longer periods, for example, during the ninety years from 1897 to 1986 studied by Lakonishok and Smidt (1988).

4.5.1 Day-of-the-Week

Monday returns measure the result of an investment for 72 hours from Friday's close to Monday's close. Expected equity returns for Mondays should therefore be higher than for 24-hour returns on other days of the week. Seemingly overwhelming evidence for US equities, following Fields (1931) and Cross (1973), shows, however, that average Monday returns have been both lower and negative from 1897 until the 1980s. This anomaly is particularly puzzling because there

Table 4.3. Percentage return statistics, given by French.

	Monday	Tuesday	Wednesday	Thursday	Friday
Mean	−0.168	0.016	0.097	0.045	0.087
s.d.	0.843	0.727	0.748	0.686	0.660

then seems to have been no compensation for accepting equity risk during the weekend and/or on Monday.

French (1980) reports the means and standard deviations (s.d.) for daily, percentage returns from the Standard & Poor Composite Index between 1953 and 1977 (see Table 4.3). The Monday returns are lower than for other days, by 0.2% on average. This is a small difference for one day but it is substantial over one year. French shows that Monday's mean was negative for 20 of the 25 years and for all five subperiods of five years. Rubinstein (2001) notes that Monday's mean was negative for all twelve five-year periods from 1928 to 1987 and that Monday always had the worst five-year average return. Lakonishok and Smidt (1988) go back even further, to 1897. There is some evidence that the period of negative mean returns has been confined to the weekend and early trading on Monday (Harris 1986; Abraham and Ikenberry 1994).

Although the negative Monday average was a persistent phenomenon in the US for many years, the empirical evidence is markedly different for recent years. Monday returns have been slightly higher than for the other days of the week after the publication of Cross (1973), from 1973 until 1996 (Sullivan et al. 2001). Furthermore, Monday was the best day in the decade from 1989 to 1998 (Rubinstein 2001).

Significant day-of-the-week effects have been found in many other countries: for Australia, Canada, Japan, and the UK by Jaffe and Westerfield (1985); for Canada, Singapore, and the UK by Condoyanni et al. (1987); for Japan from 1949 to 1988 by Ziemba (1991); and for several European countries between 1986 and 1992 by Chang, Pinegar, and Ravichandran (1993). Negative Monday averages are common for European stock indices and also occur in Japan. Negative Tuesday averages are found for Pacific Rim countries, including Japan; this Tuesday effect may reflect the earlier Monday effect in New York.

It must be appreciated that the negative mean effects are small. The Monday average return is between −0.2% and −0.1% in many studies. Selling on Friday and buying late on Monday would lose money after the historically appropriate transaction costs are deducted.

Some explanations for the day-of-the-week effects observed in older datasets are reviewed by Hawawini and Keim (1995). They are found to be unconvincing, not least because the general effect is robust across countries. Nevertheless, we may note that Abraham and Ikenberry (1994) support the idea that US individual investors have tended to sell on Mondays after reviewing their portfolios at the weekend following negative returns on Friday, that Chen and Singal (2003) show some short sellers close positions (i.e. buy) on Fridays and reopen them (i.e. sell) on Mondays, and that Penman (1987) finds that bad news about US earnings has been more likely than good news to be announced at the weekend.

Regression tests that use dummy variables for the day-of-the-week are identical to one-way ANOVA tests. These tests provide an F-statistic which is usually so large that the hypothesis of equal expected returns for all days is rejected at very low significance levels. Connolly (1989, 1991) has criticized these tests because they ignore nonnormality, conditional heteroskedasticity, and autocorrelation. Furthermore, for large samples and conventional significance levels (e.g. 5%), Type I errors can be more common than Type II errors when Bayesian methods are used to calculate the error probabilities. Connolly reinterpreted test results from a Bayesian perspective and argued that the US day-of-the-week effect had disappeared by 1975. Abraham and Ikenberry (1994) disagreed and showed that negative Monday averages were a consequence of even lower averages when Friday's return is negative. Chang et al. (1993) applied Connolly's Bayesian test methodology and found that European effects were significant after 1985.

4.5.2 Holidays

US markets have often closed for eight days in a year. Ariel (1990) shows that more than one-third of the total return from US stock market portfolios was earned on the eight days before the holidays, during the period from 1963 to 1982. The average pre-holiday return from the CRSP value-weighted index was 0.36% during this period, compared with 0.03% for other days. Statistical tests show the difference is highly significant and not a consequence of other calendar anomalies. Ariel notes that Merrill (1966) had found that the Dow Jones Industrial Average advanced more frequently on days preceding holidays during the earlier period from 1897 to 1965. Ariel analyzes possible explanations for the holiday effect but finds they all have shortcomings. Lakonishok and Smidt (1988) confirm Ariel's findings back to 1897 for individual stocks.

There is some evidence for a pre-holiday effect in Japan (Ziemba 1991) and the UK. Kim and Park (1994) estimate mean returns for the UK FT-30 index from 1972 to 1987 to be 0.22% on the day before a holiday, −0.14% for the holiday and the next day, and 0.04% on other days. Their mean estimates for the Japanese Nikkei–Dow index during the same years are 0.19% before a holiday and 0.04% on other days. The comparable estimates of the US effect, from the S&P 500 index, are further apart at 0.30% (pre-holiday) and 0.02% (others). All these estimates ignore dividends. The UK and Japanese holiday effects are not the same as the US effect because they are found when the US market is open and the other markets are closed.

Table 4.4. Average percentage daily returns, by day of the week and before and after holidays.

Series		Mon	Tue	Wed	Thu	Fri	Pre-h	Hol	F
S&P 500-share	S	−0.02	0.10*	0.13*	0.05	0.05	0.24*	−0.01	1.60
S&P 500-share	F	0.04	0.06	0.10	0.04	−0.06	0.05	−0.03	0.66
Coca Cola	S	0.12	0.24*	0.15*	0.10	0.03	0.08	−0.19	1.11
General Electric	S	0.16*	0.14*	0.04	0.01	0.02	0.21	−0.13	1.03
General Motors	S	0.20*	0.08	0.08	−0.02	−0.07	0.20	−0.07	1.25
FT 100-share	S	−0.13*X	0.06	0.09*	0.04	0.09*	0.18	0.12	3.20*
FT 100-share	F	−0.15*X	0.07	0.09	0.01	0.01	0.18	0.16	2.60*
Glaxo	S	−0.13X	0.18*	0.27*	0.19*	0.19*	0.10	0.39	2.50*
Marks & Spencer	S	−0.17*X	0.15	0.24*	−0.03	0.16*	0.12	0.03	3.23*
Shell	S	−0.19*X	0.12*	0.14*	0.10	0.16*	0.23	0.22	4.37*
Nikkei 225-share	S	−0.18*X	−0.01	0.10	0.16*	0.02	0.15	−0.08	3.09*
Treasury bonds	F	−0.02	0.09*	−0.02	0.05	0.02	0.19*	−0.03	1.89
3-month sterling bills	F	−0.01	0.00	−0.01	−0.00	−0.00	0.01	−0.03	0.86
DM/$	F	−0.03	0.02	0.03	0.03	−0.03	0.02	−0.10	0.88
Sterling/$	F	−0.02	0.05	0.04	0.01	−0.05	0.02	0.00	0.95
Swiss franc/$	F	−0.02	0.03	0.01	0.03	−0.05	0.03	−0.15	0.97
Yen/$	F	−0.02	0.03	0.03	0.05	−0.04	0.04	−0.08	1.23
Gold	F	−0.16*	0.04	−0.07	0.00	−0.11	0.34*	−0.27	2.73*
Corn	F	−0.07	−0.06	−0.01	−0.04	−0.07	0.13	0.06	0.53
Live cattle	F	−0.04	−0.05	−0.02	0.07	0.13*	0.28*	0.15	3.16*

"Pre-h" is a day that precedes a holiday. "Hol" refers to returns for a holiday period and the subsequent open-market day. Starred averages are significantly different from zero, at the 5% significance level, when the standard hypothesis test is applied. Monday averages are followed by "X" if they differ significantly from the Tuesday to Friday average, at the 5% level. F is the one-way ANOVA test statistic for a null hypothesis of equal expected returns; stars indicate values beyond 2.10, which is the 95% quantile of the relevant F-distribution.

4.5.3 Weekday Results for Twenty Series

Table 4.4 documents day-of-the-week and holiday mean returns for our twenty time series. These series are shorter than those already discussed and thus it is less easy to identify any anomalous effects. Each return is assigned to one of seven categories. Monday returns are for all 72-hour periods when the market was open on Friday, Monday, and Tuesday. Tuesday returns are for 24-hour periods when the market was open from Monday to Wednesday inclusive; likewise for Wednesday, Thursday, and Friday returns. The remaining returns are assigned either to a pre-holiday category if the market is closed on the next weekday or to a holiday category if the market is closed on the previous weekday.

The average percentage returns are followed by a star in Table 4.4 if the average for the category is significantly different from zero, using a standard two-tail test and the 5% significance level. There are six starred *negative* averages: *all* are for Mondays and are between −0.19% and −0.13%. Four of these six averages are for UK equity series. The six Monday equity averages marked with the letter "X" are significantly different from the overall averages for Tuesdays to Fridays for the same series (5% level, two-tail test). There are 25 starred positive averages including the Monday averages for General Electric and General Motors. Of the 31 starred averages, 24 are for spot equity series and only 7 are for the futures series. None of the currency futures averages are significant.

All the pre-holiday averages are positive and, with one exception, are more than the holiday averages. Also, the pre-holiday average is the highest of the seven averages for a majority of the assets considered. The significant estimate of 0.24% for the S&P 500 index, from July 1982 to June 1992, is similar to the average found by Ariel (1990) for the earlier period from 1963 to 1982.

The F-statistic in the far-right column of Table 4.4 is the ANOVA test statistic for equal expected returns across the categories. The degrees-of-freedom of the test statistic are 6 and 2400+ and hence the null distribution is approximately $\frac{1}{6}\chi_6^2$ when the usual assumptions are made. Some of the assumptions, such as normal distributions, are false although this may not be very important. The eight starred F-statistics are for the five UK equity series, the Nikkei index, gold futures, and cattle futures. Rigorous tests are possible by maximizing likelihoods within an ARCH framework, using the methodology described in Chapter 10.

The extreme returns in the week commencing on 19 October 1987 have a noticeable impact on a few of the equity averages in Table 4.4. If we exclude the five returns in the crash week, the Monday S&P 500 futures average increases from 0.04% to 0.11% and becomes significant at the 5% level; also, the Coca Cola Monday average moves up to 0.17% and is significant, two US averages fall into the insignificant region and two UK averages increase to significant positive values. The F-statistics for the US equity series change by as much as 0.44 when the crash week is removed but most of the changes in the F-statistics are small and the list of significant test statistics does not change.

4.5.4 Day-of-the-Month

Ariel (1987) reports the remarkable result that all of the US stock market's cumulative advance from 1963 to 1981 occurred in regular half-month periods. Average returns were only positive for the last trading day of the month and for trading days in the first half of the month during these years. These results still occur when large returns around the start of the year are excluded. Once more, Lakonishok and Smidt (1988) find evidence for the calendar anomaly back to 1897. They also show that positive average returns are particularly high for the four trading days that commence on the last trading day of a month. This turn-of-the-month anomaly has also been found in Japanese index returns (Ziemba 1991) and for other countries (Jaffe and Westerfield 1989), but it disappeared from the S&P 500 index after 1990 (Maberly and Waggoner 2000).

The empirical evidence might be consistent with buying pressure following the payment of monthly salaries (Ogden 1990). Also, Penman (1987) shows that

US companies have been more likely to publish their earnings information in the first two weeks of a calendar quarter if the earnings news is good. This result holds for each of the four quarters and average returns are higher in these "good news" periods. Earnings news may therefore explain some of the day-of-the-month anomaly (as well as low Monday returns), but only if investors irrationally ignore the bad signal implicit in a delayed earnings announcement.

There is no evidence for day-of-the-month effects that are statistically significant for our twenty series. Higher average returns were recorded for the eleven equity series during the period from the last day of a month until the middle of the next month, particularly for all five index series until the end of the first week of the month.

4.5.5 Month-of-the-Year

Rozeff and Kinney (1976) show that returns from equal-weighted US stock indices were significantly higher at the start of the new tax year in January than in other months, during the period from 1904 to 1974. Praetz (1973) and Officer (1975) show in earlier research that Australian return distributions depend upon the month. The international study of Gultekin and Gultekin (1983) documents monthly mean returns for seventeen countries between 1959 and 1979. Mean returns were found to be significantly higher in January than in other months for thirteen of the seventeen countries.

Small US firms have earned higher returns on average than predicted by a single-factor pricing model (Banz 1981) and these excess returns have been found to occur primarily at the start of the year (Keim 1983; Hawawini and Keim 2000). Thus the January seasonal effect interacts with a size effect, although the size premium in observed returns at the turn of the year may be exaggerated by bid–ask spreads (Keim 1989). The size effect can be seen clearly in average January returns for US indices given by Gultekin and Gultekin (1983): 5.1% for an equal-weighted index compared with only 1.0% for a value-weighted index. Tinic and West (1984, Table 7) estimate the average return in January as 4% per month, but only 1% on average for the other months, for US companies that had average-risk (unit beta) between 1935 and 1982.

The most popular explanation of the substantial January effect in the US market is the tax-loss selling hypothesis of Brown, Keim, Kleidon, and Marsh (1983). They suggest that selling pressure at the tax year-end depresses prices that rebound in January. The hypothesis is supported first by the absence of a January effect before 1917, when there was no incentive to sell for tax reasons (Schultz 1985; Jones, Lee, and Apenbrink 1991), and second by the year-end trading behavior of individual investors (Ritter 1988). The international evidence, however, is far from consistent, although other explanations are not more credible (Hawawini and Keim 1995).

The recent paper by Bouman and Jacobsen (2002) documents a new time-of-the-year anomaly. They show that monthly index returns are significantly lower during the six months from May until October than the remaining half of the year from November to April. They motivate this splitting of the year by reference to an old market saying, "Sell in May and go away," that is frequently mentioned in the European financial press. Their results are typically for the period from 1970 to 1998, which postdates the market folklore. The average index return for Nov/Apr is higher than for May/Sep for 36 of the 37 countries studied. Many of the differences are statistically significant. Bouman and Jacobsen provide evidence that the differences are not a rediscovery of the January effect. The average differences in one-month returns are 0.9%, 2.0%, and 1.5%, respectively, for the US, the UK, and Japan. The t-values for these differences are 1.95, 3.10, and 2.62. They decrease when a January dummy variable is included in their regression equation to 1.61, 2.48, and 2.23.

There is no compelling evidence for month-of-the-year effects for our twenty series. There are indications of anomalous monthly averages but the evidence from a decade of returns lacks statistical significance, as noted previously for day-of-the-month subperiods. The January averages are relatively high for the indices; for our US and UK series they are higher than for all other months and the Nikkei January average is only surpassed by the May average. However, none of the January index averages is significantly different to the average for the remaining eleven months, at the 5% level.

4.5.6 *Astronomy and Average Returns*

The number of hours of daylight depends on the calendar and upon latitude. When these hours decrease during the fall (autumn) many people are less content and a significant proportion suffer from depression. Motivated by these medical facts, Kamstra, Kramer, and Levi (2003) use regression methods to show that daylight is associated with average returns when asymmetric effects before and after the winter solstice are included in the analysis. As they expect, their effects increase with distance from the Equator and there is a phase difference of six months between the Northern and Southern Hemispheres. They give results for nine countries, finding evidence that stock market returns are lower in the fall and higher in the winter season. Related evidence about the sensitivity of returns to sunlight is provided by Hirshleifer and Shumway (2003).

The phases of the moon repeat every 29.5 days and appear to be related to stock market returns. Dichev and Janes (2003) show that the average returns from all major US stock indices around new moon dates are nearly double those around full moon dates, when seven-day windows define the periods around the lunar dates. The annualized differences between new and full moon returns are then between 5% and 8%. These large differences are not, however, significant—the probability of observing a larger difference when no lunar effect exists is 34% for their longest dataset, which contains daily Dow Jones returns from 1896 to 1999. Higher averages around new moon dates are also found for all of the other six G7 countries and for all but one of eighteen further countries. The differences between new and full moon returns average more than 9% for all 25 countries and the difference is statistically significant at the 1% level, for the period from 1973 to 2000. Yuan, Zheng, and Zhu (2001) provide further results.

4.5.7 Autocorrelation Induced by Calendar Effects

Calendar anomalies are puzzling and may have become less pronounced in recent years. On their own they have little impact on the autocorrelations of daily returns because daily means are very small compared with daily standard deviations. Appendix 4.13 provides some theoretical results when returns are the sum of a white noise process and a mean process determined solely by the calendar. The maximum autocorrelation induced by day-of-the-week effects is 0.02, at lag 5, when the daily means are the numbers reported by French (1980) and we pretend there are no holidays, so that Monday returns are always separated by five days. The maximum autocorrelation induced by either the day-of-the-month or the month-of-the-year effects is less than 0.003 for reasonable estimates of the magnitudes of these effects.

4.5.8 Standard Deviations and the Calendar

Although it is difficult to explain why expected returns depend on the calendar, it is easy to produce one plausible explanation of calendar variations in the standard deviations of returns. Standard deviations are measures of price variability and prices change more frequently when there is more news. In particular, Monday returns reflect news on three calendar days and may be expected to be more variable than other returns. Monday returns will have a variance three times as large as the variance on other weekdays if prices follow geometric Brownian motion in calendar time. Likewise, holiday returns may be expected to have additional variability.

The Monday effect is seen in the standard deviations given by French (1980). The standard deviation of Monday returns is 0.84%, compared with 0.71% for other days. The additional Monday variation is about 18% (= 0.84/0.71 − 1), which is much less than the 73% (= $\sqrt{3}$ − 1) expected when news arrives at the same rate on all days including Saturdays and Sundays. Not surprisingly, observed standard deviations of returns imply, first, that less relevant information is produced during the weekend than on weekdays and, second, that less is produced during hours when stock markets are closed (French and Roll 1986).

To compare standard deviations across days of the week, without modeling other volatility effects associated with conditional heteroskedasticity, we can use

Table 4.5. Estimated percentage proportions of weekly variance, by day of the week.

Series		Mon	Tue	Wed	Thu	Fri
S&P 500-share	S	21.3	21.2	19.3	19.3	19.0
S&P 500-share	F	20.2	22.0	19.6	19.5	18.7
Coca Cola	S	20.1	20.5	19.0	19.7	20.7
General Electric	S	21.0	20.7	18.1	18.9	21.2
General Motors	S	19.6	20.2	19.1	20.7	20.4
FT 100-share	S	23.4*	19.0	20.8	18.2	18.6
FT 100-share	F	23.8*	18.8	19.4	18.4	19.7
Glaxo	S	20.4	20.8	19.7	20.1	19.1
Marks & Spencer	S	20.2	22.3*	20.3	18.4	18.7
Shell	S	20.0	20.4	19.1	21.6	19.0
Nikkei 225-share	S	25.8*	18.6	20.0	18.3	17.2*
Treasury bonds	F	20.1	16.8*	17.1*	18.8	27.1*
3-month sterling bills	F	25.3*	18.5	17.3*	18.2	20.8
DM/$	F	23.5*	19.1	17.2*	18.9	21.3
Sterling/$	F	24.7*	20.4	16.3*	17.3*	21.3
Swiss franc/$	F	22.9*	19.5	16.9*	19.1	21.7
Yen/$	F	22.0	19.5	17.0*	19.9	21.6
Gold	F	25.1*	17.4*	17.6*	17.9*	22.0
Corn	F	26.3*	20.6	18.6	18.5	16.0*
Live cattle	F	21.8	19.9	20.0	19.5	18.7

Starred averages are significantly different from 20%, at the 5% significance level. The average standard error for the above estimated proportions is approximately 1%.

robust estimates of the proportion of weekly variance attributable to each day. Suppose a market is open for six consecutive days commencing with a particular Friday denoted by day t. Let r_{t+i} be the return for day $t + i$, as usual, and let

$$w_{t+i} = (r_{t+i} - \bar{r}_i)^2 \bigg/ \sum_{j=1}^{5} (r_{t+j} - \bar{r}_j)^2$$

with $\bar{r}_i$ the mean return for day i (Monday is $i = 1$, etc.). The quantities w_{t+i} can be averaged across weeks to give estimates of the proportion of the total variance in a week associated with each day. The estimates will be consistent but may be slightly biased.

Table 4.5 lists percentage estimates for the twenty series. The standard errors of these estimates are all approximately 1%. The starred estimates in this table are significantly different from 20%, using a 5% significance level and a two-tail test. The five possible tests for any row are not independent because the proportions must sum to one. There are no starred estimates for the US equity series and thus these estimates provide no evidence for a weekly volatility seasonal pattern. The Monday returns for the UK and Japanese index series have significantly more variability than those for other days. The high figure for the Nikkei index may reflect trading on Saturdays for some of the period considered.

The Treasury bond futures estimates indicate significantly more variability in Friday returns and this reflects the timing of US macroeconomic news announcements, many of which are made early on Friday mornings (Harvey and Huang 1991; Ederington and Lee 1993, 1995). All the currency futures series, as well as the gold and corn futures series, have significantly more variability in Monday returns. Baillie and Bollerslev (1989b) report the same conclusion for spot currency rates. Futures variability is low on Wednesdays for many series. Typical Monday and Wednesday proportions are 24% and 17% and this suggests Monday standard deviations are approximately one-fifth higher than the Wednesday numbers.

Holiday returns generally have higher standard deviations than other returns and the opposite result generally holds for pre-holiday returns. When standard deviations are ranked for the seven categories used in Table 4.4, with the crash week excluded, pre-holiday returns have the lowest rank for thirteen series and holiday returns have the highest rank for a different set of thirteen series; holiday returns outrank pre-holiday returns for nineteen of the twenty series. The holiday volatility effect is particularly marked for the S&P 500 spot series; the pre-holiday returns have standard deviation 0.57%, the Monday to Friday statistics range from 0.78% to 0.97%, and the holiday returns statistic is 1.09%.

Identifying further calendar patterns in standard deviations may not be possible for the twenty series. Estimates for subperiods of the month do not show any discernible pattern. Standard deviation estimates have been noticeably higher in some months than others (e.g. October for stocks) but this is probably a consequence of general changes in volatility that can produce higher levels of conditional variances for several weeks.

4.6   Skewness and Kurtosis

Skewness statistics are sometimes used to assess the symmetry of distributions, while kurtosis statistics are often interpreted as a measure of similarity to a normal distribution.

These statistics are sensitive to extreme observations because they make use of the third and fourth powers of the observations, respectively. This is a particular problem for stock series that include the 1987 crash. Consequently, the crash week is excluded from the stock series for the calculations of the skewness and kurtosis statistics listed in Table 4.1. The S&P 500 spot series has skewness equal to -3.58 for the entire ten years of daily returns but this figure falls to -0.67 when the crash week is excluded. The kurtosis for the same series falls from 77.0 to 10.4 when the crash week is removed. There are similar large changes for the

S&P 500 futures series and for both FTSE 100 series, with important but less dramatic changes for the individual stocks and the Nikkei index.

The three-month sterling bill futures have exceptional skewness and kurtosis values. Once more, these can be attributed to an extreme outlier. On Thursday, 17 September 1992, the day after sterling left the European Exchange Rate Mechanism, sterling interest rates fell sharply and the futures return was 2.9%, some 18 standard deviations away from the average. When the week containing this crisis is excluded, the skewness falls from 2.29 to −0.15 and the kurtosis from 59.8 to 20.8. There are further extreme outliers in January 1985.

The standard error of a skewness estimate b calculated from n returns depends on n and the population distribution. It equals $\sqrt{6/n}$ for a random sample from a normal distribution. This formula is of minimal value because returns have excess kurtosis that increases the standard error. Few of the estimates b are far from zero and hence they do not provide much evidence that the returns distributions are not symmetric. The S&P 500 index figures, however, are both less than −0.5. There is some evidence for negative skewness in US index returns (Campbell and Hentschel 1992) and for slight positive skewness in company returns (Perry 1982) that is higher, on average, for small firms and nonsurviving firms (Duffee 1995). However, almost all the evidence for unconditional skewness in US stock returns may be a consequence of very occasional negative outliers; for some evidence, see Harvey and Siddique (1999) for the S&P 500 index and Blair et al. (2002) for the constituents of the S&P 100 index.

All twenty sets of returns are *leptokurtic*, since all the estimates of kurtosis in Table 4.1 exceed 3, which is the value for normal distributions. The standard error of a kurtosis estimate k is $\sqrt{24/n}$ for a random sample from a normal distribution. This equals approximately 0.1 for our series. Nineteen of the twenty estimates in Table 4.1 exceed 3 by more than ten of these standard errors. It is very clear that the returns-generating process is not even approximately Gaussian. This is an old conclusion that may first have been established in Alexander (1961). It has since been shown for almost all series of daily and more frequent returns.

4.7 The Shape of the Returns Distribution

The first important stylized fact for daily returns is a remark about their distribution:

1. *The distribution of returns is not normal.*

Instead, we can say of the distribution that

- it is approximately symmetric;
- it has fat tails;
- it has a high peak.

Table 4.6.　Relative frequencies for samples of returns.

		Percent no change	within		beyond						
			0.25	0.5	1	1.5	2	3	4	5	6
Normal distribution			19.74	38.29	31.73	13.36	4.55	0.27	0.01	0.00	0.00
Series											
S&P 500-share	S	0.00	30.88	52.67	19.73	8.50	3.28	0.91	0.47	0.24	0.20
S&P 500-share	F	1.38	34.12	58.20	16.29	6.96	2.85	0.71	0.40	0.24	0.20
Coca Cola	S	6.64	24.87	48.24	22.74	8.82	3.91	0.95	0.47	0.20	0.12
General Electric	S	6.37	25.07	47.61	23.53	10.40	4.98	1.15	0.40	0.20	0.08
General Motors	S	6.56	24.75	45.83	24.87	10.48	4.47	0.83	0.16	0.08	0.08
FT 100-share	S	0.28	22.46	43.46	24.20	7.63	2.97	0.83	0.47	0.24	0.20
FT 100-share	F	2.53	23.37	44.33	23.49	8.26	3.32	0.99	0.47	0.28	0.16
Glaxo	S	7.12	26.70	50.44	22.82	9.69	4.75	1.66	0.44	0.24	0.12
Marks & Spencer	S	14.60	21.36	44.66	26.78	11.87	5.06	1.15	0.28	0.04	0.04
Shell	S	9.81	23.38	46.00	26.07	10.68	4.35	1.15	0.51	0.28	0.08
Nikkei 225-share	S	0.28	30.60	56.01	19.85	10.02	5.24	1.54	0.45	0.24	0.12
Treasury bonds	F	2.33	24.96	46.16	26.74	11.83	6.01	0.99	0.20	0.04	0.00
3-month sterling bills	F	6.02	37.08	60.07	16.78	7.72	4.04	1.39	0.75	0.36	0.20
DM/$	F	2.45	25.35	44.80	26.65	11.98	5.54	1.19	0.24	0.04	0.04
Sterling/$	F	2.61	26.53	46.94	26.49	11.23	5.42	1.27	0.36	0.08	0.00
Swiss franc/$	F	1.30	23.61	43.69	27.80	12.50	5.10	0.91	0.20	0.04	0.04
Yen/$	F	2.02	28.00	48.56	24.71	11.94	5.34	1.30	0.24	0.16	0.08
Gold	F	1.67	31.40	54.28	22.40	11.50	6.42	1.94	0.52	0.08	0.00
Corn	F	4.03	24.84	47.07	23.69	10.40	5.58	1.70	0.40	0.04	0.04
Live cattle	F	2.21	22.78	44.44	28.39	13.72	6.72	0.00	0.00	0.00	0.00
Averages											
Spot series			25.56	48.32	23.40	9.79	4.33	1.13	0.41	0.19	0.11
Futures series			27.46	48.96	23.95	10.73	5.12	1.13	0.34	0.12	0.07
All series			26.61	48.67	23.70	10.31	4.77	1.13	0.37	0.15	0.09
Series with crash excluded											
S&P 500-share	S	0.00	27.93	48.93	24.01	11.05	4.64	1.07	0.44	0.20	0.12
S&P 500-share	F	1.39	28.25	50.67	23.02	11.09	5.11	1.47	0.44	0.24	0.12
Coca Cola	S	6.66	22.54	44.93	26.31	11.13	4.99	1.11	0.44	0.12	0.00
General Electric	S	6.38	23.81	45.40	25.67	11.21	5.67	1.19	0.28	0.08	0.04
General Motors	S	6.58	23.97	44.06	26.66	11.49	5.15	1.11	0.24	0.00	0.00
FT 100-share	S	0.28	20.36	39.98	28.29	9.98	3.92	0.95	0.40	0.12	0.08
FT 100-share	F	2.54	21.59	41.40	27.73	10.74	4.32	1.03	0.40	0.16	0.04
Glaxo	S	7.13	25.45	48.71	24.10	10.19	5.27	1.63	0.44	0.16	0.12
Marks & Spencer	S	14.63	20.93	44.15	27.47	12.56	5.19	1.03	0.16	0.00	0.00
Shell	S	9.83	22.79	44.99	27.07	11.93	4.72	0.99	0.36	0.12	0.00
Nikkei 225-share	S	0.28	29.40	54.05	21.07	10.70	5.94	1.67	0.45	0.16	0.04
Averages, all stock series			24.28	46.12	25.58	11.10	4.99	1.20	0.36	0.12	0.05

The percentages of standardized daily returns, $(r_t - \bar{r})/s$, within various intervals are shown in Table 4.6 for the twenty illustrative series. This information is summarized in Table 4.7 by frequencies for the magnitudes of the standardized daily returns, that show averages across all series.

Table 4.7. Average frequencies for standardized daily returns.

Range	Observed	Normal	Observed minus normal
0 to 0.25	26.6%	19.7%	6.9%
0.25 to 0.5	22.1%	18.6%	3.5%
0.5 to 1	27.6%	30.0%	−2.4%
1 to 1.5	13.4%	18.4%	−5.0%
1.5 to 2	5.5%	8.8%	−3.3%
2 to 3	3.6%	4.3%	−0.6%
3+	1.1%	0.3%	0.8%

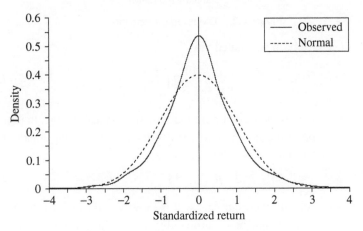

Figure 4.1.   S&P 500 returns distribution.

The first two rows of Table 4.7 show there are more observations in the range from $\bar{r} - 0.5s$ to $\bar{r} + 0.5s$ than are expected from a normal distribution, corresponding to a *high peak* in empirical distributions. The final row shows there are also more *extreme* observations, either below $\bar{r} - 3s$ or above $\bar{r} + 3s$, corresponding to two *fat tails*. The high values of kurtosis are caused by the outliers in the tails. As the frequencies total 100%, there must be fewer observations elsewhere that occur within the ranges $\bar{r} \pm 0.5s$ to $\bar{r} \pm 3s$. Note that the high peak and fat tails effects are interdependent, because extreme returns contribute large squared returns to the variance of the distribution, which implies there must be more observations near the center of the distribution than are found for a normal distribution having the same mean and variance.

Figures 4.1 and 4.2 compare kernel estimates of the probability distribution for standardized returns, $z_t = (r_t - \bar{r})/s$, with the normal distribution for the spot S&P 500 returns and the DM/$ futures returns, respectively. These density

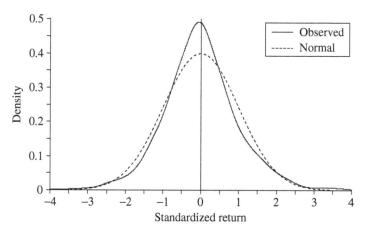

Figure 4.2. DM returns distribution.

estimates $\hat{f}(z)$ have been calculated as

$$\hat{f}(z) = \frac{1}{n} \sum_{t=1}^{n} \frac{1}{B} \phi\left(\frac{z - z_t}{B}\right) \tag{4.6}$$

with $\phi(\cdot)$ the density of the standard normal distribution and the bandwidth B a decreasing function of the sample size n (Silverman 1986). As the standardized returns have unit variance, it is acceptable to use

$$B = n^{-0.2}. \tag{4.7}$$

The figures show clearly the high peaks. It is, however, difficult to discern the fat tails because there is not much probability in the tails, although there are more observations than expected from a normal distribution. The crash week is excluded from the S&P 500 calculations; the distribution is even more peaked if this week is included. More details of the crash effect are provided in Table 4.6, where the distributions are summarized for all returns and again for the stock returns when the crash week is excluded.

A general observation about the extreme returns is that about 1% of all the daily returns in the twenty series are more than three standard deviations from the mean. This is about four times the normal figure. We could conjecture that these "3 s.d." events occur (very approximately) three times a year. The frequency of more extreme outliers is also documented in Table 4.6. The average frequency of observations more than four standard deviations distant from the mean is close to 0.4% and thus this event occurred, on average, once a year for each asset. Such events would only occur once in sixty years if daily returns were observations from a normal distribution. A typical standard deviation for a daily stock index return has been 1% and so we might expect an index to rise or fall by more than 4%, from one market close to the next, very approximately once a year. Statements like this must be interpreted as approximate results that depend on the returns process having a similar distribution in the future to that estimated from previous data.

Inferences from extreme values may be relevant for risk management, but reliable inferences require sufficient extremes and the assumption of stationarity. Extreme value theory applied to financial returns is not covered in any detail in this book. Some results are noted in Section 12.12 and some interesting references are Loretan and Phillips (1994), Longin (1996), Tsay (2002, Chapter 7), and Poon, Rockinger, and Tawn (2004).

Many returns are zero and this helps to explain the peaked centers of the empirical distributions. The percentage of days having a zero price change from the previous day is given in Table 4.6 under the heading "Percent no change." These zero changes are not simply a consequence of infrequent trading. Each of the three US stock return series has more than 6% of the returns equal to zero, but the stocks all have trading volumes measured in tens of thousands of shares every day. The US stock zeros are a consequence of the minimum price movement being relatively large compared with the standard deviation of returns. The average price for these series is about \$60 and the minimum price change was one-eighth of a dollar; thus the smallest possible positive return was typically 0.2%, which is more than 0.1 s.d. The chance of a normal variable being within 0.05 s.d. of the mean value is 4%, so the number of US stock zeros can be explained by discrete prices combined with a peaked distribution.

4.8 Probability Distributions for Returns

A satisfactory probability distribution for daily returns must have high kurtosis and be either exactly or approximately symmetric. We now review several distributions that have these properties.

Praetz (1972), Clark (1973), and many others have argued that observed returns come from a mixture of normal distributions. There is then some mixing variable, ω_t, that defines a set of *conditional* normal distributions for returns:

$$r_t \mid \omega_t \sim N(\mu, f(\omega_t)) \qquad (4.8)$$

for some function f. The quantity $\sigma_t^2 = f(\omega_t)$ is a conditional variance and, to simplify our discussion, the mean return is supposed to be the constant μ. Few assumptions are then required to guarantee that the *unconditional* distribution of returns has excess kurtosis, as is shown later in Chapters 8, 9, and 11.

The mixing variable ω_t has been associated with observable quantities such as trading volume (Clark 1973; Ghysels, Gourieroux, and Jasiak 1998) and the number of transactions (Harris 1987; Jones, Kaul, and Lipson 1994; Ané and Geman 2000). Another interpretation is that ω_t is the number of new items of relevant information absorbed by the market on day t (Beckers 1981; Tauchen and Pitts 1983; Gallant, Hsieh, and Tauchen 1991), although then there is no practical possibility of observing outcomes for ω_t. This issue is unimportant for appropriate moment tests of the mixture hypothesis (Richardson and Smith 1994a). Mixture models require further structure to ensure that they define a satisfactory model for returns, provided in Chapters 9–11. In particular, the existence of conditional heteroskedasticity shows that variables such as ω_t and ω_{t+1} are not independent.

Whatever interpretation is given to ω_t, choices can be made for the distribution of the conditional variance $\sigma_t^2 = f(\omega_t)$ that defines particular unconditional distributions for returns. Praetz (1972) favored an inverse gamma distribution for σ_t^2 so that returns have a generalized Student t-distribution with degrees of freedom $\nu > 2$. Returns then have a finite central moment of order N if and only if $N < \nu$. In particular, the unconditional kurtosis is finite when $\nu > 4$ and then equals $3 + 6/(\nu - 4)$. As $\nu \to \infty$, the generalized t-distribution converges to a normal distribution. Blattberg and Gonedes (1974) use likelihood ratios and other methods to claim that Student distributions provide a better fit than stable distributions to US stock returns. The majority of their estimates of ν are between 4 and 6. Kon (1984) has all 33 estimates of ν between 3 and 6. Bollerslev (1987) extends the mixture model to produce conditional t-distributions in an ARCH framework.

Clark (1973) supposed that σ_t^2 has a lognormal distribution and this choice has become very popular in the stochastic volatility literature. Returns are then said to have a lognormal-normal distribution. All the moments of the unconditional distribution for returns are then finite but the density function must be represented using an integral. The moments, however, can be found without difficulty, as is shown in Section 11.5. In particular, the unconditional kurtosis is $3 \exp(V)$ when $\log(\sigma_t^2)$ has variance V. Typical estimates of V are at least 0.5 (Taylor 1986; Jacquier, Polson, and Rossi 1994).

Further suggestions for the distribution of σ_t^2 are a linear function of a Poisson variable (Press 1967), an unconstrained, discrete distribution (Kon 1984; Ryden, Teräsvirta, and Asbrink 1998), and a gamma distribution (Madan and Seneta 1990). Kim and Kon (1994) make some comparisons. Others distributions used in finance research are also mixtures of normal distributions. For example, the generalized error distribution used by Nelson (1991) is a complicated mixture (Hsu 1980, 1982).

The gamma and the inverse gamma distributions for σ_t^2 mentioned above, like the inverse Gaussian (IG) distribution, are special cases of the generalized inverse Gaussian (GIG) distribution. The distribution of returns is called the normal inverse Gaussian (NIG) distribution when $\sigma_t^2 \sim$ IG and the generalized hyperbolic distribution when $\sigma_t^2 \sim$ GIG. Barndorff-Nielsen and Shephard (2001) show

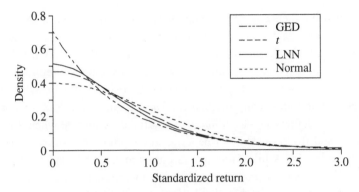

Figure 4.3. Probability density functions.

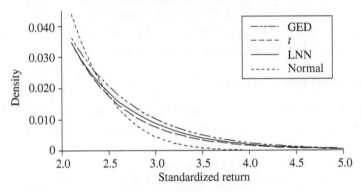

Figure 4.4. Tail densities.

that these distributions are useful for modeling returns measured over a variety of timescales.

Figures 4.3 and 4.4 compare the probability density functions of normal, Student t, lognormal-normal (LNN), and generalized error (GED) distributions. The parameters of these distributions are chosen so that they have mean 0, variance 1, and kurtosis equal to either 3 (normal) or 6 (t, LNN, GED). Definitions and mathematical results for the three fat-tailed density functions are provided in Sections 9.6 (t, GED) and 11.5 (LNN). The plotted density functions are all symmetric about 0. Figure 4.3 shows that all the nonnormal densities are more peaked than the normal and this effect is most pronounced for the GED. The normal density crosses the other density functions between 0.45 and 0.75 and is the highest between 0.8 and 2.3. Figure 4.4 shows densities for the tails of the distributions. The normal density crosses the others again between 2.3 and 2.6 and soon becomes small relative to the other densities. The GED density is the highest between 2.4 and 6.0, after which the t-density has the highest values.

Finally, we mention the infinite-variance stable (Pareto–Lévy) distribution advocated by Mandelbrot (1963) and Fama (1965), although few researchers now use it. This distribution is covered in detail by Rachev and Mittnik (2000). There is no compact formula for the general density function but it can be derived by numerical methods. The most important parameter of the stable distribution is its characteristic exponent α with $0 < \alpha \leqslant 2$. Any k-period return defined by the sum $r_t + \cdots + r_{t+k-1}$ has the same characteristic exponent when the r_t are independent and identically distributed. The exponent equals 2 for normal distributions, but defines a distribution whose variance is infinite when it is less than 2. Fama and Roll (1971) describe a quantile method for estimating α that has often been applied, while Akgiray and Lamoureux (1989) and Rachev and Mittnik (2000) survey and compare estimation methods. Studies of US stock returns, however, reject the stable distribution as a satisfactory model (Blattberg and Gonedes 1974; Hagerman 1978; Perry 1983). Hagerman shows that estimates of α steadily increase from about 1.5 for daily returns to about 1.9 for returns measured over 35 days. Monthly returns have distributions much closer to the normal shape than those of daily returns and this contradicts the stable hypothesis.

4.9 Autocorrelations of Returns

So far we have only reviewed properties of the distribution of one return. Now we consider measures of the dependence between the returns for time periods t and $t + \tau$, which are separated by τ time periods.

The correlation between returns τ periods apart is estimated from n observations by the *sample autocorrelation* at *lag* τ,

$$\hat{\rho}_{\tau,r} = \sum_{t=1}^{n-\tau}(r_t - \bar{r})(r_{t+\tau} - \bar{r}) \bigg/ \sum_{t=1}^{n}(r_t - \bar{r})^2, \quad \tau > 0, \qquad (4.9)$$

with $\bar{r}$ the sample mean of all n observations. The symbol $\hat{\rho}$ indicates that the sample statistic estimates a correlation parameter ρ of a stochastic process when the data come from a stationary process. The two subscripts τ and r respectively state the lag and the series that provide the estimates. The definition in (4.9) is standard in time series literature. It provides very similar estimates to the correlation between the $n - \tau$ pairs of observations $(r_t, r_{t+\tau})$ for long time series.

The definition is not altered here for series of futures returns taken from several contracts. Returns from a pair of futures contracts during the same period are similar because arbitrage principles imply they have a common dependence upon spot returns. Consequently, the distribution of the product of two mean-adjusted returns changes little when the two terms are for different futures contracts.

Autocorrelation estimates are calculated with the implicit assumption that expected returns, $E[r_t]$, are constant. Changes in expected returns would have to be substantial to make $\hat{\rho}_{\tau,r}$ a seriously biased estimate of the correlation between r_t and $r_{t+\tau}$. This is shown in Appendix 4.13 for day-of-the-week and other possible

Table 4.8. Autocorrelations for returns.

Series		Lags 1–5 Autocorrelations					Lags 1–30 Category frequency					
		1	2	3	4	5	1	2	3	4	5	6
S&P 500-share	S	0.101	−0.033	−0.026	−0.020	0.056	0	0	17	11	1	1
S&P 500-share	F	−0.029	−0.117	−0.023	−0.029	0.063	1	1	17	10	1	0
Coca Cola	S	−0.035	−0.100	−0.038	−0.048	0.060	1	0	16	12	1	0
General Electric	S	−0.023	−0.061	−0.035	−0.012	0.042	0	2	16	12	0	0
General Motors	S	−0.003	−0.069	−0.009	−0.044	0.027	0	1	14	15	0	0
FT 100-share	S	0.066	−0.001	0.020	0.073	0.010	0	1	12	14	3	0
FT 100-share	F	0.012	−0.030	0.023	0.046	0.004	0	0	9	21	0	0
Glaxo	S	0.080	−0.018	−0.013	−0.023	0.007	0	0	15	14	1	0
Marks & Spencer	S	0.034	−0.006	−0.044	0.003	−0.016	0	0	17	13	0	0
Shell	S	0.045	0.052	−0.001	−0.005	0.013	0	1	14	14	1	0
Nikkei 225-share	S	0.035	−0.099	−0.003	0.062	−0.027	0	1	14	14	1	0
Treasury bonds	F	0.030	0.018	−0.011	−0.016	−0.036	0	1	12	17	0	0
3-month sterling bills	F	0.056	−0.083	0.018	−0.031	0.045	0	1	12	14	3	0
DM/$	F	−0.001	0.001	0.015	−0.032	0.022	0	1	11	17	1	0
Sterling/$	F	0.027	−0.010	−0.019	−0.016	0.004	0	0	16	14	0	0
Swiss franc/$	F	−0.011	−0.004	0.006	−0.028	0.014	0	1	12	16	1	0
Yen/$	F	−0.002	0.013	0.018	−0.004	0.035	0	0	10	20	0	0
Gold	F	−0.055	0.061	0.019	−0.067	0.020	0	3	12	14	1	0
Corn	F	0.101	−0.032	0.013	−0.018	−0.023	0	0	14	13	2	1
Live cattle	F	0.011	−0.009	0.043	0.022	−0.027	0	0	16	13	1	0

Autocorrelation averages and frequency totals

Spot series	S	0.033	−0.037	−0.017	−0.001	0.019	1	6	135	119	8	1
Futures series	F	0.013	−0.017	0.009	−0.016	0.011	1	8	141	169	10	1
All series		0.022	−0.026	−0.002	−0.009	0.015	2	14	276	288	18	2
All series, crash excluded		0.024	−0.015	−0.008	−0.013	−0.000	0	11	293	282	14	0

The six categories that summarize the signs and magnitudes of the autocorrelations are (1) below −0.1, (2) between −0.1 and −0.05, (3) between −0.05 and 0, (4) between 0 and 0.05, (5) between 0.05 and 0.1, and (6) above 0.1. The final row of averages presents average values after all returns in October 1987 have been excluded.

calendar determinants of expected returns. The consequences of changes in risk-free rates and risk premia for autocorrelation estimates are also minor and are postponed until Section 6.10.

The sample autocorrelations of returns are generally close to zero, regardless of the time lag. This is the second important stylized fact for daily returns:

2. *There is almost no correlation between returns for different days.*

Statements like this can be found as far back as research by Working (1934) and Kendall (1953), before computers could be used for the statistical calculations.

4.9.1 *Lags 1–30*

Table 4.8 presents information about the autocorrelation estimates for the twenty series of daily returns, calculated for all lags τ between 1 and 30 trading days.

To summarize their signs and magnitudes, they are here assigned to one of six categories:

  (i) $\hat{\rho} < -0.1$;

  (ii) $-0.1 \leqslant \hat{\rho} < -0.05$;

  (iii) $-0.05 \leqslant \hat{\rho} < 0$;

  (iv) $0 \leqslant \hat{\rho} \leqslant 0.05$;

  (v) $0.05 < \hat{\rho} \leqslant 0.1$;

  (vi) $0.1 < \hat{\rho}$.

The numbers of autocorrelations in each of the six categories are tabulated, along with the values for the first five lags.

The estimated autocorrelations of returns are seen to be very small numbers. More than 90% of the 600 estimates summarized in Table 4.8 are between -0.05 and 0.05. Some 99% of the estimates are between -0.1 and 0.1. Any linear dependence in the stochastic process generating daily returns must be considered small. There are similar numbers of positive and negative estimates; 47% are positive for the spot series and the comparable figure is 55% for the futures series.

Figure 4.5 is a typical scatter diagram for returns in consecutive periods. The gold futures returns in periods t and $t + 1$ respectively define the variables on the horizontal and vertical axes. There appears to be no linear dependence between the variables and it is difficult to see any evidence for a form of nonlinear dependence. Patterns will be visible in a scatter diagram, however, when the price changes are usually a small multiple of the asset's effective tick size (Crack and Ledoit 1996); such patterns are created by discrete prices and are not evidence of dependence between returns.

The extreme observations at the time of the October 1987 crash have a noticeable impact on only a handful of the autocorrelation estimates. Any crash effect has been assessed by comparing the autocorrelations for complete series with the weighted averages of autocorrelations calculated first for the months until September 1987 and second for the months from November 1987; the weights are proportional to the numbers of returns in the two subsamples. The first-lag, US spot index autocorrelation changes from 0.101 to 0.099 when the crash month is excluded, the UK estimate changes from 0.066 to 0.071, and the Japanese estimate from 0.035 to 0.076. The estimate furthest from zero in Table 4.8 is -0.117, for the second-lag autocorrelation of S&P 500 futures returns. This exceptional estimate is determined by crash returns, since it changes to 0.008 when the crash month is removed from the series.

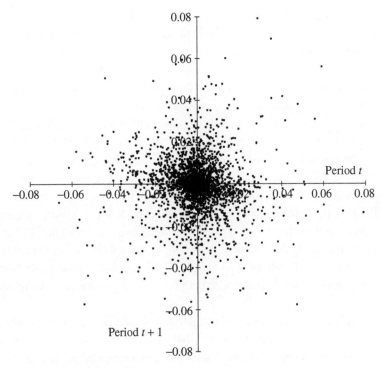

Figure 4.5. Gold returns in consecutive periods.

4.9.2 Lag 1: Daily Equity Series

Most of the first-lag equity autocorrelations in Table 4.8 confirm three results noted by several researchers for *daily* returns: large firms generally have positive estimates, portfolios and hence spot indices have higher estimates than individual securities, and futures on indices have less dependence than spot indices.

The average first-lag estimate across very large samples of US stocks is almost zero in the paper by French and Roll (1986). In their Table 3 they document an average of 0.003 for the twenty years from 1963 to 1983, while Lo and MacKinlay (1990a, p. 181) mention an average of -0.014 for the longer period from 1962 to 1987. However, French and Roll make it clear that the magnitude of the first-lag estimates increases, on average, with the size of the firm. Their average estimates for five quintiles defined by firm size are -0.064 (smallest firms), -0.017, 0.012, 0.025, and 0.054 (largest firms). This pattern of estimates is consistent with negative dependence caused by bid–ask spreads (which are wider for smaller firms) and positive dependence in a factor that is common to all stocks. Blair et al. (2002) report a median first-lag value of 0.037 for a set of large firms, defined by all firms included in the S&P 100 index between 1983 and 1992; the interquartile range of the first-lag autocorrelations is from 0.008 to 0.075 and these summary statistics are not sensitive to inclusion of the crash day in the calculations.

Fisher (1966) and Scholes and Williams (1977) observed that returns from portfolios of stocks will display positive dependence when the component stock prices depend on a common factor and are not contemporaneous. Returns from infrequently traded stocks will tend to reflect common information later than other stocks, so common information may be incorporated into portfolio returns on different days and hence induce positive autocorrelation. This issue of non-synchronous trading is analyzed in a theoretical setting by Lo and MacKinlay (1990b) with further analysis in Boudoukh, Richardson, and Whitelaw (1994). Small-firm portfolios suffer most from nonsynchronous trading and consequently display the most dependence. Conrad and Kaul (1989) report estimates for five size-based portfolios, each containing 400+ stocks. Their first-lag estimates for 1962 to 1985 are 0.46 (smallest quintile), 0.40, 0.36, 0.35, and 0.20 (largest quintile). As equal-weighted portfolios over-represent thinly traded firms they too can have substantial first-lag dependence. For example, Campbell, Lo, and MacKinlay (1997) report an estimate of 0.35 for the CRSP equal-weighted index from 1962 to 1994, that can be compared with 0.18 for the comparable value-weighted index.

Ahn et al. (2002) provide a detailed comparison of the first-lag autocorrelation for returns in recent years from 24 indices that have futures contracts written on their levels. The spot autocorrelation is higher than the corresponding futures value for each index, which is compatible with some stale prices in each index—futures prices then lead the spot index because the former is a traded asset unlike the latter. The differences between the spot and futures autocorrelations are significant at the 5% level for 21 of the 24 indices. The S&P 500 has autocorrelations 0.03 (spot) and -0.04 (futures), for the FTSE 100 they are 0.08 and 0.02 and for the Nikkei 225 the values are -0.00 and -0.02. The highest spot autocorrelations are for indices that have a large total weight on firms which trade relatively infrequently, for example, 0.22 for the Russell 2000 index of small US firms.

First-lag equity estimates for US *weekly* returns have many similarities with estimates for daily returns. They are discussed by Conrad and Kaul (1989), Lo and MacKinlay (1990a), Boudoukh, Richardson, and Whitelaw (1994), and Campbell et al. (1997).

4.9.3 Tests

The autocorrelation estimates can be used to test the hypothesis that the process generating observed returns is a series of independent and identically distributed (i.i.d.) random variables. The asymptotic theory in Section 3.9 informs us that the standard error of an autocorrelation estimate is approximately $1/\sqrt{n} = 0.02$ when there are $n = 2500$ observations from an i.i.d. process. Twenty-eight of the hundred estimates given in Table 4.8 for the first five lags of the twenty series are

Table 4.9. Q-statistics calculated from thirty
autocorrelations, for returns and transformed returns.

Series		r	$|r|$	r^2	$\log(|r - \bar{r}|)$
S&P 500-share	S	66.2	975.5	214.3	151.5
S&P 500-share	F	90.0	1179.0	213.2	321.2
Coca Cola	S	70.1	974.5	967.0	511.2
General Electric	S	53.1	1151.2	1014.2	293.0
General Motors	S	50.8	558.6	507.9	141.5
FT 100-share	S	58.3	1055.4	1365.6	150.8
FT 100-share	F	35.4	1293.3	763.7	238.0
Glaxo	S	45.0	1059.8	894.1	282.9
Marks & Spencer	S	37.8	241.5	417.8	72.0
Shell	S	43.0	594.7	653.7	130.0
Nikkei 225-share	S	71.1	2950.3	380.6	1653.9
Treasury bonds	F	41.2	926.8	643.4	371.6
3-month sterling bills	F	76.0	991.0	75.1	866.5
DM/$	F	49.3	314.6	236.3	85.5
Sterling/$	F	38.7	433.4	508.3	151.5
Swiss franc/$	F	45.7	262.6	206.5	104.9
Yen/$	F	37.1	289.9	112.0	195.4
Gold	F	67.9	1999.0	1139.4	884.8
Corn	F	84.0	3851.6	4785.0	1303.3
Live cattle	F	46.4	1128.6	1152.2	513.8

The numbers tabulated are the series length multiplied by the sum of squared autocorrelations, summing across the first thirty lags. The null hypothesis of i.i.d. returns is tested by comparing the tabulated numbers with χ^2_{30}. The null hypothesis is rejected at the 5% level if $Q > 43.77$ and at the 1% level if $Q > 50.89$.

more than two standard errors (0.04) from zero and hence are significant at the 5% level. This suggests many of the series are not generated by an i.i.d. process.

The i.i.d. hypothesis can also be tested by using the portmanteau Q-statistic of Box and Pierce (1970), calculated from the first k autocorrelations as

$$Q_{k,r} = n \sum_{\tau=1}^{k} \hat{\rho}_{\tau,r}^2. \tag{4.10}$$

The asymptotic distribution of the Q-statistic is chi-squared, with k degrees of freedom, when the process is i.i.d. The values of Q when $k = 30$ are listed in Table 4.9; they reject the i.i.d. hypothesis at the 5% level for 14 of the 20 series. Thus again it appears that many of the returns processes are not i.i.d. The i.i.d. hypothesis can be dealt with far more decisively, however, by testing the autocorrelations of transformed returns, as we will soon see.

The standard error of an autocorrelation estimate used in tests of the i.i.d. hypothesis cannot be used in tests of the interesting hypothesis that returns are uncorrelated. An appropriate standard error when there are n observations is more than $1/\sqrt{n}$ because returns are conditionally heteroskedastic. This conclusion is established in the next chapter and then followed by appropriate autocorrelation tests of the random walk hypothesis.

4.10   Autocorrelations of Transformed Returns

Functions of returns can have substantial autocorrelations even though returns have very small autocorrelations. The evidence for such nonlinear dependence is obtained here by considering the autocorrelations of various powers of absolute returns, $|r_t|$. We consider these autocorrelations for two reasons. The first is to demonstrate beyond doubt that daily returns are not produced by an i.i.d. process. The second is to document an important characteristic of daily returns that must be considered when developing models, namely the third major stylized fact:

   3. *There is positive dependence between absolute returns on nearby days, and likewise for squared returns.*

Autocorrelations are discussed for time series $\{|r_t|^\lambda\}$ with a particular interest in the two cases $\lambda = 1, 2$. These series are observations from an i.i.d. process whenever the returns come from an i.i.d. process. Consequently, the same large-sample theory is applicable to the transformed series when testing the i.i.d. hypothesis, providing the moments $E[|r_t|^{2\lambda}]$ are finite. Granger and Andersen (1978) suggested there would be informative results when $\lambda = 2$, which was confirmed in Taylor (1982b) and followed by numerous results for the powers $\lambda = 1, 2$ in Taylor (1986). All positive numbers λ are discussed by Ding, Granger, and Engle (1993).

The limit of the autocorrelations as $\lambda \to 0$ is important when developing and estimating certain volatility models, first noted by Scott (1987). The limit is the same as the autocorrelations of $\log(|r_t|)$ when considering random variables having continuous density functions, since $(|r|^\lambda - 1)/\lambda \to \log(|r|)$ as $\lambda \to 0$. The limit cannot be calculated from data when some returns are zero. To avoid this difficulty we calculate the autocorrelations from the following transformation of mean-adjusted returns, which defines "logarithmic absolute returns": $l_t = \log(|r_t - \bar{r}|)$. The autocorrelations of the series $\{l_t\}$ will be interpreted as the appropriate numbers for the special case $\lambda = 0$. When λ is positive it makes very little difference whether or not the returns are mean-adjusted.

4.10.1   Lags 1 to 5

Summaries of the autocorrelation estimates for the series $\{|r_t|\}$, $\{r_t^2\}$, and $\{l_t\}$ are respectively presented in Tables 4.10, 4.11, and 4.12. Each table presents 100 estimates for the first five lags of twenty series. Almost all the estimates are positive: 100 for absolute returns, 100 for squared returns, and 98 for logarithmic absolute returns. A substantial majority of the estimates exceed 0.04 and hence

Table 4.10. Autocorrelations for absolute returns.

Series		Lags 1–5 Autocorrelations					Lags 1–30 Category frequency					
		1	2	3	4	5	1	2	3	4	5	6
S&P 500-share	S	0.159	0.195	0.230	0.126	0.209	0	0	0	3	13	14
S&P 500-share	F	0.249	0.286	0.226	0.149	0.197	0	0	0	0	19	11
Coca Cola	S	0.329	0.162	0.145	0.159	0.158	0	0	0	3	15	12
General Electric	S	0.224	0.211	0.176	0.159	0.168	0	0	0	0	12	18
General Motors	S	0.204	0.161	0.146	0.116	0.101	0	0	0	7	15	8
FT 100-share	S	0.298	0.251	0.180	0.184	0.139	0	0	0	12	3	15
FT 100-share	F	0.277	0.265	0.205	0.150	0.160	0	0	0	3	11	16
Glaxo	S	0.247	0.163	0.138	0.150	0.169	0	0	0	2	13	15
Marks & Spencer	S	0.155	0.078	0.075	0.082	0.075	0	0	0	18	11	1
Shell	S	0.196	0.161	0.159	0.117	0.113	0	0	0	4	21	5
Nikkei 225-share	S	0.315	0.285	0.276	0.277	0.257	0	0	0	0	0	30
Treasury bonds	F	0.086	0.112	0.137	0.148	0.184	0	0	0	0	13	17
3-month sterling bills	F	0.232	0.228	0.189	0.151	0.136	0	0	0	4	13	13
DM/$	F	0.054	0.063	0.080	0.090	0.090	0	0	0	10	18	2
Sterling/$	F	0.101	0.079	0.086	0.106	0.081	0	0	0	6	20	4
Swiss franc/$	F	0.032	0.027	0.071	0.061	0.092	0	0	1	11	16	2
Yen/$	F	0.113	0.069	0.121	0.059	0.111	0	0	0	13	14	3
Gold	F	0.210	0.181	0.183	0.200	0.195	0	0	0	0	0	30
Corn	F	0.311	0.285	0.230	0.255	0.289	0	0	0	0	0	30
Live cattle	F	0.083	0.156	0.141	0.143	0.121	0	0	0	0	8	22
Autocorrelation averages and frequency totals												
Spot series	S	0.236	0.185	0.169	0.152	0.154	0	0	0	49	103	118
Future series	F	0.159	0.159	0.152	0.137	0.151	0	0	1	47	132	150
All series		0.194	0.171	0.160	0.144	0.152	0	0	1	96	235	268
All series, crash excluded		0.115	0.107	0.107	0.113	0.113	0	0	6	130	287	177

reject the i.i.d. hypothesis at the 5% significance level: 98 for absolute returns, 95 for squared returns, and 83 for logarithmic absolute returns.

These estimates are sensitive to the inclusion of the crash month (October 1987) in the calculations. As the final row in each table shows, exclusion of the crash month (as described previously for returns) lowers the average estimates. This is particularly so for absolute and squared returns at lags 1 and 2. The lower estimates are to be expected because the crash period contains a cluster of higher than usual absolute returns. Removing the crash month causes the first-lag stock index estimates for absolute returns to decrease substantially; for the US from 0.16 to 0.06 (spot) and 0.25 to 0.09 (futures); for the UK from 0.30 to 0.10 (spot) and 0.28 to 0.12 (futures); and for Japan from 0.31 to 0.25 (spot). The numbers of positive and significant estimates change little with the removal of the crash month. There are then 100, 100, and 96 positive estimates, of which 97, 93, and 72 are greater than $2/\sqrt{n} = 0.04$.

Figure 4.6 is a scatter plot of absolute returns for gold in consecutive periods. The correlation between $|r_t|$ and $|r_{t+1}|$ is 0.21 on this figure and it may not appear,

Table 4.11. Autocorrelations for squared returns.

		\multicolumn{5}{c}{Lags 1–5 Autocorrelations}	\multicolumn{6}{c}{Lags 1–30 Category frequency}
Series		1	2	3	4	5	1	2	3	4	5	6
S&P 500-share	S	0.074	0.181	0.097	0.017	0.168	0	0	2	24	2	2
S&P 500-share	F	0.082	0.258	0.058	0.011	0.067	0	0	2	24	3	1
Coca Cola	S	0.545	0.200	0.088	0.100	0.110	0	0	1	22	3	4
General Electric	S	0.303	0.365	0.217	0.105	0.185	0	0	0	12	12	6
General Motors	S	0.398	0.111	0.104	0.036	0.056	0	0	0	25	2	3
FT 100-share	S	0.603	0.274	0.140	0.153	0.107	0	0	1	15	9	5
FT 100-share	F	0.348	0.266	0.201	0.065	0.080	0	0	0	17	9	4
Glaxo	S	0.414	0.127	0.085	0.083	0.128	0	0	1	11	12	6
Marks & Spencer	S	0.288	0.149	0.077	0.092	0.077	0	0	1	18	9	2
Shell	S	0.293	0.225	0.215	0.089	0.113	0	0	0	20	5	5
Nikkei 225-share	S	0.231	0.091	0.117	0.127	0.080	0	0	0	14	13	3
Treasury bonds	F	0.123	0.131	0.111	0.123	0.197	0	0	0	2	17	11
3-month sterling bills	F	0.054	0.115	0.059	0.014	0.020	0	0	3	23	3	1
DM/$	F	0.059	0.094	0.049	0.056	0.059	0	0	0	17	12	1
Sterling/$	F	0.102	0.093	0.084	0.125	0.061	0	0	0	6	17	7
Swiss franc/$	F	0.038	0.050	0.059	0.038	0.073	0	0	0	20	9	1
Yen/$	F	0.071	0.052	0.108	0.028	0.065	0	0	3	22	4	1
Gold	F	0.180	0.149	0.168	0.158	0.167	0	0	0	0	8	22
Corn	F	0.405	0.309	0.199	0.219	0.321	0	0	0	0	0	30
Live cattle	F	0.088	0.170	0.160	0.151	0.135	0	0	0	0	10	20
Autocorrelation averages and frequency totals												
Spot series	S	0.350	0.191	0.127	0.089	0.114	0	0	6	161	67	36
Future series	F	0.141	0.153	0.114	0.090	0.113	0	0	8	131	92	99
All series		0.235	0.170	0.120	0.089	0.114	0	0	14	292	159	135
All series, crash excluded		0.099	0.096	0.086	0.093	0.091	0	0	20	232	241	107

at first sight, that there is any dependence between the variables. As $|r_t|$ increases, there is more chance of a high value of $|r_{t+1}|$ and this may be discerned in the figure. To emphasize the dependence, Figure 4.7 shows the expectation of $|r_{t+1}|$ conditional upon observing $|r_t| > c$ for various c between 0.1 and 4%. These expectations are marked by diamonds and increase almost linearly with c. The figure also shows the expectation of r_{t+1} given that $r_t > c$, marked by squares, and the expectation of r_{t+1} given $r_t < -c$, marked by triangles.

4.10.2 Lags 1 to 30

The category frequencies in Tables 4.10–4.12 summarize the estimates for the first thirty lags. The 600 estimates summarized in each table are almost all positive, the totals being 599, 586, and 586. Excluding the crash month reduces these totals to 594, 580, and 578. All estimates in categories five and six exceed 0.05 and are significant at the 1% level for tests of the i.i.d. hypothesis. The three tables have 503, 294, and 352 estimates in these classes compared with the 36 estimates for returns that fall outside the range from −0.05 to 0.05. These comparisons of

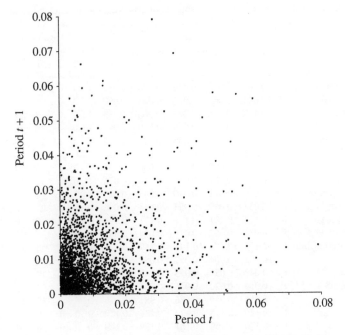

Figure 4.6. Gold returns: absolute values in consecutive periods.

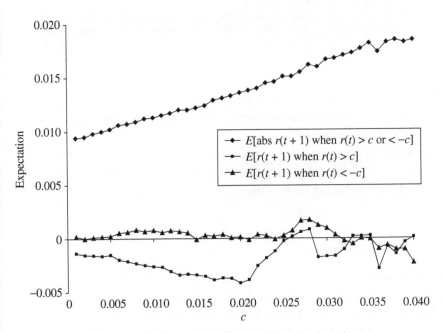

Figure 4.7. Gold returns: selected conditional expectations.

Table 4.12.   Autocorrelations for logarithms of absolute, mean-adjusted returns.

Series		1	2	3	4	5	1	2	3	4	5	6
			Lags 1–5 Autocorrelations						Lags 1–30 Category frequency			
S&P 500-share	S	0.005	0.004	0.040	0.034	0.083	0	0	0	19	11	0
S&P 500-share	F	0.024	0.068	0.077	0.063	0.090	0	0	0	6	24	0
Coca Cola	S	0.137	0.085	0.049	0.068	0.083	0	0	0	2	24	4
General Electric	S	0.078	0.073	0.060	0.070	0.081	0	0	0	10	20	0
General Motors	S	0.057	0.069	0.065	0.080	0.047	0	0	1	21	8	0
FT 100-share	S	0.039	0.073	0.043	0.055	0.056	0	0	1	19	10	0
FT 100-share	F	0.071	0.068	0.059	0.036	0.061	0	0	0	16	14	0
Glaxo	S	0.095	0.087	0.062	0.070	0.076	0	0	0	11	19	0
Marks & Spencer	S	0.060	0.012	0.046	0.043	0.028	0	0	5	22	3	0
Shell	S	0.057	0.059	0.053	0.041	0.036	0	0	0	22	8	0
Nikkei 225-share	S	0.178	0.201	0.177	0.171	0.174	0	0	0	0	0	30
Treasury bonds	F	0.034	0.062	0.071	0.094	0.081	0	0	0	5	25	0
3-month sterling bills	F	0.178	0.168	0.145	0.157	0.131	0	0	0	0	18	12
DM/$	F	0.022	−0.004	0.057	0.042	0.058	0	0	4	21	5	0
Sterling/$	F	0.048	0.053	0.055	0.048	0.067	0	0	0	19	11	0
Swiss franc/$	F	0.019	−0.020	0.026	0.035	0.066	0	0	2	23	5	0
Yen/$	F	0.085	0.050	0.076	0.081	0.076	0	0	1	17	12	0
Gold	F	0.120	0.115	0.122	0.136	0.110	0	0	0	0	10	20
Corn	F	0.170	0.150	0.151	0.139	0.169	0	0	0	0	4	26
Live cattle	F	0.054	0.067	0.109	0.066	0.076	0	0	0	1	23	6

Autocorrelation averages and frequency totals

Spot series	S	0.078	0.074	0.066	0.070	0.074	0	0	7	126	103	34
Future series	F	0.075	0.071	0.086	0.081	0.089	0	0	7	108	151	64
All series		0.077	0.072	0.077	0.076	0.082	0	0	14	234	254	98
All series, crash excluded		0.062	0.059	0.063	0.064	0.069	0	0	22	307	202	69

significant autocorrelation estimates demonstrate the validity of the third stylized fact—there is far more linear dependence among the transformed returns than among the returns themselves.

The abundant numbers of significant estimates for the transformed series inevitably ensure that the Q-statistics are very large when compared with the appropriate χ^2 distribution. Table 4.9 shows values for absolute returns,

$$Q_{30,|r|} = n \sum_{\tau=1}^{30} \hat{\rho}^2_{\tau,|r|},$$

and the other transformed series. The values of Q are always more than 240 for the series of absolute returns so the i.i.d. hypothesis must be false. Furthermore, the differences $Q_{30,|r|} - Q_{30,r}$ all exceed 200, emphasizing that there is far more linear dependence in the process generating transformed returns than in the process for returns.

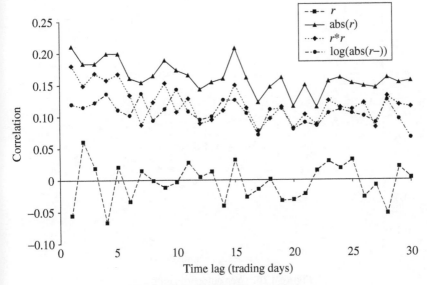

Figure 4.8. Gold autocorrelations.

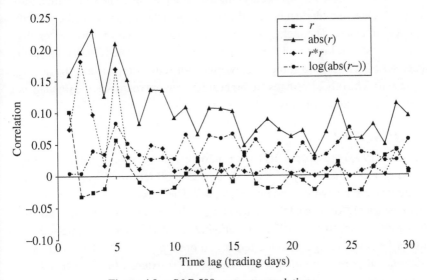

Figure 4.9. S&P 500 spot autocorrelations.

Figures 4.8–4.11 are plots of the autocorrelations of returns (marked with squares), absolute returns (triangles, joined by solid lines), squared returns (diamonds) and logarithmic absolute returns (circles). The gold estimates in Figure 4.8 show that the absolute returns and the returns respectively have the highest and lowest estimates for gold at all of the first thirty lags. The picture is less clear in Figure 4.9 for the S&P 500 spot estimates, although the absolute returns do

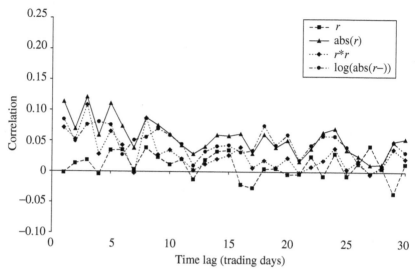

Figure 4.10.   Yen autocorrelations.

have the highest estimates for twenty-nine of the thirty lags. The yen estimates, in Figure 4.10, are smaller than in the other figures and the lines joining the symbols frequently intersect. The highest estimate is for absolute returns more often than for the other series. Figure 4.11 shows averages of the estimates obtained from the twenty series. This figure shows the averages for returns are always the average nearest zero. The other averages are highest for squared returns at the first lag and thereafter for absolute returns.

4.10.3   Lags 1 to 625

Ding et al. (1993) present results for the autocorrelations of $|r_t|^\lambda$ calculated from a series of more than sixty years of daily S&P 500 returns. Fractional powers of λ are investigated within the range 0.125–5. The maximum correlation occurs when λ is near 1, for at least the first 100 lags. The absolute returns have positive autocorrelation up to lag 2705, a remarkable result that may be largely due to a higher level of average absolute returns before the year 1940 than afterwards. A subsequent paper by Granger and Ding (1995) extends the investigation of fractional powers of λ to commodity and exchange rate series. They show that the maximum correlation often occurs when λ is close to 1.

Autocorrelations up to lag 625 have been calculated for the series discussed throughout this chapter, to obtain further results about the power λ giving the most linear dependence in each series $|r_t|^\lambda$. The Q-statistic defined by

$$Q_{k,|r|^\lambda} = n \sum_{\tau=1}^{k} [\mathrm{cor}(|r_t|^\lambda, |r_{t+\tau}|^\lambda)]^2 \qquad (4.11)$$

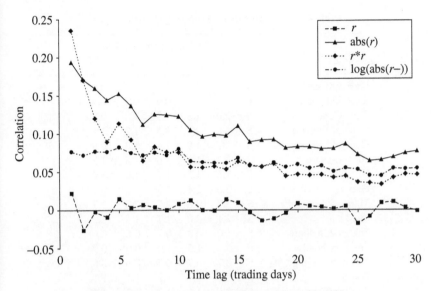

Figure 4.11. Average autocorrelations across 20 series.

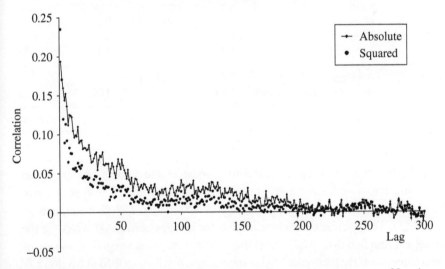

Figure 4.12. Autocorrelations of absolute and squared returns; averages across 20 series.

has been maximized for $k = 1, 5, 25, 125, 625$ by calculating Q for $\lambda = 0.1, 0.2, 0.3, \ldots, 5$. The powers λ_{max} that maximize Q are shown in Table 4.13. Three-quarters of the numbers λ_{max} are within the range 0.7–1.3 when 625 lags are used and the average value of λ_{max} is then 1.01. The numbers λ_{max} do not change much when the crash month is excluded, providing 25 or more lags are used.

Figure 4.12 shows the across-series averages of the autocorrelations for absolute and squared returns up to lag 300. The figure shows that absolute returns have

Table 4.13. Powers that maximize Q-statistics.

Series		Q calculated from lags 1 to...				
		1	5	25	125	625
S&P 500-share	S	1.2	1.2	1.0	0.9	0.8
S&P 500-share	F	1.1	1.1	0.9	0.7	0.7
Coca Cola	S	2.0	1.8	1.5	1.0	0.8
General Electric	S	1.8	1.8	1.5	1.2	1.1
General Motors	S	2.1	1.9	1.4	1.0	0.9
FT 100-share	S	2.3	1.9	1.6	1.5	1.3
FT 100-share	F	1.6	1.5	1.2	1.2	1.0
Glaxo	S	2.6	2.1	1.3	1.0	0.9
Marks & Spencer	S	3.0	2.8	2.7	2.3	1.7
Shell	S	2.1	2.0	1.7	1.5	1.3
Nikkei 225-share	S	1.0	0.8	0.7	0.6	0.6
Treasury bonds	F	5.0	1.5	1.0	0.9	0.9
3-month sterling bills	F	0.7	0.7	0.7	0.6	0.6
DM/$	F	1.7	1.1	1.2	1.1	1.1
Sterling/$	F	1.5	1.6	1.7	1.7	1.4
Swiss franc/$	F	1.9	1.3	1.2	1.2	1.2
Yen/$	F	0.8	0.9	0.7	0.6	0.7
Gold	F	1.0	1.0	0.8	0.8	0.7
Corn	F	2.2	1.7	1.8	1.7	1.4
Live cattle	F	5.0	2.8	1.6	1.1	1.1
Averages		2.03	1.58	1.31	1.13	1.01
Averages, crash excluded		1.55	1.29	1.18	1.10	1.02

Each tabulated number is the power that gives the most dependence in absolute returns raised to a positive power, with dependence summarized by the sum of squared autocorrelations, summing across the first 1, 5, 25, 125, or 625 lags.

more dependence than squared returns for a considerable number of lags. It also shows the across-series averages are positive for many lags. The first negative averages for selected λ are at lags 196 ($\lambda = 0.5, 1, 1.5$), 168 ($\lambda = 2$), and 89 ($\lambda = 2.5$). The averages are close to zero for all lags above 200 whatever the power λ. From lags 300 to 625 a majority of the averages are negative, and this is a consequence of the theoretical finite-sample bias that is described in Section 5.6. The slow decline shown by the averages in Figure 4.12 is typical of long-memory effects, but it would be wrong to conclude from the figure that the individual series have a long-memory property.

4.10.4 Characteristics of Returns Time Series

The tables and figures show that while very little autocorrelation is present in series of returns $\{r_t\}$, *substantially more* autocorrelation is found in series of absolute returns $\{|r_t|\}$. The autocorrelations of absolute returns are always positive at a lag of one day and positive dependence continues to be found for several further lags. Power transformations of absolute returns, including squared returns $\{r_t^2\}$, also display positive dependence but generally to a lesser degree. These conclusions are characteristics of all the series of returns studied here. Most and often all of these conclusions apply to any long series of daily returns from a financial asset that is traded frequently.

The high dependence in series of absolute returns proves that the returns process is not made up of independent and identically distributed random variables. It does not provide conclusions about the random walk and efficient market hypotheses. Large absolute returns are more likely than small absolute returns to be followed by large absolute returns, but this result alone cannot be used to predict the direction of price changes. Early statements of similar conclusions are made by Mandelbrot (1963) and Fama (1965).

There is a simple explanation for the dependence found in series of absolute returns, based upon the volatility clusters noted in Section 2.4. Changes in price volatility create clusters of high and low volatility, that may reflect changes in the flow of relevant information to the market. There are then some periods during which returns are relatively more variable and hence expected absolute returns are relatively high. In other periods, returns have relatively little dispersion and expected absolute returns are relatively low. The clustering of expected absolute returns causes positive dependence in the observed data. This explanation is developed in detail in Chapters 8–11.

Other explanations are less easy to motivate. Weekend and other calendar effects cannot explain the dependence in absolute and squared returns (Appendix 4.13). Neither can a linear, correlated process provide a satisfactory explanation (Section 4.11).

4.10.5 Consequences

The consequences of positive dependence between absolute (or squared) returns on nearby days are essentially the same as the consequences of volatility clustering. All econometric methods and financial applications that assume returns are i.i.d. need to be reconsidered. A few examples are mentioned here.

One example arises when testing the interesting hypothesis that returns on different days are not correlated with each other. As this version of the random walk hypothesis is weaker than the statement that returns are i.i.d., the standard errors of the estimates $\hat{\rho}_{\tau,r}$ obtained from n returns need not be $1/\sqrt{n}$ when the weaker hypothesis applies. Instead estimates of appropriate standard errors can exceed $2/\sqrt{n}$ (Chapter 5). Another example relates to estimating the density function of returns. The likelihood function is only the product of unconditional densities when returns are i.i.d. As they are not, likelihood inferences and parameter estimates must be based upon a suitable product of conditional density functions

(Chapters 9–11). As volatility is to some extent predictable, the continuous-time processes required to derive the Black–Scholes and related option pricing are incorrectly specified. More sophisticated pricing formulae, which reflect volatility expectations and dynamics, are required. These formulae are used by traders (Chapters 14–16).

4.11 Nonlinearity of the Returns Process

Recall that a stochastic process for returns is linear if it is possible to describe returns by the equation

$$r_t = \mu + \varepsilon_t + \sum_{j=1}^{\infty} b_j \varepsilon_{t-j}$$

where μ and the b_j are constants and $\{\varepsilon_t\}$ is a process of zero-mean i.i.d. random variables. We have already shown that this model is indefensible if all the coefficients b_j are zero. More effort is required to reject the general linear model, although many readers will surely be content to accept that Figures 4.8–4.12 show autocorrelations that are inconsistent with linear theory.

4.11.1 Not Linear

Let $s_t = (r_t - \mu)^2$ and assume the returns have finite kurtosis, $\kappa = E[s_t^2]/E[s_t]^2$. The autocorrelations of the stochastic process $\{s_t\}$, denoted by $\rho_{\tau,s}$, are known for stationary, Gaussian (and hence linear) processes to be the squares of the return autocorrelations $\rho_{\tau,r}$, i.e. $\rho_{\tau,s} = \rho_{\tau,r}^2$ for any lag τ (Granger and Newbold 1976). Clearly, the empirical evidence is decisively against these equalities. The mathematics is far less tidy for non-Gaussian, linear processes. Appendix 4.14 shows that for such processes there is a general result

$$\rho_{\tau,s} = \frac{2}{\kappa - 1} \rho_{\tau,r}^2 + \frac{\kappa - 3}{\kappa - 1} \alpha_\tau \tag{4.12}$$

with the positive numbers α_τ determined by the b_j alone. Thus $\rho_{\tau,s}$ is a weighted average of $\rho_{\tau,r}^2$ and α_τ with all weight given to the first term only when $\kappa = 3$.

An upper bound for sums of the α_τ can be obtained from the proportional reduction in mean square error obtained by the optimal forecasts for a linear model, denoted by $\theta = \{\mathrm{var}(r_t) - \mathrm{var}(\varepsilon_t)\}/\mathrm{var}(r_t)$. It can be shown that

$$\alpha_\tau \geqslant 0 \quad (\tau > 0) \quad \text{and} \quad \sum_{\tau=1}^{\infty} \alpha_\tau \leqslant \frac{\theta}{(1 - \theta)^2}. \tag{4.13}$$

As it is only necessary to consider leptokurtic distributions, $\kappa > 3$, and

$$\sum_{\tau=1}^{k} \rho_{\tau,s} \leqslant \max \left(\sum_{\tau=1}^{k} \rho_{\tau,r}^2, \frac{\theta}{(1 - \theta)^2} \right) \tag{4.14}$$

for any positive integer k. To complete the argument against all linear processes it is necessary to select the number of lags k and to offer a value for θ. Further rigor and significance tests do not seem necessary at this point. Table 4.11 gives autocorrelation estimates for squared returns. These estimates are almost identical to the autocorrelations of mean-adjusted squared returns, which are the natural estimates of $\rho_{\tau,s}$. Inspection of Table 4.11 shows that the sample autocorrelations contradict the inequality (4.14) for all series if $k = 5$ and $\theta = 0.15$. The contradictions remain when the crash month is excluded from the calculations. Increasing k will increase the difference between the two sums in the inequality and thus confirm that linear processes are not appropriate. The assumption $\theta < 0.15$ is innocuous since no one has found a forecast anywhere near 15% more accurate than the random walk forecast for liquid traded assets.

4.12 Concluding Remarks

Any satisfactory statistical model for daily returns must be consistent with three stylized facts that are of particular importance. First, the distribution of returns is approximately symmetric and has high kurtosis, fat tails and a peaked center compared with the normal distribution. Second, the autocorrelations of returns are all close to zero. Third, the autocorrelations of both absolute returns and squared returns are positive for many lags and they indicate substantially more linear dependence than the autocorrelations of returns.

Several models examined in the remainder of this book are compatible with these stylized facts. The density of returns is a mixture of normal densities for many of these models, with the mixture defined by variation in volatility. The dependence among absolute and squared returns is then a consequence of slow changes in volatility.

Further Reading

Ahn, D.-H., J. Boudoukh, M. P. Richardson, and R. F. Whitelaw. 2002. Partial adjustment or stale prices? Implications from stock index and futures return autocorrelations. *Review of Financial Studies* 15:655–689.

Ding, Z., C. W. J. Granger, and R. F. Engle. 1993. A long memory property of stock market returns and a new model. *Journal of Empirical Finance* 1:83–106.

Jorion, P. and W. N. Goetzmann. 1999. Global stock markets in the twentieth century. *Journal of Finance* 54:953–980.

Lakonishok, J. and S. Smidt. 1988. Are seasonal anomalies real? A ninety year perspective. *Review of Financial Studies* 1:435–455.

Sullivan, R., A. Timmermann, and H. White. 2001. Dangers of data mining: the case of calendar effects in stock returns. *Journal of Econometrics* 105:249–286.

4.13   Appendix: Autocorrelation Caused by Day-of-the-Week Effects

Suppose the process generating daily returns depends on the day of the week according to the following seasonal model:

$$r_t = \mu_t + \sigma_t \varepsilon_t, \quad \mu_t = \mu_{t+5}, \quad \sigma_t = \sigma_{t+5},$$

with $\{\varepsilon_t\}$ a stationary, zero-mean, unit-variance process. Autocorrelations calculated from a sample of returns will depend on the calendar terms $\mu_i, \sigma_i, 1 \leqslant i \leqslant 5$. The numerical consequences of these day-of-the-week terms are, however, small. Similar methods can be used to show that month-of-the-year effects are much smaller.

4.13.1   Returns

As the sample size n increases, an autocorrelation estimate $\hat{\rho}_{\tau,r,n}$ defined for n random variables r_t by $\sum(r_t - \bar{r})(r_{t+\tau} - \bar{r})/\sum(r_t - \bar{r})^2$ will converge with probability 1 to a limit. Estimates calculated from observations will converge to the same limit, which is here denoted by $\pi_{\tau,r}$. This limit would be the population autocorrelation $\rho_{\tau,r}$ if the returns process was stationary. As n increases,

$$\bar{r} = \frac{1}{n}\sum_{t=1}^{n} r_t \quad \rightarrow \quad \frac{1}{5}\sum_{i=1}^{5} \mu_i = \mu, \quad \text{say,}$$

and

$$\frac{1}{n}\sum_{t=1}^{n-\tau} r_t r_{t+\tau} \quad \rightarrow \quad \frac{1}{5}\sum_{i=1}^{5} E[r_i r_{i+\tau}].$$

Now assume ε_t is uncorrelated with $\varepsilon_{t+\tau}$ whenever $\tau \neq 0$. Then it can be shown that the daily calendar effects create the asymptotic, estimated autocorrelations:

$$\pi_{\tau,r} = \sum_{i=1}^{5}(\mu_i - \mu)(\mu_{i+\tau} - \mu) \bigg/ \sum_{i=1}^{5}(\mu_i - \mu)^2 + \sigma_i^2, \quad \tau > 0. \quad (4.15)$$

Clearly, $\pi_{\tau,r} = \pi_{\tau+5,r}$ for all positive τ; it can also be shown that $\pi_{1,r} = \pi_{4,r}$ and $\pi_{2,r} = \pi_{3,r}$.

To emphasize the small magnitudes of the numbers $\pi_{\tau,r}$, suppose the daily means and standard deviations equal the estimates of French (1980), tabulated in Section 4.5. Then (4.15) gives these values for $\pi_{\tau,r}$:

τ	π
1, 4	−0.003
2, 3	−0.005
5	0.017

4.13.2 Squared Returns

Let π_{τ,r^2} be the limit of estimates $\hat{\rho}_{\tau,r^2,n}$. Also, let $\gamma_i = E[r_i^2] = \mu_i^2 + \sigma_i^2$ and $\gamma = (\gamma_1 + \cdots + \gamma_5)/5$. Now assume the ε_t are i.i.d. with $E[\varepsilon_t^3] = 0$ and $E[\varepsilon_t^4] = \lambda$. Then it can be shown that

$$\pi_{\tau,r^2} = \sum_{i=1}^{5}(\gamma_i - \gamma)(\gamma_{i+\tau} - \gamma) \bigg/ \sum_{i=1}^{5}(\gamma_i - \gamma)^2 + 4\mu_i^2\sigma_i^2 + (\lambda - 1)\sigma_i^4, \quad \tau > 0.$$

(4.16)

Again using French's estimates, (4.16) gives the following low autocorrelations first for the Gaussian case $\lambda = 3$ and second for the leptokurtic case $\lambda = 6$:

τ	$\lambda = 3$	$\lambda = 6$
1, 4	−0.006	−0.002
2, 3	−0.003	−0.001
5	0.017	0.007

A second example is provided by averaging the variance proportions given in Table 4.8 for the four currency futures series (Monday 23.3%, Tuesday 19.6%, Wednesday 16.8%, Thursday 18.8%, Friday 21.5%) with the mean effects assumed to be zero:

τ	$\lambda = 3$	$\lambda = 6$
1, 4	0.002	0.001
2, 3	−0.005	−0.002
5	0.006	0.002

4.14 Appendix: Autocorrelations of a Squared Linear Process

Suppose $\{r_t\}$ is linear with $r_t = \mu + \sum b_i \varepsilon_{t-i}$. All sums are over the nonnegative subscript i in this appendix, unless stated otherwise. Assume that $E[r_t^4]$ is finite and, without loss of generality, that the ε_t have zero mean and unit variance and also that $b_0 = 1$. Let $\lambda = E[\varepsilon_t^4]$ and define

$$s_t = (r_t - \mu)^2 = \sum_i b_i^2 \varepsilon_{t-i}^2 + 2\sum_{i<j}\sum b_i b_j \varepsilon_{t-i}\varepsilon_{t-j}.$$

Then $E[s_t] = \sum b_i^2$. To find the autocorrelations of $\{s_t\}$ we need to evaluate $E[s_t s_{t+\tau}]$, which can be done by remembering that the ε_t are i.i.d. Straightforward algebra eventually shows that, for all $\tau \geqslant 0$,

$$\text{cov}(s_t, s_{t+\tau}) = E[s_t s_{t+\tau}] - E[s_t]^2 = (\lambda - 3)\sum b_i^2 b_{i+\tau}^2 + 2\Big(\sum b_i b_{i+\tau}\Big)^2.$$

Consequently,

$$\rho_{\tau,s} = \frac{(\lambda - 3)\sum b_i^2 b_{i+\tau}^2 + 2(\sum b_i b_{i+\tau})^2}{(\lambda - 3)\sum b_i^4 + 2(\sum b_i^2)^2}.$$

To simplify this expression, note, first, that r_t has kurtosis κ related to the kurtosis λ of ε_t by

$$\frac{\kappa - 3}{\lambda - 3} = \sum b_i^4 \Big/ \left(\sum b_i^2\right)^2$$

when $\lambda \neq 3$, second, that the autocorrelations of $\{r_t\}$ are

$$\rho_{\tau,r} = \sum b_i b_{i+\tau} \Big/ \sum b_i^2,$$

and, third, that the autocorrelations of the process $r_t^* = \sum_i b_i^2 \varepsilon_{t-i}$ are

$$\alpha_\tau = \sum b_i^2 b_{i+\tau}^2 \Big/ \sum b_i^4.$$

These three observations permit simplification of the previous equation for $\rho_{\tau,s}$, to give

$$\rho_{\tau,s} = \frac{(\kappa - 3)\alpha_\tau + 2\rho_{\tau,r}^2}{\kappa - 3 + 2}.$$

This is equation (4.12). To establish bounds for the nonnegative quantities α_τ, note that

$$\sum_{\tau=1}^{\infty}\sum_{i=0}^{\infty} b_i^2 b_{i+\tau}^2 = \frac{1}{2}\left\{\left(\sum b_i^2\right)^2 - \sum b_i^4\right\}$$

and so

$$\sum_{\tau=1}^{\infty} \alpha_\tau = \frac{1}{2}\left\{\left(\sum b_i^2\right)^2 - \sum b_i^4\right\} \Big/ \sum b_i^4.$$

Let $\theta = \{\mathrm{var}(r_t) - \mathrm{var}(\varepsilon_t)\}/\mathrm{var}(r_t)$, so $\sum b_i^2 = 1/(1-\theta)$. As $\sum b_i^4 \geqslant 1$, it follows that (4.13) is correct, i.e.

$$\sum_{\tau=1}^{\infty} \alpha_\tau \leqslant \frac{1}{2}\left\{\frac{1}{(1-\theta)^2} - 1\right\} \leqslant \frac{\theta}{(1-\theta)^2}.$$

Part II

Conditional Expected Returns

5

The Variance-Ratio Test of
the Random Walk Hypothesis

Comparisons between the variances of one-period and multi-period returns are used to test the random walk hypothesis in this chapter. This variance-ratio test is straightforward and often powerful for detecting departures from randomness. Several empirical examples are discussed, as well as theoretical properties of the test statistic. These properties depend on results about the distributions of sample autocorrelations.

5.1   Introduction

Chapters 5–7 cover tests about the conditional *first* moment properties of returns. These tests answer several questions, including, Are returns unpredictable? and Are markets weak-form efficient? Some readers may want to assume the answers are "yes" and to focus on understanding price volatility, i.e. conditional *second* moment properties; they should jump to Chapter 8.

The random walk hypothesis asserts that price changes are unpredictable in some way. The hypothesis can be defined by considering the relevance of the historical record of returns for the optimal prediction of the next return. It is true if the optimal prediction is the same number at all times and for all possible histories. Our definitions of optimality are given in Section 5.2.

Tests of the random walk hypothesis also require data, a test statistic, and the distribution of the statistic when the hypothesis is true. Several test statistics are available. Their power to identify alternatives to randomness depends on the statistic and the alternative. In this chapter we focus on the variance-ratio test of Lo and MacKinlay (1988), which is particularly powerful when the alternative is either trends in prices or mean-reversion in prices. Many further tests that can be more informative for other alternatives are evaluated in the next chapter.

The variance-ratio test compares the variances of returns measured over two different holding periods, for example, one day and one week. The test statistic, based on the ratio of variance estimates, is defined in Section 5.3. An example of the test calculations is provided in Section 5.4, using Excel, followed by a discussion of selected test results for daily, weekly, monthly, and annual returns in Section 5.5. The theoretical properties of the test statistic depend on the distributions of sample autocorrelations when returns are uncorrelated but conditionally heteroskedastic. The distributional results are covered in Section 5.6.

The power of random walk tests can be increased by reducing the level of conditional heteroskedasticity in the data used for tests. A rescaling transformation of returns that achieves this is discussed in Section 5.7. The variance-ratio test finds more evidence against randomness after the transformation, as do many of the additional tests described in Chapter 6.

5.2 The Random Walk Hypothesis

5.2.1 Definitions

There are several definitions of the random walk hypothesis (RWH). They state conditions that incorporate the idea that prices wander ("walk") in an unpredictable ("random") manner.

One definition that we do not use is that returns have independent and identical distributions (i.i.d.). The i.i.d. hypothesis is not very relevant if we are interested in the predictability of returns. It will be rejected by an appropriate test if the conditional variances of returns have sufficient variation through time, but this may tell us nothing about the predictability of returns. For example, the statistically significant autocorrelation in absolute and squared returns rejects the i.i.d. hypothesis but it does not prove that returns can be predicted. Even if we test and reject the i.i.d. hypothesis using the autocorrelations of returns, we still cannot reject the hypothesis that returns are uncorrelated at the same significance level. This fact will be illustrated in Section 6.2.

A more general RWH is defined by first replacing identical distributions by identical means and second replacing independent distributions by uncorrelated distributions. This gives our first definition of the random walk hypothesis:

$$E[r_t] = E[r_{t+\tau}] \quad \text{and} \quad \text{cov}(r_t, r_{t+\tau}) = 0 \quad \text{for all } t \text{ and all } \tau > 0. \quad \text{RWH1}$$

When RWH1 is true, the returns process is uncorrelated and hence the best linear prediction of a future return is its unconditional mean, which RWH1 assumes is a constant. Linear predictors of r_{t+1} are defined by

$$f_{t+1} = \alpha + \sum_{i=0}^{\infty} \beta_i r_{t-i}.$$

RWH1 implies that the mean squared forecast error, $E[(r_{t+1} - f_{t+1})^2]$, is minimized by the constant predictor given by setting $\alpha = E[r_{t+1}]$ and all $\beta_i = 0$.

Definition RWH1 can be found in the pioneering text by Granger and Morgenstern (1970). The assumptions are weak. For example, it is not even assumed that the returns process is stationary. Further assumptions are required if the sample autocorrelations of returns are used to test RWH1. Lo and MacKinlay (1988) list three further assumptions that permit asymptotic tests and that are satisfied by a very general category of conditionally heteroskedastic processes.

The definition RWH1 does not exclude the possibility that a nonlinear predictor is more accurate than the unconditional expectation. However, illustrations of this mathematical result do not yield plausible models for returns; an example is given at the end of Section 3.4. The unconditional mean is the best prediction when our second definition of RWH applies, namely,

$$E[r_{t+1} \mid I_t] = \mu \quad \text{for some constant } \mu \text{ and for all times } t \text{ and}$$
$$\text{all return histories } I_t = \{r_{t-i}, \ i \geqslant 0\}. \qquad \text{RWH2}$$

These conditions are the same as saying that returns have a stationary mean μ and that the process of excess returns, $\{r_t - \mu\}$, is a martingale difference. Definition RWH2 has its origins in Samuelson (1965).

RWH2 implies RWH1, whenever returns have finite variance. Most tests of the random walk hypothesis employ sample autocorrelations and are hence tests of RWH1. These tests reject RWH2 whenever they reject RWH1, as we assume returns have finite variance. The distinction between RWH1 and RWH2 is of minor importance to us and is generally ignored. Campbell et al. (1997, Section 2.1) also discuss definitions of the RWH.

A stationary mean for returns appears in the definitions to ensure that the sample autocorrelations are consistent estimates. Asset pricing models do not, of course, require expected returns to be constant through time. Some joint tests of time-varying expected returns and zero autocorrelation are given in Section 6.10. Further joint tests are possible within an ARCH-M framework and are discussed in Sections 10.4 and 10.5.

5.2.2 Random Walks and Market Efficiency

Tests of the random walk hypothesis can provide insight into issues of market efficiency. Nevertheless, random walk tests should not be considered to be tests of the weak-form efficient market hypothesis (EMH).

First, consider the situation when the RWH is false. The EMH can then be true, for some definitions of market efficiency, or it too may be false. Prices can fully reflect the information in past prices, and thus the EMH holds, as defined by Fama (1976, 1991), when the RWH is false. For example, conditional expected returns, $E[r_{t+1} \mid I_t]$, could depend on previous returns because the asset's risk premium follows a stationary, autocorrelated process. Or $E[r_{t+1} \mid I_t]$ could be a function of the conditional variance, $\text{var}(r_{t+1} \mid I_t)$. These expectations and hence returns are autocorrelated for the ARCH-M models introduced in Section 9.5. Another possibility is that some linear predictor is more accurate than prediction using a constant value but transaction costs exceed gross, risk-adjusted payoffs from trading. Then the EMH holds, as defined by Jensen (1978), yet the RWH is false. For example, returns could follow an MA(1) process with the moving-average parameter so close to zero that net trading profits are impossible. Efficiency might, however, be defined as a fair game for excess returns (LeRoy 1989) and then the EMH will be false whenever expected returns are constant and RWH2 is false.

Second, consider the situation when RWH1 is true. Then there may exist a nonlinear predictor which is more accurate than prediction using a constant value and, consequently, (i) RWH2 is false, (ii) the EMH can be false using the LeRoy definition, (iii) the EMH can be false for the Jensen definition when trading costs are sufficiently low, and (iv) the EMH can be false for Fama's definition as Jensen inefficiency implies Fama inefficiency. The existence of a successful nonlinear predictor when RWH1 is true is, however, a theoretical possibility which is unlikely to have practical relevance.

5.3 Variance-Ratio Tests

5.3.1 Theoretical Motivation

The variance of a multi-period return is the sum of single-period variances when the RWH is true. Several tests seek to exploit any divergence from this prediction, the most important being the variance-ratio test of Lo and MacKinlay (1988).

To provide some intuition for the test, initially suppose that the stochastic process generating returns is stationary, with $V(1) = \text{var}(r_t)$. Two-period returns are the sum of two consecutive returns and their variance equals

$$V(2) = \text{var}(r_t + r_{t+1}) = \text{var}(r_t) + \text{var}(r_{t+1}) + 2\,\text{cov}(r_t, r_{t+1}) = (2 + 2\rho_1)V(1),$$
(5.1)

with ρ_1 the first-lag autocorrelation of one-period returns. The two-period variance ratio is defined by

$$\text{VR}(2) = \frac{V(2)}{2V(1)} = 1 + \rho_1.$$
(5.2)

The autocorrelation term is zero when the RWH applies and then the variance ratio is one. Otherwise, the RWH is false and the ratio can be either more or less than one.

Next consider N-period returns for any integer $N \geqslant 2$. When the RWH is true,

$$V(N) = \text{var}(r_t + r_{t+1} + \cdots + r_{t+N-1})$$
$$= \text{var}(r_t) + \text{var}(r_{t+1}) + \cdots + \text{var}(r_{t+N-1}) = NV(1)$$

and thus the variance ratio is unity for all N:

$$\text{VR}(N) = \frac{V(N)}{NV(1)} = 1.$$
(5.3)

When the RWH is false, $V(N)$ equals $NV(1)$ plus the covariance terms between all pairs of distinct returns; thus

$$V(N) = NV(1) + 2\sum_{i=1}^{N-1}\sum_{j=i+1}^{N} \operatorname{cov}(r_{t+i-1}, r_{t+j-1})$$

$$= V(1)\left[N + 2\sum_{i=1}^{N-1}\sum_{j=i+1}^{N} \rho_{j-i}\right]. \tag{5.4}$$

The double summation can be simplified to give the variance ratio as

$$\mathrm{VR}(N) = 1 + \frac{2}{N}\sum_{\tau=1}^{N-1}(N - \tau)\rho_\tau. \tag{5.5}$$

The empirical test uses observed returns to decide if a sample estimate of the variance ratio is compatible with the theoretical prediction of one stated by equation (5.3). The test is most likely to reject the RWH when the ratio in equation (5.5) is far from one. This happens when a linear function of the first $N - 1$ autocorrelations, namely

$$(N - 1)\rho_1 + (N - 2)\rho_2 + \cdots + 2\rho_{N-2} + \rho_{N-1},$$

is far from zero. The multiplier is $N - \tau$ for ρ_τ. All the multipliers are positive and they decrease as the lag increases. A variance-ratio test is therefore particularly appropriate when the alternative to randomness involves autocorrelations that all have the same sign and that decrease as the lag increases. These properties are possessed by ARMA(1, 1) processes that have a positive autoregressive parameter ϕ and then $\rho_\tau = A\phi^\tau$, $\tau \geqslant 1$. Two important examples are described in Section 3.6. One example has mean reversion in prices ($A < 0$ and $\mathrm{VR}(N) < 1$), while the other has trends in prices ($A > 0$ and $\mathrm{VR}(N) > 1$).

5.3.2 The Test Statistic

The researcher must first choose a value for N. Indeed, the choice can appear to be arbitrary. Suppose a set of n observed returns has average $\bar{r}$ and variance $\hat{V}(1) = \sum(r_t - \bar{r})^2/(n - 1)$. An appropriate estimate of $V(N)$ is

$$\hat{V}(N) = \frac{n}{(n - N)(n - N + 1)}\sum_{t=1}^{n-N+1}(r_t + r_{t+1} + \cdots + r_{t+N-1} - N\bar{r})^2 \tag{5.6}$$

and then the sample variance ratio is

$$\widehat{\mathrm{VR}}(N) = \frac{\hat{V}(N)}{N\hat{V}(1)}. \tag{5.7}$$

This ratio is very similar to the linear function of sample autocorrelations, $\hat{\rho}_\tau$, that is suggested by (5.5):

$$\widehat{VR}(N) \cong 1 + \frac{2}{N} \sum_{\tau=1}^{N-1} (N - \tau)\hat{\rho}_\tau. \tag{5.8}$$

The RWH should be rejected if the sample variance ratio is significantly far from one. We can only decide what is significant if we have a distribution for $\widehat{VR}(N)$ when the RWH is true. This distribution can be obtained after making technical assumptions that are discussed later, in Section 5.6; it is not necessary to assume the returns process is stationary. An estimate of the variance of $\widehat{VR}(N)$ follows from (5.8) and estimates of the variances of the first $N - 1$ autocorrelations $\hat{\rho}_\tau$. An appropriate estimate of $n \, \text{var}(\hat{\rho}_\tau)$ is provided by

$$b_\tau = \frac{n \sum_{t=1}^{n-\tau} s_t s_{t+\tau}}{(\sum_{t=1}^{n} s_t)^2}, \quad \text{with } s_t = (r_t - \bar{r})^2, \tag{5.9}$$

and then an estimate of $n \, \text{var}(\widehat{VR}(N))$ is given by

$$v_N = \frac{4}{N^2} \sum_{\tau=1}^{N-1} (N - \tau)^2 b_\tau. \tag{5.10}$$

A useful and very accurate approximation to b_τ can be calculated from the kurtosis of returns, k, and the autocorrelations $\hat{\rho}_{\tau,s}$ of the terms $s_t = (r_t - \bar{r})^2$:

$$b_\tau \cong 1 + (k - 1)\hat{\rho}_{\tau,s}. \tag{5.11}$$

The above estimates are consistent when the RWH is true; they then converge to the parameters that they estimate as n increases. Finally, the standardized distribution of the sample variance ratio,

$$z_N = \frac{\widehat{VR}(N) - 1}{\sqrt{v_N/n}}, \tag{5.12}$$

is approximately the standard normal distribution when the RWH is true. This is an asymptotic result, so the approximation becomes perfect as $n \to \infty$.

Comparisons of z_N with $N(0, 1)$ provide satisfactory results when n/N is "large" but they can be unsatisfactory when n/N is "small." Problems are only likely to arise when returns are recorded monthly or less often. The asymptotic result should certainly be applicable when $n/N \geqslant 100$. Further details of the derivation and reliability of variance-ratio tests are given by Lo and MacKinlay (1988, 1989), Cochrane (1988), and Campbell et al. (1997).

Tests are often performed for more than one value of N. It is then necessary to avoid using hindsight to find the most interesting value of N. Chow and Denning (1993) discuss this problem and show how to perform a test by using the maximum value of $|z_N|$.

Nonparametric variations of the variance-ratio test can also be performed. These tests are evaluated using the ranks and signs of returns, and are investigated by Wright (2000) and Luger (2003).

5.4 An Example of Variance-Ratio Calculations

It is easy to calculate variance ratios and their RWH test values. We now provide our first example of calculations using elementary software, namely Excel. There are, of course, more efficient ways to organize the calculations, for example, by using Visual Basic functions, but these require some programming skill. This section can be skipped by readers who are not interested in software.

Exhibit 5.1 shows calculations for the S&P 100 index from January 1991 to December 2000. The most important Excel formulae used are listed in Table 5.1. The time series is defined and graphed in Section 2.2. It contains 2531 index levels p_t that are located in cells B12 to B2542. The results are obtained when $N = 5$.

The first steps are to calculate the returns r_t, ignoring dividends, and a few summary statistics. To avoid small numbers, we work with percentage returns and henceforth drop the percentage adjective. The return for 3 January 1991, which is period $t = 1$, is obtained by inserting into cell C13 the formula =100*LN(B13/B12). The remaining returns are obtained by selecting and copying cell C13, followed by pasting it into cells C14 to C2542. The number, average, and kurtosis of the returns are required and can be found in cells B3 to B5, making use of the functions COUNT, AVERAGE, and KURT. It is necessary to add three to the statistic supplied by KURT as Excel calculates the excess kurtosis.

Next, columns D, E, and F are respectively filled with the terms $r_t - \bar{r}$, $s_t = (r_t - \bar{r})^2$, and $r_t + r_{t+1} + \cdots + r_{t+N-1} - N\bar{r}$. After typing formulae into cells D13 and E13, namely =C13-$B$4 and =D13*D13, columns D and E are completed by copying and pasting the 1×2 rectangle C13:D13. The first five-period excess return, $r_1 + r_2 + \cdots + r_5 - 5\bar{r}$, is given by applying the SUM function to cells D13:D17, to give the result in cell F13. The remainder of column F is given by copying and pasting cell F13, stopping at cell F2538, which corresponds to period $t = n - N + 1$.

Now we can calculate the sample variance ratio. The one-period sample variance $\hat{V}(1)$ is given in cell E3 by the function VAR. The estimate $\hat{V}(N)$ of the N-period variance in cell E4 uses equation (5.6) and the function SUMSQ, which here adds the squares of the N-period excess returns. The sample ratio $\widehat{VR}(N)$ follows immediately in cell E5, and on this occasion equals 0.9050.

To calculate the test statistic z_N defined by equation (5.12), we must first find estimates b_τ of $n \operatorname{var}(\hat{\rho}_\tau)$, for $1 \leqslant \tau \leqslant N - 1$. These are calculated here by using equation (5.11). A value for the autocorrelation in that equation can be obtained from the Excel function CORREL applied to two ranges containing the terms $s_t = (r_t - \bar{r})^2$. For $\tau = 1$, the first range covers times 1 to $n - 1$ and the second

	A	B	C	D	E	F	G	H	I
1	Summary statistics	% Returns r(t)		Variance ratio statistics			Lag	b	b*(weight^2)
2	count, n	2530		N	5		1	2.7251	6.9762
3	average	0.059239		V(1)	0.9726		2	2.2233	3.2015
4	kurtosis	8.045		V(N)	4.4013		3	1.7052	1.0913
5				VR	0.9050		4	1.7289	0.2766
6				v	11.5456				
7				z	-1.4059				
8									
9									
10	Date	Index	% Return	One-period		N-periods			
11		p(t)	r(t)	r(t) - mean r	s(t)	r(t) - mean r			
12	2 Jan 91	153.36							
13	3 Jan 91	151.44	-1.2599	-1.3191	1.7400	-5.1801			
14	4 Jan 91	151.28	-0.1057	-0.1649	0.0272	-2.8104			
15	7 Jan 91	148.53	-1.8345	-1.8938	3.5864	-2.3329			
16	8 Jan 91	148.15	-0.2562	-0.3154	0.0995	-1.3248			
17	9 Jan 91	146.05	-1.4276	-1.4869	2.2108	-0.6139			
18	10 Jan 91	147.68	1.1099	1.0506	1.1038	1.7304			

Exhibit 5.1. Variance-ratio calculations for the S&P 100 index, 1991–2000.

Table 5.1. Formulae used in the variance-ratio spreadsheet.

Cell	Formula	Note
B3	=COUNT(C13:C2542)	a
B4	=AVERAGE(C13:C2542)	a
B5	=KURT(C13:C2542)+3	a
C13	=100*LN(B13/B12)	
D13	=C13-$B$4	
E3	=VAR(C13:C2542)	a
E4	=B3*SUMSQ(F13:F2538)/((B3-E2)*(B3-E2+1))	a
E5	=E4/(E2*E3)	
E6	=SUM(I2:I5)	b
E7	=(E5-1)/SQRT(E6/B3)	
E13	=D13*D13	
F13	=SUM(D13:D17)	b
H2	=1+($B$5-1)*CORREL($E$13:E2541,E14:$E$2542)	a
H3	=1+($B$5-1)*CORREL($E$13:E2540,E15:$E$2542)	a
I2	=H2*(2*($E$2-G2)/$E$2)^2	

Notes: a, assumes $n = 2530$; b, assumes $N = 5$.

covers times 2 to n. The formula for b_1, in cell H2, can be copied down column H and then edited to give the correct formulae for the other estimates b_τ. Column I contains the values of $4(N-\tau)^2 b_\tau / N^2$, whose sum defines v_N in equation (5.10). The quantity v_N can be found in cell E6. Finally, the test statistic z_N is calculated from n, $\widehat{\text{VR}}(N)$ and v_N, here giving the value -1.406 in cell E7.

These calculations rely on the correlation function CORREL, which gives numbers different from but very similar to the sample autocorrelations defined by

$$\sum (s_t - \bar{s})(s_{t+\tau} - \bar{s}) \Big/ \sum (s_t - \bar{s})^2.$$

5.5 Selected Test Results

5.5.1 Daily Returns

Some results are discussed for 22 series that each contain ten years of daily returns. The ratios of N-period to one-period variances are tested for three values of N. When $N = 2$, the test statistic z_2 gives the same results as the standardized first-lag autocorrelation, $\hat{\rho}_1/\sqrt{b_1/n}$, from equations (5.8), (5.10), and (5.12). When $N = 5$ and $N = 20$, the test statistics respectively compare approximations to weekly and monthly variances with daily variances.

First consider two series of returns, from the S&P 100 index and the spot DM/\$ exchange rate, both from 1991 to 2000. Their variance ratios $\widehat{\text{VR}}(N)$ are

	$N = 2$	$N = 5$	$N = 20$
S&P 100 index	0.976	0.905	0.759
Spot DM/\$	1.018	1.042	1.036

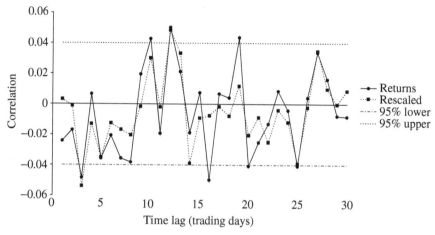

Figure 5.1.   S&P 100 autocorrelations.

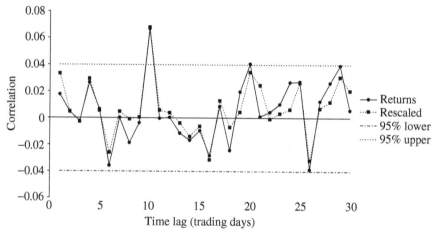

Figure 5.2.   Spot DM/$ autocorrelations.

The corresponding test statistics z_N, defined by equation (5.12), are

	$N = 2$	$N = 5$	$N = 20$
S&P 100 index	−0.73	−1.41	−1.76
Spot DM/$	0.73	0.80	0.32

All these test values accept the RWH at the 5% significance level, because they are within the symmetric range that contains 95% of the probability of the standard normal distribution (−1.96 to 1.96).

The absence of statistically significant results reflects the low autocorrelations of the returns. Figures 5.1 and 5.2 show the values of $\hat{\rho}_\tau$, marked using solid circles and joined by solid lines. Only a few of these estimates, shown beyond

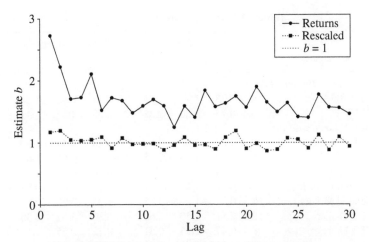

Figure 5.3.   S&P 100 autocorrelation variance estimates.

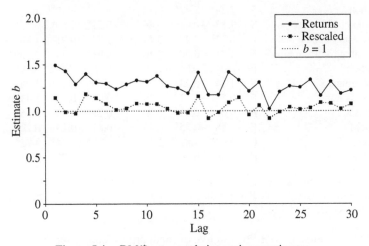

Figure 5.4.   DM/$ autocorrelation variance estimates.

the dotted lines at ± 0.04, are outside the 95% confidence interval for an i.i.d. process, namely $\pm 1.96/\sqrt{n}$. Appropriate intervals are wider, however, because the estimated sample variances of the $\hat{\rho}_\tau$ are b_τ/n with $b_\tau > 1$. Figure 5.3 shows that the values of b_τ commence above 2.5 for the index series and often exceed 1.5; the estimates are again marked by circles and are calculated from equation (5.9). The values of b_τ in Figure 5.4 are nearer one for the currency series but many of the estimates exceed 1.25.

Next consider the twenty equity, currency, and commodity series defined by Table 2.2, for which autocorrelations were documented in Section 4.9. Their test statistics z_N are listed in Table 5.2. Six of these series reject the RWH at the 5% significance level when $N = 2$. All the significant values indicate positive

Table 5.2.   Variance-ratio test values.

Test statistic		Returns			Rescaled returns		
		z_2	z_5	z_{20}	z_2	z_5	z_{20}
Series from 1991 to 2000							
S&P 100-share	S	−0.73	−1.41	−1.76	0.17	−0.92	−1.58
DM/$	S	0.73	0.80	0.32	1.59	1.55	1.41
Twenty further series							
S&P 500-share	S	4.00*	2.66*	0.62	5.20*	4.46*	1.90
S&P 500-share	F	−1.40	−1.43	−1.75	−0.75	−0.68	−1.02
Coca Cola	S	−1.24	−2.33*	−2.05*	0.16	−0.85	−1.06
General Electric	S	−0.92	−1.93	−1.27	−0.73	−0.82	−0.83
General Motors	S	0.57	−1.29	−0.75	1.34	−0.20	0.16
FT 100-share	S	2.51*	1.50	1.68	3.80*	3.57*	4.30*
FT 100-share	F	−0.47	−1.23	−0.51	0.72	0.25	2.13*
Glaxo	S	3.56*	1.85	0.48	5.88*	4.13*	2.24*
Marks & Spencer	S	1.96*	0.40	−1.44	2.80*	1.54	−0.22
Shell	S	2.34*	2.52*	0.34	4.68*	4.10*	1.13
Nikkei 225-share	S	1.83	−0.01	0.46	3.57*	2.69*	3.76*
Treasury bonds	F	0.71	0.47	0.48	1.73	0.91	1.46
3-month sterling bills	F	1.21	−0.30	0.40	4.91*	4.54*	4.70*
DM/$	F	−0.01	0.04	1.09	0.78	1.48	3.19*
Sterling/$	F	1.14	0.23	0.46	1.69	0.71	1.96
Swiss franc/$	F	−0.55	−0.57	0.49	−0.09	−0.10	1.43
Yen/$	F	−0.01	0.55	2.60*	0.29	0.94	3.36*
Gold	F	−1.88	−0.35	−0.47	−0.82	0.13	0.28
Corn	F	2.94*	1.82	2.33*	4.70*	3.14*	4.22*
Live cattle	F	0.56	0.94	−0.00	0.52	1.08	0.24

The crash week, commencing on 19 October 1987, is excluded from the time series. Stars identify test values that reject the RWH at the 5% level, for two-tailed tests. The test statistics are defined by equation (5.12).

dependence, because $z_2 \geqslant 1.96$, and five of them are for equity series, including the spot returns for the S&P 500 and the FTSE 100 indices. These results show that some series have significant dependence between consecutive returns. There are only three rejections when $N = 5$ and also three when $N = 20$. Overall, these tests do not provide much evidence against randomness.

5.5.2 Weekly Returns

Lo and MacKinlay (1988) [LM] focus on weekly returns from US indices, portfolios, and firms between 1962 and 1985. Campbell, Lo, and MacKinlay (1997) [CLM] update many of the calculations by extending the sample to 1994, to provide series of 1695 weekly returns.

CLM first consider equal and value-weighted indices calculated by pooling returns from the New York (NYSE) and American (AMEX) stock exchanges.

These market indices provide the following variance ratios for the four values of N that they used:

	$N = 2$	$N = 4$	$N = 8$	$N = 16$
Equal weighted	1.20	1.42	1.65	1.74
Value weighted	1.02	1.02	1.04	1.02

All of these variance ratios imply positive dependence, which is obviously more pronounced when the portfolio weights are all equal. The test statistics z_N are as follows:

	$N = 2$	$N = 4$	$N = 8$	$N = 16$
Equal weighted	4.53	5.30	5.84	4.85
Value weighted	0.51	0.30	0.41	0.14

The RWH is therefore rejected at very low significance levels by the equal-weighted index. The data of CLM accept the RWH for the value-weighted index, in contrast to the subset studied by LM that rejects at the 5% level for three of the four values of N ($z_N = 2.33, 2.31, 2.07, 1.38$).

Comparing the equal and value-weighted results, portfolios of smaller firms are anticipated to have more dependence than those for larger firms. CLM sort all firms by market capitalization into five size portfolios and then calculate further variance ratios. These exceed one but accept the RWH for the portfolio of large firms. They are much larger for the other portfolios and reject the RWH, with $z_N \geqslant 4$ for medium-size firms and $z_N \geqslant 7$ for small-size firms.

The rejections of the RWH for portfolio returns may merely reflect stale prices. This possibility is supported by CLM's results for individual firms. The variance ratios for the 411 firms whose securities were traded throughout their sample period are usually near one and their averages across firms are less than one. Thus the positive dependence in portfolios is not found at the level of the individual firm. Many studies have attempted to say why this has occurred. See, for example, the collection of papers by Lo and MacKinlay (1999) and the references and methods of Boudoukh et al. (1994) and Ahn et al. (2002).

5.5.3 *Monthly Returns*

Poterba and Summers (1988) include comparisons of monthly and annual variances in their Tables 2 and 4, so then $N = 12$. They tabulate the reciprocal of the standard variance-ratio definition, so we consider the inverses of their numbers. For US market returns in excess of the risk-free rate, from 1926 to 1985, the variance ratio from the value-weighted index is $\widehat{VR}(12) = 1.31$ with a similar ratio of 1.27 for the equal-weighted index. The market indices for many other countries, from 1957 (or earlier) until 1986, have values of $\widehat{VR}(12)$ that exceed unity. These ratios include 1.20 for the UK (from 1939 to 1986), 1.14 for France,

1.64 for Germany, and 1.15 for Japan. Thus there has been evidence for positive dependence in monthly market returns, although it appears that many of the test values do not reject the RWH at conventional significance levels.

5.5.4 Annual Returns

Poterba and Summers (1988) investigate the evidence for mean-reversion in annual stock returns by studying a modified variance ratio. This is calculated from monthly returns as

$$\widehat{VR}(j, 12) = \frac{\hat{V}(j)/j}{\hat{V}(12)/12}.$$

It is similar to the usual ratio $\widehat{VR}(N)$ calculated from annual returns, when $N = j/12$. The modified ratio is less than one when $j \geqslant 36$, i.e. $N \geqslant 3$, for US market indices from either 1871 or 1926 until 1985. For the sixty-year period commencing in 1926, the six-year variance ratios are 0.78 and 0.65, respectively for value- and equal-weighted excess returns. The small number of nonoverlapping N-year returns inevitably makes it difficult to find statistically significant variance ratios. Subsequent research by Kim, Nelson, and Startz (1998) and others shows that the deviations of the annual variance ratios from unity could well be compatible with the RWH. Related literature on tests for long-horizon returns includes Richardson and Stock (1989), Kim, Nelson, and Startz (1991), Richardson (1993), and Daniel (2001).

5.5.5 Markets Worldwide

Variance-ratio test results have been reported for very many markets and a few studies of daily and weekly returns are noted here. Liu and He (1991) and Luger (2003) both test five major exchange rate series, while Lee, Pan, and Liu (2001) investigate nine Australasian FX series. Peterson, Ma, and Ritchey (1992) cover seventeen commodity markets. Poon (1996) provides detailed results for the UK stock market for indices, portfolios, and individual stocks. Yilmaz (2001) gives results for twelve emerging markets (primarily in Latin America and Asia), the US, and Japan, while Gilmore and McManus (2003) cover three Central European markets.

5.6 Sample Autocorrelation Theory

The variance-ratio test and many other random walk tests rely on theoretical results about the distributions of a set of sample autocorrelations. These results can be skipped by readers who are not interested in theoretical results.

The sample autocorrelations are defined as

$$\hat{\rho}_\tau = \sum_{t=1}^{n-\tau}(r_t - \bar{r})(r_{t+\tau} - \bar{r}) \bigg/ \sum_{t=1}^{n}(r_t - \bar{r})^2, \quad \bar{r} = \frac{1}{n}\sum_{t=1}^{n}r_t. \quad (5.13)$$

We suppose the terms r_t and $\hat{\rho}_\tau$ are random variables in this section. Note that the sample autocorrelations are biased. Their sum across all lags is always

$$\sum_{\tau=1}^{n-1} \hat{\rho}_\tau = -\frac{1}{2}. \tag{5.14}$$

This shows that $E[\hat{\rho}_\tau] \neq \rho_\tau$ in general. Providing $\sum \rho_\tau$ converges as n increases, the bias is of order $1/n$. The magnitude of the bias depends on the lag. Processes with high positive values of $\sum \rho_\tau$ have the most bias.

5.6.1 Results for I.I.D. Processes

When the r_t are i.i.d. and have finite variance, the asymptotic distribution of $\sqrt{n}\hat{\rho}_\tau$ is normal with zero mean and unit variance for all positive τ. Also, $\hat{\rho}_\tau$ and $\hat{\rho}_\xi$ are asymptotically independent whenever $\tau \neq \xi$. It is not necessary to assume that the process is Gaussian (Anderson and Walker 1964).

The finite-sample expectation of $\hat{\rho}_\tau$ is proportional to the number of terms in its numerator, and thus

$$E[\hat{\rho}_\tau] = -\frac{n-\tau}{n(n-1)} \tag{5.15}$$

from (5.14). Also $\text{var}(\hat{\rho}_\tau)$ is less than $1/n$, and the covariance between sample autocorrelations at different lags is negative and of order $1/n^2$ when $n \geqslant 2\max(\tau, \xi)$. All these results follow from the methods in Moran (1967).

The bias is not always trivial when tests are performed. Consider the scaled sum of the first N autocorrelations:

$$S = \sqrt{\frac{n}{N}} \sum_{\tau=1}^{N} \hat{\rho}_\tau. \tag{5.16}$$

Then the asymptotic distribution of S is standard normal but the exact expectation of S is approximately $-\sqrt{j/n}$ when $N \ll n$; this is -0.3 when $N = 250$ and $n = 2500$. Tests based upon S are similar to the regression slope tests of Jegadeesh (1991) when single-period returns are regressed against N-period returns (Section 6.3). The obvious way to reduce the effects of the bias when testing the RWH is to increase each term $\hat{\rho}_\tau$ by $(n-\tau)/(n(n-1))$.

5.6.2 Results for Uncorrelated Processes

Next we consider uncorrelated processes that have a stationary mean, $\mu = E[r_t]$. The important consequence of relaxing the i.i.d. assumption is that we lose the general result that the asymptotic variance of $\sqrt{n}\hat{\rho}_\tau$ is unity.

Estimates of the variance can be obtained when further assumptions are made, in addition to the random walk hypothesis. Taylor (1984, 1986) assumes the uncorrelated process has a property of multivariate symmetry. For continuous distributions, this property requires the multivariate probability density function of the vector $(r_{t+1}, r_{t+2}, \ldots, r_{t+n})'$ to depend only on the n terms $|r_{t+i} - \mu|$, $1 \leqslant i \leqslant n$, for all positive integers n and t. Lo and MacKinlay (1988) do not assume symmetry and instead add different assumptions which restrict the nonlinear dependence and heterogeneity in the returns process. Their mixing assumptions are defined in White (1984). The additional assumptions of both Taylor and Lo and MacKinlay permit very general forms of conditional heteroskedasticity, including calendar terms. The estimated variance of $\sqrt{n}\hat{\rho}_\tau$ is then

$$b_\tau = n \sum_{t=1}^{n-\tau} (r_t - \bar{r})^2 (r_{t+\tau} - \bar{r})^2 \bigg/ \left(\sum_{t=1}^{n} (r_t - \bar{r})^2 \right)^2. \qquad (5.17)$$

This estimate is almost unbiased when the process has multivariate symmetry.

The asymptotic variance is defined when the following limits exist and are finite:

$$c_\tau = \lim_{n\to\infty} E\left[n^{-1} \sum_{t=1}^{n} (r_t - \mu)^2 (r_{t+\tau} - \mu)^2 \right]$$

and

$$\sigma^2 = \lim_{n\to\infty} E\left[n^{-1} \sum_{t=1}^{n} (r_t - \mu)^2 \right].$$

The asymptotic variance is then given by

$$\beta_\tau = \lim_{n\to\infty} n \operatorname{var}(\hat{\rho}_\tau) = c_\tau / \sigma^4. \qquad (5.18)$$

Also, the asymptotic distribution of $\sqrt{n}\hat{\rho}_\tau$ is $N(0, \beta_\tau)$ and the variables $\hat{\rho}_\tau$ and $\hat{\rho}_\xi$ are asymptotically independent whenever $\tau \neq \xi$ (Lo and MacKinlay 1988).

If, furthermore, the process $\{r_t\}$ is stationary with finite kurtosis,

$$k = E[(r_t - \mu)^4]/(E[(r_t - \mu)^2])^2,$$

then

$$\beta_\tau = \lim_{n\to\infty} n \operatorname{var}(\hat{\rho}_\tau) = 1 + (k - 1)\rho_{\tau,s} \qquad (5.19)$$

with $\rho_{\tau,s}$ denoting the autocorrelation function of the squares process defined by $s_t = (r_t - \mu)^2$. Realistic processes for the squares have positive autocorrelations and then $\beta_\tau > 1$. A typical kurtosis estimate is 6 and a typical autocorrelation for squares at a low lag is 0.15, for which $\beta_\tau = 1.75$. The values of β_τ can be arbitrarily large for the volatility models described in Chapters 9–11.

5.6.3 Autocorrelated Processes

The asymptotic distributions of sample autocorrelations for processes that are a linear combination of terms from an i.i.d., finite-variance process are described by many writers, including Anderson and Walker (1964), Kendall, Stuart, and Ord (1983), and Brockwell and Davis (1991). The finite-sample bias for the general linear process is given by Lomnicki and Zaremba (1957). The implications of the results in these sources for correlated returns processes are discussed in Taylor (1982a, 1986).

Asymptotic theory shows that the variance of $\sqrt{n}\hat{\rho}_\tau$ (defined for returns) can differ from one if either (i) returns are uncorrelated but squared returns are correlated, thus indicating a nonlinear process, or (ii) returns are generated by a correlated, linear process. Conditional heteroskedasticity is sufficient to produce variances far from one but realistic correlations between returns are not sufficient to do this. Consequently, asymptotic variances for an appropriate correlated, nonlinear process for returns will be predominantly determined by the nonlinear structure of the process.

5.7 Random Walk Tests Using Rescaled Returns

Returns do not have constant conditional variances and this is the primary reason for their autocorrelations having more variability than those calculated from i.i.d. processes. The excess variability can often be reduced substantially if we can find a way to rescale returns that ensures the rescaled quantities have approximately constant conditional variances.

5.7.1 Definition

Rescaled returns are defined by

$$r_t^* = \frac{r_t - \bar{r}}{\sqrt{h_t}} \tag{5.20}$$

with h_t a conditional variance for period t calculated from returns observed until period $t - 1$. When the RWH is true for the process generating returns we may also expect the hypothesis to be true for the process generating rescaled returns. When the RWH is false, the autocorrelations of the random variables that generate returns and rescaled returns can differ by important amounts. Reasons for this and some discussion of the implications are included in Sections 6.2, 6.9, and 6.13.

The ARCH models defined in Chapter 9 provide a framework for the calculation of the conditional variances h_t. Here we use a specification that has the advantage of simplicity at the cost of probably specifying a suboptimal model for h_t. Results are given for exponentially weighted moving averages, parametrized by a power p,

$$\begin{aligned} p = 1 : \quad & \sqrt{h_t} = (1 - \gamma)\sqrt{h_{t-1}} + c\gamma|r_{t-1} - \bar{r}|, \\ p = 2 : \quad & h_t = (1 - \gamma)h_{t-1} + c\gamma(r_{t-1} - \bar{r})^2. \end{aligned} \tag{5.21}$$

There are also two positive parameters, c and γ. When $p = 1$, the variance estimate is proportional to the square of the conditional mean absolute deviation (Taylor 1980, 1986, 2000). When $p = 2$ and $c = 1$, we obtain the integrated

GARCH(1, 1) model of Engle and Bollerslev (1986). The selected specification for h_t has the advantage that it is robust against nonstationarity created by changes in the unconditional variances of returns. It is also robust against outliers when $p = 1$.

The parameters p, c, γ are selected by maximizing the log-likelihood function when it is assumed that returns have conditional normal distributions with means and variances given by $\bar{r}$ and h_t. The log-likelihood function equals

$$\log L = -\frac{1}{2}\left[n \log(2\pi) + \sum_t \log(h_t) + \sum_t (r_t^*)^2\right].$$

It is defined for the general ARCH model in Section 9.5. For a given pair p and γ, the optimal c makes the average of the squared rescaled returns equal to one. Thus the maximization only involves searching for the best γ for each power p considered. The recursive equations must be initialized in some way. Here we use an appropriate average, calculated from the first twenty returns as

$$h_1^{p/2} = \frac{c}{20} \sum_{t=1}^{20} |r_t - \bar{r}|^p.$$

The log-likelihood has been maximized for the twenty-two series of daily returns discussed in Section 5.5. The most recent data are for two series covering the period from 1991 to 2000. The best choice for both is $p = 2$, with $\gamma = 0.042$ for the S&P 100 index series and $\gamma = 0.028$ for the spot Deutsche mark series. For the other twenty series, the optimal power p is one for eleven series; also, the optimal γ averages 0.05 with a range from 0.02 to 0.13.

5.7.2 Further Autocorrelation Variance Estimates

The variances of autocorrelations calculated from rescaled returns are estimated by replacing returns by rescaled returns in equation (5.9). These estimates of $n \operatorname{var}(\operatorname{cor}(r_t^*, r_{t+\tau}^*))$ are denoted by b_τ^*. We should expect these estimates to be close to one when there is no linear dependence in the squares of rescaled returns or, equivalently, when ARCH effects have been eliminated by the rescaling transformation.

Figures 5.3 and 5.4 show the estimates b_τ^*, respectively for the S&P 100 index series and the spot Deutsche mark series, marked by squares and joined by dotted lines. It can be seen that the estimates for rescaled returns are much nearer to one than the corresponding estimates b_τ for returns.

5.7.3 The Autocorrelations of Rescaled Returns

Figures 5.1 and 5.2 show the autocorrelations of the rescaled returns, again joined by dotted lines, for comparison with the autocorrelations of the returns. The two sets of autocorrelations look similar, on each figure, but they differ by enough

Table 5.3. Autocorrelations for rescaled returns.

Series		Lags 1–5 Autocorrelations					Lags 1–30 Category frequency					
		1	2	3	4	5	1	2	3	4	5	6
S&P 500-share	S	0.119	0.013	0.008	−0.017	0.004	0	0	17	12	0	1
S&P 500-share	F	0.001	−0.003	0.003	−0.026	0.000	0	0	16	14	0	0
Coca Cola	S	0.006	−0.035	−0.003	−0.025	0.003	0	0	16	14	0	0
General Electric	S	−0.012	−0.003	−0.005	−0.008	−0.002	0	0	17	13	0	0
General Motors	S	0.042	−0.041	0.010	−0.017	0.006	0	0	10	20	0	0
FT 100-share	S	0.084	0.014	0.025	0.031	0.028	0	0	13	16	1	0
FT 100-share	F	0.034	−0.013	0.006	0.030	0.036	0	0	14	16	0	0
Glaxo	S	0.125	−0.003	0.004	−0.007	0.033	0	0	14	15	0	1
Marks & Spencer	S	0.066	−0.004	−0.032	0.017	0.001	0	0	20	9	1	0
Shell	S	0.105	0.028	0.004	−0.017	0.008	0	0	15	14	0	1
Nikkei 225-share	S	0.078	0.003	0.008	0.011	0.016	0	0	6	23	1	0
Treasury bonds	F	0.039	0.013	−0.024	−0.017	−0.008	0	0	11	19	0	0
3-month sterling bills	F	0.103	0.013	0.024	0.011	0.034	0	0	12	17	0	1
DM/$	F	0.013	0.015	0.025	−0.005	0.027	0	0	9	21	0	0
Sterling/$	F	0.032	−0.021	−0.005	0.006	0.020	0	0	9	21	0	0
Swiss franc/$	F	−0.000	−0.013	0.017	−0.012	0.013	0	1	10	18	1	0
Yen/$	F	0.006	0.013	0.024	0.005	0.044	0	0	7	23	0	0
Gold	F	−0.021	0.026	0.018	−0.040	0.001	0	1	14	14	1	0
Corn	F	0.090	−0.039	0.034	0.015	0.002	0	0	6	22	2	0
Live cattle	F	0.009	−0.006	0.047	0.012	−0.018	0	0	14	16	0	0
Autocorrelation averages and frequency totals												
Spot series	S	0.068	−0.003	0.002	−0.004	0.011	0	0	128	136	3	3
Future series	F	0.028	−0.001	0.015	−0.002	0.014	0	2	122	201	4	1
All series		0.046	−0.002	0.009	−0.003	0.012	0	2	250	337	7	4
All series, crash excluded		0.041	−0.001	0.005	−0.001	0.010	0	3	255	330	9	3

The six categories that summarize the signs and magnitudes of the autocorrelations are (1) below −0.1, (2) between −0.1 and −0.05, (3) between −0.05 and 0, (4) between 0 and 0.05, (5) between 0.05 and 0.1, and (6) above 0.1. The final row of averages presents average values after all returns in the week from 19 to 23 October 1987 have been excluded.

to produce nontrivial differences between their variance ratios, as noted below. For the S&P 100 index data, it is seen that the returns have five out of thirty autocorrelations beyond the dotted lines at $\pm 1.96/\sqrt{n} = \pm 0.04$, but the rescaled returns only have two such autocorrelations. This is a consequence of the higher variability of the estimates from returns, i.e. $b_\tau > b_\tau^*$ as shown in Figure 5.3.

A comparison of the autocorrelations for the other twenty series of daily returns (Table 4.8) with those for rescaled returns (Table 5.3) shows that the latter have less dispersion and are more often positive. For returns, 20 of the 600 autocorrelations are above 0.05 at lags 1–30, but only 11 are this high for rescaled returns; 16 are less than −0.05 for returns, compared with only 2 for rescaled returns. Of the 270 autocorrelation estimates from the 9 spot series at lags 1–30, there are 128 positive autocorrelations for returns (47%) and 145 for rescaled returns (54%). For the 330 estimates from the 11 futures series, the positive estimates number 180 for returns (55%) and 206 for rescaled returns (62%).

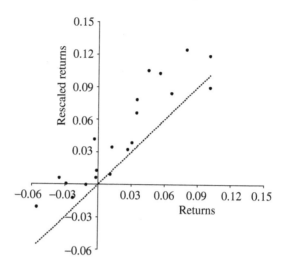

Figure 5.5. First-lag autocorrelations.

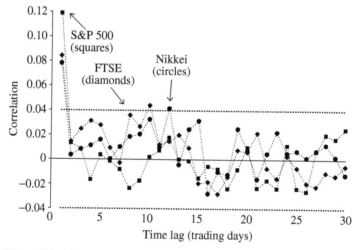

Figure 5.6. Autocorrelations for rescaled returns from three spot indices.

Figure 5.5 compares the first-lag estimates for returns and rescaled returns. Eighteen of the twenty circles are above the dotted line and hence indicate higher estimates from the rescaled data. The higher estimates demand an explanation. The simplest has two parts: first, the RWH is false for several series and, second, rescaling the returns magnifies the predictable component. The magnification effect is demonstrated for suitable autocorrelated processes by Monte Carlo and theoretical methods in Sections 6.9 and 6.13 respectively.

Figure 5.6 displays the autocorrelations of rescaled returns calculated from spot stock indices. The S&P 500, FTSE, and Nikkei series all have a substantial

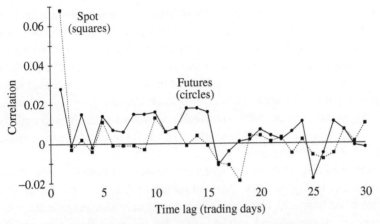

Figure 5.7. Average autocorrelations for rescaled returns.

positive estimate at the first lag, followed by much smaller estimates. Almost all of the index estimates from lag two onwards are within the dotted lines, at ±0.04, so that tests based upon only one of these estimates will probably accept the RWH. The Nikkei estimates, shown by circles, are positive for all of the first 12 lags. The Nikkei total of 24 positive estimates at lags 1–30 compares with 17 positive FTSE autocorrelations (diamonds) and only 13 positive S&P autocorrelations (squares).

Figure 5.7 emphasizes the generally positive and very small dependence in the rescaled returns for futures series. The average estimates for the eleven futures series (marked by circles) are positive for 13 of the first 15 lags. The futures averages are greater than or almost equal to the averages for the nine spot series (marked by squares) for all lags from 2 to 15 inclusive.

5.7.4 Variance-Ratio Test Results for Rescaled Returns

The variance ratios for the rescaled returns are as follows for the two most recent data series, with the ratios for the returns shown in brackets:

	$N = 2$	$N = 5$	$N = 20$
S&P 100 index	1.004 (0.976)	0.957 (0.905)	0.840 (0.759)
Spot DM/$	1.034 (1.108)	1.069 (1.042)	1.143 (1.036)

The corresponding random walk test statistics z_N also change:

	$N = 2$	$N = 5$	$N = 20$
S&P 100 index	0.17 (−0.73)	−0.92 (−1.41)	−1.58 (−1.76)
Spot DM/$	1.59 (0.73)	1.55 (0.80)	1.41 (0.32)

None of these test values rejects the RWH at the 5% significance level. The rescaling of returns increases all six test values, by amounts that range from 0.18 to 1.09.

Test values z_N for the other twenty series of daily returns are shown in Table 5.2. All but one of the sixty test values is increased by rescaling and several of the increases are substantial. These increases reflect the changes in (at least) the first-lag sample autocorrelations (noted above and in Figure 5.5) and reductions in the standard errors of the variance ratios. Eight of the test values for rescaled returns are significant at the 5% level when $N = 2$, each indicating significant positive first-lag dependence. There are seven significant values when $N = 5$ and eight when $N = 20$. The total of 23 significant test values for rescaled returns compares with a total of 12 for the returns.

Variance-ratio test statistics are tabulated for several further series of daily rescaled returns in Taylor (2000). All values are significant at the 5% level for five series of daily returns from the Dow Jones Industrial Average index, which together cover the period from 1897 to 1988. The five test values z_N range from 2.04 to 10.22 when $N = 2$, from 2.98 to 7.74 when $N = 5$ and from 4.05 to 6.42 when $N = 20$. The test values for the series covering the latest period, from 1968 to 1988, are 10.22, 7.74, and 4.16. All of these values reject the RWH at very low significance levels.

5.8 Summary

The hypothesis that the returns generating process has a constant mean and is uncorrelated can be tested by comparing variances for two investment horizons. The ratio of two variance estimates differs significantly from the random walk prediction for several time series, including equity index series. Reducing conditional heteroskedasticity in the test data enables more evidence against the random walk hypothesis to be found.

Further Reading

Chow, K. V. and K. C. Denning. 1993. A simple multiple variance ratio test. *Journal of Econometrics* 58:385–401.

Kim, C.-J., C. R. Nelson, and R. Startz. 1998. Testing for mean reversion in heteroskedastic data based on Gibbs-sampling-augmented randomization. *Journal of Empirical Finance* 5:131–154.

Lo, A. W. and A. C. MacKinlay. 1988. Stock market prices do not follow random walks: evidence from a simple specification test. *Review of Financial Studies* 1:41–66.

Poon, S. 1996. Persistence and mean reversion in UK stock returns. *European Financial Management* 2:169–196.

6

Further Tests of the
Random Walk Hypothesis

Several test statistics are defined and evaluated for twenty time series of daily returns in this chapter. Significant, positive dependence is found in a majority of the series, and almost no dependence in the remaining series. The results are consistent with substantial variation in the power of the tests to detect the small dependence present in some of the series.

6.1 Introduction

A variety of random walk tests have been motivated by particular alternatives to randomness. These alternatives include trends in prices, mean-reversion in prices, cyclical patterns, long-range dependence, and chaotic dynamics. This chapter covers several test statistics and compares their results with those of the variance-ratio tests described in the previous chapter. The tests are described in Sections 6.3–6.7, after a review of general methodological issues in Section 6.2.

Autocorrelation tests and test statistics that are asymptotically equivalent to functions of autocorrelations include the first-lag and variance-ratio tests. Further autocorrelation tests are reviewed in Section 6.3. The list of tests begins with the portmanteau Q-statistic of Box and Pierce (1970), which make no assumptions about the alternative to randomness. It continues with a test that simply counts significant autocorrelations. The third test uses the T-statistic of Taylor (1982a), which has power to detect trends and which is similar to the variance-ratio test. The fourth and fifth tests are respectively regressions of multi-period and single-period returns upon multi-period returns. These tests of Fama and French (1988) and Jegadeesh (1991) have the power to detect slow mean-reversion in prices.

Section 6.4 covers tests based upon the spectral density function. The original motivation for these tests was an alternative to randomness that incorporates cyclical patterns in returns. We consider three tests, computed first from the density at zero frequency, second from the density at the frequency of a weekly cycle in daily data, and third from the number of significant peaks and troughs in a plot of the density (Praetz 1979).

Section 6.5 describes the nonparametric runs test. It is one of the oldest tests in the literature (Fama 1965) and has power against $MA(1)$ alternatives. Section 6.6 defines rescaled range tests, first developed by Mandelbrot (1972) with the intention of discovering dependence between observations that are far apart and later revised by Lo (1991). Finally, Section 6.7 contains a discussion of the nonparametric BDS test of Brock, Dechert, and Scheinkman (1987), which has the power to detect chaotic dynamics and many other alternatives to an i.i.d. process.

The results from all the random walk tests applied to daily data are discussed together in Section 6.8 after describing all the tests. When nineteen tests are evaluated for each of the twenty series, 32% of the test values reject the random walk hypothesis (RWH) at the 5% level. The rejection frequency rises to 65% for the hybrid test of Taylor (1986), which uses the first autocorrelation $\hat{\rho}_1$ for equity series and the trend statistic T for all other series. The Monte Carlo results in Section 6.9 show that the considerable variations in rejection frequencies across tests can be explained by variations in their power to detect small levels of dependence.

Some dependence in returns can be created first by variation in equilibrium expected returns, second by bid–ask spreads, and third by any rules that limit price movements. The magnitude of the dependence is discussed in Section 6.10. Section 6.11 concludes the two chapters about tests of the RWH.

6.2 Test Methodology

6.2.1 Test Size

A test has correct size if the significance level is the maximum probability of a Type I error. The Type I error in Chapters 5 and 6 is to reject the RWH when this null hypothesis is correct. The test size will be increased if the conditional heteroskedastic (ARCH) feature of the returns process is ignored. This can be a serious problem. For example, suppose returns are uncorrelated, the first-lag autocorrelation has distribution $\hat{\rho}_1 \sim N(0, 2/n)$ for a sample of n returns, we incorrectly assume $\hat{\rho}_1 \sim N(0, 1/n)$, and the significance level is 5%. Then the probability of rejecting the RWH, when $\hat{\rho}_1$ is the (two-tailed) test statistic, is given by

$$P(\sqrt{n}|\hat{\rho}_1| > 1.96), \quad \text{with } \sqrt{n}\hat{\rho}_1 \sim N(0, 2).$$

With $Z \sim N(0, 1)$, this probability equals $P(|Z| > 1.96/\sqrt{2}) = 17\%$. The true size of the test is then more than three times the nominal size. Thus, if we test that returns have independent and identical distributions (i.i.d.) using the autocorrelations of returns, and reject i.i.d., then we cannot reject the RWH at the same significance level.

There are at least three ways to eliminate the consequences of ARCH effects from random walk tests. First, standard errors of test variables can be estimated with the assumption that the RWH is true and then these standard errors can be built into the test statistics. This strategy has already been seen for variance-ratio tests in Section 5.3. Second, returns can be transformed to rescaled returns with the intention of obtaining a time series for which asymptotic linear theory is more applicable, as in Section 5.7. This second method is compared with the first in Section 6.8. Third, an ARCH model can be developed that contains time-varying conditional means and then the RWH can be associated with parameter restrictions that can be tested using robust tests. The ARCH strategy is complicated by the necessity of modeling the conditional variance process. Some typical results are given in Sections 10.4 and 10.5.

Test procedures that contain an unspecified parameter will have spurious size if the parameter is chosen to make the test statistic as extreme as possible. For example, a comparison of the variances of N-period and single-period returns requires selection of N. Chow and Denning (1993) document the consequences for test size when the most extreme variance-ratio test statistic is selected and they show how an appropriate test can then be performed. Likewise, Richardson (1993) shows that tests based on the first-lag correlation of N-period returns have spurious size if N is chosen to maximize the correlation observed. His Monte Carlo results show some evidence for dependence in annual stock returns may be spurious. A variation on the theme of focusing on extreme results is the confusing situation when some autocorrelations are significant but several are not; a selective choice of lags can then determine the test result.

The choice of significance level is always arbitrary. A 5% level is used for all of the tests in this chapter. There is the possibility that Type I errors are more likely than Type II errors for long series. For example, suppose 2500 returns come from an MA(1) process and that the RWH is rejected when the first-lag autocorrelation exceeds $1.65/\sqrt{n} = 0.033$. Also, suppose standard i.i.d. theory applies. Then the probability of a Type I error when the moving-average parameter is zero is 5%, but the probability of a Type II error when the parameter equals 0.07 is less than 5%.

6.2.2 Test Power

A test has optimal power if the probability of a Type II error is minimized. The Type II error in Chapters 5 and 6 is to accept the RWH when the hypothesis is false. Optimal tests can only be designed for specific alternatives to a random process, for example, an MA(1) process with positive dependence. Many alternatives encompass too many parameters (or even model specifications) to permit the development of optimal tests. For example, the ARMA(1, 1) models that follow from price-trend models (Taylor 1982a) or from mean-reversion models (Poterba and Summers 1988) have too many parameters for the construction of uniformly most powerful tests. It is necessary to aim lower and to seek tests that have relatively high power for plausible returns processes and parameter levels.

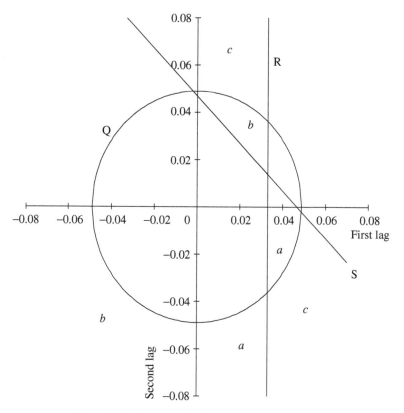

Figure 6.1.   Accept and reject regions for three tests.

Test power depends on the test statistic, the alternative to randomness, the significance level, and the number of observations. Power values can vary substantially across test statistics because they reject the RWH under different circumstances.

To illustrate some of the issues, consider the task of building a test statistic from the first two sample autocorrelations, $\hat{\rho}_1$ and $\hat{\rho}_2$. If we have no idea how returns may depart from randomness, then we may decide to reject the RWH for large values of $Q = \hat{\rho}_1^2 + \hat{\rho}_2^2$. If we believe the only credible alternative is an MA(1) process with positive dependence, then we will reject the RWH for large values of $R = \hat{\rho}_1$. We may, however, believe the alternative to randomness is positive dependence at two or more lags and then reject the RWH for large values of $S = \hat{\rho}_1 + \hat{\rho}_2$. Figure 6.1 shows the regions in which the three test statistics, Q, R, and S, accept or reject the RWH when there are 2500 observations, the autocorrelations have standard errors equal to 0.02 under the null hypothesis, and each test has a 5% significance level. In this figure, the RWH is rejected if the pair $(\hat{\rho}_1, \hat{\rho}_2)$ is outside the circle marked Q, or is to the right of the line marked R, or is above the line marked S. The number of tests that reject the RWH can be any number between 0 and 3, depending on the outcome $(\hat{\rho}_1, \hat{\rho}_2)$. At the two points marked a, exactly one of Q and R rejects the RWH; likewise, exactly one of two tests rejects at the points marked b for Q and S and at the points marked c for R and S. It would be wrong to look at the figure and say that Q is best because it rejects the RWH in a larger fraction of the diagram than the other tests. The important criterion is the probability of being within a rejection region and these probabilities will vary depending on the alternative to randomness.

Test power also depends on the strategy used to remove ARCH effects. To illustrate this, suppose the RWH is tested using the first-lag autocorrelation of returns and that $\hat{\rho}_1 \sim N(\rho, b/n)$ with $b > 1$ a known number that does not depend on $\rho \geqslant 0$. Then the RWH can be rejected at the 5% level if $\hat{\rho}_1 > 1.65\sqrt{b/n}$ and the probability of a Type II error is

$$p_1(\rho) = \Phi(1.65 - \rho\sqrt{n/b})$$

with $\Phi(\cdot)$ the cumulative distribution function of $N(0, 1)$. Another strategy is to calculate the first-lag autocorrelation of rescaled returns, $\hat{\rho}_1^*$, and to hope that this reduces the variability of the estimate, to give $\hat{\rho}_1^* \sim N(\rho^*, 1/n)$ for some ρ^* that depends on ρ and the process that generates returns. The probability of a Type II error is then

$$p_2(\rho) = \Phi(1.65 - \rho^*\sqrt{n}).$$

The rescaling method will enhance the test's power if $p_2(\rho) < p_1(\rho)$. This condition is equivalent to $\rho < \rho^*\sqrt{b}$. As $b > 1$ and there is evidence that $\rho^* > \rho > 0$ when the RWH is false (e.g. Table 5.2), it follows that rescaling will probably increase test power. The number of observations required to obtain a power of 50% is proportional to b/ρ^2. If rescaling halves b and doubles ρ, then the 50% power level can be attained with only one-eighth of the number of observations.

6.2.3 Multiple Tests

It is fairly inevitable that people will try many methods on the same data. Usually, the RWH is rejected for some tests but not for others. An obvious solution is to reduce the significance level for each test and then to reject the RWH if one or more tests gives a significant result. The correct way to do this is typically unknown because the various test statistics do not provide independent results. The special case when all test statistics are linear combinations of autocorrelations is studied in Richardson and Smith (1994b).

A classical methodology would avoid multiple tests altogether. The researcher would identify a preferred alternative to random behavior, then develop a powerful test, and finally apply it. However, few researchers would not be interested in the results from other tests. A compromise methodology is followed in this chapter.

Favored alternative hypotheses are selected for each series and the respective powerful tests are given first priority in Section 6.8.

6.3 Further Autocorrelation Tests

Many random walk test statistics are a function of k autocorrelation estimates $\{\hat{\rho}_1, \hat{\rho}_2, \ldots, \hat{\rho}_k\}$ calculated from n returns. We now review several tests that supplement the first-lag and variance-ratio tests described in Chapter 5. It is supposed that the returns also provide estimates b_τ of n var$(\hat{\rho}_\tau)$ that are asymptotically consistent when the RWH is true. All the following test statistics can be easily adapted when rescaled returns are used instead of returns.

6.3.1 The General Q-Test

The Q-statistic of Box and Pierce (1970) evaluated in Chapter 4 is defined as

$$Q_k = n \sum_{\tau=1}^{k} \hat{\rho}_\tau^2.$$

The asymptotic distribution of Q_k is χ_k^2 when the returns process is i.i.d., because the estimates $\hat{\rho}_\tau$ are asymptotically independent. The expected value of Q_k exceeds $E[\chi_k^2] = k$ when the RWH is true and the process is conditionally heteroskedastic. The Q-test is then inappropriate. A revised statistic that has a satisfactory size is given by

$$Q_k^* = n \sum_{\tau=1}^{k} \frac{R_\tau^2}{b_\tau}. \tag{6.1}$$

This statistic does have asymptotic distribution χ_k^2 when the RWH is true. The revised Q-statistic will have relatively low power for specific alternatives because it is intended to have power for any alternative to randomness that can be detected using autocorrelations.

The choice of k is arbitrary. Results are given for $k = 10, 30$, and 50. A single Q-statistic rejects the RWH at the 5% level if $Q_{10} > 18.31$, $Q_{30} > 43.77$, or $Q_{50} > 67.50$.

6.3.2 The Number of Significant Autocorrelations

Given many autocorrelations, some will probably appear to be significant regardless of whether or not the RWH is true. Finding a few significant values does not tell us much, unless their lags have a theoretical explanation or some overall test is significant. A simple test rejects the RWH if N or more of the first k autocorrelations are significant at the 5% level, with N chosen to ensure the test has correct size. It can be assumed that the number of significant autocorrelations has a binomial distribution when the RWH is true.

Results are given later when $k = 28$ and $N = 4$. Let N_r count the number of times we observe $|\hat{\rho}_\tau| > 1.96\sqrt{b_\tau/n}$ for lags 1–28 inclusive. Then the RWH is rejected at the 5% level if $N_r \geqslant 4$.

6.3.3 The Price-Trend Test T

The price-trend hypothesis described in Section 3.6 states that the returns generating process has the positive autocorrelations $\rho_\tau = A\phi^\tau$. Taylor (1982a) develops a powerful test of the RWH against this alternative by considering the logarithms of likelihood ratios for the vector $\hat{\rho} = (\hat{\rho}_1, \hat{\rho}_2, \ldots, \hat{\rho}_k)'$. These are

$$l(A, \phi) = \log L(\hat{\rho} \mid \rho_\tau = A\phi^\tau) - \log L(\hat{\rho} \mid \rho_\tau = 0).$$

An accurate approximation to the ratio, when A is small and the returns process is linear, is provided by

$$l = nA \sum_{\tau=1}^{k} \phi^\tau \hat{\rho}_\tau + l_0$$

with l_0 a constant that does not depend on $\hat{\rho}$. The RWH should then be rejected if

$$T_{k,\phi} = \sum_{\tau=1}^{k} \phi^\tau \hat{\rho}_\tau$$

is sufficiently large.

The number of autocorrelations k and the test parameter ϕ must be preselected. Taylor (1982a, 1986) recommended the choices $k = 30$ and $\phi = 0.92$, because these values deliver high test power for the ranges $0.01 \leqslant A \leqslant 0.04$ and $0.8 \leqslant \phi \leqslant 0.975$. These choices are retained here. Conditional heteroskedasticity can be accommodated by adjusting the variance of the test statistic. The asymptotic distribution of

$$T = \sqrt{n}\frac{\sum_{\tau=1}^{30} 0.92^\tau \hat{\rho}_\tau}{(\sum_{\tau=1}^{30} 0.92^{2\tau} b_\tau)^{0.5}} \tag{6.2}$$

is $N(0, 1)$ when the RWH is true. The null hypothesis is rejected at the 5% significance level using a one-tail test whenever $T \geqslant 1.65$. When the autocorrelation variances can be assumed to be $1/n$, so $b_\tau = 1$, the test statistic becomes

$$T = 0.4274\sqrt{n} \sum_{\tau=1}^{30} 0.92^\tau \hat{\rho}_\tau.$$

This version of the test rejected the RWH for rescaled returns from currencies and commodities in Taylor (1982a, 1986). The test and several others are evaluated in the very detailed analysis of Japanese markets by Kariya, Tsukuda, Maru, Matsue, and Omaki (1995).

6.3.4 The Multi-Period Autocorrelation Test

Fama and French (1988) demonstrate that mean-reverting price components will induce more first-lag dependence in appropriate long-horizon returns than in short-horizon returns. This insight motivates their random walk test.

The theoretical correlation between consecutive j-period returns is

$$\rho_1^{(j)} = \text{cor}(r_{t+1} + \cdots + r_{t+j}, r_{t+j+1} + \cdots + r_{t+2j}) = \sum_{i=1}^{j} \sum_{l=1}^{j} \frac{\text{cov}(r_{t+i}, r_{t+j+l})}{V(j)},$$

where $V(j)$ continues to denote the j-period variance. This expression simplifies to the following function of the first $2j - 1$ autocorrelations of single-period returns:

$$\rho_1^{(j)} = \frac{\sum_{\tau=1}^{j} \tau \rho_\tau + \sum_{\tau=j+1}^{2j-1} (2j - \tau) \rho_\tau}{j + 2 \sum_{\tau=1}^{j-1} (j - \tau) \rho_\tau}.$$

Multi-period first-lag autocorrelations calculated from observed data are thus expected to be similar to a linear function of single-period autocorrelations.

The test is implemented here by evaluating the sample estimate of the linear function in the numerator of $\rho_1^{(j)}$ divided by its estimated standard error; thus,

$$w_\tau = \min(\tau, 2j - \tau),$$

$$F(j) = \frac{\sum_{\tau=1}^{2j-1} w_\tau \hat{\rho}_\tau}{(\sum_{\tau=1}^{2j-1} w_\tau^2 b_\tau / n)^{0.5}}. \tag{6.3}$$

The test statistic $F(j)$ has an asymptotic standard normal distribution when the RWH is true. An alternative implementation of the test estimates $\rho_1^{(j)}$ from overlapping j-period returns and then divides by a consistent standard error.

Fama and French (1988) show that the first-lag autocorrelations of 36-, 48-, and 60-month returns calculated from monthly returns on US stock portfolios from 1926 to 1985 are negative and often less than -0.3. The significance of the results has been debated by Richardson (1993), who investigates the distribution of the maximum of $|\hat{\rho}_1^{(j)}|$.

The choice of j requires an understanding of plausible parameters for mean-reverting models. As the test was designed for long-horizon returns, results using daily data are given later for $j = 125$, so that the test results are similar to a test for dependence in six-month returns.

6.3.5 A Multi-Period Regression Test

Jegadeesh (1991) considered the general regression test of the RWH given by regressing the k-period return, from times t to $t + k - 1$, upon the latest j-period return, from times $t - j$ to t. Jegadeesh assumed the alternative to the RWH is mean-reversion in prices and then showed that, asymptotically, $k = 1$ maximizes the ratio of the regression slope divided by its standard error. This ensures that $k = 1$ maximizes the power of the test for sufficiently large samples (Geweke 1981). A large value of j is appropriate when any mean-reversion in prices occurs slowly.

The population regression slope from a regression of returns on j-period returns is

$$\beta^{(j)} = \frac{\text{cov}(r_t, r_{t-1} + \cdots + r_{t-j})}{V(j)} = \frac{2\sum_{\tau=1}^{j-1} \rho_\tau}{j + 2\sum_{\tau=1}^{j-1}(j - \tau)\rho_\tau},$$

for a stationary process. This suggests a test based upon the sum of the first $j - 1$ autocorrelations of single-period returns that defines the test statistic:

$$J(j) = \frac{\sum_{\tau=1}^{j-1} \hat{\rho}_\tau}{(\sum_{\tau=1}^{j-1} b_\tau/n)^{0.5}}. \tag{6.4}$$

A test could also be performed by estimating the regression slope divided by a standard error estimate that is consistent under conditional heteroskedasticity. The test statistic $J(j)$ has an asymptotic standard normal distribution when the RWH is true. Values of $J(j)$ are provided later for daily returns with the choice $j = 250$.

Jegadeesh (1991) presents test results for regressions of monthly returns on US stock portfolios against total returns during the previous four to nine years. Evidence for mean-reversion is found, even in the post-war period from 1947 to 1988. The dependence in returns, however, is entirely concentrated in the predictability of January returns.

6.3.6 Linear Test Functions

The T-test of Taylor (1982a), the VR-test of Lo and MacKinlay (1988), the F-test of Fama and French (1988), and the J-test of Jegadeesh (1991) are all based upon either an exact or an approximate linear function of k autocorrelations. The general linear test function is $\sum w_\tau \hat{\rho}_\tau$. The correlation between any two linear functions can be substantial. The asymptotic correlation, for i.i.d. data, is

$$\text{cor}\left(\sum c_\tau \hat{\rho}_\tau, \sum d_\tau \hat{\rho}_\tau\right) = \sum c_\tau d_\tau \Big/ \left\{\left(\sum c_\tau^2\right)\left(\sum d_\tau^2\right)\right\}^{0.5}.$$

The maximum correlations between the T-test statistic, with $k = 30$ and $\phi = 0.92$, and the other linear functions are 0.987 when $k = 25$ for the VR-test, 0.91 when $k = 15$ for the J-test, and 0.79 when $k = 13$ for the F-test. Figure 6.2 shows the autocorrelation weights w_τ for the four tests specified in the previous sentence when these weights are scaled to make their totals one for each test.

The optimal selection of weights in a linear test statistic should be proportional to the autocorrelations expected when the returns are not random (Richardson and Smith 1994b; Daniel 2001). The autocorrelations are $\rho_\tau = A\phi^\tau$ when the

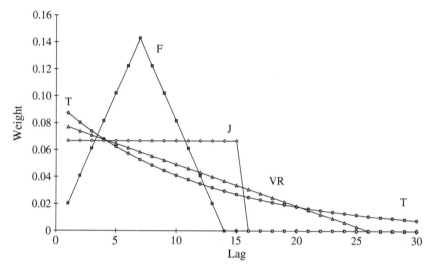

Figure 6.2. Autocorrelation weights for four tests.

alternative to randomness is either trends or mean-reversion. It then follows that the weights w_τ should be proportional to ϕ^τ, *if* a meaningful guess at the value of ϕ is possible. The T-test is then a particularly appropriate test.

6.4   Spectral Tests

Spectral analysis is particularly appropriate when cycles in returns are the preferred alternative to random behavior. A typical cyclical model is

$$r_t = \mu + \sum_{j=1}^{J} \alpha_j \cos(\omega_j t - \beta_j) + \varepsilon_t.$$

Cycle j then has frequency ω_j and is repeated every $2\pi/\omega_j$ time units. The evidence for cycles in financial time series is not impressive and consequently our discussion of spectral methods is brief. Granger and Newbold (1986, Chapter 2) describe relevant spectral theory for economic series, while Praetz (1979) highlights practical issues when testing returns for a flat spectral density.

The spectral density function for a covariance stationary process is here defined by

$$s(\omega) = \frac{\sigma^2}{2\pi} \left[1 + 2 \sum_{\tau=1}^{\infty} \rho_\tau \cos(\tau\omega) \right], \quad 0 \leqslant \omega \leqslant 2\pi, \tag{6.5}$$

with σ^2 and ρ_τ denoting the variance and the autocorrelations of the process. The integral of $s(\omega)$ from 0 to 2π equals σ^2. As $s(\omega) = s(2\pi - \omega)$, it is only necessary to consider frequencies from 0 to π. The density at $\omega = 0$ is only finite for short memory processes.

Suppose the spectral density function is scaled as follows:

$$f(\omega) = 2\pi s(\omega)/\sigma^2. \tag{6.6}$$

Then $f(\omega) = 1$ for all ω when the RWH is true. There will be peaks in a plot of $f(\omega)$ at the frequencies ω_j for the cyclical model. If, however, the autocorrelations are those of an ARMA(1, 1) process, so that $\rho_\tau = A\phi^\tau$, $\tau > 0$, then

$$f(\omega) = 1 - A + \frac{A(1 - \phi^2)}{1 - 2\phi\cos(\omega) + \phi^2}. \tag{6.7}$$

The function $f(\omega)$ varies monotonically from $f(0) = 1 + 2A\phi/(1 - \phi)$ to $f(\pi) = 1 - 2A\phi/(1 + \phi)$. For the price-trend hypothesis, A is positive and the function is decreasing, with a single thin peak at zero frequency ($\omega = 0$) when ϕ is almost one. For the mean-reversion hypothesis, A is negative and the function is increasing, with $f(0) = 1 - B$, where B is the proportion of returns variance due to incorrectly interpreted information.

To test the RWH it is necessary to first estimate $f(\omega)$ and then apply some test for a constant spectral density. Appropriate estimates of $f(\omega)$ are

$$\hat{f}(\omega) = 1 + 2\sum_{\tau=1}^{M} w_\tau \hat{\rho}_\tau \cos(\tau\omega) \tag{6.8}$$

with M an increasing function of the sample size n and with the positive multipliers w_τ chosen to ensure consistent estimates of $f(\omega)$. The Parzen multipliers are used here, defined by

$$w_\tau = \begin{cases} 1 - 6\tau^2(M - \tau)/M^3, & 0 < \tau \leqslant M/2, \\ 2(M - \tau)^3/M^3, & M/2 \leqslant \tau \leqslant M. \end{cases}$$

It is seen that spectral density estimates are linear functions of the first $M - 1$ autocorrelations. Plots of the autocorrelations $\hat{\rho}_1, \hat{\rho}_2, \ldots, \hat{\rho}_{M-1}$ and the estimated spectral shape, $\hat{f}(\omega)$, $0 \leqslant \omega \leqslant \pi$, provide the same information. The spectral picture will be more helpful either when there are cycles or when some of the linear functions are particularly informative.

Praetz (1979) shows that estimates $\hat{f}(\omega_1)$ and $\hat{f}(\omega_2)$ are correlated for nearby frequencies, with negligible correlation when $|\omega_1 - \omega_2| \geqslant 4\pi/M$. Consequently, tests are here based on $\hat{f}(\omega)$ calculated at frequencies separated by $4\pi/M$. Standardized test statistics are given by the following equation, when the autocorrelations have estimated variances b_τ/n, for $j = 0, 1, \ldots, M/4$:

$$f_j = [\hat{f}(4\pi j/M) - 1] \bigg/ \left\{ 4\sum_{\tau=1}^{M-1} b_\tau n^{-1}[w_\tau \cos(4\pi j\tau/M)]^2 \right\}^{0.5}. \tag{6.9}$$

The statistics f_j can be treated as independent observations from $N(0, 1)$ when the RWH is true and asymptotic theory is applicable to the sample autocorrelations.

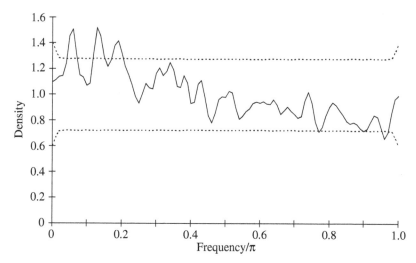

Figure 6.3.   Spectral density for spot S&P returns.

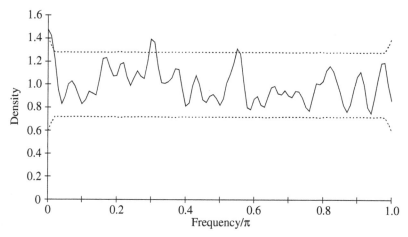

Figure 6.4.   Spectral density for Treasury bond returns.

The most plausible cyclical period is one week when studying daily returns. The corresponding frequency when there are no holidays is $\omega = 2\pi/5$ and the standardized spectral statistic has $j = M/10$. This statistic will be denoted by f_{w} to emphasize the period tested. A one-tail test is appropriate.

Another test counts the number of significant peaks and troughs in the estimated spectral density (Praetz 1979). Let N_s count the number of times that $|f_j|$ exceeds some threshold number. Then N_s has an asymptotic binomial distribution when the RWH is true. Here we let $M = 100$ and test the RWH using a 5% significance level. It is then appropriate to reject the RWH if $|f_j|$ exceeds 1.93 for four or more of the twenty-six statistics f_j.

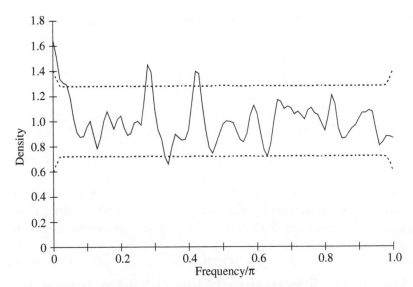

Figure 6.5. Spectral density for DM/$ returns.

The statistic f_0 is of particular interest. Any process that has an autocorrelation pattern similar to that of the price-trend hypothesis will have a spectral density function that is maximized at zero frequency. A one-tail test is appropriate.

Figures 6.3, 6.4, and 6.5 are three examples of plots of the estimated spectral shape, $\hat{f}(\omega)$, $0 \leqslant \omega \leqslant \pi$, respectively for returns calculated from the spot S&P 500 index, Treasury bond futures, and DM futures. The dots on these figures define confidence bands when the RWH is true; on average, 95% of the spectral estimates are within the bands when the RWH holds. There are an insignificant number of peaks on each of these figures, but it is instructive to note that the highest density estimates are at zero frequency for the two futures series. The other peaks can be interpreted as chance outcomes.

6.5 The Runs Test

As returns have a nonnormal and perhaps nonstationary distribution, nonparametric tests can be appropriate. The runs test applied by Fama (1965) is a simple example. It is similar to a first-lag autocorrelation test.

A positive run is a sequence of consecutive positive returns, a no-change run is a sequence of zero returns, and a negative run has a similar definition. Let q_t be the sign of the return r_t, thus q_t is 1, 0, or -1, respectively for positive, zero, or negative r_t. Also, let c_t be 1 if $q_t \neq q_{t+1}$ and 0 otherwise. Then $c_t = 1$ indicates that r_{t+1} commences a new run and thus the total number of runs of all types is

$$C = 1 + \sum_{t=1}^{n-1} c_t.$$

Suppose there are n_1 positive returns, n_2 zero returns, and n_3 negative returns in a series of n returns. Then the mean and variance of the random variable generating C, conditional upon n_1, n_2, and n_3, are

$$E[C] = n + 1 - \frac{1}{n}\sum n_j^2$$

and

$$\text{var}(C) = \left\{ \sum n_j^2 \left(n + n^2 + \sum n_j^2 \right) - n^3 - 2n \sum n_j^3 \right\} \Big/ (n^3 - n)$$

when the signs q_t are generated by i.i.d. variables (Mood 1940). All the above summations are over $j = 1, 2, 3$. Let RWH* represent the null hypothesis that the q_t are i.i.d. It is usual to assume that there is no difference between RWH and RWH*, although neither hypothesis implies the other. The statistic C has an approximate normal distribution, for large n. Tests can then be decided by evaluating

$$K = (C - E[C])/\sqrt{\text{var}(C)}, \tag{6.10}$$

with RWH* (and RWH) rejected at the 5% level if $|K| > 1.96$. Trends in prices would give fewer runs than expected while a tendency towards price reversals would give more runs.

The runs test is easy to perform and it avoids all the problems created by conditional heteroskedasticity. A possible handicap, however, is a reduction in test power due to the loss of information in the transformation from returns to their signs. To show this and to further understand the test, let us now assume that there are no zero returns. Then the total number of runs becomes

$$C = 1 + \frac{1}{4}\sum_{t=1}^{n-1}(q_t - q_{t+1})^2 = \tfrac{1}{2}(n+1) - \frac{1}{2}\sum_{t=1}^{n-1} q_t q_{t+1}.$$

As the average of the q_t is approximately zero, and we have assumed $q_t^2 = 1$, their first-lag autocorrelation is approximately $\sum q_t q_{t+1}/n$. Therefore, C is essentially a linear function of a first-lag autocorrelation. However, the first-lag autocorrelation of the stochastic process that generates $\{q_t\}$ can be less than for $\{r_t\}$. For example, a zero-mean, stationary, Gaussian process has

$$\rho_{1,q} = E[q_t q_{t+1}] = P(q_t = q_{t+1}) - P(q_t \neq q_{t+1})$$
$$= 2P(q_t = q_{t+1}) - 1 = (2/\pi)\arcsin(\rho_{1,r})$$
$$\cong 0.64\rho_{1,r}. \tag{6.11}$$

We see that the runs test is like a special first-lag test that may have less power than a conventional first-lag test because the runs test uses less information.

The test is problematic whenever there is thin trading in the asset, because there may then be several instances of consecutive zero returns. These may be responsible for fewer total runs than expected, thereby permitting rejection of the independence assumption (and RWH*) even when there is no serial correlation.

6.6 Rescaled Range Tests

Alternatives to uncorrelated processes possess some linear dependence, that can be classified as having either a short or a long memory. Short memory processes, including ARMA processes, have autocorrelations that converge rapidly to zero. Long memory processes, such as the ARFIMA processes mentioned in Section 3.8, have autocorrelations that converge at a slower rate to zero; these processes can have autocorrelations ρ_τ that are approximately proportional to τ^{2d-1}, $0 < d < 0.5$, for high lags τ. Range statistics that have power to detect long-term dependence were first developed for hydrological data (Hurst 1951) and later applied to financial returns (Mandelbrot 1972). Lo (1991) provides many references and a rigorous description of appropriate tests when the preferred alternative to randomness is long-term dependence.

The range defined by a set of returns $\{r_1, \ldots, r_n\}$ is similar to the range of the price logarithms. It is defined using partial sums of deviations from the average $\bar{r}$ to be

$$M_n = \left[\max_{1 \leqslant T \leqslant n} \sum_{t=1}^{T} (r_t - \bar{r}) \right] - \left[\min_{1 \leqslant T \leqslant n} \sum_{t=1}^{T} (r_t - \bar{r}) \right].$$

R/S-test statistics are ranges divided by scaled standard deviations,

$$\frac{R}{S} = \frac{1}{\sqrt{n}\hat{\sigma}} M_n, \tag{6.12}$$

where $n\hat{\sigma}^2$ is a constant multiplied by some consistent estimate of the variance of M_n. Two special cases define Mandelbrot's and Lo's test statistics; thus,

$$\hat{\sigma} = s \quad \text{defines } (R/S)_{\text{Man}}, \tag{6.13}$$

$$\hat{\sigma}^2 = s^2 \left[1 + 2 \sum_{j=1}^{q} \left(1 - \frac{j}{q+1} \right) \hat{\rho}_j \right] \quad \text{defines } (R/S)_{\text{Lo}},$$

with s^2 the sample variance of returns. Lo's expression for $\hat{\sigma}^2$ is proportional to an estimate of the spectral density at zero frequency calculated using the first q autocorrelations of the returns. Under certain assumptions, the distributions of these statistics converge, as n and q increase, to that of the range of a Brownian bridge on the unit interval. We use $q = 20$ for our tests.

The null hypothesis of an uncorrelated process can be tested using $(R/S)_{\text{Man}}$, with some restrictions on moments and heterogeneity. This test has power against short memory dependence. Lo focuses on the null hypothesis of a short memory process, with explicit additional restrictions on the degree of dependence, and then the appropriate test statistic is $(R/S)_{\text{Lo}}$. The asymptotic results are applicable to many stationary, ARCH processes. A two-tailed test rejects the null hypothesis at the 5% significance level when an R/S statistic is below 0.809 or above 1.862.

Lo (1991) reports results for daily returns from US stock indices and concludes that the returns process is characterized by short-term dependence because the values of $(R/S)_{Man}$ reject the RWH but the values of $(R/S)_{Lo}$ are insignificant and therefore do not support long-term dependence. The same conclusion is consistent with the results of Greene and Fielitz (1977) and Hiemstra and Jones (1997) for daily returns from large samples of individual US stocks. Goetzmann (1993) applies rescaled range tests to annual index returns, as far back as 1700 for the London market, and concludes that there may be long-term dependence over very long horizons.

6.7 The BDS Test

Chaotic dynamics motivates the BDS test of Brock et al. (1987, 1996). The BDS test has the power to detect many alternatives to an i.i.d. process, so that it is of interest regardless of beliefs about chaotic effects.

Chaotic processes are nonlinear and deterministic. They can have occasional large changes and periods of extraordinary volatility. Their sample autocorrelations can converge to zero for increasingly large datasets and thus the realizations of a chaotic process can mimic many important features of financial time series. Several examples are presented by Hsieh (1991), along with several results for the application of the BDS test to financial time series. Gleick (1987) provides a nontechnical introduction to chaos while Baumol and Benhabib (1989) show how economic models could produce chaotic dynamics.

6.7.1 Correlation Integrals

For a sample of n observations $\{x_1, \ldots, x_n\}$, an embedding dimension m, and a distance ε, the correlation integral $C_m(n, \varepsilon)$ is estimated by

$$I(x_s, x_t, \varepsilon) = \begin{cases} 1 & \text{if } |x_s - x_t| < \varepsilon, \\ 0 & \text{otherwise}, \end{cases}$$

$$I_m(x_s, x_t, \varepsilon) = \prod_{k=0}^{m-1} I(x_{s+k}, x_{t+k}, \varepsilon), \tag{6.14}$$

$$C_m(n, \varepsilon) = \frac{2}{(n-m)(n-m+1)} \sum_{s=1}^{n-m} \sum_{t=s+1}^{n-m+1} I_m(x_s, x_t, \varepsilon).$$

The function $I(\cdot)$ indicates whether or not the observations at times s and t are near each other, as determined by the distance ε. The product $I_m(\cdot)$ is only one when the two m-period histories $(x_s, x_{s+1}, \ldots, x_{s+m-1})$ and $(x_t, x_{t+1}, \ldots, x_{t+m-1})$ are near each other in the sense that each term x_{s+k} is near x_{t+k}. The estimate of the correlation integral is the proportion of pairs of m-period histories that are near each other.

For observations from many processes, including stationary processes, we can define the limit

$$C_m(\varepsilon) = \lim_{n \to \infty} C_m(n, \varepsilon).$$

When the observations are from an i.i.d. process, the probability of m consecutive near pairs of observations is simply the product of m equal probabilities and hence

$$C_m(\varepsilon) = C_1(\varepsilon)^m.$$

When the observations are from a chaotic process, however, the conditional probability of x_{s+k} being near x_{t+k}, given that x_{s+j} is near x_{t+j} for $0 \leqslant j < k$, is higher than the unconditional probability and hence

$$C_m(\varepsilon) > C_1(\varepsilon)^m.$$

The conditional probabilities can be much higher than the unconditional probabilities when m is large compared with the correlation dimension defined by Grassberger and Procaccia (1983), because the m-period histories of chaotic processes fill less space in m dimensions than i.i.d. processes (Hsieh 1991).

6.7.2 The Test Statistic

These properties of correlation integrals led BDS to consider the random variable $\sqrt{n}(C_m(n, \varepsilon) - C_1(n, \varepsilon)^m)$. For an i.i.d. process, the distribution of this variable converges to a normal distribution as n increases, with mean zero and variance V_m determined by the distribution of the i.i.d. random variables. The BDS test statistic is given by

$$W_m(\varepsilon) = \sqrt{\frac{n}{\hat{V}_m}}(C_m(n, \varepsilon) - C_1(n, \varepsilon)^m) \tag{6.15}$$

with $\hat{V}_m$ a consistent estimate of V_m. The statistic $W_m(\varepsilon)$ is compared with $N(0, 1)$ and it is conventional to perform a two-tail test, as certain (nonchaotic) alternatives to i.i.d. will often give negative values of the test statistic. There are many equations for a consistent estimator of V_m (in, for example, Hsieh 1989). Following Brock, Dechert, Scheinkman, and LeBaron (1996), the results here are calculated using

$$\hat{V}_m = 4\left(K^m + (m-1)^2 C^{2m} - m^2 K C^{2m-2} + 2\sum_{j=1}^{m-1} K^{m-j} C^{2j} \right), \tag{6.16}$$

with $C = C_1(n, \varepsilon)$ and

$$K = \frac{6}{(n-m-1)(n-m)(n-m+1)}$$

$$\times \sum_{s=2}^{n-m} \left(\left[\sum_{r=1}^{s-1} I_m(x_r, x_s) \right] \left[\sum_{t=s+1}^{n-m+1} I_m(x_s, x_t) \right] \right).$$

6.7.3 Properties

Hsieh (1991) provides simulation evidence that shows the BDS test has power to detect chaotic processes and many other alternatives to i.i.d. when the parameters of the alternative processes are sufficiently far from zero. These alternatives include linear AR(1) and MA(1) processes, processes with step changes in their mean and/or variance, nonlinear moving-average processes, threshold autoregressive processes, and, most important, ARCH processes. The intuition for power against ARCH alternatives is as follows. These alternatives display volatility clustering. Then, when a set of variables x_{s+j} are near x_{t+j} for $0 \leqslant j < k$, it is more likely than at other times that the k pairs come from periods of low volatility. Volatility clustering then implies that the next pair, (x_{s+k}, x_{t+k}), is more likely to come from low volatility periods and thus be near than at other times.

An extension of the BDS test that tests the null hypothesis of a linear process involves replacing the original data by the residuals from an estimated linear model. The asymptotic distribution of the BDS test statistic is unchanged by this filtering operation (Brock 1987). Unfortunately, there does not appear to be a similar result for standardized residuals from uncorrelated ARCH processes, that is, for returns minus their mean divided by the conditional standard deviations given by an estimated model. Hsieh (1991) shows that routine comparison of test results with a normal distribution can be inappropriate for 1000 standardized residuals from an ARCH process.

6.7.4 Results

The BDS test has often rejected the i.i.d. hypothesis for returns but the test values are nearly always much smaller, and frequently insignificant, for standardized residuals from ARCH models. See, for example, Hsieh (1989) for daily foreign exchange returns, Hsieh (1991) for weekly, daily, and 15-minute returns from US stock indices and decile portfolios, and Abhyankar, Copeland, and Wong (1995, 1997) for 5-minute and more frequent returns from several stock indices.

The BDS test has two parameters: the length m of the m-period histories that are compared and the distance measure ε. It is commonplace to report a table of test results with $m = 2, 3, 4, \ldots$ and ε equal to various multiples of the data's standard deviation s. Multiples such as 0.5, 1, and 1.5 are often chosen. All entries in the table of test values may give the same conclusion, especially when testing returns, but this is unlikely when testing standardized residuals. We focus here on test results when (i) $m = 2$, $\varepsilon = 0.75s$, (ii) $m = 4$, $\varepsilon = s$, and (iii) $m = 8$, $\varepsilon = 1.25s$. The corresponding test statistics are called W_2, W_4, and W_8.

6.8 Test Results for the Random Walk Hypothesis

The RWH is now evaluated for the test statistics described in Sections 6.3–6.7 and comparisons are made with the first-lag and variance-ratio tests defined in

Table 6.1. Rejection frequencies for random walk tests. (The tabulated numbers are the number of series, out of 20, that reject the RWH at the 5% significance level.)

	Returns				Rescaled returns			
Estimates of b included in the test	No	No	Yes	Yes	No	No	Yes	Yes
Crash week	In	Out	In	Out	In	Out	In	Out
Column	1	2	3	4	5	6	7	8
Test								
First autocorrelation, $\hat{\rho}_1$	7	10	2	6	9	8	9	8
Number of significant autocorrelations, N_r	9	6	0	0	3	1	2	3
Portmanteau, to lag 10, Q_{10}	12	9	2	6	8	8	6	7
Portmanteau, to lag 30, Q_{30}	14	11	0	0	7	7	5	6
Portmanteau, to lag 50, Q_{50}	15	15	1	2	4	5	3	4
Trend test, T	4	3	3	2	12	11	12	11
Variance ratio, week/day, z_5	9	7	0	3	7	7	7	7
Variance ratio, month/day, z_{20}	5	5	2	3	9	9	8	8
Multi-period first autocorrelation, $F(125)$	2	2	2	1	3	3	3	3
Multi-period regression, $J(250)$	3	5	3	4	8	7	8	8
Spectral density at zero frequency, f_0	4	2	2	2	9	8	10	8
One-week cycle, f_w	4	3	1	1	2	2	2	2
Number of spectral peaks, N_s	7	4	0	0	2	2	2	2
Runs test, K	9	9						
Rescaled range, $(R/S)_{\text{Man}}$	6	6						
Modified rescaled range, $(R/S)_{\text{Lo}}$	1	1						
BDS test, 2-period histories, W_2	19				10			
BDS test, 4-period histories, W_4	19				10			
BDS test, 8-period histories, W_8	20				7			
Stocks first autocorrelation, others trend test	6	8	3	7	14	13	13	13

Rescaled returns are returns minus their sample mean divided by an estimate of their conditional standard deviation. The tests are robust against conditional heteroskedasticity when estimates of $b_\tau = n\,\mathrm{var}(\hat{\rho}_\tau)$ are included in the tests. Crash week out indicates that returns during the crash week, commencing 19 October 1987, are excluded. The following tests reject the null hypothesis in only one tail: N_r, Q_{10}, Q_{30}, Q_{50}, T, f_0, f_w, N_s.

Chapter 5. Results are discussed for the set of twenty time series introduced in Chapter 2. Each series contains approximately 2500 daily returns and results are also obtained from the rescaled returns defined in Section 5.7.

As far as is possible, RW test statistics have been calculated from a selection of formulae depending on three choices: (a) either returns or rescaled returns are used; (b) the variances of autocorrelations at lag τ are either assumed to be $1/n$ or estimated to be b_τ/n; and (c) either all the (rescaled) returns are used or the crash week, commencing on 19 October 1987, is excluded. All the sample autocorrelations used in the tests are adjusted for the bias predicted under the null hypothesis by equation (5.15); the quantity $(n - \tau)/(n(n - 1))$ is added to the usual estimate of the autocorrelation $\hat{\rho}_\tau$.

Table 6.1 presents an overview of the test results for nineteen test statistics, with the eight columns showing how the three choices impact on the number of significant test results. The tabulated numbers show how many series reject the RWH at the 5% significance level. Only one series (on average) should reject the null hypothesis when it is true for all the assets and the size of the test is correct. The rejection frequency is clearly much higher in all columns of the table. We first discuss the information conveyed by Table 6.1 and follow this by a discussion of the results by test and then by asset.

6.8.1 Sensitivity to Specification of the Tests

The highest rejection frequencies are found in the first two columns, for returns when there are no corrections for conditional heteroskedasticity (ARCH effects). These high frequencies are evidence against the hypothesis that returns are i.i.d.; they are not, however, evidence against the more general RWH. The rejection of the i.i.d. hypothesis is most decisive using the BDS test. This is an interesting observation, although it must be remembered that the autocorrelations of absolute returns also reject the i.i.d. hypothesis convincingly (see Section 4.10).

The third and fourth columns of Table 6.1 show that the numbers of significant test results are much reduced when estimated variances b_τ/n are incorporated into the autocorrelation tests. This is particularly apparent for the portmanteau statistic Q_{50}. This statistic rejects the i.i.d. hypothesis for fifteen of the twenty series but rejects the RWH for only one or two series. This happens because the squares of autocorrelation estimates, $\hat{\rho}_\tau^2$, have expectations that are often far above $1/n$ because of the ARCH effects; hence Q-statistics calculated from k lags have expectations far above k when ARCH effects are ignored.

Comparisons between the third and fourth columns show that some of the rejection frequencies are particularly sensitive to the numbers in the crash week when tests use returns. The seventh and eighth columns show that this effect is not observed for the rescaled returns.

The four columns for rescaled returns in Table 6.1 show that the autocorrelation test results for this type of data are not sensitive to the other two choices. The estimated variances b_τ/n are then similar to $1/n$ and so either variance measure gives similar test results. The rescaling of returns reduces the relative magnitude of the equity numbers in the crash week and this explains why few test decisions change when the crash week is removed.

There are many more significant results from rescaled returns than from returns when ARCH effects are eliminated from the tests, as can be seen by comparing column four with column eight. Linear dependence is more likely to be significant if rescaling (i) reduces the variability of autocorrelations, and/or (ii) increases the average estimate of the magnitude of the dependence. The first explanation is true for my data and the second is supported by Figure 5.5 and the Monte Carlo results

Table 6.2. Results of the BDS test.

		Returns			Rescaled returns		
m		2	4	8	2	4	8
ε/s		0.75	1.00	1.25	0.75	1.00	1.25
S&P 500-share	S	2.31	4.87	8.91	−1.49	−1.28	−0.13
S&P 500-share	F	3.79	6.60	11.89	−1.34	−1.43	0.35
Coca Cola	S	8.50	10.67	14.39	4.11	3.72	3.94
General Electric	S	6.66	8.73	12.54	2.08	1.23	1.06
General Motors	S	4.84	8.12	11.20	1.30	2.23	2.42
FT 100-share	S	3.68	7.05	11.28	−1.65	0.02	1.00
FT 100-share	F	5.69	8.99	13.41	−0.68	0.46	0.86
Glaxo	S	6.93	11.37	16.86	2.24	2.87	3.32
Marks & Spencer	S	5.51	6.57	9.16	2.84	3.33	4.05
Shell	S	6.91	9.49	11.27	2.92	3.41	2.91
Nikkei 225-share	S	17.01	26.60	39.05	1.60	3.69	4.22
Treasury bonds	F	3.49	6.72	12.39	−1.95	−2.44	−0.89
3-month sterling bills	F	13.35	19.53	24.89	1.96	2.95	3.51
DM/$	F	1.96	4.46	9.13	−1.52	−1.24	0.01
Sterling/$	F	3.78	5.48	8.85	0.67	0.58	1.54
Swiss franc/$	F	1.52	2.90	6.54	−1.11	−1.71	−0.53
Yen/$	F	5.86	8.52	13.42	3.35	4.42	6.33
Gold	F	9.66	12.21	16.54	2.03	1.60	1.93
Corn	F	11.72	17.45	26.62	0.30	0.94	1.69
Live cattle	F	3.84	9.96	18.08	−1.97	−0.47	1.05

m is the embedding dimension, ε is a distance that is used to decide if returns are near each other, s is the standard deviation of the returns after excluding the crash week. The BDS test statistics are calculated using all the returns, including those in the crash week. The asymptotic null distribution of the test statistics is $N(0, 1)$. Monte Carlo methods are used to obtain quantiles for tests applied to rescaled returns. The 2.5% and 97.5% quantiles used for the tests are −1.25 and 2.72 when m is 2, −0.78 and 3.00 when m is 4, −0.36 and 3.39 when m is 8.

in Section 6.9. LeBaron (1992) also considers the empirical relationship between linear dependence and volatility.

6.8.2 Results by Test

Now we discuss the results of thirteen autocorrelation tests evaluated from rescaled returns with the crash week excluded, the runs test, two rescaled range tests evaluated using all the returns, and three BDS tests evaluated from all the rescaled returns. The results from these specifications of nineteen tests reject the RWH for 32% of the tests performed, at the 5% significance level. Test values are listed for the BDS test in Table 6.2 and for the first-lag and variance-ratio tests in Table 5.2.

The final row of Table 6.1 shows the rejection frequency for the hybrid test recommended after the tests in my previous book (Taylor 1986, p. 171). The hybrid test applied to an equity series uses the first autocorrelation $\hat{\rho}_1$ and for all other assets it uses the trend statistic T. As the final row shows, the hybrid test procedure rejects more often than any of the nineteen tests; it rejects the RWH for thirteen of the twenty series. The $\hat{\rho}_1$-test rejects for six of the eleven equity series, and the T-test rejects for seven of the remaining nine series.

The highest rejection frequency for a single test is eleven using the trend test T. The next highest frequency is ten for two of the BDS tests, followed by nine for the runs test, and eight for the $\hat{\rho}_1$-test, the twenty-day variance-ratio test, z_{20}, the zero frequency spectral test, f_0, and the regression test of returns against lagged annual returns, $J(250)$. However, the high scores for the BDS tests may be unreliable and misleading in view of the Monte Carlo results discussed in the next section.

The test statistics are allocated into three sets. First, there is the T-test and statistics whose rejections of the RWH are frequently for series that are also found to be nonrandom by the T-test. The three statistics z_{20}, f_0, and $J(250)$, like T, are all linear functions of a large number of positively weighted autocorrelations, with the weights either decreasing or constant as the lag increases. Each of these three statistics rejects the RWH for eight series. They respectively reject the RWH for eight, seven, and six of the eleven series for which T rejects the RWH. The test values for T and z_{20} are very similar and the correlation between the twenty pairs of values exceeds 0.99. The rejection count for z_{20} increases to ten if one-tailed tests are performed.

The T-test rejects for seven of the eleven futures series (including three of the four currency series) and all three spot stock index series, but for only one of the six individual stock series. The f_0- and $J(250)$-tests also reject for seven futures series, but for only the Nikkei from among the spot series. The number of significant autocorrelations N_r can be allocated to the first set; T rejects for two of the three series for which N_r rejects randomness.

The second set contains the first autocorrelation statistic $\hat{\rho}_1$ and tests whose rejections of the RWH are frequently for series that are also found to be nonrandom by $\hat{\rho}_1$. The three Q-statistics have a total of seventeen rejections. The $\hat{\rho}_1$-test rejects on sixteen of these occasions. The five-day variance-ratio test, z_5, rejects for seven series and on every occasion $\hat{\rho}_1$ also rejects the RWH. The runs test, K, rejects for nine series, six of which are also rejected by $\hat{\rho}_1$, and then the numbers of runs are less than expected for a random process. The number of significant spectral estimates N_s and the test for a weekly cycle f_w can both be allocated to the second set as, in each case, $\hat{\rho}_1$ rejects for the two series for which the test rejects randomness.

The statistic $\hat{\rho}_1$ rejects the RWH for all three spot stock indices, all three UK stock series, and two of the futures series. All these rejections indicate significant, positive first-lag dependence. There are no significant, negative test values and there are no rejections for the three US stock series.

The remaining tests form a third set. The three BDS tests reject the RWH for ten, ten, and seven series; the $\hat{\rho}_1$- and T-tests reject the hypothesis for between three and five of these series. The rescaled range tests in their original form reject the RWH for six series with significant evidence of positive dependence found for all four currencies; T rejects for three of the six series and $\hat{\rho}_1$ for one of the six. Only one series rejects the RWH when Lo's modification is used so the dependence may be classified as short term. Finally, the test based upon the first-lag autocorrelation of semi-annual returns, $F(125)$, rejects the RWH for three series, only one of which is rejected by either T or $\hat{\rho}_1$.

6.8.3 Results by Asset

A simple count of how many times the nineteen tests reject randomness for each asset allows classification into three groups. In the first group, with the most rejections, are corn futures (11), three-month sterling bill futures (10), and Shell (10). In the second group, with between six and nine rejections, we find the spot stock indices and the exchange rates. The rejection counts are 9 for the Nikkei 225 index, the yen and Glaxo, 8 for the S&P 500 index, the Deutsche mark and the Swiss franc, 7 for the FTSE 100 index and 6 for sterling and Marks & Spencer. In the third group, with five or less rejections, are the other series: all three large US firms (Coca Cola (3), General Electric (0), General Motors (2)) and futures for Treasury bonds (5), the S&P 500 (4), the FTSE 100 (2), live cattle (2), and gold (1).

It is not surprising that there is more dependence in spot indices than in index futures because spot indices are not traded assets. The equity dependence is found by the $\hat{\rho}_1$-test and by tests that frequently reject when $\hat{\rho}_1$ also rejects randomness. The currency dependence is detected by the T-test and other tests that are linear functions of many autocorrelations.

There are interdependencies between the twenty time series of returns that imply some dependence between their test values. This dependence is potentially substantial for the spot indices and their futures (Ahn et al. 2002) and also for the four currencies. Appendix 6.12 provides theoretical results about the dependence of test values from a pair of cross-correlated time series when the RWH is true for both series.

6.8.4 Dependence through Time

The hybrid test procedure uses the first autocorrelation $\hat{\rho}_1$ for all equity series and the T-test for all other series. It rejected randomness at the 5% significance level for all forty series in Taylor (1986). Here, however, the hybrid test only rejects randomness for thirteen series out of twenty. Dependence among returns therefore appears to be diminishing as time progresses.

Returns on General Electric and General Motors stock from 1966 to 1976 have significant positive values of $\hat{\rho}_1$ in Taylor (1986), but not here from 1984 to 1993. Returns on sterling, Deutsche mark, and Swiss franc futures all have lower test values for T and f_0 here, for the period from 1982 to 1991, than for the earlier period from 1974 to 1981 covered in Taylor (1986). Campbell, Lo, and MacKinlay (1997, Section 2.8) also report a decline in dependence though time, for daily and weekly returns from the CRSP value- and equal-weighted indices.

6.9 The Size and Power of Random Walk Tests

The random walk tests have been performed with critical values obtained from asymptotic theory. The test results for rescaled returns use ARCH models that are probably mis-specified. Asymptotic theory and/or rescaling the returns might distort the size of a test. Monte Carlo simulations help to clarify the size of the tests.

Table 6.1 shows that the rejection frequency is firstly far higher for some tests than for others and is secondly higher for rescaled returns than for returns, once the tests are adjusted for ARCH effects. These variations in the rejection rates call for some explanation. Monte Carlo estimates of test power for special alternatives to randomness show that there are stochastic processes that can explain many features of the observed test results.

6.9.1 A Returns Model for Simulations

Simulated uncorrelated returns are obtained from the product of two independent processes; thus,

$$r_t = \sigma_t \varepsilon_t.$$

The stochastic volatility (SV) process $\{\sigma_t\}$ is defined by supposing $\{\log(\sigma_t)\}$ is AR(1) and Gaussian, with mean α, standard deviation β, and autocorrelations ϕ^τ. The variables ε_t are i.i.d., standard normal variables. This SV model for returns is discussed at length in Chapter 11.

Simulated correlated returns are obtained by introducing a third independent stochastic process $\{\mu_t\}$, which specifies the mean component:

$$r_t = \mu_t + \sigma_t \varepsilon_t.$$

The μ_t are all zero for the size calculations but are generated by some linear process for the power calculations. All of the nonlinear effects are then in the uncorrelated component $\sigma_t \varepsilon_t$. This rather curious assumption can explain why rescaled returns have more dependence than returns.

6.9.2 Size

Estimates of the size of the tests have been obtained by simulating series of 2500 returns with volatility parameters $\alpha = -5.15$, $\beta = 0.422$, and $\phi = 0.973$. These have been realistic values for currency returns (Taylor 1994a,b).

The first two columns of Table 6.3 show the empirical sizes of the tests when the significance level is 5%; the autocorrelation tests incorporate finite-sample bias corrections and variance estimates b_τ/n. First, consider all the tests except the BDS tests. For the 40 000 simulated series the estimated size figures have standard errors close to 0.1%. The size estimates range from 3.3% to 6.5%. The highest values are for the test statistics T and f_0. These tests reject in only one tail. The z_{20} statistic is very highly correlated with T, here rejects in two tails and has size very close to 5%. We conclude that asymptotic theory is only approximately valid when there are 2500 returns and the tests must be adjusted for ARCH effects.

The BDS size figures are calculated from only 500 series, because calculations of BDS test statistics are relatively slow. All the series reject the i.i.d. hypothesis for returns. The rescaled returns are closer to an i.i.d. process but the high empirical sizes show that the test is not reliable. This can be explained by the failure of asymptotic theory when volatility parameters are estimated (Hsieh 1991) and by mis-specification of the conditional variances when the rescaled returns are calculated. The critical values of the test can be adjusted to obtain a more correct size, but the values depend on the process assumed to generate returns and on the embedding dimension m. Appropriate 2.5% and 97.5% quantiles, for the stochastic volatility model simulated here, are -1.25 and 2.72 when m is 2, -0.78 and 3.00 when m is 4, and -0.36 and 3.39 when m is 8. These quantiles are used in Table 6.1, when counting significant results from the BDS test applied to rescaled returns.

6.9.3 Power against an ARMA(1, 1) Alternative

Test power has been estimated when the mean component $\{\mu_t\}$ is assumed to be AR(1) with autoregressive parameter 0.95 and with variance equal to 2% of the variance of the returns. These two parameters have been credible for currencies for long periods during past years (Taylor 1992, 1994b). The volatility parameters are unchanged. The simulated returns have an ARMA(1, 1) representation and are from a process whose autocorrelation is $0.02(0.95^\tau)$ at a lag of τ periods. Again series of 2500 returns are simulated and tests are performed using a 5% significance level.

The third and fourth columns of Table 6.3 show empirical power figures calculated from 10 000 series, except for the BDS tests when 500 series are used. Ignoring the BDS figures for returns, the highest power figures are for those test

Table 6.3. Percentage size and power of random walk tests for three stochastic processes. (Simulated returns are the sum of a linear process $\{\mu_t\}$ plus an uncorrelated, nonlinear process $\{\sigma_t \varepsilon_t\}$. The process $\{\log(\sigma_t)\}$ is Gaussian and AR(1), and $\{\varepsilon_t\}$ is Gaussian white noise.)

Component μ_t	Zero		AR(1)		MA(1)	
Autocorrelations of returns at						
Lag 1:	0		0.019		0.05	
Lag 2:	0		0.018		0	
Lag 5:	0		0.015		0	
Lag 20:	0		0.007		0	
Test evaluated using:						
returns (R) or rescaled returns (RR)	R	RR	R	RR	R	RR
Column	1	2	3	4	5	6
Test						
First autocorrelation, $\hat\rho_1$	5.0	5.1	12	29	50	90
Number of significant autocorrelations, N_r	4.9	5.0	17	47	10	14
Portmanteau, to lag 10, Q_{10}	5.2	5.2	22	61	21	58
Portmanteau, to lag 30, Q_{30}	5.5	5.3	21	57	15	37
Portmanteau, to lag 50, Q_{50}	5.8	5.2	19	50	12	29
Trend test, T	6.0	6.2	66	94	21	37
Variance ratio, week/day, z_5	5.1	5.1	25	62	31	65
Variance ratio, month/day, z_{20}	4.9	5.1	53	90	14	26
Multi-period first autocorrelation, $F(125)$	4.0	4.2	19	27	6	6
Multi-period regression, $J(250)$	3.3	3.7	23	34	5	6
Spectral density at zero frequency, f_0	6.0	6.5	65	91	12	18
One-week cycle, f_w	6.0	5.6	5	4	9	10
Number of spectral peaks, N_s	3.3	4.1	8	15	10	27
Runs test, K	5.2		22		73	
Rescaled range, $(R/S)_{\mathrm{Man}}$	5.7		20		6	
Modified rescaled range, $(R/S)_{\mathrm{Lo}}$	3.6		7		4	
BDS test, 2-period histories, W_2	100	11.2	100	4.4	100	6.8
BDS test, 4-period histories, W_4	100	16.8	100	4.8	100	5.8
BDS test, 8-period histories, W_8	100	21.6	100	4.6	100	4.0

The mean, standard deviation, and autoregressive parameter of the Gaussian, AR(1) process $\{\log(\sigma_t)\}$ are respectively $\alpha = -5.15$, $\beta = 0.422$, and $\phi = 0.973$. The size estimates in columns 1 and 2 are obtained from 40 000 simulations and the power estimates in columns 3–6 are obtained from 10 000 simulations, except for the BDS figures obtained from 500 simulations. Each simulation provides a series of 2500 simulated returns. All tests are evaluated with a significance level equal to 5%. Except for the BDS tests, all the test statistics have asymptotic size equal to the significance level for the processes simulated. The BDS results in columns 4 and 6 are obtained using the critical values listed in Table 6.2. The following tests reject the null hypothesis in only one tail: N_r, Q_{10}, Q_{30}, Q_{50}, T, f_0, f_w, N_s. Rescaled returns are returns minus their sample mean divided by an estimate of their conditional standard deviation.

statistics that are linear functions of autocorrelations with weights that are monotonically decreasing. The high power estimates for returns are 66% for T, 65% for f_0, and 53% for z_{20}. The next highest figure is far lower at 25%. Note that rejection in two tails reduces the power of z_{20} by about 12%.

Test power is substantially increased by using rescaled returns and in some instances the increase is remarkable. The three high estimates improve to 94%, 91%, and 90%. The next highest figure is 62% for z_5 compared with only 25% when returns are not rescaled. The considerable increases in test power are caused by two effects already discussed in Section 6.2. The first is a reduction in the standard errors of autocorrelations. The second is the creation of more dependence by rescaling (Taylor 1986, p. 177). A mathematical explanation of the second effect is given in Appendix 6.13.

The BDS test is powerless according to the simulations reported here for rescaled returns. The power estimates are almost identical to the significance level when the appropriate quantiles are used. Higher rejection frequencies are obtained if the standard normal distribution is used instead, but even then the rejection frequencies are only a few per cent more than the numbers listed for the size calculations in the second column of Table 6.3.

6.9.4 *Power against an MA(1) Alternative*

The test having most power depends, of course, on the assumed alternative to randomness. Suppose now that the mean component $\{\mu_t\}$ is MA(1) and has moving-average parameter 1 and variance equal to 10% of the variance of returns. The simulated returns then follow an MA(1) process with first-lag population autocorrelation equal to 0.05. The volatility parameters, series length, and significance level are as before.

The fifth and sixth columns of Table 6.3 show, as should be expected, that test power is higher when fewer autocorrelations are used. The runs test K is a type of first-lag test and outperforms $\hat{\rho}_1$ for returns to a remarkable extent; in general, K is more powerful than $\hat{\rho}_1$ for returns whenever there is sufficient variation in conditional variances. However, the runs test is second to $\hat{\rho}_1$ for rescaled returns. Runs test values cannot be increased by rescaling but the values of $\hat{\rho}_1$ generally increase and their standard errors generally decrease. The three highest power estimates for returns are 73%, 50%, and 31%, respectively for K, $\hat{\rho}_1$, and z_5. The corresponding power estimates for rescaled data are 73%, 90%, and 65%. Once more, the rescaling transformation can substantially increase test power.

The BDS test is again found to be powerless for rescaled returns. The low power from Monte Carlo results contrasts with the empirical power of 50% in Table 6.1 for two of the tests applied to 20 real time series. There are at least two possible explanations. The BDS test may detect nonrandom behavior that is sufficiently different to that simulated. Alternatively, the quantiles used to test the real time series may be misleading because they are obtained by simulating a volatility process that is sufficiently different to those of real series.

6.10 Sources of Minor Dependence in Returns

Dependence among observed returns can be caused by time-varying expected returns, bid–ask spreads, price measurement errors, and rules that limit price changes. Any such dependence is small and less than that found in the series tested in this chapter.

6.10.1 Time-Varying Expected Returns

The null hypothesis of a random walk includes the assumption that returns have a stationary mean. Some variation in expected returns is compatible with market equilibrium. Finance theory does not require risk-free rates and risk premia to be constant through time and it would be surprising if they did not vary.

Suppose now that the returns process is the sum of two independent stationary components, $\{\mu_t\}$ and $\{e_t\}$, with the second a zero-mean uncorrelated process. Then the autocorrelations of returns are

$$\rho_\tau = \text{cov}(\mu_t, \mu_{t+\tau})/\text{var}(r_t), \quad \tau > 0,$$

and hence bounds on the autocorrelations at all positive lags are given by

$$|\rho_\tau| \leqslant \text{var}(\mu_t)/\text{var}(r_t) = \rho^*. \tag{6.17}$$

A few more assumptions provide an estimate for ρ^*. The expected return in annual terms, equivalent to μ_t, is $\exp(250\mu_t + 125\sigma^2) - 1$ when the uncorrelated component is Gaussian with variance σ^2 and there are 250 trading days in a year. Over a few years the range for annual expected returns might be at most 20%. The range for μ_t, say μ' to μ'', is then constrained by $250(\mu'' - \mu') < \log(1.2)$. A bound for the variance of μ_t is given by a uniform distribution, namely $(\mu'' - \mu')^2/12$. A typical US stock has returns variance 0.016^2 (see Table 4.1). Thus one estimate of ρ^* is

$$\rho^* = [\log(1.2)/250]^2/[12(0.016)^2] = 0.0002.$$

Another way of producing a value for ρ^* is to follow Merton (1980) and suppose returns are a constant risk-free rate r_f plus a risk premium that is a function of volatility plus an uncorrelated residual; thus,

$$r_t = r_f + a_j\sigma_t^j + \sigma_t\varepsilon_t.$$

When the risk premium is 10% per annum for the median level of volatility and $\log(\sigma_t)$ has a normal distribution with plausible parameters for stocks, ρ^* is 0.0001 when the risk premium equals $0.025\sigma_t$ and ρ^* is 0.0007 when the premium is $1.6\sigma_t^2$ (Taylor 1986).

Further simulation results for the components model $r_t = \mu_t + e_t$ are reported in Table 6.4 for five different ways of defining μ_t and with e_t either i.i.d. or defined by

Table 6.4. Simulation estimates of the impact of expected return models on test statistics.

Model for μ_t	Volatility	$\Delta\hat{\rho}_1$ Returns	$\Delta\hat{\rho}_1$ Rescaled returns	ΔT Returns	ΔT Rescaled returns
$a_0 t$	C	0.0004 (0.0006)	0.0004 (0.0006)	0.07 (0.12)	0.08 (0.12)
	V	0.0004 (0.0005)	0.0007 (0.0007)	0.09 (0.11)	0.13 (0.15)
$a_1 \sigma_t$	V	0.0004 (0.0007)	0.0005 (0.0007)	0.07 (0.13)	0.09 (0.12)
$a_2 \sigma_t^2$	V	0.0016 (0.0036)	0.0011 (0.0015)	0.28 (0.70)	0.21 (0.28)
Day effects	C	−0.0031 (0.0028)	−0.0029 (0.0027)	0.01 (0.09)	0.00 (0.09)
	V	−0.0028 (0.0022)	−0.0045 (0.0033)	0.07 (0.11)	−0.03 (0.12)
Month effects	C	0.0009 (0.0009)	0.0007 (0.0012)	0.10 (0.15)	0.10 (0.16)
	V	0.0005 (0.0009)	0.0020 (0.0018)	0.04 (0.11)	0.25 (0.23)

The models for expected returns are defined in Section 6.10. The unexpected component of returns has volatility that is either constant (C) or variable (V) with its logarithm AR(1) and Gaussian. $\Delta\hat{\rho}_1$ is the value of $\Delta\hat{\rho}_1$ for returns minus $\Delta\hat{\rho}_1$ for the uncorrelated component of returns. ΔT has a similar definition. The tabulated numbers are averages for samples of 40 series, with sample standard deviations in brackets. All autocorrelations are calculated from 2000 simulated returns. The results are taken from Taylor (1986).

the stochastic volatility process described in Section 6.9. The tabulated numbers summarize changes in statistics caused by time-varying expectations. Thus, for example, $\Delta\hat{\rho}_1$ is $\hat{\rho}_1$ calculated from returns r_t minus $\hat{\rho}_1$ calculated from the uncorrelated component e_t.

The specifications of μ_t are from Taylor (1986). First, results are given for a long trend in expected returns, $\mu_t = a_0 t$, with a_0 chosen to make the expected annual return increase by 20% over eight years. Second, the risk premium is linear in volatility, with $\mu_t = 0.025\sigma_t$. Third, the premium is the quadratic function $\mu_t = 1.6\sigma_t^2$. Fourth, day-of-the-week effects are specified by supposing that Monday's expected return is 0.23% less than the expectations on all other days. Finally, a month effect is given by supposing μ_t on any day in January is 0.18% higher than μ_t on any day in any other month.

The simulation results show that the changes in test results caused by the assumed levels of variation in expected returns are very small. The calendar effects induce more dependence than can be attributed to a reasonable equilibrium model. None of the simulation results can explain the large observed increases in the variance ratio and T-statistics when rescaled returns replace returns in the tests.

Random walk tests can be revised to test the null hypothesis that there is zero autocorrelation among excess returns, $r_t - \mu_t$. Revised tests use an estimate $\hat{\rho}$ of the upper bound ρ^*. For example, the revised test based upon the first-lag autocorrelation rejects the null hypothesis at the 5% level if

$$\frac{|\hat{\rho}_1|}{\sqrt{b_1/n}} > 1.96 + \frac{\rho^*}{\sqrt{b_1/n}}.$$

The amount added to 1.96 is then 0.10 if there are 2500 returns, b_1 is 1, and ρ^* is 0.0020 (the highest first-lag, positive average in Table 6.4). Likewise, a revised T-test rejects the null hypothesis at the 5% level if

$$T > 1.65 + 4.51\rho^*\sqrt{n}$$

and all the autocorrelation variances can be assumed to be at least $1/n$. The amount added to 1.65 could then be as much as 0.45 for a series of 2500 returns when ρ^* is 0.0020.

6.10.2   Bid–Ask Spreads

Suppose each reported price p_t is either a bid or an ask price when a market closes. Let p_t^* be the bid–ask average. Let δ_t be the measure of the discrepancy between the reported and midpoint prices, defined by

$$\log(p_t) = \log(p_t^*) + \delta_t.$$

Also, let r_t and r_t^* be returns series calculated from price series p_t and p_t^*. Then

$$r_t = r_t^* + \delta_t - \delta_{t-1}.$$

It may be assumed that the δ_t are uncorrelated and are independent of all terms in the series r_t^*. Then

$$\mathrm{cov}(r_t, r_{t+1}) = \mathrm{cov}(r_t^*, r_{t+1}^*) - \mathrm{var}(\delta_t).$$

For stationary processes, the relationship between the theoretical autocorrelations of reported and midpoint returns, respectively ρ_τ and ρ_τ^*, depends on the ratio $\psi = \mathrm{var}(\delta_t)/\mathrm{var}(r_t)$; thus,

$$\rho_1 = -\psi + (1 - 2\psi)\rho_1^*, \qquad \rho_\tau = (1 - 2\psi)\rho_\tau^* \quad \text{for } \tau \geqslant 2. \qquad (6.18)$$

The amount of spurious correlation is negative and essentially $-\psi$ at the first lag. As the effect is negative, bid–ask spreads cannot explain the positive dependence documented here for several series.

   To illustrate the spurious correlation, consider exchange rate futures for which the spread is less than 0.05% of the bid–ask average price. Then, if the δ_t average zero, $|\delta_t| < 0.0005$ implies $\mathrm{var}(\delta_t) < 0.00025^2$. From Table 4.1, $\mathrm{var}(r_t) > 0.007^2$ and hence the spurious theoretical autocorrelation is between -0.0013 and zero.

6.10.3   Random Data Errors

Likewise, random data errors reduce the first-lag autocorrelation. The term p_t^* then refers to the correct price, δ_t is occasionally nonzero and then indicates an error and p_t is the price used by the researcher. Estimation of the effect $-\psi$ is difficult although it is obviously negative.

6.10.4 Limit Rules

Some years ago, many futures contracts could not be traded at prices differing by more than a predetermined amount from the previous day's close or settlement price. There are now far less of these constraints. Some price series contain a high frequency of limited prices. Roll (1984) reported that orange juice futures contracts had limited prices on more than 10% of the days in his sample.

Limit restrictions create spurious positive dependence among returns. When a market closes limit-up, subsequent prices must move higher on average to reflect the information that caused prices to rise on the limit day. The opposite pattern occurs for limit-down events.

Simulations provide approximate estimates of the autocorrelation induced by limit rules. Let $\{p_t^*\}$ be a simulated random walk and, for convenience, let market-limited prices $\{p_t\}$ be defined using some limit parameter θ by

$$
p_t = \begin{cases}
p_t^* & \text{if } (1+\theta)p_{t-1} \geqslant p_t^* \geqslant (1-\theta)p_{t-1}, \\
(1+\theta)p_{t-1} & \text{if } p_t^* > (1+\theta)p_{t-1}, \\
(1-\theta)p_{t-1} & \text{if } p_t^* < (1-\theta)p_{t-1}.
\end{cases} \tag{6.19}
$$

This definition of $\{p_t\}$ ignores intraday price movements that hit limits. The autocorrelation induced by the limit rule is a function of the ratio θ/σ, with σ^2 the variance of the uncorrelated returns r_t^*.

Table 6.5 summarizes some simulation results when the process $\{r_t^*\}$ is first Gaussian white noise and is second defined by the stochastic volatility process described in Section 6.9. The impact of limit rules is small and occurs almost entirely at the first lag. The limits create more spurious dependence among returns than among rescaled returns, when there are changes in conditional variances. Limited prices and hence extreme returns are more likely to occur in periods of high volatility when their impact on tests is likely to be reduced by dividing returns by volatility estimates.

The number of limited prices in the eleven futures series studied here are 99 for cattle contracts, 45 for corn, 16 for Treasury bonds, 14 for gold, 2 for the yen, and none in the other series. Only the corn series is both constrained by limits and has a significant test value for $\hat{\rho}_1$, for either returns or rescaled returns. These test values remain significant at the 5% level if they are revised downwards using the information in Table 6.5. None of the rejections of randomness for the futures series can be explained solely by limit rules.

6.11 Concluding Remarks

The results from a variety of tests show that many of the twenty time series tested in Chapters 5 and 6 contradict the RWH while some of the series provide little

Table 6.5. Simulation estimates of the impact of a simple limit rule on test statistics.

		Average values of:			
θ/σ	Per cent limit days	$\Delta\hat{\rho}_1$ Returns	$\Delta\hat{\rho}_1$ Rescaled returns	ΔT Returns	ΔT Rescaled returns
Gaussian noise					
1.5	14.6	0.10	0.09	2.10	1.83
2	4.9	0.04	0.03	0.66	0.56
2.5	1.3	0.01	0.01	0.17	0.13
3	0.3	0.00	0.00	0.03	0.03
Stochastic volatility					
1.5	10.6	0.14	0.07	4.59	1.82
2	5.2	0.09	0.03	2.59	0.86
2.5	2.7	0.06	0.02	1.57	0.44
3	1.5	0.04	0.01	0.99	0.24

The limit rule is defined in Section 6.10.4. Limited prices can only change by a proportion θ, or less, from day to day. σ is the standard deviation of returns when there are no limits. Unlimited returns are either Gaussian and i.i.d. or they are uncorrelated with a volatility process whose logarithm is AR(1) and Gaussian, with standard deviation 0.6 and AR parameter 0.985. $\Delta\hat{\rho}_1$ is the value of $\hat{\rho}_1$ for limited returns minus $\hat{\rho}_1$ for unlimited returns. ΔT has a similar definition. All autocorrelations are calculated from 2000 simulated returns. The results are taken from Taylor (1986).

evidence, if any, against the hypothesis. There is evidence against randomness for the spot stock indices and the futures on foreign exchange rates, but less evidence for the futures on indices.

The dependence that is found in many series of daily returns is *positive* dependence. For these series, the random variables that generate returns on consecutive days are positively correlated and, in some cases, these variables are also positively correlated beyond consecutive time periods. The dependence among daily returns is extremely small, as seen for example in Figures 5.5–5.7, and it appears to have decreased in recent years. Nevertheless it is more than can be explained by time-varying risk premia.

Test power is relatively high for both the first autocorrelation test and the runs test evaluated on either equity series or simulations of MA(1) processes. Test power is also relatively high for linear functions of autocorrelations evaluated either on foreign exchange series or on simulations of ARMA(1, 1) processes that have positive dependence at all lags. Powerful linear functions have weights that decrease as the lag increases. Appropriate examples are defined by the T-test for trends, variance-ratio tests, and the estimated spectral density at zero frequency.

Further Reading

Fama, E. F. and K. R. French. 1988. Permanent and temporary components of stock prices. *Journal of Political Economy* 96:246–273.

Goetzmann, W. N. 1993. Patterns in three centuries of stock market prices. *Journal of Business* 66:249–270.

Hsieh, D. A. 1991. Chaos and nonlinear dynamics: application to financial markets. *Journal of Finance* 46:1839–1877.

Richardson, M. and T. Smith. 1994. A unified approach to testing for serial correlation in stock returns. *Journal of Business* 67:371–399.

Taylor, S. J. 1982. Tests of the random walk hypothesis against a price-trend hypothesis. *Journal of Financial and Quantitative Analysis* 17:37–61.

6.12 Appendix: the Correlation between Test Values for Two Correlated Series

Suppose $\{r_{1,t}\}$ and $\{r_{2,t}\}$ are two uncorrelated, cross-correlated processes, whose linear interdependence is entirely contemporaneous, so that

$$\text{cor}(r_{1,s}, r_{2,t}) = \begin{cases} \lambda & \text{if } s = t, \\ 0 & \text{otherwise.} \end{cases}$$

General results are presented for martingale differences, after results are first derived for the simpler situation when the vectors $(r_{1,t}, r_{2,t})'$ follow a zero-mean i.i.d. process. The univariate processes are assumed to have unit variance without loss of generality.

To obtain the asymptotic correlation between the sample autocorrelations $\hat{\rho}_{1,\tau}$ and $\hat{\rho}_{2,\tau}$, defined here for positive lags τ by

$$\hat{\rho}_{i,\tau} = \sum_{t=1}^{n-\tau} r_{i,t} r_{i,t+\tau} \bigg/ \sum_{t=1}^{n} r_{i,t}^2,$$

consider the variables

$$A_n = \frac{1}{n} \sum_{s=1}^{n-\tau} \sum_{t=1}^{n-\tau} r_{1,s} r_{1,s+\tau} r_{2,t} r_{2,t+\tau} \quad \text{and} \quad B_{i,n} = \frac{1}{n} \sum_{t=1}^{n} r_{i,t}^2,$$

so that

$$n \hat{\rho}_{1,\tau} \hat{\rho}_{2,\tau} = A_n / (B_{1,n} B_{2,n}).$$

As n increases, $B_{i,n} \to 1$ and, applying the i.i.d. assumption,

$$E[A_n] \to E[r_{1,t} r_{1,t+\tau} r_{2,t} r_{2,t+\tau}] = E[r_{1,t} r_{2,t}] E[r_{1,t+\tau} r_{2,t+\tau}] = \lambda^2.$$

Hence

$$n E[\hat{\rho}_{1,\tau} \hat{\rho}_{2,\tau}] \to \lambda^2, \qquad n \, \text{cov}(\hat{\rho}_{1,\tau}, \hat{\rho}_{2,\tau}) \to \lambda^2,$$

and since $n \operatorname{var}(\hat{\rho}_{i,\tau}) \to 1$, from the i.i.d. assumption, it follows that

$$\operatorname{cor}(\hat{\rho}_{1,\tau}, \hat{\rho}_{2,\tau}) \to \lambda^2, \quad \text{also.}$$

Similar steps show that there is no asymptotic correlation between $\hat{\rho}_{1,\tau}$ and $\hat{\rho}_{2,\xi}$ whenever $\tau \neq \xi$. It then follows that for any constants a_τ the linear combinations L_1 and L_2 defined by $L_i = \sum a_\tau \hat{\rho}_{i,\tau}$ (summing over some range $1 \leqslant \tau \leqslant k$) also have correlation λ^2.

The preceding results can be extended to a bivariate, stationary, martingale difference process, that has $E[r_{2,t+\tau} \mid r_{2,t}, r_{1,s}r_{1,s+\tau}] = 0$ for $t \geqslant s$ and $\tau > 0$, and likewise for the conditional expectation of $r_{1,t+\tau}$. Assuming $n \operatorname{var}(\hat{\rho}_{i,\tau}) \to \beta_{i,\tau}$, the general result also depends on the autocorrelations $\rho_{\tau,p}$ of the products $p_t = r_{1,t}r_{2,t}$ and the variance term $\kappa = \operatorname{var}(r_1 r_2)/(\operatorname{var}(r_1)\operatorname{var}(r_2))$:

$$\operatorname{cor}(\hat{\rho}_{1,\tau}, \hat{\rho}_{2,\tau}) \to \frac{\lambda^2 + \kappa \rho_{\tau,p}}{(\beta_{1,\tau}\beta_{2,\tau})^{0.5}}.$$

Some estimates of λ exceed 0.9, for example, for (rescaled) spot and futures returns from the same index and for some pairs of (rescaled) currency returns. High estimates imply that sample autocorrelations are then highly correlated across series when the random walk hypothesis is true for both series.

6.13   Appendix: Autocorrelation Induced by Rescaling Returns

Suppose returns r_t are the sum of an autocorrelated component μ_t and an uncorrelated component $\sigma_t \varepsilon_t$, as in Section 6.9, with σ_t representing volatility. It is shown here that rescaling will increase measures of dependence when appropriate assumptions are made. We compare the autocorrelations of the processes defined by

$$r_t = \mu_t + \sigma_t \varepsilon_t \quad \text{and} \quad y_t = \frac{r_t}{\sigma_t} = \frac{\mu_t}{\sigma_t} + \varepsilon_t.$$

Assuming the three processes $\{\mu_t\}$, $\{\sigma_t\}$, and $\{\varepsilon_t\}$ are stationary and stochastically independent of each other, that μ_t has mean zero, and that the ε_t are i.i.d. with mean zero and variance one, the autocorrelations are

$$\rho_{\tau,r} = \frac{E[\mu_t \mu_{t+\tau}]}{E[\mu_t^2] + E[\sigma_t^2]} \quad \text{and} \quad \rho_{\tau,y} = \frac{E[\mu_t \mu_{t+\tau}]E[\sigma_t^{-1}\sigma_{t+\tau}^{-1}]}{E[\mu_t^2]E[\sigma_t^{-2}] + 1}.$$

Let

$$A = \frac{\operatorname{var}(\mu_t)}{\operatorname{var}(r_t)}, \quad \omega = E[\sigma_t^2]E[\sigma_t^{-2}], \quad \text{and} \quad C = \frac{\omega}{1 + A(\omega - 1)}.$$

Then the ratio of the autocorrelations simplifies to

$$\frac{\rho_{\tau,y}}{\rho_{\tau,r}} = C\frac{E[\sigma_t^{-1}\sigma_{t+\tau}^{-1}]}{E[\sigma_t^{-2}]} \geqslant C\rho_{\tau,\sigma^{-1}}.$$

The term ω is at least one by Jensen's inequality (and as $\omega = 1 - \text{cov}(\sigma_t^2, \sigma_t^{-2})$). Since realistic values of A are almost zero, we anticipate that C exceeds one. Appropriate autocorrelations for the process $\{\sigma_t^{-1}\}$ are almost one for daily variables (Chapters 11 and 12) and so we may anticipate that $\rho_{\tau,y}/\rho_{\tau,r} > 1$.

To illustrate a lower bound for the ratio, suppose $A = 0.05$ and $\{\log(\sigma_t)\}$ is Gaussian with variance $\beta^2 = 0.25$. Then $\omega = \exp(4\beta^2) = e$ and $C \cong 2.5$.

7

Trading Rules and Market Efficiency

Trend-following trading rules have the potential to exploit any positive autocorrelation in the stochastic process that generates returns. Four of these rules are evaluated in this chapter. There have been long periods in the past when trading rules would have provided valuable information about future prices. However, their value has not been demonstrated in recent years.

7.1 Introduction

Trading rules are numerical methods that use a time series of prices to decide the quantity of an asset owned by a market participant. This chapter considers the information that can be obtained from trading rules. Both the paradigm of efficient markets and the low levels of autocorrelation among daily returns can motivate prior beliefs that trading rules cannot achieve anything of practical value. Nevertheless, it will be seen that trading rules have sometimes been able to generate profitable investment decisions, particularly for trading foreign exchange, that challenge the efficient market hypothesis.

Four trading rules are evaluated in some depth in this chapter. The double moving-average rule and the channel rule are two elementary rules that are popular in the literature of technical analysts, while the filter rule is an elementary rule that has often been tried in academic research. The fourth rule is designed around ARMA(1, 1) forecasts of future returns. These rules are defined in Section 7.2. They all aspire to identify trends in recent prices that persist into the future.

There are many other trading rules that are not analyzed here. Several further rules based upon technical analysis are defined rigorously and investigated by Lo, Mamaysky, and Wang (2000). They claim that some technical patterns provide useful information about the prices of US stocks. However, expected returns following their patterns are similar to unconditional expectations (Jegadeesh 2000) and the same conclusion applies to UK firms (Dawson and Steeley 2003). Lukac and Brorsen (1990) find that many rules applied to commodity and financial futures prices make profits, but they do not conclude that these futures markets have been inefficient.

Research into trading rules has a long history, which initially focused on efforts to refute the notion of an efficient market. More recent research, pioneered by Brock, Lakonishok, and LeBaron (1992), instead uses trading rules to learn about the conditional means and variances of future returns. Their methods are described in Section 7.3 and are then evaluated for equity, currency, and other markets in Sections 7.4 and 7.5. Significant information about conditional means is uncovered by elementary rules, although its importance has diminished in recent years. Section 7.6 describes an Excel spreadsheet that implements the calculations of Brock et al.

The weak form of the efficient market hypothesis is defined in Section 7.7 by a statement that says trading rules cannot outperform passive investment strategies, after considering trading costs and risk. Trading costs appear to have been sufficient to eliminate profit opportunities at major equity markets (Section 7.8), but not at currency markets (Section 7.9). Net trading profits at spot and futures foreign exchange markets during the 1970s and the 1980s can be explained in many ways, but the possibility of an inefficient market is shown to be credible in Section 7.10. Finally, the Monte Carlo results summarized in Section 7.11 show that very low levels of positive dependence among returns can be exploited by trend-following trading rules.

7.2   Four Trading Rules

A *trading rule* is a method for converting the history of prices into investment decisions. A typical decision variable at time t is the quantity q_{t+1} of an asset that is owned from the time of price observation t until the next observation at time $t+1$. The quantity q_{t+1} is some function of the price history $I_t = \{p_t, p_{t-1}, p_{t-2}, \ldots\}$. The time counter t refers to trading days throughout this chapter, unless stated otherwise.

Most rules restrict the quantities to a few possible levels. At time t we consider a maximum of three levels, whose values might depend on I_t. We call day $t+1$ a Buy day if the quantity is the highest possible, a Sell day if it is the lowest possible, and a Neutral day if the quantity is some intermediate value. Typical values of the three quantities are 1, 0, and -1 for futures contracts and 2, 1, and 0 for equities.

Trading actions are determined by the classifications of days and vice versa. For example, consider two scenarios when day t is a Buy and day $t+1$ is a Sell. First, a futures trader will liquidate a long position and initiate a short position at the close of day t, perhaps with $q_t = 1$ and $q_{t+1} = -1$. Alternatively, if the asset is a stock that cannot be sold short, a trader will sell all he or she owns and invest the proceeds in a deposit account, again at the close of day t, so $q_t > 0$ and $q_{t+1} = 0$.

The ambitions of traders have inevitably led to the creation of a multitude of trading rules. These rules have the objective of owning more of the asset when expected returns are higher. There is some predictability in the returns process whenever these expectations are fulfilled. The four trading rules investigated in this chapter are all designed to identify the current trend in prices, typically up or down. The rules will be profitable if prices generally move in the direction of the current trend for a sufficiently long period of time. The most attention will be given to the first of the four rules.

7.2.1 The Moving-Average Rule

A comparison of two moving averages defines one of the rules most frequently mentioned in market literature. Two averages of lengths S (a short period of time) and L (a longer period) are calculated at time t from the most recent price observations, including p_t:

$$a_{t,S} = \frac{1}{S} \sum_{j=1}^{S} p_{t-S+j}, \qquad a_{t,L} = \frac{1}{L} \sum_{j=1}^{L} p_{t-L+j}. \tag{7.1}$$

We consider the relative difference between the short- and long-term averages, measured by

$$R_t = \frac{a_{t,S} - a_{t,L}}{a_{t,L}}. \tag{7.2}$$

Brock et al. (1992) includes a statement that the most popular parameter combinations have $S \leqslant 5$ and $L \geqslant 50$.

When the short-term average is above [below] the long-term average, recent prices are higher [lower] than older prices and it may be imagined that prices are following an upward [downward] trend. When the two averages are similar, it may be argued that the information is not precise enough to form a view about the trend. Consequently, Brock et al. (1992) classify time period $t + 1$, which is the time from the close on day t until the close on day $t + 1$, as

$$\text{Buy if } R_t > B, \quad \text{Neutral if } -B \leqslant R_t \leqslant B, \quad \text{Sell if } R_t < -B. \tag{7.3}$$

This classification algorithm has three parameters: S, L, and B. The bandwidth B can be zero and then (almost) all days are either Buys or Sells.

Figure 7.1 shows moving averages for the S&P 100 index from July to December 2000 when $S = 1$ and $L = 50$, respectively marked by filled diamonds and empty circles. When B is zero, most days in July and August are Buys, and most days in October, November, and December are Sells. The two dotted curves are 1% above and below the long-term average. A few index levels are between these curves and hence there are a few Neutral days when $B = 0.01$.

The calculations for all the rules may be misleading if they are applied to price series that contain predictable jumps, particularly series that are constructed from

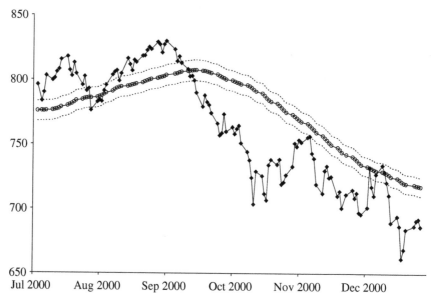

Figure 7.1. Moving averages for the S&P 100 index.

several futures contracts. A satisfactory way to apply the rules to futures data replaces the price series $\{p_t\}$ by a wealth series $\{w_t\}$, constructed from returns $\{r_t\}$ using the definition $w_t = w_{t-1}\exp(r_t)$.

7.2.2 The Channel Rule

Lukac, Brorsen, and Irwin (1988) found that a channel rule performed best in their study of several technical trading systems. Their version of the channel trading rule assumes that a futures trader is always in the market. The description here adapts the rule so that neutral positions can be taken when a bandwidth parameter B is positive.

By analogy with the moving-average rule, the short-term average is replaced by the most recent price (so $S = 1$) and the long-term average is replaced by either a minimum or a maximum of the L previous prices, respectively defined by

$$m_{t-1} = \min(p_{t-L}, \ldots, p_{t-2}, p_{t-1}),$$
$$M_{t-1} = \max(p_{t-L}, \ldots, p_{t-2}, p_{t-1}). \tag{7.4}$$

A person who believes prices have been following an upward [downward] trend may be willing to believe the trend has changed direction when the latest price is less [more] than all recent previous prices.

The rule has two parameters: the channel length L and the bandwidth B. The algorithm to classify day $t + 1$ depends on the classification of the previous day.

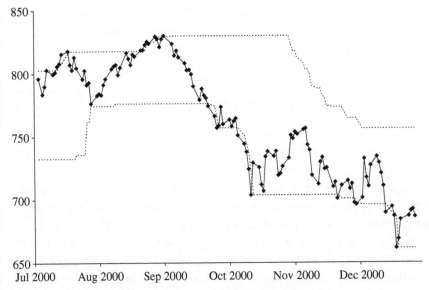

Figure 7.2.   Channels for the S&P 100 index.

If day t is a Buy, then day $t + 1$ is

$$\text{Buy if } p_t \geqslant (1 + B)m_{t-1}, \quad \text{Sell if } p_t < (1 - B)m_{t-1}, \quad \text{Neutral otherwise.}$$
$$(7.5)$$

Likewise, if day t is a Sell, then symmetric principles classify day $t + 1$ as

$$\text{Sell if } p_t \leqslant (1 - B)M_{t-1}, \quad \text{Buy if } p_t > (1 + B)M_{t-1}, \quad \text{Neutral otherwise.}$$
$$(7.6)$$

For a Neutral day t, day $t + 1$ is

$$\text{Buy if } p_t > (1 + B)M_{t-1}, \quad \text{Sell if } p_t < (1 - B)m_{t-1}, \quad \text{Neutral otherwise.}$$
$$(7.7)$$

Figure 7.2 shows values of p_t, M_{t-1}, and m_{t-1} for the S&P 100 index when $L = 40$. When B is zero, all the days until late September are Buys, as $p_t > m_{t-1}$. The first Sell day is identified on 22 September when $p_t < m_{t-1}$ and the remaining days are all Sells as then $p_t < M_{t-1}$.

7.2.3 The Filter Rule

Alexander (1961) invented a filter rule that has often been used in academic studies to separate days into two sets based upon a trader's market position. Sweeney (1986, 1988) used the filter rule to challenge market efficiency, respectively for foreign exchange and US firms. The rule is adapted here to allow for a band within which neutral positions are taken.

An analogy with the moving-average rule can again be attempted: the short-term average is replaced by the most recent price and the long-term average is

162 7. *Trading Rules and Market Efficiency*

replaced by some multiple of the maximum or minimum since the most recent trend is believed to have commenced. The terms m_t and M_t are now defined, for a positive filter size parameter f and a trend commencing at time s, by

$$m_{t-1} = (1 - f)\max(p_s, \ldots, p_{t-2}, p_{t-1}),$$
$$M_{t-1} = (1 + f)\min(p_s, \ldots, p_{t-2}, p_{t-1}). \tag{7.8}$$

A person may now believe an upward [downward] trend has changed direction when the latest price has fallen [risen] by a fraction f from the highest [lowest] price during the upward [downward] trend.

The parameters of the rule are the filter size f and the bandwidth B. Classification of days follows almost the same methods as for the channel rule. If day t is a Buy, then $s + 1$ is the earliest Buy day for which there are no intermediate Sell days and day $t + 1$ is classified using (7.5); it is possible that $s + 1 = t$. Likewise, if day t is a Sell, then $s + 1$ is the earliest Sell day for which there are no intermediate Buy days and day $t + 1$ is classified using (7.6). If day t is Neutral, then find the most recent non-Neutral day and use its value of s: if this non-Neutral day is a Buy, then apply (7.5) and otherwise apply (7.6). To start classification, the first non-Neutral day is identified when either $p_t > (1 + B)M_{t-1}$ or $p_t < (1 - B)m_{t-1}$, with $s = 1$.

7.2.4 A Statistical Rule

Trading rules based upon ARMA(1, 1) models for rescaled returns are investigated in several publications, commencing with Taylor (1983, 1986). The particular rule used in Taylor (1992) is discussed in this chapter and evaluated for futures contracts. It would have made profits for currency trades in the 1980s, to be discussed further in Sections 7.9 and 7.10. Note immediately, however, that these profits are slightly less than those from the simpler moving-average, channel, and filter rules.

The ARMA(1, 1) process is defined by equation (3.23) and its autocorrelations are $A\phi^\tau$. The parameter A is positive for the price-trend model introduced by equation (3.42). From A and the autoregressive parameter ϕ we can obtain the moving-average parameter θ from equation (3.27). The statistical trading rule uses ARMA forecasting theory applied to rescaled returns defined by $r_t/\sqrt{h_t}$, with the conditional standard deviation $\sqrt{h_t}$ obtained from a special case of the simple ARCH specification introduced in Section 5.7.

The rule relies on a standardized forecast k_{t+1}, given by the one-day-ahead forecast divided by an estimate of its standard error,

$$k_{t+1} = f_{t,1}/\hat{\sigma}_f. \tag{7.9}$$

This is evaluated using the equations

$$f_{t,1} = (h_{t+1}/h_t)^{1/2}\{(\phi + \theta)r_t - \theta f_{t-1,1}\},$$
$$\hat{\sigma}_f = \sqrt{h_{t+1}}\{A\phi(\phi + \theta)/(1 + \phi\theta)\}^{1/2}, \tag{7.10}$$
$$\sqrt{h_{t+1}} = 0.9\sqrt{h_t} + 0.1253|r_t|.$$

An upward [downward] trend is predicted when k_{t+1} is positive [negative].

A nonnegative threshold parameter k^* determines the classification of days. If day t is a Buy, then day $t + 1$ is

$$\text{Buy if } k_t > 0, \quad \text{Sell if } k_t \leqslant -k^*, \quad \text{Neutral otherwise.} \tag{7.11}$$

Likewise, if day t is a Sell, then day $t + 1$ is

$$\text{Sell if } k_t < 0, \quad \text{Buy if } k_t \geqslant k^*, \quad \text{Neutral otherwise.}$$

The day after a Neutral day t is

$$\text{Buy if } k_t \geqslant k^*, \quad \text{Sell if } k_t \leqslant -k^*, \quad \text{Neutral otherwise.}$$

7.3 Measures of Return Predictability

Trading rules provide information about future returns whenever the returns on Buy days have a different distribution to the returns on Sell days. We define two sets of time indices I and J as follows:

t is in I, denoted by $t \in I$, if period $t + 1$ is classified as a Buy,

t is in J, denoted by $t \in J$, if period $t + 1$ is classified as a Sell.

Then we may say that a trading rule applied to a stationary stochastic process representing prices is *uninformative* if the conditional densities $f(r_{t+1} \mid t \in I)$ and $f(r_{t+1} \mid t \in J)$ are identical; the rule is *informative* if these conditional densities are different.

A trading rule will be informative if expected returns depend on the Buy/Sell information, i.e.

$$E[r_{t+1} \mid t \in I] \neq E[r_{t+1} \mid t \in J]. \tag{7.12}$$

Given a time series of observed prices it is natural to assess the evidence about this inequality by using a difference between sample means. Let the number of time indices in the Buy and Sell sets be denoted by n_I and n_J respectively. The average returns for Buy and Sell days are

$$\bar{r}_I = \frac{1}{n_I} \sum_{t \in I} r_{t+1} \quad \text{and} \quad \bar{r}_J = \frac{1}{n_J} \sum_{t \in J} r_{t+1} \tag{7.13}$$

and hence a measure of predictability is $\bar{r}_I - \bar{r}_J$.

An obvious test of the null hypothesis that the rule is uninformative requires calculation of standard deviations s_I and s_J, respectively from the Buy returns and the Sell returns, followed by a comparison of

$$z = (\bar{r}_I - \bar{r}_J)\left(\frac{s_I^2}{n_I} + \frac{s_J^2}{n_J}\right)^{-0.5} \qquad (7.14)$$

with the standard normal distribution. Brock et al. (1992) obtain highly significant positive values of a similar statistic, which are reviewed in the next section.

A second way to find evidence for predictability is to show that the probability of the price rising depends on the trading rule information. Buy and Sell probabilities can be estimated, after removing any zero returns, by

$$\bar{p}_I = P(r_{t+1} > 0 \mid t \in I \text{ and } r_{t+1} \neq 0), \qquad (7.15)$$

and likewise $\bar{p}_J$, and hence the difference $\bar{p}_I - \bar{p}_J$ can be calculated. A binomial test is used by Brock et al. to show that their sample differences are highly significant.

Brock et al. also show that something can be learnt about conditional second moments from trading rules. Evidence for such predictability is measured by the difference between standard deviations, $s_J - s_I$, which indicates whether or not volatility is higher when Sell classifications are made than when Buy classifications occur.

7.3.1 Interpretation of the Test Statistic z

It is instructive to clarify the most general null hypothesis about returns that can be tested by the methodology that leads to the z-test based upon equation (7.14). We now show that z can be used to test the null hypothesis that returns in excess of a stationary mean are generated by a stationary martingale difference. This null hypothesis is the definition of the random walk hypothesis given by definition RWH2 on p. 101, with the additional assumption of stationarity. Distributional assumptions are unimportant when z is evaluated for large samples, as a version of the central limit theorem will ensure that the distribution of z is approximately normal.

Let i_t be 1 if the information up to time t is used to classify period $t + 1$ as a Buy, i.e. $t \in I$, and otherwise let i_t be 0. Likewise, j_t is 1 if $t \in J$ and it is 0 otherwise. Then the difference between Buy and Sell averages, for classifications of times $t = 1, 2, \ldots, n$, is

$$\bar{r}_I - \bar{r}_J = \frac{1}{n_I}\sum_{t=1}^{n} i_t r_{t+1} - \frac{1}{n_J}\sum_{t=1}^{n} j_t r_{t+1}$$

$$= \sum_{t=1}^{n}\left(\frac{i_t}{\sum_s i_s} - \frac{j_t}{\sum_s j_s}\right) r_{t+1}. \qquad (7.16)$$

Now assume stationarity and let $E[r_t] = \mu$. Then the large sample properties of $\bar{r}_I - \bar{r}_J$ are unaltered if we replace $\sum i_t/n$ by $E[i_t]$. Defining

$$F_t = (i_t/E[i_t]) - (j_t/E[j_t]),$$

we have $E[F_t] = 0$ and

$$F_t = \begin{cases} 1/E[i_t], & t \in I, \\ -1/E[j_t], & t \in J, \\ 0, & \text{otherwise.} \end{cases}$$

The large sample properties of $\bar{r}_I - \bar{r}_J$ are thus the same as those of

$$d = \frac{1}{n} \sum_{t=1}^{n} F_t(r_{t+1} - \mu). \tag{7.17}$$

The expectation of d is zero when the excess returns $r_t - \mu$ are a martingale difference (MD), because then $E[r_{t+1} - \mu \mid F_t] = 0$. The variance of d, multiplied by n, simplifies to $E[F_t^2 (r_{t+1} - \mu)^2]$, by applying the MD and stationarity assumptions, and this expectation is consistently estimated by $n(s_I^2/n_I + s_J^2/n_J)$. It follows that the asymptotic distribution of z is $N(0, 1)$ when the process generating excess returns is a stationary martingale difference. Such processes are white noise and are hence uncorrelated. Many examples are given in Chapter 9 when we define ARCH specifications that have constant conditional means.

7.3.2 Power of the Test Statistic z

A sample value of d calculated from a sample of returns is almost identical to $\text{cov}(r_{t+1}, F_t)$, when μ, $E[i_t]$, and $E[j_t]$ are respectively replaced by $\bar{r}$, n_I/n, and n_J/n. Thus a sample value of d essentially equals the sample covariance of r_{t+1} with a nonlinear function of returns (up to time t), determined by the trading rule, which has only three possible values. The variance-ratio test of the random walk hypothesis, presented in Section 5.3, which compares single- and N-period variances, is essentially a test based upon the following covariance:

$$\text{cov}\left(r_{t+1}, \sum_{\tau=1}^{N-1}(N - \tau)r_{t+1-\tau}\right).$$

Consequently, the trading rule z-test is only likely to be more powerful than a variance-ratio test when r_{t+1} correlates more highly with the nonlinear, trading rule function $F_t(r_t, r_{t-1}, \dots)$ than with the linear function $\sum(N - \tau)r_{t+1-\tau}$.

Acar (1993, 2002) has presented several related results for the single moving-average rule without a band (so $S = 1$ and $B = 0$). When expected returns are zero, the quantity $\frac{1}{2}F_t$ is then approximately the sign ($+1$ or -1) of a linear function of returns. It seems probable in these circumstances that the z-test is less powerful than an appropriate variance-ratio test. This prediction is supported by empirical test results for US and UK equity returns (Taylor 2000). Acar (1993) also shows that the single moving-average rule has optimal properties when returns follow a Gaussian ARMA(1, 1) process.

The Monte Carlo study of test power in Section 6.9 shows that selected variance-ratio and autocorrelation tests of the random walk hypothesis have power above 90% when applied to 2500 returns defined by an ARMA(1, 1) process whose autocorrelations are $0.02(0.95^\tau)$. Further simulations show that the power of the trading rule z-test is also high when the trading rule parameters are chosen appropriately: 74% for the moving-average rule when $S = 1$, $L = 30$, and $B = 0.01$; 67% for the channel rule when $L = 10$ and $B = 0$; and 74% for the filter rule when $f = 0.02$ and $B = 0.01$, all for one-tail tests.

7.4 Evidence about Equity Return Predictability

7.4.1 US Equities

Brock et al. (1992) use various technical rules to identify Buy and Sell days for the Dow Jones Industrial Average (DJIA) from 1897 to 1986. The DJIA does not include any dividend payments and this index has contained thirty stocks since 1928. Brock et al. document significant, positive values of the mean return and probability differences, $\bar{r}_I - \bar{r}_J$ and $\bar{p}_I - \bar{p}_J$, and of the standard deviation differences, $s_J - s_I$. Thus the first and second moments of these returns have been predictable to some degree and hence technical rules have been informative. Four conclusions are particularly interesting, and are discussed here for the moving-average rule. Ten parameter combinations are evaluated by Brock et al., all of which have $1 \leqslant S \leqslant 5$, $50 \leqslant L \leqslant 200$, and $B = 0$ or 1%.

First, "buy signals consistently generate higher returns than sell signals." The average returns on Buy and Sell days, across all parameter combinations, are respectively equivalent to 12% and -7% per annum (p.a.) (Brock et al., Table II). Tests on the differences between Buy and Sell average returns, using the z-statistic in equation (7.14), provide highly significant values of z for each of the ten parameter combinations evaluated, ranging from 3.79 to 6.04. The null hypothesis is also rejected at the 5% significance level for each subperiod considered: 1897–1914, 1915–1938, 1939–1962, and 1962–1986. The respective subperiod differences between annualized Buy and Sell returns are 18%, 27%, 11%, and 12%.

Second, "returns following sell signals are negative, which is not easily explained by any of the currently existing equilibrium models." All four subperiods have negative Sell averages, which cannot be explained by calendar anomalies because about 40% of all days are Sell days.

Third, "returns following buy signals are less volatile than returns following sell signals." Standard deviations of 0.89% and 1.34% are reported, respectively for Buy and Sell days (Brock et al., p. 1749). Consequently, if volatility measures risk, then changes in risk levels do not explain the higher average returns for Buy days than for Sell days.

Fourth, "returns from these...strategies are not consistent with...popular models." The most credible model assessed is the exponential ARCH model of Nelson (1991), incorporating MA(1) and conditional variance terms in the specification of the conditional mean, to be defined later in Sections 9.5 and 10.2. The bootstrap *p*-values for the difference between Buy and Sell average returns are all less than 0.5% for this ARCH model. Although it cannot explain the difference between the average returns, the exponential ARCH model appears to explain some of the observed difference between Buy volatility and Sell volatility.

Several further research studies have applied the rules and parameter values of Brock et al. Bessembinder and Chan (1995a) reconsider the DJIA evidence. After including dividend yields in the calculation of returns, they find that negative expected returns on Sell days only occur before 1939. They claim that realistic transaction costs have always exceeded the amount required to eliminate gross trading profits. The predictability of the DJIA could then be a consequence of transactions costs, varying risk premia, bandwagon effects, and/or other explanations. The bandwagon concept is rejected by showing that there is as much useful information in CRSP indices, which are not followed by the market, as there is in the DJIA. Also, the moving-average rule can predict returns from individual equities but not their abnormal returns with respect to market models.

Sullivan, Timmermann, and White (1999) discuss the problem of data-snooping. This will occur if researchers copy rules from market literature that only promotes those technical rules that have the best historical returns. Sullivan et al. reanalyze the data of Brock et al., for more rules and for many more parameter combinations. They confirm that there is statistically significant evidence that trading rules provide information about the conditional mean of the DJIA, until 1986. However, they find no evidence that the rules are informative during the subsequent decade until 1996, for either the DJIA or for futures on the S&P 500 index. We obtain the same conclusion in Section 7.6 for the S&P 100 index, from 1991 to 2000.

Day and Wang (2002) show that the evidence for predictability may arise because the prices of the component stocks in the index are not always synchronous. They find that the differences between Buy and Sell average returns from 1962 to 1986 are much less for (i) a value-weighted index constructed from the DJIA stocks, which gives less weight to smaller firms whose stocks may trade less often, and (ii) "true" levels of the DJIA given by modeling returns as an MA(1) process, which is consistent with nonsynchronous prices. Trading volumes were much higher from 1987 to 1996, when the average returns on Buy and Sell days are similar for the moving-average rule.

Fang and Xu (2003) compare DJIA average returns for the moving-average rule with a time series rule based upon forecasting returns using an AR(1) process, from 1896 to 1996. Their average difference between Buy and Sell returns for the time series rule is more than double the figure for the moving-average rule. This is an interesting result, although estimation of the AR(1) parameter from all the data may enhance the performance of the time series rule.

7.4.2 Other Equity Markets

Bessembinder and Chan (1995b) replicate the methods of Brock et al. for six Asian equity indices, from 1975 to 1989. The annualized difference between Buy and Sell returns for the moving-average rule averages 8% for Hong Kong, Japan, and Korea and a massive 52% for the emerging markets of Malaysia, Thailand, and Taiwan. Ito (1999) provides further evidence that indices for developed (Canada, Japan) and emerging markets (Indonesia, Mexico, Taiwan) have been predictable, for the period from 1980 to 1996.

Hudson, Dempsey, and Keasey (1996) is possibly the only study that applies the methodology of Brock et al. to a very long series of index levels from another country. They investigate the UK FT-30 index from 1935 to 1994. All their average Buy returns are significantly higher than average Sell returns, at low significance levels. The overall averages are equivalent to annual rates of 16% on Buy days and −6% on Sell days. Significant differences are reported for subperiods until 1981 but not for the most recent subperiod from 1981 to 1994. Any profits from the trading rules are less than transaction costs.

Taylor (2000) provides results for several UK series recorded from 1972 to 1991: the Financial Times All-Share (FTA) index, calculated from the prices of more than 600 stocks, the prices of twelve large firms, and indices calculated from these prices. The moving-average rule produces values of the z-statistic that are significant at the 5% level for the FTA index, the 12-share indices, and four of the twelve firms. The most predictability is found in the FTA index. The values of the z-statistic correlate much more highly with linear combinations of autocorrelations, such as variance ratios, than they do with the first-lag auto-correlations.

Our first conclusion about equity returns is that their conditional means have depended on trading rule information for long periods of time. Our second is that the degree of predictability has decreased substantially in recent years.

7.5 Evidence about the Predictability of Currency and Other Returns

We next consider the predictability of the twenty equity, currency, and commodity return series defined by Table 2.2 and tested for randomness in Chapters 5 and 6.

7.5.1 *The Moving-Average Rule*

The issue of parameter optimization is deliberately avoided by Brock et al., who report the results for all the parameter combinations that they evaluated. We do the same and initially discuss results for all 24 combinations of short averaging periods S, long averaging periods L, and bandwidths B given by $S = 1, 2,$ or 5, $L = 10, 100, 150,$ or 200, and $B = 0$ or 1%. For all combinations, classification of days as Buy, Sell, or Neutral commences at time 201. To avoid any impact from extreme outliers, the days in the crash week (commencing on 19 October 1987) are excluded from the Buy and Sell sets when the summary statistics are calculated.

The columns of Table 7.1 present the averages of quantities across all 24 parameter combinations. These quantities are the numbers of Buy and Sell days n_I, n_J, the average returns $\bar{r}_I, \bar{r}_J$, the probabilities of price rises $\bar{p}_I, \bar{p}_J$, the differences in average returns $\bar{r}_I - \bar{r}_J$, the standardized test statistics z, and the standard deviations s_I, s_J. Table 7.1 also shows how many of the combinations produce values of z below -1.96 or above 1.96 that reject the null hypothesis of a stationary martingale difference for excess returns at the 5% level.

It is very clear from Table 7.1 and perhaps surprising that far more evidence is found for predictability in each of the four currency series than in any other series. For the yen, 15 of the 24 z-values exceed 1.96, with higher counts of 18 for the Deutsche mark and the Swiss franc and 19 for sterling. We should note, however, that many of the z-values for currencies are near 1.96 and that the 24 test values for a currency do not provide 24 independent test results. There are only seven values of z above 1.96 in total for the other sixteen series and there are no values below -1.96. The average probabilities for the currencies of price rises on Buy days are 5–6% higher than the statistics on Sell days. The differences $\bar{p}_I - \bar{p}_J$ are much less for most of the other series.

The differences $s_J - s_I$ between the Sell and Buy standard deviations are generally higher for the equity series than for the other series. There is some evidence that volatility is higher following falling prices than following rising prices, but only for equities. The Buy standard deviations are less than the Sell standard deviations for all the stock indices and all three US stock firms. The difference is most pronounced for the Nikkei series, with averages of 0.92% and 1.79% respectively for Buy and Sell days. Almost no difference is detected for the three UK firms, although Taylor (2000) finds $s_I < s_J$ for all twelve UK firms analyzed for the longer period from 1972 to 1991.

The values of the longer averaging period, L, used to produce Table 7.1 follow Brock et al. and are much higher than those used in some other studies, e.g. Taylor (1992). Repeating the calculations, with the only change being that $L = 10, 20, 30,$ or 40, produces 100 significant values of z at the 5% level (21% of the 480 test values) compared with 77 significant values in Table 7.1 (16% of the test

Table 7.1. Trading results for the moving-average trading rule.

Series		Days Buy	Days Sell	Means (%) Buy	Means (%) Sell	Chance positive Buy	Chance positive Sell	Mean (%) Buy-Sell	z	Counts z < −1.96	Counts z > 1.96	s.d. (%) Buy	s.d. (%) Sell
S&P 500-share	S	1685	492	0.0548	0.0619	0.5468	0.5557	−0.0071	−0.14	0	0	0.76	1.13
S&P 500-share	F	1461	695	0.0116	0.0642	0.5164	0.5521	−0.0526	−0.99	0	0	0.95	1.25
Coca Cola	S	1487	741	0.1170	0.1075	0.5206	0.5148	0.0095	0.14	0	0	1.44	1.86
General Electric	S	1502	696	0.0678	0.1070	0.5037	0.5182	−0.0393	−0.56	0	0	1.29	1.77
General Motors	S	1216	1019	0.0679	0.0501	0.4965	0.5070	0.0178	0.24	0	0	1.62	1.81
FT 100-share	S	1448	717	0.0508	0.0436	0.5238	0.5319	0.0073	0.17	0	0	0.80	1.07
FT 100-share	F	1267	895	0.0248	0.0338	0.5131	0.5343	−0.0090	−0.18	0	0	0.91	1.23
Glaxo	S	1699	557	0.1465	0.0696	0.5399	0.5372	0.0769	0.90	0	1	1.72	1.74
Marks & Spencer	S	1404	807	0.0264	0.1295	0.5592	0.6051	−0.1031	−1.44	0	0	1.67	1.56
Shell	S	1478	700	0.0769	0.1040	0.5381	0.5590	−0.0271	−0.46	0	0	1.23	1.28
Nikkei 225-share	S	1318	827	0.0651	−0.0314	0.5526	0.4824	0.0966	1.43	0	1	0.92	1.79
Treasury bonds	F	1367	752	0.0373	0.0020	0.5287	0.5078	0.0353	1.01	0	0	0.74	0.77
3-month sterling bills	F	762	1330	−0.0028	−0.0083	0.4882	0.4696	0.0055	0.81	0	0	0.11	0.19
DM/$	F	1145	1022	0.0400	−0.0281	0.5108	0.4586	0.0681	2.10	0	18	0.75	0.75
Sterling/$	F	1118	1058	0.0469	−0.0226	0.5375	0.4844	0.0695	2.10	0	19	0.77	0.77
Swiss franc/$	F	1082	1103	0.0402	−0.0332	0.5205	0.4711	0.0734	2.10	0	18	0.85	0.77
Yen/$	F	1146	974	0.0493	−0.0112	0.5216	0.4571	0.0605	2.03	0	15	0.71	0.65
Gold	F	683	1462	−0.0494	−0.0395	0.4803	0.4774	−0.0099	−0.15	0	0	1.55	1.16
Corn	F	819	1379	0.0333	−0.0578	0.5051	0.4751	0.0912	1.59	0	5	1.41	1.10
Live cattle	F	1493	672	0.0495	0.0161	0.5283	0.5206	0.0334	0.66	0	0	0.87	1.22
Averages across all series		1279	895	0.0471	0.0262	0.5216	0.5110	0.0209	0.57	0	4	1.08	1.23

The twenty series are defined in Table 2.2. The numbers for each series are averages of the day frequencies, means, standard deviations, z-statistics, and probabilities across parameter combinations, except for the numbers that count how many z-statistics are significant at the 5% level. The 24 parameter combinations are given by combining $B = 0$, 1%, $S = 1, 2, 5$, and $L = 50, 100, 150, 200$. Returns in the crash week commencing on 19 October 1987 are excluded.

values). For the lower values of L, there are ten or more significant z-statistics for the S&P 500 futures returns, the FTSE 100 spot returns and the yen and corn futures returns; the significant values for these series are negative for the S&P and positive for the other assets.

7.5.2   The Channel and Filter Rules

The initial channel rule results are for the eight combinations of channel lengths L and bandwidths B given by $L = 50, 100, 150$, or 200 and $B = 0$ or 1%, once more motivated by Brock et al. Classification commences with time period 202 using prices up to time 201 and a neutral position at time 200. The proportion of significant test values z (6%) is similar to the significance level (5%). The currencies again have the majority of the significant results. A slight fall in the overall average mean difference, $\bar{r}_I - \bar{r}_J$, for the currencies from 0.068% for the moving-average rule to 0.055% for the channel rule has a considerable impact on the proportion of significant currency mean differences. Shorter channel lengths L are recommended in Taylor (1994b), for example. Once more, repeating the calculations with $L = 10, 20, 30$, or 40 produces similar numbers, both for the number of significant results and for the currency mean differences.

For the filter rule, appropriate filter sizes f have been selected by considering the standard deviations of daily returns and the sizes assessed by Sweeney (1986). Results have been obtained for all eight combinations of f and bandwidths B given by $f = 2\%, 4\%, 6\%$, or 8% and $B = 0$ or 1%. Classification commences with time period 3, assuming a neutral position at time 1. Overall, 23% of the z-statistics are significant at the 5% level: 25 of them are above 1.96 and of these 14 are for currency series, while 10 values of z for US equity series are below -1.96. The overall currency mean difference, $\bar{r}_I - \bar{r}_J$, is now 0.053% and hence very similar to the average level for the channel rule that has fewer significant results.

7.5.3   Comparisons with Random Walk Tests

The various random walk tests applied to the same data in Chapter 6 reject the null hypothesis for 32% of the tests when the significance level is 5%. This rejection frequency exceeds that for all three trading rules. The correlations between the average values of z in Table 7.1 and the twenty-day variance-ratio test statistics in Table 5.2 are 0.69 for returns and 0.60 for rescaled returns, while the correlations are almost zero for two- and five-day variance ratios. Similar correlations are reported in Taylor (2000) for a different set of time series.

7.5.4   Currencies

There is clearly something noteworthy about the series for the four currencies, from 1982 to 1991, that is detected by a comparison of the average Buy return with the average Sell return. The average difference $\bar{r}_I - \bar{r}_J$ across currencies is always between 0.05% and 0.07% for the five specifications of rules and parameter combinations mentioned in this section, and this is enough to be of economic importance. Based upon Table 7.1, an average year contains 112 Buy days that provided a return of 4.9%, and 104 Sell days that provided a return of -2.5%. Thus a trader who was long (short) on Buy (Sell) days would have made more than 7% p.a. before transactions costs. Very similar results are documented in Kho (1996) for weekly returns from currency futures, from 1981 to 1991.

As we will see in Section 7.10, the 1980s was a decade when currency speculation would have been particularly successful. During the later period from 1991 to 2000, the average difference $\bar{r}_I - \bar{r}_J$ for the spot DM/$ rate is between 0.02% and 0.05% for many values of the moving-average parameter L but none of the test values z are significant at the 5% level.

7.6 An Example of Calculations for the Moving-Average Rule

We now present a spreadsheet that shows how we can classify days for the moving-average rule and then test the null hypothesis that returns (in excess of their mean level) are a stationary martingale difference. The illustrative results are for the S&P 100-share index from January 1991 to December 2000. This section can be skipped by readers who are not interested in trading rule software.

We first have to select the three parameters of the trading rule. A reasonable method maximizes the difference between average Buy returns and average Sell returns for a relevant series that predates the data to be tested. This motivates the choices $S = 1$, $L = 50$, and $B = 1\%$, obtained by selecting the best values for the DJIA series from 1897 to 1968 for the 24 combinations evaluated in Section 7.5 (Taylor 2000).

Exhibit 7.1 shows Excel calculations, with the key Excel formulae listed in Table 7.2. The 2531 index levels p_t are located in cells B3 to B2533. We work with percentage returns and henceforth drop the percentage adjective. The first return in cell C4 is given by 100*LN(B4/B3). The squared returns are also used in the calculations, with the first value placed in cell D4. Columns C and D are completed by copying and pasting the 1×2 rectangle C4:D4 as far as row 2533.

The three parameters of the trading rule are in cells F38, G38, and H38. Each day is classified as belonging to one of three classes whose names are inserted into cells G40, H40, and I40. As $S = 1$, it is not necessary to calculate any short-term moving averages.

The next step is to fill the seven cells E52, F52, and E53 to I53. The function AVERAGE provides the long-term moving-average values shown in E52 and E53, while the relative differences R_t defined by equation (7.2) commence with F52 and F53. Each day is classified by using the previous relative difference. Cell G53 shows that 14 March is classified as a Buy, since the short-term average

	A	B	C	D	E	F	G	H	I	J
1	Date	Index	% Return	Squared % r		Returns p.a.				
2		p(t)	r(t)	r(t)*r(t)		253				
3	2-Jan-91	153.36								
4	3-Jan-91	151.44	-1.260	1.587						
5	4-Jan-91	151.28	-0.106	0.011		Trading parameters			Test result	
37	20-Feb-91	172.84	-1.191	1.417		S	L	% B	z	% breakeven C
38	21-Feb-91	172.76	-0.046	0.002		1	50	1	-1.47	-0.22
39	22-Feb-91	173.21	0.260	0.068						
40	25-Feb-91	173.99	0.449	0.202			Buy	Sell	Neutral	All
41	26-Feb-91	171.73	-1.307	1.709		count	1352	460	669	2481
42	27-Feb-91	174.64	1.680	2.823		sum r	34.37	59.42	41.11	134.90
43	28-Feb-91	174.04	-0.344	0.118		sum r*r	959.6	946.1	490.0	2395.7
44	1-Mar-91	175.73	0.966	0.934		mean	0.0254	0.1292	0.0614	0.0544
45	4-Mar-91	174.88	-0.485	0.235		variance	0.7097	2.0445	0.7298	0.9631
46	5-Mar-91	178.30	1.937	3.751		st dev	0.8424	1.4298	0.8543	0.9814
47	6-Mar-91	178.10	-0.112	0.013		mean p.a.	6.43	32.68	15.55	13.76
48	7-Mar-91	178.07	-0.017	0.000		trades	116	68		
49	8-Mar-91	177.56	-0.287	0.082		av. duration	11.66	6.76		
50	11-Mar-91	176.97	-0.333	0.111						
51	12-Mar-91	175.68	-0.732	0.535	Avge(L)	% R(t)	Class	New buy	New sell	
52	13-Mar-91	178.13	1.385	1.918	164.56	8.25				
53	14-Mar-91	177.65	-0.270	0.073	165.04	7.64	Buy	Yes	No	
54	15-Mar-91	177.94	0.163	0.027	165.57	7.47	Buy	No	No	
55	18-Mar-91	177.04	-0.507	0.257	166.09	6.59	Buy	No	No	
56	19-Mar-91	173.70	-1.905	3.628	166.59	4.27	Buy	No	No	
84	29-Apr-91	176.74	-1.522	2.316	177.37	-0.36	Buy	No	No	
85	30-Apr-91	177.71	0.547	0.300	177.43	0.16	Neutral	No	No	
86	1-May-91	180.42	1.513	2.291	177.54	1.62	Neutral	No	No	
87	2-May-91	180.30	-0.067	0.004	177.69	1.47	Buy	Yes	No	
88	3-May-91	180.27	-0.017	0.000	177.84	1.37	Buy	No	No	

Exhibit 7.1. Predictability calculations for the S&P 100 index, 1991–2000.

Table 7.2.   Formulae used in the spreadsheet for the moving-average rule.

Cell	Formula
C4	`=100*LN(B4/B3)`
D4	`=C4*C4`
E52	`=AVERAGE(B3:B52)`
F52	`=100*(B52-E52)/E52`
G41	`=COUNTIF($G$53:$G$2533,G40)`
G42	`=SUMIF($G$53:$G$2533,G40,$C$53:$C$2533)`
G43	`=SUMIF($G$53:$G$2533,G40,$D$53:$D$2533)`
G44	`=G42/G41`
G45	`=(G43-G41*G44*G44)/(G41-1)`
G46	`=SQRT(G45)`
G47	`=$F$2*G44`
G48	`=COUNTIF(H53:H2533,"Yes")`
G49	`=G41/G48`
G53	`=IF(F52>$H$38,$G$40,IF(F52<-$H$38,$H$40,$I$40))`
H53	`=IF(($G$53=$G$40)*AND($G$52<>$G$40),"Yes","No")`
I38	`=(G44-H44)/SQRT((G45/G41)+(H45/H41))`
I53	`=IF(($G$53=$H$40)*AND($G$52<>$H$40),"Yes","No")`
J38	`=0.5*(G44-H44)/((1/G49)+(1/H49))`

on 13 March is more than 1% above the long-term average. The classification formula uses the IF function twice to make comparisons between the percentage relative difference and the percentage bandwidth found in H38. Columns H and I also employ the IF function, to respectively determine when sequences of Buys and Sells commence that correspond to the commencement of trades, as will be explained in Section 7.8. Thus H53 and I53 respectively contain Yes and No because a Buy sequence commences in row 53.

Columns E to I are completed by copying and pasting the 1×5 rectangle E53:I53 as far as the final row of the spreadsheet.

The returns for the Buy days are summarized in cells G41 to G49. The number of Buy days is obtained using the COUNTIF function, which here counts how many of the cells in G53:G2533 are the same as cell G40. The sum of the Buy returns is given by the SUMIF function, which here sums all the numbers in C53:C2533 for which the matched cell in column G is the same as cell G40. Likewise, we obtain the sum of the squared Buy returns, followed by the one-day mean, variance, and standard deviation, the annualized mean, the number of trades, and their average duration in trading periods. The Sell and Neutral summary statistics are given by copying and pasting the Buy formulae. Finally, we calculate the test statistic z of equation (7.14) and the breakeven transaction cost C^* of equation (7.19).

The results show that the annualized average Sell return of 33% is much higher than the annualized average Buy return of 6%, which is interesting when compared with the low Sell returns of Brock et al. However, the z-statistic is -1.47 so that the difference between the averages is not significant at the 10% level. Another interesting result is that the standard deviation of the Buy returns (0.84%) is much lower than those of the Sell returns (1.43%).

7.7 Efficient Markets: Methodological Issues

Significant evidence of price predictability does not necessarily imply that a market is inefficient. Rather, to argue that a market is inefficient it is necessary to find a trading rule that has superior performance when it is compared with a passive benchmark. A suitable passive benchmark could be to buy and hold an asset or it could be risk-free investment. The risk-adjusted returns from these two passive strategies are both equal to the risk-free interest rate. Superior performance is then equivalent to a risk-adjusted return, net of all costs, that exceeds the risk-free rate. Like Jensen (1978), we define the weak form of the efficient market hypothesis by the following statement:

> No trading rule has an expected, risk-adjusted, net return greater than that provided by risk-free investment.

Convincing evidence against the hypothesis requires superior performance that is both statistically and economically significant.

Many issues arise for the above definition of market efficiency. Trading costs, resources, opportunities to diversify, and risk aversion vary considerably among individuals and among institutional investors. Hence performance from the same trading rule varies across traders and a market could be efficient for some and not for others.

Measuring performance requires risk adjustments. These are straightforward when all investment is in domestic equities and only one risk factor is priced. It is far from clear how the adjustments should be performed, however, when investment opportunities are international and include currencies, commodities, bills, bonds, and real estate.

Trading rules are usually evaluated after some form of optimization. It is well known that trading decisions have a favorable bias when parameters are selected after (*ex post*) finding the values that give the best results. Instead, parameters should be selected using only the information available before (*ex ante*) the outcomes from decisions are known. The amount of data used for optimizations is often subjective—using approximately one-third of the available prices is fairly common (e.g. Sweeney 1986), while three years of daily prices can be sufficient to obtain satisfactory parameter values for a simple rule (Taylor 1994b).

Bias can appear in many other ways. The rule itself can be chosen *ex post*, possibly by unintentional "data snooping" (Sullivan et al. 1999). This possibility can be avoided by using past prices to define the structure of the trading rule, by using the genetic algorithm methodology of Allen and Karjalainen (1999), Ready (2002), Neely, Weller, and Dittmar (1997), and Neely and Weller (2001). Lukac et al. (1988) and Lukac and Brorsen (1990) find that their best *ex post* rule is much better than the rule selected *ex ante* as time progresses. Also, Elton, Gruber, and Rentzler (1987) show that speculative funds possessing superior prospectus performance have indifferent subsequent performance. At present most academic researchers find superior performance more interesting than inferior results, so there is a potential selection bias in academic literature. This effect can be nullified by replicating published studies on later data, providing the results are published regardless of the outcome.

It is important to realize that all trading rule evaluations assume that it is possible to trade without altering the path taken by subsequent prices. This presumes first that there is a sufficient level of liquidity and second that any superior trader can avoid other traders copying a successful rule.

Trading rules are often evaluated for the prices of futures contracts. The evaluation of trading performance is then complicated by the small amount of collateral needed to initiate trades. If the margin deposit is essentially zero, then the calculation of returns and adjustments for risk are problematic. A practical resolution of these issues is given in Section 7.9. The possibility of a geared position in futures does not affect the efficiency of a market as gearing simply magnifies expected excess returns, risk adjustments, and the standard deviation of excess returns by the same amount.

Two methodologies for assessing efficiency are now described. The method in Section 7.8 is particularly appropriate for stocks and stock indices. The asset traded then has substantial systematic risk, short selling may be difficult and the natural benchmark is buy and hold. The other method, to be described in Section 7.9, is appropriate for trading futures. Trading rules can then have minimal or no systematic risk, even when the underlying asset is a stock index, because short positions are often as common as long positions. The natural benchmark is then risk-free investment.

7.8 Breakeven Costs for Trading Rules Applied to Equities

Significant differences between the average returns on Buy and Sell days are only evidence against market efficiency if transaction costs are sufficiently low and special assumptions can be made about risk. A standard assumption, made here following Sweeney (1986), is that the risk premium for holding an asset is the same on Buy days as on Sell days. There is always a possibility that trading rules seek out a time-varying risk premium, so that Buy days have a higher average premium than Sell days.

7.8.1 A Breakeven Formula

The breakeven cost for a trading rule is the level of transaction costs that ensures the average daily risk-adjusted profit, in excess of risk-free interest payments, equals the average daily expenditure on trading. Breakeven costs depend on the quantity of the asset held on Buy days, on any Neutral days, and on Sell days. Formulae for calculating average risk-adjusted returns are provided by Sweeney (1986, 1988), Day and Wang (2002), and Olson (2004) when the three quantities are integers, such as $(1, 0, 0)$ and $(1, 0, -1)$. We may note that $(1, 0, -1)$ and $(2, 1, 0)$ have identical risk-adjusted returns, because adding a fixed quantity to a portfolio will not change its risk-adjusted return.

In general, we may decide that the benchmark strategy is "buy and hold" and that this strategy owns some quantity $q_{t,\text{BH}}$ from the close on day t to the close on day $t + 1$. During the same time period suppose someone who follows a trading rule holds the quantity:

$$q_t = \begin{cases} (1 + Q_I)q_{t,\text{BH}} & \text{if period } t + 1 \text{ is classified as Buy,} \\ q_{t,\text{BH}} & \text{if period } t + 1 \text{ is classified as Neutral,} \\ (1 + Q_J)q_{t,\text{BH}} & \text{if period } t + 1 \text{ is classified as Sell.} \end{cases} \tag{7.18}$$

The specific choices $Q_I = n_J/n_I$ and $Q_J = -1$, with n_I and n_J the numbers of Buy and Sell days observed, have two advantages. First, the *ex post* risks of the benchmark and trading strategies are the same and, second, short selling is not necessary. The total risk-adjusted return for these choices, in excess of the risk-free rate, is simply

$$Q_I n_I (\bar{r}_I - \bar{r}_{f,I}) + Q_J n_J (\bar{r}_J - \bar{r}_{f,J}) = n_J (\bar{r}_I - \bar{r}_{f,I} - (\bar{r}_J - \bar{r}_{f,J}))$$

with $\bar{r}_I$ and $\bar{r}_J$ the average Buy and Sell returns, and $\bar{r}_{f,I}$ and $\bar{r}_{f,J}$ denoting the average risk-free rates for Buy and Sell days.

Now also assume that transaction costs are a proportion C of the price of the goods bought or sold. Also let D_I and D_J be the average durations of Buy and Sell trades, with a Buy (Sell) trade defined in the obvious way as a sequence of consecutive Buy (Sell) days. Then the reduction in the total return caused by transaction costs is

$$2C|Q_I|\frac{n_I}{D_I} + 2C|Q_J|\frac{n_J}{D_J} = 2Cn_J\left(\frac{1}{D_I} + \frac{1}{D_J}\right).$$

This reduction equals the total risk-adjusted return, in excess of the risk-free rate, when C equals the breakeven cost:

$$C^* = \frac{(\bar{r}_I - \bar{r}_J) - (\bar{r}_{f,I} - \bar{r}_{f,J})}{2(1/D_I + 1/D_J)}. \tag{7.19}$$

This formula assumes capital is required to finance trades. This is not the case for futures and then the interest-rate terms should be removed.

When $C < C^*$, a trader could have outperformed the benchmark strategy. It is not possible to use a sample value of C^* to perform a simple test of the null hypothesis of market efficiency; for our definition of efficiency, the autocorrelations of returns can all be positive and hence they can inflate the standard errors of terms like $\bar{r}_I$ above s_I^2/n_I, which is only the appropriate value for the random walk hypothesis.

7.8.2 Estimates

Bessembinder and Chan (1995a, 1998) use the same rules and parameter combinations as Brock et al. (1992) to estimate breakeven costs for the DJIA from 1926 to 1991. Across all combinations, they state that the breakeven cost equals 0.39% when a "double or out" strategy is followed, so that

$$Q_I = 1 \quad \text{and} \quad Q_J = -1;$$

they assume this strategy has the same risk as "buy and hold." The breakeven cost falls to 0.22% for their most recent subsample, from 1976 to 1991. They report bid–ask spreads of 0.12% (Knez and Ready 1996) and commission costs of 0.13% for institutional traders (Chan and Lakonishok 1993), for the later years of their sample, giving a total cost of 0.25%. Bessembinder and Chan (1998) conclude that there is little reason to view the differences between Buy and Sell average returns as indicative of market inefficiencies. They apply the same methodology to Asian equity indices in Bessembinder and Chan (1995b).

Taylor (2000) uses optimized parameters that give the least breakeven cost for the DJIA from 1897 to 1968. For the moving-average rule this gives a zero bandwidth and the highest levels of the averaging periods considered: 5 and 200 days. These choices minimize the number of transactions, in contrast to the choices that maximize measures of predictability and simultaneously also maximize transactions. The breakeven cost C^* equals 1.07% for the DJIA, from 1968 to 1988. This suggests profit opportunities for traders able to learn from the information available in 1968. However, they would have had to trade the thirty constituent stocks simultaneously at the prices used for index calculations, which is not very plausible (Day and Wang 2002). Taylor (2000) also finds the average of C^* across twelve UK firms is a mere 0.08% for the optimized parameters and concludes that there is no evidence that the market for UK stocks was inefficient in the 1970s and 1980s.

Most of the values of C^* for the twenty series discussed in Section 7.5 are near zero when the moving-average rule is applied with the optimized parameters given above. The average breakeven cost equals 0.31% for the sixteen noncurrency series, but the four breakeven currency costs are more substantial and range from 0.59% to 2.25%.

7.9 Trading Rule Performance for Futures Contracts

7.9.1 A Measure of Trading Performance

Trading rules have often been assessed by applying them to futures contracts. Trading costs are then often lower than for spot transactions and less capital is required to finance decisions. The amount of capital required is actually irrelevant when a trader has sufficient resources to deposit Treasury bills as margin collateral. We assume a representative trader can do so and that the total cost of opening and later closing a futures position is a fixed proportion c of the initial price of the goods traded. With these assumptions, Taylor (1988, 1992) derives the following performance measure for N trades in some futures contract, with trade j begun at price p_j and concluded at price p_j^* and with π_j equal to either 1 or -1, respectively if the trader is long or short for trade j:

$$R = \sum_{j=1}^{N} \left\{ \pi_j \left(\frac{p_j^* - p_j}{p_j} \right) - c \right\}. \tag{7.20}$$

This measure is positive whenever the average proportional price movement during trades (in the direction wanted by the trader) exceeds the proportional transaction cost.

The quantity R is interpreted as the return from a risky investment minus the return from a risk-free investment. To see why, suppose a trading rule produces trading positions (long, short, or neutral) from time t_1 to time t_2. The risk-free investment is the purchase at time t_1, at a price B_1, of a T-bill that matures at (or soon after) time t_2, followed by its sale at time t_2. The corresponding risky investment is identical except the T-bill is the margin deposit for all N trades and the number of contracts traded is $B_1/(Qp_j)$ for trade j with Q the quantity of goods per contract. The risky investment will be called a *risky bill*. Then R is the return from a risky bill minus the return from the corresponding risk-free T-bill and thus R is an *excess return*. The definition of the excess return ignores minor cash flows, including interest paid on reinvested profits and losses, interest foregone on funds used to pay transaction costs and any cash flows from daily settlement of profits and losses. These neglected terms are not important (Taylor 1988, 1992).

The excess return measure R can be used to discuss the efficiency of a futures market if we suppose a representative trader manages a well-diversified portfolio that includes short-maturity bills and equities. This trader will buy and sell futures contracts if this improves the distribution of portfolio returns, for example, by reducing the portfolio variance without reducing the portfolio mean. The trader will include risky bills in the managed portfolio if their expected return exceeds the level offered by comparable risky assets. In particular, a futures market can be called inefficient if expected excess returns on risky bills are positive and the systematic risk ("beta") of risky bills with respect to a market portfolio is zero or negative. When these conditions apply, the trader can form a portfolio including risky bills that improves upon any benchmark portfolio that invests only in risk-free bills and the market portfolio. It may be possible for the T-bill collateral to be used to finance a geared futures position but this will merely multiply the excess return by the gearing factor, which has no impact on the efficiency of the futures market.

7.9.2 Examples of Positive Excess Returns

Positive average excess returns are obtained for the US Treasury bond futures market in Taylor (1988), but the averages are not significantly different from zero at the 5% level; the betas of the excess returns are essentially zero.

The double moving-average, channel, filter, and statistical rules of Section 7.2 are evaluated using *ex ante* parameter values for sterling, Deutsche mark, Swiss franc, and yen futures in Taylor (1992), for the highly profitable six-year period from December 1981 to November 1987. The futures trading positions can be obtained using the classification algorithms; for example, a long trade is initiated and concluded at the closing prices on days s and t respectively if days $s + 1$ to t are all Buy days, but both days s and $t + 1$ are not Buy days.

The overall excess return, obtained by averaging across rules, currencies, and contracts, is 7.2% p.a. when $c = 0.2\%$. The rules average 7.8 trades p.a. so the gross excess return is 8.8% p.a. From the average excess return across rules and currencies, for each of twelve six-month trading periods, a t-ratio of 4.40 can be calculated that is highly significant. The same twelve numbers are regressed upon S&P 500 index returns minus T-bill returns to produce a beta estimate of 0.04 and a 95% confidence interval from -0.09 to 0.18. The beta estimate is very similar for a global equity index. It is concluded that the currency futures market appears to have been inefficient.

For the sixteen combinations of rule and currency, all the average excess returns are positive and ten of their t-ratios are significant at the 5% level using a one-tail test. ANOVA tests do not find significant differences in average excess returns, either between currencies or between rules. It is, of course, wrong to select the trading rule parameters *ex post*. The average portfolio excess return when this is done equals 11.7% p.a. and hence *ex post* optimization adds 4.5% to the *ex ante* average of 7.2%.

7.9.3 Further Results

Average excess returns have also been calculated for the four rules applied to the eleven futures series whose predictability was considered in Section 7.5. However, the results do not provide any additional evidence against the efficiency of futures markets.

The selection of ranges used for parameter optimizations is subjective to some extent. The bandwidth B is set to zero. The short-term average of the moving-average rule is always the latest price ($S = 1$) and the long-term averaging period L is between 2 and 60. The channel rule length L is chosen from the same set. The percentage filter size f is selected from $\{0.5, 1, 1.5, \ldots, 25\}$. The parameters of the statistical rule are given by jointly optimizing A from $\{0.01, 0.02, 0.03, 0.04\}$, ϕ from $\{0.91, 0.93, 0.95, 0.97, 0.99\}$ and k^* from $\{0.2, 0.4, 0.6, 0.8, 1\}$. Except for the filter rule, the parameter levels can be selected without considering the standard deviation of returns. As the sterling bill returns have much smaller standard deviations, all the candidate filter sizes are then divided by five.

Each futures series spans ten years. For each asset, the first three years are used to obtain optimized parameters for the first contract traded and, thereafter, contracts are traded across a seven-year period with parameters optimized *ex ante* separately for every contract using all the available *ex ante* price information. The optimized parameters maximize the average excess return, for some proportional cost c. As before, c is set to 0.2% except for bill futures when it is set to 0.04%. Most retail speculators in the 1980s would have had lower transaction costs (commission plus bid–ask spreads) than assumed here (Fink and Feduniak 1988) and institutional traders would pay less.

The overall average excess return for the four currencies is 5.7% p.a. for the seven-year period that ends in November 1991. The average is very high for the first three years, which are part of the Taylor (1992) study, but it is only 1.3% p.a. for the final four years. The average figure for the other seven assets is 1% p.a. before transaction costs, but it is negative after costs are deducted. The annual averages for each of these seven assets are then between -1.5% and 0.3%.

7.10 The Efficiency of Currency Markets

7.10.1 Trading Profits

Simple trading rules applied to dollar exchange rates have generally found evidence for trading profits in the 1970s and the 1980s, but the evidence from the 1990s is less encouraging for speculators. Dooley and Shafer (1983), Sweeney (1986), Taylor (1986, 1992), Levich and Thomas (1993), Kho (1996), Szakmary and Mathur (1997), and LeBaron (1999) all report currency trading profits for dollar rates. Furthermore, Okunev and White (2003) show that momentum strategies derived from moving averages of monthly rates, which buy strong currencies and sell weak currencies, would have been profitable from 1980 to 2000.

The magnitude of trading profits for ungeared futures trades can be measured by the excess return measure given by equation (7.20). Some studies use spot rates and suppose the trader switches between holding domestic and foreign currency. Doubling the trading profits from long/neutral spot positions gives the same profits as from long/short futures positions, providing (a) spot results are adjusted for differences between domestic and foreign interest rates and (b) there are no arbitrage opportunities between the spot and futures markets.

We now consider the magnitude of annual excess returns for various time periods. Initially, we consider five studies that cover the second half of the 1970s and the 1980s. These studies indicate that average excess returns were very approximately 7% p.a. during this fifteen-year period, before transaction costs.

Sweeney (1986) evaluates the filter rule for ten series of spot dollar exchange rates. From his Table V, an average annual profit of 2.5% is obtained from 1976 to 1980, for filter sizes that give significant profits before 1976. Doubling 2.5% gives an excess return of 5% above the dollar risk-free interest rate, which may reduce to 4% after transaction costs. The futures trades in Taylor (1986) give net excess returns of 7% from 1979 to 1981. The trades described in Section 7.9 and Taylor (1992) have average net excess returns of 4% from 1982 to 1984 and 10% from 1984 to 1987. Levich and Thomas (1993) evaluate filter and moving-average rules for the daily futures prices of five currencies. They do not optimize parameters. Their average gross excess returns for the filter rule, across all filter sizes and all currencies, are 7% from 1976 to 1980, 7% from 1981 to 1985, and 4% from 1986 to 1990. Kho (1996) obtains higher gross excess returns when the moving-average rule of Brock et al. (1992) is applied to weekly prices for futures on four currencies from 1981 to 1991. The average return is 10%, across all currencies and parameter combinations.

The comprehensive analysis by Olson (2004) of daily spot rates for eighteen dollar exchange rates from 1971 to 2000 shows that currency trading profits have declined in the 1990s. He applies the double moving-average rule, without a bandwidth parameter, and reports results for moving-average parameters optimized over five-year periods. After deducting roundturn transaction costs of 0.1% and then doubling his long/neutral spot excess returns, his Tables 4–8 provide the following out-of-sample (i.e. *ex ante*) net excess returns, firstly for all eighteen currencies and secondly for the four major currencies (sterling, Deutsche mark, Swiss franc, and yen) used in many prior studies:

	All 18	Major 4
1976–1980	8%	17%
1981–1985	2%	4%
1986–1990	10%	15%
1991–1995	0%	2%
1996–2000	−3%	−3%

The profits until 1990 are surprisingly high, when they are compared with previous studies, and they do not continue into the 1990s. Adjusting the excess returns for a constant risk premium, estimated from the buy-and-hold return for foreign currency in the same period, as in Sweeney (1986), gives the following risk-adjusted results:

	All 18	Major 4
1976–1980	7%	10%
1981–1985	6%	7%
1986–1990	2%	4%
1991–1995	1%	1%
1996–2000	0%	0%

Olson (2004) concludes that the trading profits before 1991 may have been a temporary inefficiency that has now disappeared. It is therefore intriguing that Okunev and White (2003) report trading profits from their momentum strategy during the 1990s.

7.10.2 Explanations

The positive average excess returns from currency trading before the 1990s are significantly different from zero (Taylor 1992; Levich and Thomas 1993; Kho 1996). They cannot be explained by a single, priced risk factor that is identified with an equity market portfolio (Taylor 1992; Okunev and White 2003; Olson 2004). The most popular explanations of the excess returns refer to either a time-varying risk premium (TVRP) or to central bank intervention.

The TVRP explanation can be motivated by international asset pricing models, but the magnitude of the premium in forward exchange rates required to explain trading profits is considerable. Taylor (1992) uses Monte Carlo methods to claim that trading rule profits can only be explained if the average reward for accepting the risky side of a one-month forward transaction is at least 2% of the forward price, which leads to an implausibly high reward-to-risk ratio.

Bessembinder and Chan (1992) regress monthly returns from currency futures contracts on a constant and the lagged values of three instrumental variables: the equity dividend yield, the yield on three-month T-bills, and a "junk" bond yield premium. Significant dependence is found, from which monthly conditional expected returns are estimated. These are usually between -1% and 1% and are consistent with a TVRP, although market inefficiency is an alternative explanation. Conditional expectations within the same range are obtained by Bams, Walkowiak, and Wolff (2004), by applying the Kalman filter to one-month forward prediction errors.

Kho (1996) estimates a bivariate model for futures returns and excess returns from a world equity index that allows both the futures "beta" and the price of risk to vary through time. Between one-third and one-half of the excess returns obtained from trading rules can then be explained by the TVRP for futures returns. As excess returns adjusted for the estimated TVRP are not significantly different from zero, the trading results do not provide a clear-cut conclusion about the efficiency of the currency futures market.

Central bank explanations are motivated by the possibility that these banks delay adjustments to fundamental factors by "leaning against the wind," so that profits can be made by trading rules that seek out trends (Szakmary and Mathur 1997). LeBaron (1999) demonstrates that a large proportion of the trading profits from a single moving-average rule were earned on the days that the Federal Reserve intervened in the currency markets. From 1979 to 1992, the daily average excess return from the trading rule is 0.033% for the mark/dollar rate. This average falls to 0.008% when the 12% of days on which the Fed intervened are removed. Likewise, the yen/dollar average falls from 0.040% to 0.017% when 6% of the days are removed.

Saacke (2002) evaluates interventions by both the Fed and the Bundesbank. Neely (2002) also includes interventions by the monetary authorities in Switzerland and Australia and he uses the same trading rule as LeBaron (1999), but from 1983 to 1998. The average annual excess return for the rule applied to the mark/dollar is 6.0% and it falls to 2.6% when Fed intervention days are removed. The Bundesbank intervened on more than twice as many days as the Fed; removing these days reduces the average further, to 1.3%. By using several exchange rates per day, Neely concludes that high trading rule returns precede interventions. It appears that the monetary authorities intervene in response to short-term trends from which trading rules have recently profited.

In conclusion, currency trading profits can be explained in many ways. The possibility that some of the profit opportunities available in the 1970s and the 1980s were the result of an inefficient market cannot be dismissed.

7.11 Theoretical Trading Profits for Autocorrelated Return Processes

It may appear that the claimed excess returns for currency trades are contradicted by a lack of correlation between currency returns. From Chapters 4–6 we know that there is almost no correlation between the returns from exchange rate futures on different dates. However, there is some relevant evidence that challenges the random walk hypothesis: a variance-ratio test rejects the hypothesis for two of the four currency futures series at the 5% level (Table 5.2, final column) and the trend test statistic T rejects the hypothesis for three of these series, again at the 5% level (Section 6.8). There are also several rejections at the same level of the similar hypothesis that daily returns are generated by a stationary martingale difference plus a constant (Section 7.5).

The results from these hypothesis tests, together with the evidence for profitable currency futures trades, imply that trading rules may be able to exploit low levels of linear dependence between returns. This is confirmed in Taylor (1994b), by applying the channel trading rule to the prices of several thousand simulated futures contracts obtained from an ARMA(1, 1) process. The channel rule is preferred as it consistently outperformed the double moving-average and filter rules in a small simulation study contained in Taylor (1992), thereby supporting its prior endorsement by Lukac et al. (1988). We now define the simulated process and then summarize some of the simulated trading outcomes.

7.11.1   Monte Carlo Model

As in Section 6.9, a correlated returns process $\{r_t\}$ is simulated by supposing that

$$r_t = \mu_t + \sigma_t \varepsilon_t. \tag{7.21}$$

The trend component $\{\mu_t\}$ is a Gaussian AR(1) process that has mean zero, variance $A\omega^2$, and autocorrelations ϕ^τ, while the residual component $\{\sigma_t \varepsilon_t\}$ is uncorrelated and has variance $(1 - A)\omega^2$. The stochastic volatility process $\{\sigma_t\}$, to be discussed in Chapter 11, is defined by supposing $\{\log(\sigma_t)\}$ is Gaussian and AR(1), with mean α, standard deviation β, and autocorrelations Φ^τ. The variables ε_t are i.i.d. and normal with mean zero and variance $1 - A$. The three processes $\{\mu_t\}$, $\{\sigma_t\}$, and $\{\varepsilon_t\}$ are independent of each other.

As explained in Sections 3.5 and 3.6, the simulated returns process is an ARMA(1, 1) process with autocorrelations $A\phi^\tau$. The parameter values $A = 0.02$ and $\phi = 0.95$ are used in Taylor (1992, 1994b) because they have been compatible with the autocorrelations of daily and monthly currency returns. The correlation between consecutive returns is then a mere 0.019. More important, however, is that the sum of the autocorrelations over all positive lags is 0.38. It is this high sum which explains the high level of the simulated trading profits. The remaining simulation parameters are compatible with the average level and the autocorrelations of squared daily currency returns: $\alpha = -5.15$, $\beta = 0.422$, and $\Phi = 0.973$.

7.11.2   Monte Carlo Results

We consider the expected value of the excess return from trading, defined by equation (7.20), for the channel rule described in Section 7.2 without a bandwidth parameter. The maximum expected value of 7.6% p.a. occurs for the above model parameters when the channel length parameter L is 14 days and there are no transaction costs.

Higher values of L are optimal when trading is costly. When the proportional trading cost c equals 0.2%, the optimal L is 23 days and then the maximum expected net excess return is 5.6% p.a. More realistic results are obtained by supposing L is chosen *ex ante* after learning from a few years of trading results. Selecting the best L using a learning period of one, two, or four years gives expected net excess returns respectively equal to 4.0%, 4.4%, and 4.6% p.a.

The expected net excess returns from the simulations when $A = 0.02$ and $\phi = 0.95$ are slightly less than the typical 7% p.a. for historical series of exchange rates discussed in Section 7.10. The high historical level may be fortuitous, although it can be matched by slightly increasing either A or ϕ.

It is concluded that a simple trading rule can exploit very low levels of autocorrelation when all the theoretical autocorrelations are positive. From simulations for various values of A and ϕ, the expected gross excess return is approximately a positive constant multiplied by $-A \log(1 - \phi)$. The multiplicative constant depends primarily upon the standard deviation of the returns process.

The success of the channel trading rule applied to the simulated ARMA(1, 1) process must imply that the channel rule often correctly identifies the direction of the current trend, represented by the process $\{\mu_t\}$. Suppose q_t is either 1 or -1, respectively if the trading rule is long or short during period t, and let s_t be either 1 or -1, respectively if μ_t is positive or negative. The proportion of days for which $q_t = s_t$ is denoted by P. It is a measure of directional forecasting accuracy, which equals 50% for rules applied to random walks. The proportion P is between 61% and 63% for many values of L and many learning periods when $A = 0.02$ and $\phi = 0.95$. This level of accuracy is particularly impressive when it is compared with the 64% that can be attained by using the optimal ARMA(1, 1) forecast of the trend component.

7.12 Concluding Remarks

There is plenty of evidence that trading rules have been able to reveal information about the conditional distributions of future returns. Furthermore, some of this information has been sufficiently precise to allow trading rules to make profits that are several per cent per annum, after deducting transaction costs and adjusting for risk.

The successful applications of trading rules are, however, generally restricted to prices recorded before the 1990s. Higher trading volumes, the arrival of cheap and almost instantaneous communication of information around the world, and the inexorable tendency for competition to eliminate price imperfections have probably all contributed to higher levels of market efficiency in recent years.

Further Reading

Brock, W., J. Lakonishok, and B. LeBaron. 1992. Simple technical trading rules and the stochastic properties of stock returns. *Journal of Finance* 47:1731–1764.

Day, T. E. and P. Wang. 2002. Dividends, nonsynchronous prices, and the returns from trading the Dow Jones Industrial Average. *Journal of Empirical Finance* 9:431–454.

Neely, C. J. 2002. The temporal pattern of trading rule returns and exchange rate intervention: intervention does not generate technical trading profits. *Journal of International Economics* 58:211–232.

Olson, D. 2004. Have trading rule profits in the currency markets declined over time? *Journal of Banking and Finance* 28:85–105.

Sweeney, R. J. 1986. Beating the foreign exchange market. *Journal of Finance* 41:163–182.

Taylor, S. J. 1992. Rewards available to currency futures speculators: compensation for risk or evidence of inefficient pricing? *Economic Record* 68(supplement):105–116.

Part III

Volatility Processes

8

An Introduction to Volatility

Asset price volatility is central to the following seven chapters, in which we cover volatility measurement and modeling, continuous-time processes, option pricing formulae, and volatility forecasting. This short introductory chapter commences with definitions of volatility and continues with a general discussion of explanations for volatility changes. It is then shown that volatility changes explain the major stylized facts for time series of asset returns.

8.1   Definitions of Volatility

Volatility is a measure of price variability over some period of time. It typically describes the standard deviation of returns, in a particular context that depends on the definition used. Alternatively, we can say that volatility is the standard deviation of the change in the logarithm of a price or a price index during a stated period of time. Volatility can be defined and interpreted in five different ways. Various interpretations appear in phrases such as:

(i) The volatility of Microsoft stock is 30% per annum.

(ii) The annualized volatility of the sterling/dollar exchange rate was 12% in 2004.

(iii) The volatility of tomorrow's price is 1%, given our observations of recent prices.

(iv) The volatility of prices follows a mean-reverting stochastic process.

(v) The market volatility for the FTSE 100 index during the next three months is 15% per annum.

In the first phrase *volatility* is simply a parameter, which is invariably denoted by σ. The standard deviation of the continuously compounded return during any T-year period is then $\sigma\sqrt{T}$, whatever the prior history of the asset's price. This definition is applicable whenever prices are assumed to follow geometric Brownian motion (GBM), defined in Chapter 13. The variance of a change in the price's logarithm, $\log(p(T_2)) - \log(p(T_1))$, is then proportional to the time difference, $T_2 - T_1$ years, and equals $\sigma^2(T_2 - T_1)$. The assumption of GBM is unrealistic when describing market prices because future price variability does depend on the recent history of prices. Nevertheless, it can be a useful approximation to reality for other purposes, particularly when defining a parameter that permits the determination of rational option prices. Statement (i) could then describe one of the parameters used to value Microsoft options.

Realized volatility, also called *historical volatility*, is the standard deviation of a set of previous returns. For n trading periods, and returns $r_{t-n}, \ldots, r_{t-1}$, whose average is $\bar{r}$, the historical standard deviation

$$ s = \sqrt{\frac{1}{n-1} \sum_{i=1}^{n} (r_{t-i} - \bar{r})^2}, $$

provides a simple estimate of the standard deviation of the return for trading period t. This volatility measure can be stated in annual units as $s\sqrt{N}$, with N denoting the number of trading periods in one year. Statement (ii) may then follow from a hypothetical calculation that finds the set of 252 daily returns in that year have standard deviation 0.007 56 so that $s\sqrt{N} = 0.12$. Recent research into realized volatility has considered trading periods measured in minutes, with n chosen to provide a one-day history of intraday returns. Some properties of this high-frequency volatility measure are described in Chapter 12.

Conditional volatility is the standard deviation of a future return that is conditional on known information such as the history of previous returns. Unlike realized volatility, the expectation for the next period is calculated using a time-series model that has been selected and estimated using appropriate data. Convenient and accurate equations for volatility expectations are provided by ARCH models, described in detail in Chapters 9 and 10. These autoregressive, conditional heteroskedastic models specify the conditional variance h_t of the return in period t, using prior information I_{t-1}. A popular example is a weighted sum of squared excess returns, defined by the recursive equation

$$ h_t = \omega + \alpha (r_{t-1} - \mu)^2 + \beta h_{t-1}, $$

with the parameters α, β, μ, and ω estimated from a long time series of returns. Statement (iii) might be made if we had estimated these parameters using daily returns until 23 November 2005 (day $t-1$) and had then found $h_t = (0.01)^2$ for the return from the 23rd to the 24th (day t).

Stochastic volatility processes are motivated by noting that volatility is not constant and hence it is interesting to seek to specify how volatility changes through time. Typical discrete-time models suppose that volatility is unobservable and then its stochastic properties may be inferred from either absolute or squared returns. A first-order autoregressive process provides a parsimonious description of the logarithm of volatility, which is evaluated in Chapter 11. Continuous-time models are used to price options when the assumption of constant volatility is relaxed. A square-root process for volatility, discussed in Chapter 13, permits the rapid calculation of appropriate option prices. Statement (iv) indicates that high volatility levels are expected to be followed by lower levels; conversely, when the current level of volatility is low it is expected that volatility will increase.

Implied volatility is a value calculated from an option price. It equals the volatility parameter σ for which an option's market price equals its theoretical price according to a pricing formula. The Black–Scholes pricing formula provides theoretical prices for European call options, say $c(\sigma)$, and assumes that the asset price process is GBM with annual variance rate σ^2. As $c(\sigma)$ is an increasing function of σ, for any market price c_M between the lower and upper bounds that exclude arbitrage profits there is a unique solution to the equation

$$c_M = c(\sigma)$$

that defines the implied volatility. These volatility measures depend on the time until expiry and the exercise price of the option, as will be seen in Chapter 14. Thus statement (v) might be made if the implied volatility of an European at-the-money option on 17 September 2004 that expires on 17 December 2004 equals 0.15. Option markets are competitive and prices must incorporate the market's expectations about future volatility. It is therefore reasonable to conjecture that implied volatilities are the best source of information when forecasting volatility. This hypothesis is investigated in Chapter 15.

At any time the values of realized volatility, conditional volatility, unobservable stochastic volatility, and implied volatility will usually all be different, because different data and assumptions are employed when these values are calculated. To illustrate some differences, Figure 8.1 shows a year of annualized volatility numbers for the S&P 500 index, calculated once every day from June 2003 until May 2004. The three curves show annualized, percentage standard deviations for realized volatility (dark, continuous curve) defined by the 100-day standard deviation, conditional volatility (light, continuous) estimated from the GJR-GARCH model, to be introduced in Section 9.7, and implied volatility (dots) defined by a new version of the VIX index, which is calculated from S&P 500 option prices.

8.2 Explanations of Changes in Volatility

The volatility of asset prices is not the same at all times. Volatility clustering is seen in periods of high and low volatility when returns are plotted in time order (Chapter 2). Furthermore, the stylized fact that squared returns are positively autocorrelated (Chapter 4) is indicative of positive autocorrelation in the volatility process. In later chapters we will see that the parameters of ARCH and stochastic volatility models reject the hypothesis of constant volatility. We will also see

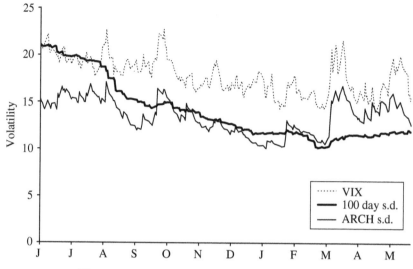

Figure 8.1. A year of annualized volatility numbers.

that traders do not believe volatility is constant, because implied volatilities vary considerably through time.

So why does volatility change? There is no complete and satisfactory answer to this fundamental question. There are partial answers that explain some of the variation in volatility, but much variation remains unexplained.

Stock market volatility increases during crises and then decreases in due course. The economic crisis known as the Great Depression was accompanied by fears of social unrest (Voth 2003) and very high volatility from 1929 to 1934, attaining levels that have rarely been observed in later years (Officer 1973; Schwert 1990a). The political crisis triggered by the Watergate tapes in March 1973 created uncertainty about the US administration that was eventually resolved by the resignation of President Nixon in August 1974. Volatility increased substantially when the existence of the tapes became public knowledge (Hsu 1982). The stock market crash of October 1987 was a financial crisis that was followed by a short period of extraordinary high volatility (Schwert 1990a,b). There are no satisfactory economic explanations for this crisis, although we may note that volatility was high immediately before the crash. Volatility was high before the terrorist attacks on 11 September 2001 and went much higher when the US markets reopened six days later.

Macroeconomic variables, such as inflation, employment, and GNP, have an impact upon the volatility of stock, foreign exchange and interest-rate markets. Scheduled macroeconomic news releases in the US coincide with the commencement of a few minutes of much higher volatility, both in the US (Ederington and Lee 1993; Fleming and Remolona 1999) and in the UK (Areal and Taylor 2002).

Inflation, money growth, and industrial production explain a small proportion of the variability of stock market volatility over longer periods of time (Schwert 1989), so that most of the variation in volatility remains unexplained.

Stock volatility is dependent, to some degree, on the level of the market. When prices fall, the value of firm equity relative to debt decreases and hence financial leverage increases. At the same time volatility increases on average (Black 1976b; Christie 1982). This phenomenon is discussed in Sections 9.7 and 10.2. It may, however, be a volatility effect that is not attributable to changes in debt/equity ratios (Duffee 1995).

Theoretical asset pricing models can explain some variation in volatility, for example, models that assume investors have asymmetric information (Brock and LeBaron 1996; Timmermann 2001). Several theoretical models are mentioned by Johnson (2001), who proposes a novel theory that rational agents must infer the degree of persistence of fundamental shocks. More empirical research is needed to decide if theoretical models can explain the magnitude of day-to-day changes in volatility.

Volatility is positively correlated with trading volume (Karpoff 1987; Gallant, Rossi, and Tauchen 1992). This does not imply that changes in volume cause changes in volatility, or vice versa. Indeed, it can be argued that it is more plausible that there is no causal relationship between volatility and volume; whatever factors determine volatility may, simultaneously, also determine volume.

Trading decisions and hence volatility must, at least in part, be determined by the information that reaches the market. A simple economic model is presented below that shows volatility increases as the amount of information increases. The market efficiently interprets information in this model.

Empirical analysis of the relationship between volatility and information is difficult because we can only identify some of the relevant information. US stock market volatility has a weak relationship with daily counts of headlines reported by Dow Jones in the Broadtape and the Wall Street Journal (Mitchell and Mulherin 1994) and an insignificant dependence on the number of news releases by Reuters on its North American Securities News wire (Berry and Howe 1994). The total number of news headlines provided by Reuters only has a minor impact upon foreign exchange volatility; however, counts of appropriate headlines selected using economic keywords have a more discernible impact (Melvin and Yin 2000; Chang and Taylor 2003).

8.3 Volatility and Information Arrivals

The following economic model shows that volatility can be related to a stochastic number of intraday price revisions. The origins of this model are in Clark (1973) and Epps and Epps (1976), followed by a rigorous economic analysis of information arrivals, volatility, and volume in Tauchen and Pitts (1983). The market is assumed to be efficient with daily returns r_t having expected value μ. The number of news items on day t is represented by a random variable, denoted by N_t. When news item i reaches the market, the price logarithm changes by $\varepsilon_{i,t}$ and these changes are assumed to have zero mean. Then

$$r_t = \mu + \sum_{i=1}^{N_t} \varepsilon_{i,t}. \tag{8.1}$$

Now suppose further that the $\varepsilon_{i,t}$ are i.i.d., normal random variables, which are independent of N_t. Let θ^2 be the variance of $\varepsilon_{i,t}$. Then the distribution of the return conditional on n_t news items is normal with variance

$$\text{var}(r_t \mid N_t = n_t) = n_t \theta^2. \tag{8.2}$$

It is then appropriate to define the stochastic volatility process by

$$\sigma_t^2 = N_t \theta^2 \tag{8.3}$$

and then

$$r_t = \mu + \sigma_t u_t \tag{8.4}$$

with u_t a standard normal random variable that is independent of the random variable σ_t.

From equation (8.2) it can be seen that volatility changes when the amount of relevant news changes. Also, volatility clustering will then occur if there is sufficient positive autocorrelation in the process of news counts to ensure that there are some periods of several consecutive days that have high news counts and others that have low counts. With further assumptions, expected trading volume is proportional to the number of news items and hence volatility and volume are positively correlated variables (Tauchen and Pitts 1983).

The above information arrivals model does show why volatility can change, even if some of the assumptions can be criticized; for example, prices may change even when there is no new information. Further methods and results are provided in several papers. Harris (1987) considers empirical transaction counts, Lamoureux and Lastrapes (1990) include volume in an ARCH model, Gallant, Hsieh, and Tauchen (1991) consider the implications of temporal dependence in daily news counts, and Andersen (1996) utilizes a microstructure framework that includes noise traders. Blair, Poon, and Taylor (2001a) propose and investigate multivariate extensions of the information arrival model. Luu and Martens (2003) show that intraday returns provide new insights into the relationship between volatility and volume, which support information arrival models.

8.4 Volatility and the Stylized Facts for Returns

The three major stylized facts for daily returns presented in Chapter 4 can all be explained by assuming that volatility follows a stochastic process that has the property that today's volatility is positively correlated with the volatility on any future day. We suppose in this section that daily returns can be described by the equation

$$r_t = \mu + \sigma_t u_t \tag{8.5}$$

with six assumptions, which are:

(i) the expected return μ is a constant;

(ii) σ_t is a positive random variable, that has more than one possible realized value;

(iii) the stochastic process $\{\sigma_t\}$ is stationary, $E[\sigma_t^4]$ is finite and all the autocorrelations of $\{\sigma_t^2\}$ are positive;

(iv) u_t is a standard normal random variable, so $u_t \sim N(0, 1)$;

(v) the u_t are i.i.d. variables;

(vi) the processes $\{\sigma_t\}$ and $\{u_t\}$ are stochastically independent, i.e. the vector variables $(\sigma_1, \sigma_2, \ldots, \sigma_n)$ and $(u_1, u_2, \ldots, u_n)$ are independent for all positive integers n.

Equation (8.5) is identical to (8.4), but it is not necessary to make any of the intraday assumptions used to derive (8.4).

The first stylized fact is that the distribution of returns is not normal. From (8.5) the distribution of returns is a mixture of normal distributions, with the mixture determined by the distribution of volatility. This mixture distribution has higher kurtosis than that of a normal distribution, since

$$\mathrm{var}(r_t) = E[(r_t - \mu)^2] = E[\sigma_t^2 u_t^2] = E[\sigma_t^2]E[u_t^2] = E[\sigma_t^2],$$
$$E[(r_t - \mu)^4] = E[\sigma_t^4 u_t^4] = E[\sigma_t^4]E[u_t^4] = 3E[\sigma_t^4],$$
$$\mathrm{kurtosis}(r_t) = \frac{3E[\sigma_t^4]}{E[\sigma_t^2]^2} = 3\left(1 + \frac{\mathrm{var}(\sigma_t^2)}{E[\sigma_t^2]^2}\right) > 3. \tag{8.6}$$

The second stylized fact is that returns are almost uncorrelated. The autocorrelations are zero at all positive lags τ when the assumptions apply, because

$$\mathrm{cov}(r_t, r_{t+\tau}) = \mathrm{cov}(\sigma_t u_t, \sigma_{t+\tau} u_{t+\tau})$$
$$= E[\sigma_t u_t \sigma_{t+\tau} u_{t+\tau}] - E[\sigma_t u_t]E[\sigma_{t+\tau} u_{t+\tau}]$$
$$= E[\sigma_t \sigma_{t+\tau}]E[u_t]E[u_{t+\tau}] - E[\sigma_t]E[\sigma_{t+\tau}]E[u_t]E[u_{t+\tau}]$$
$$= 0 - 0$$
$$= 0. \tag{8.7}$$

The third stylized fact is that both absolute returns and squared returns are positively autocorrelated. Let $s_t = (r_t - \mu)^2$. Then, for all positive lags τ,

$$
\begin{aligned}
\operatorname{cov}(s_t, s_{t+\tau}) &= \operatorname{cov}(\sigma_t^2 u_t^2, \sigma_{t+\tau}^2 u_{t+\tau}^2) \\
&= E[\sigma_t^2 u_t^2 \sigma_{t+\tau}^2 u_{t+\tau}^2] - E[\sigma_t^2 u_t^2] E[\sigma_{t+\tau}^2 u_{t+\tau}^2] \\
&= E[\sigma_t^2 \sigma_{t+\tau}^2] E[u_t^2] E[u_{t+\tau}^2] - E[\sigma_t^2] E[\sigma_{t+\tau}^2] E[u_t^2] E[u_{t+\tau}^2] \\
&= \operatorname{cov}(\sigma_t^2, \sigma_{t+\tau}^2) \\
&> 0.
\end{aligned}
\tag{8.8}
$$

Consequently, positive dependence in the volatility process implies positive dependence in squared excess returns. Likewise, it can be shown that there is also positive dependence in absolute excess returns, $a_t = |r_t - \mu|$.

The six assumptions that follow equation (8.5) suffice to provide a framework within which volatility changes explain the major stylized facts for returns. This framework is developed further in Chapter 11, by considering specific stochastic processes for $\{\sigma_t\}$. Some of the assumptions can be relaxed, as indeed they are in Chapter 9 for ARCH models, without altering the conclusion that volatility changes explain the stylized facts.

8.5 Concluding Remarks

The sources of volatility changes are elusive. Time-series models for volatility can be estimated from asset returns without knowing why volatility changes, and this is the path that we take in the next four chapters. Later we consider volatility forecasting, and then take into account the additional volatility information that is revealed by option prices.

Further Reading

Andersen, T. G. 1996. Return volatility and trading volume: an information flow interpretation of stochastic volatility. *Journal of Finance* 51:169–204.

Schwert, G. W. 1989. Why does stock market volatility change over time? *Journal of Finance* 44:1115–1153.

Tauchen, G. E. and M. Pitts. 1983. The price variability–volume relationship on speculative markets. *Econometrica* 51:485–505.

9

ARCH Models: Definitions and Examples

Examples of models for the conditional variances of returns are described and estimated in this chapter. These models are easy to estimate from a time series of returns and provide insights into the movement of volatility through time. The models belong within a general class of ARCH models that is also defined.

9.1 Introduction

ARCH stands for *autoregressive conditional heteroskedasticity*. Changes in the scale of a variable give us the word *heteroskedastic*. A scale parameter is a standard deviation or a variance and the variable of interest here is the return from an asset. The variance of a return, *conditional* on the information in previous returns, is found to depend on this information. Engle (1982) defined a stochastic process whose variables have conditional mean zero and conditional variance given by a linear function of previous squared variables. The squared variables follow an *autoregressive* process in his pioneering and influential research, as we will see in Section 9.2.

Subsequent research has provided many alternative functions that specify the conditional variance of a variable at time t as a function of information known at time $t - 1$. For any specification that also gives us the conditional density function at time t, we will call the stochastic process an ARCH model provided that the standardized residuals of the process are independent and identically distributed. In particular, we allow the conditional mean to vary though time, unlike some authors who prefer to restrict the acronym ARCH to processes whose conditional means are always zero.

There is a multitude of ARCH specifications and many of them have their own acronyms, the best known being GARCH (generalized ARCH) from Bollerslev (1986) and EGARCH (exponential, generalized ARCH) from Nelson (1991). The popularity of the models can be explained by their compatibility with the major stylized facts for asset returns, by efficient methods for estimating model parameters and by the availability of useful volatility forecasts. The specification of conditional densities provides the likelihood function for a dataset, which can be maximized to give optimal parameter estimates. Several software packages will maximize the likelihood function and thus estimation of an ARCH model is now a routine activity. Likelihood theory allows specifications to be compared and choices to be made from among the many functions that have been proposed for conditional variances.

The literature on ARCH models is considerable. Bollerslev, Chou, and Kroner (1992) provide a review of theory and ten years of empirical evidence for financial markets, which covers applications to equities, foreign exchange, and interest rates. The authors describe an impressive number of interesting studies without requiring the reader to understand many equations. The subsequent survey by Bollerslev, Engle, and Nelson (1994) is suitable for those readers who wish to see more theory than is presented in this book. It also contains detailed examples of the specification of conditional densities for daily returns from US equity indices, going back as far as 1885. A neglected precursor to the ARCH literature is a working paper by Rosenberg (1972), while early likelihood estimates of an integrated ARCH specification can be found in Taylor and Kingsman (1979).

Some basic ARCH models and the general ARCH framework are described in this chapter, followed by more complex models, likelihood theory, and modeling strategies in the next chapter. We primarily consider models for daily returns in these two chapters and also note some studies of weekly and monthly returns. Models for intraday returns require additional parameters to represent intraday volatility patterns, as will be explained in Chapter 12. There are many applications of ARCH methods in finance research, including investigations into asset pricing, hedging, and microstructure effects. Option pricing, volatility forecasting, and density estimation are also important application areas, that are described in Chapters 14, 15, and 16 respectively.

This chapter continues with a brief account of the ARCH(1) model in Section 9.2. This is followed by a detailed description of the popular GARCH(1, 1) model in Section 9.3 and an example of its estimation and results for foreign exchange returns in Section 9.4. The general ARCH framework is explained in Section 9.5, with the assumption that the conditional distributions are normal. This assumption is relaxed in Section 9.6. GARCH models are much less satisfactory for equities than for foreign exchange, because the direction of price changes is relevant when modeling equity volatility. An asymmetric volatility model is described in Section 9.7 and estimated for a series of index returns in Section 9.8.

9.2 ARCH(1)

The simplest example of an ARCH process is the ARCH(1) specification presented by Engle (1982). The distribution of the return for period t, conditional on all previous returns, is normal with constant mean μ and time-varying conditional variance h_t defined by

$$r_t \mid r_{t-1}, r_{t-2}, \ldots \sim N(\mu, h_t) \tag{9.1}$$

and

$$h_t = \omega + \alpha(r_{t-1} - \mu)^2. \tag{9.2}$$

The volatility parameters are $\omega > 0$ and $\alpha \geqslant 0$. The volatility of the return in period t then depends solely on the previous return. Either a large positive or a large negative return in period $t - 1$ implies higher than average volatility in the next period when α is positive; conversely, returns near the mean level μ imply lower than average future volatility.

The residual at time t is

$$e_t = r_t - \mu$$

and the forecast error when predicting squared residuals is

$$v_t = e_t^2 - E[e_t^2 \mid r_{t-1}, \ldots] = e_t^2 - h_t.$$

These forecast errors are uncorrelated. Replacing h_t in (9.2) by $e_t^2 - v_t$ gives

$$e_t^2 = \omega + \alpha e_{t-1}^2 + v_t$$

and hence squared residuals follow an AR(1) process. This explains the AR part of the ARCH acronym.

The ARCH(1) model is stationary when $\alpha < 1$. It cannot describe the returns process successfully, because squared residuals have autocorrelations that cannot be approximated by the autocorrelation function $\rho_\tau = \alpha^{|\tau|}$; these autocorrelations are defined when e_t^2 has finite variance, which requires $3\alpha^2 < 1$. Any satisfactory AR(p) process for squared residuals must have a high order p. A natural alternative is an ARMA process and this explains the interest in GARCH models.

9.3 GARCH(1, 1)

The GARCH(1, 1) model with conditional normal distributions is the most popular ARCH specification in empirical research, particularly when modeling daily returns. The letter "G" appears in the acronym of this model because it is *generalized* from ARCH(1) by including a lagged variance term in the conditional variance equation. The popularity of GARCH(1, 1) may be explained by three observations. First, the model has only four parameters and these can be estimated easily. Second, it provides an explanation of the major stylized facts for daily returns. Third, it is often found that the volatility forecasts from this specification have similar accuracy to forecasts from more complicated specifications. Initially, we assume conditional normal distributions following Bollerslev (1986) and Taylor (1986), who independently defined and derived properties of the GARCH(1, 1) model.

9.3.1 Definitions

The distribution of the return for period t, conditional on all previous returns, is defined by

$$r_t \mid r_{t-1}, r_{t-2}, \ldots \sim N(\mu, h_t)$$

with

$$h_t = \omega + \alpha(r_{t-1} - \mu)^2 + \beta h_{t-1}. \tag{9.3}$$

There are four parameters, namely μ, α, β, and ω. The constraints $\omega \geqslant 0$, $\alpha \geqslant 0$, and $\beta \geqslant 0$ are required to ensure that the conditional variance is never negative. The possibility $\alpha = 0$ is of no interest and so we assume α is positive. The model is styled GARCH(1, 1) because one previous squared residual and one previous value of the conditional variance are used to define the conditional variance for period t. Calculations of conditional variances from the recursive definition (9.3) are straightforward, providing an initial value is available for the first time period. Numerical examples are provided in Section 9.4.

The major properties of a GARCH(1, 1) stochastic process can be summarized in one sentence. The process is stationary if $\alpha + \beta < 1$ and then

- the unconditional variance is finite;
- the unconditional kurtosis always exceeds three and can be infinite;
- the correlation between the returns r_t and $r_{t+\tau}$ is zero for all $\tau > 0$; and
- the correlation between the squared residual $s_t = (r_t - \mu)^2$ and $s_{t+\tau}$ is positive for all $\tau > 0$ and equals $C(\alpha + \beta)^\tau$, with C positive and determined by both α and β.

The process is now discussed in some detail, commencing with a second definition and then covering stationarity, an ARCH(∞) representation, selected moments of the process, its autocorrelations, an integrated specification, and finally prediction of future variances.

The residuals of the process are

$$e_t = r_t - \mu$$

and the standardized residuals are defined to be

$$z_t = \frac{r_t - \mu}{\sqrt{h_t}} = \frac{e_t}{\sqrt{h_t}}. \tag{9.4}$$

The distribution of z_t conditional on previous returns is then

$$z_t \mid r_{t-1}, r_{t-2}, \ldots \sim N(0, 1)$$

and thus it does not depend on the past history of returns. With minor additional assumptions, it follows that the z_t are independent and identically distributed (i.i.d.). The formal definition of GARCH(1, 1) with conditional normal distributions used here is based on the i.i.d. assumption; thus,

$$r_t = \mu + h_t^{1/2} z_t, \tag{9.5}$$

$$z_t \sim \text{i.i.d. } N(0, 1), \tag{9.6}$$

and

$$h_t = \omega + \alpha (r_{t-1} - \mu)^2 + \beta h_{t-1}. \tag{9.7}$$

9.3.2 Stationarity

From (9.5) and (9.7),

$$h_t = \omega + (\alpha z_{t-1}^2 + \beta) h_{t-1}, \tag{9.8}$$

and hence

$$E[h_t] = \omega + (\alpha + \beta) E[h_{t-1}] \tag{9.9}$$

whenever these expectations are finite, because z_{t-1} is independent of h_{t-1}. From (9.9) it can be anticipated that the process is covariance stationary if and only if $\alpha + \beta < 1$. Bollerslev (1986) proves this result, assuming ω is positive and that the process starts indefinitely far in the past. The process is also strictly stationary when $\alpha + \beta < 1$ and the same assumptions apply (Nelson 1990a). The constraints $\alpha + \beta < 1$ and $\omega > 0$ are now assumed until stated otherwise.

9.3.3 Another Representation

The conditional variance depends on all previous returns when β is positive, so that the covariance stationary GARCH(1, 1) process has an ARCH(∞) representation. From (9.7) applied one time period earlier, $h_{t-1} = \omega + \alpha (r_{t-2} - \mu)^2 + \beta h_{t-2}$, and hence (9.7) can be rewritten as

$$\begin{aligned} h_t &= \omega + \alpha (r_{t-1} - \mu)^2 + \beta (\omega + \alpha (r_{t-2} - \mu)^2 + \beta h_{t-2}) \\ &= \omega + \beta \omega + \alpha (r_{t-1} - \mu)^2 + \alpha \beta (r_{t-2} - \mu)^2 + \beta^2 h_{t-2}. \end{aligned}$$

Repeated substitutions then show that

$$\begin{aligned} h_t &= \frac{\omega}{1 - \beta} + \alpha (r_{t-1} - \mu)^2 + \alpha \beta (r_{t-2} - \mu)^2 \\ &\quad + \alpha \beta^2 (r_{t-3} - \mu)^2 + \alpha \beta^3 (r_{t-4} - \mu)^2 + \cdots, \end{aligned} \tag{9.10}$$

where it is assumed that the process has an infinite past history. This equation shows that the conditional variance for period t is a linear function of the past squared residuals $(r_{t-\tau} - \mu)^2$, $\tau > 0$, and that the weight given to past information diminishes as the lag τ increases. The conditional variance is an increasing function of each squared residual so that volatility clusters will occur. A high average for recent squared returns will make the conditional variance high so that a high squared return is more likely in the next period and vice versa for a low recent average. Equation (9.10) also shows that the conditional variances have a minimum level, that equals $\omega/(1-\beta)$.

9.3.4 Moments

Properties of the stochastic process $\{r_t\}$ are derived from the assumption that the standardized residuals $\{z_t\}$ are i.i.d. and also from the fact that h_t is a function of the previous values $\{z_{t-1}, z_{t-2}, z_{t-3}, \ldots\}$. The unconditional mean return is

$$E[r_t] = \mu + E[h_t^{1/2}]E[z_t] = \mu$$

and the unconditional variance, denoted by σ^2, equals

$$\sigma^2 = \text{var}(r_t) = E[(r_t - \mu)^2] = E[h_t]E[z_t^2] = E[h_t] = \frac{\omega}{1-\alpha-\beta}, \quad (9.11)$$

from (9.9). The conditional variance equation, (9.7), can be rewritten using (9.11) as

$$h_t = (1-\alpha-\beta)\sigma^2 + \alpha(r_{t-1} - \mu)^2 + \beta h_{t-1}.$$

Thus h_t is a weighted combination of the unconditional variance σ^2, the previous squared residual $(r_{t-1} - \mu)^2$, and the previous conditional variance h_{t-1}, with respective weights $1-\alpha-\beta$, α, and β.

The unconditional fourth moment is finite if and only if

$$2\alpha^2 + (\alpha + \beta)^2 < 1 \quad (9.12)$$

and then

$$E[(r_t - \mu)^4] = E[h_t^2]E[z_t^4] = 3E[h_t^2].$$

The unconditional expectation of h_t^2 can be derived by squaring both sides of equation (9.8), followed by taking expectations of both sides. This leads to the result that the kurtosis of returns is

$$\text{kurtosis}(r_t) = \frac{3E[h_t^2]}{\sigma^4} = 3\left[\frac{1-(\alpha+\beta)^2}{1-2\alpha^2-(\alpha+\beta)^2}\right] > 3 \quad (9.13)$$

when $2\alpha^2 + (\alpha + \beta)^2 < 1$; otherwise, the kurtosis is infinite. Returns therefore have more kurtosis than the normal distribution, which is a consequence of the unconditional distribution being a mixture of normals.

9.3.5 Autocorrelations

The returns process is uncorrelated, because the conditional mean of the return at time t is constant, whatever the returns before time t. Formally, for all positive lags τ,

$$\text{cov}(r_t, r_{t+\tau}) = \text{cov}(e_t, e_{t+\tau}) = E[h_t^{1/2}z_t h_{t+\tau}^{1/2}z_{t+\tau}]$$
$$= E[h_t^{1/2}z_t h_{t+\tau}^{1/2}]E[z_{t+\tau}] = 0. \quad (9.14)$$

The returns process is not, of course, a sequence of i.i.d. variables because conditional variances are a function of previous returns.

The autocorrelations of the squared residuals,

$$s_t = (r_t - \mu)^2 = e_t^2 = h_t z_t^2$$

are only defined when the kurtosis of returns is finite, which we now assume. Let

$$v_t = e_t^2 - h_t = h_t(z_t^2 - 1) \tag{9.15}$$

be the forecast error when predicting squared residuals. Then the process $\{v_t\}$ is white noise, since its mean is zero, it is covariance stationary and its autocovariances are

$$\begin{aligned}
\text{cov}(v_t, v_{t+\tau}) &= E[v_t v_{t+\tau}] = E[h_t(z_t^2 - 1)h_{t+\tau}(z_{t+\tau}^2 - 1)] \\
&= E[h_t(z_t^2 - 1)h_{t+\tau}]E[z_{t+\tau}^2 - 1] = 0
\end{aligned}$$

for all positive lags. From (9.7) and (9.15) it follows that the squared residuals s_t follow an ARMA(1, 1) process with innovations provided by the forecast errors v_t; thus,

$$s_t = \omega + (\alpha + \beta)s_{t-1} + v_t - \beta v_{t-1}. \tag{9.16}$$

The autocorrelations of an ARMA(1, 1) process are derived in Section 3.5. From equation (3.26) it follows that the autocorrelations of the process $\{s_t\}$ are

$$\text{cor}(s_t, s_{t+\tau}) = C(\alpha, \beta)(\alpha + \beta)^\tau, \quad \tau > 0, \tag{9.17}$$

with

$$C(\alpha, \beta) = \frac{\alpha(1 - \alpha\beta - \beta^2)}{(\alpha + \beta)(1 - 2\alpha\beta - \beta^2)}. \tag{9.18}$$

The term $C(\alpha, \beta)$ is positive whenever the kurtosis is finite. Hence the autocorrelations of the squared residuals are all positive and decline geometrically, whenever these autocorrelations are defined. For the typical values $\alpha = 0.06$ and $\beta = 0.92$, $C = 0.139$ and the autocorrelations at lags 1, 10, 25, and 50 are respectively 0.137, 0.114, 0.084, and 0.051.

When the kurtosis of returns is infinite, the sample autocorrelations of a very long series of data $\{s_t\}$ are still given by the geometric decay formula, (9.17), but with $C(\alpha, \beta) = \frac{1}{3}(3\alpha + \beta)/(\alpha + \beta)$ (see Ding and Granger 1996).

The arguments used to show that the GARCH(1, 1) model can explain the major stylized facts for returns are similar to, yet different from, those given in Section 8.4. The first five assumptions in Section 8.4 are satisfied by a stationary GARCH(1, 1) model, with $\sigma_t^2 = h_t$, but the sixth assumption is not. Although the random variables h_t and z_t are independent, the stochastic processes $\{h_t\}$

and $\{z_t\}$ are not stochastically independent; in particular, h_t is a function of $\{z_{t-1}, z_{t-2}, \dots\}$, stated as follows by Nelson (1990a):

$$\frac{h_t}{\omega} = 1 + \sum_{k=1}^{\infty} \left(\prod_{i=1}^{k} (\alpha z_{t-i}^2 + \beta) \right).$$

9.3.6 Integrated Specification

Empirical estimates of the sum of the parameters α and β are often near one and sometimes the sum exceeds one if the parameters are not constrained. Consequently, Engle and Bollerslev (1986) consider the *integrated* specification when $\alpha + \beta = 1$, known as IGARCH(1, 1), with ω only constrained to be nonnegative:

$$h_t = \omega + \alpha (r_{t-1} - \mu)^2 + (1 - \alpha) h_{t-1}. \tag{9.19}$$

Nelson (1990a) discusses the mathematical properties of the integrated process. Although it is not covariance stationary, it is, however, strictly stationary when ω is positive and the process has an indefinite past; also, the unconditional variance of returns is then infinite, but this does not prevent the calculation of conditional variances. Furthermore, strictly stationary models can also be defined when $\alpha + \beta > 1$ providing $E[\log(\alpha z_t^2 + \beta)] < 0$.

9.3.7 Forecasts

The history of returns is irrelevant when forecasting returns, because the standardized returns are i.i.d. The best forecast of r_{t+n}, given a history of returns $\{r_t, r_{t-1}, \dots\}$, is thus the constant mean μ for all positive forecast horizons n, when accuracy is measured by the expected squared forecast error.

The history of returns can instead be used to calculate the conditional variances for all horizons. These are denoted by $\hat{s}_{t+n}$, because they also equal the conditional expectation of the squared residual $s_{t+n} = (r_{t+n} - \mu)^2$. At time t, the history provides

$$\hat{s}_{t+1} = h_{t+1} = \operatorname{var}(r_{t+1} \mid r_t, r_{t-1}, \dots) = E[s_{t+1} \mid r_t, r_{t-1}, \dots].$$

Initially, suppose $\alpha + \beta < 1$. Then we can obtain

$$\begin{aligned}
\hat{s}_{t,2} &= \operatorname{var}(r_{t+2} \mid r_t, r_{t-1}, \dots) = E[s_{t+2} \mid r_t, r_{t-1}, \dots] \\
&= E[h_{t+2} z_{t+2}^2 \mid r_t, r_{t-1}, \dots] = E[h_{t+2} \mid r_t, r_{t-1}, \dots] \\
&= E[\omega + (\alpha z_{t+1}^2 + \beta) h_{t+1} \mid r_t, r_{t-1}, \dots] \\
&= \omega + (\alpha + \beta) h_{t+1} = (1 - \alpha - \beta)\sigma^2 + (\alpha + \beta) h_{t+1} \\
&= \sigma^2 + (\alpha + \beta)(h_{t+1} - \sigma^2)
\end{aligned}$$

with σ^2 the unconditional variance of the process, given in (9.11). Likewise, for $n > 2$,

$$\hat{s}_{t,n} = \text{var}(r_{t+n} \mid r_t, r_{t-1}, \ldots) = E[h_{t+n} \mid r_t, r_{t-1}, \ldots]$$
$$= \omega + (\alpha + \beta)E[h_{t+n-1} \mid r_t, r_{t-1}, \ldots] = \omega + (\alpha + \beta)\hat{s}_{t,n-1}$$
$$= \sigma^2 + (\alpha + \beta)(\hat{s}_{t,n-1} - \sigma^2).$$

Hence, for all $n \geqslant 1$,

$$\text{var}(r_{t+n} \mid r_t, r_{t-1}, \ldots) = \sigma^2 + (\alpha + \beta)^{n-1}(h_{t+1} - \sigma^2). \tag{9.20}$$

This result can also be derived from the ARMA representation given previously by equation (9.16). Expectations of future volatility, as measured by the conditional variance of returns, are seen to revert geometrically towards the unconditional variance as the forecast horizon increases. The sum $\alpha + \beta$ determines the rate of reversion and is often referred to as the *persistence* parameter of the process.

Similar methods provide results for the integrated case when $\alpha + \beta = 1$, these being

$$\text{var}(r_{t+n} \mid r_t, r_{t-1}, \ldots) = (n - 1)\omega + h_{t+1}. \tag{9.21}$$

Conditional variances for the total return over n periods are simply sums of one-period conditional variances, thus

$$\text{var}(r_{t+1} + \cdots + r_{t+n} \mid r_t, r_{t-1}, \ldots) = \sum_{j=1}^{n} \hat{s}_{t,j}$$
$$= n\sigma^2 + \frac{1 - (\alpha + \beta)^n}{1 - \alpha - \beta}(h_{t+1} - \sigma^2) \tag{9.22}$$

for the stationary process and

$$\text{var}(r_{t+1} + \cdots + r_{t+n} \mid r_t, r_{t-1}, \ldots) = \tfrac{1}{2}n(n - 1)\omega + nh_{t+1} \tag{9.23}$$

for the integrated process.

9.4 An Exchange Rate Example of the GARCH(1, 1) Model

The GARCH(1, 1) model, with conditional normal distributions, is defined by equations (9.5)–(9.7). Prices p_t, returns r_t, conditional variances h_t, and standardized residuals z_t are connected by the system of equations

$$r_t = \log(p_t/p_{t-1}) = \mu + h_t^{1/2} z_t \tag{9.24}$$

and

$$h_t = \omega + \alpha(r_{t-1} - \mu)^2 + \beta h_{t-1} = \omega + (\alpha z_{t-1}^2 + \beta)h_{t-1}, \tag{9.25}$$

here ignoring any dividends when defining the returns. Numerical values have to be assigned to μ, α, β, and ω.

Calculation of the conditional variances and estimation of the model parameters is easy for this ARCH specification, and can be accomplished without difficulty using Excel software. An example is provided here for the daily DM/$ exchange rate from January 1991 to December 2000, defined and graphed in Section 2.2. Readers who are not interested in ARCH calculations should skip to the subsection headed "DM/$ results" on p. 209.

9.4.1 Conditional Variances

Exhibit 9.1 illustrates the calculation of conditional variances and shows the results for a few days. First, the time series of 2591 daily exchange rates is located in cells B17 to B2607. These rates are the Deutsche mark price of one dollar. Next, returns are calculated. The return for 3 January 1991, which is period $t = 1$, equals 0.000 536 and is obtained by inserting =LN(B18/B17) into cell C18. Returns for the subsequent periods are obtained by selecting and copying cell C18, followed by pasting it into cells C19 to C2607. Some summary statistics for the set of 2590 returns are given in cells B3 to B10, obtained from the functions AVERAGE, STDEV, SKEW, KURT, CORREL, MIN, and MAX. The returns range from -4.0% to 3.4%, have more kurtosis than a normal distribution, and a sample standard deviation of 0.67%. The correlation between consecutive returns is 0.018 and provides no evidence of significant correlation.

The only technical issue in the calculations is the value of the conditional variance for the first period. The variance of the complete sample of returns is used in Exhibit 9.1, to give the contents of cell D18 as $h_1 = 4.501 \times 10^{-5}$. Alternative possibilities are either to set h_1 equal to the unconditional variance, $\sigma^2 = \omega/(1 - \alpha - \beta)$, or to include h_1 in the set of parameters that are to be estimated. The formulae for selected cells, including D18, are given in Table 9.1.

The calculations in Exhibit 9.1 are for the values $\mu = 0.0001$, $\alpha = 0.06$, $\beta = 0.92$, and $\sigma^2 = 4 \times 10^{-5}$, so that $\omega = 8 \times 10^{-7}$. The four parameter values of the model are in cells G3 to G6. The values of μ and σ^2 are based upon summary statistics, while the values of α and β are typical values in the literature. Returning to the calculations in row 18, the first standardized residual, z_1, is given by the formula =(C18-$G$3)/SQRT(D18) in cell E18; here the "absolute reference" $G$3 is used to ensure that subsequent copying and pasting gives the correct results. The remaining cell in the row, G18, is explained later.

The calculations for time period $t = 2$ commence with $h_2 = \omega + (\alpha z_1^2 + \beta)h_1$. This can be obtained by inserting into cell D19 the formula given in Table 9.1, where again absolute references are used to refer to the model's parameters. Then z_2 is given by copying and pasting cell E18 into cell E19.

	A	B	C	D	E	F	G
1	Summary stats.					Parameter	Value
2		Returns r(t)				Model	
3	Mean	0.0001290				Mu	0
4	Standard deviation	0.006709				Omega	8.000E-07
5	Skewness	-0.141				Alpha	0.0600
6	Kurtosis	5.277				Beta	0.9200
7	Lag 1 correlation	0.0176				*Reparametrized*	
8						Mu*1000	0.1000
9	Minimum	-0.0403				Alpha	0.0600
10	Maximum	0.0340				Persistence	0.9800
11						Variance*10000	0.4000
12							
13						log L	9389.09
14							
15	Date	Price	Return	Variance	Standardized residual		Log density
16		p(t)	r(t)	h(t)	z(t)		l(t)
17	2 Jan 91	1.4915					
18	3 Jan 91	1.4923	0.000536	4.5014E-05	0.0649		4.0832
19	4 Jan 91	1.5025	0.006813	4.2224E-05	1.0331		3.5837
20	7 Jan 91	1.5323	0.019638	4.2350E-05	3.0024		-0.3912
21	8 Jan 91	1.5340	0.001108	6.2667E-05	0.1274		3.9118
22	9 Jan 91	1.5145	-0.012793	5.8515E-05	-1.6854		2.5338

Exhibit 9.1. An example of GARCH(1, 1) calculations for the DM/$ rate.

It is now possible to evaluate all the remaining conditional variances, for times $t \geqslant 3$; select cells D19 and E19, then copy and paste them into the rectangle D20:E2607, whose corners are D20, E20, D2607, and E2607.

Table 9.1. Formulae used in the GARCH(1, 1) spreadsheets.

Cell	Formula
C18	=LN(B18/B17)
D18	=B4*B4
D19	=$G$4+(($G$5*E18*E18)+$G$6)*D18
E18	=(C18-$G$3)/SQRT(D18)
G3	=0.001*G8
G4	=G11*(1-G10)/10000
G5	=G9
G6	=G10-G9
G18	=-0.5*(LN(2*PI())+LN(D18)+(E18*E18))

9.4.2 Parameter Estimation

The parameters μ, α, β, and ω can be estimated from the returns data by seeking the values giving the maximum likelihood of obtaining the observed data. The theory of maximum likelihood estimation for ARCH models is introduced in Section 9.5 and reviewed in some detail in Section 10.4. For the present time we simply note that appropriate estimates for n returns are given by maximizing the log-likelihood function,

$$\log L = \sum_{t=1}^{n} l_t, \qquad (9.26)$$

with

$$l_t = -\tfrac{1}{2}[\log(2\pi) + \log(h_t) + z_t^2]. \qquad (9.27)$$

Each term l_t is a function of μ, α, β, and ω.

Column G of Exhibit 9.1 includes the values of l_t. The formula for l_1, in cell G18, is given in Table 9.1. Copying and pasting provides G19, etc. The value of the log-likelihood is then SUM(G18:G2607) and is shown in cell G13 to be 9389.09. Higher values of the log-likelihood are obtained by maximizing the contents of cell G13 by changing the values in cells G3 to G6.

Perhaps the easiest way to maximize the log-likelihood function is to reparametrize the function. Maximizing over μ, α, β, and ω is the same as maximizing over μ, α, the persistence $\alpha + \beta$, and the unconditional variance $\sigma^2 = \omega/(1 - \alpha - \beta)$. Scaling some of these terms makes their magnitudes comparable, which can make it easier to perform the maximization. Results are given here when the maximization is over the "optimization parameters" defined as $10^3\mu$, α, $\alpha + \beta$, and $10^4\sigma^2$. The original spreadsheet is modified slightly to find the parameter estimates. The values of the "optimization parameters" are placed in cells G8 to G11 and then μ, α, β, and ω are calculated in cells G3 to G6.

Maximization of the log-likelihood function can be achieved by use of the Excel tool called Solver. The constraints $\alpha \geqslant 0.0001$, $\alpha + \beta \leqslant 0.9999$, and $\sigma^2 \geqslant 0$ are appropriate when estimating the stationary version of the GARCH(1, 1) model. Solver is used to maximize cell G13 with the constraints applied to cells G9, G10, and G11. Commencing the maximization at the parameter values given in Exhibit 9.1 produces the optimal values shown in Exhibit 9.2. A highly desirable property of any maximization algorithm is that the answer does not depend on the initial values. This is indeed the case for the combination of algorithm, model, and data discussed here.

9.4.3 DM/$ results, 1991–2000

The maximum likelihood estimates $\hat{\mu}$ and $\hat{\sigma}^2 = \hat{\omega}/(1-\hat{\alpha}-\hat{\beta})$ of the unconditional mean and variance of the returns process are respectively close to the sample mean and variance. The parameter estimates shown in Exhibit 9.2 also include $\hat{\alpha} = 0.0354$, $\hat{\beta} = 0.9554$, and the persistence estimate $\hat{\alpha} + \hat{\beta} = 0.9908$. Robust standard errors for these three estimates, calculated using matrices given later in Section 10.4, are 0.0081, 0.0097, and 0.0048 respectively. The unit root hypothesis $\alpha + \beta = 1$ is rejected at the 5% level in Section 10.5. The theoretical kurtosis of returns is found to be finite for the parameter estimates, by checking the inequality in equation (9.12).

It is notable that the persistence estimate is nearer to one than values reported for daily observations of the DM/$ rate in earlier periods. Taylor (1994a) estimates $\hat{\alpha} = 0.099$, $\hat{\beta} = 0.871$, and $\hat{\alpha} + \hat{\beta} = 0.970$ for the period from December 1977 to November 1990, while Bollerslev et al. (1994) estimate $\hat{\alpha} = 0.068$, $\hat{\beta} = 0.880$, and $\hat{\alpha} + \hat{\beta} = 0.948$ for the period from January 1981 to July 1992. Both studies reject a unit root at low significance levels.

Exhibit 9.2 shows summary statistics for the standardized residuals in cells D3 to D10, based upon the estimated parameters. Their sample mean and variance are very near to the theoretical values of 0 and 1 respectively. Their skewness and kurtosis, however, both show that these standardized returns are not a sample from a normal distribution. Instead, the kurtosis (4.61), the minimum (−4.99), and the maximum values (4.35) suggest a fat-tailed distribution is more appropriate.

Figure 9.1 shows the ten-year time series of volatility estimates from 1991 to 2000 given by the annualized conditional standard deviations, $\sigma_t = \sqrt{259h_t}$; the scaling constant (259) is the average number of returns per annum in the time series. The volatility estimates are plotted as percentages and range from 6.5% in July 1996 to 19.1% in August 1991. Half of the estimates are inside the interquartile range, from 8.8% to 11.7%. The median and mean values are 10.3% and 10.6% respectively. The early estimates depend on the value of h_1. If h_1 is treated as an additional parameter, then firstly σ_1 becomes 13.7%, rather than the 10.8% shown in Figure 9.1, and secondly the estimates of the original parameters change by negligible amounts.

	A	B	C	D	E	F	G
	Summary stats.	Returns r(t)	Standardized z(t)			Parameter / *Model*	Value
1							
2	Mean	0.0001290		-0.0018		Mu	0.0001377
3	Standard deviation	0.006709		1.0015		Omega	4.242E-07
4	Skewness	-0.141		-0.217		Alpha	0.0354
5	Kurtosis	5.277		4.612		Beta	0.9554
6	Lag 1 correlation	0.0176		0.0323		*Reparametrized*	
7						Mu*1000	0.1377
8	Minimum	-0.0403		-4.99		Alpha	0.0354
9	Maximum	0.0340		4.35		Persistence	0.9908
10						Variance*10000	0.4610
11							
12						log L	9396.06
13							
14							
15	Date	Price p(t)	Return r(t)	Variance h(t)	Standardized residual z(t)		Log density l(t)
16							
17	2 Jan 91	1.4915					
18	3 Jan 91	1.4923	0.000536	4.5014E-05	0.0593		4.0836
19	4 Jan 91	1.5025	0.006813	4.3437E-05	1.0129		3.5902
20	7 Jan 91	1.5323	0.019638	4.3501E-05	2.9567		-0.2685

Exhibit 9.2.　GARCH(1, 1) parameter estimates for the DM/$ rate, 1991–2000.

Figures 9.2 and 9.3 show the annualized conditional standard deviations in more detail, respectively for one year of high volatility and for one year of low volatility. These figures also show the annualized percentage returns, clustered around the horizontal axis. The scales are the same for the two figures, to emphasize the differences between volatility during the two highlighted years.

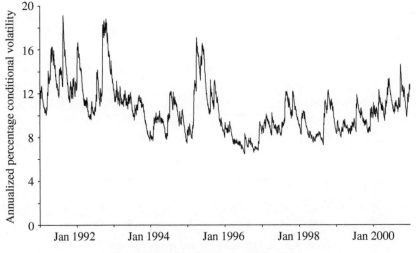

Figure 9.1. DM/$ volatility 1991–2000.

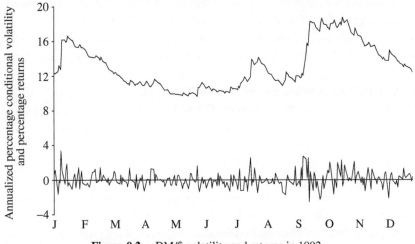

Figure 9.2. DM/$ volatility and returns in 1992.

Figure 9.2 shows high levels of Deutsche mark volatility throughout 1992, with a range from 9.6% to 18.7%. An extreme return of 3.4% on 9 January is responsible for the sudden increase of σ_t from 12.8% to 16.2%. After a week of very high volatility, the estimates generally decline and fall below the median level in May. Much more dispersion can be seen in the returns during September and October and this translates into higher levels of volatility. These months coincide with a crisis in the management of the European exchange rate mechanism, which included the withdrawal of the British pound from this mechanism on 16 September. There were four notable returns on 11, 14, 16, and 17 September, all

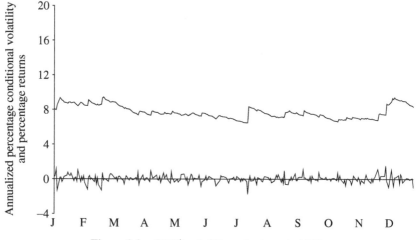

Figure 9.3. DM/$ volatility and returns in 1996.

beyond $\pm 2.3\%$, which raised the volatility estimates from 12.0% to 18.3%. The period above the very high level of 17% lasts for about six weeks and is followed by a steady decline in volatility, to a year-end value of 12.4%.

Figure 9.3, in contrast, shows much lower levels of volatility in 1996. The lowest level of 6.5% is followed by 8.3% on the next day, responding to a return of -1.7% on 16 July. The highest volatility estimate is 9.4% and hence volatility throughout the year is below the ten-year median level.

Volatility forecasts for the stationary GARCH(1, 1) model revert towards a constant as the forecast horizon increases. The conditional annualized standard deviation at time t, for time period $t + n$, is given by $\sigma_{t,n} = \sqrt{259\hat{s}_{t,n}}$ with $\hat{s}_{t,n}$ defined by equation (9.20). Figure 9.4 shows forecasts up to six months into the future, when $\sigma_{t,1}$ is either 8% or 14%. These forecast functions converge to $\sqrt{259\hat{\sigma}^2} = 10.9\%$ as $n \to \infty$. The rate of convergence depends on the persistence parameter, $\alpha + \beta$. When $n = H + 1$, with $H = \log(0.5)/\log(\alpha + \beta)$, variance forecasts are halfway between the first forecast and the eventual limit. The half-life H is estimated to be 75 trading periods, which equals 3.47 months.

9.5   A General ARCH Framework

There are very many specifications of ARCH models in finance literature. The next two sections summarize their common features and provide some examples. The essential ingredients of ARCH models are conditional density functions, which describe the density of the next return conditional on information that is known at the present time. These densities are often assumed to be normal, as they are in this section. More flexibility is provided by permitting nonnormal conditional densities, which are illustrated in the next section.

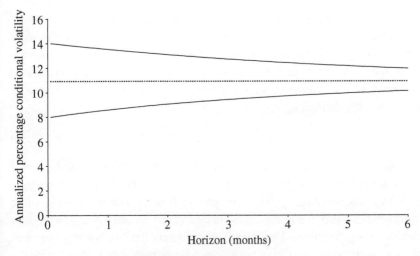

Figure 9.4. Volatility forecasts.

The general set-up makes use of trading periods indexed by t, returns r_t, relevant information I_{t-1} known at time $t - 1$, a vector of parameters denoted by θ, conditional mean functions μ_t, and conditional variance functions h_t. The conditional functions for time t are defined using the information known at time $t - 1$ and the parameters θ. Naturally I_{t-1} includes r_{t-1} and all the prior information I_{t-2}. For the GARCH(1, 1) example considered in Sections 9.3 and 9.4, I_{t-1} is the history of returns $\{r_{t-1}, r_{t-2}, \dots\}$, μ_t is a constant value μ, $h_t = \omega + \alpha(r_{t-1} - \mu)^2 + \beta h_{t-1}$, and $\theta = (\mu, \omega, \alpha, \beta)'$.

In the general set-up, with conditional normality assumed,

$$r_t \mid I_{t-1} \sim N(\mu_t, h_t), \tag{9.28}$$

with both μ_t and h_t functions of I_{t-1} and θ. We will often refer to the *residual*

$$e_t = r_t - \mu_t, \tag{9.29}$$

which has conditional distribution

$$e_t \mid I_{t-1} \sim N(0, h_t),$$

and to the *standardized residual*

$$z_t = \frac{r_t - \mu_t}{\sqrt{h_t}}, \tag{9.30}$$

which has conditional distribution

$$z_t \mid I_{t-1} \sim N(0, 1).$$

As I_{t-1} suffices to determine z_{t-1} and all previous values of the z-process, it follows that the standardized residuals are independent and identically distributed (i.i.d.).

Equation (9.28) can be interpreted in two ways. First, it provides a way to use observed time series to calculate numbers μ_t and h_t at time $t - 1$ and hence a specific conditional distribution for the random variable r_t. The observations are then assumed to start at time $t = 1$ and some initial information I_0 is assumed to be available. Second, equation (9.28) can be viewed as summarizing a stochastic process, formally defined by

$$r_t = \mu_t + h_t^{1/2} z_t, \quad z_t \sim \text{i.i.d.} \, N(0, 1). \tag{9.31}$$

This process could start at time $t = 1$, when initial information is required, or it could be defined for all integer times (including negative t) whenever the process is stationary. The stochastic process perspective is used to define models, while the time series perspective is used to estimate and test parameters and to produce predictive density functions. The general set-up is very flexible. Some of the more important specifications that have been used are now mentioned, after stating the criterion used to estimate parameters.

9.5.1 Estimation

The complete specification of conditional densities by (9.28) explains why ARCH models are a convenient way to model volatility. The product of conditional densities $f(r_t \mid I_{t-1}, \theta)$ can be maximized to provide an appropriate estimate of the parameters θ from a set of n observed returns $\{r_1, r_2, \ldots, r_n\}$. The product, as a function of θ, is

$$L(\theta) = f(r_1 \mid I_0, \theta) f(r_2 \mid I_1, \theta) \cdots f(r_n \mid I_{n-1}, \theta) \tag{9.32}$$

and its logarithm equals

$$\begin{aligned}
\log L(\theta) &= \sum_{t=1}^{n} \log f(r_t \mid I_{t-1}, \theta) \\
&= \sum_{t=1}^{n} -\tfrac{1}{2} \log(2\pi) - \tfrac{1}{2} \log(h_t(\theta)) - \frac{(r_t - \mu_t(\theta))^2}{2 h_t(\theta)} \\
&= -\frac{1}{2} \left[n \log(2\pi) + \sum_{t=1}^{n} \log(h_t(\theta)) + z_t^2(\theta) \right]
\end{aligned} \tag{9.33}$$

because the conditional densities have normal distributions. Equation (9.32) is simply the multivariate density of the returns, $f(r_1, r_2, \ldots, r_n \mid I_0, \theta)$, when the information sets are the histories of the observed returns and then $L(\theta)$ is the likelihood function. We will also use this name for $L(\theta)$ when more information is used to define the conditional densities. Maximization of (9.33) provides the maximum likelihood estimate $\hat{\theta}$, whose properties are described in Section 10.4.

9.5.2 Information

The information set I_{t-1} is very often restricted to the history of returns $\{r_{t-1}, r_{t-2}, \dots\}$. It is sometimes augmented by calendar information, so that calendar effects can be modeled. Additional market information known at time $t-1$ can be included. Interest rates can help to specify time-varying expected returns. Options information is a particularly interesting source of volatility information that is investigated in detail in Chapter 15. Trading volume information has also been considered but with less success.

9.5.3 Conditional Means

Relatively few specifications have been suggested for conditional means, compared with the variety investigated for conditional variances. This reflects the general lack of important correlation in returns. The simplest specification for μ_t is a constant. Some people include day-of-the-week and other dummy variables to capture calendar anomalies. Many people use an MA(1) specification to model the very weak correlation in the returns process; then

$$\mu_t = \mu + \Theta e_{t-1} \tag{9.34}$$

and the two parameters μ and Θ are included in the vector θ.

It is intuitive to suppose that expected returns increase as risk increases. The conditional variance is one measure of risk, so that a plausible specification of the conditional mean is

$$\mu_t = \xi + \lambda h_t^{1/2}. \tag{9.35}$$

This is an example of the ARCH-in-mean model of Engle, Lilien, and Robins (1987). An asset that has zero conditional variance is risk-free so it is logical to identify ξ with the risk-free interest rate and to require this parameter to be positive. The price of risk parameter, λ, should also be positive for many assets. Both ξ and λ are included in the vector θ. The assumption of a constant risk-free rate can be removed when interest-rate data $\{i_t\}$ are available, by then specifying $\mu_t = i_t + \lambda h_t^{1/2}$. Any model that represents μ_t as a function of h_t is called an ARCH-M model. These models have autocorrelation in the returns process, because conditional variances and hence conditional means are autocorrelated; details are given in Hong (1991).

9.5.4 Conditional Variances

The passage of time has seen increasingly sophisticated attempts to describe conditional variances. The GARCH(p, q) model of Bollerslev (1986) generalizes the original ARCH(p) model of Engle (1982). The conditional variance then depends on the p most recent squared residuals and the q most recent conditional variances, thus

$$h_t = \omega + \sum_{i=1}^{p} \alpha_i e_{t-i}^2 + \sum_{j=1}^{q} \beta_j h_{t-j}. \qquad (9.36)$$

In many empirical studies it is found that $p = q = 1$ is appropriate. The residuals process is covariance stationary when $\alpha_1 + \cdots + \alpha_p + \beta_1 + \cdots + \beta_q < 1$. The autocorrelations of squared residuals are described in Bollerslev (1988), conditions for nonnegative conditional variances are provided by Nelson and Cao (1992), aggregation results are given in Drost and Nijman (1993), and option pricing formulae are derived by Duan (1995).

The signs of the residuals e_{t-i} are irrelevant in the GARCH model. Nelson (1991) shows that the symmetric treatment of positive and negative residuals is not appropriate for US stock market returns. His exponential GARCH model is one of the first of many specifications that involve asymmetric functions of the residuals (Engle 1990; Glosten, Jagannathan, and Runkle 1993; Zakoïan 1994; Sentana 1995). Some of these specifications are described in Sections 9.7 and 10.2 and one of them is estimated in Section 9.8. In some cases the specifications can be considered to represent two regimes, corresponding to either a rising or a falling price. More complicated regime switching models are defined from either price information (Fornari and Mele 1996; Anderson, Nam, and Vahid 1999) or from unobservable states (Cai 1994; Hamilton and Susmel 1994).

The autocorrelations of the squared residuals decay rapidly towards zero for GARCH and many other specifications. There is evidence, however, that the empirical autocorrelations decay slowly so that long memory specifications deserve consideration. Long memory ARCH models are introduced in Baillie, Bollerslev, and Mikkelsen (1996) and in Bollerslev and Mikkelsen (1996) and they will be considered in Section 10.3.

Linear functions of squared residuals appear in many specifications of the conditional variance, as in the GARCH model. An equally plausible starting point is a linear function of absolute residuals that defines the conditional standard deviation, for example,

$$h_t^{1/2} = \omega + \sum_{i=1}^{p} \alpha_i |e_{t-i}| + \sum_{j=1}^{q} \beta_j h_{t-j}^{1/2}, \qquad (9.37)$$

with special cases in Taylor and Kingsman (1979), Taylor (1986), and Schwert (1989). Absolute values, rather than squares, are employed in the EGARCH model of Nelson (1991), described in Section 10.2, and in several other specifications.

Finally, the impact of nontrading periods can be modeled by multiplicative effects. For daily data, let h_t^* be the appropriate conditional variance for a return calculated over a 24-hour period. A higher level is often appropriate if trading period t includes the weekend and/or holidays for which the market is closed;

the multiplier $m_t = h_t / h_t^*$ then exceeds 1. One adaptation of the GARCH(1, 1) model is

$$r_t = \mu + h_t^{1/2} z_t, \quad z_t \sim \text{i.i.d. } N(0, 1),$$

$$h_t = m_t h_t^*, \tag{9.38}$$

$$h_t^* = \omega + (\alpha + \beta z_{t-1}^2) h_{t-1}^*, \tag{9.39}$$

$$m_t = 1 + W w_t + V v_t, \tag{9.40}$$

with w_t and v_t respectively counting the number of weekend days (Saturdays and Sundays) and the number of vacation days during trading period t. The parameter vector is then $\theta = (\mu, \omega, \alpha, \beta, W, V)'$. Similar multipliers m_t are defined and estimated in Nelson (1991), Bollerslev et al. (1994), and Taylor (1994a).

The ARCH family is well populated and its variety can be bewildering, particularly when considering the specification of the conditional variance. Bollerslev et al. (1994, p. 2971) aptly remark, "The richness of the family of parametric ARCH models is both a blessing and a curse. It certainly complicates the search for the 'true' model, and leaves quite a bit of arbitrariness in the model selection stage. On the other hand, the flexibility of the ARCH class of models means that in the analysis of structural economic models with time varying volatility, there is a good chance that an appropriate parametric ARCH model can be formulated that will make the analysis tractable." Methods for guiding the selection of a specific model are presented later, particularly in Sections 10.5 and 10.6.

9.6 Nonnormal Conditional Distributions

Empirical evidence, commencing with Engle and Bollerslev (1986) and Bollerslev (1987), has often contradicted the assumption that returns have conditional normal distributions. Very often the distribution of the estimated standardized residuals, $\hat{z}_t$, obtained from observed returns and a parameter estimate $\hat{\theta}$, has excess kurtosis. The assumption $z_t \sim N(0, 1)$ is then untenable when seeking a satisfactory description of the returns process. This is important if a researcher requires a model that is compatible with empirical evidence, for example, when attempting to derive the density of future prices by Monte Carlo methods.

A false assumption of normality is not serious, however, when estimating ARCH model parameters that are only used to calculate conditional variances or when testing parameter restrictions. Indeed, for econometric reasons, it can be beneficial to assume normal distributions when the assumption is known to be false, as discussed in Section 10.4. Consequently, for some purposes, modeling nonnormal conditional distributions is not necessary.

The most general ARCH set-up that we now consider supposes that the standardized residuals are i.i.d. with zero mean, unit variance, and a distribution that depends on one or more parameters. This distribution is denoted by $D(0, 1)$ and now

$$r_t = \mu_t + h_t^{1/2} z_t, \quad z_t \sim \text{i.i.d. } D(0, 1). \tag{9.41}$$

The conditional distributions of returns are now represented by

$$r_t \mid I_{t-1} \sim D(\mu_t, h_t), \tag{9.42}$$

and, as before, μ_t and h_t are functions of information I_{t-1} and the parameter vector θ.

9.6.1 Examples

The two most popular choices for the distribution $D(0, 1)$ are the standardized t-distribution (Bollerslev 1987) and the generalized error distribution (Nelson 1989, 1991). Figures 4.3 and 4.4 display examples of their density functions.

The density function of the standardized t-distribution is determined by one parameter, the degrees-of-freedom ν; thus,

$$f(z \mid \nu) = c(\nu) \left[1 + \frac{z^2}{\nu - 2} \right]^{-(\nu+1)/2} \tag{9.43}$$

with $c(\nu)$ defined in terms of the gamma function, $\Gamma(\cdot)$, by

$$c(\nu) = \frac{\Gamma(\frac{1}{2}(\nu + 1))}{\Gamma(\frac{1}{2}\nu)\sqrt{\pi(\nu - 2)}}. \tag{9.44}$$

The parameter ν must exceed 2. The condition for a finite moment of order n is $n < \nu$. In particular, the kurtosis is finite when $\nu > 4$ and then equals $3(\nu - 2)/(\nu - 4)$. As $\nu \to \infty$, the density function converges to that of the standard normal distribution. The gamma function is defined by an integral as

$$\Gamma(u) = \int_0^\infty x^{u-1} e^{-x} \, dx, \quad u > 0.$$

Some useful results are $\Gamma(\frac{1}{2}) = \sqrt{\pi}, \Gamma(1) = 1, \Gamma(u+1) = u\Gamma(u)$, and $\Gamma(n) = (n - 1)!$ for positive integers n.

The density function of the generalized error distribution (GED) is also determined by one parameter, the tail-thickness η; thus,

$$f(z \mid \eta) = C(\eta) \exp\left[-\frac{1}{2} \left| \frac{z}{\lambda(\eta)} \right|^\eta \right], \tag{9.45}$$

with

$$\lambda(\eta) = 2^{-(1/\eta)} \left[\frac{\Gamma(\eta^{-1})}{\Gamma(3\eta^{-1})} \right]^{1/2} \quad \text{and} \quad C(\eta) = \frac{\eta}{2} \left[\frac{\Gamma(3\eta^{-1})}{\Gamma(\eta^{-1})^3} \right]^{1/2}. \tag{9.46}$$

The parameter η is positive. The distribution is standard normal when $\eta = 2$ and has thicker tails than the normal when $\eta < 2$; it is double exponential when

$\eta = 1$. All the moments of the distribution are finite and the kurtosis equals $\Gamma(5\eta^{-1})\Gamma(\eta^{-1})/\Gamma(3\eta^{-1})^2$.

Both the above densities can be represented as mixtures of normal distributions (Praetz 1972; Hsu 1982) and hence standardized returns can be factorized as

$$z_t = m_t^{1/2} u_t \quad \text{with } E[m_t] = 1 \text{ and } u_t \sim N(0, 1).$$

It is then possible to fit ARCH models into the information arrivals framework of Section 8.3, with m_t measuring the news arrivals in period t divided by the number expected at time $t - 1$ (Taylor 1994a).

Further possibilities for the distribution $D(0, 1)$ are the two-parameter generalized t-distribution of Bollerslev et al. (1994, p. 3018) and the nonparametric specification of Engle and González-Rivera (1991).

9.6.2 Estimation

Parameters such as the degrees-of-freedom ν or the tail-thickness η are included in the parameter vector θ. Typically, h_t and z_t are functions of some subset θ^* of θ and the density function of z_t is determined by the remaining elements, $\theta^\bullet$, of θ. The conditional density of observation t is

$$f(r_t \mid I_{t-1}, \theta) = \frac{f(z_t(\theta^*) \mid \theta^\bullet)}{\sqrt{h_t(\theta^*)}} \tag{9.47}$$

and the log-likelihood function is now

$$\log L(\theta) = \sum_{t=1}^{n} \log f(r_t \mid I_{t-1}, \theta)$$

$$= \sum_{t=1}^{n} -\tfrac{1}{2} \log(h_t(\theta^*)) + \log(f(z_t(\theta^*) \mid \theta^\bullet)). \tag{9.48}$$

Maximization of (9.48) provides the maximum likelihood estimate $\hat{\theta}$ of all the parameters.

9.6.3 Nonnormal GARCH(1, 1)

Many formulae for the stationary GARCH(1, 1) process do not depend on the distribution of the standardized residuals z_t. These include the unconditional variance, the autocorrelations of the squared residuals when the kurtosis of returns is finite, and the forecasts of future volatility, provided by equations (9.11), (9.17), (9.18), and (9.20). The conditions for returns to have finite kurtosis, however, are firstly that

$$\text{kurtosis}(z_t) = E[z_t^4] = k_z$$

is finite and secondly that

$$(\alpha + \beta)^2 + \alpha^2(k_z - 1) < 1, \tag{9.49}$$

proved by Nelson (1990a, equation 29). The kurtosis equals

$$\text{kurtosis}(r_t) = k_z \frac{1 - (\alpha + \beta)^2}{1 - (\alpha + \beta)^2 - \alpha^2 (k_z - 1)} \tag{9.50}$$

when it is finite (He and Teräsvirta 1999, equation 8).

9.7 Asymmetric Volatility Models

The conditional variance of future asset prices is not a symmetric function of changes in prices at some markets, particularly at equity markets. An $x\%$ rise in the price today typically has a different impact on future volatility to an $x\%$ fall in the price today, whatever the value of x. Nelson (1991) shows that a fall in the US stock market has a much larger impact on the next day's volatility than a rise of the same magnitude. In this situation, squared residuals, $e_{t-1}^2 = (r_{t-1} - \mu_{t-1})^2$, do not provide all the relevant new information at time $t - 1$ about volatility at time t. Instead, there is some additional information in e_{t-1}.

Much research has focused on the sign of the residual e_{t-1}, which is identical to the sign of the standardized residual z_{t-1}. The additional information is then summarized by the indicator variable

$$S_{t-1} = \begin{cases} 1 & \text{if } e_{t-1} < 0, \\ 0 & \text{if } e_{t-1} \geqslant 0. \end{cases} \tag{9.51}$$

Sometimes e_{t-1} in (9.51) is replaced by the return r_{t-1} in empirical work, which makes little difference to results because conditional means μ_t are very near zero. Engle and Ng (1993) describe hypothesis tests that can be used to decide if volatility is an asymmetric function. Their sign bias tests involve regressing z_t^2 on explanatory variables such as S_{t-1} and $S_{t-1} e_{t-1}$. A significant t-ratio from an ordinary least squares regression is then evidence of asymmetry.

We now consider a popular asymmetric specification for the conditional variance h_t, followed by numerical examples in Section 9.8. Further asymmetric specifications, a summary of the magnitude of the asymmetric effect, and a review of explanations for this effect follow later in Section 10.2.

9.7.1 GJR-GARCH

The GARCH(1, 1) model states that μ_t is a constant and h_t is a linear function of e_{t-1}^2 and h_{t-1}. Asymmetry can be introduced by weighting e_{t-1}^2 differently for negative and positive residuals; thus,

$$h_t = \omega + \alpha e_{t-1}^2 + \alpha^- S_{t-1} e_{t-1}^2 + \beta h_{t-1}. \tag{9.52}$$

This is a straightforward way to model asymmetry, here called the GJR(1, 1) model following the work of Glosten, Jagannathan, and Runkle (1993). The squared residual is multiplied by $\alpha + \alpha^-$ when the return is below its conditional expectation ($S_{t-1} = 1$) and by α when the return is above or equal to the expected value ($S_{t-1} = 0$). The parameters are usually constrained by $\omega \geqslant 0$, $\alpha > 0$, $\alpha + \alpha^- > 0$, and $\beta \geqslant 0$. The GJR(p, q) model is defined by adding p terms to the right side of equation (9.36), so that

$$h_t = \omega + \sum_{i=1}^{p} (\alpha_i + \alpha_i^- S_{t-1}) e_{t-i}^2 + \sum_{j=1}^{q} \beta_j h_{t-j}.$$

To obtain theoretical results we will assume that the standardized residuals have symmetric, continuous distributions. Then $E[S_{t-1}] = \frac{1}{2}$, and S_{t-1} is independent of z_{t-1}^2. Some formulae for the GJR(1, 1) model can be obtained by replacing α in the corresponding GARCH(1, 1) formulae by the average weight on the term e_{t-1}^2, i.e. by $\alpha + \frac{1}{2}\alpha^-$. For example, the persistence parameter of the process can be deduced by writing

$$h_{t+1} = \omega + ((\alpha + \alpha^- S_t) z_t^2 + \beta) h_t \tag{9.53}$$

and then taking expectations at time $t - 1$:

$$E[h_{t+1} \mid I_{t-1}] = \omega + (\alpha + \tfrac{1}{2}\alpha^- + \beta) h_t.$$

Therefore, the persistence parameter is $\phi = \alpha + \frac{1}{2}\alpha^- + \beta$. Also, forecasts of volatility are provided by (9.20) with α replaced by $\alpha + \frac{1}{2}\alpha^-$.

The process is both covariance stationary and strictly stationary when $\phi < 1$ and then the unconditional variance is $\sigma^2 = \omega/(1 - \phi)$. Replacing α in the GARCH(1, 1) equations by $\alpha + \frac{1}{2}\alpha^-$ does not provide correct fourth moments. It can be shown that the kurtosis of returns for the GJR(1, 1) process is finite when $k_z = E[z_t^4]$ is finite and

$$\gamma = (\alpha + \tfrac{1}{2}\alpha^- + \beta)^2 + (\alpha + \tfrac{1}{2}\alpha^-)^2 (k_z - 1) + \tfrac{1}{4} k_z (\alpha^-)^2 \tag{9.54}$$

is less than one. The kurtosis then equals

$$\text{kurtosis}(r_t) = k_z \frac{1 - (\alpha + \tfrac{1}{2}\alpha^- + \beta)^2}{1 - \gamma} \tag{9.55}$$

and the autocorrelations of squared residuals, $s_t = (r_t - \mu)^2$, decrease geometrically, at the persistence rate $\phi = \alpha + \frac{1}{2}\alpha^- + \beta$; thus,

$$\rho_\tau = \text{cor}(s_t, s_{t+\tau}) = \phi^{\tau-1}\rho_1, \qquad \tau > 0,$$
$$\rho_1 = \frac{(\phi - \beta)(1 - \beta\phi) + \delta\phi}{1 - 2\beta\phi + \beta^2 + \delta}, \tag{9.56}$$

with

$$\delta = \frac{k_z (\alpha^-)^2}{4(k_z - 1)}.$$

These results can be derived from formulae for a family of extended GARCH(1, 1) processes proved by He and Teräsvirta (1999, equations 8 and 21) and by Ling and McAleer (2002).

9.8   Equity Examples of Asymmetric Volatility Models

One of the simplest asymmetric volatility models to estimate is the GJR(1, 1) model. This model can be estimated without difficulty using Excel software, by adapting the methods for the GARCH(1, 1) model presented in Section 9.4. Estimation and results are illustrated here for the daily observations of the S&P 100-share index from January 1991 to December 2000, defined and graphed in Section 2.2.

Researchers often specify the conditional mean to be a function of previous returns, so we include both MA(1) and ARCH-M terms in the model to illustrate how these features can be included in estimation software. The GJR(1, 1)-MA(1)-M model estimated here is defined by combining equations (9.34), (9.35), and (9.52). Prices p_t, returns (ignoring dividends) r_t, conditional means μ_t, conditional variances h_t, residuals e_t, and standardized residuals z_t are connected by the system of equations

$$r_t = \log(p_t/p_{t-1}) = \mu_t + e_t = \mu_t + h_t^{1/2} z_t, \tag{9.57}$$

$$\mu_t = \mu + \lambda h_t^{1/2} + \Theta e_{t-1}, \tag{9.58}$$

$$S_{t-1} = \begin{cases} 1 & \text{if } e_{t-1} \leqslant 0, \\ 0 & \text{if } e_{t-1} > 0, \end{cases} \tag{9.59}$$

and

$$h_t = \omega + \alpha e_{t-1}^2 + \alpha^- S_{t-1} e_{t-1}^2 + \beta h_{t-1}. \tag{9.60}$$

Readers who are not interested in the calculations for this model should skip to the subsection headed "S&P 100 results" on p. 225.

9.8.1   Calculations

Less detail about the calculations is given here than for the GARCH(1, 1) example presented in Section 9.4. The focus here is on those aspects of the calculations that are not required for the simpler GARCH(1, 1) model.

Initially, we suppose the conditional distribution is normal and then there are seven terms in the parameter vector,

$$\theta = (\mu, \lambda, \omega, \Theta, \alpha, \alpha^-, \beta)'. \tag{9.61}$$

The parameters are estimated by maximizing the log-likelihood, given by equation (9.33), which is a function of θ. This can be done directly or by maximizing over a reparametrized vector. The results here are obtained by maximizing over

$$\theta^* = (10^3(\mu + \lambda s), \lambda, \Theta, \alpha, A, \phi, 10^4 \sigma^2)' \tag{9.62}$$

	A	B
1	**Summary stats.**	Returns r(t)
2	Mean	0.0005924
3	Standard deviation	0.0098623
4	Skewness	-0.286
5	Kurtosis	8.045
6	Lag 1 correlation	-0.0242
7		
8	Minimum	-0.0752
9	Maximum	0.0561

	F (Parameter / Model)	G (Value)
2	Mu	0.0000995
3	Lambda	0.0500
4	Theta	-0.0200
5	Omega	1.000E-06
6	Alpha	0.0200
7	Alpha minus	0.0400
8	Beta	0.9500
11	*Reparametrized*	
12	(Mu+Lambda*s)*1000	0.5926
13	Lambda	0.0500
14	Theta	-0.0200
15	Alpha	0.0200
16	Asymmetry A	3.0000
17	Persistence	0.9900
18	Variance*10000	1.0000
	log L	8417.42

Date	Index p(t)	Return r(t)	Mean mu(t)	Variance h(t)	Residual e(t)	St resid z(t)	Sign S(t)	Log density l(t)
2 Jan 91	153.36							
3 Jan 91	151.44	-0.012599	0.000592	0.00009726	-0.013191	-1.3375	1	2.8056
4 Jan 91	151.28	-0.001057	0.000873	0.00010384	-0.001930	-0.1894	1	3.6494
7 Jan 91	148.53	-0.018345	0.000638	0.00009987	-0.018983	-1.8995	1	1.8828
8 Jan 91	148.15	-0.002562	0.001021	0.00011750	-0.003583	-0.3305	1	3.5510
9 Jan 91	146.05	-0.014276	0.000704	0.00011340	-0.014980	-1.4067	1	2.6339
10 Jan 91	147.68	0.011099	0.000952	0.00012219	0.010147	0.9179	0	3.1647

Exhibit 9.3. An example of calculations for the S&P 100 index, 1991–2000, GJR(1, 1)-MA(1)-M model with conditional normal distributions.

Table 9.2. Formulae used in the GJR(1, 1)-MA(1)-M spreadsheets.

Cell	Formula
Exhibits 9.3–9.6	
D26	=B3
D27	=$G$3+($G$4*SQRT(E27))+($G$5*F26)
E26	=B4*B4
E27	=$G$6+(($G$7+$G$8*H26)*F26*F26)+($G$9*E26)
F26	=C26-D26
G3	=0.001*G12-(G13*B4)
G4	=G13
G5	=G14
G6	=G18*(1-G17)/10000
G7	=G15
G8	=(G16-1)*G15
G9	=G17-G7-0.5*G8
G26	=F26/SQRT(E26)
H26	=IF(G26<0,1,0)
Exhibits 9.3 and 9.4	
I26	=-0.5*LN(2*PI())-0.5*LN(E26)-0.5*G26*G26
Exhibit 9.5	
B14	=G10
B15	=B14-2
B16	=(B14+1)/2
B17	=GAMMALN(B16)-GAMMALN(B14/2)-0.5*LN(PI()*B15)
G10	=IF(G19>0.00001,1/G19,"infinity")
I26	=$B$17-0.5*LN(E26)-$B$16*LN(1+(G26*G26/$B$15))
Exhibit 9.6	
B14	=G10
B15	=GAMMALN(1/B14)
B16	=GAMMALN(3/B14)
B17	=0.5*(B15-B16)-(LN(2)/B14)
B18	=0.5*(B16-3*B15)+LN(B14/2)
G10	=G19
I26	=$B$18-0.5*LN(E26)-0.5*IF(ABS(G26)>0, EXP($B$14*(LN(ABS(G26))-$B$17)),0)

with s the sample standard deviation of the observed returns, $A = (\alpha + \alpha^-)/\alpha$, $\phi = \alpha + \frac{1}{2}\alpha^- + \beta$, and $\sigma^2 = \omega/(1 - \phi)$. The first component of θ^* is approximately a multiple of the conditional mean when the conditional variance is at its median level.

Exhibit 9.3 shows some of the calculations for an initial guess at the optimal value of θ^*. The initial guess is in cells G12 to G18 and the corresponding vector θ is in cells G3 to G9. The terms in θ are used to calculate the conditional means and variances, etc. At time t we know μ_t and h_t, because they are calculated from information known at time $t-1$. We then use the return r_t to calculate e_t, z_t, S_t, l_t,

h_{t+1}, and μ_{t+1}, in that order. The quantity l_t is the contribution of observation t to the log-likelihood function and is defined by equation (9.27). The initial values for the mean and variance in cells D26 and E26 are given by the summary statistics for the whole sample. After formulae are entered into cells F26, G26, H26, I26, E27, and D27, all of the remaining cells can be filled by copying and pasting. Table 9.2 provides a list of the relevant formulae.

The Excel tool Solver can find the maximum of the log-likelihood function. Suitable constraints on θ^* when estimating the stationary GJR(1, 1) model are $\alpha \geqslant 0.0001, A \geqslant 0, \phi \leqslant 0.9999$, and $\sigma^2 \geqslant 0$. The maximum likelihood estimates are shown in Exhibit 9.4 and are discussed in Section 9.8.2.

Next suppose we are also interested in estimating the model with nonnormal conditional distributions. We first assume the conditional distribution is the standardized t-distribution with ν degrees of freedom. There are then eight parameters to estimate and $\theta = (\mu, \lambda, \omega, \Theta, \alpha, \alpha^-, \beta, \nu)'$. As ν can be anywhere between 2 and infinity it is easier to estimate its reciprocal, which is between 0 and $\frac{1}{2}$. Then ν^{-1} is the eighth term in θ^* and the additional constraint $0.001 \leqslant \nu^{-1} \leqslant 0.499$ is appropriate when estimating the parameters using Solver. The only change that needs to be made to the calculations concerns the terms l_t. From equations (9.43) and (9.48),

$$l_t = -\tfrac{1}{2}\log(h_t) + \log(c(\nu)) - \frac{\nu+1}{2}\log\left(1 + \frac{z_t^2}{\nu-2}\right) \qquad (9.63)$$

with $c(\nu)$ defined by (9.44). Exhibit 9.5 shows the result of maximizing the log-likelihood function. Cells B14 to B17 are used to hold functions of ν. In particular, $\log(c(\nu))$ is in B17, with the values of $\log(\Gamma(\cdot))$ provided by the function GAMMALN. The spreadsheet formulae for l_t and $\log(c(\nu))$ are included in Table 9.2.

Similar methods provide the results when the conditional distribution is the generalized error distribution with tail-thickness parameter η. The eighth term in both θ and θ^* is η, and the constraint $\eta \geqslant 0.01$ is appropriate. The expression for l_t becomes

$$l_t = -\tfrac{1}{2}\log(h_t) + \log(C(\eta)) - \tfrac{1}{2}(|z_t|/\lambda(\eta))^\eta \qquad (9.64)$$

with $C(\eta)$ and $\lambda(\eta)$ defined by (9.46). Exhibit 9.6 shows the result of maximizing the log-likelihood function. Cells B14–B18 contain functions of η. In particular, $\log(C(\eta))$ and $\log(\lambda(\eta))$ are respectively in B18 and B17. Once more, relevant spreadsheet formulae are included in Table 9.2.

9.8.2 S&P 100 Index Results, 1991–2000

Table 9.3 lists the GJR(1, 1)-MA(1)-M parameter estimates for the three conditional distributions, normal, t, and GED. Standard errors are shown in brackets and are calculated using the methods described later in Section 10.4.

Summary stats.	Returns r(t)	Standardized z(t)			Parameter — Model	Value		
Mean	0.0005924	-0.007			Mu	-0.0006073		
Standard deviation	0.0098623	1.0021			Lambda	0.1377		
Skewness	-0.286	-0.489			Theta	0.0110		
Kurtosis	8.045	5.501			Omega	1.150E-06		
Lag 1 correlation	-0.0242	0.0065			Alpha	0.0108		
					Alpha minus	0.0869		
Minimum	-0.0752	-7.02			Beta	0.9324		
Maximum	0.0561	3.92						
					Reparametrized			
					(Mu+Lambda*s)*1000	0.7503		
					Lambda	0.1377		
					Theta	0.0110		
					Alpha	0.0108		
					Asymmetry A	9.0429		
					Persistence	0.9867		
					Variance*10000	0.8627		
					log L	8430.94		

Date	Index p(t)	Return r(t)	Mean mu(t)	Variance h(t)	Residual e(t)	St resid z(t)	Sign S(t)	Log density l(t)
2 Jan 91	153.36							
3 Jan 91	151.44	-0.012599	0.000592	0.00009726	-0.013191	-1.3375	1	2.8056
4 Jan 91	151.28	-0.001057	0.000683	0.00010884	-0.001740	-0.1668	1	3.6300
7 Jan 91	148.53	-0.018345	0.00077	0.00010293	-0.019116	-1.8841	1	1.8968
8 Jan 91	148.15	-0.002562	0.000768	0.00013282	-0.003330	-0.2889	1	3.5026
9 Jan 91	146.05	-0.014276	0.000902	0.00012608	-0.015178	-1.3517	1	2.6568
10 Jan 91	147.68	0.011099	0.000861	0.00014122	0.010238	0.8615	0	3.1426

Exhibit 9.4. Parameter estimates for the S&P 100 index, 1991–2000, GJR(1, 1)-MA(1)-M model with conditional normal distributions.

	A	B	C	D	E	F	G	H	I
1	**Summary stats.**								
2		Returns r(t)	Standardized z(t)			Parameter / Model	Value		
3	Mean	0.0005924	-0.021			Mu	-0.0002560		
4	Standard deviation	0.0098623	1.0046			Lambda	0.1112		
5	Skewness	-0.286	-0.494			Theta	-0.0111		
6	Kurtosis	8.045	5.566			Omega	7.521E-07		
7	Lag 1 correlation	-0.0242	0.0255			Alpha	0.0123		
8						Alpha minus	0.0784		
9	Minimum	-0.0752	-7.08			Beta	0.9398		
10	Maximum	0.0561	3.92			nu (d.o.f.)	6.616		
11						*Reparametrized*			
12						(Mu+Lambda*s)*1000	0.8409		
13	**Student terms**					Lambda	0.1112		
14	nu	6.6160				Theta	-0.0111		
15	nu - 2	4.6160				Alpha	0.0123		
16	(nu + 1)/2	3.8080				Asymmetry A	7.3827		
17	log of c(nu)	-0.7766				Persistence	0.9913		
18						Variance*10000	0.8654		
19						1/nu (inverse d.o.f.)	0.1511		
20									
21						log L	8495.13		
22									
23									
24	Date	Index p(t)	Return r(t)	Mean mu(t)	Variance h(t)	Residual e(t)	St resid z(t)	Sign S(t)	Log density l(t)
25	2 Jan 91	153.36							
26	3 Jan 91	151.44	-0.012599	0.000592	0.00009726	-0.013191	-1.3375	1	2.5952
27	4 Jan 91	151.28	-0.001057	0.001057	0.00010795	-0.002104	-0.2025	1	3.7567
28	7 Jan 91	148.53	-0.018345	0.000894	0.00010260	-0.019240	-1.8994	1	1.6167
29	8 Jan 91	148.15	-0.002562	0.001230	0.00013077	-0.003792	-0.3316	1	3.6048
30	9 Jan 91	146.05	-0.014276	0.001029	0.00012495	-0.015306	-1.3693	1	2.4192
31	10 Jan 91	147.68	0.011099	0.001228	0.00013944	0.009871	0.8359	0	3.1256

Exhibit 9.5. Parameter estimates for the S&P 100 index, 1991–2000, GJR(1, 1)-MA(1)-M model with conditional *t*-distributions.

	Returns r(t)	Standardized z(t)	Parameter (Model)	Value
Summary stats.				
Mean	0.0005924	-0.011	Mu	-0.0003306
Standard deviation	0.0098623	1.0065	Lambda	0.1092
Skewness	-0.286	-0.495	Theta	-0.0163
Kurtosis	8.045	5.547	Omega	8.419E-07
Lag 1 correlation	-0.0242	0.0303	Alpha	0.0119
			Alpha minus	0.0789
Minimum	-0.0752	-7.05	Beta	0.9389
Maximum	0.0561	3.94	eta	1.362
			Reparametrized	
			(Mu+Lambda*s)*1000	0.7465
GED terms			Lambda	0.1092
eta	1.3619		Theta	-0.0163
log G(eta inv)	0.2207		Alpha	0.0119
log G(3* eta inv)	0.0985		Asymmetry A	7.6581
log lambda	-0.4479		Persistence	0.9902
log C	-0.6660		Variance*10000	0.8614
			eta	1.362
			log L	8487.82

Date	Index p(t)	Return r(t)	Mean mu(t)	Variance h(t)	Residual e(t)	St resid z(t)	Sign S(t)	Log density l(t)
2 Jan 91	153.36							
3 Jan 91	151.44	-0.012599	0.000592	0.00009726	-0.013191	-1.3375	1	2.5857
4 Jan 91	151.28	-0.001057	0.001019	0.00010796	-0.002076	-0.1998	1	3.7982
7 Jan 91	148.53	-0.018345	0.000809	0.00010260	-0.019155	-1.8911	1	1.7349
8 Jan 91	148.15	-0.002562	0.001229	0.00013048	-0.003791	-0.3318	1	3.6013
9 Jan 91	146.05	-0.014276	0.000950	0.00012466	-0.015227	-1.3638	1	2.4249
10 Jan 91	147.68	0.011099	0.001205	0.00013893	0.009894	0.8394	0	3.0497

Exhibit 9.6.   Parameter estimates for the S&P 100 index, 1991–2000, GJR(1, 1)-MA(1)-M model with conditional GED distributions.

Table 9.3.   Parameter estimates for a GJR model estimated from the S&P 100 index. (The GJR(1, 1)-MA(1)-M model is defined by equations (9.57)–(9.60). The conditional distributions are either normal or nonnormal as defined in Section 9.6. The data are the daily values of the S&P 100 index from January 1991 to December 2000. Standard errors are shown in brackets.)

Parameter	Normal	Distribution t	GED
$\mu \times 10^4$	−6.07 (5.44)	−2.56 (4.45)	−3.31 (4.35)
λ	0.1377 (0.0687)	0.1112 (0.0577)	0.1092 (0.0566)
Θ	0.0110 (0.0203)	−0.0111 (0.0207)	−0.0163 (0.0199)
$\omega \times 10^6$	1.150 (0.338)	0.752 (0.214)	0.842 (0.217)
α	0.0108 (0.0097)	0.0123 (0.0106)	0.0119 (0.0113)
α^-	0.0869 (0.0219)	0.0784 (0.0153)	0.0789 (0.0151)
β	0.9324 (0.0114)	0.9398 (0.0088)	0.9389 (0.0088)
ν		6.616 (0.771)	
η			1.362 (0.020)
$A = (\alpha + \alpha^-)/\alpha$	9.043	7.383	7.658
$\phi = \alpha + 0.5\alpha^- + \beta$	0.9867 (0.0054)	0.9913 (0.0041)	0.9902 (0.0042)
$\sigma^2 \times 10^4$	0.8627	0.8654	0.8614
$\log(L)$	8430.94	8495.13	8487.82

Most of the estimates are similar across the distributions and the numbers discussed in this paragraph are for the normal specification. Of primary interest are the estimates of α^- in comparison with the estimates of α. With $\hat{\alpha}^- = 0.0869$ and $\hat{\alpha} = 0.0108$, negative residuals have much more impact on the conditional variance than do positive residuals. The squares of negative and positive residuals are respectively multiplied by 0.0977 and 0.0108. The estimated asymmetry ratio is remarkably high, being $\hat{A} = 0.0977/0.0108 = 9.0$. The review of asymmetry ratios in Section 10.2 will show that the level of estimated asymmetry for 1991–2000 is higher than for previous time periods. Adding half of $\hat{\alpha}^-$ to $\hat{\alpha}$ and to the estimate $\hat{\beta} = 0.9342$ gives the persistence estimate $\hat{\phi} = 0.9867$. Variance forecasts then have half-life $H = \log(0.5)/\log(\hat{\phi}) = 52$ trading periods, which

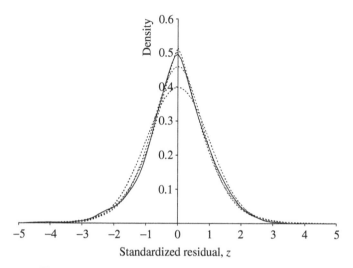

Figure 9.5. Density estimates for standardized residuals.

is two and a half months. The estimates of the three parameters that determine the conditional mean are $\hat{\Theta} = 0.0108$, which is insignificantly different from zero, $\hat{\mu} = -6.073 \times 10^{-4}$, and $\hat{\lambda} = 0.1377$. The positive sign for $\hat{\lambda}$ is plausible, while the negative sign for $\hat{\mu}$ is not; the null hypothesis $\lambda = 0$ is tested in Section 10.5 and just rejected at the 5% level.

The levels of kurtosis calculated from the standardized residuals are 5.50, 5.57, and 5.55 for the three conditional distributions. The standard errors of these estimates are 0.10 when the conditional distribution is normal and hence that hypothesis is unsustainable. The estimated shape parameters are $\hat{\nu} = 6.62$ for the t-distribution and $\hat{\eta} = 1.362$ for the GED, implying kurtosis levels of 5.29 and 4.13 for the standardized residuals. The t-distribution matches the sample kurtosis better and it also has a higher maximum value for the log-likelihood than the GED. Figure 9.5 shows a kernel estimate of the density of the standardized residuals from the normal specification (solid curve), for comparison with the standard normal density, the estimated t density and the estimated GED (three dotted curves); the kernel estimate is defined by equation (4.6) with bandwidth equal to 0.2. The nonnormal densities provide a much better fit to the kernel density than the normal density. The maxima of the densities are 0.40 (normal), 0.46 (t), 0.50 (kernel), and 0.51 (GED).

The condition for the models to have finite kurtosis for the returns is $\gamma < 1$, with γ defined by (9.54). The estimates of γ are 1.002 for the t-distribution and 0.995 for the GED, indicating that any appropriate model may have an infinite fourth moment for returns.

Figure 9.6 shows the ten-year time series of volatility estimates from 1991 to 2000 given by the annualized conditional standard deviations, $\sigma_t = \sqrt{253 h_t}$;

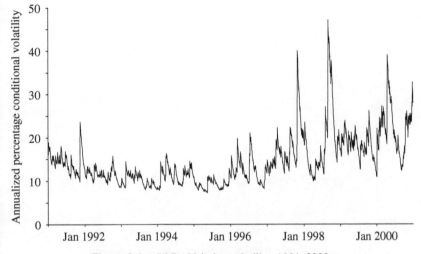

Figure 9.6. S&P 100 index volatility, 1991–2000.

the scaling constant (253) is the average number of returns per annum in the time series. These estimates of σ_t are for the conditional normal specification and differ only slightly from the estimates for the t-specification. The volatility estimates are plotted as percentages and range from 7.3% in May 1995 to 47.1% in September 1998. Half of the estimates are inside the interquartile range, from 10.5% to 17.6%. The median and mean values are 13.0% and 14.6% respectively. Figure 9.6 shows that the second half of the returns series was more volatile than the first half, with average levels of 11.3% from 1991 to 1995 and 17.9% from 1996 to 2000. This might be evidence either that the index returns process was not stationary throughout the decade or that the volatility process has a long memory. Ignoring the MA(1) term, the conditional mean is determined by the conditional variance as $\mu_t = \mu + \lambda h_t^{1/2}$. The annualized values, $253\mu_t$, vary considerably, with minimum 0.7% and interquartile range from 7.7% to 23.2%.

Figures 9.7 and 9.8 show the annualized conditional standard deviations and the annualized percentage returns for one year of high volatility and for one year of low volatility. The scales are the same for the two figures.

Figure 9.7 shows high levels of index volatility throughout nearly all of the year 2000. The new millennium commences with volatility at 11% and then shoots up to 22% following a fall in the index of 3.8% on 4 January. Thereafter, volatility remains above the median level for the decade. It is, of course, the large market falls that increase the volatility of this series dramatically. The largest fall during the year was 6.0% on 14 April, which moves the volatility estimate from 25% to 39%. The fall was more than reversed after the weekend by rises of 4.1% and 3.0% on 17 and 18 April, despite which volatility fell slightly because little weight is given by the estimated model to the squares of positive residuals. Five months

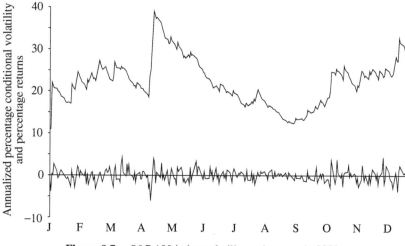

Figure 9.7.   S&P 100 index volatility and returns in 2000.

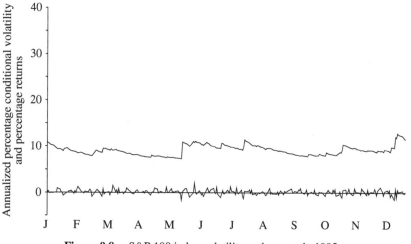

Figure 9.8.   S&P 100 index volatility and returns in 1995.

later volatility had declined to 13%, to be followed by a general increase in the final quarter of the year. Falls of 3.0% and 3.8% on 15 and 20 December move the volatility back up to 33%.

Figure 9.8 shows much lower levels of volatility in 1995. The lowest level of 7.3% is near the estimated lower bound for the model, which is equal to $253\hat{\omega}/(1 - \hat{\beta}) = 6.1\%$. It is followed by 10.9% on the next day, responding to the lowest return during the year, equal to -1.6% on 18 May. The highest volatility estimate is 12.9% on 21 December and hence volatility throughout the year is below the ten-year median level.

9.9 Summary

ARCH models define conditional distributions for returns that are characterized by time-varying conditional variances. The parameters of these models can be estimated by maximizing the likelihood of observed returns and hence the volatility of returns can be calculated. Many choices can be made in selecting a model, so that an accurate description of the process generating observed returns becomes a realistic aspiration. Additional accuracy may require models that are more complex than those presented so far. Further models, likelihood theory, and methods for selecting a model are the major topics in the next chapter.

Further Reading

Bollerslev, T. 1986. Generalized autoregressive conditional heteroscedasticity. *Journal of Econometrics* 31:307–327.

Bollerslev, T., R. Y. Chou, and K. F. Kroner. 1992. ARCH modeling in finance: a review of the theory and empirical evidence. *Journal of Econometrics* 52:5–59.

Engle, R. F. 1982. Autoregressive conditional heteroscedasticity with estimates of the variance of United Kingdom inflation. *Econometrica* 50:987–1007.

Glosten, L. R., R. Jagannathan, and D. Runkle. 1993. Relationship between the expected value and the volatility of the nominal excess return on stocks. *Journal of Finance* 48:1779–1801.

10
ARCH Models: Selection and Likelihood Methods

Several additional ARCH models are described in this chapter. Methods for selecting a model from the many possibilities are given, including hypothesis tests that use maximum likelihood estimates and their standard errors.

10.1 Introduction

There seem to be few limits to the complexity that can be built into an ARCH model. The simple examples described in Chapter 9 suffice for many purposes. There are, however, applications that require more complicated structures, as does the search for more accurate descriptions of observed returns. The exponential GARCH model of Nelson (1991) is another asymmetric volatility model. It is described in Section 10.2, where we consider asymmetric specifications and evidence in some detail. The long memory extension of EGARCH investigated by Bollerslev and Mikkelsen (1996) is presented in Section 10.3. It is a significant advance in the search for a better model.

Deciding if one model is better than another often requires hypothesis tests that involve parameter estimates and their standard errors. The appropriate likelihood theory for estimates, standard errors, and tests is documented in Section 10.4, with examples from the research literature discussed in Section 10.5. The final selection of an ARCH model may either reflect pragmatic concerns or a belief that no further useful progress can be made. Section 10.6 provides details of diagnostic checks that are often used to assess the adequacy of a model.

Section 10.7 mentions additional interesting specifications that are beyond the scope of this chapter, including multivariate models. Finally, Section 10.8 concludes the two ARCH chapters.

10.2 Asymmetric Volatility: Further Specifications and Evidence

We recall some notation: returns r_t have conditional means and variances respectively denoted by μ_t and h_t, the residuals are $e_t = r_t - \mu_t$, and the standardized residuals are $z_t = e_t/\sqrt{h_t}$.

10.2.1 EGARCH

Another popular way to introduce asymmetry into conditional variances was developed by Nelson (1991). He proposed ARMA models for the logarithm of h_t. To appreciate why these might be plausible, consider the special case of the integrated GARCH(1, 1) model (9.19) when $\omega = 0$; then

$$h_t = \alpha e_{t-1}^2 + (1 - \alpha)h_{t-1},$$

which implies

$$(h_t - h_{t-1})/h_{t-1} = \alpha(z_{t-1}^2 - 1).$$

When α is small, this process is similar to a random walk with i.i.d. steps for $\log(h_t) \cong (h_t - h_{t-1})/h_{t-1}$. Thus a family of processes in some ways similar to GARCH(1, 1) can be defined by supposing that $\log(h_t)$ is an AR(1) process with residuals that are an appropriate symmetric function of the standardized residuals z_{t-1}. Nelson (1991) goes beyond this symmetric framework by employing a particular asymmetric function $g(z_{t-1})$ for the volatility residuals.

Nelson's simplest stationary EGARCH model assumes returns have conditional distributions that are normal with constant mean and with variances given by

$$\log(h_t) = \mu_{\log(h)} + \Delta(\log(h_{t-1}) - \mu_{\log(h)}) + g(z_{t-1}) \qquad (10.1)$$

and

$$g(z_{t-1}) = \vartheta z_{t-1} + \gamma(|z_{t-1}| - \sqrt{2/\pi}). \qquad (10.2)$$

The four variance parameters are the mean $\mu_{\log(h)}$ of the process $\log(h_t)$, the autoregressive parameter Δ, and the two parameters, ϑ and γ, that appear in the function g. The terms $g(z_{t-1})$ have zero mean, because $\sqrt{2/\pi}$ is the expectation of $|z_{t-1}|$ when z_{t-1} has a normal distribution. The terms $g(z_{t-1})$ are also i.i.d., since the variables z_{t-1} have the same properties. Thus equations (10.1) and (10.2) define an AR(1) process for $\log(h_t)$ that is stationary when $-1 < \Delta < 1$. As h_t is the exponential of an AR(1) process, the model for returns is called EGARCH(1).

The volatility residual function $g(z)$ is defined by two straight lines that join at $z = 0$. The function has slope $\vartheta - \gamma$ when z is negative (the market falls) and slope $\vartheta + \gamma$ when z is positive (the market rises). Figure 10.1 shows $g(z)$ as dotted lines when $\vartheta = -0.11$ and $\gamma = 0.22$, as estimated by Nelson (1989) for an index of 90 US stocks from 1928 to 1956. The estimated function for a later period is also shown, by solid lines, using $\vartheta = -0.12$ and $\gamma = 0.16$, from estimates in Nelson (1991) for the CRSP value-weighted US market index from 1962 to 1987. It can be seen that a large standardized residual will increase conditional volatility, but by much more when the market moves down.

EGARCH models with nonnormal conditional distributions are defined by a small change to equation (10.2). The constant $\sqrt{2/\pi}$ is replaced by the expectation

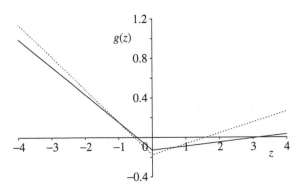

Figure 10.1. Examples of the function $g(z)$.

of $|z_{t-1}|$ to ensure that the expectation of $g(z_{t-1})$ is zero; thus,

$$g(z_{t-1}) = \vartheta z_{t-1} + \gamma (|z_{t-1}| - E[|z_{t-1}|]). \tag{10.3}$$

The required expectation for the standardized t-distribution with ν degrees of freedom is

$$E[|z_{t-1}|] = \frac{2\sqrt{\nu - 2}\,\Gamma[(\nu + 1)/2]}{\sqrt{\pi}(\nu - 1)\Gamma[\nu/2]}, \tag{10.4}$$

while for the GED distribution, with thickness parameter η, it equals

$$E[|z_{t-1}|] = \Gamma(2\eta^{-1})/\{\Gamma(\eta^{-1})\Gamma(3\eta^{-1})\}^{1/2}.$$

The general EGARCH(p, q) model of Nelson (1991) represents $\log(h_t)$ as an ARMA(p, q) process, with residuals defined by (10.3). He proves many results. In particular, the returns process is strictly stationary if and only if the ARMA process is strictly stationary. Returns are covariance stationary when they are both strictly stationary and have finite variance. Strictly stationary processes with conditional normal distributions or conditional GED distributions, with $\eta > 1$, have all moments finite. However, conditional t-distributions typically have no finite unconditional moments for returns. The autocorrelations of squared residuals (when they exist) are given by very complicated formulae. A geometric decay formula can be obtained for the EGARCH(1) model, for the autocorrelations of the logarithms of squared residuals (when they exist), because

$$\log((r_t - \mu)^2) = \log(h_t) + \log(z_t^2)$$

is the sum of AR(1) and white noise processes (Taylor 1994a).

10.2.2 Further Examples

There are many more asymmetric volatility models in the literature (e.g. in Hentschel 1995), three of which are mentioned here. Franses and van Dijk (2000) discuss these and other specifications in some detail. The conditional variance in the GJR(1, 1) model includes the squared residual multiplied by a function of the residual; thus,

$$h_t = \omega + w(e_{t-1})e_{t-1}^2 + \beta h_{t-1} \tag{10.5}$$

with

$$w(e_{t-1}) = \begin{cases} \alpha + \alpha^- & \text{if } e_{t-1} < 0, \\ \alpha & \text{if } e_{t-1} \geqslant 0. \end{cases} \tag{10.6}$$

Changing the weighting function to

$$w(e_{t-1}) = \alpha + \frac{\gamma}{e_{t-1}} \tag{10.7}$$

defines the quadratic GARCH(1, 1) model of Sentana (1995), that has

$$h_t = \omega + \gamma e_{t-1} + \alpha e_{t-1}^2 + \beta h_{t-1} = \omega - \frac{\gamma^2}{4\alpha} + \alpha \left[e_{t-1} + \frac{\gamma}{2\alpha} \right]^2 + \beta h_{t-1}.$$

This specification is more flexible in one respect than some others because it does not assume that the next period's variance is minimized when the latest residual is zero; rather, h_t is symmetric around $e_{t-1} = -\gamma/(2\alpha)$.

Function (10.6) changes abruptly at $e_{t-1} = 0$, while function (10.7) has identical limits as $e_{t-1} \to \pm\infty$. Both drawbacks are avoided by a smooth transition specification (Hagerud 1997; González-Rivera 1998), such as

$$w(e_{t-1}) = \alpha + \frac{\delta}{1 + \exp(\zeta e_{t-1})}, \quad \zeta > 0. \tag{10.8}$$

The weight then changes monotonically as e_{t-1} increases, from $\alpha + \delta$ (as $e_{t-1} \to -\infty$) to α (as $e_{t-1} \to \infty$) and it equals the mid value $\alpha + \frac{1}{2}\delta$ when $e_{t-1} = 0$. The additional parameter ζ controls the rate at which the weights change. As $\zeta \to \infty$, the GJR(1, 1) specification is obtained with $\alpha^- = \delta$.

Weighted combinations of absolute residuals can also be used to define conditional variances. The threshold GARCH(1, 1) model of Zakoïan (1994) defines conditional standard deviations $h_t^{1/2}$ by

$$h_t^{1/2} = \omega + \alpha |e_{t-1}| + \alpha^- S_{t-1} |e_{t-1}| + \beta h_{t-1}^{1/2}, \tag{10.9}$$

with S_{t-1} equal to 1 when e_{t-1} is negative and equal to 0 otherwise. This is similar to the GJR(1, 1) model, but with h and e^2 in (9.52) respectively replaced by $\sqrt{h}$ and $|e|$. The symmetric special case, when $\alpha^- = 0$, is the absolute value GARCH(1, 1) model of Taylor (1986).

10.2.3 News Impact Curves

The various asymmetric volatility specifications provide different functional relationships between the next period's conditional variance h_t and the information known at time $t - 1$. The new information at time $t - 1$ is summarized by the

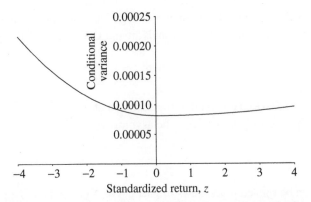

Figure 10.2. News impact curve, GJR model, S&P 100 index.

residual e_{t-1}, while old information is summarized by h_{t-1} and perhaps other variables known at time $t-2$. The news impact curve of Engle and Ng (1993) is defined by considering how h_t varies with e_{t-1}, when all variables known at time $t-2$ are replaced by their unconditional values. The notation $N(e_{t-1})$ is used to represent the curve here.

For variations of GARCH(1, 1) it is sufficient to replace h_{t-1} by the unconditional variance σ^2. Consider, for example, the GJR(1, 1) model defined by (9.52). Then

$$N(e_{t-1}) = h_t(e_{t-1} \mid h_{t-1} = \sigma^2) = \omega + \beta\sigma^2 + (\alpha + \alpha^- S_{t-1})e_{t-1}^2. \quad (10.10)$$

This curve can be written more compactly as two quadratic functions, joined to each other at the vertical axis; thus,

$$N(x) = \begin{cases} N(0) + (\alpha + \alpha^-)x^2 & \text{when } x < 0, \\ N(0) + \alpha x^2 & \text{when } x \geqslant 0, \end{cases} \quad (10.11)$$

with $N(0) = \omega + \beta\sigma^2$. Figure 10.2 is an example of the curve when the parameters are the values given in Exhibit 9.4 for the S&P 100 index. For the EGARCH(1) model, defined by (10.1) and (10.2), the corresponding curve is

$$N(x) = \begin{cases} N(0) \exp((\vartheta + \gamma)x/\sigma) & \text{when } x \geqslant 0, \\ N(0) \exp((\vartheta - \gamma)x/\sigma) & \text{when } x < 0, \end{cases} \quad (10.12)$$

with $N(0) = \sigma^{2\Delta} \exp[(1 - \Delta)\mu_{\log(h)} - \gamma\sqrt{2/\pi}]$ when the conditional distribution is normal. Engle and Ng (1993) provide further examples and also document a nonparametric estimate of the news impact curve. Franses and van Dijk (2000) illustrate the curves for many specifications.

10.2.4 How Much Asymmetry?

The magnitude of the asymmetric volatility effect can be measured by the ratio of the weights given to positive and negative residuals that have the same absolute value. For the GJR(1, 1) model, the squares of negative residuals are multiplied by $\alpha + \alpha^-$ while the squares of positive residuals are multiplied by α. The asymmetry ratio is then defined as

$$A = \frac{\alpha + \alpha^-}{\alpha}. \tag{10.13}$$

Likewise, for the EGARCH(1) model, standardized absolute residuals are multiplied by either $\gamma - \vartheta$ or $\gamma + \vartheta$ so that the asymmetry ratio is

$$A = \frac{\gamma - \vartheta}{\gamma + \vartheta}. \tag{10.14}$$

These ratios can be related to the news impact curve $N(x)$ and its first derivative $N'(x)$. For GJR(1, 1),

$$A = \frac{N(-x) - N(0)}{N(x) - N(0)} = \frac{-N'(-x)}{N'(x)}$$

for all positive x, while the same relation is a good approximation for EGARCH(1) when x is near zero. For other specifications, the function

$$A(x) = \frac{-N'(-x)}{N'(x)}$$

can be used to attempt to summarize the asymmetric effect.

Estimates of A can be inferred from the results in many papers, although the models estimated are often extensions of those mentioned above. Estimates greater than one are frequently found for equity markets. There is no evidence, however, for asymmetric volatility at foreign exchange markets (Taylor 1994a). As DM/\$ and \$/DM volatility are identical, symmetric specifications are then plausible.

Estimates for US stock indices are more than one for samples of daily returns throughout the twentieth century. The estimates of A vary considerably, perhaps reflecting the difficulty of estimating A precisely. The pioneering work of Nelson (1989, 1991) provides $A = 3.2$ for the Standard 90-share index from 1928 to 1956 and $A = 7.2$ for the CRSP value-weighted market index from 1962 to 1987. Brock et al. (1992) estimate $A = 2.3$ for a ninety-year Dow Jones Industrial Average series from 1896 to 1986. Bollerslev et al. (1994) present complicated news impact curves that include more parameters than the examples discussed above. Their results indicate that $A(x)$ is very approximately 2 in each of four periods, 1885–1914, 1914–1928, 1928–1952, and 1953–1990. Bollerslev and Mikkelsen (1996, 1999) estimate long memory EGARCH models for the S&P 500 index and have $A = 3.1$ from 1953 to 1990 and $A = 6.0$ from 1961 to 1991. Evidence for asymmetric effects is also found in monthly US returns from 1815 to 1925, by Goetzmann, Ibbotson, and Peng (2001).

Next, considering more recent years, Blair et al. (2002) show that one extreme return can have a substantial impact on the estimate of A. They find $A = 4.1$ for the S&P 100-share index from 1983 to 1992 and the lower estimate $A = 2.1$ when a dummy variable is used to remove the crash return on 19 October 1987. For the same S&P index, Blair et al. (2001a) report the high value $A = 8.5$ for the GJR model from 1993 to 1998 while Taylor (2002) finds $A = 5$ for a long memory EGARCH model estimated from 1989 to 1998.

Asymmetric volatility effects have been found for individual US firms by Christie (1982), Cheung and Ng (1992), Duffee (1995), and Jubinski and Tomljanovich (2003). Blair et al. (2002) compare volatility results from GJR(1, 1) models for the S&P 100 index with results for all firms that were included in the index at some time during the same decade, from 1983 to 1992. The median estimate of A is 2.3, compared with 4.1 for the index, with the estimated asymmetry for the index exceeding that for 83% of the firms. The estimates of A exceed 1 (i.e. $\alpha^- > 0$) for 95% of the firms, although only 14% of the estimates reject the hypothesis of symmetry (i.e. $A = 1$, $\alpha^- = 0$) at the 5% level.

There is also convincing evidence for asymmetric equity volatility in Japan. Engle and Ng (1993) present many results for the Japanese TOPIX index from 1980 to 1988, including $A = 2.6$ for the GJR model and $A = 1.8$ for the EGARCH model. Their evidence for asymmetry remains significant when the series of returns is truncated to exclude the 1987 crash. Bekaert and Wu (2000), for the overlapping period from 1985 to 1994, find $A = 2.8$ as part of a multivariate model for the Nikkei 225 index and three portfolios.

The evidence is less consistent for the UK. Poon and Taylor (1992) report $A = 1.3$ for the UK FT All-Share index from 1969 to 1989. Taylor (2000) gives estimates for indices and twelve UK firms from 1972 to 1991. The estimates for the firms range from 1 to 1.6 and the majority do not reject the hypothesis $A = 1$ at the 5% level. In contrast, substantial asymmetry ($A = 5.4$) is estimated for the FTSE 100 index in Section 16.2, for the later period from 1992 to 2002.

10.2.5 Explanations

Any economic explanation of asymmetric volatility effects cannot rely on features of modern trading habits, such as the demand for portfolio insurance, because effects are found throughout the last century. The asymmetric effect has often been referred to as a "leverage effect," following Black (1976b), who noted that volatility rises when the market falls and debt/equity ratios increase. However, the asymmetric effect is large while daily changes in leverage are small. Duffee (1995) uses simple methods applied to all 2494 US firms included in a set of CRSP tapes to show that the degree of asymmetry is related to neither debt/equity ratios nor firm size. Bekaert and Wu (2000) show asymmetry is not related to changes in leverage for Japanese portfolios. Their detailed study provides the explanation of covariance asymmetry for the asymmetry in firm volatility: negative market shocks increase conditional covariances between market and stock returns substantially, unlike positive shocks.

Another explanation has been called the "volatility feedback effect" and involves a contemporaneous negative relationship between returns and volatility. Assuming volatility risk is priced, an increase in volatility will raise the required equity return and cause an immediate price decline. Campbell and Hentschel (1992) develop a price model that displays volatility feedback, with the dividend shock being their only state variable. Wu (2001) extends the modeling framework to two state variables, dividend growth and dividend volatility, and provides empirical evidence for weekly and monthly market returns. Both dividend news and volatility feedback are found to be important components of the process that generates returns.

A trading explanation for asymmetric effects in daily volatility at the level of the firm is investigated by Avramov, Chordia, and Goyal (2004). They use transaction databases to identify buyer and seller initiated trades in their study of 2232 NYSE firms. They then show that selling activity governs the asymmetric effect. Their results support their argument that "herding" or uninformed traders sell when prices fall, leading to an increase in volatility, while "contrarian" or informed traders sell after prices rise leading to a reduction in volatility.

10.3   Long Memory ARCH Models

The specific examples of ARCH models presented so far can all explain the stylized fact that the autocorrelations of both absolute returns and squared returns are positive. However, the rate at which such autocorrelations decay towards zero may be incompatible with GARCH and similar models. Stationary GARCH and EGARCH models have a property known as *short memory* and, in particular, the theoretical autocorrelations ρ_τ of conditional variances and squared returns are then geometrically bounded, i.e. $|\rho_\tau| \leqslant C\phi^\tau$ for some $C > 0$ and $1 > \phi > 0$. Empirical autocorrelations for absolute returns and squared returns provide evidence that their theoretical counterparts decay more slowly so that they are not geometrically bounded (Dacorogna, Müller, Nagler, Olsen, and Pictet 1993; Ding et al. 1993; Bollerslev and Mikkelsen 1996). A *long memory* model is then appropriate. Further evidence for long memory effects comes from high-frequency data, as we will see later in Chapter 12, where more detail is provided about the mathematics of long memory processes.

Short memory ARCH models are typically special cases of long memory ARCH models. The special cases correspond to setting a long memory parameter d to zero. It is rather surprising that there are relatively few studies of long memory specifications, because estimates of d usually reject the null hypothesis $d = 0$

comprehensively. This is relevant when pricing options because prices are shown to be sensitive to the parameter d in Section 14.7.

As previously discussed in Section 3.8, long memory models are usually defined by applying the filter $(1 - L)^d$ to a process followed by assuming the filtered process is a stationary ARMA(p, q) process. The lag operator L shifts any process $\{y_t\}$ backwards by one time period, so $Ly_t = y_{t-1}$, while the differencing parameter d is between zero and one for volatility applications. The filter then represents *fractional differencing* and it is defined by the binomial expansion

$$(1 - L)^d = 1 - dL + \frac{d(d - 1)}{2!}L^2 - \frac{d(d - 1)(d - 2)}{3!}L^3 + \cdots . \quad (10.15)$$

The infinite series cannot be simplified when $0 < d < 1$, which may explain why long memory ARCH studies are sparse.

Baillie (1996) and Bollerslev and Mikkelsen (1996) both show how to use the filter $(1 - L)^d$ to define a long memory process for the conditional variance h_t, by making either the GARCH or EGARCH model more general. The GARCH generalization cannot be recommended because the returns process then has infinite variance for all positive values of d, which is incompatible with the stylized facts for asset returns. The EGARCH generalization may not have this drawback, as then $\log(h_t)$ is covariance stationary for $d < \frac{1}{2}$ and it may be conjectured that the returns process has finite variance for some specifications and parameter values.

10.3.1 FIEGARCH$(1, d, 1)$

From Section 10.2, the EGARCH$(1, 1)$ model defines the conditional variance by

$$\log(h_t) = \mu_{\log(h)} + (1 - \Delta L)^{-1}(1 + \psi L)g(z_{t-1})$$

and

$$g(z_{t-1}) = \vartheta z_{t-1} + \gamma(|z_{t-1}| - E[|z_{t-1}|]). \quad (10.16)$$

Inserting the additional filter $(1 - L)^{-d}$ into the function of L that multiplies past values of the volatility shocks $g(z_{t-1})$ gives a model investigated by Bollerslev and Mikkelsen (1996, 1999):

$$\log(h_t) = \mu_{\log(h)} + (1 - \Delta L)^{-1}(1 - L)^{-d}(1 + \psi L)g(z_{t-1}). \quad (10.17)$$

Fractional differencing of $\log(h_t) - \mu_{\log(h)}$ then gives an ARMA$(1, 1)$ process, hence $\log(h_t)$ can be defined by *fractional integration* (FI) of the ARMA process, i.e. it is an ARFIMA$(1, d, 1)$ process. The acronym adopted for the returns process is then FIEGARCH$(1, d, 1)$.

10.3.2 Calculations

Fractional differencing creates computational issues because the expansion in (10.15) must be truncated at some point. The coefficients of the powers L^j are provided by

$$(1-L)^d = 1 - \sum_{j=1}^{\infty} a_j L^j, \quad a_1 = d, \quad a_j = \frac{j-d-1}{j} a_{j-1}, \quad j \geqslant 2, \quad (10.18)$$

and they decay slowly, being asymptotically proportional to $j^{-(1+d)}$. This suggests truncation after a large number of terms, although the truncation limit N must not be too large compared with the number of available observations. The limit $N = 1000$ has often been selected.

Given a choice for N, the conditional variances for the FIEGARCH$(1, d, 1)$ model can be computed from

$$\log(h_t) = \mu_{\log(h)} + \sum_{j=1}^{N} b_j [\log(h_{t-j}) - \mu_{\log(h)}] + g(z_{t-1}) + \psi g(z_{t-2}) \quad (10.19)$$

with the coefficients b_j defined by

$$(1-\Delta L)(1-L)^d = 1 - \sum_{j=1}^{\infty} b_j L^j, \quad b_1 = d + \Delta, \quad b_j = a_j - \Delta a_{j-1}, \quad j \geqslant 2.$$

$$(10.20)$$

For data indexed by times $t \geqslant 1$, some of the times $t - j$ in (10.19) will precede time 1. The terms $\log(h_{t-j})$ can be replaced by $\mu_{\log(h)}$ whenever $t - j \leqslant 0$. To commence calculations, set $\log(h_1) = \mu_{\log(h)}$ and $g(z_0) = 0$. All the conditional variances are influenced by these substitutions. When data are plentiful it may then be advisable to estimate parameters by maximizing the likelihood function for a subperiod that excludes the first 1000 or so observations.

10.3.3 Examples

FIEGARCH$(1, d, 1)$ and more complicated structures are evaluated in Bollerslev and Mikkelsen (1996), using 9559 daily returns of the S&P 500 index from 1953 to 1990. The maximum likelihood estimate of d is 0.633, with a standard error of 0.063, when the conditional distributions are assumed to be normal for the purpose of estimating the parameters. As the estimate is ten standard errors above zero, the null hypothesis $d = 0$ is rejected and hence the ARCH model provides evidence against short memory specifications. Likewise, the null hypothesis $d = 1$ is also rejected, which indicates that an integrated process is not appropriate. Similar results are obtained by Bollerslev and Mikkelsen (1999). For the later period from 1989 to 1998 and the same specification of the variance process, Taylor (2002) estimates d to be 0.57 for daily returns from the S&P 100 index.

All three studies find $d > 0.5$ when the likelihood of the data is maximized for the FIEGARCH$(1, d, 1)$ model. Thus the ARFIMA process for $\log(h_t)$ appears to have an infinite variance. However, we will see evidence in Chapter 12 that high-frequency returns support the claim that d is less than 0.5 for the volatility process of both exchange rates and equity indices.

10.4 Likelihood Methods

In addition to estimating the parameters of a model by maximizing the likelihood function, it is also of interest to test hypotheses about the parameters and to estimate the standard errors of the parameter estimates. Appropriate likelihood theory is presented in Bollerslev and Wooldridge (1992) and in Bollerslev et al. (1994), building on results provided by Engle (1982) and Weiss (1984, 1986). Likelihood theorems are proved for the GARCH$(1, 1)$ model, including the integrated specification IGARCH$(1, 1)$, by Lee and Hansen (1994) and Lumsdaine (1996). Theorems for general ARCH(p) and GARCH(p, q) models are respectively proved by Kristensen and Rahbek (2004) and Ling and McAleer (2003).

The methods and results depend on the specification of the distribution of the standardized residuals. First we consider the maximum likelihood estimate (MLE) when it is necessary to choose a distribution. Then we consider the quasi-MLE (QMLE) approach, which obtains results by maximizing the likelihood when the distribution is assumed normal but this assumption is not made when estimating the standard errors. Finally, some results for the models estimated in Chapter 9 are discussed.

In this section, θ denotes the p parameters of the model, so that $\theta = (\theta_1, \ldots, \theta_p)'$ is a $p \times 1$ vector, and θ_0 denotes the true value of θ. The model states that the conditional mean and variance, $\mu_t(\theta)$ and $h_t(\theta)$, of the return r_t are known at time $t - 1$ from information I_{t-1}. The standardized residuals $z_t = (r_t - \mu_t)/\sqrt{h_t}$ are i.i.d. observations from a distribution whose density function is $f(z \mid \theta)$. The mean and variance functions are assumed to be differentiable as often as necessary.

It is not necessary to assume that the process $\{r_t\}$ is strictly stationary. Many results simplify when it is strictly stationary, however, to classical results for i.i.d. observations that are stated and derived in standard texts (e.g. Greene 2000).

10.4.1 MLE

The likelihood function $L(\theta)$ is the product of conditional densities. Its logarithm is the sum of the logarithms of the conditional densities, which are denoted by $l_t(\theta)$; thus,

$$\log L(\theta) = \sum_{t=1}^{n} l_t(\theta)$$

with

$$l_t(\theta) = \log f(r_t \mid I_{t-1}, \theta) = -\tfrac{1}{2} \log h_t(\theta) + \log f(z_t(\theta)). \qquad (10.21)$$

The partial derivatives of $l_t(\theta)$ define the $p \times 1$ score vector, $s_t(\theta)$, by

$$s_t(\theta_i) = \frac{\partial l_t(\theta)}{\partial \theta_i}, \quad 1 \leqslant i \leqslant p. \qquad (10.22)$$

The MLE, denoted by $\hat{\theta}_{n,\mathrm{ML}}$, maximizes $\log(L(\theta))$, which requires solving the p equations

$$\sum_{t=1}^{n} s_t(\theta_i) = 0, \quad 1 \leqslant i \leqslant p.$$

The MLE is consistent and its asymptotic distribution is normal when θ_0 is not on the boundary of its parameter space, the conditional density is correctly specified and regularity conditions apply.

Define the $p \times p$ information matrix A_0 by

$$(A_0)_{i,j} = \lim_{n \to \infty} -\frac{1}{n} \sum_{t=1}^{n} E\left[\frac{\partial^2 l_t}{\partial \theta_i \partial \theta_j} \right], \quad 1 \leqslant i, j \leqslant p, \qquad (10.23)$$

evaluated at the true parameters θ_0, which simplifies for a strictly stationary process to

$$(A_0)_{i,j} = -E\left[\frac{\partial^2 l_t}{\partial \theta_i \partial \theta_j} \right].$$

Then the distribution of $\sqrt{n}(\hat{\theta}_{n,\mathrm{ML}} - \theta_0)$ converges to a p-variate normal distribution as $n \to \infty$, written here as

$$\sqrt{n}(\hat{\theta}_{n,\mathrm{ML}} - \theta_0) \to N(0, A_0^{-1}). \qquad (10.24)$$

Consistent estimates of the terms in the matrix A_0 are calculated from n observations by

$$\hat{A}_{i,j} = -\frac{1}{n} \sum_{t=1}^{n} \frac{\partial^2 l_t}{\partial \theta_i \partial \theta_j} = -\frac{1}{n}\left(\frac{\partial^2 \log L}{\partial \theta_i \partial \theta_j} \right), \qquad (10.25)$$

with the derivatives evaluated at the MLE.

The matrix A_0 equals the expected value of the outer product of the scores when the conditional density is correctly specified. Then $A_0 = B_0$ with

$$(B_0)_{i,j} = \lim_{n \to \infty} \frac{1}{n} \sum_{t=1}^{n} E[s_t(\theta_i)s_t(\theta_j)], \qquad (10.26)$$

evaluated at θ_0, which again simplifies to the standard result for i.i.d. observations when the ARCH process is strictly stationary. The terms in this matrix are consistently estimated by

$$\hat{B}_{i,j} = \frac{1}{n} \sum_{t=1}^{n} s_t(\theta_i)s_t(\theta_j), \qquad (10.27)$$

evaluated at $\hat{\theta}_{n,\text{ML}}$. Only first derivatives are required to compute $\hat{B}$, which can be useful when it is difficult to calculate satisfactory second derivatives and hence $\hat{A}$.

The BHHH algorithm (Berndt, Hall, Hall, and Hausman 1974) maximizes the log-likelihood by an iterative method that calculates $\hat{B}$ at each iteration. Thus this popular algorithm only requires first derivatives to find the MLE and to compute its covariance matrix. Numerical derivatives are routinely calculated by software. However, analytic derivatives are generally preferable and can be calculated easily for many models (Fiorentini, Calzolari, and Panatoni 1996); examples are presented later and in the appendix to this chapter.

Hypothesis tests about one of the p parameters can be performed by constructing the usual ratio statistic. For example, consider testing the null hypothesis that the first parameter is a particular value, say $H_0 : \theta_1 = \theta_1^*$. First find the MLE and an estimate $\hat{C}$ of its covariance matrix (either $n^{-1}\hat{A}^{-1}$ or $n^{-1}\hat{B}^{-1}$). Then the first element of the MLE and its estimated variance, say $\hat{\theta}^{(1)}$ and $\hat{C}_{1,1}$, define the ratio

$$t = \frac{\hat{\theta}^{(1)} - \theta_1^*}{\sqrt{\hat{C}_{1,1}}} \qquad (10.28)$$

whose asymptotic distribution is the standard normal distribution, $N(0, 1)$, assuming θ_1^* is inside the set of feasible values for θ_1. General Wald tests, of a parameter constraint $H_0 : c(\theta_0) = 0$, for a function c, can be performed using a formula given by Bollerslev et al. (1994, p. 2982).

Likelihood-ratio (LR) tests can also be used to test a constraint on the true parameter vector θ_0. For example, consider the following null hypothesis that specifies $k < p$ of the parameter values:

$$H_0 : \theta_i = \theta_i^*, \quad 1 \leqslant i \leqslant k. \qquad (10.29)$$

The MLE under the null hypothesis is provided by maximizing the log-likelihood function over the $p - k$ unconstrained parameters to give a maximum value L_0. Denote the maximum of the unconstrained log-likelihood by L_1. Then the usual likelihood-ratio result can be used to decide the hypothesis test, namely that

$$2(L_1 - L_0) \overset{a}{\sim} \chi_k^2 \qquad (10.30)$$

with $\overset{a}{\sim}$ indicating that this is an asymptotic result. A large value of the test statistic indicates that the alternative hypothesis is much more likely than the null hypothesis to describe the data and then the null is rejected.

The LR and Wald tests are asymptotically equivalent, but they can of course provide different results when evaluated for a finite sample of observations. Note that the asymptotic test theory does requires modification when the null hypothesis restricts θ to be on the boundary of its parameter space. As defined here, the LR and

Wald tests are then conservative and reject a true null hypothesis less often than the significance level of the test. For example, if the null hypothesis is a normal distribution and the alternative is a t-distribution with ν degrees of freedom, then the null is $H_0 : \nu^{-1} = 0$, for which θ_0 is on the boundary. Bollerslev (1987) notes that the LR test is then conservative.

10.4.2   QMLE

The distribution of the standardized residuals is generally unknown. If we specify a particular density function and we are wrong, then there is no guarantee that the MLE and its standard errors are consistent. Newey and Steigerwald (1997) show the MLE is consistent if the true and assumed densities are both symmetric. They also show the MLE is inconsistent if the true density is asymmetric, the assumed density is symmetric, and the conditional mean is not always zero.

The QMLE methodology guarantees the consistency of estimates and standard errors by assuming normal distributions. There are then no distribution parameters in θ. The logarithms of the conditional densities are now

$$l_t(\theta) = -\tfrac{1}{2}[\log(2\pi) + \log(h_t(\theta)) + z_t^2(\theta)] \tag{10.31}$$

and maximizing the log-likelihood function provides the QMLE, denoted by $\hat{\theta}_{n,\text{QML}}$.

The QMLE is consistent whatever the true distribution of the standardized residuals, assuming that the conditional mean and variance functions have been correctly specified. However, the covariance matrix of $\sqrt{n}\hat{\theta}_{n,\text{QML}}$ is not consistently estimated in general by the sample counterpart of either A_0^{-1} or B_0^{-1}. The asymptotic result is now

$$\sqrt{n}(\hat{\theta}_{n,\text{QML}} - \theta_0) \overset{a}{\sim} N(0, A_0^{-1} B_0 A_0^{-1}). \tag{10.32}$$

The matrix $A_0^{-1} B_0 A_0^{-1}$ is in general different to both A_0^{-1} and B_0^{-1} when the conditional distributions that define the observations are not normal.

The QMLE is less accurate than the MLE when the conditional distributions are known and are not normal. Engle and González-Rivera (1991) quantify the reduction in efficiency for the GARCH(1, 1) model with conditional t-distributions. The ratios $\text{var}(\hat{\alpha}_{\text{ML}})/\text{var}(\hat{\alpha}_{\text{QML}})$ and $\text{var}(\hat{\beta}_{\text{ML}})/\text{var}(\hat{\beta}_{\text{QML}})$ are both asymptotically equal to 0.41 when the degrees of freedom parameter is 5; the ratios increase to 0.82 when the degrees of freedom parameter is 8.

The matrices A_0 and B_0 can be estimated, as before, by (10.25) and (10.27). The second derivatives in (10.25) can be avoided by using the following alternative consistent estimate of A_0, given by Bollerslev and Wooldridge (1992),

$$(\hat{A}_{\text{BW}})_{i,j} = \frac{1}{n} \sum_{t=1}^{n} \frac{1}{h_t}\left(\frac{\partial \mu_t}{\partial \theta_i}\right)\left(\frac{\partial \mu_t}{\partial \theta_j}\right) + \frac{1}{2h_t^2}\left(\frac{\partial h_t}{\partial \theta_i}\right)\left(\frac{\partial h_t}{\partial \theta_j}\right). \tag{10.33}$$

The standard errors provided by estimating $A_0^{-1} B_0 A_0^{-1}$, using (10.27) and either (10.25) or (10.33) are called *robust standard errors*, to emphasize that they are applicable when the assumption of conditional normal distributions is known to be wrong. Robust Wald tests are performed in the obvious way using the QMLE and the robust standard errors.

Differentiation of (10.31) and some algebra shows that the score vector is

$$s_t(\theta_i) = \frac{z_t}{\sqrt{h_t}} \left(\frac{\partial \mu_t}{\partial \theta_i} \right) + \frac{z_t^2 - 1}{2h_t} \left(\frac{\partial h_t}{\partial \theta_i} \right). \tag{10.34}$$

To compare the magnitudes of robust and nonrobust standard errors, suppose the conditional mean is a constant. Then $\partial \mu_t / \partial \theta_i \equiv 0$,

$$(\hat{A}_{BW})_{i,j} = \frac{1}{n} \sum_{t=1}^{n} \frac{1}{2h_t^2} \left(\frac{\partial h_t}{\partial \theta_i} \right) \left(\frac{\partial h_t}{\partial \theta_j} \right) \tag{10.35}$$

and

$$\hat{B}_{i,j} = \frac{1}{n} \sum_{t=1}^{n} \frac{(z_t^2 - 1)^2}{4h_t^2} \left(\frac{\partial h_t}{\partial \theta_i} \right) \left(\frac{\partial h_t}{\partial \theta_j} \right). \tag{10.36}$$

Then the limit of the ratio $\hat{B}_{i,j}/(\hat{A}_{BW})_{i,j}$, as n increases, is

$$\kappa = (B_0)_{i,j}/(A_0)_{i,j} = \tfrac{1}{2}E[(z_t^2 - 1)^2] = \tfrac{1}{2}E[z_t^4 - 1] \quad \text{for all } i \text{ and } j \tag{10.37}$$

(Pagan 1996). Since observed z_t are leptokurtic, $\kappa > 1$. The covariance matrices, in descending order of magnitude, are then approximately $n^{-1}\kappa A_0^{-1}$ for the robust method, $n^{-1}A_0^{-1}$ for the information matrix, and $n^{-1}\kappa^{-1}A_0^{-1}$ for the outer product of the scores. These results show that the robust standard errors of parameters in the variance equation will exceed the values provided by the alternative standard methods, when normal distributions are assumed but the z_t are leptokurtic. Standard errors that are not robust will often be unreliable, because the excess kurtosis is often substantial.

All of the above theory is asymptotic. There are few Monte Carlo investigations into the accuracy of the theory for samples of hundreds or thousands of observations. Bollerslev and Wooldridge (1992), Lumsdaine (1995), and Fiorentini et al. (1996) provide some results for relatively short time series, while Bollerslev and Mikkelsen (1996) give results for long series from GARCH models and long memory extensions.

10.4.3 GARCH(1, 1) Example

The GARCH(1, 1) model has four parameters, with $\theta = (\mu, \omega, \alpha, \beta)'$. Assuming symmetric distributions, the matrices A_0 and B_0 are block diagonal, with the mean parameter μ in one block and the three variance parameters in the other block (Engle 1982). Thus we set all terms outside the diagonal blocks of $\hat{A}$ and $\hat{B}$ to zero.

The robust covariance matrix for $(\hat{\omega}, \hat{\alpha}, \hat{\beta})'$ can be obtained after evaluating the 3×3 matrices in equations (10.35) and (10.36). This can be done using analytic derivatives of h_t, by evaluating

$$\frac{\partial h_t}{\partial \omega} = 1 + \beta \frac{\partial h_{t-1}}{\partial \omega},$$

$$\frac{\partial h_t}{\partial \alpha} = (r_{t-1} - \mu)^2 + \beta \frac{\partial h_{t-1}}{\partial \alpha},$$

$$\frac{\partial h_t}{\partial \beta} = h_{t-1} + \beta \frac{\partial h_{t-1}}{\partial \beta},$$

at the QMLE. The initial partial derivatives can be set either to their unconditional expectations,

$$\frac{\partial h_1}{\partial \omega} = \frac{1}{1 - \beta}, \qquad \frac{\partial h_1}{\partial \alpha} = \frac{\partial h_1}{\partial \beta} = \frac{\omega}{(1 - \beta)(1 - \alpha - \beta)},$$

or to zero (when h_1 is not a function of the parameters).

The QMLE for the DM/\$ from 1991 to 2000 was obtained in Section 9.4 using Excel. Further Excel calculations that utilize Visual Basic code provide the terms in the matrices and the following robust standard errors for the estimates:

Parameter	Estimate	Robust standard error
μ	1.38×10^{-4}	1.23×10^{-4}
ω	4.24×10^{-7}	1.90×10^{-7}
α	0.0354	0.00806
β	0.9554	0.00966

The robust estimate of the correlation between $\hat{\alpha}$ and $\hat{\beta}$ is -0.867 and the robust standard error of the persistence estimate $\hat{\phi} = \hat{\alpha} + \hat{\beta} = 0.9908$ is 0.00482.

The t-ratio for the null hypothesis $\mu = 0$ equals 1.12, so this hypothesis is accepted at conventional significance levels. The interesting null hypothesis of a unit root in the variance process, i.e. $\phi = 1$, produces a t-ratio equal to $(0.9908 - 1)/0.00482 = -1.91$, which is discussed further in Section 10.5.

The robust standard errors of the variance parameters exceed those from the information matrix and the products of the scores by amounts that are similar to those predicted by (10.37). The standardized residuals have kurtosis equal to 4.61, so that κ is estimated to be 1.80. The values of $\hat{B}_{i,j}/(\hat{A}_{\mathrm{BW}})_{i,j}$ are near $\hat{\kappa}$ and range from 1.77 to 2.03. Dividing the standard errors from the products of the scores by the robust standard errors gives 1.80, 1.82, and 1.64, again approximately equal to $\hat{\kappa}$.

10.4.4   GJR(1, 1)-MA(1)-M Example

The GJR(1, 1)-MA(1)-M model defined in Section 9.8 has three mean parameters and four variance parameters. Parameter estimates for the S&P 100 index series are given in Table 9.3, with normal, t-, and GED distributions. The nonnormal specifications add an eighth parameter to θ. The standard errors of the parameter estimates are also provided in Table 9.3. They are all calculated using the outer product matrix $\hat{B}$ of equation (10.27), and for the normal specification they are robust and also use the matrix $\hat{A}_{BW}$ from (10.33). These matrices contain first derivatives that are evaluated analytically, using the formulae in the appendix to this chapter. The analytic calculations are not difficult if Visual Basic code is used. Numerical first derivatives may give less accurate results, while satisfactory numerical second derivatives could not be obtained when an attempt was made to evaluate the matrix $\hat{A}$ in (10.25).

Tests about the values of λ and the persistence ϕ are deferred to the next section. The negative estimates of μ are counterintuitive. However, their standard errors are seen to be relatively large and 95% confidence intervals for μ include sensible positive values. The MA(1) parameter estimates are insignificant at conventional significance levels. The t-ratios for the null hypothesis $\Theta = 0$ are 0.54, -0.54, and -0.82 for the three distributions.

The robust correlations between the parameter estimates for the normal specification include $\text{cor}(\hat{\mu}, \hat{\lambda}) = -0.95$. The only other correlation outside the range ± 0.6 is $\text{cor}(\hat{\omega}, \hat{\beta}) = -0.62$. Also, $\text{cor}(\hat{\alpha}, \hat{\alpha}^-) = -0.47$, $\text{cor}(\hat{\alpha}, \hat{\beta}) = -0.36$, and $\text{cor}(\hat{\alpha}^-, \hat{\beta}) = -0.54$.

10.5 Results from Hypothesis Tests

The selection of an ARCH model can be guided by hypothesis tests based upon the likelihood theory summarized in the previous section. We review methods and results for some important tests, about the shape of the conditional distribution, about the dependence of the conditional mean on the conditional variance, and about the persistence of the conditional variance.

10.5.1 Tests for Conditional Normality

The null hypothesis that the conditional distribution of daily returns is normal is usually rejected comprehensively, commencing with the likelihood-ratio (LR) test results of Taylor and Kingsman (1979) for two commodity series and of Bollerslev (1987) for two exchange rate series. The LR test is decided by the value of $2(L_1 - L_0)$ with L_0 the maximum log-likelihood for conditional normal distributions and with L_1 the maximum value for a larger class of conditional distributions, which includes the normal as a special case. The two most popular standardized alternatives are the standardized t-distribution and the generalized error distribution (GED) (see Section 9.6), which each have a single shape parameter, respectively the degrees of freedom ν and the tail-thickness η. When $1/\nu \to 0$ or $\eta = 2$ the distribution is normal. As these alternative distributions have one extra parameter, the test statistic is then compared with a critical value from the

χ_1^2 distribution; for example, the null hypothesis is rejected at the 5% level if the statistic exceeds 3.84. This test gives conservative results for the t-distribution alternative, because zero is a boundary value for $1/\nu$ (Bollerslev 1987).

Table 9.3 lists the maximum log-likelihoods for the S&P 100 dataset and the GJR(1, 1)-MA(1)-M model estimated in Section 9.8. The LR test values are respectively 128.4 and 113.8 for the t- and GED alternatives. These values fall in the far right tail of the χ_1^2 distribution and thus reject the conditional normal hypothesis decisively. This is a standard result in the literature and I am unaware of any study of daily data that accepts the conditional normal hypothesis. Taylor (1994a) is one of many studies that reject the normal hypothesis for foreign exchange, with all LR test values exceeding 120 for the DM/$ rate from 1977 to 1990.

A second test procedure requires the standard errors (s.e.) of the shape parameters. For the GED alternative, $t = (\hat{\eta} - 2)/\text{s.e.}(\hat{\eta})$ is compared with a standard normal distribution which gives -31.2 for the S&P 100 dataset. With $\zeta = \nu^{-1}$, $t = \hat{\zeta}/\text{s.e.}(\hat{\zeta})$ can be evaluated and interpreted with caution; this statistic is $0.1512/0.0186 = 8.13$ for the S&P 100 dataset.

10.5.2 Do Expected Returns Depend on Volatility?

A positive relationship between the conditional mean μ_t and the conditional variance h_t might appear plausible, particularly when the asset approximates the market portfolio. The evidence for such a relationship can be assessed by estimating an ARCH-M model that includes h_t in the equation that defines μ_t. For our S&P 100 example,

$$\mu_t = \mu + \lambda h_t^{1/2} + \Theta e_{t-1}, \tag{10.38}$$

and the relevant null hypothesis is $\lambda = 0$. The alternative of interest, $\lambda > 0$, is essentially an econometric hypothesis, because asset pricing theory neither prescribes the functional relationship between μ_t and h_t nor requires it to be constant through time (see Glosten et al. 1993). A popular alternative relationship, used in much of the literature cited below, replaces $h_t^{1/2}$ in (10.38) by h_t. Then λ can be interpreted as a measure of relative risk aversion.

Several methods are available for testing a hypothesis such as $\lambda = 0$ in (10.38). Two of these are the LR test and the usual Wald test, which requires specification of the shape of the conditional distribution; a third is the robust Wald test that assumes normal distributions and then utilizes robust standard errors. For our S&P 100 example, first consider results for conditional t-distributions when the value of L_1 is given in Table 9.3 as 8495.13. When the constraint $\lambda = 0$ is applied we obtain $L_0 = 8493.91$. Hence the LR test value is $2 \times 1.82 = 3.64$ and we accept the null hypothesis at the 5% level, because 3.64 is less than the 95th percentile of χ_1^2, which is 3.84. Again from Table 9.3, the MLE of λ is 0.1112, with standard error 0.0577, giving a Wald test value of $0.1112/0.0577 = 1.93$. Once more we narrowly accept $\lambda = 0$ at the 5% level, since 1.93 is within ± 1.96. These conclusions might be considered suspect if we thought the true conditional density was far from the assumption of a t-density. To avoid such doubts, we can use the QMLE of λ and its robust standard error, 0.1377 and 0.0687 respectively, to obtain the robust Wald test value of 2.00. On this occasion the robust test just rejects $\lambda = 0$ at the 5% level, in contrast to the other tests.

The literature about the sign and the significance of λ does not provide simple conclusions for the US equity market. Bollerslev et al. (1992, p. 25) state that almost all of the early studies find λ is positive and significantly different from zero at the 5% level, examples including French, Schwert, and Stambaugh (1987) and Chou (1988). These studies predate the use of asymmetric volatility specifications. As incorrect specification of the conditional variance equation generally leads to inconsistent estimates of λ (noted, for example, by Pagan and Ullah 1988), the early evidence may be unreliable.

The EGARCH and GJR-GARCH studies of Nelson (1991) and Glosten et al. (1993) report negative estimates of λ for excess returns from the CRSP value-weighted market portfolio; these are returns in excess of the risk-free rate. Nelson gives $t = -3.36/2.03 = -1.66$ using daily returns from 1962 to 1987 and the GED density, while Glosten et al. give the robust test values $t = -2.83$ and $t = -2.43$ for their models 5 and 5-L, using monthly returns from 1951 to 1989.

The intensive study of US index returns by Bollerslev et al. (1994) uses a variant of the EGARCH model and finds that the estimates of λ (their parameter μ_3) are positive for daily returns in all four periods, 1885–1914, 1914–1928, 1928–1952, and 1953–1990. The respective values of t are 0.03, 0.71, 2.79, and 0.23 so that the null hypothesis $\lambda = 0$ is rejected at the 5% level only for the period from 1928 to 1952. We may also note that Blair et al. (2002) estimate that λ is positive for daily returns from the S&P 100 index and 70% of its constituent firms, from 1983 to 1992, with the null hypothesis $\lambda = 0$ accepted at the 10% level for the index and 90% of the firms. Their index result contrasts with the significant estimates of λ (at the 10% level) that are documented in Table 9.3 for the same index in the later period from 1991 to 2000.

In conclusion, if there is a relationship between the conditional daily mean μ_t and the conditional daily variance h_t for the US market, then it appears to vary through time, with either positive or negative dependence being possible.

A different conclusion is obtained by Ghysels, Santa-Clara, and Valkanov (2004a) for the conditional monthly mean return of the CRSP value-weighted index from 1928 to 2000. They document significant evidence for a positive risk-return trade-off when the conditional monthly variance is estimated by using a function of squared daily returns.

Studies of UK index volatility have not produced significant values of λ. All estimates of λ are positive but insignificant at the 5% level for the FT All-Share index from 1965 to 1989 (Poon and Taylor 1992) and all estimates are insignificant for the FTSE 100 index from 1985 to 1994 (Taylor 2000).

10.5.3 Tests for a Unit Root in Volatility

We next consider tests of the null hypothesis that the volatility process has a unit root. First suppose the alternative hypothesis is a stationary, short memory process for volatility. The null hypothesis is often stated as $\phi = 1$, with ϕ the persistence parameter that equals $\alpha + \beta$ for the GARCH(1, 1) model, $\alpha + \frac{1}{2}\alpha^- + \beta$ for the GJR(1, 1) model, and Δ for the EGARCH(1) model. The alternative hypothesis is $\phi < 1$. For models with more autoregressive parameters, ϕ is defined as the largest root of a polynomial equation. For example, in an EGARCH(2, q) model the filter $(1 - \Delta_1 L - \Delta_2 L^2)$ multiplies $\log(h_t)$ and typically it can be factored as $(1 - \phi L)(1 - \phi_1 L)$ with ϕ and ϕ_1 real numbers and $|\phi| > |\phi_1|$, as in Nelson (1991).

Estimates of ϕ very often exceed 0.97 for series of daily returns, but since estimated standard errors of ϕ are often less than 0.02 it is necessary to perform hypothesis tests.

The restriction $\phi = 1$ defines models that are not covariance stationary. The GARCH(1, 1) model is, however, strictly stationary when $\phi = 1$. The results of Lee and Hansen (1994) and Lumsdaine (1995, 1996) show that the robust Wald test of the unit root hypothesis does not need to be modified in the GARCH(1, 1) context, but Lumsdaine shows the likelihood ratio and Lagrange multiplier tests are unreliable. Generally, the Wald test is performed without worrying about its properties in a unit root context, which may be dubious for the EGARCH model in particular.

The evidence against a unit root in foreign exchange volatility is fairly strong and quite different to the evidence for equity volatility. The robust t-ratio for the daily DM/$ series from 1991 to 2000, modeled by GARCH(1, 1), equals $(0.9908 - 1)/0.00482 = -1.91$. A one-tailed test is reasonable and then the null hypothesis is rejected at the 5% level. The unit root hypothesis is rejected for the same exchange rate in earlier years. Taylor (1994a) gives results from 1977 to 1990. His robust t-ratios are $(0.9702 - 1)/0.0111 = -2.68$ for GARCH(1, 1) and $(0.9607 - 1)/0.0117 = -3.36$ for the symmetric EGARCH(1) model. When nonnormal specifications are estimated the t-ratios vary from -2.28 to -3.93, while subperiod robust t-ratios are -2.96 (1977–1983) and -2.34 (1984–1990). All these test values reject the unit root hypothesis at low significance levels. Bollerslev et al. (1994) produce a more significant result for the similar period from 1981 to 1992, namely $(0.948 - 1)/0.0138 = -3.78$. There is less evidence against a unit root in the initial years of floating exchange rates. Engle and Bollerslev (1986) estimate ϕ is 0.996 for weekly observations of the Swiss franc rate against the dollar from 1973 to 1985, while Engle and González-Rivera (1991) give estimates of 0.998 and 1.050 for daily observations of the £/$ rate from 1974 to 1983, respectively for normal and t-distributions.

The volatility of US equity indices often appears to contain a unit root. Bollerslev et al. (1992) state that the unit root null hypothesis is accepted by French et al. (1987), Chou (1988), Pagan and Schwert (1990), and Schwert and Seguin (1990). The EGARCH estimate of Nelson (1991) is $\hat{\phi} = 0.99962$, with standard error 0.00086 and $t = -0.00038/0.00086 = -0.45$, for a CRSP value-weighted index from 1962 to 1987. Bollerslev et al. (1994) have three estimates of ϕ out of four very near to 1 in their study of indices from 1885 to 1990. The estimates of their parameter Δ_1 are 0.9942, 0.9093, 0.9994, and 0.9979, respectively for 1885–1914, 1914–1928, 1928–1952, and 1953–1990. These long series have small standard errors for ϕ, so that the robust t-ratios are not close to zero; they equal -1.76, -5.27, -0.67, and -1.91.

The persistence estimates given in Table 9.3 for the S&P 100 index in the more recent years from 1991 to 2000 are not so near to unity. These GJR(1, 1) persistence estimates $\hat{\phi}$ are respectively 0.9867, 0.9913, and 0.9902 for the normal, t- and GED conditional distributions. Computation of the standard errors of these estimates requires either the 3×3 covariance matrix of $(\hat{\alpha}, \hat{\alpha}^-, \hat{\beta})'$ or the variance of $\hat{\phi}$ for a reparametrization of the model (say with ϕ replacing β). The two methods will provide slightly different answers. The 3×3 matrix is used here and then the robust t-ratio is -2.48 for the normal specification, and -2.10 and -2.30 for the t- and GED specifications. All these t-ratios reject a unit root at the 5% significance level. Blair et al. (2002) have a much lower persistence estimate for the same index and model from 1983 to 1992, that is highly sensitive to the crash return on 19 October 1987. They report $\hat{\phi} = 0.9289$ for the GJR(1, 1) model, but $\hat{\phi} = 0.9755$ when a crash dummy variable is included in the conditional variance equation. The median estimate of $\hat{\phi}$ is 0.9732 for the constituent stocks of the index when the dummy is included. A few of these estimates exceed 1. There is no correlation between $\hat{\phi}$ and the size of the S&P 100 firms. The impact of crashes on persistence was also noted by Friedman and Laibson (1989) in a study of quarterly returns.

A second possible statement of the alternative hypothesis is a stationary, long memory process for volatility. In the notation of Section 10.3, the null and alternative hypotheses are then $d = 1$ and $d < 1$ respectively. There are few examples of this hypothesis test for ARCH models. Bollerslev and Mikkelsen (1996) perform the test for the S&P 500 index from 1953 to 1990, and from the FIEGARCH(1, d, 1) model obtain

$$t = (\hat{d} - 1)/\text{s.e.}(\hat{d}) = (0.633 - 1)/0.063 = -5.83.$$

This is very strong evidence against the unit root hypothesis. It contrasts with $t = -1.91$ when the volatility alternative for the same series is the best short memory EGARCH process of Bollerslev et al. (1994). As the fractionally integrated (FI) model has a much higher likelihood than the simpler EGARCH specification, it is natural to prefer the FI test result. The difference between the test values (-5.83 against -1.91) is presumably a consequence of the long memory alternative defining a more powerful test of the unit root hypothesis on this occasion.

The long memory test is evidently important and it merits more research. Further series should be tested and the reliability of the Wald test for a unit root in a FIEGARCH model should be assessed.

10.6 Model Building

The choice of ARCH model in an empirical study will depend on many factors, such as the purpose of the modeling exercise, the expertise of the researcher, the time that can be devoted to the exercise, and the available software and data. Conditional variances and volatility forecasts that are fairly accurate can be obtained from simple models. Option prices that avoid the assumption of constant volatility can also be obtained from simple models (see Chapter 14). Models with more parameters and/or a more complicated mathematical structure are necessary when attempting to describe the stochastic process followed by prices as accurately as possible. The additional effort required to understand and estimate a more detailed model can provide more incisive tests of interesting hypotheses. For example, including long memory possibilities in the modeling framework can provide different and relevant evidence about the hypothesis of a unit root in volatility, as noted in Section 10.5.

A model can be selected either from a fixed set of candidate models or by following a sequential procedure. Models are compared using the maximum values of the log-likelihood function, by testing special cases against more general possibilities and by evaluating diagnostic tests. Out-of-sample predictions can also be used to select a model, particularly when forecasting is the goal of the modeling exercise.

Methods developed initially for models that have i.i.d. residuals are often applied in the ARCH context even if their exact properties are then unknown. For example, a quick way to select a model from a fixed set is to optimize the information criterion of either Akaike (1974) or Schwarz (1978), respectively denoted AIC and SIC. For ARCH models this requires maximizing either $2 \log L(\hat{\theta}) - 2P$ for AIC or $2 \log L(\hat{\theta}) - P \log(n)$ for SIC, with $\hat{\theta}$ the MLE for a model that has P parameters estimated from n observations. As the SIC criterion consistently estimates the orders p and q of a GARCH(p, q) model, SIC may be preferred to AIC. Bollerslev and Mikkelsen (1996) show that these criteria usually find the correct model in their Monte Carlo study of GARCH(1, 1), IGARCH(1, 1), and the fractionally integrated extension of GARCH(1, 1).

10.6.1 Diagnostic Checks

ARCH models are constructed from an i.i.d. sequence of standardized residuals $z_t = (r_t - \mu_t)/\sqrt{h_t}$. From returns data $\{r_t\}$ and an estimated model we can calculate the estimated standardized residuals $\hat{z}_t$, by replacing the parameter θ in the equations for μ_t and h_t by the MLE $\hat{\theta}$. These terms $\hat{z}_t$ will almost be observations from an i.i.d. sequence when the model is correctly specified; they will not be exactly i.i.d. because $\hat{\theta} \neq \theta$. As the autocorrelations of either $|r_t|$ or r_t^2 are the most direct evidence for conditional heteroskedasticity, it is logical to examine the autocorrelations of $|\hat{z}_t|$ and/or $\hat{z}_t^2$ to see if there is any predictability in the terms $\hat{z}_t$.

The most popular diagnostic test statistic is a Q-statistic, which is defined in the same way as the Box and Pierce (1970) statistic computed from the residuals of a homoskedastic ARMA model. For autocorrelations $R_{\tau,|\hat{z}|}$ and $R_{\tau,\hat{z}^2}$ calculated from n observations of $|\hat{z}_t|$ and $\hat{z}_t^2$,

$$Q_k^A = n \sum_{\tau=1}^{k} R_{\tau,|\hat{z}|}^2 \tag{10.39}$$

and

$$Q_k^{(2)} = n \sum_{\tau=1}^{k} R_{\tau,\hat{z}^2}^2. \tag{10.40}$$

The statistic Q_k can also be calculated from the autocorrelations of the $\hat{z}_t$, although large values are unlikely because returns are almost uncorrelated.

The asymptotic distributions of Q_k^A and $Q_k^{(2)}$ are often assumed to be chi-squared distributions, by analogy with the theory for homoskedastic processes. Li and Mak (1994) show the analogy is imperfect. They prove that comparing $Q_k^{(2)}$ with χ_k^2 is a conservative test procedure and they present an alternative quadratic form of the autocorrelations $R_{\tau,\hat{z}^2}$ whose asymptotic distribution is χ_k^2. The popular and simpler method is to follow the Box–Pierce approach and compare Q_k^A and/or $Q_k^{(2)}$ against χ_{k-m}^2 with m counting a relevant number of estimated parameters, assuming $k > m$. The theoretical results of McLeod and Li (1983) suggest the estimated parameters in the conditional mean equation can be ignored and thus m can be the number of estimated parameters in the conditional variance equation. The Monte Carlo evidence of Bollerslev and Mikkelsen (1996) shows that this ad hoc adjustment can be recommended when the fraction m/k is small.

The value of k is rather arbitrary. When $k = 20$, the statistics Q_k, Q_k^A, and $Q_k^{(2)}$ for the DM/\$ data and the GARCH(1, 1) model estimated in Section 9.4

are respectively 27.17, 35.94, and 14.74. Then Q_{20}^A exceeds the 5% critical value of 27.59 from χ_{17}^2, although a simple explanation of this result is not available by inspecting the autocorrelations of the quantities $|\hat{z}_t|$. For the S&P 100 index data and the GJR(1, 1)-MA(1)-M model estimated in Section 9.8, the statistics Q_{20}, Q_{20}^A, and $Q_{20}^{(2)}$ are respectively 27.22, 15.24, and 13.49. None of these values suggests the model is unsatisfactory, although the results in Taylor (2002) indicate that a long memory ARCH model is superior for S&P 100 index returns.

An alternative to the portmanteau test procedure described above is to assess moment conditions one at a time, as in Nelson (1991) and Bollerslev et al. (1994). There are several relevant functions f for which

$$E[f(z_t)] = 0 \tag{10.41}$$

when the model is correctly specified, including z_t, $z_t^2 - 1$, $z_t z_{t+\tau}$, $z_t(z_{t+\tau}^2 - 1)$, and $(z_t^2 - 1)(z_{t+\tau}^2 - 1)$ with τ positive. An elementary test for a correct specification is given by comparing $\sqrt{n}\bar{x}/s$ against the standard normal distribution, with $\bar{x}$ and s the average and the standard deviation of $x_t = f(\hat{z}_t)$, providing the variance of $f(z_t)$ is finite. This test procedure ignores the impact of parameter estimation error and hence is only approximately valid; estimation error is likely to be a serious issue when $f(z_t)$ is either z_t or $z_t^2 - 1$. Diagnostic tests about the distribution of the z_t can also be performed. Symmetry can be assessed by setting $f(z_t)$ to either z_t^3 or $z_t|z_t|$ and particular distributions can be assessed using $f(z_t) = |z_t| - E[|z_t|]$, etc.

Lagrange multiplier (LM) tests provide diagnostic information for particular alternatives to a candidate model and avoid the effort of maximizing the likelihood function for the alternative model. Robust LM tests are described by Bollerslev and Wooldridge (1992). LM tests and theory are also covered in Engle and Ng (1993), Bollerslev et al. (1994), and Franses and van Dijk (2000).

ARCH models are usually estimated from prices recorded during several years. It is then possible that the parameters of the most appropriate model vary within the time period considered. Splitting the dataset into two sections and then comparing parameter estimates across the two subperiods provides some information about the constancy of parameters. The sum of the maximized log-likelihoods for the subperiods minus the maximum for the complete dataset can be used to find a likelihood-ratio statistic and hence to assess the hypothesis of constant parameters.

10.6.2 Foreign Exchange Example

A model for DM/$ volatility is selected in Taylor (1994a) after comparing plausible specifications, testing various hypotheses, and obtaining diagnostic information. The data are daily returns from futures contracts traded in Chicago, defined as changes in the price logarithm. There are 3283 returns in the complete dataset, from December 1977 to November 1990.

The conditional mean depends on the day of the week and is defined by five dummy variables, one for each day of the week. The conditional variance is higher for returns that include either a weekend or vacation period. Let h_t^* be the appropriate conditional variance if period t defines a 24-hour return. Then suppose the trading period conditional variance h_t is the following multiple of h_t^*,

$$\frac{h_t^*}{h_t} = \begin{cases} 1 & \text{if close } t \text{ is 24 hours after close } t - 1, \\ M & \text{if } t \text{ falls on a Monday and } t - 1 \text{ on a Friday}, \\ V & \text{if a vacation occurs between close } t \text{ and close } t - 1, \end{cases}$$

with M and V parameters. A standard specification for h_t^* then completes the model. This is defined by writing one of the standard specifications for h_t as a function of previous terms h_{t-i} and z_{t-i}, $i > 0$, followed by replacing all terms h_{t-j} by h_{t-j}^*, $j \geqslant 0$. See equation (9.39) for the GARCH(1, 1) case, while for the EGARCH(1) case replace terms h_{t-j} by h_{t-j}^* in (10.1).

The initial comparisons of maximized log-likelihoods are made between the GARCH(1, 1) model (parameters ω, α, β) and the symmetric EGARCH(1) model (parameters $\mu_{\log(h)}, \gamma, \Delta$) and between conditional normal, t- and GED distributions. The normal models all have ten parameters, three in the conditional variance equation and seven calendar parameters; the nonnormal models have an additional shape parameter. The GED is superior to the t-distribution for this dataset. The maximum log-likelihood is 10.5 more for GARCH-GED than for GARCH-t and it is 9.3 more for EGARCH(1)-GED than for EGARCH(1)-t. The exponential specification fits the data more accurately than the GARCH specification. The log-likelihood advantage of the EGARCH(1) model is 5.0 and 6.2 respectively for GED and t-distributions. These comparisons and others for subperiods all favor the EGARCH(1)-GED specification, which is now called the benchmark model. Its parameter estimates for the complete dataset include tail-thickness $\hat{\eta} = 1.32$, persistence $\hat{\Delta} = 0.9658$, Monday multiplier $\hat{M} = 1.41$, and vacation multiplier $\hat{V} = 1.69$.

The benchmark model is compared with alternatives by using the maximum likelihood for the alternative minus the maximum likelihood for the benchmark, denoted AL. The simpler alternative of conditional normal distributions has AL = -73.27, hence the likelihood ratio test statistic is $-2\,\text{AL} = 146.54$, which rejects the normal hypothesis when compared with χ_1^2. Another simpler alternative is a unit root in volatility, $\Delta = 1$. The statistic $-2\,\text{AL} = 38.22$ is against the unit root hypothesis, although it is preferable to draw this conclusion from the robust Wald test as documented in Section 10.5. The benchmark model has a symmetric response to volatility shocks and has $\vartheta = 0$ in the more general equation

$$g(z_{t-1}) = \vartheta z_{t-1} + \gamma(|z_{t-1}| - E[|z_{t-1}|]). \tag{10.42}$$

The asymmetric model has AL $= 0.55$, which provides no evidence that the shocks are asymmetric. The use of two linear functions in the volatility shock function merely follows tradition. However, the smoother quadratic function,

$$g(z_{t-1}) = \vartheta z_{t-1} + \gamma (z_{t-1}^2 - 1),$$

fits the data worse, with AL $= -10.5$. Finally, EGARCH(p, q) models with more parameters than the benchmark do not provide a significantly better result. For example, when $p = 2$ and $q = 1$, the test statistic is $2\,\mathrm{AL} = 1.10$, which is less than the median of the χ_2^2 distribution.

The benchmark model passes tests of the moment condition hypothesis, (10.41), for the functions z_t, $z_t^2 - 1$, z_t^3, $z_t z_{t+\tau}$, and $(z_t^2 - 1)(z_{t+\tau}^2 - 1)$, $1 \leqslant \tau \leqslant 10$. A more demanding diagnostic test compares benchmark parameter estimates for 1977 to 1983 with those for 1984 to 1990. Adding the maximized log-likelihoods for the subperiods and then subtracting the maximum when the parameters are held constant throughout the sample period gives a test value equal to $2\,\mathrm{AL} = 33.08$, which exceeds the 5% critical value of 19.68 in the right-hand tail of χ_{11}^2. Tests on the individual parameters suggest four changes from the first to the second subperiod: a fall in the variance of volatility shocks, a rise in the median level of volatility, and changes to two of the calendar parameters.

10.6.3 Equity Index Example

A model for the volatility of the S&P 500 index is selected in Bollerslev and Mikkelsen (1996) by comparing the values of AIC and SIC across models, performing robust Wald tests and evaluating the portmanteau statistics Q_k, Q_k^A, and $Q_k^{(2)}$. The data are 9559 daily changes in the logarithm of the index, from January 1953 to December 1990.

The conditional mean is specified as AR(3), so that

$$\mu_t = \mu + \xi_1 r_{t-1} + \xi_2 r_{t-2} + \xi_3 r_{t-3}.$$

The estimates of ξ_1, ξ_2, ξ_3 are not sensitive to the specification of the conditional variance and equal 0.184, -0.057, and 0.021 for the preferred model, each with robust standard error equal to 0.011 approximately. The conditional variance incorporates a term N_t that counts the number of nontrading days that are included in trading period t; N_t is 0 for most periods, equals 1 if the market closes for a one-day holiday on the day before day t, and equals 2 when day t is a Monday that follows trade on Friday. GARCH specifications of the conditional variance are far inferior to EGARCH specifications, judged by the AIC and SIC criteria, which is a consequence of the volatility shocks having an asymmetric impact. The EGARCH specifications that are discussed are all special cases of the FIEGARCH$(2, d, 1)$ model including the nontrading variable,

$$\log \left(\frac{h_t}{1 + \delta N_t} \right) = \mu_{\log(h)} + \frac{(1 + \psi L)g(z_{t-1})}{(1 - \phi_1 L)(1 - \phi_2 L)(1 - L)^d}, \tag{10.43}$$

where g is the usual volatility shock function, (10.3), and the AR(2) term has been factorized as $(1 - \phi_1 L)(1 - \phi_2 L)$. The authors' preferred model has $\hat{\delta} = 0.22$.

Model selection commences by supposing $d = 0$ and considering EGARCH(1). The $Q_k^{(2)}$-statistic rejects this specification, by finding serial correlation in the squares of its standardized residuals. Furthermore, the AIC and SIC criteria are much higher for EGARCH(2, 1) and indeed the likelihood ratio test easily rejects $\phi_2 = \psi = 0$ when $d = 0$. The related study of the same data by Bollerslev et al. (1994) finds the 2, 1 model maximizes SIC. The largest AR root of the EGARCH(2, 1) model is $\hat{\phi}_1 = 0.997$. This model is rated higher than the integrated special case by AIC and SIC, but a robust Wald test probably accepts the unit root hypothesis at the 5% level.

The integrated EGARCH(2, 1) model has $\phi_1 = 1$ and $d = 0$, or equivalently $\phi_2 = 0$ and $d = 1$. It is a special case of the long memory model, FIEGARCH(1, d, 1), given by $\phi_2 = 0$ in (10.43). This long memory model has $\hat{d} = 0.633$ and the highest values of AIC and SIC for the set of models discussed. The values of Q_{10} and Q_{100} are 10.0 and 100.5 respectively, which provide no evidence against the specification of the conditional mean when compared with χ_7^2 and χ_{97}^2. The value of Q_{10}^A is 15.1. There are seven estimated variance parameters and a comparison against χ_3^2 rejects the model at the 1% level, although the test procedure may be suspect when there are so few remaining degrees of freedom. For Q_{100}^A, the test value of 122.7 just rejects the conditional variance specification at the 5% level.

10.7 Further Volatility Specifications

The ARCH specifications already discussed necessarily exclude many other specifications, because the ARCH literature is vast. We now mention further specifications that are relevant because they have the potential to answer interesting economic questions.

10.7.1 Univariate Specifications

The separation of a time series into temporary and permanent components allows the impact of transient and fundamental information to be identified. Engle and Lee (1999) suppose the conditional variance h_t reverts rapidly towards a permanent component that is highly persistent. Then h_t is the sum of two components, each of which is determined by past information and the latest standardized residual z_{t-1}. An empirical example is included in Engle and Mezrich (1995). The autocorrelations of squared returns for stationary components models decay rapidly at low lags and then relatively slowly at higher lags. Component models may therefore be a satisfactory alternative to long memory models. However, Bollerslev and Mikkelsen (1996) prefer long memory to components in perhaps the only empirical comparison of these concepts in an ARCH context.

The information set I_{t-1} used to define conditional distributions at time t has been restricted to the history of returns and calendar variables in the specific examples presented so far. Exogenous variables can also be included in the relevant information and in general we may have $I_{t-1} = \{r_{t-i}, x_{t-i}, i \geqslant 1\}$ with x_t either univariate or a vector variable.

A simple example is given by a dummy variable x_t that is 1 when $t \geqslant T$ and 0 when $t < T$. Time T refers to an event such as listing options on a stock. An additional term δx_{t-1} can be added to the right side of any of the previously defined equations for h_t. A test of the null hypothesis $\delta = 0$ then indicates whether or not the event has a permanent impact on the level of volatility. Taylor (1994c) evaluates the test when the event is listing options in the UK on Shell stock and finds no evidence for a permanent effect. Similar tests by St. Pierre (1998) and Jubinski and Tomljanovich (2003) for large samples of US firms show that volatility either decreases or remains constant after options are listed. The alternative methodology that compares the variance of returns before and after the event is unsatisfactory if options are listed when volatility is not at its mean level.

A very important example occurs when the additional information x_t is a measure of asset volatility obtained from the prices of options on the asset. Several studies have shown that there is incremental information in option prices that can be used to provide more accurate predictions of subsequent volatility, commencing with Day and Lewis (1992). A logical adaptation of GARCH(1, 1), for example, is

$$h_t = (1 - \beta L)^{-1}(\omega + \alpha(r_{t-1} - \mu)^2) + (1 - \delta L)^{-1}x_{t-1} \qquad (10.44)$$

with L the lag operator and x_{t-1} the square of an implied volatility. We defer our discussion of options information and ARCH models until Chapter 15, following the definition of implied volatility in Chapter 14.

Information about trading volume could be used to define x_t (e.g. Lamoureux and Lastrapes 1990, 1994). It is essential that lagged volume, and not contemporaneous volume, is used to define h_t. A measure of unexpected volume as a proportion of expected volume may be advisable, because aggregate volume is usually not stationary. Specifications like (10.44) can then be tried.

The standardized residuals z_t are independent and identically distributed variables in the general ARCH framework described in Section 9.5 and in all the examples already described. The assumption of identical distributions can be relaxed by permitting the shape of the distribution to depend on the information I_{t-1}. Hansen (1994) lets the degrees of freedom of a t-distribution be a function of I_{t-1}. Dueker (1997), Harvey and Siddique (1999), Rockinger and Jondeau (2002), and Jondeau and Rockinger (2003) also relate the shape to the information. Such research is difficult because the single variable z_t has to be used to define the conditional mean, variance, and shape. Successful applications may enhance value-at-risk calculations, which depend in part on the shape of the left tail of the distribution of z_t.

Switching ARCH models also have standardized residuals that are not identically distributed. The economy oscillates between unobservable states in these models. There are occasional changes in the state and then the parameters that determine the conditional variance also change. Two states could be used to distinguish a normal market from a market experiencing a crisis or to distinguish a strong economy from a weak economy. An example of a switching ARCH model is

$$h_t = \omega(S_t) + \alpha(r_{t-1} - \mu)^2 + \beta h_{t-1} \tag{10.45}$$

with $\{S_t\}$ a Markov chain process that is stochastically independent of the standardized residuals. Estimation of the model provides the probabilities of the states at time t conditional on the information provided by observed returns (see Cai 1994; Hamilton and Susmel 1994; Dueker 1997). Although these authors refer to "switching ARCH," they could also locate their models in a stochastic volatility (SV) framework. Indeed, the special case of (10.45) that has $\alpha = \beta = 0$ is a well-known SV model; its literature and properties are described in Section 11.4.

10.7.2 Multivariate Specifications

ARCH models for the conditional variances and covariances of the returns from two or more assets have many applications. They can be used to see how common information affects related assets, such as market indices in different countries or the spot and futures price of the same asset. They can also be used to compute time-varying risk factors and hedge ratios, from appropriate functions of covariances and variances. Bollerslev et al. (1994) and Engle and Kroner (1995) describe several multivariate specifications and a similar account is given in Franses and van Dijk (2000). Kroner and Ng (1998) and Bekaert and Wu (2000) cover multivariate asymmetric models. Bollerslev et al. (1992) survey the early empirical research.

For N assets, let ε_t now represent the $N \times 1$ vector of residuals and let H_t represent the $N \times N$ conditional covariance matrix, $H_t = E[\varepsilon_t \varepsilon_t' \mid I_{t-1}]$. As H_t is symmetric, there are $\frac{1}{2}N(N + 1)$ terms that need to be defined using the information I_{t-1}. We now consider multivariate generalizations of the GARCH(1, 1) model. The most general model, which represents each element of H_t as a linear combination of all the elements of $\varepsilon_{t-1}\varepsilon_{t-1}'$ and all the elements of H_{t-1}, requires $\frac{1}{2}N(N + 1) \times (1 + N(N + 1))$ parameters and it is called a *vec* model (Engle and Kroner 1995). There are 21 parameters when $N = 2$.

The large number of parameters in *vec* models and the requirement that the parameters define positive semi-definite covariance matrices motivates several special cases. One of these is the *diagonal* model of Bollerslev, Engle, and

Wooldridge (1988), for which element (i, j) of H_t is simply a linear combination of elements (i, j) from $\varepsilon_{t-1}\varepsilon'_{t-1}$ and H_{t-1}. This reduces the number of covariance parameters to $\frac{3}{2}N(N+1)$, i.e. to 9 when $N = 2$. The additional simplification that the conditional correlations are time-invariant gives the *constant correlation* model of Bollerslev (1990), which has only $\frac{1}{2}N(N+5)$ parameters, i.e. 7 when $N = 2$. These simplifications have the drawback that, for example, the residual for asset 1 does not appear in the variance equation for asset 2 and hence some relevant information about asset 2 may not be used. A parsimonious compromise between the *vec* and *diagonal* representations, which avoids this drawback, is the *BEKK* model (Baba, Engle, Kraft, and Kroner 1991). It is defined by quadratic forms as

$$H_t = W + A'\varepsilon_{t-1}\varepsilon'_{t-1}A + B'H_{t-1}B \qquad (10.46)$$

with W, A, and B being $N \times N$ matrices. Matrix W is symmetric and positive semi-definite, which guarantees H_t has the same properties. There are $\frac{1}{2}N(5N+1)$ parameters, i.e. 11 when $N = 2$.

Recently, Engle (2002) has popularized simple multivariate models that have *dynamic conditional correlations*. Another modeling strategy commences by assuming expected returns are linear functions of factors and that the factor returns follow ARCH processes (see Engle, Ng, and Rothschild 1990; Ng, Engle, and Rothschild 1992; King, Sentana, and Wadhwani 1994).

10.8 Concluding Remarks

ARCH modeling has rapidly become a dominant paradigm when discrete-time models are used to describe the prices of financial assets. It is easy to obtain maximum likelihood estimates of parameters and to compare alternative model specifications. This explains why ARCH models are often preferred to other volatility models that can also explain the stylized facts for returns.

The selection of a specific model for the returns from a financial asset involves choices that can be guided by estimating models for a sample of returns. A long memory model should be considered if the objective is to obtain a high likelihood value from a dataset by fitting a model that has few parameters. The FIEGARCH model described in Section 10.3 is a promising example. Relevant standard errors, hypothesis tests, and diagnostic criteria should always be evaluated, as surveyed in Sections 10.4–10.6. Successful new specifications may well emerge in the future.

There is much more that can be written about ARCH models. A detailed description of multivariate models is beyond the scope of this text and the interested reader should see Engle and Kroner (1995), Kroner and Ng (1998), and Engle (2002). ARCH models for intraday returns are important and are covered in Chapter 12. The continuous-time limits of discrete-time models are also important and they are documented in Chapter 13. Applications to option pricing, volatility forecasting and density estimation are evaluated in Chapter 14–16.

Further Reading

Bollerslev, T., R. F. Engle and D. B. Nelson. 1994. ARCH models. In *Handbook of econometrics*, vol. IV, pp. 2959–3038 (North-Holland).

Bollerslev, T. and H. O. Mikkelsen. 1996. Modeling and pricing long memory in stock market volatility. *Journal of Econometrics* 73:151–184.

Engle, R. F. and V. Ng. 1993. Measuring and testing the impact of news on volatility. *Journal of Finance* 48:1749–1778.

Nelson, D. B. 1991. Conditional heteroskedasticity in asset returns: a new approach. *Econometrica* 59:347–370.

Pagan, A. R. 1996. The econometrics of financial markets. *Journal of Empirical Finance* 3:15–102.

Taylor, S. J. 1994. Modeling stochastic volatility: a review and comparative study. *Mathematical Finance* 4:183–204.

10.9 Appendix: Formulae for the Score Vector

Suppose there are p parameters and that only the first m of these appear in the equations that define $\mu_t(\theta)$ and $h_t(\theta)$, with the remaining parameters (if any) defining the density function of the standardized residuals $z_t(\theta)$. Analytic standard errors can be calculated from the $p \times 1$ score vector, $s_t(\theta) = \partial l_t / \partial \theta$, if analytic formulae are available for $\partial \mu_t / \partial \theta$ and $\partial h_t / \partial \theta$. The general formula for the first m terms in the score vector is

$$s_t(\theta_i) = \frac{\partial l_t}{\partial \theta_i} = \frac{a(z_t) z_t}{\sqrt{h_t}} \left(\frac{\partial \mu_t}{\partial \theta_i} \right) + \frac{a(z_t) z_t^2 - 1}{2 h_t} \left(\frac{\partial h_t}{\partial \theta_i} \right), \quad 1 \leqslant i \leqslant m, \quad (10.47)$$

with the function $a(\cdot)$ determined by the density function of the z_t. When this density is normal,

$$a = 1,$$

when it is the standardized t with ν degrees of freedom,

$$a = \frac{\nu + 1}{\nu - 2 + z_t^2},$$

and when it is the generalized error distribution with tail-thickness parameter η,

$$a = \begin{cases} \dfrac{\eta |z_t|^{\eta-2}}{2\lambda(\eta)^\eta}, & \text{if } z_t \neq 0, \\ 0, & \text{when } z_t = 0, \end{cases}$$

with $\lambda(\cdot)$ defined by (9.46). The final term in the score vector for the standardized t is

$$\frac{\partial l_t}{\partial \nu} = \frac{d \log c(\nu)}{d\nu} - \tfrac{1}{2} \log(x_t) + \frac{(\nu + 1) z_t^2}{2 x_t (\nu - 2)^2}, \quad x_t = 1 + \frac{z_t^2}{\nu - 2},$$

and for the GED it equals

$$\frac{\partial l_t}{\partial \eta} = \frac{d \log C(\eta)}{d\eta} - \tfrac{1}{2}(\log |z_t| - \log \lambda(\eta)) \frac{|z_t|}{\lambda(\eta)^{\eta}},$$

with $c(\cdot)$ and $C(\cdot)$ defined by (9.44) and (9.46).

Recursive formulae for

$$\frac{\partial \mu_t}{\partial \theta} \quad \text{and} \quad \frac{\partial h_t}{\partial \theta}$$

can be written down for the GARCH model and many of its extensions. For example, for the GJR(1, 1)-MA(1)-M model defined and estimated in Section 9.8, with residuals e_{t-1} and conditional normal distributions, $m = p = 7$,

$$\theta = (\mu, \lambda, \Theta, \omega, \alpha, \alpha^-, \beta)',$$

$$\frac{\partial \mu_t}{\partial \theta} = (1, \sqrt{h_t}, e_{t-1}, 0, 0, 0, 0)' - \Theta \frac{\partial \mu_{t-1}}{\partial \theta} + \frac{\lambda}{2\sqrt{h_t}} \frac{\partial h_t}{\partial \theta}, \qquad (10.48)$$

and

$$\frac{\partial h_t}{\partial \theta} = (0, 0, 0, 1, e_{t-1}^2, S_{t-1} e_{t-1}^2, h_{t-1})'$$

$$- 2(\alpha + \alpha^- S_{t-1}) e_{t-1} \frac{\partial \mu_{t-1}}{\partial \theta} + \beta \frac{\partial h_{t-1}}{\partial \theta}. \qquad (10.49)$$

When an additional parameter defines the density of the standardized residuals, equations (10.48) and (10.49) define the first seven terms of the vectors and the eighth terms are zero.

11
Stochastic Volatility Models

Stochastic processes for volatility and hence returns are defined and investigated in this chapter. These models have a simple structure and can explain the major stylized facts for asset returns. Their parameters can be estimated in many ways, although the most efficient methods are rather complicated.

11.1 Introduction

Volatility changes are so frequent that it is appropriate to model volatility by a random variable. We now do this in a discrete-time framework, although it is also instructive to consider continuous-time models when pricing options as we will see later in Chapter 14. Volatility cannot be observed directly from discrete-time returns data because it is a latent variable that is not traded. It can, however, be estimated fairly accurately from high-frequency data, as is shown in the next chapter. All estimates are imperfect and we have to interpret volatility as a latent variable that can be modeled and predicted through its direct influence on the magnitude of returns.

Stochastic volatility (SV) models involve specifying a stochastic process for volatility. They therefore differ from ARCH models that specify a process for the conditional variance of returns. The SV literature has its origins in Rosenberg (1972), Clark (1973), Taylor (1982b), and Tauchen and Pitts (1983) and has grown less rapidly than the comparable ARCH literature that developed from Engle (1982) and Bollerslev (1986). The reason for the greater popularity of ARCH models is quite simply that maximum likelihood estimation is easy for ARCH but difficult for SV models. Nevertheless, SV models arise naturally when pricing options in a world of changing volatility. SV and ARCH models explain the same stylized facts and have many similarities. Each family of models has constructive applications, so that efforts to solve the difficult problem of deciding which is best are probably misguided.

Shephard (1996) provides an excellent introductory survey of SV and ARCH models. He remarks that the properties of SV models are easier to find, understand, manipulate, and generalize to the multivariate case. Subsequent developments in the SV literature have largely concentrated on methods for estimating model parameters and the unobservable volatility variable. A variety of ingenious algorithms are reviewed in Sections 11.6 and 11.9. Ghysels, Harvey, and Renault (1996) provide a more mathematical survey of SV models, which covers both discrete and continuous-time formulations. They also include a detailed discussion of option prices motivated by the SV framework. Shephard (2005) is a recent collection of important SV papers, which contains a review of the SV literature.

Further motivation for SV models and a general definition are provided in Section 11.2. Excess returns are defined to be the product of volatility and an i.i.d. standardized variable. Mathematical analysis is much easier when the two variables in the product are stochastically independent. General results for this assumption are given in Section 11.3 and applied to very different volatility processes in Sections 11.4 and 11.5. The first volatility process is a finite-state Markov chain while the second is a Gaussian AR(1) process for the logarithm of volatility. The Gaussian specification defines what we call the standard SV model because it appears in the most SV studies, commencing with Taylor (1982b). There is a variety of methods, discussed in Section 11.6, for estimating the parameters of the standard model. A foreign exchange example is provided in Section 11.7 for a straightforward estimation method that applies the Kalman filter.

The assumptions of the standard SV model are relaxed in Sections 11.8 and 11.9. First we permit heavier tails in the distribution of returns than are given by conditional normal distributions. Then we introduce asymmetric effects into the volatility process by relaxing the assumption of stochastic independence between the volatility and standardized processes. The chapter continues with a description of long memory specifications in Section 11.10 and multivariate SV models in Section 11.11, followed by some notes on comparing and combining SV and ARCH models in Section 11.12.

11.2 Motivation and Definitions

Stochastic volatility models suppose the volatility on day t, denoted by σ_t, is partially determined by unpredictable events on the same day. Volatility is proportional to the square root of the number of news items in the information arrivals model of Section 8.3. There is then an unpredictable component in σ_t as invariably some news is not scheduled (Taylor 1986). Volatility in this framework will be autocorrelated whenever the news counts are autocorrelated and then the stochastic properties of $\{\sigma_t\}$ merit investigation.

Related motivation comes from the concept of time deformation, for which the trading clock runs at different rates on different days with the clock represented by either transaction counts or trading volume (Clark 1973; Ghysels et al. 1998; Ané and Geman 2000). Shocks to volume then create an unpredictable volatility component.

A third source of motivation comes from approximations to diffusion processes for a continuous-time volatility variable. Volatility diffusion processes are plausible when deriving option pricing formulae without the assumption of constant volatility. Some of these formulae can only be evaluated by simulation of discrete-time volatility processes (Hull and White 1987).

The above remarks motivate study of stochastic volatility (SV) models, which we require to have two properties. First, returns in excess of a constant mean μ can be factorized as

$$r_t - \mu = \sigma_t u_t \tag{11.1}$$

with σ_t positive. Second, there is an unpredictable component in volatility, i.e. $\text{var}(\sigma_t \mid r_{t-1}, r_{t-2}, \ldots) > 0$. The random variables u_t are assumed to be independent and identically distributed (i.i.d.) with zero mean and unit variance. Often, it is also assumed that the u_t are normally distributed, otherwise the factorization may not be unique, as noted below. We consider various stochastic processes for $\{\sigma_t\}$ in subsequent sections. We could replace the mean μ in (11.1) by a function of previous returns if we wished to incorporate autocorrelation among returns into the model, although this is not done here.

SV models are characterized by two random shocks per unit time, one of which is u_t. The other shock, say η_t, partially determines σ_t. For example, η_t may be the residual in an ARMA model for some function of σ_t. As there are twice as many shocks as observed returns it is impossible to deduce the realized values of σ_t and u_t from returns r_t. Volatility is then latent and unobservable, which certainly complicates the estimation of model parameters.

Analysis of the factorization (11.1) requires some assumptions about the relationship between the stochastic processes $\{\sigma_t\}$ and $\{u_t\}$. We call the SV model *independent* if these two processes are stochastically independent. Independent SV models are considered in Sections 11.3–11.8 and then we consider models that allow some dependence between the processes. General dependent processes are defined in Ghysels et al. (1996) with an assumption that each process does not Granger-cause the other process.

The general ARCH model for uncorrelated returns also factorizes excess returns, but as

$$r_t - \mu = h_t^{1/2} z_t \tag{11.2}$$

with $z_t \sim$ i.i.d. $D(0, 1)$ and the conditional variance h_t a function of information known before time t. It does not follow that ARCH models are SV models, by substituting $\sigma_t^2 = h_t$, because there is no unpredictable volatility component in h_t, since $\text{var}(h_t \mid I_{t-1}) = 0$. However, when z_t is a mixture of normal distributions, we can write $z_t = m_t^{1/2} u_t$ with $E[m_t] = 1$, $\text{var}(m_t) > 0$, and m_t independent of both $u_t \sim N(0, 1)$ and I_{t-1}, as noted in Section 9.6. Then $\sigma_t = (h_t m_t)^{1/2}$ makes (11.1) and (11.2) equivalent, with $E[\sigma_t^2 \mid I_{t-1}] = h_t$ and

$\text{var}(\sigma_t^2 \mid I_{t-1}) = h_t^2 \, \text{var}(m_t) > 0$. Thus ARCH models with appropriate fat-tailed conditional distributions are SV models in our terminology.

The typical conditional variance function h_t is a very intricate function of I_{t-1} for SV models, with $h_t \neq \sigma_t^2$. The standardized residuals $z_t = (r_t - \mu)/\sqrt{h_t}$ always have zero mean and unit variance, but $z_t \neq u_t$. Generally the z_t are not i.i.d., which is shown for certain independent SV models in Section 11.4. It follows that there are SV models which are not ARCH models, since the z_t are i.i.d. for ARCH models.

11.3 Moments of Independent SV Processes

Now suppose $\{\sigma_t\}$ is strictly stationary and stochastically independent of $\{u_t\}$. The independence assumption allows us to derive general formulae for the moments of $r_t - \mu = \sigma_t u_t$. Any expectation $E[f_1(\sigma_t, \sigma_{t-1}, \dots) f_2(u_t, u_{t-1}, \dots)]$ is simply the product of $E[f_1]$ and $E[f_2]$. The assumption that the u_t are i.i.d. with zero mean and unit variance will help to simplify $E[f_2]$. The mean, variance, and kurtosis of returns are

$$E[r_t] = \mu, \quad \text{var}(r_t) = E[\sigma_t^2], \quad \text{and} \quad \text{kurtosis}(r_t) = k_r = k_u \frac{E[\sigma_t^4]}{E[\sigma_t^2]^2}$$

$$(11.3)$$

with k_u the kurtosis of u_t, which is 3 for normal distributions. The formula for k_r is given by adapting equation (8.6). These expressions and those that follow are only defined when all the relevant moments are finite. For example, the kurtosis of returns is finite if and only if both k_u and $E[\sigma_t^4]$ are finite.

The returns process is uncorrelated, from (8.7). Furthermore, the excess returns, $r_t - \mu$, are a martingale difference process. The squares of the excess returns

$$s_t = (r_t - \mu)^2 = \sigma_t^2 u_t^2$$

have the same covariances as the squares of volatility, i.e.

$$\text{cov}(s_t, s_{t+\tau}) = \text{cov}(\sigma_t^2, \sigma_{t+\tau}^2), \quad \tau > 0,$$

from (8.8). The autocorrelations of the s_t are thus a multiple of the autocorrelations of the σ_t^2, respectively denoted by $\rho_{\tau,s}$ and ρ_{τ,σ^2}, as follows:

$$\rho_{\tau,s} = \left[\frac{\text{var}(\sigma_t^2)}{\text{var}(s_t)} \right] \rho_{\tau,\sigma^2}, \quad \tau > 0.$$

Then

$$\rho_{\tau,s} = \left[\frac{E[\sigma_t^4] - E[\sigma_t^2]^2}{k_u E[\sigma_t^4] - E[\sigma_t^2]^2} \right] \rho_{\tau,\sigma^2} = \frac{k_r - k_u}{k_u(k_r - 1)} \rho_{\tau,\sigma^2}, \quad \tau > 0, \quad (11.4)$$

whenever the kurtosis of returns is finite. High persistence in the volatility process will cause $\rho_{1,s}$ to be almost $(k_r - k_u)/(k_u(k_r - 1))$, which is bounded above by $1/k_u$.

Similar results can be derived for any positive power p of the absolute excess returns,

$$a_t = |r_t - \mu| = \sigma_t |u_t|.$$

Let

$$A(p) = \frac{E[\sigma_t^{2p}]}{E[\sigma_t^p]^2} \quad \text{and} \quad B(p) = \frac{E[|u_t|^{2p}]}{E[|u_t|^p]^2}. \tag{11.5}$$

Then by modifying (8.8) and (11.4) we can obtain the autocorrelations of a_t^p as a multiple of those of σ_t^p; thus,

$$\rho_{\tau,a^p} = C(p)\rho_{\tau,\sigma^p}, \quad \tau > 0,$$

with

$$C(p) = \frac{A(p) - 1}{A(p)B(p) - 1} \leqslant \frac{1}{B(p)}. \tag{11.6}$$

Note that $A(p)$ and $C(p)$ are functions of p and the parameters of the process $\{\sigma_t\}$. Taylor (1986) derives (11.6) when p is either 1 or 2.

For normally distributed u_t,

$$E[|u_t|^p] = 2^{p/2} \pi^{-1/2} \Gamma((p+1)/2) \tag{11.7}$$

and hence $B(p)$ can be evaluated. In particular, $E[|u_t|] = \sqrt{2/\pi}$, $E[|u_t|^3] = 2\sqrt{2/\pi}$, $B(1) = \pi/2$, and $B(2) = 3$, as $\Gamma(1) = \Gamma(2) = 1$.

11.4 Markov Chain Models for Volatility

A discrete probability distribution that has only two possible outcomes defines the simplest nontrivial distribution for volatility. A two-state Markov chain then defines the simplest stochastic process for volatility. This volatility model can explain the major stylized facts for returns and it is constructive in two ways. First, it provides some intuition for models and likelihood methods when volatility has a continuous distribution. Second, it illustrates some of the differences between ARCH and SV models. The two-state Markov chain model is quite popular in research literature, although it describes returns less successfully than models that have a continuous distribution for volatility. We present a detailed collection of results when volatility has two states and then illustrate parameter estimation for DM/\$ returns. Finally, we mention extensions that consider three or more states.

A two-state model for volatility is derived in Ball and Torous (1983) by supposing prices contain occasional jumps. A two-state Markov chain for volatility is evaluated in Hamilton (1988) and Pagan and Schwert (1990). Further theoretical and empirical results are provided by Pagan (1996) and Taylor (1999).

Models with several volatility states are investigated by Ryden et al. (1998) and the moments of these and more complex models are described by Timmermann (2000). The model for returns is often called a hidden Markov model (HMM), as the Markov variable is unobservable volatility. Many theoretical results for HMMs are provided by Lindgren (1978) and Hamilton (1994, Chapter 22).

11.4.1 Definition of the Two-State Model

The volatility σ_t for period t has distribution given by

$$\sigma_t = \begin{cases} \sigma_L \text{ with probability } p, \\ \sigma_H \text{ with probability } 1 - p, \end{cases} \tag{11.8}$$

with the subscripts "L" and "H" referring to low and high volatility states, so $\sigma_L < \sigma_H$. Volatility oscillates between the two states as time passes. The probability of a change in the state only depends on the latest state when $\{\sigma_t\}$ is a Markov process. The probabilities of up and down changes are respectively denoted by

$$p_{LH} = P(\sigma_t = \sigma_H \mid \sigma_{t-1} = \sigma_L) \quad \text{and} \quad p_{HL} = P(\sigma_t = \sigma_L \mid \sigma_{t-1} = \sigma_H). \tag{11.9}$$

The expected numbers of up and down changes are equal, as the volatility process is stationary, and hence the constraint

$$p \times p_{LH} = (1 - p) \times p_{HL} \tag{11.10}$$

applies to the change probabilities.

The return for period t is

$$r_t = \mu + \sigma_t u_t, \tag{11.11}$$

with μ a constant and with the u_t independent and identically distributed as $N(0, 1)$. The model for returns has five parameters, μ, σ_L, σ_H, p, and either p_{LH} or p_{HL}. The processes $\{\sigma_t\}$ and $\{u_t\}$ are assumed to be stochastically independent. Returns have distribution $N(\mu, \sigma_L^2)$ when volatility is low and distribution $N(\mu, \sigma_H^2)$ when volatility is high. Their unconditional variance is

$$\sigma^2 = \text{var}(r_t) = E[\sigma_t^2] = p\sigma_L^2 + (1 - p)\sigma_H^2 \tag{11.12}$$

and their unconditional density is a mixture of normal densities,

$$f(r_t) = p\psi(r_t \mid \mu, \sigma_L^2) + (1 - p)\psi(r_t \mid \mu, \sigma_H^2), \tag{11.13}$$

with $\psi(r \mid \mu, \Sigma^2)$ here representing the density of $N(\mu, \Sigma^2)$. The symmetric density $f(r_t)$ is leptokurtic because it is a normal mixture. The kurtosis of returns is

$$k = \text{kurtosis}(r_t) = \frac{3(p\sigma_L^4 + (1 - p)\sigma_H^4)}{\sigma^4} \tag{11.14}$$

from equation (8.6). An appropriate density for daily returns is obtained when $p = 3/4$, $\sigma_L^2 = \sigma^2/2$, and $\sigma_H^2 = 5\sigma^2/2$, from Taylor (1999). The kurtosis then equals 5.25.

11.4.2 Autocorrelations

The returns process satisfies all the assumptions made in Section 11.3. Consequently, the returns are uncorrelated and the autocorrelations of squared excess returns can be obtained directly from those of squared volatility.

Results for the variables σ_t^2 can be derived easily from results for the variables $(\sigma_t^2 - \sigma_L^2)/(\sigma_H^2 - \sigma_L^2)$, whose outcomes are either 0 or 1. In particular,

$$E[\sigma_t^2 \mid \sigma_{t-1}^2, \sigma_{t-2}^2, \ldots] = \sigma^2 + (1 - p_{LH} - p_{HL})(\sigma_{t-1}^2 - \sigma^2).$$

Then we can deduce

$$\sigma_t^2 = \sigma^2 + (1 - p_{LH} - p_{HL})(\sigma_{t-1}^2 - \sigma^2) + \xi_t \qquad (11.15)$$

for variables ξ_t that are white noise. This follows from the Wold decomposition of a stationary process, although the residuals ξ_t are not i.i.d. (Pagan 1996). Thus $\{\sigma_t^2\}$ is an AR(1) process, with autoregressive parameter

$$\phi = 1 - p_{LH} - p_{HL} \qquad (11.16)$$

and autocorrelations

$$\rho_{\tau,\sigma^2} = \phi^\tau, \quad \tau > 0.$$

Hence, from (11.4), the autocorrelations of the squared excess returns, $s_t = (r_t - \mu)^2$, are

$$\rho_{\tau,s} = \frac{k-3}{3(k-1)}\phi^\tau, \quad \tau > 0, \qquad (11.17)$$

with the kurtosis of returns k given by (11.14). We may also note that $\{\sigma_t^\lambda\}$ is an AR(1) process with AR parameter ϕ for all positive λ and hence the autocorrelations of $s_t^{\lambda/2}$ can be derived from (11.6).

The persistence parameter ϕ must be almost 1 for daily returns, as already seen in Chapters 9 and 10. Therefore both of the change probabilities, p_{LH} and p_{HL}, must be small because their sum is $1 - \phi$. Consequently, changes of state must be rare if the model is applied to daily returns (Pagan 1996). For the illustrative values $\phi = 0.98$ and $p = 3/4$, equation (11.10) gives $p_{LH} = 0.005$ and $p_{HL} = 0.015$. The expected time until an up change is then $1/p_{LH} = 200$ time units when the volatility is low, which is about ten months for daily returns. Also supposing that $\sigma_H^2 = 5\sigma_L^2, k = 5.25$, and the autocorrelations of the squared excess returns decay geometrically from $\rho_{1,s} = 0.173$.

11.4.3 Conditional State Probabilities

It is impossible to identify the volatility state at any time if the only data we have are provided by returns. Instead, we have to settle for conditional probabilities. Let H be a set of n returns, $\{r_1, \ldots, r_n\}$, let $I_t = \{r_1, \ldots, r_t\}$ be the usual history up to and including time t, and let $J_t = \{r_t, \ldots, r_n\}$ be the current and future values at time t. Then conditional probabilities for the low state, $P(\sigma_L \mid A)$, can be obtained when A is any of H, I_{t-1}, I_t, J_t, J_{t+1}, and $I_{t-1} + J_{t+1}$, from equations in Lindgren (1978), Hamilton (1988), and Taylor (1999).

We focus on the conditional state probabilities, given prior returns, denoted

$$p_t = P(\sigma_t = \sigma_L \mid I_{t-1}) \quad \text{and} \quad q_t = P(\sigma_t = \sigma_H \mid I_{t-1}). \tag{11.18}$$

The derivation supposes we already have p_{t-1} and q_{t-1} from I_{t-2}. These prior probabilities for σ_{t-1} can be updated by Bayes' theorem when r_{t-1} becomes available, to give the posterior probabilities

$$
\begin{aligned}
p_{t-1}^* &= P(\sigma_{t-1} = \sigma_L \mid I_{t-1}) \\
&= \frac{p_{t-1}\psi(r_{t-1} \mid \mu, \sigma_L^2)}{p_{t-1}\psi(r_{t-1} \mid \mu, \sigma_L^2) + q_{t-1}\psi(r_{t-1} \mid \mu, \sigma_H^2)}
\end{aligned}
\tag{11.19}
$$

and $q_{t-1}^* = 1 - p_{t-1}^*$, with $\psi(\cdot)$ again the normal density function. The next pair of prior probabilities follow from the transition probabilities of the Markov chain. In particular,

$$p_t = p_{t-1}^*(1 - p_{LH}) + q_{t-1}^* p_{HL}.$$

Combining the two previous equations provides the recursive formula,

$$p_t = \frac{p_{t-1}\psi(r_{t-1} \mid \mu, \sigma_L^2)(1 - p_{LH}) + q_{t-1}\psi(r_{t-1} \mid \mu, \sigma_H^2)p_{HL}}{p_{t-1}\psi(r_{t-1} \mid \mu, \sigma_L^2) + q_{t-1}\psi(r_{t-1} \mid \mu, \sigma_H^2)}, \tag{11.20}$$

which commences with $p_1 = p$.

These probabilities cluster around 0 and 1 for daily returns data, because volatility rarely changes state. Long sequences of returns from the same state give a high probability of correctly identifying the state on most days. When future returns are also used, 85% of the conditional probabilities are either below 0.01 or above 0.99 for realistic parameters (Taylor 1999).

11.4.4 Conditional Return Distributions

The conditional density of r_t given the previous returns I_{t-1} is a normal mixture,

$$f(r_t \mid I_{t-1}) = p_t\psi(r_t \mid \mu, \sigma_L^2) + (1 - p_t)\psi(r_t \mid \mu, \sigma_H^2), \tag{11.21}$$

which is almost normal when p_t is almost 0 or 1. The conditional variance is simply

$$h_t = p_t\sigma_L^2 + (1 - p_t)\sigma_H^2. \tag{11.22}$$

Clearly, h_t is neither σ_{t-1}^2 nor σ_t^2, which is a general feature of stochastic volatility models. As h_t is a linear function of p_t, it follows from (11.20) that h_t is an intricate nonlinear function of h_{t-1} and $(r_{t-1} - \mu)^2$. The standardized residual at time t is

$$z_t = \frac{r_t - \mu}{\sqrt{h_t}} = \left[\frac{\sigma_t^2}{p_t\sigma_L^2 + (1 - p_t)\sigma_H^2}\right]^{1/2}.$$

Table 11.1. Formulae used in the two-state volatility spreadsheet.

Cell	Formula
B12	`=1/SQRT(2*PI())`
D19	`=((D18*G18*(1-$H$9))+((1-D18)*H18*$H$10))/` `((D18*G18)+((1-D18)*H18))`
E18	`=D18*$H$4*$H$4+(1-D18)*$H$5*$H$5`
F18	`=(C18-$H$3)/SQRT(E18)`
G18	`=$B$12*EXP(-0.5*((((C18-$H$3)/$H$4)^2))/$H$4`
H9	`=(1-H6)*(1-H7)`
H10	`=H6*(1-H7)`
H13	`=SUM(I18:I2607)`
H18	`=$B$12*EXP(-0.5*(((C18-$H$3)/$H$5)^2))/$H$5`
I18	`=LN(D18*G18+(1-D18)*H18)`

The variables $\{z_t\}$ have zero mean, unit variance, and are uncorrelated. They are not i.i.d., however, as their conditional kurtosis is a function of past values of the process:

$$\text{kurtosis}(z_t \mid I_{t-1}) = \text{kurtosis}(r_t \mid I_{t-1}) = \frac{3(p_t\sigma_L^4 + (1-p_t)\sigma_H^4)}{h_t^2}.$$

Consequently, the two-state volatility model is not an ARCH model according to the definition we have adopted in Section 9.5.

Conditional variances for any future period, i.e. $\text{var}(r_{t+n} \mid I_t), n \geqslant 1$, are given by the same methods as in Section 9.3 and equal

$$\sigma^2 + (1 - p_{LH} - p_{HL})^{n-1}(h_{t+1} - \sigma^2).$$

11.4.5 Parameter Estimation

The likelihood L of a set of returns is the product of the conditional densities, given by (11.21). It is easy to evaluate, in contrast to the situation when volatility has a continuous distribution. The function $L(r_1, \ldots, r_n \mid \mu, \sigma_L, \sigma_H, p_{LH}, p_{HL})$ is unbounded when μ equals any of the values r_t, because then $L \to \infty$ as $\sigma_L \to 0$. Consequently, the maximum likelihood estimate (MLE) of all five parameters does not exist. The MLE of the four volatility parameters can be obtained with the constraint that μ is the sample mean. This method provides consistent parameter estimates, although care is required to avoid local maxima of the likelihood function (Ryden et al. 1998).

11.4.6 Currency Examples

The MLE for the ten years of daily DM/\$ returns from 1991 to 2000 is given by $\sigma_L = 0.00496$, $\sigma_H = 0.00912$, $p = 0.646$, and $\phi = 0.924$, with variance ratio $\sigma_H^2/\sigma_L^2 = 3.38$ and transition probabilities $p_{LH} = 0.0270$ and $p_{HL} = 0.0493$. The maximum log-likelihood of 9410.04 exceeds the maximum of 9396.06 for

#	A	B	C	D	E	F	G	H	I
1	Summary stats.						Parameter	Estimate	
2		Returns r(t)		Prior prob. p(t)	Standardized z(t)				
3	Mean	0.000129		0.6549	0.0008		Mu	0.000129	
4	Standard deviation	0.006709		0.2918	1.0062		Sigma low	0.00496	
5	Lag 1 correlation	0.0176		0.9010	0.0268		Sigma high	0.00912	
6	Skewness	-0.141			-0.169		p	0.6464	
7	Kurtosis	5.277			4.592		Phi	0.9237	
8									
9	Minimum	-0.0403		0.0493	-5.05		P(low to high)	0.0270	
10	Maximum	0.0340		0.9434	4.65		P(high to low)	0.0493	
11									
12	1/sqrt(2*pi)	0.3989							
13							log L	9410.04	
14									
15	Date	Price	Return r(t)	Prob(low) Prior p(t)	Cond. Var. h(t)	St. resid. z(t)	Density In low state	Density In high state	Log density
16									
17	2 Jan 91	1.4915							
18	3 Jan 91	1.4923	0.000536	0.6464	4.529E-05	0.0604	80.18	43.71	4.2089
19	4 Jan 91	1.5025	0.006813	0.7608	3.859E-05	1.0759	32.44	33.44	3.4867
20	7 Jan 91	1.5323	0.019638	0.7469	3.941E-05	3.1077	0.04	4.43	0.1385
21	8 Jan 91	1.5340	0.001108	0.0704	7.901E-05	0.1102	78.89	43.50	3.8285
22	9 Jan 91	1.5145	-0.012793	0.1609	7.371E-05	-1.5050	2.70	16.03	2.6307
23	10 Jan 91	1.5287	0.009332	0.0782	7.855E-05	1.0383	14.38	26.29	3.2331

Exhibit 11.1. Two-state Markov chain parameter estimates for the DM/$ rate, 1991–2000.

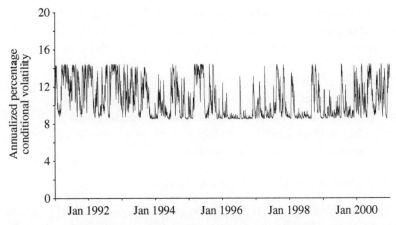

Figure 11.1. DM/$ volatility from the two-state model.

the GARCH(1, 1) model estimated from the same data in Section 9.4. However, the Markov chain model has one more parameter than the GARCH model and therefore it is inappropriate to use the higher likelihood as evidence that ARCH models are inferior. The persistence estimates are rather different for the Markov chain and GARCH models, being respectively 0.924 and 0.991. The estimate of ϕ has a high standard error and a conventional 95% confidence interval for ϕ includes 0.96. A low persistence level for the Markov chain model is also noted in Taylor (1999), where ten years of daily £/$ returns from 1982 to 1991 provide the estimates $\sigma_H^2/\sigma_L^2 = 3.73$, $p = 0.726$, $\phi = 0.880$, $p_{LH} = 0.0329$, and $p_{HL} = 0.0871$.

Exhibit 11.1 shows part of an Excel spreadsheet that was used to find the MLE for the DM/$ series, with a selection of the cell formulae provided in Table 11.1. The log-likelihood, $\log L(\sigma_L, \sigma_H, p, \phi)$, is maximized with the constraints $\sigma_L \geq 0.0001$, $\sigma_H \geq \sigma_L$, and $1 > p, \phi > 0$.

A time series of volatility estimates, given by the annualized conditional standard deviations $\tilde{\sigma}_t = \sqrt{259h_t}$, is shown in Figure 11.1. These estimates come from (11.22) and their range, from 8.5% to 14.4%, reflects a range for the conditional probabilities p_t from 0.049 to 0.943. Figure 11.1 can be compared with the equivalent Figure 9.1 for the GARCH(1, 1) model. There is a tendency for the conditional standard deviations of the Markov chain model to cluster around the extreme values σ_L and σ_H, which contrasts with the unimodal distribution of $\tilde{\sigma}_t$ for GARCH(1, 1).

11.4.7 Extensions

Markov chain models for volatility can be made more realistic by increasing the number of states. The conditional state probabilities can then be obtained by adapting equation (11.20) and hence it is feasible to obtain the MLE for the volatility parameters. Ryden et al. (1998) show how the most appropriate number of states can be inferred by using likelihood methods. They find that a three-state model is preferable to a two-state model for several series of daily S&P 500 index returns.

A Markov chain can be used to select an ARCH model instead of a volatility state. This idea defines the switching ARCH models, which we mentioned in Section 10.7. They are a hybrid of ARCH and SV specifications. In a similar manner, a Markov chain can be used to specify the parameters of a SV process; this is explained at the end of the next section.

11.5   The Standard Stochastic Volatility Model

The simplest credible continuous distribution for the stochastic volatility σ_t is log-normal when returns are observed daily or less often. Then $\log(\sigma_t) \sim N(\alpha, \beta^2)$, with α and β parameters. The lognormal distribution is the standard choice when a continuous distribution is used for volatility. This choice is pragmatic. It guarantees positive outcomes for volatility (unlike a normal distribution), it permits calculation of moments and it allows any level of excess kurtosis in returns. It appears in Taylor (1980, 1982b) and Tauchen and Pitts (1983) and it is supported by the early empirical study of Clark (1973). The recent evidence from several studies of high-frequency returns provides strong empirical support for the lognormal distribution, several years after its adoption for daily volatility; this evidence is discussed in the next chapter.

The autocorrelations of volatility are proportional to those of absolute excess returns for independent SV processes (equation (11.6)). This indicates that the autocorrelations of volatility must decrease slowly, because this occurs for samples of absolute excess returns (Section 4.10). Therefore, the simplest appropriate stationary stochastic process for volatility is a Gaussian AR(1) process for its logarithm,

$$\log(\sigma_t) - \alpha = \phi(\log(\sigma_{t-1}) - \alpha) + \eta_t. \tag{11.23}$$

The parameter ϕ represents volatility persistence, with $-1 < \phi < 1$. The i.i.d. volatility residuals η_t have distribution $N(0, \sigma_\eta^2)$, with $\sigma_\eta^2 = \beta^2(1 - \phi^2)$.

The *standard SV model* of Taylor (1986) is given by (11.23),

$$r_t = \mu + \sigma_t u_t, \tag{11.24}$$

and two further assumptions. First the i.i.d. variables u_t are distributed as $N(0, 1)$ and second the processes $\{\sigma_t\}$ and $\{u_t\}$ are stochastically independent. The returns process is strictly stationary, since it is the product of independent strictly stationary processes. It is also covariance stationary, because the returns have finite variance, as shown later.

The standard model has received more attention than any other SV specification. Its major properties are as follows.

- All the moments of returns are finite.
- The kurtosis of returns equals $3\exp(4\beta^2)$.
- The correlation between the returns r_t and $r_{t+\tau}$ is zero for all $\tau > 0$.
- The correlation between the squared excess return $s_t = (r_t - \mu)^2$ and $s_{t+\tau}$ is positive for all $\tau > 0$ when ϕ is positive. The correlation approximately equals $C\phi^\tau$ with C a positive function of β.
- The autocorrelation function of $a_t^p = |r_t - \mu|^p$ has approximately the same shape as that of s_t for all positive p.

More flexible models are obtained by allowing excess kurtosis in the u_t and/or dependence between $\sigma_{t'}$ and u_t for some values of $t' - t$, as discussed later in Sections 11.8 and 11.9. It should be noted that the standard SV model does not permit volatility to react asymmetrically to price falls and price rises, because σ_t is independent of the signs of all previous returns. It may also be noted that some writers avoid referring to σ_t and instead consider either $h_t = \sigma_t^2$ or $h_t = \log(\sigma_t^2)$, with h_t being their notation for a function of σ_t. Such notation would be confusing if it were used here, as we reserve the notation h_t for the conditional variance given by $\mathrm{var}(r_t \mid r_{t-1}, r_{t-2}, \ldots)$.

We now describe several properties of the standard SV model, including a state space representation, its moments, and its autocorrelations. We then provide an overview of the methods that can be used to estimate the parameter vector, which is $\theta = (\mu, \alpha, \beta, \phi)'$, in Section 11.6. This is followed by a survey of typical parameter estimates.

11.5.1 State Space Representation

For additional variables defined by

$$l_t = \log(|r_t - \mu|), \quad L_t = \log(\sigma_t), \quad \text{and} \quad \xi_t = \log(|u_t|),$$

there exists a linear state space representation for the process $\{l_t\}$. The measurement equation is

$$l_t = L_t + \xi_t$$

and the transition equation is

$$L_t = (1 - \phi)\alpha + \phi L_{t-1} + \eta_t. \tag{11.25}$$

The logarithm of volatility is then the unobservable state variable and application of the Kalman filter provides information about its distribution conditional on observed returns (Scott 1987; Nelson 1988; Harvey, Ruiz, and Shephard 1994). The state space model is not Gaussian because ξ_t is not a normal variable. The distribution of ξ_t has mean $\mu_\xi = -0.63518\ldots$ and variance $\sigma_\xi^2 = \pi^2/8$ (Wishart 1947; Scott 1987). It is skewed with a long left-hand tail. The process $\{l_t\}$ is an ARMA(1, 1) process, since it is the sum of an AR(1) process and an independent i.i.d. process.

11.5.2 Density and Moments

The unconditional density function of returns is symmetric about its mean μ. Called the LNN density in Section 4.8, it is given by integrating over the latent volatility variable,

$$f(r_t) = \int_0^\infty \psi(r_t \mid \mu, \sigma^2) \Lambda(\sigma \mid \alpha, \beta^2) \, d\sigma,$$

with $\psi(\cdot)$ the normal density function and $\Lambda(\cdot)$ the lognormal density function defined by equation (3.4). This integral can only be evaluated numerically. Figures 4.3 and 4.4 display an example of the density.

For any positive number p,

$$E[|r_t - \mu|^p] = E[\sigma_t^p] E[|u_t|^p]. \tag{11.26}$$

As $\log(\sigma_t^p) = p \log(\sigma_t)$, the distribution of $\log(\sigma_t^p)$ is $N(p\alpha, p^2\beta^2)$ and thus

$$E[\sigma_t^p] = \exp(p\alpha + \tfrac{1}{2}p^2\beta^2). \tag{11.27}$$

All the moments given by (11.26) can be evaluated using (11.7) and (11.27). In particular,

$$E[|r_t - \mu|] = \sqrt{2/\pi} \exp(\alpha + \tfrac{1}{2}\beta^2),$$
$$\mathrm{var}(r_t) = \exp(2\alpha + 2\beta^2), \tag{11.28}$$
$$\mathrm{kurtosis}(r_t) = 3\exp(4\beta^2).$$

11.5.3 Autocorrelations

The excess returns $r_t - \mu$ are a martingale difference and are hence uncorrelated.

The autocorrelations of $l_t = \log(|r_t - \mu|)$ can be derived easily from the state space equations (11.25). The variance of l_t is $\beta^2 + (\pi^2/8)$, because the variances of L_t and ξ_t are respectively β^2 and $\pi^2/8$. The covariance of l_t with $l_{t+\tau}$ is the same as that of L_t with $L_{t+\tau}$ when $\tau > 0$ and equals $\beta^2\phi^\tau$. Thus $\{l_t\}$ has autocorrelations

$$\rho_{\tau,l} = C(0, \beta)\phi^\tau, \quad \tau > 0,$$

with

$$C(0, \beta) = \frac{8\beta^2}{8\beta^2 + \pi^2}. \tag{11.29}$$

These autocorrelations are all positive (assuming that ϕ is positive) and they decay geometrically at the rate ϕ.

The autocorrelations of $a_t = |r_t - \mu|$ and $s_t = (r_t - \mu)^2$ have approximately the same shape, although they decay from different constants. The following approximations are good when β^2 is small and/or ϕ^τ is near 1:

$$\rho_{\tau,a} \cong C(1, \beta)\phi^\tau, \quad \rho_{\tau,s} \cong C(2, \beta)\phi^\tau, \quad \tau > 0,$$

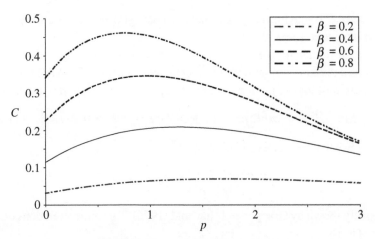

Figure 11.2. The function $C(p, \beta)$.

with

$$C(1, \beta) = \frac{\exp(\beta^2) - 1}{(\pi/2)\exp(\beta^2) - 1} \quad \text{and} \quad C(2, \beta) = \frac{\exp(4\beta^2) - 1}{3\exp(4\beta^2) - 1}. \tag{11.30}$$

For the typical value $\beta = 0.4$, the constants $C(0, \beta)$, $C(1, \beta)$, and $C(2, \beta)$ are respectively 0.115, 0.206, and 0.191.

These geometric decay formulae have the same shape as the autocorrelations of both s_t from a GARCH(1, 1) model and l_t from an EGARCH(1) model (Taylor 1994a). The standard SV model has many similarities with GARCH(1, 1), yet it is more similar to the special case of EGARCH(1) given by symmetric reactions to price falls and rises. This remark is made more precise in Section 13.4 when we consider the diffusion limits of the SV, GARCH, and EGARCH models when observations are obtained more and more frequently.

The above approximations extend to the autocorrelations of a_t^p for any positive value of p. From (11.5), (11.7), and (11.27), $A(p, \beta) = \exp(p^2\beta^2)$,

$$B(p) = \sqrt{\pi}\,\Gamma(p + \tfrac{1}{2})\Gamma(\tfrac{1}{2}p + \tfrac{1}{2})^{-2}, \tag{11.31}$$

$$C(p, \beta) = \frac{\exp(p^2\beta^2) - 1}{B(p)\exp(p^2\beta^2) - 1}, \quad p > 0, \tag{11.32}$$

and there is the approximation

$$\rho_{\tau,a^p} \cong C(p, \beta)\phi^\tau, \quad \tau > 0. \tag{11.33}$$

As $p \to 0$, $C(p, \beta)$ converges to $C(0, \beta)$ given in (11.29).

Figure 11.2 shows $C(p, \beta)$ as a function of p, when $\beta = 0.2$, 0.4, 0.6, and 0.8. When β is held constant, it can be seen that C increases monotonically as p increases until a maximum value is attained and then C decreases monotonically as p continues to increase. The dependence within the process $\{a_t^p\}$ is maximized when the term C is maximized. These maxima occur at $p = 1.70, 1.27, 0.97$, and 0.75 as β increases from 0.2 to 0.8.

The *exact* formulae for the autocorrelations of a_t^p can be obtained from (11.6) once we know the autocorrelations of σ_t^p. As $\log(\sigma_t^p)$ is a Gaussian AR(1) process, the distribution of $\log(\sigma_t^p) + \log(\sigma_{t+\tau}^p)$ is $N(2p\alpha, 2(1 + \phi^{|\tau|})p^2\beta^2)$ and hence

$$E[\sigma_t^p \sigma_{t+\tau}^p] = \exp(2p\alpha + (1 + \phi^\tau)p^2\beta^2), \quad \tau \geqslant 0. \tag{11.34}$$

It then follows that the autocorrelations of σ_t^p are

$$\rho_{\tau,\sigma^p} = \frac{\exp(p^2\beta^2\phi^\tau) - 1}{\exp(p^2\beta^2) - 1}, \quad \tau \geqslant 0, \tag{11.35}$$

as previously shown by Granger and Newbold (1976). The autocorrelations of a_t^p are, from (11.6),

$$\rho_{\tau,a^p} = \frac{\exp(p^2\beta^2\phi^\tau) - 1}{B(p)\exp(p^2\beta^2) - 1}, \quad \tau > 0. \tag{11.36}$$

This equation is in Ghysels et al. (1996), while the results for $p = 1$ and $p = 2$ are in Taylor (1986).

When $p^2\beta^2$ is small and/or ϕ^τ is near 1, we can approximate $\exp(p^2\beta^2\phi^\tau) - 1$ by $\phi^\tau(\exp(p^2\beta^2) - 1)$, to obtain the approximations given in equations (11.30) and (11.33). The exact result when $p = 2$ is

$$\rho_{\tau,s} = \frac{\exp(4\beta^2\phi^\tau) - 1}{3\exp(4\beta^2) - 1}, \quad \tau > 0. \tag{11.37}$$

When $\beta = 0.4$ and $\phi = 0.98$ the first autocorrelation of squared excess returns is 0.1860 and the approximate value from (11.30) is 0.1873; at lag 20 the approximation is much less accurate, the exact and approximate values being 0.114 and 0.128 respectively.

11.5.4 *Markov Chain Alternatives and Extensions*

The variance of returns conditional upon previous returns, denoted by h_t, is a complicated function for the standard SV model. As the density of σ_t is unimodal, it is safe to assume that the density of h_t has the same property. This contrasts with the situation for the two-state volatility model described in Section 11.4. The distribution of h_t is bimodal for that model, with most outcomes near to one of the two volatility levels whenever the persistence of volatility is near one. The marked difference in the distribution of h_t can then be used to decide between the standard SV model and the two-state volatility model.

Taylor (1999) essentially proposes estimating the regression model

$$E[r_t^2] = \beta_0 + \beta_1 h_t^{(2V)} + \beta_2 h_t^{(GARCH)}.$$

The conditional variance $h_t^{(2V)}$ for the two-state model is given by (11.22), while $h_t^{(GARCH)}$ obtained by estimating the GARCH(1, 1) model is used as a good approximation to the unknown conditional variance for the standard SV model. The two-state model is then preferred if and only if $\hat{\beta}_1 > \hat{\beta}_2$. A Monte Carlo investigation shows that this procedure has high power to select the correct model. When applied to ten years of daily returns from the rate of exchange between sterling and the dollar, $\hat{\beta}_1$ is almost zero while $\hat{\beta}_2$ is near one so that the standard SV model is overwhelmingly favored for the data considered.

So, Lam, and Li (1998) add Markov switching to the standard SV model. They replace the mean α of $\log(\sigma_t)$ by a term α_t that is determined by a finite-state Markov chain. This model is estimated in their paper with three states for α_t, using weekly observations of the S&P 500 index.

11.6 Parameter Estimation for the Standard SV Model

Many methods have been proposed for estimating the parameters of the standard SV model, $\theta = (\mu, \alpha, \beta, \phi)'$, from a set of n observed returns $I_n = \{r_1, \ldots, r_n\}$. We suppose μ is estimated by the average return $\bar{r}$ and focus on estimating α, β, and ϕ. MLEs can only be obtained by complicated methods and hence many alternative estimates have been proposed. The likelihood function is the product of conditional densities $f(r_t \mid I_{t-1})$, with $I_{t-1} = \{r_1, \ldots, r_{t-1}\}$, but tractable expressions for these densities are not known. An obvious modification of equations (11.20) and (11.21) provides the densities when the number of volatility states is finite. It is probable that these equations can be adapted to approximate the standard SV model using a large number of volatility states and hence the likelihood can be approximated.

A formula for the likelihood is given by integrating the product of (a) the conditional density of the returns given the volatilities and (b) the density of the volatilities. This defines the n-dimensional integral

$$L(r_1, \ldots, r_n \mid \theta)$$
$$= \int_{\sigma_1} \int_{\sigma_2} \cdots \int_{\sigma_n} f(r_1, \ldots, r_n \mid \sigma_1, \ldots, \sigma_n) f(\sigma_1, \ldots, \sigma_n \mid \theta) \, d\sigma_1 \cdots d\sigma_n.$$
$$(11.38)$$

Both terms inside the integral can be evaluated with ease, but the exact value of the integral can only be evaluated by numerical methods. Fridman and Harris (1998) outline an efficient method for calculating an approximation to the integral that is based upon a discrete approximation to the distribution of σ_t.

There is a trade-off between the accuracy of the parameter estimates and the sophistication of the methods. Elementary moment matching and quasi-maximum likelihood (or Kalman filter) methods are straightforward. The generalized method of moments (GMM) methodology is a more complicated technique. The MCMC (or Bayesian) method advocated by Jacquier, Polson, and Rossi (1994) and the simulated likelihood methods of Daníelsson (1994) and Sandmann and Koopman (1998) are more accurate, but they are even more complicated. All these methods can be adapted to estimate some of the more complicated SV models discussed later in this chapter.

The quasi-ML and MCMC methods also provide information about the distributions of the unobservable volatilities conditional on the observed returns, which is required if volatility is to be forecast into the future. Diagnostic tests for the adequacy of the standard SV model are fairly easy to perform for the GMM and quasi-ML methods.

11.6.1 Elementary Moment Estimates

The mean α and the standard deviation β of $\log(\sigma_t)$ can be estimated by matching two moments of the returns distribution. For example, from the sample second and fourth moments we obtain the standard deviation s and kurtosis k and hence $\hat{\beta}^2 = \frac{1}{4}\log(k/3)$ and $\hat{\alpha} = \log(s) - \hat{\beta}^2$ from (11.28), assuming $k > 3$. The sample kurtosis is inaccurate and sensitive to outliers. A more robust method equates the sample means $\bar{a}$ and $\bar{s}$ of the observed quantities $a_t = |r_t - \bar{r}|$ and $s_t = (r_t - \bar{r})^2$ with the theoretical mean absolute deviation and variance. This provides $\hat{\alpha} = \log(\pi \bar{a}^2/(2\sqrt{\bar{s}}))$ and $\hat{\beta}^2 = \log(2\bar{s}/(\pi \bar{a}^2))$, again from (11.28). The autoregressive parameter ϕ can be estimated by minimizing a goodness-of-fit measure for selected sample autocorrelations. One possibility is to minimize $f(K, \phi) = \sum(\hat{\rho}_{\tau,a} - K\phi^\tau)^2$, summing over $\tau = 1, \ldots, 50$ with $\hat{\rho}_{\tau,a}$ the sample autocorrelations of the quantities a_t. This possibility is motivated by equation (11.30) and we might hope that $\hat{K} \cong C(1, \hat{\beta})$. The above estimators are probably relatively inaccurate. They are evaluated in Taylor (1982b, 1986) and provide estimates that are generally similar to those in more recent studies.

11.6.2 GMM

The generalized method of moments seeks parameter values that provide theoretical moments that are close to the empirical moments, using more moments than there are parameters. Melino and Turnbull (1990) is an early example of the application of the method to estimating SV parameters. Jacquier et al. (1994) and particularly Andersen and Sørensen (1996) provide a detailed investigation of the finite sample properties of GMM estimates for the standard SV model. The first four moment conditions they consider are

$$g_i(\theta) = \left(\frac{1}{n}\sum_{t=1}^{n}(|r_t - \bar{r}|)^i\right) - E[\sigma_t^i]E[|u_t^i|]$$

and the remainder are of the form

$$g_j(\theta) = \left(\frac{1}{n} \sum_{t=1}^{n} (|r_t - \bar{r}|)^k (|r_{t+\tau} - \bar{r}|)^k \right) - E[\sigma_t^k \sigma_{t+\tau}^k] E[|u_t^k|]^2 \quad (11.39)$$

with i and j counting the moment conditions, $k = 1$ or 2 and $\tau > 0$. All the terms in (11.39) can be evaluated using (11.7), (11.27), and (11.34). The GMM estimate of θ is given by minimizing the quadratic form $g'Wg$ for an appropriate weighting matrix W (see Hansen (1982) and Hamilton (1994, Chapter 14) for general theoretical results for the GMM method).

Andersen and Sørensen (1996) find a total of fourteen moment conditions is appropriate for the parameter values that they consider in their simulation study. They also evaluate many methods for choosing W. They encounter some numerical problems when $\phi = 0.98$, which casts doubts on the usefulness of the method when applied to daily returns. Shephard (1996) lists several criticisms of GMM in the SV context. The ad hoc selection of moment conditions can be avoided by using the efficient method of moments technique, applied by Gallant, Hsieh, and Tauchen (1997), but this is a very technical methodology.

11.6.3 QML

The state space representation given by (11.25) can be used to derive conditional means and variances for the variables $l_t = \log(|r_t - \mu|)$ and $L_t = \log(\sigma_t)$, after replacing μ by the average return $\bar{r}$ and employing the Kalman filter. The model parameters can then be estimated by maximizing a likelihood function. This easy method is illustrated in the next section. Harvey (1989) is an authoritative text about the filter; its equations are provided in the appendix to this chapter.

Harvey et al. (1994) apply the Kalman filter to obtain the best predictions of l_t and L_t that are linear combinations of the information $J_{t-1} = \{l_1, \dots, l_{t-1}\}$. The best linear predictor of l_t, given J_{t-1}, is here denoted by $l_{t-1,1}$ and the mean square error of the prediction error $v_t = l_t - l_{t-1,1}$ is denoted by F_t. The updating equations for the predictions are particularly simple for the standard SV model and take the same form as ARMA(1, 1) predictions when the filter is in its steady state.

The distribution of the observations l_t is negatively skewed. The quasi-MLE (QMLE) of α, β, and ϕ is given by pretending the l_t have conditional normal distributions,

$$l_t \mid J_{t-1} \sim N(l_{t-1,1}, F_t), \quad (11.40)$$

and then maximizing

$$\log L = -\frac{1}{2} \sum_{t=1}^{n} \left(\log(2\pi) + \log(F_t) + \frac{v_t^2}{F_t} \right). \quad (11.41)$$

The QMLE is consistent and asymptotically normal. The likelihood theory for ARCH models described in Section 10.4 applies to the QMLE for the SV model. In particular, the covariance matrix of the QMLE is given by equation (10.32), for reasons outlined by Harvey et al. (1994) and Harvey and Shephard (1996).

The Kalman filter also provides a prediction of L_t, namely $l_{t-1,1} - \mu_\xi$ with mean square error $F_t - (\pi^2/8)$. This can be used to obtain an approximately unbiased prediction of σ_t from J_{t-1}, given by $\exp(l_{t-1,1} - \mu_\xi + \frac{1}{2}(F_t - (\pi^2/8)))$. Also, the Kalman smoothing algorithm can be used to estimate σ_t from all the observations J_n.

Diagnostic checks for the QML methodology rely on the result that the terms $z_t = v_t/\sqrt{F_t}$ are uncorrelated, with zero mean and unit variance, when the model is correctly specified. One disadvantage of QML is that the variables l_t are sensitive to small values of r_t, so that the residual v_t is a negative outlier when $r_t \cong 0$. This sensitivity can be reduced by using a transformation of Breidt and Carriquiry (1996) discussed by Ghysels et al. (1996) and defined in Section 11.7.

11.6.4 Simulated ML

The QML methodology can only provide an approximation to the likelihood function. This function can be evaluated by a variety of Monte Carlo methods. Simulated likelihood values can then be maximized to provide an exact MLE for the standard SV model. The first Monte Carlo method was developed by Daníelsson and Richard (1993) and Daníelsson (1994), who use importance sampling. A conceptually simpler and faster algorithm is presented in Sandmann and Koopman (1998). They write the exact log-likelihood of the variables l_t as the quasi-log-likelihood (given in (11.41)) plus a remainder function. This remainder function can be calculated by a small number of simulations that use the Kalman smoother. Similar techniques are described by Durbin and Koopman (2000).

11.6.5 MCMC

Another way to obtain the information provided by the likelihood function uses Bayesian analysis. Bayesian estimation methods make use of data $r = (r_1, \ldots, r_n)$ and a prior density $f(\theta)$ for the parameters θ to find the posterior density $f(\theta \mid r)$. Likewise, although we do not observe the latent volatility process, we can seek the posterior density $f(\sigma \mid r)$, with $\sigma = (\sigma_1, \ldots, \sigma_n)$. These posterior densities can be obtained by the Markov chain Monte Carlo (MCMC) methodology, whose principles are explained and illustrated by Chib (2001) and Tsay (2002).

MCMC methods provide the joint posterior density $f(\sigma, \theta \mid r)$, from which we can obtain both $f(\theta \mid r)$ and $f(\sigma \mid r)$. The Markov chain, here denoted by $\{X_k\}$, can be generated by Monte Carlo methods that deliver an outcome $X_{k+1} = (\sigma^{(k+1)}, \theta^{(k+1)})$ from X_k and a transition density $f(X_{k+1} \mid X_k)$. A technical problem is to define a transition density that ensures the chain $\{X_k\}$ is ergodic with the required stationary distribution, namely $f(\sigma, \theta \mid r)$. All solutions to this problem involve complicated algorithms that are beyond the scope of this book. The early algorithm of Jacquier et al. (1994) has a high level of dependence in the Markov chain so that very long Monte Carlo sequences are required to estimate the posterior density. Details are also provided in Jacquier, Polson, and Rossi (2004). More efficient algorithms are described by Shephard (1996), Shephard and Pitt (1997), and Kim, Shephard, and Chib (1998). These papers also discuss the selection of the prior density $f(\theta)$. An approximation to the likelihood $L(r \mid \theta)$ is provided by the methods of Kim, Shephard, and Chib (1998).

The logical point estimate of θ is given by the mean of its posterior density, which can be estimated from a long realization of N outcomes from the Markov chain by

$$\hat{\theta} = \frac{\theta^{(M+1)} + \cdots + \theta^{(N)}}{N - M},$$

with the first M outcomes discarded to diminish the influence of the arbitrary starting value X_1. Jacquier et al. (1994) provide simulation results that support their claim that the MCMC estimate is much more accurate than the GMM and QMLE estimates. The covariance matrix of $\hat{\theta}$ can be estimated after first estimating the autocorrelations of the terms $\theta^{(k)}$, as in Shephard and Pitt (1997).

11.6.6 Typical Estimates

We only review estimates for daily returns from foreign exchange here. The standard SV model has also been estimated for daily equity returns. However, the results are of limited interest for equities because the model does not allow volatility to respond asymmetrically to price falls and price rises.

Estimates of the persistence parameter ϕ are usually between 0.95 and 0.99, just as they are for measures of persistence from ARCH models. Taylor (1986, p. 89) uses an elementary moment matching method and reports 0.985, 0.987, and 0.989 for the DM/\$, £/\$, and SF/\$ rates, from 1974 to 1981. The same method gives 0.969 for the DM/\$ from 1977 to 1990, compared with 0.938 for the QMLE method (Taylor 1994a). Harvey et al. (1994) apply QMLE to DM/\$, £/\$, SF/\$, and yen/\$ rates for the shorter period from 1981 to 1985 and obtain the estimates 0.965, 0.991, 0.957, and 0.995, with respective standard errors equal to 0.021, 0.007, 0.002, and 0.005.

MCMC estimates are given by Jacquier et al. (1994) for the DM/\$ and £/\$ rates from 1980 to 1990. The point estimates are 0.95 and 0.96 respectively and 95% posterior intervals are 0.92–0.97 and 0.94–0.98 respectively. Further MCMC estimates are provided by Pitt and Shephard (1999) for the longer and more recent period from 1981 to 1998. They study DM/\$, £/\$, FF/\$, SF/\$, and yen/\$ rates and their persistence estimates are 0.965, 0.970, 0.947, 0.953, and

0.841 respectively, with standard errors all below 0.004. The low estimate for the yen series is surprising.

Estimates of the standard deviation β of $\log(\sigma_t)$ are usually between 0.3 and 0.7. This is the case for all of the estimates from DM/\$ series that are mentioned above. The logarithm of the unconditional standard deviation of returns is $\alpha + \beta^2$ from (11.28), with α the mean of $\log(\sigma_t)$. As the standard deviation is near 0.7% for FX returns, estimates of α are usually between -5.4 and -5.0.

11.7   An Example of SV Model Estimation for Exchange Rates

This section can be skipped by readers who are not interested in Excel calculations. The QML method is a straightforward method for estimating the parameters of the standard SV and related models. It is easy to implement within Excel, unlike other methods that instead have the advantage that they produce more accurate estimates of the parameters. We illustrate the QML calculations for the standard SV model because the calculations are easy to understand; we do not consider QML to be superior to alternative methods.

Exhibit 11.2 shows part of the relevant spreadsheet for our DM/\$ data from 1991 to 2000. The expected return μ is estimated by the average observed return $\bar{r}$. The mean, standard deviation, and autoregressive parameters of the process $\log(\sigma_t)$, respectively denoted by α, β, and ϕ, are estimated by maximizing the quasi-likelihood of the observed quantities $l_t = \log(|r_t - \bar{r}|)$, defined by equations (11.40) and (11.41). At time t we already know the conditional mean $l_{t-1,1}$ and the conditional variance F_t for l_t. We then observe the outcome for l_t and find the prediction error v_t, followed by calculating the next conditional mean and variance, $l_{t,1}$ and F_{t+1}, using the filtering equations given in the appendix to this chapter. The spreadsheet row for time t is completed by calculating the standardized error $z_t = v_t/\sqrt{F_t}$ and the contribution to the log-likelihood, namely $-\frac{1}{2}(\log(2\pi) + \log(F_t) + v_t^2/F_t)$.

The model parameters are in cells H3, H4, and H5 of Exhibit 11.2. The quantities $\bar{r}$, μ_ξ, $\alpha + \mu_\xi$, $H_t \equiv \pi^2/8$, and $\sigma_\eta^2 = \beta^2(1 - \phi^2)$ are located in cells H10–H14. The initial values $l_{0,1} = \alpha + \mu_\xi$ and $F_1 = H_1 + \beta^2$ are placed in cells E20 and G20. It is then only necessary to create formulae for cells D20, F20, H20, I20, E21, and G21 before copying and pasting can be used to complete the filtering calculations. The most important cell formulae are provided in Table 11.2.

Exhibit 11.2 shows the results when the log-likelihood (in cell H7) is maximized with the constraints $\beta \geqslant 0.0001$ and $|\phi| \leqslant 0.9999$. The estimate $\hat{\alpha} = -5.16$ is in line with previous DM/\$ estimates but the "volatility of volatility" estimate $\hat{\beta} = 0.288$ is relatively low. Alternative estimates are given by matching the standard deviation of returns and either the mean absolute deviation ($\hat{\alpha} = -5.16$, $\hat{\beta} = 0.409$) or the kurtosis of returns ($\hat{\alpha} = -5.15$, $\hat{\beta} = 0.376$), using formulae given in Section 11.6. The QML estimate of the persistence parameter is

	A	B	C	D	E	F	G	H	I
	Summary stats.	r(t)	l(t) data	l(t) model	z(t)		Parameter	Estimate	
1									
2	Mean	0.000129	-5.8008	-5.7903	-0.0016		Alpha	-5.1551	
3	Standard deviation	0.006709	1.1625	1.1475	1.0140		Beta	0.2883	
4	Lag 1 correlation	0.0176	0.0578	0.0621	-0.0026		Phi	0.9839	
5	Skewness	-0.141	-1.154		-1.206				
6	Kurtosis	5.277	5.786		5.974		log L	-4026.268	
7									
8	Minimum	-0.0403	-14.47		-7.69		Average return	0.000129	
9	Maximum	0.0340	-3.21		2.07		E[log(abs(u))]	-0.6352	
10							alpha + E[...]	-5.7903	
11							H	1.2337	
12							var(eta)	0.0026	

Date	Price p(t)	Return r(t)	Log abs ret l(t)	Prediction l(t-1,t)	Error v(t)	MSE F(t)	Stand. Error z(t)	Like. Term
2 Jan 91	1.4915							
3 Jan 91	1.4923	0.000536	-7.8078	-5.7903	-2.0175	1.3168	-1.7581	-2.602
4 Jan 91	1.5025	0.006813	-5.0080	-5.9156	0.9076	1.3118	0.7924	-1.369
7 Jan 91	1.5323	0.019638	-3.9369	-5.8605	1.9236	1.3074	1.6823	-2.468
8 Jan 91	1.5340	0.001108	-6.9285	-5.7526	-1.1759	1.3037	-1.0299	-1.582
9 Jan 91	1.5145	-0.012793	-4.3488	-5.8153	1.4665	1.3005	1.2860	-1.877
10 Jan 91	1.5287	0.009332	-4.6882	-5.7408	1.0526	1.2977	0.9240	-1.476

Exhibit 11.2. QML parameter estimates for the standard SV model, from the DM/$ rate, 1991–2000.

Table 11.2.   Formulae used in the standard SV model spreadsheet.

Cell	Formula
D20	=LN(ABS(C20-$H$10))
E20	=H12
E21	=(1-$H$5)*$H$12+($H$5*D20)-($H$5*$H$13*F20/G20)
F20	=D20-E20
G20	=H4*H4+H13
G21	=$H$13+($H$5*$H$5*$H$13*(G20-$H$13)/G20)+$H$14
H7	=SUM(I20:I2609)
H12	=H3+H11
H13	=PI()*PI()/8
H14	=H4*H4*(1-H5*H5)
H20	=F20/SQRT(G20)
I20	=-0.5*(LN(2*PI())+LN(G20)+H20*H20)

$\hat{\phi} = 0.9839$ and it is slightly less than the GARCH(1, 1) persistence estimate of 0.9908 for the same data, calculated in Section 9.4.

Summary statistics for the data l_t are similar to the theoretical values for the standard SV model when the QML estimates are inserted into the theoretical equations. This is seen in cells C3–D5 for the mean, standard deviation, and first autocorrelation of l_t. The standardized errors z_t have satisfactory summary statistics, with the minimum value of -7.69 reflecting the outliers that occur in the left tail for the QML method. The outliers can be trimmed by the method of Breidt and Carriquiry (1996). If we redefine $2l_t$ to be $\log(r_t^2 + cs^2) - cs^2/(r_t^2 + cs^2)$, with s the standard deviation of the returns, then the minimum value of z_t increases to -3.69 when $c = 0.0002$ and the QMLE is almost unchanged with $\hat{\phi} = 0.9847$; some writers recommend $c = 0.02$ but this produces unsatisfactory summary statistics for the DM/\$ data.

The filtering equations converge to a steady state. The series F_t is independent of the data and converges to 1.2754 for the estimated parameters. The quantity $\phi H_t / F_t$ is also independent of the data and converges to the moving-average parameter of l_t when it is rewritten as an ARMA(1, 1) process with innovations v_t; the limit is 0.9518 for the estimated parameters.

Figure 11.3 shows annualized percentage predictions of σ_t for the SV model that are joined by dark lines. These can be compared with GARCH(1, 1) predictions that are shown by light dots on the same figure. The SV prediction at time $t - 1$ is a constant multiplied by $\exp(l_{t-1,1})$, with the constant chosen to eliminate bias, with the average value of the squared predictions equal to the sample variance of the returns. It can be seen that the SV and GARCH predictions are usually similar. The standard deviation of the difference between the annualized values from the two methodologies is 1.1%.

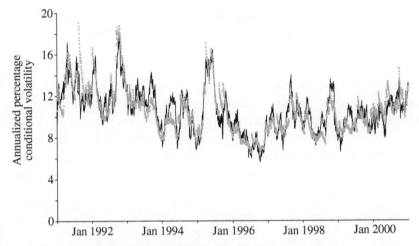

Figure 11.3. DM/\$ volatility from the SV model.

11.8 Independent SV Models with Heavy Tails

The standard SV model supposes $r_t - \mu$ is the product of independent variables, $u_t \sim N(0, 1)$ and σ_t, whose logarithm is given by a Gaussian, AR(1) process. Heavier tails for the returns can be modeled by now assuming that the u_t have a standardized t-distribution with $\nu > 2$ degrees of freedom, the density function being given by (9.43). This modification of the standard SV model will be called the *standard SVt* model. It was first investigated by Harvey et al. (1994).

From the definition of the Student t-distribution, u_t is the product of independent variables

$$u_t = v_t \sqrt{w_t} \quad \text{with } v_t \sim N(0, 1) \text{ and } (\nu - 2)w_t^{-1} \sim \chi_\nu^2. \tag{11.42}$$

Excess returns are then a mixture of normal distributions,

$$r_t - \mu = \sigma_t u_t = (\sigma_t \sqrt{w_t})v_t = \sigma_t^* v_t \tag{11.43}$$

with $\log(\sigma_t^*)$ following a non-Gaussian, ARMA(1, 1) process.

11.8.1 State Space Representation

The state space equations, (11.25), also apply for the SVt model but the distribution of

$$\xi_t = \log(|u_t|) = \log(|v_t|) + \tfrac{1}{2}\log(w_t) \tag{11.44}$$

now has mean and variance respectively given by

$$\mu_\xi = \tfrac{1}{2}(\psi(\tfrac{1}{2}) - \psi(\tfrac{1}{2}\nu) + \log(\nu - 2)) \tag{11.45}$$

and

$$\sigma_\xi^2 = \tfrac{1}{8}(\pi^2 + 2\psi'(\tfrac{1}{2}\nu)), \tag{11.46}$$

where $\psi(x) = \mathrm{d}\log\Gamma(x)/\mathrm{d}x$ and $\psi'(x) = \mathrm{d}\psi/\mathrm{d}x$ are the digamma and tri-gamma functions; similar formulae can be found in Ruiz (1994).

11.8.2 Moments

The expectation of r_t^p is finite only when $p < \nu$, which contrasts with finite moments of all orders for the standard SV model. All the finite moments can be obtained from equations (11.26) and (11.27). Recall the notation defined by $\log(\sigma_t) \sim N(\alpha, \beta^2)$. Now $E[|r_t - \mu|] = E[|u_t|]\exp(\alpha + \frac{1}{2}\beta^2)$, with $E[|u_t|]$ given by (10.4). Also, the variance of r_t is $\exp(2\alpha + 2\beta^2)$, as before, since the u_t have unit variance, and the kurtosis of r_t is $3(\nu - 2)\exp(4\beta^2)/(\nu - 4)$ when $\nu > 4$.

11.8.3 Autocorrelations

Approximate and exact formulae for the autocorrelations of $a_t^p = |r_t - \mu|^p$, $p > 0$, are respectively given in (11.33) and (11.36) for the standard SV model. These equations remain valid for the standard SVt model when $2p < \nu$, with the function $B(p)$ defined by (11.5) given by Ghysels et al. (1996) as

$$B(p, \nu) = \frac{\Gamma(p + \frac{1}{2})\Gamma(-p + \frac{1}{2}\nu)\Gamma(\frac{1}{2})\Gamma(\frac{1}{2}\nu)}{[\Gamma(\frac{1}{2}p + \frac{1}{2})\Gamma(-\frac{1}{2}p + \frac{1}{2}\nu)]^2}, \quad \nu > 2p > 0. \quad (11.47)$$

The approximate formula becomes

$$\rho_{\tau,a^p} \cong C(p, \nu, \beta)\phi^\tau = \frac{\exp(p^2\beta^2) - 1}{B(p, \nu)\exp(p^2\beta^2) - 1}\phi^\tau, \quad \nu > 2p > 0, \tau > 0. \quad (11.48)$$

Ghysels et al. (1996) observe that $B(p, \nu)$ declines as ν increases so that the above autocorrelations are less than those when $u_t \sim N(0, 1)$, which corresponds to the limit $\nu \to \infty$. There is still a simple formula for the exact autocorrelations of $l_t = \log(|r_t - \mu|)$, namely

$$\rho_{\tau,l} = \frac{\beta^2}{\beta^2 + \sigma_\varepsilon^2}\phi^\tau, \quad \tau > 0, \quad (11.49)$$

with σ_ε^2 the function of ν defined by (11.46).

11.8.4 Parameter Estimates

All the estimation methods for the standard SV model can be adapted to estimate the parameters of the standard SVt model. The easiest estimation method uses the Kalman filter applied to the state space representation to obtain the quasi-maximum likelihood function. The additional degrees-of-freedom parameter ν changes the constants μ_ξ and $H_t \equiv \sigma_\xi^2$ that appear in the Kalman filtering equations, but the equations themselves are unchanged; they are provided in the appendix to this chapter. The QML method then estimates the additional parameter ν, constrained to be at least 2. Harvey et al. (1994) estimate ν to be near 6 for two exchange rate series and to be infinity for two others.

The QMLE of ν for our benchmark DM/\$ series of daily returns is 15.9, implying a distribution for the shocks u_t that is close to normal. The quasi-log-likelihood is only 0.53 more than for the standard SV model estimated in the previous section. Therefore, the likelihood values do not provide any evidence against the simpler model. The other QML estimates for the SVt model are $\hat{\alpha} = -5.12$, $\hat{\beta} = 0.284$, and $\hat{\phi} = 0.9849$.

MCMC methods for SVt models are provided by Chib, Nardari, and Shephard (2002) and Jacquier et al. (2004) while simulated MLE is implemented by Sandmann and Koopman (1998). These researchers estimate ν to be between 7 and 13 for daily S&P 500 index returns, although the standard SVt model estimated by some of them is mis-specified because it is not an asymmetric volatility model.

11.9 Asymmetric Stochastic Volatility Models

The independent SV models considered in previous sections do not allow volatility to depend on the direction of price changes. Asymmetric volatility effects can be modeled within the SV framework by supposing that there is some dependence between the shocks to volatility and the standardized shocks in the logarithms of prices. Such dependence is a feature of bivariate diffusion models for price and volatility that have been used to price options, to be discussed in Sections 13.4 and 14.6. The particular diffusion models of Scott (1987, 1991), Wiggins (1987), and Chesney and Scott (1989) lead directly to the two equations that we have already employed for the standard SV model:

$$r_t = \mu + \sigma_t u_t \quad \text{and} \quad \log(\sigma_t) - \alpha = \phi(\log(\sigma_{t-1}) - \alpha) + \eta_t. \quad (11.50)$$

Asymmetric volatility effects occur in this model if there is appropriate dependence between η_t and one or more of the standardized price shocks $\{u_t, u_{t-1}, \ldots\}$. One possibility is to assume the vector variables $(u_t, \eta_t)'$ are i.i.d. with a bivariate normal distribution. This *contemporaneous SV model* is rather unsatisfactory as the returns process is no longer uncorrelated when u_t is correlated with η_t, which is incompatible with the motivation from diffusion processes (Taylor 1994a); also, the expected return ceases to equal μ.

11.9.1 The General SV Model

Another way to incorporate asymmetry, which has proved far more popular, assumes the variables $(u_t, \eta_{t+1})'$ have bivariate normal distributions with

$$\begin{pmatrix} u_t \\ \eta_{t+1} \end{pmatrix} \sim \text{i.i.d. } N\left(\begin{pmatrix} 0 \\ 0 \end{pmatrix}, \begin{pmatrix} 1 & \delta\sigma_\eta \\ \delta\sigma_\eta & \sigma_\eta^2 \end{pmatrix} \right), \quad (11.51)$$

so that δ is the correlation between u_t and η_{t+1}. Equations (11.50) and (11.51) define the *general SV model*, which is the Euler approximation to the motivating diffusion process. The excess returns $r_t - \mu$ are a martingale difference and hence are uncorrelated, because the variable u_t is independent of all subsets of $\{\sigma_t, \sigma_{t-1}, \sigma_{t-2}, \ldots, u_{t-1}, u_{t-2}, \ldots\}$. A negative correlation δ induces a negative correlation between r_t and $\sigma_{t+1} - \sigma_t$ and then the model generates asymmetric volatility effects in a manner similar to that of the EGARCH(1) model of Section 10.2.

We next review some theoretical results for the general SV model.

11.9.2 Moments

The expectations of univariate functions of returns do not depend on the correlation δ, as u_t is independent of σ_t. Consequently, the moments of returns (variance, kurtosis, etc.) are as already given in Section 11.5. Likewise, with $l_t = \log(|r_t - \mu|)$ the expectation of $l_t l_{t+\tau}$ does not depend on the correlation δ because η_{t+1} and $\log(|u_t|)$ are uncorrelated (Harvey et al. 1994). However, the expectations of other products do depend on δ. For example, with $s_t = (r_t - \mu)^2$,

$$E[s_t s_{t+\tau}] = \exp(4\alpha + 4(1 + \phi^\tau)\beta^2)[1 + 4\delta^2 \sigma_\eta^2 \phi^{2(\tau-1)}], \quad \tau > 0, \quad (11.52)$$

with β^2 the variance of $\log(\sigma_t)$. This result and others that follow can be derived by applying the assumption that the vector variables $(u_t, \gamma_{t+1})'$ are i.i.d., for $\gamma_{t+1} = \exp(\eta_{t+1})$, with $E[\gamma_{t+1}] = \exp(\sigma_\eta^2/2) = \lambda$, $E[u_t \gamma_{t+1}] = \delta \sigma_\eta \lambda$, and $E[u_t^2 \gamma_{t+1}] = (1 + \delta^2 \sigma_\eta^2)\lambda$.

Estimation of the model parameters by GMM requires moments that distinguish between positive and negative values of δ. Chesney and Scott (1989) apply the result

$$\mathrm{cov}(r_t, l_{t+1} - \phi l_t) = \delta \sigma_\eta \exp(\alpha + \tfrac{1}{2}\beta^2), \quad (11.53)$$

while Melino and Turnbull (1990) make use of the covariances between returns and subsequent absolute excess returns, the first being

$$\mathrm{cov}(r_t, |r_{t+1} - \mu|) = \delta \sigma_\eta \sqrt{2/\pi} \exp(2\alpha + \beta^2(1 + \phi)). \quad (11.54)$$

The covariance between r_t and s_{t+1} is also proportional to δ, as noted later in (11.58). The return r_t is more highly correlated with $|r_{t+1} - \mu|$ than with $l_{t+1} - \phi l_t$. For the typical values $\beta = 0.4$ and $\phi = 0.98$, the covariances in (11.53) and (11.54) respectively imply correlations equal to 0.047δ and 0.094δ.

11.9.3 Autocorrelations

The autocorrelations of l_t are

$$\rho_{\tau,l} = \frac{8\beta^2}{8\beta^2 + \pi^2}\phi^\tau, \quad \tau > 0, \quad (11.55)$$

for any δ (Harvey et al. 1994), while those of s_t are (Taylor 1994a):

$$\rho_{\tau,s} = \frac{[1 + 4\delta^2\sigma_\eta^2\phi^{2(\tau-1)}]\exp(4\beta^2\phi^\tau) - 1}{3\exp(4\beta^2) - 1}, \quad \tau > 0. \tag{11.56}$$

11.9.4 Parameter Estimates

The most straightforward method for estimating the parameters of the *general* SV model has been developed by Harvey and Shephard (1996). They modify the quasi-maximum likelihood estimation methodology, based upon the state space representation, to enable QMLE to deliver an estimate of the correlation δ. They exploit the fact that the sign of the excess return, $S_t = \text{sgn}(r_t - \mu) = \text{sgn}(u_t)$, provides some information about the distribution of η_{t+1}, since $E[\eta_{t+1} \mid S_t] = \sqrt{2/\pi}\delta\sigma_\eta S_t$ for the general SV model. The Kalman filter can then be applied after conditioning the terms l_t on the signs S_t. Harvey and Shephard (1996, Table 3) estimate $\delta = -0.66$, with a standard error of 0.05, and $\phi = 0.988$ (s.e. 0.003) for the daily CRSP returns used by Nelson (1991) to estimate EGARCH models. Their methods can also be revised to estimate the general SVt model. Note, however, that my notation is similar to, but different from, theirs.

Two other papers have also used Nelson's data to estimate asymmetric specifications, but in both a *contemporaneous* SV model is estimated. Sandmann and Koopman (1998) use their simulated MLE method to estimate $\delta = -0.375$, with a reported standard error of only 0.004, and $\phi = 0.985$ (s.e. 0.003). Jacquier et al. (2004) find posterior distributions for a contemporaneous SVt model. Their point estimate of δ is -0.48, with a 95% posterior interval from -0.54 to -0.42; for ϕ the point estimate is 0.988 with a 95% interval from 0.984 to 0.992. Their estimates of the degrees-of-freedom parameter ν, defined in Section 11.7, vary from 10 to 32 for the six series that they consider.

Yu (2004) estimates both the general and the contemporaneous SV models by the MCMC method for two US stock index series. He finds very strong empirical evidence that the general specification provides the more accurate description of his data. The preferred estimates of the correlation δ are -0.32 and -0.39, respectively for a few years of S&P 500 and CRSP returns.

11.9.5 Aggregation

A variety of theoretical results for sums of returns are included in Ghysels et al. (1996). We only discuss distributional results. The distribution of returns is symmetric for the general SV model because u_t has a symmetric distribution that is independent of σ_t. The distribution of aggregated returns is, however, negatively skewed when the correlation δ is negative. Then volatility tends to increase after a fall in prices and hence the probability of a large fall over more than one period exceeds the probability of a corresponding large rise.

Let N-period returns and their central moments be defined by

$$r_{t,N} = r_t + \cdots + r_{t+N-1} \quad \text{and} \quad m_{N,p} = E[(r_{t,N} - N\mu)^p]. \tag{11.57}$$

Then the N-period skewness is

$$\text{skewness}(N) = m_{N,3}/m_{N,2}^{1.5},$$

which can be evaluated using the results

$$m_{N,2} = N\exp(2\alpha + 2\beta^2) \quad \text{and} \quad m_{N,3} = 3\sum_{j=1}^{N-1}(N-j)a_j \quad \text{for } N \geqslant 2,$$

with

$$a_j = \text{cov}(r_t, (r_{t+j} - \mu)^2) = 2\delta\sigma_\eta\phi^{j-1}\exp(3\alpha + \tfrac{1}{2}(5 + 4\phi^j)\beta^2) \quad \text{for } j \geqslant 1. \tag{11.58}$$

The skewness is proportional to the correlation δ. When the persistence ϕ is 0.98 and the standard deviation of volatility is $\beta = 0.4$, the skewness is zero when $N = 1$ and 0.213δ when $N = 2$. Assuming δ is negative, the skewness declines as N increases until attaining its minimum value of 1.54δ when $N = 95$; thereafter the skewness is an increasing function of N, with limit zero as $N \to \infty$ from a central limit theorem.

The kurtosis of multi-period returns can be found from the further equations:

$$\text{kurtosis}(N) = m_{N,4}/m_{N,2}^2,$$

$$m_{N,4} = 3N\exp(4\alpha + 8\beta^2) + 6\sum_{j=1}^{N-1}(N-j)b_j + 12\sum_{1\leqslant i<j<k\leqslant N}c_{i,j,k},$$

$$b_j = E[s_t s_{t+j}],$$

$$c_{i,j,k} = E[(r_{t+i} - \mu)(r_{t+j} - \mu)(r_{t+k} - \mu)^2]$$
$$= 2\delta^2\sigma_\eta^2\phi^{k-i-2}(1 + 2\phi^{k-j})\exp(4\alpha + \tfrac{1}{2}\beta^2 d_{i,j,k}),$$

and

$$d_{i,j,k} = (1+\phi^{2k+j-3i})^2 + (1+2\phi^{k-j})^2(1-\phi^{2(j-i)}) + 4(1-\phi^{2(k-j)}), \tag{11.59}$$

with b_j given by (11.52). Consequently, the kurtosis is a quadratic function of the correlation δ. Using the same illustrative parameter values as before, the kurtosis equals 5.69 when $N = 1$, $5.65 + 0.07\delta^2$ when $N = 2$, $5.25 + 0.86\delta^2$ when $N = 21$, and $4.19 + 2.15\delta^2$ when $N = 126$; it is a decreasing function of N when $\delta = 0$ or $\delta = -0.5$, but has a maximum kurtosis of 6.53 at $N = 75$ when $\delta = -1$.

11.10 Long Memory SV Models

In Sections 11.5–11.9 we have only considered a first-order autoregressive process for the logarithm of volatility. The autocorrelations of volatility then decay geometrically and volatility is said to have a short memory. The same property of a short memory carries over to the process of absolute returns and its power transformations. We noted in Section 10.3 that empirical autocorrelations for absolute returns and squared returns provide evidence that short memory volatility processes may be unsatisfactory. Instead, long memory may be a necessary feature of a satisfactory volatility model. We discuss the evidence for long memory in volatility in much more detail in the next chapter, where the context is high-frequency data analysis. Here we consider long memory models of volatility that have been motivated by studies of daily returns. These models have similar properties to the long memory ARCH models described in Section 10.3.

11.10.1 The FISV Model

Breidt, Crato, and de Lima (1998), Harvey (1998), and Arteche (2004) define and investigate independent SV models for returns that have the logarithm of volatility following the ARFIMA(p, d, q) process that originates in Granger (1980) and Hosking (1981). The special case when $p = 1$ and $q = 0$ has received the most attention. It is presented here as an extension of the standard SV model of Section 11.5 and called the FISV model. The returns and volatility processes are defined by

$$r_t = \mu + \sigma_t u_t$$

and

$$\log(\sigma_t) = \alpha + (1 - \phi L)^{-1}(1 - L)^{-d}\eta_t \qquad (11.60)$$

with L the usual lag operator. This simplifies to the standard SV model when d is zero. Both returns and volatility have a long memory and are covariance stationary when $0 < d < \frac{1}{2}$.

The autocorrelations of $\log(\sigma_t)$ can be evaluated from formulae in Baillie (1996), Breidt et al. (1998), and Harvey (1998). They are asymptotically proportional to τ^{2d-1}, assuming $0 < d < \frac{1}{2}$, and the same asymptotic result is applicable to σ_t, $a_t = |r_t - \mu|$, and $s_t = (r_t - \mu)^2$ (Andersen and Bollerslev 1997a).

11.10.2 Estimation

When the variables $\log(\sigma_t)$ follow an ARFIMA process, the logarithms of absolute excess returns, $l_t = \log(|r_t - \mu|)$, also follow an ARFIMA process. Furthermore, the differencing parameter d is the same for $\log(\sigma_t)$ and l_t. The spectral densities of these processes are approximately proportional to ω^{-2d} for small positive ω.

Consequently, d can be estimated from observations of l_t (after replacing μ by $\bar{r}$) using some version of the spectral estimator proposed by Geweke and Porter-Hudak (1973), without first specifying values for p and q. Bollerslev and Wright (2000) investigate a suitable estimator of d using Monte Carlo methods. They document its downward bias when low-frequency data are used.

Breidt et al. (1998) describe spectral quasi-likelihood estimation for the FISV model defined by (11.60). Estimation from the process for l_t is not practical in the time domain but the quasi-likelihood function for this process has a simple form when it is stated in the frequency domain. A Monte Carlo study of the QML estimates shows they are accurate and almost unbiased for a series of 4096 observations, when d is the typical value 0.4 and ϕ is 0, 0.4, or 0.8. The estimates are less satisfactory for a series of 1024 observations. Asymmetric extensions of the FISV model can also be partially estimated by maximizing the spectral quasi-likelihood. The method then estimates all of the parameters except the correlation δ defined in (11.51). Breidt et al. (1998) estimate $d = 0.444$ and $\phi = 0.932$ for the daily returns from a value-weighted CRSP index between 1962 and 1989. They permit the variance of $\log(u_t^2)$ to be an additional parameter, whose estimate suggests a distribution with a heavy tail.

Gallant et al. (1997) use their efficient method of moments technique to estimate several SV models, including a long-memory model. Their estimates of d range from 0.48 to 0.55 for a very long series of adjusted daily returns from the S&P composite price index.

11.11   Multivariate Stochastic Volatility Models

Two ways to model the volatility of several assets by using component SV models have been investigated. The first methodology specifies each of N return processes as a standard SV model and incorporates parameters that permit general covariances between asset returns and asset volatilities. A general multivariate model, based upon remarks in Ghysels et al. (1996), is given by

$$r_{i,t} = \mu_i + \sigma_{i,t} u_{i,t},$$
$$L_{i,t} = \log(\sigma_{i,t}),$$
$$L_t = (L_{1,t}, \ldots, L_{N,t})' = \alpha + \Phi(L_{t-1} - \alpha) + \eta_t. \tag{11.61}$$

The vector AR(1) process L_t has i.i.d. residuals η_t that are stochastically independent of the i.i.d. vector of shocks u_t; the distributions of η_t and u_t are multivariate normal, with covariance matrices Σ_η and Σ_u, and the diagonal entries in Σ_u are all unity. The matrix Σ_η can be singular, so that each asset's volatility is a linear combination of less than N common terms.

Harvey et al. (1994) estimate a special case of this model for four dollar exchange rates by using the multivariate extension of the QML method, which only requires applying the Kalman filter to a vector process. They assume Φ is the identity matrix and then a principal components analysis of the estimate of Σ_η shows that two factors explain the volatilities of the four rates. Mahieu and Schotman (1994) use QML estimation for all six bilateral rates obtained from the dollar and three other currencies, thus avoiding the selection of a numeraire currency. Both of these studies show how to find the covariance matrix of $\xi_t = \log(|u_t|)$ from Σ_u. Daníelsson (1997) describes a multivariate simulated MLE algorithm and obtains higher likelihoods than for multivariate ARCH models.

A second methodology explicitly assumes a factor structure for volatility. Kim, Shephard, and Chib (1998) propose that the $N \times 1$ vector of returns r_t depends on an unobservable $k \times 1$ factor f_t and an idiosyncratic $N \times 1$ residual ε_t; thus,

$$r_t = \mu + Bf_t + \varepsilon_t \tag{11.62}$$

for some $N \times k$ matrix of factor loadings B. Each component of f_t and ε_t is assumed to follow a standard SV model and these $N + k$ models are independent of one another. The model is identifiable when $b_{i,i} = 1$ and $b_{i,j} = 0$ for $i \leqslant k$ and $j > i$, giving a total number of volatility and factor parameters equal to $3(N + k) + Nk - k(k + 1)/2$.

Pitt and Shephard (1999) use MCMC methods to estimate this model for five dollar exchange rates and two factors, finding that one- and two-factor models give similar results for daily returns from 1981 to 1998. The persistence parameter of the volatility in the one-factor model is 0.970. Chib, Nardari, and Shephard (2005) enhance the MCMC method and use their algorithm to estimate a more complicated factor model.

11.12 ARCH versus SV

11.12.1 Comparisons

Several volatility models are similar in the sense that they can explain the major stylized facts for asset returns. It is natural to seek tests that can decide which of these models provides the best description of asset returns. There is a powerful test for comparing the two-state Markov chain model for volatility with the standard SV model, as noted in Section 11.5. This test provides strong empirical evidence against the two-state model for the £/$ exchange rate (Taylor 1999).

The more interesting comparison for symmetric volatility models is between the standard SV model and either the GARCH(1, 1) model or the symmetric version of the EGARCH(1) model. We have to be aware, however, that there may be no useful way to discriminate between these models. The mathematical reason is that the limit of EGARCH(1) for higher-frequency data is the diffusion process that motivates the general SV model (see Section 13.4 and Nelson (1990a)). Consequently, debating the advantages of these models as descriptions of data may be pointless.

Kim, Shephard, and Chib (1998) compare the likelihoods of standard SV models with those of GARCH(1, 1) models that have either (a) conditional normal or (b) conditional t-distributions. For comparison (a), the three-parameter SV model has higher likelihoods than the three-parameter ARCH model for daily observations of four exchange rates from 1981 to 1985. Nonnested likelihood-ratio tests strongly favor the SV model. For comparison (b), the ARCH model has an extra parameter and is within the SV family as defined in Section 11.2. It also has higher likelihoods than the standard SV model. Empirical likelihood comparisons between GARCH(1, 1)-t and SVt would be helpful but none are known. Given that degrees-of-freedom estimates are higher for SV than for ARCH, we may anticipate that the likelihood advantage of SV when comparing three-parameter models may disappear when comparing models that have four volatility parameters.

An esoteric difference between standard SV models and ARCH models is based upon the concept of reversing time. A stochastic process is reversible if and only if the likelihood function $L(r_{t+1}, r_{t+2}, \ldots, r_{t+n})$ equals $L(r_{t+n}, r_{t+n-1}, \ldots, r_{t+1})$ for all n and t. Gaussian AR(1) processes are reversible and hence the standard SV model also has this property. The EGARCH(1) model is not reversible. Taylor (1994a) states that it is difficult to make constructive use of this insight when the ARCH model is not conditionally normal.

11.12.2 SARV

It is possible to combine parametric ARCH and SV models into a general structure. Andersen (1994) defines a flexible general stochastic process that includes popular ARCH and SV specifications as special cases. His *polynomial stochastic autoregressive volatility* (SARV) model is defined by the following equations when conditional expected returns are constant:

$$r_t = \mu + g(K_t)z_t$$

and

$$K_t = \omega + \beta K_{t-1} + (\gamma + \alpha K_{t-1})\xi_t \qquad (11.63)$$

with $z_t \sim$ i.i.d. $D_z(0, 1)$, $\xi_t \sim$ i.i.d. $D_\xi(1, \sigma_\xi^2)$ and with z_t independent of ξ_{t-j}, $j \geqslant 0$. These equations simplify to the GARCH(1, 1) model when $\gamma = 0$, $\xi_t = z_{t-1}^2$, and $g(K_t) = \sqrt{K_t}$, with K_t then being the conditional variance. There is also a simplification to the standard SV model when $\alpha = 0$, $\xi_t = \eta_t + 1$, and $g(K_t) = \exp(K_t)$, with K_t then representing the SV variable $\log(\sigma_t)$. Andersen (1994) also shows that the EGARCH(1) and the general SV models are members of the SARV family. He recommends estimating the SARV parameters by the generalized method of moments and he provides formulae for evaluating appropriate moments. An illustration of the methodology is provided for a bivariate dataset of returns and trading volumes. Further discussion of the SARV family can be found in Ghysels et al. (1996) and Meddahi and Renault (2004).

11.13 Concluding Remarks

Stochastic volatility models provide alternative models and methodologies to ARCH models. SV models give more prominence to volatility because these models specify a process for volatility, rather than for conditional variances. The downside of the central role of volatility in SV models is that the conditional variances are very complicated functions, so that maximum likelihood estimation is far from straightforward.

High-frequency data provides useful volatility information that cannot be extracted from daily returns. We consider this information in the next chapter and see that it offers further methods for estimating the parameters of SV models and the unobservable volatility process. Later, the continuous-time versions of SV models are defined in Chapter 13 and their option pricing formulae are presented and discussed in Chapter 14.

Further Reading

Clark, P. K. 1973. A subordinated stochastic process model with finite variance for speculative prices. *Econometrica* 41:135–155.

Ghysels, E., A. C. Harvey, and E. Renault. 1996. Stochastic volatility. In *Handbook of statistics*, vol. 14, *Statistical methods in finance* (ed. C. R. Rao and G. S. Maddala), pp. 119–191. Amsterdam: North-Holland.

Harvey, A. C., E. Ruiz, and N. Shephard. 1994. Multivariate stochastic variance models. *Review of Economic Studies* 61:247–264.

Ryden, T., T. Teräsvirta, and S. Asbrink. 1998. Stylized facts of daily return series and the hidden Markov model. *Journal of Applied Econometrics* 13:217–244.

Shephard, N. 1996. Statistical aspects of ARCH and stochastic volatility. In *Likelihood, time series with econometric and other applications* (ed. D. R. Cox, D. V. Hinkley, and O. E. Barndorff-Nielsen), pp. 1–67. London: Chapman & Hall.

Taylor, S. J. 1994. Modeling stochastic volatility: a review and comparative study. *Mathematical Finance* 4:183–204.

11.14 Appendix: Filtering Equations

The standard SV model has the linear state space representation given by (11.25):

$$l_t = L_t + \xi_t \quad \text{and} \quad L_t = (1 - \phi)\alpha + \phi L_{t-1} + \eta_t,$$

with $E[\xi_t \eta_t] = 0$. This can be rewritten in a conventional form after defining zero-mean variables by $\varepsilon_t = \xi_t - \mu_\xi$ and $L_t^* = L_t - \alpha$, so that

$$l_t = L_t^* + \alpha + \mu_\xi + \varepsilon_t \quad \text{and} \quad L_t^* = \phi L_{t-1}^* + \eta_t.$$

Following Sandmann and Koopman (1998), let

$$Z_t = \begin{pmatrix} 1 & 1 \end{pmatrix}, \qquad H_t = \tfrac{1}{8}\pi^2, \qquad \alpha_t = \begin{pmatrix} L_t^* \\ \alpha + \mu_\xi \end{pmatrix},$$

$$T_t = \begin{pmatrix} \phi & 0 \\ 0 & 1 \end{pmatrix}, \qquad Q_t = \begin{pmatrix} \sigma_\eta^2 & 0 \\ 0 & 0 \end{pmatrix}, \qquad \tilde{\eta}_t = \begin{pmatrix} \eta_t \\ 0 \end{pmatrix}.$$

Then

$$l_t = Z_t \alpha_t + \varepsilon_t \quad \text{and} \quad \alpha_t = T_t \alpha_{t-1} + \tilde{\eta}_t$$

with $\mathrm{var}(\varepsilon_t) = H_t$, $\mathrm{var}(\tilde{\eta}_t) = Q_t$, $E[\varepsilon_t \tilde{\eta}_t] = 0$, and $(\varepsilon_t, \tilde{\eta}_t')'$ i.i.d.

From a_t and P_t known at time $t - 1$, which are the conditional mean and variance of α_t for Gaussian state space models, the Kalman filter provides the best linear predictor $l_{t-1,1} = Z_t a_t$ and

$$v_t = l_t - Z_t a_t, \qquad F_t = Z_t P_t Z_t' + H_t, \qquad K_t = T_{t+1} P_t Z_t' F_t^{-1},$$

$$a_{t+1} = T_{t+1} a_t + K_t v_t, \qquad P_{t+1} = T_{t+1} P_t (T_{t+1} - K_t Z_t)' + Q_{t+1},$$

as in Sandmann and Koopman (1998), whose notation differs slightly from that in the reference text by Harvey (1989). These recursive equations can be initialized with

$$a_1 = \begin{pmatrix} 0 \\ \alpha + \mu_\xi \end{pmatrix} \quad \text{and} \quad P_1 = \begin{pmatrix} \sigma_\eta^2/(1 - \phi^2) & 0 \\ 0 & 0 \end{pmatrix}.$$

The preceding equations simplify because of the zeros in the matrices Q_t and T_t. In particular, the filter calculations can be reduced to

$$v_t = l_t - l_{t-1,1},$$

$$l_{t,1} = (1 - \phi)(\alpha + \mu_\xi) + \phi l_t - \phi H_t v_t F_t^{-1},$$

$$F_{t+1} = H_t + \phi^2 (F_t - H_t) H_t F_t^{-1} + \sigma_\eta^2, \tag{11.64}$$

from which the quasi-likelihood can be calculated, as stated in (11.41), commencing with $l_{0,1} = \alpha + \mu_\xi$ and $F_1 = H_1 + \sigma_\eta^2/(1 - \phi^2)$.

The filtering equations are the same for the standard SVt model, although μ_ξ and $H_t = \sigma_\xi^2$ must be replaced respectively by the mean and variance given in (11.45) and (11.46). For the more general set-up when there is a nonzero correlation between u_t and either η_t or η_{t+1}, the Kalman filter can be applied either as above or to the same process conditional on the signs of excess returns. See Sandmann and Koopman (1998) and Harvey and Shephard (1996) for the relevant formulae when the information in the signs is used, respectively for dependence of u_t on η_t and of u_t on η_{t+1}.

Part IV

High-Frequency Methods

12

High-Frequency Data and Models

Prices recorded several times each hour generate large datasets. Several properties and applications of these high-frequency datasets are described in this chapter, for both equity and foreign exchange markets. Special attention is given to the more precise volatility estimates obtained from high-frequency return data.

12.1 Introduction

High-frequency is the adjective used to indicate that prices are recorded more often than daily. The more prices a day, the higher is the frequency of the observations. Complete datasets contain all prices and/or quotes, for which Engle (2000) uses the phrase ultra-high frequency. Most research, however, employs regularly sampled data and the most common frequency is probably one price every five minutes.

High-frequency data have their advantages but they present new challenges. On the plus side, the additional price observations allow us to learn more about how prices react to information. More observations also enable us to estimate and forecast volatility more accurately, which benefits derivatives traders and risk and portfolio managers. On the other hand, microstructure effects (such as the spread between buying and selling prices) become more important, intraday patterns in trading behavior have to be modeled and the size of datasets can become daunting. Nevertheless, analysis of high-frequency data is rewarding and well worth the additional effort.

It is more difficult to obtain cheap high-frequency data than it is to obtain comparable daily data. There were few high-frequency studies before the 1990s, notable examples being Wood, McInish, and Ord (1985), Harris (1986), and Kawaller, Koch, and Koch (1987) for the US equity market. The problem of data availability disappeared when Olsen & Associates (O&A) gave away a year of their ultra-high-frequency exchange rate data, leading to several studies that were presented at the O&A conference in 1995. Section 12.2 describes these data and their properties are a recurring subject in this chapter. The results of fifteen years of FX research by the O&A organization are presented in the impressive book by Dacorogna, Gençay, Müller, Olsen, and Pictet (2001). The most studied high-frequency equity data are probably those in the Trade and Quotation database of

NYSE, AMEX, and NASDAQ prices, which can be bought from the New York Stock Exchange.

Some general features of high-frequency data are covered in Section 12.2, including the market microstructures that define price data, the selection of a frequency, and the aforementioned O&A dataset. A single day of stock index prices is then discussed in Section 12.3, to illustrate some characteristics of ultra-high-frequency price records.

The stylized facts for high-frequency returns are similar to but distinct from those for daily returns. Five general facts are described in Section 12.4. Of particular importance are variations in the average level of volatility throughout the day, some of which can be explained by major macroeconomic news announcements. Estimates of the intraday volatility pattern are discussed in Section 12.5. These estimates appear in some of the intraday methodologies for modeling volatility that are covered in Section 12.6. Intraday trading rules are reviewed quickly in Section 12.7.

Volatility can be estimated and modeled more precisely by using high-frequency returns data. Recent research has focused on the properties of *realized volatility*, which is defined as the square root of the sum of the squares of intraday returns. Section 12.8 outlines the theory of this volatility estimate and then Section 12.9 covers its empirical properties in some detail. The evidence for long memory effects in volatility is found to be particularly striking when high-frequency data are used.

Some studies that assess the impact of information on prices are reviewed in Section 12.10. Comparisons of the rates at which different markets reflect the same information in their prices are of particular interest. Models for the times that elapse between trades are described in Section 12.11. The distribution of extreme returns, at all frequencies, is the subject of Section 12.12.

Sometimes only summary values for the intraday price record are known. Section 12.13 covers volatility estimation using intraday high and low prices. Finally, Section 12.14 concludes this high-frequency chapter.

12.2 High-Frequency Prices

12.2.1 Microstructure

Trading at financial markets around the world is organized in several ways and the precise microstructure of a market often determines the form of available data. Equities have been primarily traded at exchanges that have a physical location, while most currency trading has been over-the-counter (OTC) consisting of inter-bank deals. Whether exchange traded or OTC, asset prices may be determined by either a quote-driven or an order-driven structure. These structures differ in the method that establishes a price between buyers and sellers. Quotes are issued by market makers who are prepared to be both buyers and sellers of the asset. Either there is a monopolist specialist who makes the market or the task is competitive. Alternatively, orders can be matched automatically by electronic systems, thereby removing intermediaries from the dealing process. Trading mechanisms do change and recent years have seen much more electronic trading and more use of order-driven structures.

Goodhart and O'Hara (1997) includes a detailed discussion of microstructure and consequences for high-frequency research, which supplements the textbook on microstructure by O'Hara (1995). Gourieroux and Jasiak (2001) provide numerical examples of the operation of markets at the micro level.

12.2.2 Price Types

Price data are often only available as either quotes or transaction prices. Quotes may be firm up to a specified amount or they may only be indicative so that further negotiation is required if a quotation is acceptable to some counterparty. A market maker usually quotes both a *bid* and an *ask* price, and is willing to sell at the ask a and to buy at the bid b. The *spread*, $a - b$, provides an income to the market maker in return for supplying liquidity, which is a risky activity. At order-driven markets a typical order book contains a set of limit orders from which the most competitive bid and ask prices are determined.

The best databases include both a and b, although some only provide the *midpoint*, $(a + b)/2$. The midpoint need not reflect beliefs about the current value of the asset when quoters prefer to trade one side of the market. Spreads emphasize that assets have more than one price for those people who wish to trade immediately, with immediate buyers paying more than immediate sellers receive for the same goods. Transactions need not occur at an endpoint of the spread if a deal can be agreed at some interior point.

Transaction price datasets can reflect a spread even when the market is order-driven, because orders can be of varying types with some requiring an immediate transaction that will generally occur at a worse price. Transaction prices are often recorded without supplementary information about the best bid and ask contemporaneously on offer. Prices may exhibit a bid–ask bounce effect for a period of time, during which the best bid and ask are constant with transactions prices bouncing between the two levels.

High-frequency datasets include prices and the times at which they are recorded, often accurate to the nearest second. They may also include quantities traded.

Errors are more likely to occur in the very large datasets that arise when information is collected about all trades and/or quotes. The impact of errors is more severe than in daily price records, since intraday returns have smaller standard deviations and hence return outliers created by price errors are more extreme. Dacorogna et al. (2001) describe algorithms for detecting suspect prices. Their

Table 4.6 shows that fewer than 0.1% of recent Reuters real-time data for major FX rates were classified as outliers. In a study of FTSE futures transactions, Areal and Taylor (2002) found 56 suspicious prices in a set of 2.85 million, by inspecting the major return outliers, but could not, of course, expect to find all incorrectly recorded prices.

12.2.3 Selection of a Frequency

Complete records of transactions and/or quotes are usually so numerous that they are sampled at some intraday frequency. Higher frequencies provide more information but contain relatively more noise from the bid–ask spread. Sampling prices every five minutes is probably the most popular choice, following Andersen and Bollerslev (1997b).

In volatility studies it is often appropriate to choose the frequency to avoid bias caused by microstructure effects. This motivates the selection of the thirty-minute frequency in some of the research by Andersen, Bollerslev, Diebold, and Labys (2000, 2003). In contrast, Bandi and Russell (2004a,b) find that the optimal frequency is near to five minutes.

12.2.4 Clocks and Trading Hours

Precise times are important for intraday studies. Clocks are reset twice a year in the US and Europe, but not in Japan. When the most important US macro-economic news is released in the North American winter, it is 07:30 Central Standard Time (CST) in Chicago, 08:30 Eastern Standard Time (EST) in New York, 13:30 Greenwich Mean Time (GMT) in London, 14:30 in Paris, and 22:30 in Tokyo. In the summer these times are the same in the US, but are usually 13:30 British Summer Time in London and always 21:30 in Tokyo. A further complication is that the US and the UK change their clocks at different times in spring and autumn so there are a few days every year when London is not five hours ahead of New York.

The OTC foreign exchange market never shuts—it is a 24-hour market. Stock markets open during local business hours. These times may well change in the future, but recent local times have been from 09:30 to 16:00 in New York, from 08:00 to 16:30 in London and from 09:00 to 15:00 in Tokyo, with slightly different times for index futures trading.

12.2.5 The FX Database of Olsen & Associates

Much high-frequency research has been stimulated by the one-year database of spot DM/$ and yen/$ quotations collected and distributed by Olsen & Associates, which will be called the O&A database throughout this chapter. Published research includes Acar and Lequeux (1999), Andersen and Bollerslev (1997a,b, 1998a), Chang and Taylor (1998), Daníelsson and de Vries (1997), DeGennaro

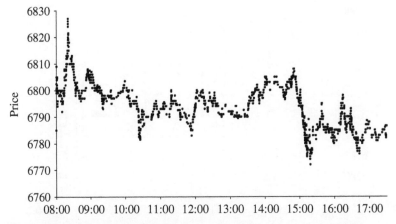

Figure 12.1. FTSE 100, March futures trades on 22 December 1999.

and Shrieves (1997), Engle and Russell (1997), Ghysels et al. (1998), Kanzler (1998), Peiers (1997), Ramsey and Zhang (1997), Taylor and Xu (1997), and Zhou (1996). Most attention has been given to the DM/$ dataset, which contains more than 1 400 000 quotations on the interbank network for the year between October 1992 and September 1993 inclusive, time stamped using GMT.

This dataset is a good example of the massive amount of available data and of their limitations. The quotes are merely indicative. Their precise source is unclear. It is widely believed that almost all Reuters quotations are included, but it is less well known firstly that some of the data came from Knight Ridder and Telerate and secondly that there are nine gaps in the data due to technical failures, each lasting several hours (Kanzler 1998). Less than 0.1% of the quotes are made between 21:00 GMT on Friday and 21:00 GMT on Sunday. Following Andersen and Bollerslev (1997b), most researchers ignore this weekend period. The quotation rate is also low on Christmas Day and New Year's Day.

12.3 One Day of High-Frequency Price Data

We consider one day of London futures prices for the FTSE 100 index to illustrate some of the general characteristics of price records that are intended to be complete. The day selected is Friday, 22 December 1999, when futures trading was essentially electronic and order-driven; any very large deals at the "upstairs" market are not recorded in the illustrative dataset.

A total of 1741 electronic transaction prices, times, and volumes were recorded for the March 2000 contract by the LIFFE exchange during the nine-and-a-half hours that the futures market was open, from 08:00 to 17:30 GMT. There were 3.0 transactions per minute on average, with a median interval between transactions of five seconds. Twenty of the inter-transaction times exceed three minutes and the longest is almost seven minutes. The transactions rate was particularly high around

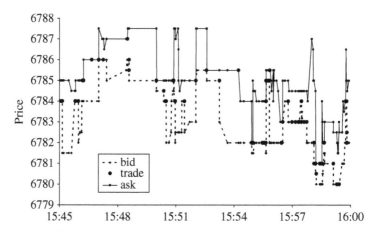

Figure 12.2.   Bids, asks, and trades for fifteen minutes.

the market open, with 197 between 08:00 and 08:30. It was also relatively high in the hour after US equity markets opened at 14:30 GMT, with 323 transactions in that hour. More than two-thirds of the transactions were for either one or two contracts, while the largest decile has trades of ten or more contracts.

Figure 12.1 shows each transaction price during the day. The market opened at 6785 and traded between 6772 and 6827, with a final price of 6786.5 eleven seconds before the market closed. These prices have a tick size of 0.5, although only 19% of them are not integers. Some 45% of the prices were identical to the preceding price and 17% of the price changes were one tick.

The records sold by LIFFE also include 2206 bid and 2162 ask prices on the same day, which are the most competitive prices at the time they were submitted to the order book. A closer look at some of the prices can be obtained from Figure 12.2, which shows fifteen minutes of bid, ask, and transaction prices, commencing at 15:45. The order prices are shown by small dots and joined by lines, while the transaction prices are shown by large dots and are not joined together. One-third of the prices are for trades, with 52 trades at the bid price and 22 at the ask. The first eight trades are at the bid, although less than eight dots can be seen for these trades as some are recorded at identical times. After them, the next five trades are at the ask.

Only a fifth of the bid and ask order prices can be matched using the criterion that they occur at identical times. Figure 12.3 shows the 437 values of the spread that can be calculated from contemporaneous orders. The mode, median, and average of these spreads are respectively 1, 2, and 2.2, with a range from 0.5 to 12.

12.4   Stylized Facts for Intraday Returns

Intraday returns have stylized facts that are similar to but distinct from those presented for daily returns in Chapter 4. General statements that apply to almost

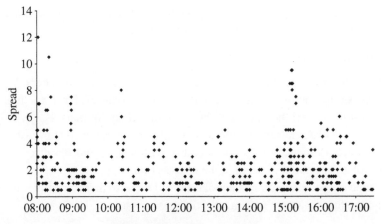

Figure 12.3. Bid–ask spreads.

all high-frequency datasets must take account of the variation in frequencies and microstructure effects found in such datasets. Five general statements are made in this section.

12.4.1 Returns

An intraday return is defined in exactly the same way as a daily return. It is simply the change in the logarithm of the price during an interval of time, assuming there are no dividend payments during the interval. Suppose we consider five-minute returns. Then we require one price for each five-minute interval and it is conventional to use the last price from the interval. When the price data are bid and ask prices, it is normal to calculate returns from midpoint prices.

Reliance on latest prices will lead to returns that are measured over periods that are not exactly five minutes as many of the prices will not be recorded at exactly the end of an interval. This will be unimportant when the average time between available prices is short, say a minute or less. There may be no prices in some intervals, in which case it is necessary to use the most recent price. As an alternative to using latest prices, a return over exactly five minutes can be obtained by linear interpolation between the last price in an interval and the first price in the next interval, as in Andersen and Bollerslev (1997b), although this can create spurious predictability.

Equity and many other markets are not open continuously. Overnight and week-end returns are often ignored in high-frequency studies as they occur over much longer intervals of time and must have different statistical properties to intraday returns. Closed-market returns are nevertheless often relevant. For example, Areal and Taylor (2002) note that the aggregate intraday return from a long position in FTSE 100 futures is −3% per annum from 1990 to 1998 but the aggregate return is 12% per annum. Thus all the equity risk premium was earned when the market was closed during these years. They also find that more than 30% of the variance of daily returns is attributable to the hours when the market is closed.

12.4.2   The Distribution of Intraday Returns

The means and variances of intraday returns are necessarily small numbers. Mean returns are similar across the trading day. There is some evidence for higher average returns around the open and the close of US equity markets, given by Harris (1986) and Andersen and Bollerslev (1997b) respectively for cash and futures markets. Variances vary considerably within days and we discuss the intraday volatility pattern in detail in the next section.

The shape of the distribution is leptokurtic and more so than for daily returns. We adapt the first major stylized fact for daily returns to:

1. *Intraday returns have a fat-tailed distribution, whose kurtosis increases as the frequency of price observations increases.*

This result is to be expected when returns have a finite fourth moment. It is then almost inevitable when intraday returns are uncorrelated and daily returns have excess kurtosis, while the central limit theorem implies the distribution converges to the normal as the inter-price interval increases.

Dacorogna et al. (2001, Table 5.1) document a kurtosis of 38 for ten-minute DM/$ returns from 1987 to 1993 and declining values for decreasing frequencies: 27 for hourly returns, 12.4 for six-hourly returns, 6.3 for daily returns, and 3.7 for weekly returns. They also find the skewness of the distributions is near zero. Andersen and Bollerslev (1997b) report summary statistics for S&P 500 futures from 1986 to 1989, but excluding a month around the 1987 crash. Their kurtosis estimates are 29, 33, and 16 for 5-, 25-, and 200-minute returns, with skewness estimates -0.6, -1.8, and -1.5 for these frequencies. Areal and Taylor (2002) estimate the kurtosis as 25 for five-minute returns from FTSE 100 futures between 1990 and 1998.

The distributions of high-frequency returns often show a sharp spike at zero, which can simply reflect the feasible set of discrete prices rather than few trades per interval. For example, some 22% of the five-minute returns of Areal and Taylor (2002) are zero but less than 3% of their five-minute intervals contain no transactions.

12.4.3   Autocorrelations of Intraday Returns

More dependence might be anticipated in intraday returns than in daily returns for two reasons. First, bid–ask bounce in transaction prices or a midpoint bounce induced by dealers with order imbalances will show most clearly at higher frequencies. The negative autocorrelation created by bouncing prices is proportional to the variance of the spread divided by the variance of returns (see equation (6.18));

the numerator is constant while the denominator decreases as the frequency of returns increases. Second, the exploitation of any dependence is more difficult when expected profits per trade decline as data frequency increases, but costs do not. The magnitude of observed dependence is, however, often remarkably small. Our second stylized fact is:

2. *Intraday returns from traded assets are almost uncorrelated, with any important dependence usually restricted to a negative correlation between consecutive returns.*

Some estimates of negative first-lag autocorrelation for foreign exchange returns from quotes are (i) around -0.18 for a few days of one-minute returns (Goodhart and Figliuoli 1991), (ii) -0.040 for one year of five-minute DM/\$ returns (Andersen and Bollerslev 1997b), with -0.070, -0.082, and -0.043 for 10-, 20-, and 30-minute returns, and (iii) -0.108 for one year of five-minute yen/\$ returns (Chang and Taylor 2003), with -0.093, -0.066, and -0.018 for 10-, 30-, and 60-minute returns. The autocorrelations of the longer time series of six years of one-minute DM/\$ graphed by Dacorogna et al. (2001, Figure 5.1) are -0.16 at lag 1, -0.02 at lag 2, -0.01 at lag 3, and are thereafter negligible. Much more dependence is found in tick-by-tick returns by Zhou (1996).

Estimates of the first-lag autocorrelation for returns from equity index futures are almost zero. A value of 0.009 is given for four years of five-minute S&P 500 returns by Andersen and Bollerslev (1997b), increasing to 0.039 for hourly returns, while 0.001 is the value for eight years of five-minute FTSE 100 returns in Areal and Taylor (2002). Substantial positive autocorrelation can occur, however, for nontraded assets such as spot indices whose component prices are not continually updated. Stoll and Whaley (1990) report first-lag autocorrelations for five-minute returns equal to 0.24 for the Major Market Index (MMI) of 20 highly active stocks and 0.45 for the broad-based S&P 500 index, from 1984 to 1986.

Stale prices provide a satisfactory explanation for spot index dependence as positive dependence is not found in the returns from the component stocks. Instead, several researchers have reported significant negative dependence for individual stock returns. One example is the median first-lag autocorrelation of -0.21 for five-minute returns from the thirty stocks in the DJIA index, from 1993 to 1998 (Andersen, Bollerslev, Diebold, and Ebens 2001). More extreme examples are median estimates of -0.27 and -0.48 for daily sets of one-minute transaction returns, respectively for IBM traded at the NYSE and Intel traded at NASDAQ in 1994 (Lin, Knight, and Satchell 1999).

12.4.4 Autocorrelations of Intraday Absolute Returns

The significant positive autocorrelation among daily absolute returns across many lags can be attributed to volatility clusters. There will be similar clusters in intraday

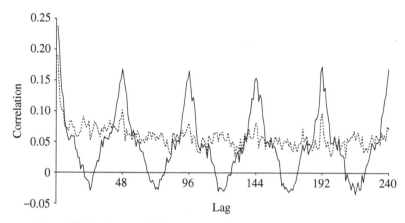

Figure 12.4. Autocorrelations for DM/$ thirty-minute absolute returns.

returns but their durations may appear to be shorter if there is an interaction with a strong intraday volatility pattern. The third stylized fact is revised for intraday returns to:

3. *There is substantial positive dependence among intraday absolute returns, which occurs at many low lags and also among returns separated by an integer number of days.*

A clear example is given by Andersen and Bollerslev (1997a, Figure 2, 1997b, Figure 4a) for the O&A year of five-minute absolute DM/$ returns. There it is seen that the autocorrelations commence with 0.31 at lag 1, decline to −0.02 at lag 144 (twelve hours) and then rise to 0.15 at lag 288 (one day). The U-shaped pattern is then repeated for lags 289 to 576 with a peak autocorrelation of 0.14 at lag 576 (two days). Peaks then recur at multiples of 288 lags with the autocorrelation at these peaks declining slowly. A 48-hour weekend period is removed prior to these calculations.

Figure 12.4, from Chang and Taylor (2003), shows these peaks for the same dataset when the frequency is thirty minutes; the autocorrelations are joined by solid lines.

Dacorogna et al. (1993, Figure 4, 2001, Figure 7.4) include the weekend in their calculations for four years of twenty-minute absolute DM/$ returns. The seasonal pattern is then across weeks instead of days and there are autocorrelations of 0.40 at lag 1, 0.15 at lag 72 (one day), and 0.24 at lag 504 (one week). Negative autocorrelations occur in these studies, at lags around one-half the seasonal period, because intraday volatility variation then dominates the persistence in daily volatility.

Similar features are found in intraday equity absolute returns. Andersen and Bollerslev (1997b, Figure 4b) find all of the first 400 autocorrelations are positive for their five-minute data for S&P 500 futures. They commence with 0.29 at lag 1,

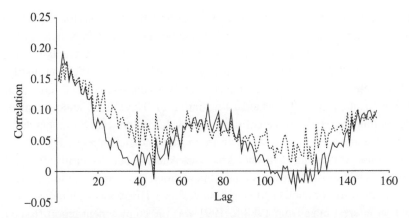

Figure 12.5. Autocorrelations for intraday absolute S&P returns.

fall to 0.07 at lag 40 (half a trading day), and rise to 0.14 at lag 80 (one day), again with a clear U-shaped pattern that repeats once a day. The general pattern can be seen in Figure 12.5, which shows the autocorrelations (as a solid line) for five-minute returns on the spot S&P 100 index (from July to October 1999) up to lag 154 (two days).

The periodic (or diurnal) behavior of intraday volatility, visible in the auto-correlations of absolute returns, was first identified by calculating the standard deviations of returns at the NYSE for intraday periods. For example, the pioneering study of Wood et al. (1985) found volatility was highest around the open and the close. The periodic effect is so marked that it is our fourth stylized fact:

4. *The average level of volatility depends on the time of day, with a significant intraday variation.*

Methods for estimating this important effect are described in the next section.
Incidentally, Müller, Dacorogna, and Pictet (1998) calculate the first ten auto-correlations of $|r_t|^p$ for various powers p, from thirty-minute DM/$ returns. The maximum dependence occurs when p is near one-half, with similar autocorrelations for absolute returns that are more than twice the values for squared returns. The same results can be seen in Dacorogna et al. (2001, Figure 5.11).

12.4.5 The Impact of Macroeconomic News on Volatility

Markets that are open respond rapidly to official US macroeconomic announcements. The most important monthly US announcements are made at 08:30 EST and less important news releases are made at later times. Ederington and Lee (1993, 1995) consider the price impact of reports about nineteen macroeconomic variables for Treasury bond, Eurodollar and Deutsche mark futures, whose markets opened at 08:20 EST during their studies.

Their first paper compares five-minute return standard deviations for announcement and nonannouncement days, with an announcement day defined as a day for which at least one of the nineteen reports was released. They find that the return from 08:30 to 08:35 on announcement days is much more volatile than, firstly, all other five-minute returns on announcement days and, secondly, all returns on nonannouncement days. The standard deviation of 08:30/08:35 announcement returns is four to five times the corresponding value on nonannouncement days. Furthermore, the announcement effects are most pronounced on Fridays.

Prices adjust very rapidly to the news releases. Analysis of tick data in the second paper shows that most of the reaction occurs within forty seconds, although there is higher volatility for another fifteen minutes or so. The report with the greatest impact on interest rates from 1988 to 1991 was the employment report (issued on Fridays), followed by reports on the Producer Price Index (PPI), the consumer price index, and durable goods orders. The employment report also had the most impact on exchange rates, followed by reports on the merchandise trade deficit, PPI, durable goods, GNP, and retail sales.

Further US evidence is provided by Andersen and Bollerslev (1998a) and Fleming and Remolona (1999). Macroeconomic news released in other countries also has a significant impact upon local volatility. Examples include Ito and Roley (1987) for Japan, Becker, Finnerty, and Kopecky (1993, 1995) for the UK, and Andersen and Bollerslev (1998a) for Germany. Generally both US and domestic announcements are found to be important at non-US markets. Our final stylized fact is:

5. *There are short bursts of high volatility in intraday prices that follow major macroeconomic announcements.*

12.5   Intraday Volatility Patterns

12.5.1   Estimation

Intraday volatility patterns are often modeled by multiplicative factors, which may vary across the days of the week. We outline estimation methods when the periodic pattern is diurnal, so it repeats every day; these methods can easily be adapted for more general patterns that repeat once a week. We suppose the return r_t for day t is the sum of N intraday returns $r_{t,j}$, $1 \leqslant j \leqslant N$. If the market has a closed period, then $j = 1$ represents that period and $r_{t,1}$ is the return from the close on day $t - 1$ to the open on day t. The latent volatility for day t is denoted by σ_t and we have

$$r_t = \sum_{j=1}^{N} r_{t,j} \quad \text{and} \quad \text{var}(r_t \mid \sigma_t) = \sigma_t^2. \tag{12.1}$$

Intraday volatility factors λ_j are defined by supposing

$$\text{var}(r_{t,j} \mid \sigma_t) = \lambda_j \sigma_t^2 \quad \text{with} \quad \sum_{j=1}^{N} \lambda_j = 1. \tag{12.2}$$

Thus λ_j is the proportion of a trading day's return variance that is attributed to period j, here assuming that intraday returns are uncorrelated and that the factors are the same for all days t. When there is a closed market period, the proportions of open-market variance are defined by

$$\kappa_j = \frac{\lambda_j}{1 - \lambda_1}, \quad j \geqslant 2 \quad \text{with} \quad \sum_{j=2}^{N} \kappa_j = 1. \tag{12.3}$$

The above factors sum to one. Another convention is to make their average one, which is relevant when defining intraday ARCH models. Factors that average one are defined by

$$\lambda_j^* = N\lambda_j. \tag{12.4}$$

Simple estimates of the variance proportions, when expected returns can be assumed to be zero, are given by

$$\hat{\lambda}_j = \frac{\sum_t r_{t,j}^2}{\sum_t \sum_{k=1}^{N} r_{t,k}^2} \quad \text{and} \quad \hat{\kappa}_j = \frac{\sum_t r_{t,j}^2}{\sum_t \sum_{k=2}^{N} r_{t,k}^2}, \tag{12.5}$$

following Taylor and Xu (1997). The above summations are over all days t in some set S. The set S might be all days or might be some subset, for example, all Fridays or all Fridays that have a macroeconomic news release. The simple estimates can be sensitive to outliers and it may be preferable to make the estimates a smooth function of the intraday time j. Andersen and Bollerslev (1997b) recommend flexible Fourier functions (FFFs) whose time-invariant specification is

$$\lambda_j = \exp\left(\mu_0 + \mu_1 j + \mu_2 j^2 + \sum_{i=1}^{D} \alpha_i I_{j=d_i} \right.$$
$$\left. + \sum_{k=1}^{P} \gamma_k \cos\left(\frac{2\pi j k}{N}\right) + \delta_k \sin\left(\frac{2\pi j k}{N}\right)\right), \tag{12.6}$$

with D dummy variables for intervals that do not fit into a smooth pattern (perhaps because of news announcement effects) and with P sinusoidal functions. Their more general specification permits an interaction between σ_t and the periodic pattern. Smooth estimates $\tilde{\lambda}_j$ are given by regressing $\hat{\lambda}_j$ on the explanatory variables in (12.6) or by the more sophisticated methods described by Andersen and Bollerslev (1997b, 1998a) and Martens, Chang, and Taylor (2002).

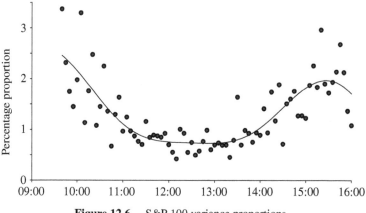

Figure 12.6.   S&P 100 variance proportions.

12.5.2 Equity Examples

Figure 12.6 shows the estimated open-market variance proportions as percentages for the four months of spot S&P 100 five-minute returns considered in Section 12.4.4. Here the first period commences at 09:35 EST to avoid any unusual effects around the open at 09:30. The estimates $\hat{\kappa}_j$ are shown by dots. The smooth curve $\tilde{\kappa}_j$ shown by a continuous trace is obtained by regressing the $\hat{\kappa}_j$ on two polynomial terms and two sinusoidal functions. The intraday volatility pattern has a clear U-shape that can also be seen in Wood et al. (1985) and Andersen and Bollerslev (1997b). The autocorrelations of scaled intraday absolute returns, $|r_{t,j}|/\hat{\kappa}_j$, are free of periodic effects, as can be seen from the dotted curve in Figure 12.5. The variance proportion from 16:00 until 09:35 EST on the next trading day is estimated as $\hat{\lambda}_1 = 0.23$ for the data used to produce Figures 12.5 and 12.6.

A second equity index example is given by five-minute FTSE 100 futures returns from November 1993 to July 1998. Figure 12.7, reproduced from Areal and Taylor (2002), shows simple estimates $\hat{\kappa}_j$ and smooth values $\tilde{\kappa}_j$ for the open-market period from 08:35 until 16:10 local time. The intraday pattern has a high initial value when the futures market opens, a minor peak in the interval from 09:30 to 09:35 when UK macro news is announced, a major peak at 13:30 when US macro news is released, and a generally higher level once US equity markets open at 14:30. Similar patterns are seen in the shorter UK datasets of ap Gwilym, Buckle, and Thomas (1999) and Tse (1999).

Further insight into the periodic pattern can usually be obtained by estimating it for the five days of the trading week. Figure 12.8 shows that the UK pattern is similar through the week except at the open and at the time of US announcements. More than 7% of the intraday variance occurs in the first five minutes on Mondays, compared with 4% to 6% on the other days. The 13:30 announcement effect is much more pronounced on Fridays than on other days. As all Fridays are included in the calculations, the effect is even greater on announcement Fridays. There

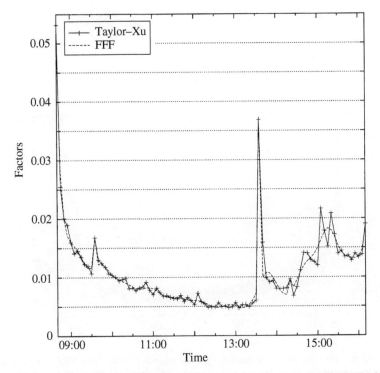

Figure 12.7. Five-minute fitted open-market variance proportions for the FTSE 100 futures index, using all days of the week, for the period from 18 November 1993 to 17 July 1998. This figure and Figures 12.8 and 12.11–12.16 are taken from *Journal of Futures Markets*, N. M. P. C. Areal and S. J. Taylor, Copyright © (2002). Reprinted by permission of John Wiley & Sons, Inc.

is also a minor volatility peak during the final minutes of trading before the weekend. The closed-market proportion is highest for the weekend period and equals 38% for the three days from Friday 16:10 until Monday 16:10, compared with $\hat{\lambda}_1 = 31\%$ when all days are analyzed together.

12.5.3 FX examples

Volatility patterns for exchange rates are described by Müller, Dacorogna, Olsen, Pictet, and Schwarz (1990), Dacorogna et al. (1993, 2001), and Andersen and Bollerslev (1997b, 1998a).

We illustrate the typical DM/\$ pattern by discussing Figure 12.9, which is reproduced from Taylor and Xu (1997). They use five-minute DM/\$ returns to estimate hourly volatility factors from the year of O&A quotations, after deleting the standard 48-hour weekend period. Factors are found for each of the 1440 five-minute periods during a five-day week using equation (12.5). Sums of twelve consecutive five-minute factors define hourly variance factors that are scaled to average one. The derived standard deviation multipliers are shown in Figure 12.9.

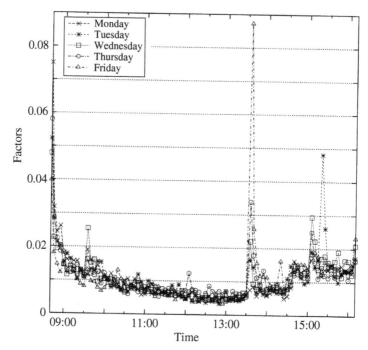

Figure 12.8. Five-minute open-market variance proportions for the FTSE 100 futures index, by day of the week, for the period from 18 November 1993 to 17 July 1998.

The clock used for the calculations is Eastern Standard Time, rather than GMT, because the periodic pattern changes when US clocks are reset in the spring and the autumn (Andersen and Bollerslev 1998a). The first interval in Figure 12.9 is for the hour from 14:30 to 15:30 EST and the last is from 13:30 to 14:30 EST on the next day. The Friday symbol, for example, is used for the 24 hours from 14:30 on Thursday until 14:30 on Friday. The reason for the unusual definition of a day is that the research study used days that ended when the FX options market closed in Philadelphia.

DM/$ volatility is seen to be relatively high during the twelve hours when European dealers are active (07:30 to 19:30 in London, 02:30 to 14:30 EST), with the highest levels when both US and European dealers are active (07:30 to 13:30 EST). The peak in interval 19 shows the importance of US macro news, with Friday and then Thursday being the most important days. Half the Fridays in the sample had an announcement about a significant macroeconomic variable so the peak would be much higher if the nonannouncement Fridays were not used in the calculations. The local maximum in interval 13 occurs when trade accelerates in Europe around 07:30 local time in London (08:30 in Frankfurt). There is also a spike on Mondays in interval 6, which is around the start of a new week in the Far East, while the lowest volatility levels were at lunchtime in Tokyo around intervals 9 and 10.

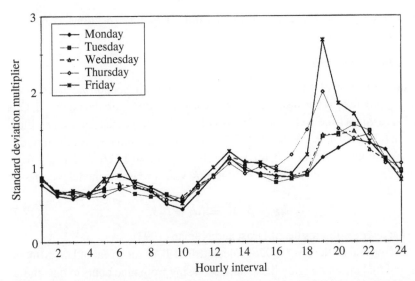

Figure 12.9. DM/$ intraday standard deviation multipliers. Reprinted from *Journal of Empirical Finance*, volume 4, S. J. Taylor and X. Xu, The incremental volatility information in one million foreign exchange quotations, pp. 317–340, Copyright © (1997), with permission from Elsevier.

The autocorrelations of scaled intraday absolute returns, $|r_{t,j}|/\hat{\lambda}_j$, do not contain periodic effects for the O&A DM/$ data, shown by Andersen and Bollerslev (1997b) for five-minute returns and by the dotted curve in Figure 12.4 for thirty-minute returns, from Chang and Taylor (2003).

12.5.4   θ-time

Another methodology for removing periodic effects from the volatility of intraday returns redefines the timescale so that the average volatility is the same for all intraday intervals during a fixed period of time, typically one day or one week. This new timescale is called θ-time by Dacorogna et al. (1993, 2001). The θ-clock runs faster during the most volatile trading hours so returns are then calculated from shorter time intervals. Thus, for example, a day of five-minute returns on the θ-clock will contain 288 intraday returns calculated from irregularly spaced prices. There will be volatility persistence present in such returns but periodic volatility effects are eliminated from the autocorrelations of absolute returns (Dacorogna et al. 2001, Figures 7.5 and 7.6).

12.6   Discrete-Time Intraday Volatility Models

Intraday returns can be used to model and forecast *intraday* volatility by adapting the ARCH models of Chapters 9 and 10 and the stochastic volatility models of Chapter 11. We now discuss a few methods. Later we cover ways to use high-frequency data to model and predict *daily* volatility (Sections 12.8, 12.9, and 15.7).

12.6.1 Intraday GARCH

Routine estimation of the GARCH(1, 1) model defined in Section 9.3 gives unsatisfactory predictions because the periodic volatility effects are then ignored. One way to see this is to consider the half-lives of variance forecasts, defined and illustrated in Section 9.4. When the GARCH(1, 1) model is estimated from K intraday returns per trading day, the half-life is given by $H_K = \log(0.5)/(K \log(\alpha_K + \beta_K))$ trading days. These values will be similar as K varies when the model is correctly specified, i.e.

$$(\alpha_K + \beta_K)^K \cong (\alpha_1 + \beta_1), \qquad (12.7)$$

from the aggregation results of Drost and Nijman (1993).

Andersen and Bollerslev (1997b) calculate half-lives for a year of DM/\$ quotations and find they are highly irregular, decreasing from nine hours to one-and-a-half hours as the frequency of returns decreases from fifteen to ninety minutes and then increasing to levels around twelve days for four-hourly and lower frequencies. They also estimate $\alpha_K + \beta_K > 1$ for the five- and ten-minute frequencies. More satisfactory results are obtained by estimating the GARCH(1, 1)-MA(1) model from sums of scaled five-minute returns,

$$R_{t,j} = r_{t,j}/\tilde{\lambda}_j, \qquad (12.8)$$

with $r_{t,j}$ a five-minute return, t counting days, j counting five-minute periods within day t, and the scale factor $\tilde{\lambda}_j$ based upon (12.6). Their GARCH model for aggregated scaled returns measured over $5k$ minutes can be written as

$$R_{t,n}^{(k)} = \sum_{j=(n-1)k+1}^{nk} R_{t,j} = e_{t,n}^{(k)} + \theta_k e_{t,n-1}^{(k)}, \qquad 1 \leqslant n \leqslant K, \qquad (12.9)$$

with $K = 288/k$ and conditional variances given by

$$h_{t,n}^{(k)} = \omega_K + \alpha_K (e_{t,n-1}^{(k)})^2 + \beta_K h_{t,n-1}^{(k)}. \qquad (12.10)$$

The estimated persistence measures, $\alpha_K + \beta_K$, then define half-lives that are fairly similar at frequencies of two hours or lower but they remain rather unsatisfactory at the highest frequencies. The measures are 0.971 for the five-minute frequency, 0.917 for twenty minutes, 0.989 for two hours and 0.980 for eight hours, with respective half-lives of approximately two hours, three hours, five days, and eleven days.

Taylor and Xu (1997) analyze the same DM/\$ data and model hourly conditional variances using both five-minute and hourly returns. Now let $r_{t,j}$ denote a five-minute return with t counting five-day weeks rather than days. Then their Table 3 includes results for the hourly returns described by the specification

$$r_{t,n}^{(12)} = \sum_{j=12(n-1)+1}^{12n} r_{t,j} = \sqrt{h_{t,n}^{(12)}} z_{t,n}, \quad z_{t,n} \sim \text{i.i.d. } D(0,1), \qquad (12.11)$$

with

$$h_{t,n}^{(12)} = \lambda_n^* \omega + \left(\frac{\lambda_n^*}{\lambda_{n-1}^*}\right)\left(\alpha (r_{t,n-1}^{(12)})^2 + \beta h_{t,n-1}^{(12)} + \gamma \sum_{j=12(n-2)+1}^{12(n-1)} r_{t,j}^2\right),$$

$$1 \leqslant n \leqslant 120. \quad (12.12)$$

Here the variance multipliers λ_n^* average 1 and their square-roots were previously discussed as Figure 12.9. When j is zero or negative the pair of subscripts t, j refers to time period $t-1, n-j$. For conditional normal distributions the parameter estimates include $\alpha = 0.0045$, $\beta = 0.9480$, and $\gamma = 0.0319$. Thus much more weight is given to the last hour of squared five-minute returns (through parameter γ) than is given to the most recent one-hour return (by parameter α). Hypothesis tests accept $\alpha = 0$ and reject $\gamma = 0$ at low significance levels. Similar results are obtained for conditional GED distributions, with the tail-thickness parameter estimated as 1.15, and for specifications having variance multipliers that differ on announcement Fridays from those on the other Fridays. In all cases, the persistence $\alpha + \beta + \gamma$ is estimated to be between 0.984 and 0.985, giving a half-life of two days, which matches the results in Andersen and Bollerslev (1997b).

A third way to estimate the GARCH(1, 1) model from intraday returns uses return intervals defined by the θ-clock described in the previous section. Dacorogna et al. (2001, Table 8.2) do this for seven years of DM/\$ quotes. They emphasize that their persistence estimates are incompatible with the aggregation formula (12.7), which fails for frequencies higher than six hours. Their estimates of $\alpha_K + \beta_K$ are 0.992 for the θ-time equivalent of ten-minute returns, only 0.968 for thirty-minute returns, and 0.988 for hourly returns.

12.6.2 HARCH

The short half-lives of volatility shocks from high-frequency data certainly appear to contradict the longer half-lives estimated from daily data. They show that a GARCH(1, 1) model, with periodic volatility effects, oversimplifies the volatility dynamics. A more accurate volatility model will contain several components. These components may be defined by a variety of economic factors, such as macro news that has low persistence and technological variables that have high persistence, leading to a long memory volatility model if enough assumptions are made (Andersen and Bollerslev 1997a).

Alternatively, the components might also reflect the actions of traders whose decision horizons vary widely, from arbitrageurs who seek very rapid gains to long-term investors who may only consider prices once a month. Müller, Dacorogna, Davé, Olsen, Pictet, and von Weizsäcker (1997) discuss the heterogeneity of traders in detail and thereby motivate their heterogeneous ARCH model. Now suppose r_t represents intraday returns measured in θ-time. Then the basic HARCH model specifies conditional variances by

$$h_t = c_0 + \sum_{j=1}^{n} c_j \left(\sum_{i=1}^{j} r_{t-i} \right)^2. \tag{12.13}$$

The square of the latest j-period return has weight c_j in this model. The number n is taken to be large so that returns measured over very many horizons are able to have an impact upon future volatility. Müller et al. (1997) estimate the model for thirty-minute returns with $n = 4096$, which corresponds to twelve weeks. They reduce the number of free parameters to eight by making blocks of the c_j equal, using $c_{j+1} = c_{j+2} = \cdots = c_{4j}$ for $j = 1, 4, 16, \ldots, 1024$. All the parameter estimates are highly significant for seven years of DM/\$ quotes and the model has a much higher log-likelihood than GARCH(1, 1).

Dacorogna, Müller, Olsen, and Pictet (1998) modify the HARCH specification, reducing the number of j-period intervals from 4096 to 7 in their empirical work and thereby speeding up the estimation of the parameters. Their EMA-HARCH model aggregates volatility components defined by exponentially weighted moving averages of squared j-period returns; thus,

$$h_t = C_0 + \sum_{j=1}^{7} C_j h_{j,t},$$

$$h_{j,t} = a_j h_{j,t-1} + (1 - a_j) \left(\sum_{i=1}^{k_j} r_{t-i} \right)^2, \tag{12.14}$$

$$a_j = \exp\left(\frac{2}{k_{j+1} - k_j} \right),$$

and they choose $k_1 = 1$ and $k_j = 1 + 4^{j-2}$ for $j \geqslant 2$. This model has a higher log-likelihood than its predecessor, for ten years of prices separated by thirty minutes of θ-time, for each of the DM/\$, £/\$, SF/\$, yen/\$, and DM/yen rates. The estimates of the parameters C_j are strikingly similar across currencies. The seven estimates of $k_j C_j$ equal 0.15 ($j = 1$), 0.19, 0.18, 0.05, 0.14, 0.11, and 0.11 ($j = 7$) for the DM/\$ series, all with standard errors near 0.01.

12.6.3 Intraday SV

There are few studies that have estimated a variant of the standard stochastic volatility model from high-frequency data. The standard SV model of Section 11.5 represents $\log(\sigma_t)$ as an AR(1) process with mean α, innovation variance σ_η^2, and autoregressive parameter ϕ. Ghysels, Gourieroux, and Jasiak (1998) restate the SV model in operational time which is driven by market activity. Their timescale is dynamic, unlike θ-time, and its increments are functions of expected activity variables $\hat{y}_{t-1}$ and surprises in those variables, $y_{t-1} - \hat{y}_{t-1}$. They summarize activity by quotation counts, bid–ask spreads, and absolute returns. Their method essentially replaces α, ϕ, and σ_η for period t in the calendar-time SV model by functions of $\exp(\beta_1 \hat{y}_{t-1} + \beta_2 (y_{t-1} - \hat{y}_{t-1}))$, for parameters β_1 and β_2. As α is a function of market activity, periodic volatility effects can appear in the calendar-time model which is estimated for the O&A dataset by the QMLE method of Harvey et al. (1994) using twenty-minute returns. Ghysels et al. conclude that absolute returns are probably the most satisfactory of the activity variables for the DM/\$ data.

A continuous-time SV model is estimated in Barndorff-Nielsen and Shephard (2001) from five-minute DM/\$ returns. This model is described in Section 13.6, where it is noted that their four-component volatility model contains a dominant short-term component and three persistent components.

12.7 Trading Rules and Intraday Prices

The apparent abundance of information offered by high-frequency price datasets may tempt us to hope that technical trading rules will then be more successful than when applied to daily prices. The principles that motivate the efficient market hypothesis are, of course, unaffected by the frequency of available data. Competition among traders will tend to eliminate profitable methods because traders generally share the same information. Furthermore, the prospect of more frequent trades from more frequent data is no advantage when transaction costs must be paid.

Central bank interventions were noted in Section 7.10 that may permit profitable currency trading. It would then be potentially valuable to review prices more often than daily, particularly if some traders learn about interventions before others (Peiers 1997; Chang and Taylor 1998; Frenkel, Pierdzioch, and Stadtmann 2001).

12.7.1 Methods

Standard moving-average trading rules for daily data can also be applied to more frequent observations, as discussed and investigated by Acar and Lequeux (1999). It is not surprising, however, that more complicated methods have been tried that seek to extract patterns from the large price histories available.

Nearest neighbor methods produce forecasts by seeking past periods that have returns similar to those recently observed. These methods essentially provide nonparametric predictors. Although they are often motivated by chaos theory, the predictors do not require chaotic dynamics to be successful. The predictors should be as successful as the best alternatives whenever the price process is stationary and there is a long price history.

Neural network methods provide price forecasts from within a general family of functions that can approximate any nonlinear function to a stated degree of accuracy. The approximating function may have many parameters that can easily be estimated from a large dataset. Alexander (2001) describes both neural network and nearest neighbor methods.

Genetic algorithms develop trading rules by optimization during a learning period. Flexible decision rules can evolve through time by discarding the least successful rules and permitting random variation within the retained rules. For further details see Neely et al. (1997) and Allen and Karjalainen (1999). These methods can be expected to thrive on large datasets if they have any potential.

12.7.2 Results

All the methodological issues emphasized in Section 7.7 for trading rules applied to daily prices are relevant for high-frequency data. It is essential that research studies reserve some data that are not used to design rules and optimize their parameters. Also note that the assumption that we can trade at recorded prices without changing the price path must become less realistic as trades become more frequent.

There is not much evidence from high-frequency trading rules against the efficient market hypothesis in the research literature. Acar and Lequeux (1999) find that none of their moving-average style trading rules produces significant profits, after transaction costs, when applied to the O&A dataset described in Section 12.2. Even traders paying marginal transaction costs appear unable to earn excess returns. Toulson, Toulson, and Sinclair (1999) apply neural networks and wavelet transform methods to two years of tick data for futures trading of five assets at LIFFE. They claim returns "modestly in excess" of those from buy and hold strategies. Alexandré, Girerd-Potin, and Taramasco (1998) evaluate nearest neighbor forecasts for two exchange rate series with disappointing results. Likewise, Dunis, Gavridis, Harris, Leong, and Nacaskul (1998) explore the potential of genetic algorithms based upon momentum and relative strength indicators for two FX series. They discover that in-sample optimized profits do not recur in their out-of-sample period. Neely and Weller (2003) evaluate the performance of an autoregressive forecasting method and a genetic program. Their FX results are consistent with an efficient market after realistic transaction costs are taken into account.

Dacorogna et al. (2001) present the case for profitable foreign exchange trading based upon the extensive research of Olsen & Associates. Perhaps we should expect any profitable opportunities to be exploited by O&A, given their considerable investment in data acquisition and research. Dacorogna et al. (2001, p. 296) tell us: "The purpose of this chapter is not to provide *ready-to-use* trading strategies, but to give a description of the main ingredients needed in order for any real-time trading model to be usable for actual trading on financial markets." And then: "Our models anticipate price movements in the foreign exchange market sufficiently well to be profitable for many years yet with acceptable risk behavior, and they have been used by many banks." The ingredients of their trading methodology include genetic algorithms and strict optimization and testing procedures.

Chapter 11 of their book includes plenty of detail about the methodology of genetic algorithms and their literature. Among their results are out-of-sample annual returns of 3–6%, using hourly data from 1987 to 1995 (their Table 11.2 and Chopard, Pictet, and Tomassini 2000), 11–13% for the period 1986–1993 (Table 11.3), and 5% per annum from 1993 to 1997 (Table 11.12). As far as I can tell, these returns are approximately in excess of the domestic risk-free rate. The critical figure, however, is the excess return on capital invested with O&A in more recent years. Some related research is described in Gençay, Ballochi, Dacorogna, Olsen, and Pictet (2002) for simpler trading rules that have also been profitable net of transaction costs.

12.8 Realized Volatility: Theoretical Results

12.8.1 Realized Volatility

Volatility during a period of time can be estimated more and more precisely as the frequency of returns increases, providing intraperiod returns are uncorrelated and certain other conditions apply. We suppose the periods are trading days with daily returns r_t that are the sum of N intraday returns $r_{t,j,N}$; thus,

$$r_t = \sum_{j=1}^{N} r_{t,j,N}. \tag{12.15}$$

For $N = 1, 2, 3, \ldots$ we define the *realized variance* for day t as

$$\hat{\sigma}_{t,N}^2 = \sum_{j=1}^{N} r_{t,j,N}^2, \tag{12.16}$$

and we refer to $\hat{\sigma}_{t,N}$ as the *realized volatility*. This and related measures of volatility appear in several high-frequency studies, early examples including Schwert (1990b), Hsieh (1991), Zhou (1996), and Taylor and Xu (1997). The quantity $\hat{\sigma}_{t,N}^2$ is simply N times the sample variance of N intraday returns (assuming a zero mean) and hence it is a natural estimate of daily variance.

Figure 12.10 illustrates annualized values of $\hat{\sigma}_{t,N}$, for the single day of FTSE transaction data described in Section 12.3. A logarithmic scale is used for N. An estimate of $\hat{\sigma}_{t,N}$ is marked by a dot for all values of N that are factors of 540 (between 3 and 540 inclusive), for the nine-hour period commencing at 08:15.

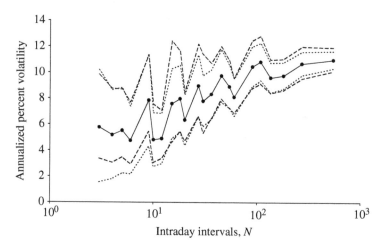

Figure 12.10. Realized volatilities for one day.

Andersen and Bollerslev (1998b), Barndorff-Nielsen and Shephard (2001), and Comte and Renault (1998) concurrently and independently showed that random variables $\hat{\sigma}^2_{t,N}$ converge to a limit σ^2_t, as $N \to \infty$, that represents the squared volatility for period t, when various assumptions are made. Subsequently, Andersen, Bollerslev, Diebold, and their co-authors used sample values of $\hat{\sigma}^2_{t,N}$, for large N, to infer interesting results about the distributional and autocorrelation properties of σ^2_t. We now provide some theoretical intuition and results for their empirical methods, including results about the accuracy of the estimator $\hat{\sigma}^2_{t,N}$. A discussion of the empirical evidence then follows in the next section. Expected returns are assumed to be zero in the theory that follows and proofs are given in the appendix to this chapter. For a mathematical survey of the theory of volatility measurement, see Andersen, Bollerslev, and Diebold (2005).

12.8.2 A Simple Example

First, consider the simplest situation when σ_t is a number that represents the latent volatility for day t and the intraday returns are conditionally Gaussian and i.i.d. for all N:

$$r_{t,j,N} \mid \sigma_t \sim \text{i.i.d. } N(0, \sigma^2_t/N), \quad 1 \leqslant j \leqslant N. \tag{12.17}$$

Then $r_t \mid \sigma_t \sim N(0, \sigma^2_t)$. Here the number σ_t is any possible outcome of a random volatility variable, while the terms $r_{t,j,N}$ are random variables.

Each of the N random quantities $Nr^2_{t,j,N}$ provides an independent and unbiased estimate of σ^2_t. The variance of their average is proportional to $1/N$, so this average will converge to σ^2_t as N increases. We have

$$E[\hat{\sigma}^2_{t,N} \mid \sigma_t] = \sigma^2_t \tag{12.18}$$

and

$$\text{var}(\hat{\sigma}_{t,N}^2 \mid \sigma_t) = \frac{2\sigma_t^4}{N}. \tag{12.19}$$

Consequently, as $N \to \infty$ the realized variance $\hat{\sigma}_{t,N}^2$ converges to the squared latent volatility σ_t^2.

If, instead, we let σ_t represent a random variable, with $r_{t,j,N} = \sigma_t u_{t,j,N}/\sqrt{N}$ and σ_t independent of $u_{t,j,N} \sim$ i.i.d. $N(0,1)$, then

$$E[\hat{\sigma}_{t,N}^2 - \sigma_t^2] = 0 \tag{12.20}$$

and

$$\text{var}(\hat{\sigma}_{t,N}^2 - \sigma_t^2) = \frac{2E[\sigma_t^4]}{N}. \tag{12.21}$$

Again $\hat{\sigma}_{t,N}^2 - \sigma_t^2 \to 0$ as $N \to \infty$, with the convergence being in mean square and hence in probability.

12.8.3 An Example with Periodic Effects

A more realistic theoretical framework includes an intraday periodic volatility pattern. For some number σ_t and for each N, now assume

$$r_{t,j,N} \mid \sigma_t \sim N(0, \lambda_{j,N}\sigma_t^2), \quad \lambda_{j,N} \geqslant 0, \quad \text{and} \quad \sum_{j=1}^{N} \lambda_{j,N} = 1 \tag{12.22}$$

with $r_{t,j,N} \mid \sigma_t$ independent of $r_{t,k,N} \mid \sigma_t$ whenever $j \neq k$. The realized variance is again unbiased and now

$$\text{var}(\hat{\sigma}_{t,N}^2 \mid \sigma_t) = 2\sigma_t^4 \sum_{j=1}^{N} \lambda_{j,N}^2. \tag{12.23}$$

This again decreases to zero, as $N \to \infty$, *providing* the multipliers $\lambda_{j,N}$ diminish at a sufficiently rapid rate. A necessary and sufficient condition is that

$$\lambda_N^* = \max_{1 \leqslant j \leqslant N} \lambda_{j,N} \to 0 \quad \text{as } N \to \infty. \tag{12.24}$$

Thus, when the maximum of the multipliers converges to zero as $N \to \infty$, the realized variance $\hat{\sigma}_{t,N}^2$ converges to σ_t^2.

There are, however, reasonable conditions for which this convergence result fails. For example, if $j = 1$ corresponds to an overnight period when the market is closed then $\lambda_{1,N}$ is the same for all N and $\text{var}(\hat{\sigma}_{t,N}^2 \mid \sigma_t) \geqslant 2\lambda_{1,N}^2\sigma_t^4 > 0$ when $\lambda_{1,N} > 0$. Likewise, if there is scheduled news that produces an instantaneous jump in the price logarithm, conditionally distributed as $N(0, \tilde{\lambda}\sigma_t^2)$, then $\text{var}(\hat{\sigma}_{t,N}^2 \mid \sigma_t) \geqslant 2\tilde{\lambda}^2\sigma_t^4$ for all N.

The realized volatility is not the most accurate estimator of σ_t^2 when the periodic pattern is known for each day t. A more general unbiased estimator is

$$\tilde{\sigma}_{t,N}^2 = \sum_{j=1}^{N} w_{j,N} r_{t,j,N}^2 \quad \text{with} \quad \sum_{j=1}^{N} w_{j,N}\lambda_{j,N} = 1. \tag{12.25}$$

Its conditional variance is

$$\text{var}(\tilde{\sigma}_{t,N}^2 \mid \sigma_t) = 2\sigma_t^4 \sum_{j=1}^{N} w_{j,N}^2 \lambda_{j,N}^2, \tag{12.26}$$

which is minimized when $w_{j,N} = 1/(N\lambda_{j,N})$ (Areal and Taylor 2002) and then

$$\text{var}(\tilde{\sigma}_{t,N}^2 \mid \sigma_t) = \frac{2\sigma_t^4}{N}. \tag{12.27}$$

This is the same variance as in (12.19). Thus the optimally weighted estimator converges to σ_t^2 as N increases.

12.8.4 A General SV Result

Our most general result supposes that intraday returns follow a general stochastic volatility process for all N. Suppose $r_{t,j,N} = \sigma_{t,j,N} u_{t,j,N}/\sqrt{N}$, $u_{t,j,N} \sim N(0,1)$, and $u_{t,j,N}$ is independent of $\sigma_{t,j,N}$ and all variables $u_{.,.,N}$ and $\sigma_{.,.,N}$ that are determined before time t, j. We assume the average squared volatility is the same for all N; thus,

$$\frac{1}{N} \sum_{j=1}^{N} \sigma_{t,j,N}^2 = \sigma_t^2. \tag{12.28}$$

Then daily returns have the SV factorization $r_t = \sigma_t u_t$ with σ_t independent of $u_t \sim N(0,1)$. In the special context of a continuous-time diffusion model for prices, σ_t^2 equals both the *integrated variance* defined by $\int_{t-1}^{t} \sigma^2(s)\,ds$ and the *quadratic variation* (QV) of the logarithms of prices during day t.

We now have

$$\text{var}(\hat{\sigma}_{t,N}^2 - \sigma_t^2) = \frac{2}{N} E\left[\frac{1}{N} \sum_{j=1}^{N} \sigma_{t,j,N}^4\right]. \tag{12.29}$$

This variance tends to zero as N increases providing the day's volatility is not concentrated around any particular time. A sufficient condition is

$$\max_i \left(\sigma_{t,i,N}^2 \Big/ \sum_j \sigma_{t,j,N}^2\right) \to 0 \quad \text{as } N \to \infty.$$

Another sufficient condition is a finite limit for $N^{-1}\sum_j \sigma_{t,j,N}^4$. Assuming one of these conditions is met, $\hat{\sigma}_{t,N}^2 \to \sigma_t^2$.

This conclusion holds for continuous-time models of prices that are diffusion processes, but not when there are jumps in the price process. The limit of the realized variance for a pure jump process is its quadratic variation, which equals the sum of squared jumps, but this is not a function of a latent volatility variable. Further theoretical discussion can be found in Andersen, Bollerslev, Diebold, and Labys (2001), Barndorff-Nielsen and Shephard (2002a), Andersen, Bollerslev, and Diebold (2003), and the appendix to this chapter.

12.8.5 Measurement Error

The convergence of $\hat{\sigma}_{t,N}^2$ to a limit σ_t^2 is a theoretical ideal. Trading is not continuous and microstructure issues such as bid–ask spreads and price discreteness ensure that realized volatility always contains some measurement error.

From (12.19), a naive estimate of the standard deviation of the measurement error $\hat{\sigma}_{t,N}^2 - \sigma_t^2$ is $\sqrt{2/N}\hat{\sigma}_{t,N}^2$. A typical high value of N is 288, for five-minute returns with no market closures, and then the naive standard error equals one-twelfth of the estimate $\hat{\sigma}_{t,N}^2$. Periodic intraday volatility effects increase the standard error, as the variance given by (12.23) exceeds that given by (12.19). Any excess conditional kurtosis in intraday returns will also increase standard errors.

Barndorff-Nielsen and Shephard [BNS] (2002a) and Meddahi (2002) emphasize and illustrate the magnitude of measurement errors. BNS (2002a,b) provide asymptotic convergence results to the standard normal distribution for a class of general, continuous-time stochastic volatility models. Their results can be used to estimate standard errors from

$$\frac{\hat{\sigma}_{t,N}^2 - \sigma_t^2}{(\frac{2}{3}\sum_{j=1}^N r_{t,j,N}^4)^{1/2}} \xrightarrow{D} N(0,1) \tag{12.30}$$

and

$$\frac{\log(\hat{\sigma}_{t,N}^2) - \log(\sigma_t^2)}{\{\frac{2}{3}\sum_{j=1}^N r_{t,j,N}^4/(\sum_{j=1}^N r_{t,j,N}^2)^2\}^{1/2}} \xrightarrow{D} N(0,1). \tag{12.31}$$

The second of these results provides the better approximation for practical values of N. The estimated standard error of $\log(\hat{\sigma}_{t,N}^2)$ is approximately $\sqrt{2k_N/(3N)}$ with k_N the sample kurtosis of the N intraday returns $r_{t,j,N}$.

Figure 12.10 shows two sets of 95% confidence intervals for one day of estimates $\hat{\sigma}_{t,N}^2$. One set is obtained from the naive standard errors and critical points of the χ_N^2 distribution, while the other set is given by (12.31). The intervals are generally wider for the more accurate standard errors given by (12.31) and they are shown by the longer dashed lines.

The above standard errors ignore microstructure noise and hence they will underestimate the variability of measurement errors. Microstructure effects will also introduce bias into the estimates $\hat{\sigma}_{t,N}^2$, which becomes more severe as N

increases. Bandi and Russell (2004a,b) show how the impact of microstructure noise can be eliminated and the optimal sampling frequency can be derived. Their average estimate of the optimal frequency for stock volatility calculations suggests that returns should be calculated every four minutes. Aït-Sahalia, Mykland, and Zhang (2005) provide further results about the impact of microstructure noise when volatility is constant.

12.8.6 Bipower Estimates

An alternative estimate of σ_t^2 is provided by the realized bipower, which can be defined by

$$\frac{\pi}{2} \sum_{j=2}^{N} |r_{t,j-1,N}| \, |r_{t,j,N}|.$$

The realized variance and the realized bipower converge to the same limit when the price process is continuous and has martingale properties. The limits are different, however, when there are jumps in the price process. Comparisons between sample variance and bipower estimates can then be used to make inferences about the jump component (Barndorff-Nielsen and Shephard 2004a,b; Andersen, Bollerslev, and Diebold 2003; Huang and Tauchen 2004).

12.9   Realized Volatility: Empirical Results

We now review a few empirical studies of realized variance (RV), in which the researchers select a specific number of intraday periods N and then calculate RV for day t from intraday returns $r_{t,j}$ as

$$\hat{\sigma}_t^2 = \sum_{j=1}^{N} r_{t,j}^2. \tag{12.32}$$

Their intention is to obtain an accurate estimate $\hat{\sigma}_t$ of the latent volatility for day t, denoted by σ_t. The intraday returns could be mean-adjusted in (12.32), but the impact of such adjustments is negligible for large values of N. We summarize results selected from Andersen, Bollerslev, Diebold, and Labys (2000, 2001), Andersen, Bollerslev, Diebold, and Ebens (2001), Ebens (1999), and Areal and Taylor (2002), and refer to their work as ABDL, ABDE, E, and AT. There are three major conclusions, that are obtained in all four studies:

- the distribution of standardized returns $r_t/\hat{\sigma}_t$ is almost normal;
- the distribution of $\log(\hat{\sigma}_t)$ is approximately normal;
- realized volatility has a long memory feature, which can be modeled by a fractionally integrated process.

12.9.1 Data

All four studies make use of five-minute returns and all exclude weekends and holidays. ABDL use DM/$ and yen/$ quotes for the ten years from December 1986 to November 1996. Quotes are used for all twenty-four hours of the day and then $N = 288$. However, they calculate RV from thirty-minute returns in their first paper. ABDE study the transaction prices for all thirty stocks in the DJIA from January 1993 until May 1998. Their transaction data come from records that extend from 09:30 EST to 16:05 EST, thus they have 79 five-minute returns per day. The returns when the market is closed are ignored, so that RV then measures the open-market variance, which is less than total daily variance. Both ABDL and ABDE also report interesting research into realized covariances and correlations. Ebens investigates the DJIA index for the same period that ABDE study the component stocks. It appears that he studies the open-market RV and presumably $N = 79$ again.

Areal and Taylor obtain returns from transaction prices for FTSE 100 futures, primarily for the period from March 1990 to July 1998 when trading was from 08:35 to 16:10 London time. They use the overnight return as well as the 91 intra-day returns when calculating the total RV. They also calculate RV as a weighted sum of squared returns, as shown by equation (12.25). This makes the open-market RV slightly more accurate and the total RV much more accurate. Figure 12.11 shows the annualized total RV as a standard deviation, namely $\sqrt{251}\hat{\sigma}_t$, for a longer period and plotted on a logarithmic scale. The exceptional value of 365% occurs on the day following the US crash on 19 October 1987.

It is desirable that RV is an unbiased estimate of the latent volatility. Bias will occur when the intraday returns are autocorrelated and can be substantial, as noted by Blair et al. (2001b) for the spot S&P 100 index. ABDE use the residuals from an MA(1) model to avoid systematic bias induced by bid–ask bounce effects. To check for bias, the expectation of σ_t^2 can be estimated by the variance of daily returns and compared with the sample mean of estimates $\hat{\sigma}_t^2$. AT find that the daily variance is 92% of the average RV when the closed-market returns are included in the calculations. The corresponding ratios for the DM/$ and the yen/$ rates are 0.95 and 0.92 from numbers tabulated by ABDL.

12.9.2 The Distribution of Standardized Returns

First we consider the distribution of daily returns standardized by their estimated volatility,

$$z_t = \frac{r_t - \hat{\mu}}{\hat{\sigma}_t}, \tag{12.33}$$

with $\hat{\mu}$ an estimate of expected returns, which is set to zero in some studies. The mean and standard deviation of the standardized returns should be respectively

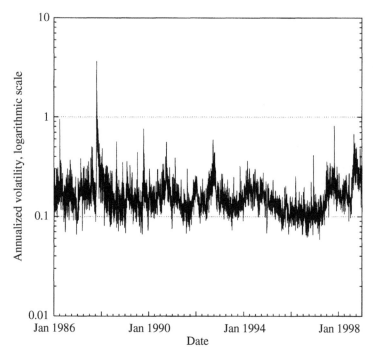

Figure 12.11.   Annualized FTSE 100 volatility calculated each
day from optimally weighted squared five-minute returns.

near to zero and one when the measurement error in $\hat{\sigma}_t^2$ is small. This occurs in
ABDL, E, and AT but ABDE have standard deviations below one for all thirty
stocks, with the median value being 0.81.

A striking result in all these studies is the distribution of the standardized returns
z_t. It is approximately normal. This can be seen from density plots in all the studies
and in Figure 12.12 for the FTSE data of AT. This shows a histogram for the z_t, a
normal density (which matches the mean and variance of the z_t) as a dotted curve,
and the kernel density estimate as a solid curve (defined by (4.6) and a bandwidth
of 0.25).

The skewness of the z_t is approximately zero, with estimates of 0.02 and 0.00
for the two currencies in ABDL, 0.03 in E, 0.16 in AT, and a median stock value
of 0.11 in ABDE. The kurtosis of the z_t is near the normal value of three and the
estimates are 2.41 and 2.41 in ABDL, 2.75 in E, 2.77 in AT, and a median of 3.13
in ABDE. These kurtosis estimates are, of course, less than for the returns r_t and
they are also less than for returns that are standardized by conditional standard
deviations from ARCH or SV models.

The high-frequency data allow us to get closer to the latent volatility variable
than methods that only use daily data and this is revealed in the closer approximation of the standardized returns to a normal distribution. The approximation is

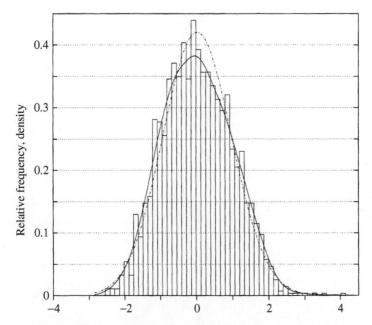

Figure 12.12. The distribution of the daily standardized returns of
FTSE 100 index futures from March 1990 to July 1998.

good but not perfect, reflecting some measurement error and also the discreteness
of price changes. It does appear reasonable to model daily returns as a mixture
of normal distributions, mixing across different values of the time-varying latent
volatility σ_t. The unconditional distribution of returns then follows from the distribution of the mixing variable σ_t, which we now consider.

12.9.3 The Distribution of Realized Volatility

The empirical distribution of $\hat{\sigma}_t^2$ is strongly skewed to the right and has very high
kurtosis, which reflects notable high outliers. The kurtosis estimates are 24 and
67 in ABDL and the median is 66 in ABDE. The distribution of the standard
deviation estimate $\hat{\sigma}_t$ is less skewed and less kurtotic, but the kurtosis estimates
remain far above three: 7.8 and 10.4 in ABDL, 17 in E, and 19 in AT.

As popular stochastic volatility models assume $\log(\sigma_t)$ has a normal distribution (as in Section 11.5), it is interesting to consider the empirical distribution
of $\log(\hat{\sigma}_t)$. These empirical distributions are approximately normal. As $\log(\hat{\sigma}_t)$
equals the latent term $\log(\sigma_t)$ plus a relatively small error, the distribution of
$\log(\sigma_t)$ is also near to normal. This implies that the distribution of returns is
approximately the lognormal–normal distribution advocated by Clark (1973),
Tauchen and Pitts (1983), and Taylor (1986).

Density plots in all four studies support an approximate normal approximation
for $\log(\hat{\sigma}_t)$. Figure 12.13 shows a histogram for the FTSE data of AT and the

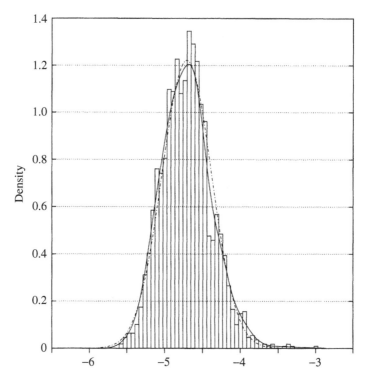

Figure 12.13.   The distribution of the logarithm of realized
volatility for the FTSE 100 index from 1990 to 1998.

matching normal density as a dotted curve. The kernel density estimate, with
bandwidth 0.1, is shown as a solid curve. The skewness of $\log(\hat{\sigma}_t)$ is generally
positive: 0.35 and 0.26 in ABDL, a median of 0.19 in ABDE, 0.75 in E, and 0.44
in AT. These values are significantly different from zero at low significance levels.
Likewise, the kurtosis estimates for $\log(\hat{\sigma}_t)$ are significantly above three: 3.26 and
3.53 in ABDL, a median of 3.89 in ABDE, 3.78 in E, and 3.71 in AT.

    Thus $\log(\hat{\sigma}_t)$ only has an approximate normal distribution, which is the most
that can be expected as there is no theoretical reason why volatility should have
a lognormal distribution. There are several possible explanations for the excess
kurtosis in the distribution of $\log(\hat{\sigma}_t)$, including measurement error and extreme
high outliers. It is possible that occasional crises create excess probability in the
right tail relative to the normal distribution. AT note that the annualized values for
the FTSE index from 1990 to 1998 have a maximum value of $\sqrt{251}\hat{\sigma}_t$ equal to
81% on 28 October 1997 and that Ebens reports exceptional values for the DJIA
index on both the 27th and the 28th. Also, three of the highest FTSE estimates
are for the day that sterling left the European Exchange Rate Mechanism and the
two following days, with all three annualized estimates above 50%.

    The various studies also provide estimates of the mean α and standard deviation

β of $\log(\hat{\sigma}_t)$. These can be compared with the typical estimates of α and β for $\log(\sigma_t)$ in the standard SV model that are mentioned in Section 11.6. The high-frequency estimates of α are -5.05 for currencies in ABDL, -4.71 for the equity index in AT, and -4.13 for the median stock in ABDE. The estimates of β include the impact of measurement errors and are 0.35 for currencies, 0.33 for the index, and 0.26 for the median stock. The FX estimates are comparable to the low-frequency FX estimates given in Sections 11.6 and 11.7.

12.9.4 *The Autocorrelations of Realized Volatility*

We should expect to find substantial positive autocorrelation in realized volatility, because RV is a fairly accurate estimate of volatility that is known to be highly persistent from our consideration of ARCH and SV models. We should also expect the positive dependence in RV to exceed that of squared daily returns because the latter quantity is a much more noisy estimate of volatility than is RV. These expectations are confirmed by the empirical evidence. All four studies estimate the first autocorrelation of $\log(\hat{\sigma}_t)$ to be between 0.60 and 0.65 and they all find that the first 100 autocorrelations are all positive.

It is important to remember that measurement error reduces autocorrelations. The autocorrelations of $\log(\hat{\sigma}_t)$ and $\log(\sigma_t)$ are proportional to each other for stationary processes; thus,

$$\mathrm{cor}(\log(\hat{\sigma}_t), \log(\hat{\sigma}_{t+\tau})) = \delta\, \mathrm{cor}(\log(\sigma_t), \log(\sigma_{t+\tau})), \quad \tau \geqslant 1, \qquad (12.34)$$

with

$$\delta = \mathrm{var}(\log(\sigma_t)) / \mathrm{var}(\log(\hat{\sigma}_t)) < 1, \qquad (12.35)$$

assuming the terms $\log(\hat{\sigma}_t/\sigma_t)$ are i.i.d. Hence the correlation between consecutive values of $\log(\sigma_t)$ is estimated to be more than 0.6. Values exceeding 0.7 appear to be plausible.

Figure 12.14 shows the autocorrelations of $\log(\hat{\sigma}_t)$ obtained by AT at lags 1–250. They decay slowly, as previously emphasized by ABDL and ABDE, and suggest we should consider a long memory model for volatility. A clear minor calendar effect can be seen in Figure 12.14, with the local maxima at lags 5, 10, 15, and 20 indicating variation in equity volatility across the five days of the week. Taylor and Xu (1997) show that average realized DM/$ volatility increases from Monday to Friday, presumably reflecting the timing of macroeconomic announcements.

12.9.5 *Fractional Integration of Realized Volatility*

A fractionally integrated process can explain the slow decay in the autocorrelations of realized volatility. The degree of fractional integration, denoted by d, is then between zero and one. We have already encountered the parameter d

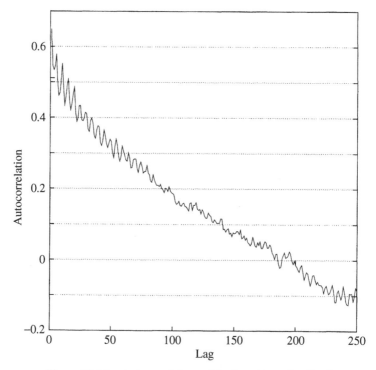

Figure 12.14.   Autocorrelations of the logarithm of realized
volatility for the FTSE 100 index from 1990 to 1998.

in Sections 10.3 and 11.10, where evidence of long memory volatility effects
in low-frequency returns was noted. The evidence is particularly impressive for
high-frequency returns, both in the four studies of realized volatility and also in
the related work of Andersen and Bollerslev (1997a) and Bollerslev and Wright
(2000).

The fractional parameter d appears in the asymptotic shapes of autocorrelations,
spectral densities, and variance ratios, as explained in Section 3.8. The variance S_T
of the sum of T consecutive observations has the scaling law $T^{-(2d+1)} S_T \to c$ as
$T \to \infty$ for a positive constant c. Thus $\log(S_T)$ is asymptotically a linear function
of $\log(T)$. The empirical data rather remarkably support a linear relationship for
small values of T. Figure 12.15 shows this for the data of AT over the range
$1 \leqslant T \leqslant 128$, from which d is estimated to be 0.42. Likewise, ABDL estimate d
as 0.39 and 0.36 and ABDE have a median estimate of 0.39, from regressions over
$1 \leqslant T \leqslant 30$. These estimates are for the logarithms of realized volatility, $\log(\hat{\sigma}_t)$.
Measurement error has no effect on the asymptotic result, so the estimates can
be used for $\log(\sigma_t)$. The estimates are also applicable to σ_t and σ_t^2, from theory
in Andersen and Bollerslev (1997a). The regressions do not, however, provide
standard errors for d.

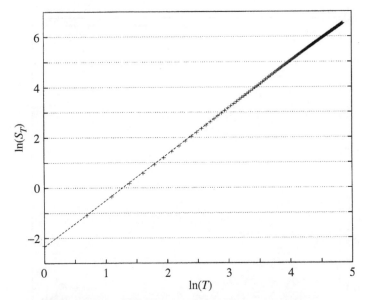

Figure 12.15. Scaling plot for daily logarithms of realized volatility, S_T is the variance of T consecutive observations.

The estimate of d devised by Geweke and Porter-Hudak (1983) relies on the unbounded shape of the spectral density $f(\omega)$ for low frequencies ω. The theoretical density is proportional to ω^{-2d} as $\omega \to 0$ and then $\omega^{2d} f(\omega) \to C$ for some positive C. The GPH estimate is obtained from n observations and $m \ll n$ values of the sample periodogram $I(\omega_j)$ that estimate $f(\omega_j)$ at the frequencies $\omega_j = 2\pi j/n$, $j = 1, 2, \ldots, m$. The least squares regression of $\log(I(\omega_j))$ on ω_j produces a slope estimate $\hat{\beta}$, from which d is estimated by $\hat{d} = -\hat{\beta}/2$. The distribution of $\hat{d}$ is approximately normal with mean d and standard deviation equal to $\pi/\sqrt{24m}$, providing m is small relative to n. The standard error of $\hat{d}$ can also be estimated from the standard OLS value for $\hat{\beta}$. The selection of m is problematic and involves a trade-off between bias and variation in $\hat{d}$. Bias is a problem if m is too large, while $\hat{d}$ is inaccurate if m is too small. Most researchers set $m = n^\theta$ for a power θ between 0.5 and 0.8. For further details of the theory of the GPH test, see Baillie (1996) and Bollerslev and Wright (2000).

An additive measurement error does not change the shape of the spectral density at low frequencies. Therefore the GPH estimates of d obtained from $\log(\hat{\sigma}_t)$ are also applicable to $\log(\sigma_t)$, σ_t, and σ_t^2. ABDL graphed $\hat{d}$ against $m = n^\theta$, looking for a region in which $\hat{d}$ is not sensitive to the choice, as suggested by Taqqu and Teverovsky (1996). ABDL estimate d to be 0.42 and 0.45 when $\theta = 0.8$, with standard errors below 0.03. ABDE prefer $\theta = 0.6$ and obtain a median estimate of d equal to 0.35, with all their estimates having a standard error of 0.07. Ebens and AT both use $\theta = 0.8$ to respectively obtain equity index estimates of 0.40

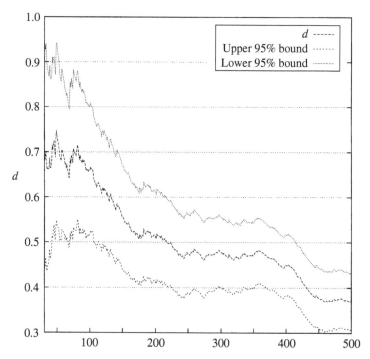

Figure 12.16. GPH estimates of the degree of fractional integration, d, as a function of the number of periodogram ordinates, n^{θ}, used in their calculations.

(s.e. 0.04) and 0.43 (s.e. 0.03). It is notable that these estimates are all in the range from 0.35 to 0.45. They are also close to the unsophisticated estimates given by the scaling law methodology. All the GPH estimates comprehensively reject $d = 0$, if we can rely on an asymptotic hypothesis test applied when m is a significant proportion of n. Figure 12.16 shows the estimates of d (and 95% confidence intervals) for the AT data, as m increases from 40 to 500, with $n = 2075$.

The filtered series

$$y_t = (1 - L)^{\hat{d}} \log(\hat{\sigma}_t) \tag{12.36}$$

is examined by ABDE and E to see if realized equity volatility responds asymmetrically to price rises and falls. They find that the sign of the return for day $t - 1$ provides information about the expected value of y_t, which is higher after a price fall than a price rise. AT observe that their values of y_t appear to be almost white noise.

12.9.6   Short or Long Memory?

The empirical evidence discussed here for RV shows that fractionally integrated processes are plausible for volatility, supporting similar empirical evidence for ARCH and SV models noted in Sections 10.3 and 11.10. Granger (1980) proved that long memory processes can arise when short memory processes are aggregated. Specifically, when AR(1) components are aggregated and the AR(1) parameters are drawn from a beta distribution then the aggregated process converges to a long memory process as the number of components increases. Andersen and Bollerslev (1997a) develop the theoretical results in more detail when the context is aggregating volatility components. It is certainly credible to assert that volatility reflects several sources of news, that the persistence of shocks depends on the sources, and hence that total volatility has a long memory property.

There are, however, alternatives to the long memory conclusion. Gallant, Hsu, and Tauchen (1999) estimate a volatility process for daily IBM returns that is the sum of only two short memory components yet the sum is able to mimic long memory. They also show that the sum of a particular pair of AR(1) processes has a spectral density very close to that of fractionally integrated white noise with $d = 0.4$ for frequencies $\omega \geqslant 0.01\pi$.

A sum of two AR(1) components is preferred for volatility in Alizadeh, Brandt, and Diebold (2002). Barndorff-Nielsen and Shephard (2001, 2002b) analyze ten years of DM/$ five-minute returns, adjusted for intraday volatility periodicity, and show that the sum of four short memory processes provides an excellent match to the autocorrelations of squared five-minute returns, which appear to display the long memory property of hyperbolic decay. Pong, Shackleton, Taylor, and Xu (2004) show that a sum of two AR(1) components forecasts currency volatility as accurately as a long memory model.

Occasional structural breaks, from one short memory process to another, are a second alternative to the long memory conclusion. Diebold and Inoue (2001) illustrate how regime switches can mimic long memory properties. Andreou and Ghysels (2002) show how to identify the number and location of multiple breaks in the volatility process. Granger and Hyung (2004) demonstrate that it is difficult to distinguish between break and long memory models, using simulations and analysis of absolute returns.

Ohanissian, Russell, and Tsay (2004) develop and investigate a test of the null hypothesis that a process has a long memory. Their test compares estimates of the long memory parameter d for a set of data frequencies; it accepts the null hypothesis for ten years of five-minute FX returns at the 5% significance level.

12.9.7 Applications

The literature on realized volatility (RV) is growing rapidly and many interesting applications can be expected in the future, in addition to the few noted here. Maheu and McCurdy (2002) estimate time-series models for FX volatility from RV that incorporate semi-Markov switching between regimes. Bollerslev and Zhou (2002) use RV to estimate a continuous-time model for FX rates that contains two short memory volatility components and a jump component; more details of the price process are given in Section 13.6. Fleming, Kirby, and Ostdiek (2003) show that RV has economic value, as better portfolios can be constructed when the covariance matrix of asset returns is estimated from RV instead of from daily returns. They show that higher expected returns can be obtained, for the same level of portfolio variance, when RV is used to select a portfolio invested in cash, a stock index, Treasury bonds, and gold. The accurate measurement of volatility by RV can be exploited when forecasting volatility (see Blair et al. 2001b; Maheu and McCurdy 2002; ABDL 2003), and the specific forecasting results described in Section 15.7.

12.10   Price Discovery

High-frequency data are ideal for making inferences about how information is reflected by prices. As information is reflected rapidly, much more can be learnt from high-frequency records. We have already noted the impact of scheduled macroeconomic news in Section 12.4.

Some news is not revealed publicly and has to be inferred from prices. Currency interventions by central banks are often not announced. Peiers (1997) finds that Bundesbank interventions are associated with Deutsche Bank making informed quotations, which precede quotations by other banks, up to one hour before Reuters announces the interventions. Chang and Taylor (1998) estimate ARCH models that incorporate dummy variables for interventions by the Bank of Japan. They infer that volatility increases thirty or more minutes before Reuters reports the interventions. Dominguez (2003) finds that some traders typically know that the Fed is intervening at least one hour before the public release of this information in newswire reports.

Several research studies have compared the relative impact of information upon two markets. Many assets are simultaneously traded in different places. Comparisons of prices for the same assets at different US equity markets have been made by Hasbrouck (1995, 2003), first for individual securities and more recently for equity indices. Two examples of price discovery research for European stocks that are simultaneously traded at domestic and US markets are Hupperets and Menkveld (2002) and Grammig, Melvin, and Schlag (2004). A few years ago, Bund futures were traded both on the floor of LIFFE and electronically by the Deutsche Terminbourse and then the relative price discovery of these two markets depended on the level of volatility (Martens 1998). Nikkei futures have been traded in Japan and Singapore, providing an opportunity for traders in Osaka to learn about prices from the foreign market when limit rules close the domestic market (Martens and Steenbeek 2001).

Spot and futures prices for the same asset have been compared to see which market first reveals information and to measure how long it takes for the slower market to catch up. Some representative contributions to this literature are Kawaller et al. (1987), Stoll and Whaley (1990), Yadav and Pope (1990), De Jong and Nijman (1997), and Taylor, van Dijk, Franses, and Lucas (2000). It has often been concluded that equity futures prices lead spot index levels and hence that price discovery occurs first in the futures market. Another strand of research compares the impact of the same information on different assets, for example, on the prices of US and UK stocks as in Kofman and Martens (1997).

12.11 Durations

The times that elapse between events such as trades or price changes can be used to predict the times of future events and to explore microstructure theories. Engle and Russell (1997, 1998) define *autoregressive conditional duration* (ACD) models for durations that are analogous to ARCH models for returns. Let x_i be the time duration between events $i - 1$ and i. Then an ACD model specifies conditional expectations for the times,

$$\psi_i = E[x_i \mid x_{i-1}, x_{i-2}, \dots], \qquad (12.37)$$

and a probability density function for the scaled times x_i/ψ_i. The scaled times are assumed to be i.i.d., so that

$$x_i = \psi_i \varepsilon_i \qquad (12.38)$$

with the random variables ε_i being i.i.d. with unit mean. A simple example is given by the WACD(1, 1) model, which has

$$\psi_i = \omega + \alpha x_{i-1} + \beta \psi_{i-1} \qquad (12.39)$$

and a Weibull distribution for the ε_i, whose density is determined by a positive parameter γ. The conditional densities of the times are then

$$f(x_i \mid \psi_i) = \frac{\gamma}{x_i} y_i \exp(-y_i) \quad \text{with } y_i = \left(\frac{x_i \Gamma(1 + \gamma^{-1})}{\psi_i} \right)^{\gamma}. \qquad (12.40)$$

The special case $\gamma = 1$ defines conditional exponential distributions, for which $f(x_i \mid \psi_i) = \exp(-x_i/\psi_i)/\psi_i$. Also, the variables ε_i^{γ} have exponential distributions with a mean that depends on γ. Much of the theory of GARCH(1, 1) models can be adapted for WACD(1, 1) models. In particular, the parameters can be estimated by maximizing the product of the conditional densities and standard errors can be obtained from the logarithm of this likelihood function (Engle and Russell 1998).

Duration times have intraday periodic patterns that can be incorporated into the conditional expectations ψ_i. Engle and Russell (1997) use multiplicative adjustment factors for the O&A dataset. They work with a subset of the DM/$ quotation times and find that the adjusted durations are autocorrelated. Their Table 3 includes the estimates $\hat{\alpha} = 0.07$, $\hat{\beta} = 0.90$, and $\hat{\gamma} = 0.91$ for the WACD(1, 1) model and they reject the null hypothesis $\gamma = 1$. Diagnostic tests are performed by checking the distribution and autocorrelations of the transformed estimated residuals $\hat{\varepsilon}_i^{\gamma}$, with fairly satisfactory results. The WACD model is used to investigate microstructure hypotheses. One conclusion is that the bid–ask spread can be used to improve predictions of durations; higher spreads reduce durations, consistent with an asymmetric information model. Another hypothesis, that traders follow a price leader, is not supported by the data.

Engle and Russell (1998) provide more theory and estimate similar models for three months of IBM transactions ending in 1991. Their parameter estimates include $\hat{\alpha} = 0.06$, $\hat{\beta} = 0.93$, and $\hat{\gamma} = 0.91$ for the WACD(1, 1) model. These are similar values to the currency estimates except that the persistence estimate $\hat{\alpha} + \hat{\beta}$ is almost one. They also report results for the more general WACD(2, 2) model and test hypotheses about the sources of the clustering of transaction times. They present evidence that clustering occurs when either informed traders or liquidity traders are active. Engle (2000) provides further analysis of the same IBM dataset and covers several microstructure theories. Evidence is found to support a model of Easley and O'Hara (1992), interpreted as no trade means no news. Longer durations are associated with lower volatility, while higher bid–ask spreads and higher volume both predict rising volatility.

Dufour and Engle (2000) is a more comprehensive study of equity transactions for eighteen firms during the same three-month period. They review the literature about asymmetric information models. These models imply that trades convey information and thus duration data may contain relevant information about prices. They then generalize a vector model of Hasbrouck (1991), for trades and quote revisions, that separates the impact of public and private information. They find that short inter-trade durations (and hence high trading activity) are related to both larger quote revisions and stronger positive autocorrelation of trades. For example, when a buy order is executed immediately after a previous order it is more likely to be followed by another buy. High trading activity is associated with large spreads, high volume, a high price impact of trades, and hence high informational content.

Duration models can also be defined by analogy with stochastic volatility models. Examples of SV duration models can be found in Gourieroux and Jasiak (2001), Bauwens and Veredas (2004), and Ghysels, Gourieroux, and Jasiak (2004).

12.12 Extreme Price Changes

It is difficult to estimate the probabilities of extreme price changes from low-frequency data because few extremes are then observed. High-frequency data provide more data in the extreme percentiles of the empirical distributions, which can be used to estimate the asymptotic shape of the distribution of returns. Extremal theory is covered in the books of Leadbetter, Lindgren, and Rootzén (1983) and Embrechts, Klüppelberg, and Mikosch (1997).

Unbounded distributions have only two possible asymptotic shapes. Their densities either decline exponentially or they follow a power law in the tails of the distribution. The former possibility applies to the standard stochastic volatility model of Section 11.5, for which all moments are finite. The other possibility occurs for general ARCH models, even when the conditional distributions are normal. It also occurs for SV models that have heavy tails, as in Section 11.8.

When a power law applies, the cumulative distribution function for returns r has the following approximate form for the right-hand tail:

$$F(r) \cong 1 - ar^{-\alpha}, \tag{12.41}$$

for a positive power α and a positive constant a that depends on the scale parameter of the distribution. More precisely,

$$F(r) = 1 - r^{-\alpha} G(r), \tag{12.42}$$

where G is a function that varies slowly as r increases, i.e. the limit of $G(\lambda r)/G(r)$ as $r \to \infty$ is one for all positive λ. A similar definition applies to the left-hand tail, although the two tails can have different values of the *tail index* α for an asymmetric distribution.

Assuming symmetry, α determines the range of finite moments. A finite moment of order p exists if and only if $p < \alpha$. This result shows that the value of α is invariant to aggregation. Thus we have a very constructive role for high-frequency returns—if we can estimate α from them, then the same value can be used to characterize extreme returns for daily returns and other low frequencies.

The estimate of α given by Hill (1975) uses the m most extreme of n observations, which are arranged in descending order, so that $r_{(1)} \geqslant r_{(2)} \geqslant \cdots \geqslant r_{(n)}$. We may suppose the observations are returns, adjusted by subtracting the sample mean. For i.i.d. data, and assuming equality in (12.41), the maximum likelihood estimate of the tail index (in the right tail) is then $\hat{\alpha}$ defined by

$$\frac{1}{\hat{\alpha}} = \frac{1}{m-1} \sum_{i=1}^{m-1} \log(r_{(i)}) - \log(r_{(m)}). \tag{12.43}$$

The left-tail estimate for return data is given by multiplying the observations by minus one and then arranging the data in descending order.

There are technical issues to face when using the Hill estimate, including the selection of m, bias in the MLE $\hat{\alpha}$, and the correct calculation of the standard error when the data contain ARCH effects and are hence not i.i.d. Daníelsson and de Vries (1997) solve these technical problems and estimate the tail indices for the O&A database. They find $\hat{\alpha}$ is between 3.5 and 4.5 for either tail of ten-minute returns for the DM/\$ and yen/\$ rates. They also estimate that a 1% (or more) increase in the DM/\$ rate during a ten-minute period will occur at an average frequency of once per year.

Dacorogna et al. (2001) apply similar methods to many series. Their Table 5.3 includes estimates of $\hat{\alpha}$ for thirty-minute returns (measured in θ-time) from seven dollar exchange rates during the decade from 1987 to 1996. The seven estimates range from 3.18 to 3.58, with a maximum standard error of 0.26. Therefore, models with infinite kurtosis appear credible for exchange rates. Their once-a-year event is a 1.7% (or more) increase in an exchange rate during a six-hour period.

12.13 Daily High and Low Prices

There are many databases of daily high, low, open, and close prices, particularly for futures markets. Although the daily high and low are only two numbers, they can provide much of the information that can be discovered about volatility from a complete intraday price record. Parkinson (1980) provided one of the first estimators of volatility from high and low prices, respectively h_t and l_t, defined by

$$\hat{\sigma}_t^2 = \frac{(\log(h_t) - \log(l_t))^2}{4 \log(2)}. \tag{12.44}$$

Assuming intraday prices follow geometric Brownian motion (defined in the next chapter), this estimator is much more accurate than the squared daily return and it is unbiased when expected returns are zero.

Parkinson's estimator is more accurate than the sum of five squared intraday returns. More accurate estimators are given by Garman and Klass (1980), who also use daily open and close prices to find a quadratic estimator that is as accurate as the sum of eight squared intraday returns. Further results appear in Beckers (1983), Rogers and Satchell (1991), and Yang and Zhang (2000). The assumptions of continuous trading, constant volatility, and a martingale for the price logarithm are, however, all theoretical ideals so that estimators like (12.44) will be biased.

12.13.1 *Models for the Daily Range*

Daily ranges can be modeled either by conditional distributions, using methods similar to those described for durations in Section 12.11, or directly from stochastic volatility models. We focus on the latter methodology, while Chou (2004) develops the alternative approach.

Suppose now that expected returns are zero and that daily returns have the stochastic volatility representation studied in Chapter 11:

$$r_t = \sigma_t u_t \tag{12.45}$$

with the latent volatility σ_t independent of $u_t \sim N(0, 1)$. As in (12.44), we can consider modeling and predicting σ_t by studying the logarithm of the daily range, namely

$$R_t = \log(h_t) - \log(l_t). \tag{12.46}$$

Assuming a diffusion process for intraday prices, with constant intraday volatility, the daily range can also be factorized to give

$$R_t = \sigma_t v_t, \tag{12.47}$$

with v_t independent of σ_t. Equation (12.47) is also applicable when there is a fixed periodic pattern in intraday volatility. These patterns change the distribution of the times at which highs and lows occur but they do not change the distribution of the range.

Taylor (1987) shows that the autocorrelations of R_t, like those of $|r_t|$, are proportional to the autocorrelations of σ_t. The constant of proportionality is much higher for the ranges R_t, because the coefficient of variation is much less for v_t than it is for $|u_t|$; the former value is $E[v_t^2]/E[v_t]^2 \cong 1.09$ and the latter is $\cong 1.57$ for geometric Brownian motion. The higher autocorrelation for ranges predicted by theory is found in four years of exchange rate data. At lags 1, 10, and 50 they are 0.51, 0.42, and 0.26 for ranges, compared with 0.25, 0.16, and 0.06 for absolute returns. The high dependence in the ranges is then used to predict volatility. Byers and Peel (2001) also document substantial positive autocorrelation among daily ranges, which leads them to recommend and estimate fractionally integrated processes.

We now consider several results presented in Alizadeh et al. (2002). They make the important observation that the distribution of $v_t = R_t/\sigma_t$ is close to lognormal when intraday prices follow a driftless geometric Brownian motion process. Equivalently, the conditional distribution of $R_t \mid \sigma_t$ is nearly lognormal. They evaluate the density of $\log(v_t)$ and find that it is almost normal, with skewness and kurtosis approximately equal to 0.17 and 2.80 respectively. This implies that the state space representation for the logarithm of the range is almost Gaussian, for the standard SV model. The measurement equation is then

$$\log(R_t) = \log(\sigma_t) + \xi_t, \tag{12.48}$$

the residual term is $\xi_t = \log(v_t)$ and the transition equation is the same as in Section 11.5:

$$\log(\sigma_t) = (1 - \phi)\alpha + \phi \log(\sigma_{t-1}) + \eta_t.$$

Parameter estimation by quasi-maximum likelihood is now much more efficient than when applied to the logarithms of absolute returns, for two reasons. The first is the approximate normality of the measurement errors in (12.48) that contrasts with the skewed and very leptokurtic distribution that occurs in (11.25). The second is a very substantial reduction in the standard deviation of the residual terms, from 1.11 to 0.29.

Alizadeh et al. (2002) also observe that bid–ask effects are almost irrelevant when calculating ranges but they can have a significant impact on the realized volatility measure discussed in Sections 12.8 and 12.9. Thus volatility prediction from ranges may be as good as from realized volatility. Their empirical results are for currency futures traded on five exchange rates in Chicago from 1978 to 1998. Estimation of the parameters of the standard stochastic volatility model from ranges gives persistence estimates that are much lower than those produced by the methods described in Chapter 11. This is attributed to model mis-specification. Both long memory and two-factor models for volatility may instead be satisfactory. They prefer a two-factor transition equation, which can be stated as

$$\log(\sigma_t) = \alpha + \log(\sigma_{1,t}) + \log(\sigma_{2,t}) \tag{12.49}$$

with

$$\log(\sigma_{i,t}) = \phi_i \log(\sigma_{i,t-1}) + \eta_{i,t}, \quad i = 1, 2. \tag{12.50}$$

Their estimates indicate that one factor is highly persistent, with $\hat{\phi}_1 = 0.97$ or 0.98, and that the other is almost uncorrelated, with $0 < \hat{\phi}_2 < 0.2$. The estimated variances of the two factors are similar. Note that the special case $\phi_2 = 0$ defines a volatility model similar to the SVt model given by equations (11.42) and (11.43).

12.14   Concluding Remarks

High-frequency data are essential for some research and provide answers to several questions that cannot be answered using daily data. The very rapid response of prices to new information requires study of frequent prices in order to both understand the impact of scheduled news and major events and to see the effects predicted by microstructure theories. It seems probable that the major insights from future research into market prices will come from high-frequency analysis.

High-frequency prices have statistical properties that are unique to intraday data, the most notable being periodic effects in transactions, volatility, and trading volume, which repeat from day to day yet vary across markets. The significant size of high-frequency datasets is beneficial when estimating daily volatility and the frequency of extreme price movements. Measures of realized volatility, in particular, have recently clarified many of the stochastic properties of volatility. The deeper understanding of volatility that is obtained can be utilized by volatility forecasters, derivatives traders, and portfolio and risk managers.

Further Reading

Alizadeh, S., M. W. Brandt, and F. X. Diebold. 2002. Range-based estimation of stochastic volatility models. *Journal of Finance* 57:1047–1091.

Andersen, T. G. and T. Bollerslev. 1997. Intraday periodicity and volatility persistence in financial markets. *Journal of Empirical Finance* 4:115–158.

Andersen, T. G., T. Bollerslev, F. X. Diebold, and H. Ebens. 2001. The distribution of realized stock return volatility. *Journal of Financial Economics* 61:43–76.

Dacorogna, M. M., R. Gençay, U. A. Müller, R. B. Olsen, and O. V. Pictet. 2001. *An introduction to high-frequency finance.* San Diego, CA: Academic Press.

Goodhart, C. A. E. and M. O'Hara. 1997. High frequency data in financial markets: issues and applications. *Journal of Empirical Finance* 4:73–114.

Wood, R. A., T. H. McInish, and J. K. Ord. 1985. An investigation of transactions data for NYSE stocks. *Journal of Finance* 40:723–739.

12.15 Appendix: Formulae for the Variance of the Realized Volatility Estimator

The most general SV model defined in Section 12.8 has $r_{t,j,N} = \sigma_{t,j,N} u_{t,j,N}/\sqrt{N}$ and $u_{t,j,N} \sim N(0,1)$, with $u_{t,j,N}$ independent of $\sigma_{t,j,N}$ and all variables $u_{.,.,N}$ and $\sigma_{.,.,N}$ that are determined before time t, j. The weaker assumption that the $u_{t,j,N}$ are i.i.d. with mean zero, variance one, and kurtosis k_N is made here.

To derive (12.29), let

$$y_{t,j,N} = r_{t,j,N}^2 - \frac{1}{N}\sigma_{t,j,N}^2 = \frac{1}{N}\sigma_{t,j,N}^2(u_{t,j,N}^2 - 1)$$

and note that the variables $y_{t,j,N}$ have mean zero and are uncorrelated, with

$$\mathrm{var}(y_{t,j,N}) = \frac{1}{N^2}E[\sigma_{t,j,N}^4]E[u_{t,j,N}^4 - 2u_{t,j,N}^2 + 1].$$

Thus

$$\hat{\sigma}_{t,N}^2 - \frac{1}{N}\sum_{j=1}^{N}\sigma_{t,j,N}^2 = \sum_{j=1}^{N} y_{t,j,N}$$

has mean zero and variance

$$\frac{k_N - 1}{N^2}E\left[\sum_{j=1}^{N}\sigma_{t,j,N}^4\right]. \tag{12.51}$$

Substituting $k_N = 3$ for conditional normal distributions gives (12.29). The special cases $\sigma_{t,j,N} = \sigma_t$ and $\sigma_{t,j,N}^2 = N\lambda_{j,N}\sigma_t^2$ respectively give (12.21) and (12.23).

The variance in (12.51) converges to zero as N increases if further assumptions are made. One set of sufficient conditions is that k_N is bounded, and that

$$\lambda_{t,N}^* = \max_{1 \leqslant j \leqslant N} \sigma_{t,j,N}^2 \Big/ \sum_{j=1}^{N}\sigma_{t,j,N}^2 \to 0 \quad \text{as } N \to \infty. \tag{12.52}$$

Then

$$\frac{k_N - 1}{N^2} \sum_{j=1}^{N} \sigma_{t,j,N}^4 \leqslant (k_N - 1)\lambda_{t,N}^* \left(\frac{1}{N} \sum_{j=1}^{N} \sigma_{t,j,N}^2\right)^2$$

and the upper bound converges to zero as N increases. For the special case of periodic volatility effects, defined by (12.22), the random variables $\lambda_{t,N}^*$ equal the constants λ_N^* given in (12.24).

The variance in (12.51) does not converge to zero when the day's volatility is concentrated around some parts of the day, i.e. when condition (12.52) does not hold. Following an example in Barndorff-Nielsen and Shephard (2002a), consider the special situation when all price changes are jumps with

$$r_{t,j,N} \mid k \text{ jumps } \sim N(0, k\xi^2).$$

Then let $J_{t,j,N}$ be the number of jumps in period t, j and let J_t be the total number for day t, assumed to be finite. The latent volatility variables are then

$$\sigma_t^2 = \xi^2 J_t \quad \text{and} \quad \sigma_{t,j,N}^2 = N\xi^2 J_{t,j,N}.$$

Assume $\xi^2 > 0$ and $E[J_t] > 0$. The variance in (12.51) now equals

$$\frac{2}{N^2} E\left[\sum_{j=1}^{N} \sigma_{t,j,N}^4\right] = 2\xi^4 \sum_{j=1}^{N} E[J_{t,j,N}^2] \geqslant 2\xi^4 \sum_{j=1}^{N} E[J_{t,j,N}] = 2\xi^4 E[J_t]$$

and consequently the realized variance does not converge to σ_t^2. Instead, realized variance converges to the sum of the squared jumps which defines the quadratic variation. The difference between the squared latent volatility and the quadratic variation may then be small, however, when the expected number of jumps in a day is large.

Part V

Inferences from Option Prices

13
Continuous-Time Stochastic Processes

Diffusion and jump processes that are defined for a continuous range of times are described in this chapter and used to construct a variety of processes for prices and their stochastic volatility. These processes are of particular importance when option prices are considered in later chapters.

13.1 Introduction

The stochastic processes that describe prices in the previous chapters only provide probability distributions for asset prices at discrete moments in time, typically once every day or once every five minutes. Processes defined for a continuous range of times are also interesting. They are important when pricing option contracts, whose prices can help us to learn more about future asset prices, as we will see in the remainder of this book.

This chapter provides an introduction to the definitions and properties of several continuous-time stochastic processes, which are encountered in the chapters that follow. A rigorous discussion of these processes requires far more mathematics than is deployed here. More theory can be found in the texts by Baxter and Rennie (1996), Cont and Tankov (2003), Etheridge (2002), and Mikosch (1998).

We consider processes of increasing complexity, concluding in Section 13.6 with bivariate processes that provide a fairly realistic description of prices and their stochastic volatility. We commence with diffusion processes that contain no jumps as time progresses. The Wiener process, also called Brownian motion, is described in Section 13.2. It is used to construct univariate and bivariate diffusions, respectively in Sections 13.3 and 13.4. Processes that only contain jumps are defined in Section 13.5. Mixed processes that incorporate both diffusion and jump components conclude the chapter.

The continuous-time processes used in finance are more often motivated by theoretical convenience than by empirical analysis. Consequently, it is common to ignore stylized facts such as the periodic intraday variation in volatility described in Section 12.5. To simplify our descriptions, we do the same. Volatility processes that are more realistic can be created by using a deterministic multiplier that represents the periodic effect.

Several notational changes are introduced in this chapter. The time variable t previously counted trading periods. The symbol t is now used differently, to refer to a time on a continuous scale. The units of t are not important, although the conventional units are years for finance applications. A typical random variable defined for a continuous timescale is represented by a capital letter with the time shown in brackets, e.g. $X(t)$, while time subscripts are reserved for a discrete timescale. Prices are now denoted by $S(t)$, as the letter P will be used to refer either to a particular probability or to a probability measure.

13.2 The Wiener Process

13.2.1 Properties

A *Wiener* or *standard Brownian motion* process is initially denoted by $\{W(t)\}$ and it consists of a random variable $W(t)$ for all times t that are nonnegative real numbers. A *sample path* from the process until time T is any realization of all the random variables for $0 \leqslant t \leqslant T$.

A Wiener process has four defining properties:

- $W(0) = 0$;
- $W(t) - W(s) \sim N(0, t - s)$ whenever $t > s$;
- $W(v) - W(u)$ is independent of $W(t) - W(s)$ whenever $v > u \geqslant t > s$;
- $W(t)$ is a continuous process—there are no jumps in its sample paths.

The independence of the *increments* $W(v) - W(u)$ and $W(t) - W(s)$ is a random walk property. For any time step Δ, the discrete-time process defined by $y_n = W(n\Delta)$, for integers n, follows a random walk. Figure 13.1 shows a realization of $\{y_n\}$ when $\Delta = 10^{-3}$ and $0 \leqslant n \leqslant 10^3$ obtained by simulating the random walk $y_n = y_{n-1} + \sqrt{\Delta} z_n$ with $z_n \sim$ i.i.d. $N(0, 1)$. This realization is merely an approximation to a sample path from a Wiener process, because it only defines sample values for a finite number of times.

A sample path from a Wiener process is not a differentiable function of time, even though it is continuous. This is only one of many properties that may be surprising when they are first encountered. The existence of a process satisfying the defining properties is outlined in the appendix to this chapter for the benefit of any skeptical readers.

13.2.2 Remarks about Stochastic Calculus

The notation dW often appears in equations. Although writers employ it in many ways, the only rigorous usage is within stochastic integrals. A detailed discussion of these integrals is outside the scope of this book. A simple example is

$$\int_0^T dW(t) = W(T).$$

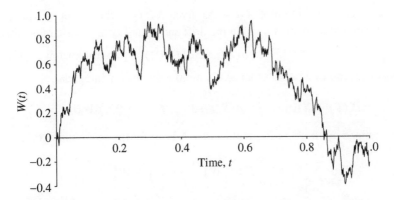

Figure 13.1. One approximation to a sample path from a Wiener process.

A less obvious result is

$$\int_0^T W(t)\, \mathrm{d}W(t) = \tfrac{1}{2}(W(T)^2 - T), \qquad (13.1)$$

which is obtained by finding the limit of

$$\sum_{j=0}^{n-1} W\!\left(\frac{j}{n}T\right)\!\left[W\!\left(\frac{j+1}{n}T\right) - W\!\left(\frac{j}{n}T\right)\right]$$

as n increases (Baxter and Rennie 1996, Section 3.3). This result emphasizes that stochastic integration is different to ordinary integration, since the latter gives $\int y\, \mathrm{d}y = T^2/2$ when the integral's limits are 0 and T.

From (13.1) we can deduce that $\mathrm{d}(W(t)^2) \neq 2W(t)\, \mathrm{d}W(t)$. A more important example for us of stochastic differentiation differing from ordinary differentiation occurs in the next section when we encounter a consequence of the following inequality:

$$\mathrm{d}(\log W(t)) \neq \mathrm{d}W(t)/W(t).$$

13.3 Diffusion Processes

13.3.1 General Processes

A general time-invariant *diffusion process*, also called an *Itô process*, is denoted by $\{X(t)\}$ in this section. It is constructed from a *drift function* $a(X(t))$, a *volatility function* $b(X(t))$, and a Wiener process. The general diffusion process can be written as a *stochastic differential equation* (SDE),

$$\mathrm{d}X(t) = a(X(t))\, \mathrm{d}t + b(X(t))\, \mathrm{d}W(t),$$

or more compactly as

$$\mathrm{d}X = a(X)\, \mathrm{d}t + b(X)\, \mathrm{d}W. \qquad (13.2)$$

The conditional distribution of $X(t + \Delta)$ given $X(t)$ can then be approximated for small increments Δ by assuming the drift and volatility are constant, so that

$$X(t + \Delta) - X(t) \mid X(t) \sim N(a(X(t))\Delta, b(X(t))^2\Delta) \text{ approximately.} \quad (13.3)$$

An equivalent representation of an SDE employs stochastic integrals,

$$X(T) - X(0) = \int_0^T a(X(t))\,dt + \int_0^T b(X(t))\,dW(t),$$

that are defined by limits of Riemann sums. A limit for the second integral is

$$\lim_{n\to\infty} \sum_{j=0}^{n-1} b\left(X\left(\frac{j}{n}T\right)\right)\left[W\left(\frac{j+1}{n}T\right) - W\left(\frac{j}{n}T\right)\right].$$

13.3.2 Arithmetic Brownian Motion

This process is outlined in the famous thesis by Bachelier (1900) on a "Theory of speculation." The drift and volatility functions are simply constants, respectively μ and σ. The SDE is therefore

$$dX = \mu\,dt + \sigma\,dW$$

and

$$X(t) - X(0) = \mu t + \sigma W(t).$$

Then $X(t) - X(s) \sim N(\mu(t - s), \sigma^2(t - s))$, whenever $t > s$. This process cannot be recommended for asset prices because $X(t)$ has a positive probability of a negative outcome, for any initial value $X(0)$.

13.3.3 Geometric Brownian Motion

Replacing X by its logarithm in the above equations will ensure that the process always has positive outcomes. We change the drift rate for $\log(X)$ to $\mu - \sigma^2/2$ and define $\{X(t)\}$ to be geometric Brownian motion (GBM) when

$$\log X(t) - \log X(0) = (\mu - \tfrac{1}{2}\sigma^2)t + \sigma W(t). \quad (13.4)$$

The distribution of $X(t)$ given $X(s)$ is then lognormal and its conditional expectation equals $X(s)\exp(\mu(t - s))$. GBM is often used as a simple description of asset price dynamics, for example, in the derivation of the Black–Scholes option pricing formula.

The corresponding SDE is

$$d(\log X) = (\mu - \tfrac{1}{2}\sigma^2)\,dt + \sigma\,dW.$$

The famous lemma of Itô (1951), explained in the textbooks listed in Section 13.1, produces the result

$$d(\log X) = dX/X - \tfrac{1}{2}\sigma^2\,dt.$$

An equivalent SDE for GBM is therefore

$$dX/X = \mu\,dt + \sigma\,dW. \quad (13.5)$$

13.3.4 The CEV Process

The volatility function of dX/X equals σ for GBM. The constant elasticity of variance (CEV) process of Cox and Ross (1976) permits this function to vary inversely with the level of asset prices; thus,

$$dX/X = \mu\, dt + \sigma X^{-\beta}\, dW, \quad 0 \leqslant \beta < 1.$$

A deterministic relationship between the asset price and its volatility is very restrictive. The continuous-time price and volatility processes described in Sections 13.4 and 13.6 are more realistic.

13.3.5 The OU Process

All the previous examples describe nonstationary processes that have a random walk property. Stationary processes require the drift function $a(X)$ to be positive when X is below its mean level and to be negative otherwise. The simplest example is the Ornstein–Uhlenbeck (OU) process, whose SDE is

$$dX = \kappa(\alpha - X)\, dt + \sigma\, dW. \tag{13.6}$$

The positive parameter κ determines the rate at which this process is pulled back towards the mean parameter α. The OU process has been used to model the logarithm of volatility (Scott 1987; Wiggins 1987), because the OU process is a continuous-time extension of the AR(1) process. Figure 13.2 shows a sample path for an OU process that reverts towards a mean level of 100; the other parameters are explained in the paragraph after equation (13.8).

The distribution of X at time t, conditional on its value at an earlier time s, is normal. The conditional mean is given by

$$E[X(t) \mid X(s)] = \alpha + e^{-\kappa(t-s)}(X(s) - \alpha). \tag{13.7}$$

These conditional expectations converge to α as t increases; they are mid-way between $X(s)$ and α when $t - s$ equals the half-life parameter defined by $\Phi = \log(2)/\kappa$. The conditional variance is independent of $X(s)$ and equals

$$\mathrm{var}(X(t) \mid X(s)) = \frac{\sigma^2}{2\kappa}(1 - e^{-2\kappa(t-s)}).$$

The limit of the conditional distributions as $t \to \infty$ is $N(\alpha, \omega^2)$ with $\omega^2 = \sigma^2/(2\kappa)$. When $X(0)$ has this distribution, firstly it is also the unconditional distribution of each random variable $X(t)$ and secondly the correlation between $X(s)$ and $X(t)$ equals $\exp(-\kappa|t - s|)$.

The OU process is the continuous-time equivalent of the AR(1) process. For a selected time increment Δ, let $\phi = \exp(-\kappa\Delta)$. Then

$$X(s + \Delta) \mid X(s) \sim N(\alpha + \phi(X(s) - \alpha), (1 - \phi^2)\omega^2). \tag{13.8}$$

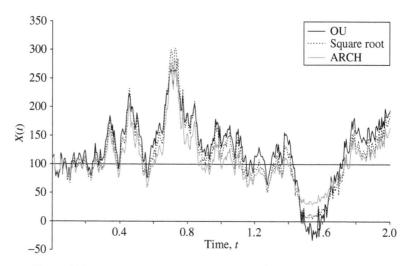

Figure 13.2.   Sample paths for three mean-reverting diffusion processes.

Consequently, the discrete-time process $y_n = X(n\Delta)$ is a Gaussian, AR(1) process with autoregressive parameter ϕ, mean α, and variance ω^2, assuming $y_0 \sim N(\alpha, \omega^2)$.

13.3.6 Simulated Paths

The three curves in Figure 13.2 show simulated paths for three mean-reverting diffusion processes that might be considered as models for the annualized variance of prices. All these processes are stationary with mean equal to 100, corresponding to an annualized volatility of 10%. Each process has standard deviation equal to 80 and a half-life of three months, so that $\Phi = 0.25$ and $\kappa = 2.77$. They all have conditional expectations defined by equation (13.7). The path for the OU process is shown by the dark, solid curve. It is obtained by simulating the distributions specified by equation (13.8), with $\Delta = 0.005$ and $\phi = 0.986$. The same realizations of a sequence of standard normal variables are used to construct all three sample paths.

13.3.7 The Square-Root Process

The OU process can attain negative values, so it is inappropriate for modeling positive variables. Reducing the volatility function $b(X)$ as X approaches zero can ensure that X remains positive. If we retain the drift function of the OU process and change the volatility function to $\xi\sqrt{X}$, we obtain the square-root process of Cox, Ingersoll, and Ross (1985):

$$dX = \kappa(\alpha - X)\,dt + \xi\sqrt{X}\,dW. \tag{13.9}$$

The realizations of the random variables $X(t)$ are always positive when the process commences at a positive value. The constraint $2\kappa\alpha \geqslant \xi^2$ is required to avoid sample paths that converge to zero.

The conditional distribution $X(t) \mid X(s)$ is now a noncentral chi-squared distribution. The conditional mean is again given by equation (13.7). The conditional variance is a linear function of $X(s)$:

$$\text{var}(X(t) \mid X(s)) = (2\kappa)^{-1}\xi^2(1 - e^{-\kappa(t-s)})[\alpha + e^{-\kappa(t-s)}(2X(s) - \alpha)].$$

As $t \to \infty$, the mean and variance respectively converge to α and $\psi^2 = \alpha\xi^2/(2\kappa)$. The limit of the conditional distributions is a *gamma* distribution, whose density is

$$f(x) = \frac{\delta^\gamma}{\Gamma(\gamma)}z^{\gamma-1}e^{-\delta z}, \quad z \geqslant 0, \tag{13.10}$$

with $\gamma = 2\kappa\alpha/\xi^2$ and $\delta = 2\kappa/\xi^2$ (Cox et al. 1985).

The dotted curve in Figure 13.2 shows a simulated path from the square-root process, for the parameter values $\alpha = 100$, $\kappa = 2.77$, and $\xi = 18.8$.

13.4 Bivariate Diffusion Processes

13.4.1 The Bivariate Wiener Process

Suppose that $\{W(t)\}$ is a Wiener process that is independent of a second Wiener process $\{Y(t)\}$. For any value of a correlation parameter ρ between -1 and 1, let us define a third Wiener process by

$$Z(t) = \rho W(t) + \sqrt{1 - \rho^2}Y(t). \tag{13.11}$$

The stochastic process whose variables are the column vector

$$B(t) = (W(t), Z(t))'$$

defines the general bivariate Wiener process. The parameter ρ then equals the correlation between the increments of the component processes:

$$\text{cor}(W(t) - W(s), Z(t) - Z(s)) = \rho.$$

The correlation parameter is often stated within a more compact equation:

$$dW\,dZ = \rho\,dt.$$

13.4.2 Examples

The stochastic volatility (SV) models of Chapter 11 specify a volatility equation and then employ the volatility variable in an equation that defines returns. An SV model is an approximation to a bivariate diffusion process for prices $S(t)$ and their stochastic variance $V(t)$, defined by the pair of equations:

$$dS/S = \mu\,dt + \sqrt{V}\,dW \tag{13.12}$$

and

$$dV = a(V) \, dt + b(V) \, dZ. \tag{13.13}$$

The price equation above combined with an OU process for $\{\log V(t)\}$ can be approximated by the asymmetric SV model of Section 11.9, which simplifies to the standard SV model of Section 11.5 when $\rho = 0$. The alternative specification of a square-root process for $\{V(t)\}$ has the advantage that closed-form option prices can then be calculated for any value of ρ, as we will see in Section 14.6. A negative correlation ρ is appropriate for equity indices, as volatility tends to increase when index levels fall.

13.4.3 Limits of ARCH Processes

ARCH models are also approximations to bivariate diffusion processes. To illustrate this, we follow Nelson (1990b) and consider a sequence of GARCH(1, 1)-M models. The symbols μ, λ, ω, α, β now represent ARCH model parameters.

Let δ be a specific time increment measured in years, which might represent one day, and let discrete-time prices $\{S_{t,\delta}, t = 0, \delta, 2\delta, \ldots\}$ and their conditional variances $\{h_{t,\delta}\}$ be represented by

$$\log(S_{t,\delta}) - \log(S_{t-\delta,\delta}) = \mu\delta + \lambda h_{t,\delta} + \sqrt{h_{t,\delta}} \, z_{t,\delta}$$

and

$$h_{t,\delta} = \omega + h_{t-\delta,\delta}(\alpha z_{t-\delta,\delta}^2 + \beta)$$

with $z_{t,\delta} \sim$ i.i.d. $N(0, 1)$. For a general time increment $\Delta \leqslant \delta$, we construct a related model for a process $\{S_{t,\Delta}\}$ and its conditional variances $\{h_{t,\Delta}\}$, defined by

$$\log(S_{t,\Delta}) - \log(S_{t-\Delta,\Delta}) = \mu\Delta + \lambda h_{t,\Delta} + \sqrt{h_{t,\Delta}} \, z_{t,\Delta} \tag{13.14}$$

and

$$h_{t,\Delta} = \omega_\Delta + h_{t-\Delta,\Delta}(\alpha_\Delta z_{t-\Delta,\Delta}^2 + \beta_\Delta) \tag{13.15}$$

with

$$\omega_\Delta = \omega(\Delta/\delta)^2, \qquad \alpha_\Delta = \alpha\sqrt{\Delta/\delta}, \qquad \beta_\Delta = 1 - \alpha_\Delta - ((1 - \alpha - \beta)\Delta/\delta)$$

and $z_{t,\Delta} \sim$ i.i.d. $N(0, 1)$. The annualized conditional variance,

$$V_{t,\Delta} = h_{t,\Delta}/\Delta,$$

can then be shown to change as follows:

$$V_{t,\Delta} - V_{t-\Delta,\Delta} = \left[\frac{\omega}{\delta^2} - \frac{(1 - \alpha - \beta)V_{t-\Delta,\Delta}}{\delta} \right]\Delta$$
$$+ \alpha\left(\frac{2}{\delta}\right)^{1/2} V_{t-\Delta,\Delta}[(\tfrac{1}{2}\Delta)^{1/2}(z_{t-\Delta,\Delta}^2 - 1)].$$

The quantity inside the second square bracket has mean and variance respectively equal to zero and Δ.

A continuous-time model for time increment Δ can be defined by supposing that prices and conditional variances only change at times that are multiples of Δ. Nelson (1990b) proves that these continuous-time models converge as $\Delta \to 0$, in distribution, to the bivariate diffusion

$$d(\log S) = (\mu + \lambda V)\,dt + \sqrt{V}\,dW \qquad (13.16)$$

and

$$dV = \frac{1}{\delta}\left[\frac{\omega}{\delta} - (1 - \alpha - \beta)V\right]dt + \alpha\left(\frac{2}{\delta}\right)^{1/2}V\,dZ. \qquad (13.17)$$

The Wiener processes W and Z are independent, because there is no correlation between the innovation terms $z_{t,\Delta}$ and $z_{t,\Delta}^2 - 1$ (Gourieroux and Jasiak 2001, p. 258).

The variance process V given by the limit of GARCH(1, 1) models has the same linear drift function as the OU and the square-root processes, but the term that multiplies the differential dZ is now proportional to V. The light, solid curve in Figure 13.2 shows a sample path for the process $X = 10^4 V$ when the parameters of V are chosen so that the mean, standard deviation, and half-life of X are respectively 100, 80, and 0.25. With $\delta = 1/250$, the ARCH parameters are $\omega = 4.43 \times 10^{-7}$, $\alpha = 0.066$, and $\beta = 0.923$.

Likewise, it can be shown that a sequence of EGARCH(1) models, based upon equation (10.1), converges to a bivariate diffusion with the logarithm of the variance process V following an OU process (Nelson 1990b; Bollerslev et al. 1994). We note that the same diffusion limit arises for stochastic volatility models, as mentioned after equation (13.13). For the volatility residual function described by equation (10.2), say

$$g_\Delta(z_\Delta) = \vartheta_\Delta z_\Delta + \gamma_\Delta(|z_\Delta| - \sqrt{2/\pi})^{1/2}$$

for time increment Δ, the correlation between the limiting Wiener processes W and Z is equal to

$$\rho = \mathrm{cor}(z_\Delta, g_\Delta(z_\Delta)) = \vartheta_\Delta/[\vartheta_\Delta^2 + \gamma_\Delta^2(1 - 2/\pi)]^{1/2}, \qquad (13.18)$$

assuming that the ratio $\vartheta_\Delta/\gamma_\Delta$ is a constant. Consequently, correlated Wiener processes occur in diffusion limits when the ARCH volatility residual function is asymmetric. Diffusion limits for some other ARCH processes are provided in Duan (1997).

13.5 Jump Processes

The sample paths of diffusion processes are continuous functions of time. In contrast, the sample paths of jump processes only change at discrete jump times.

13.5.1 Finite Activity Processes

The *Poisson* process is the simplest example of a jump process. The random variable $N_\lambda(t)$ counts the number of jump times between times 0 and t inclusive, for some finite *intensity* rate λ. The process has the following properties.

- The expected number of jumps in any time interval of length Δ is equal to $\lambda\Delta$.
- $N_\lambda(t) - N_\lambda(s)$ has a Poisson distribution, with mean $\lambda(t-s)$ for all $t > s \geq 0$.
- $N_\lambda(v) - N_\lambda(u)$ is independent of all random variables obtained from $\{N_\lambda(t), 0 \leq t \leq u\}$ for all $v > u$. In particular, it is independent of $N_\lambda(t) - N_\lambda(s)$ whenever $v > u \geq t > s$.

For any sample path from time zero until any time t, the duration of time until the next jump has an *exponential* distribution, with mean equal to $1/\lambda$ and density function

$$f(z) = \lambda e^{-\lambda z}, \quad z \geq 0. \tag{13.19}$$

The *compound Poisson* process, here denoted by $\{X(t)\}$, commences at $X(0) = 0$ and has a general distribution for the jump sizes. The jump size is an i.i.d. variable j_n when jump n occurs for a Poisson process $\{N_\lambda(t)\}$. Let $J(t)$ be the appropriate random jump j_n if there is a jump at time t and otherwise let $J(t)$ be zero. Then

$$X(t) = \sum_{0 \leq s \leq t} J(s)$$

and the SDE for X is given by

$$dX(t) = J(t)\,dN_\lambda(t). \tag{13.20}$$

It is assumed that the jump size process $\{j_n\}$ is independent of $\{N_\lambda(t)\}$.

A specific example of a jump process for the logarithm of asset prices is given by

$$d(\log S(t)) = \mu\,dt + J(t)\,dN_\lambda(t), \tag{13.21}$$

with

$$J(t) \sim N(\mu_J, \sigma_J^2) \text{ when } t \text{ is a jump time.}$$

The SDE in (13.21) is identical to

$$dS/S = \mu\,dt + (e^J - 1)\,dN_\lambda, \tag{13.22}$$

as the price is multiplied by $\exp(J(t))$ at a jump time. Also $E[S(t) \mid S(s)]$ equals $S(s)\exp(\xi(t-s))$ with $\xi = \mu + \lambda(E[\exp(j_n)] - 1)$. The corresponding discrete-time process for prices is similar to the compound events model of Press (1967) and it is also a special case of the information arrivals model of Section 8.3.

Compound Poisson processes are *finite activity* processes, as they have a finite number of jumps within any finite time interval. Suppose now that the jump sizes j_n are continuous random variables with density function $f(y)$. Then $g(y) = \lambda f(y)$ is called the Lévy measure of the process by some writers and the Lévy density by others; the arrival (or intensity) rate of jumps that have sizes between $y - \delta/2$ and $y + \delta/2$ is approximately equal to $\delta g(y)$, when δ is small.

13.5.2 *Infinite Activity Processes*

It is possible to define jump processes that have an infinite number of jumps within any finite time interval. The Lévy measure $g(y)$ can still be defined for jump sizes that have continuous distributions by the property that the arrival rate of jumps of sizes between a and b is given by

$$\int_a^b g(y) \, dy,$$

when zero is outside the range from a to b; the arrival rate is infinite whenever $a < 0 < b$, so the process has infinitely many "small" jumps.

Several examples of Lévy measures are provided in Table 1 of Carr and Wu (2004). One example is the four-parameter measure of Carr, Geman, Madan, and Yor (2002), defined by

$$g(y) = \begin{cases} Ce^{-My} y^{-(1+Y)}, & y > 0, \\ Ce^{Gy} (-y)^{-(1+Y)}, & y < 0, \end{cases}$$

with $C > 0$, $G \geqslant 0$, $M \geqslant 0$, and $Y < 2$. The CGMY jump process has infinite activity when $Y \geqslant 0$ and finite activity when $Y < 0$.

13.6 Jump-Diffusion Processes

13.6.1 *Lévy Processes*

Arithmetic Brownian motion and the compound Poisson process are examples of continuous-time random walks. Random walks have stationary and independent increments. Any continuous-time random walk $\{X(t)\}$ is called a *Lévy process*; it commences at $X(0) = 0$, the increment $X(t) - X(s)$ is independent of $\{X(r), 0 \leqslant r \leqslant s\}$, and the distribution of $X(t) - X(s)$ is identical to that of $X(t - s)$, with $0 \leqslant s \leqslant t$. The most general Lévy process can be expressed as the sum of an arithmetic Brownian motion process and an independent jump process; see Cont and Tankov (2003) for further discussion of this result and many others for Lévy processes.

Recently, several interesting jump-diffusion processes for asset prices have been constructed from Lévy processes. Typically, at least two Lévy processes are used, to ensure that price models incorporate stochastic volatility effects. These

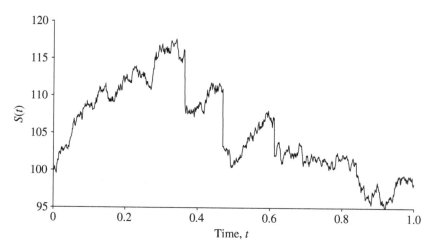

Figure 13.3.   Sample path from a jump-diffusion process.

constructions are interesting for two reasons. First, they offer new insights into the dynamics of observed prices (Barndorff-Nielsen and Shephard 2001, 2005a,b; Eraker, Johannes, and Polson 2003). Second, they provide flexible and convenient mathematical structures when option contracts are priced. These structures involve a time-change of a Lévy process, from calendar time to a new timescale that represents cumulative economic activity (Carr, Geman, Madan, and Yor 2003; Carr and Wu 2004; Huang and Wu 2004).

13.6.2 Examples

Sample paths that are continuous, except for jumps that occur at a finite rate, are obtained from the sum of a diffusion process and a finite-activity jump process. An example for the logarithm of prices, proposed in Merton (1976), is given by the sum of an arithmetic Brownian motion process and a compound Poisson process,

$$\mathrm{d}(\log S) = (\mu - \tfrac{1}{2}\sigma^2)\,\mathrm{d}t + \sigma\,\mathrm{d}W + J\,\mathrm{d}N_\lambda, \qquad (13.23)$$

for a Wiener process $\{W(t)\}$ that is independent of a compound Poisson process $\{J(t), N_\lambda(t)\}$. Figure 13.3 shows a sample path for $\{S(t)\}$ when $\mu = 0.21$, $\sigma = 0.1$, $\lambda = 3$ and the jumps are normally distributed with mean and standard deviation equal to -0.05 and 0.03. There are four jumps on this path, three of which are clearly visible near times 0.36, 0.47, and 0.61.

A realistic continuous-time model must also incorporate a stochastic process for the volatility of prices. Motivated by the existence of closed-form theoretical option prices, Bates (1996) and Scott (1997) add price jumps to a bivariate diffusion process for prices $S(t)$ and their stochastic variance $V(t)$, with the variance defined by a square-root process:

$$d(\log S) = (\mu - \tfrac{1}{2}V)\,dt + \sqrt{V}\,dW + J\,dN_\lambda, \qquad (13.24)$$

$$dV = \kappa(\alpha - V)\,dt + \xi\sqrt{V}\,dZ,$$

and $J(t) \sim N(\mu_J, \sigma_J^2)$ when t is a jump time.

Now $\{W(t), Z(t)\}$ is a bivariate Wiener process that is independent of the jump process. This bivariate process for the price and its variance has parameters μ, κ, α, ξ, λ, μ_J, σ_J, and $\rho = \mathrm{cor}(W(t), Z(t))$.

When model structures based upon (13.24) are estimated from US stock index data, as in Bakshi, Cao, and Chen (1997), Bates (2000), and Pan (2002), evidence of mis-specification is found, according to Eraker et al. (2003). This problem can be attributed to the diffusion specification for volatility, which does not permit the rapid increases in volatility that are often estimated from ARCH models. Similar models are estimated by Andersen, Benzoni, and Lund (2002), who suppose the jump intensity rate λ is a linear function of the variance V. A specification that adds a second volatility factor to (13.24) is estimated from the realized volatility of DM/\$ rates by Bollerslev and Zhou (2002).

Duffie, Pan, and Singleton (2000) propose a more general model for prices and their variances that includes finite-activity jumps in both prices and volatility. The volatility jumps are always positive. Three types of jumps are proposed: jumps in $\log(S)$, jumps in V, and simultaneous correlated jumps in both $\log(S)$ and V. Special cases of an almost identical model are estimated in the interesting paper by Eraker et al. (2003). These special cases are all defined by

$$d(\log S) = \mu\,dt + \sqrt{V}\,dW + J^S\,dN_\lambda^S \qquad (13.25)$$

and

$$dV = \kappa(\alpha - V)\,dt + \xi\sqrt{V}\,dZ + J^V\,dN_\eta^V.$$

The volatility jumps arrive at a rate η and their sizes $J^V(t)$ have an exponential distribution. The SVIJ model has independent price jumps that arrive at a rate λ and the sizes $J^S(t)$ once more have a normal distribution. The SVCJ model, in contrast, has contemporaneous price and volatility jumps, so that $N_\lambda^S(t) = N_\lambda^V(t)$ for all times t. The distribution of the price jump then has a conditional mean that is a linear function of the volatility jump.

Eraker et al. (2003) apply MCMC estimation methodology to daily returns from the S&P 500 index, from 1980 to 1999. This methodology provides posterior distributions for all the parameters and also for the outcomes from all the jump variables. For the SVCJ model, the estimate of the jump frequency λ is 1.5 jumps per annum. Most of the price jumps are negative and their average level reduces the index by 3%. An average volatility jump, when volatility is near its median level, lifts the annualized volatility from 15% to 24%. The posterior probability of jumps on a few days exceeds 0.9. It is almost one on the crash day of 19 October 1987, when it is estimated that the price jump reduces the index by 14% and the contemporaneous volatility jump lifts volatility from 40% to 50%.

Chernov, Gallant, Ghysels, and Tauchen (2003) estimate several jump-diffusion models, using daily returns on the DJIA index from 1953 to 1999. They observe that abrupt changes in volatility are an essential ingredient of a successful model.

Barndorff-Nielsen and Shephard (2001, 2002b) develop a theoretical framework that allows the volatility jump sizes, $J^V(t)$, to have a general positive distribution instead of the exponential distribution of Duffie et al. (2000). It is assumed that all increases in volatility occur at the jump times, with volatility decaying exponentially between the jumps. The price jumps are assumed to be perfectly correlated with the volatility jumps.

Barndorff-Nielsen and Shephard (2001) recommend a general volatility process that defines $\{V(t)\}$ to be a weighted sum of several independent processes $\{V_i(t)\}$ that have differing drift rates, jump intensity rates, and jump distributions. They provide an impressive empirical analysis of one year of five-minute returns from the DM/\$ exchange rate. Their estimates for a four-component volatility model identify a dominant short-term component and three persistent components that have long half-lives. This model provides a satisfactory explanation of the autocorrelations of squared five-minute returns, for time lags varying from five minutes to 100 days.

Further Reading

Eraker, B., M. Johannes, and N. G. Polson. 2003. The impact of jumps in volatility and returns. *Journal of Finance* 58:1269–1300.

13.7 Appendix: a Construction of the Wiener Process

The existence of a Wiener process can be demonstrated in many ways. We do this by considering the limit of a sequence of interdependent step processes, all defined for $0 \leqslant t \leqslant 1$.

The n-step process, denoted by $\{W_n(t)\}$, consists of a random variable $W_n(t)$ for all times in the unit interval, with steps at the times $t = 1/n, 2/n, \ldots, 1$. The process starts at zero. At each step, the random variable changes by an independent quantity $z_{n,j}$, that has a normal distribution with mean zero and variance $1/n$. Between the steps, the random variables are identical. Thus,

$$W_n(0) = 0,$$

$$W_n\left(\frac{j}{n}\right) = W_n\left(\frac{j-1}{n}\right) + z_{n,j}, \quad z_{n,j} \sim \text{i.i.d.} \, N\left(0, \frac{1}{n}\right), \quad 1 \leqslant j \leqslant n,$$

$$W_n(t) = W_n\left(\frac{j}{n}\right) \quad \text{whenever } \frac{j}{n} \leqslant t < \frac{j+1}{n} \text{ with } 0 \leqslant j \leqslant n-1.$$

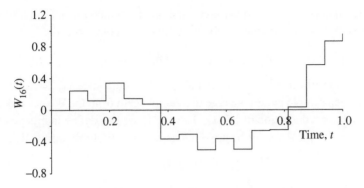

Figure 13.4. One path from a 16-step process.

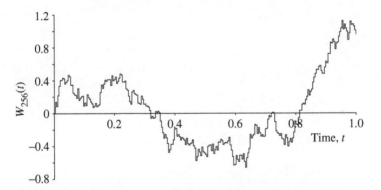

Figure 13.5. One path from a 256-step process.

Figure 13.4 shows one sample path from the 16-step process that contains 16 jumps, obtained by replacing the random steps by sample values taken from $N(0, 1/16)$.

It is constructive to focus on the sequence of processes defined by $n = 2^m$ for positive integers m. We define these processes to be interdependent, by requiring W_n and W_{2n} to be identical at the step times of W_n:

$$W_n(t) = W_{2n}(t) \quad \text{for } t = 1/n, 2/n, \ldots, 1.$$

The necessary collection of constraints is

$$z_{n,j} = z_{2n,2j-1} + z_{2n,2j}, \quad 1 \leqslant j \leqslant n, \; n = 2^m, \; m \geqslant 1.$$

The conditional distribution of $z_{2n,2j-1}$, given $z_{n,j}$, is then normal with mean $z_{n,j}/2$ and variance $1/(4n)$. Figures 13.4 and 13.5 show sample paths for the interdependent processes W_{16} and W_{256}. It may be agreed that these paths will converge to some limit if we continue to increase m.

The Wiener process $\{W(t), 0 \leqslant t \leqslant 1\}$ is here defined as the limit of the step processes $\{W_n(t)\}$, $n = 2^m$, as $m \to \infty$. Although there are several ways to define convergence for random variables, the precise method is not important in this context. All the multivariate probability functions converge, so

$$P(W_n(t_1) \leqslant x_1, \ldots, W_n(t_k) \leqslant x_k) \to P(W(t_1) \leqslant x_1, \ldots, W(t_k) \leqslant x_k)$$

as $m \to \infty$, for all times $t_1, \ldots, t_k$ and all possible outcomes $x_1, \ldots, x_k$. Similarly, the n-step sample paths converge to a sample path from the Wiener process.

Once we have a definition of $\{W(t), 0 \leqslant t \leqslant 1\}$ we can define interdependent step processes $\{W_n(t)\}$ for *all* positive integers n by simply requiring $W_n(t) = W(t)$ for $t = 1/n, 2/n, \ldots, 1$.

14

Option Pricing Formulae

This chapter reviews the determination of rational option prices for a variety of stochastic processes for the underlying asset price. These option prices often depend on a volatility risk premium. The chapter also covers the inverse problem of using observed asset and option prices to obtain implied levels of future volatility.

14.1 Introduction

Option prices are a source of valuable information about the distributions of future asset prices. This motivates our interest in option pricing formulae, which are needed to extract and interpret predictive information from the market prices of options. This chapter includes several pricing formulae for European options, all of which can be obtained by a risk-neutral valuation methodology. Rational option prices were first derived by Black and Scholes (1973) and Merton (1973), who assumed asset prices follow a geometric Brownian motion (GBM) process. An option price reveals the future level of volatility when all their assumptions are correct.

Option pricing formulae that are consistent with the empirical stylized facts for asset prices were subsequently derived. An essential property that needs to be incorporated into the option pricing framework is stochastic volatility. This was accomplished by Hull and White (1987), among others. Stochastic volatility solutions incorporate a volatility risk premium parameter. This is necessary because an option cannot be replicated by a dynamic hedge portfolio, constructed from the underlying asset and a risk-free security, when volatility is stochastic.

Section 14.2 reviews standard definitions and notation for option contracts. Section 14.3 presents the famous Black–Scholes formulae and explains how they can be derived from risk-neutral price dynamics. Information about the organization of options trading and a comprehensive analysis of Black–Scholes pricing can be found in several textbooks, including Hull (2000) and Kolb (1999).

The levels of volatility implied by a Black–Scholes formula and empirical option prices are defined in Section 14.4 and their stylized facts are also discussed. Section 14.5 covers pricing formulae when volatility follows a continuous-time stochastic process. It also covers some implications for the interpretation of

Black–Scholes implied volatilities. The pricing formulae can be evaluated rapidly for special asset price dynamics using the numerical methods introduced in Heston (1993), which are explained in Section 14.6. Formulae are also available for discrete-time price dynamics. Section 14.7 provides the equations and some illustrative results for ARCH models.

14.2   Definitions, Notation, and Assumptions

14.2.1   Terminology

An *option* is a derivative security that is assumed to be traded. Someone who buys an option has the opportunity to make a transaction of an *underlying asset* at a later date. The counterparty to any later transaction will be an option seller. The owner of a *call* option has the opportunity to buy the underlying asset, while the owner of a *put* option has the opportunity to sell. The option contract will specify an *exercise* (or strike) price and one or more times at which the opportunity can be *exercised*.

For example, on 15 February someone might pay $5 a share to buy a call option on a stock with exercise price $50 and only one permitted exercise time, say 15 March. This person will choose to exercise the option on 15 March if the share price is then above $50, as this allows a purchase below the current market price. If, however, the share price is below $50 on 15 March, then the owner of the call option will have a worthless opportunity which will not be exercised.

The option is said to be *European* in the above example because there is only one permitted exercise time. In contrast, an *American* option allows the owner to exercise at any time until a final date specified in the contract. Both European and American options are traded at major markets and sometimes both types are traded on the same underlying asset.

14.2.2   Prices and Times

Time is measured in years when we discuss options and we adopt the convention that the present time is zero. An option contract then includes the exercise price X and the time T at which the option expires, this time marking the final opportunity to exercise the option. During the interval from time 0 until the expiry time T the price of the underlying asset will fluctuate and we denote the price at time t by S_t. To simplify notation, the time subscript is often discarded when $t = 0$, thus $S = S_0$. During the same time interval a call price will commence at $c = c_0$, have price c_t at time t, and conclude at c_T. Likewise a put price will move from $p = p_0$ to p_T.

In the remainder of this book we concentrate on two problems. First, we are interested in methods for determining fair market prices c and p for given inputs that include S, T, X, and the dynamics of the continuous-time stochastic process $\{S_t\}$. Second, we are also interested in the inverse problem of using one or more observed option prices to infer one or more properties of the asset price process $\{S_t\}$.

14.2.3 Interest Rates and Dividends

Option prices depend on risk-free interest rates. We will generally assume that these are constant, which is a pragmatic assumption for options on stocks, stock indices, currencies, and commodities. It is at best a dubious assumption when valuing options on debt securities, but these are beyond the scope of this book. The continuously compounded, constant, risk-free interest rate is denoted by r, so that \$1 deposited now is worth $\$e^{rT}$ at time T. It is also assumed that borrowing and lending are possible at the same rate.

Option prices also depend on dividends paid to the owners of the underlying asset. We will assume that dividends are paid at a constant rate, denoted by q. A foreign exchange deposit will earn the constant risk-free foreign rate of interest, which then defines q. Thus, if sterling is the foreign currency, £1 will accumulate to $£e^{qT}$ at time T. The dividend assumption is trivially applicable to a stock that pays no dividends up to time T and then $q = 0$. It is a reasonable assumption for a stock index that contains many stocks that pay dividends at different times. The assumption then implies that one unit of the stock (index) becomes e^{qT} units of the stock (index) at time T, after reinvesting all the dividends at zero cost in the stock (index). For options on commodities, q can be identified with the convenience yield (if any) minus storage costs.

Options can also be written on futures contracts. A long position in the underlying asset can then be acquired by buying futures, without investing capital which can instead be invested at the rate r. Thus we set $q = r$ when we value options on futures. Hull (2000) provides more discussion of the parameter q. He also describes the valuation of options when the dividend assumption is false.

14.2.4 Forward Prices

It is well known that the forward foreign exchange rate F, at time 0 for exchange at time T, is given by the following function of the spot rate S, the domestic interest rate r, and the foreign interest rate q:

$$F = Se^{(r-q)T}. \tag{14.1}$$

Arbitrage profits can be made if F is not obtained from this equation, assuming transaction costs can be ignored. The same conclusion holds for any other asset for which forward contracts exist and our dividend assumption applies (Hull 2000, Appendix 3A). We will define a forward price F by (14.1) even when forward contracts do not exist. Any futures price is also given by (14.1), because we assume constant interest rates (Cox, Ingersoll, and Ross 1981).

14.2.5 Put–Call Parity

A second no-arbitrage equation is given by the put–call parity equation for European options. This shows the difference between the prices of calls and puts that have the same exercise price and time to expiry:

$$c - p = Se^{-qT} - Xe^{-rT} = (F - X)e^{-rT}. \tag{14.2}$$

This equation must apply (when there are no transaction costs) to prevent arbitrageurs making money without using any capital (Hull 2000, p. 275). As $c \geqslant 0$ and $p \geqslant 0$, (14.2) gives lower bounds for c and p. We deduce that

$$c \geqslant \max(Se^{-qT} - Xe^{-rT}, 0) \quad \text{and} \quad p \geqslant \max(Xe^{-rT} - Se^{-qT}, 0) \tag{14.3}$$

for European options, whatever the price dynamics for S_t. The function "max" selects the maximum of the terms inside the brackets, in (14.3) and in similar subsequent expressions. The upper bounds for European options can also be deduced from no-arbitrage arguments, and they are

$$c \leqslant Se^{-qT} \quad \text{and} \quad p \leqslant Xe^{-rT}. \tag{14.4}$$

14.2.6 Boundary Conditions

At expiry, c_T must be $S_T - X$ if $S_T > X$, and it must be zero if $S_T \leqslant X$. Thus

$$c_T = \max(S_T - X, 0). \tag{14.5}$$

Likewise,

$$p_T = \max(X - S_T, 0). \tag{14.6}$$

American options have the further boundary conditions $c_t \geqslant \max(S_t - X, 0)$ and $p_t \geqslant \max(X - S_t, 0)$ for $0 \leqslant t < T$.

14.3 Black–Scholes and Related Formulae

14.3.1 Price Dynamics

The famous formulae of Black and Scholes (1973) for the fair prices of European options follow from several assumptions, which are also discussed in Merton (1973). Asset prices $\{S_t\}$ are assumed to follow a GBM, defined in Section 13.3 and represented by the equation

$$dS = \mu S \, dt + \sigma S \, dW. \tag{14.7}$$

Here μ and σ are constants that represent the expected return and volatility per unit time. All the random variation in the asset prices comes from the Wiener process $\{W_t\}$.

14.3.2 Assumptions

The formulae are derived from the assumed price dynamics and several further assumptions. These include constant interest rates and dividend yields, short selling opportunities, no transaction costs, no taxes, and continuous trading of the asset and the option. The key insight that leads to the formulae is the assumption that no one can make arbitrage profits by owning a portfolio that contains variable quantities of the asset and the option. The impossibility of arbitrage profits from dynamic portfolios leads to a partial differential equation (PDE) that is satisfied by the price of any European derivative security. A specific derivative defines particular boundary conditions and hence a particular solution to the fundamental PDE.

We do not state or solve the PDE here, because we prefer to emphasize the derivation of option prices from risk-neutral price dynamics. This is explained after presenting and illustrating the formulae for call and put options.

14.3.3 The General Black–Scholes Formulae

The fair price of a European call option is given by a function of six parameters: the asset price S, the time until expiry T, the exercise price X, the risk-free interest rate r, the dividend yield q, and the volatility σ. The original formulae in Black and Scholes (1973) assume there are no dividends and hence omit q; these formulae are given by replacing q by zero in the equations that follow.

The option price does not depend on μ. This term does not appear in the PDE, because the return to a riskless portfolio constructed from the option and the underlying asset only depends on r.

The formula includes cumulative probabilities for the standard normal distribution. Let $N(d)$ be the probability that a standard normal variate is less than or equal to d. Then the general Black–Scholes call formula is

$$c_{\text{BS}}(S, T, X, r, q, \sigma) = Se^{-qT}N(d_1) - Xe^{-rT}N(d_2)$$

with

$$d_1 = \frac{\log(S/X) + (r - q + \frac{1}{2}\sigma^2)T}{\sigma\sqrt{T}} \quad \text{and} \quad d_2 = d_1 - \sigma\sqrt{T}. \tag{14.8}$$

The owner of one call option can create a riskless portfolio by short selling $\partial c_{\text{BS}}/\partial S$ units of the underlying asset. This *hedge ratio* is given by

$$\frac{\partial c_{\text{BS}}}{\partial S} = e^{-qT}N(d_1) \tag{14.9}$$

at time zero.

The put–call parity equation, (14.2), applies to formula prices. Thus,

$$p_{\text{BS}}(S, T, X, r, d, \sigma) = c_{\text{BS}}(S, T, X, r, d, \sigma) - Se^{-qT} + Xe^{-rT}. \tag{14.10}$$

	A	B	C	D	E
1	**Black–Scholes calculations**				
2					
3	Inputs				
4	S, time 0	6000		sigma*(T^0.5)	0.0750
5	T	0.25		log(S/X)	-0.0328
6	X	6200		d1	-0.2997
7	r	0.06		d2	-0.3747
8	q	0.03		N(d1)	0.3822
9	sigma	0.15		N(d2)	0.3539
10				S*exp(-qT)	5955.17
11	**Option prices**			X*exp(-rT)	6107.69
12	c	114.32			
13	p	266.84			

Exhibit 14.1. Black–Scholes calculations.

Table 14.1. Formulae used in the Black–Scholes spreadsheet.

Cell	Formula
E4	=B9*SQRT(B5)
E5	=LN(B4/B6)
E6	=(E5+((B7-B8)*B5)+0.5*E4*E4)/E4
E7	=E6-E4
E8	=NORMSDIST(E6)
E9	=NORMSDIST(E7)
E10	=B4*EXP(-B8*B5)
E11	=B6*EXP(-B7*B5)
B12	=E10*E8-E11*E9
B13	=E11*(1-E9)-E10*(1-E8)

The general Black–Scholes put formula is therefore

$$p_{BS}(S, T, X, r, d, \sigma) = Xe^{-rT}N(-d_2) - Se^{-qT}N(-d_1) \qquad (14.11)$$

as $N(-d) = 1 - N(d)$. Also the hedge ratio is negative and given by

$$\frac{\partial p_{BS}}{\partial S} = -e^{-qT}N(-d_1). \qquad (14.12)$$

14.3.4 Examples

Exhibit 14.1 shows the calculation of Black–Scholes option prices when $S = 6000$, $T = 0.25$, $X = 6200$, $r = 0.06$, $q = 0.03$, and $\sigma = 0.15$. The call and put prices are then $c = 114.3$ and $p = 266.8$. Table 14.1 provides the Excel formulae for these calculations. The entire calculation for an option price could be done using one very long formula, but then it is easy to make mistakes. Alternatively, an Excel VBA user-defined function could be used.

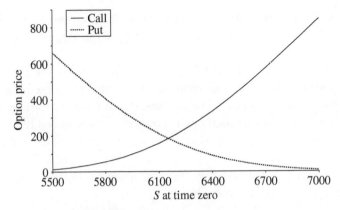

Figure 14.1. Option prices as S varies.

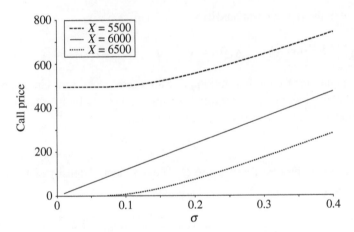

Figure 14.2. Call option prices as σ varies.

Figure 14.1 shows how the formula prices vary as S varies, with all the other inputs as stated above. The first derivatives of the two functions on this figure are the hedge ratios defined by (14.9) and (14.12).

Figure 14.2 shows the call price c as a function of σ when $S = 6000$, $T = 0.25$, $r = q = 0.04$, and X is either 5500 (dashed curve), 6000 (continuous curve), or 6500 (dotted curve). It can be seen that the call price is almost a linear function of the volatility when X equals S.

14.3.5 Risk-Neutral Pricing

In the real world of risky assets, the asset price dynamics are

$$\mathrm{d}S = \mu S \, \mathrm{d}t + \sigma S \, \mathrm{d}W \tag{14.13}$$

and we refer to the *real-world* probability measure P. The measure P is used to calculate the probabilities of events and the expectations of random variables in the real world. For example, the P-expectation of S_T equals $S \exp(\mu T)$, as $\log(S_T) - \log(S_0)$ is normal with mean $(\mu - \frac{1}{2}\sigma^2)T$ and variance $\sigma^2 T$ when the probability measure is P.

The drift rate μ is irrelevant in the Black–Scholes framework. This means that the market price of risk for the underlying asset is irrelevant. Consequently, the theoretical price of an option would be the same if the option and the underlying asset were both traded in a fictitious *risk-neutral* economy (Cox and Ross 1976). A different probability measure Q is used to calculate probabilities in the risk-neutral world.

An option's price at time zero equals the present value of the expectation of its future price in a risk-neutral world. Thus

$$c = e^{-rT} E^Q[c_T]. \tag{14.14}$$

Let f_Q denote the risk-neutral density of S_T. Then

$$c = e^{-rT} E^Q[\max(S_T - X, 0)] = e^{-rT} \int_X^\infty (x - X) f_Q(x) \, dx. \tag{14.15}$$

These two equations for the fair option price are used several times in this book.

In a risk-neutral world, the drift rate is determined solely by the risk-free rate and the dividend yield. The price dynamics are then

$$dS = (r - q)S \, dt + \sigma S \, d\tilde{W} \tag{14.16}$$

and $\tilde{W}_t$ is a Wiener process for measure Q. The risk-neutral density of S_T for the GBM process in (14.16) is the following lognormal density:

$$f_Q(x) = \frac{1}{x\sigma\sqrt{2\pi}} \exp\left(-\frac{1}{2}\left(\frac{\log(x) - [\log(S) + (r - q - \frac{1}{2}\sigma^2)T]}{\sigma\sqrt{T}}\right)^2\right). \tag{14.17}$$

The integrals needed to simplify (14.15) are then

$$\int_X^\infty f_Q(x) \, dx = N(d_2) \quad \text{and} \quad \int_X^\infty x f_Q(x) \, dx = S e^{(r-q)T} N(d_1). \tag{14.18}$$

The first of these integrals is simply the risk-neutral probability of the event $S_T > X$, while the second can be evaluated by making the substitution $y = \log(x)$. Inserting the above expressions for the integrals into (14.15) gives us the Black–Scholes call price formula.

14.3.6 Approximations

The Black–Scholes formulae can be simplified by using the forward price F instead of the underlying asset price S. From (14.1), $S \exp(-qT) = F \exp(-rT)$ and so

$$c_{BS} = e^{-rT}[FN(d_1) - XN(d_1 - \sigma\sqrt{T})]$$

with

$$d_1 = \frac{\log(F/X) + \frac{1}{2}\sigma^2 T}{\sigma\sqrt{T}}. \tag{14.19}$$

The cumulative function $N(d)$ can be approximated by the first two terms in a series expansion when d is near zero, thus:

$$N(d) \cong N(0) + dN'(0) = \frac{1}{2} + \frac{d}{\sqrt{2\pi}}. \tag{14.20}$$

This approximation implies that the formula price is almost a linear function of d_1 when both d_1 and $d_1 - \sigma\sqrt{T}$ are close to zero. This occurs in particular for *at-the-money* (ATM) options, defined by $X = F$. ATM options have $d_1 = \frac{1}{2}\sigma\sqrt{T}$ and $d_2 = -d_1$. Assuming $\sigma\sqrt{T}$ is not large, the approximate price of an ATM call option is

$$c_{\text{BS}} \cong \sqrt{\frac{T}{2\pi}} F e^{-rT} \sigma. \tag{14.21}$$

By put–call parity, the same approximation is valid for ATM put options. ATM option prices are therefore approximately linear functions of σ when $\sigma\sqrt{T}$ is not large.

14.3.7 Deterministic Volatility

The assumption of constant volatility can be relaxed to permit volatility to be a deterministic function of time, which might reflect intraday periodic effects. If we now replace σ by σ_t in the price dynamics equations, we can redefine the quantity σ^2 to be the average variance per unit time:

$$\sigma^2 = \frac{1}{T} \int_0^T \sigma_t^2 \, dt. \tag{14.22}$$

The new quantity σ given by (14.22) is a constant. The risk-neutral density of S_T is still given by (14.17) and thus the Black–Scholes formulae remain applicable.

14.3.8 American Formulae

Numerical methods are required to price American options. There are many methods available, including the accurate analytic approximations of Barone-Adesi and Whaley (1987). Assuming q is positive, their call price formula first requires an iterative calculation of the critical price S^*, above which a call option should be exercised at time zero. The approximate American price is then

$$c_{\text{American}} \begin{cases} \cong c_{\text{European}} + A(S/S^*)^{\gamma} & \text{if } S < S^*, \\ = S - X & \text{if } S \geqslant S^*. \end{cases} \tag{14.23}$$

The terms S^*, A, and γ are functions of all the input parameters except S. Their formula for the approximate American put price has a similar structure.

14.4   Implied Volatility

14.4.1   Definition

All the inputs to the Black–Scholes formulae are observable except the volatility parameter σ. Anyone using a formula to price a specific option only needs to choose a value for σ. Conversely, any appropriate market price will reveal a value of σ that equates the market and formula prices. This revealed value is of particular interest to us because it is a natural forecast of future volatility. The accuracy of such forecasts is covered in Chapter 15.

The *implied volatility* for a European call option, traded at the price c_{market}, is the number σ_{implied} that solves the equation:

$$c_{\text{market}} = c_{\text{BS}}(S, T, X, r, q, \sigma_{\text{implied}}), \tag{14.24}$$

whenever a solution exists. Note first that any solution is unique. This follows from the fact that c_{BS} increases when σ increases, keeping all other inputs fixed. The *vega* of the option is the following partial derivative (Hull 2000, p. 328):

$$\frac{\partial c_{\text{BS}}}{\partial \sigma} = Se^{-qT}\sqrt{T}\phi(d_1), \tag{14.25}$$

with $\phi(\cdot)$ the density function of the standard normal distribution. Vega is positive for all $\sigma > 0$, because it is the product of positive terms. Note second that a solution always exists whenever the market price is inside the bounds given by (14.3) and (14.4). This happens because the limit of c_{BS} as $\sigma \to 0$ is the lower bound, while the limit as $\sigma \to \infty$ is the upper bound.

The implied volatility for a European put option is defined by solving

$$p_{\text{market}} = p_{\text{BS}}(S, T, X, r, q, \sigma_{\text{implied}}). \tag{14.26}$$

A unique solution again exists when the market price is within the rational bounds. From the put–call parity relationship for formula prices, (14.10), firstly $\partial p_{\text{BS}}/\partial \sigma = \partial c_{\text{BS}}/\partial \sigma$ and secondly the implied volatilities of call and put options are equal whenever their market prices satisfy put–call parity (Hull 2000, p. 436). As observed market prices at least approximately satisfy the parity equation, we should expect to see similar implied volatilities for call and put options that have a common exercise price X and a common time until expiry T.

An approximate formula for the implied volatility is available for ATM options. From (14.21) there is the proportional approximation

$$\sigma_{\text{implied}} \cong \sqrt{\frac{2\pi}{T}}\,\frac{e^{rT}}{F}c_{\text{market}} \tag{14.27}$$

when the exercise price X equals the forward price F.

The implied volatility for an American option is defined by replacing the Black–Scholes formulae in (14.24) and (14.26) by the appropriate American pricing formulae.

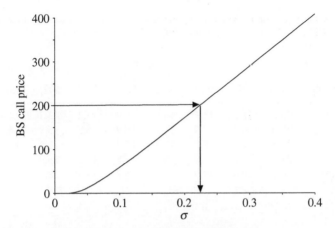

Figure 14.3. The implied volatility solution.

14.4.2 Calculation

Suppose, for example, that c_{market} is 200 when $S = 6000$, $T = 0.25$, $X = 6200$, $r = 0.06$, and $q = 0.03$. Figure 14.3 shows how c_{BS} then depends on σ. The implied volatility could be found by locating the market price on the vertical axis and then reading off the volatility value on the horizontal axis. This gives an answer of approximately 22%. The exact solution requires a numerical method, because the required inverse function cannot be stated compactly. Excel's Solver function could be used, for example, to give an implied volatility of 22.41%.

Other numerical methods are also fast, including interval subdivision and the Newton–Raphson method using the derivative in (14.25). The subdivision algorithm might start by noting that the solution to our example is obviously between 10% and 30%. Then find the formula price at the midpoint, 20%, and see that it is below the market price. The solution must therefore be in the shorter interval from 20% to 30%. Try the new midpoint, 25%, to discover that a shorter range is 20–25% and then repeat the process until a desired level of accuracy is achieved.

14.4.3 The Implied Volatility Matrix

Options are traded for several pairs of the contract parameters (T, X) at any time. Each call option has an implied volatility, from which a matrix can be formed with rows defined by T and columns defined by X. There will be a similar matrix for put options. We might expect identical numbers in a matrix if traders believe and act on the assumptions of the Black–Scholes formulae. This does not occur in empirical matrices, so that a unique volatility forecast is not provided by a matrix of option prices.

Table 14.2 is a typical example, for the settlement prices of FTSE 100 options on 4 March 2002. The lives T of the options range from 18 to 200 days. The matrix terms are the averages of call and put implieds. On the illustrative day they

Table 14.2. A matrix of implied volatilities. The tabulated numbers are percentage implied volatilities for FTSE 100 options on 4 March 2002. The settlement price of March futures was 5241 on this day.

Expiry month	4825	4925	5025	Exercise price 5125	5225	5325	5425	5525
March	20.5	18.2	15.7	14.5	13.9	13.2	13.7	14.4
April	22.0	20.4	18.9	17.7	16.9	16.3	15.9	15.6
May	21.3	20.0	19.2	18.4	17.7	17.1	16.6	16.6
June	21.0	20.0	19.0	18.6	17.8	17.2	16.9	16.5
September	20.9	20.4	19.9	19.5	18.9	18.5	18.2	17.6

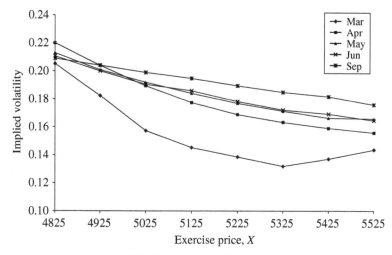

Figure 14.4. FTSE implied volatilities on 4 March 2002.

generally increase as T increases and decrease as X increases. This can also be seen from Figure 14.4.

The variation among empirical implied volatilities at any moment in time is explained by data limitations, microstructure effects, and the models used to set prices. Implieds contain measurement error if the inputs are not contemporaneous, in particular if c_{market} and S are not measured at the same time. This occurs when options and the underlying asset trade at different times. It also occurs when there are stale prices in a spot stock index. Even when individual implieds come from contemporaneous prices, the entries in the matrix may not be for identical times. Microstructure effects arise because options have discrete bid and ask prices, which define different implieds. There will be variation in the matrix entries whenever some option trades are at the bid and others are at the ask.

Even if we are able to eliminate measurement error and microstructure effects from the implied volatility matrix we will still find significant variation among

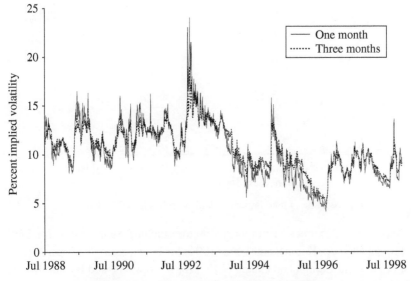

Figure 14.5. Sterling/dollar implied volatilities.

the implied volatilities. Traders are smart people and they know that asset prices do not follow a GBM. Consequently, when they value options they consider more complicated dynamics for asset prices, which leads to more complicated pricing formulae and variation within the implied matrix. Their formulae may well include premia for risks that cannot be hedged. For example, equity implieds can reflect fears that the stock market may crash.

14.4.4 Term Effects

A term structure of implied volatilities is given by varying the time T for a fixed level of either the exercise price X or the ratio X/F. The shape of the term structure generally reflects expected changes in future volatility. As volatility appears to be a mean-reverting process, the same characteristic often appears in the term structure. Thus the term structure usually declines as T increases when short-term implieds are high, and conversely when they are low.

Figure 14.5 shows daily time series of one-month and three-month ATM implied volatilities for the sterling/dollar rate from July 1988 to December 1998. On day n let $\sigma_{n,1}$ and $\sigma_{n,3}$ denote the ATM implieds when T respectively equals one month and three months. The one-month series, $\{\sigma_{n,1}\}$, has average 10.4%, minimum 4.1%, maximum 24.0%, and high values around the sterling debacle in September 1992. The three-month series, $\{\sigma_{n,3}\}$, averages 10.6% with extremes at 4.6% and 19.0%. The spread, $\sigma_{n,3} - \sigma_{n,1}$, has a standard deviation of 0.9%. It is nearly always positive when $\sigma_{n,1}$ is below 8% and is nearly always negative when $\sigma_{n,1}$ is above 14%.

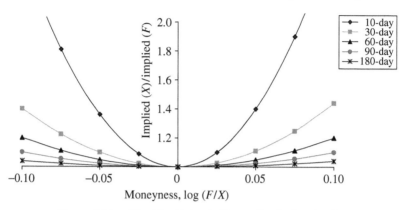

Figure 14.6.   Fitted implied volatility smiles for DM/\$ calls.

Studies of the dynamics of the term structure include Stein (1989) for S&P 100 options, Heynen, Kemna, and Vorst (1994) for Dutch equity options, Xu and Taylor (1994) and Campa and Chang (1995) for FX options, and Byoun, Kwok, and Park (2003) for FX and S&P 500 options.

14.4.5 Smile Effects

Two contrasting pictures for implied volatilities have been obtained by varying the exercise price X for a fixed time T. First, currency options generally produce a U-shape, or "smile," with the minimum implied near the forward price. Second, equity index options generally give a steady decline in implieds as X increases, sometimes called a "smirk." These shapes can be attributed to the demand for options and/or to traders incorporating assumptions about the distribution of asset prices into option prices (Bates 2003; Bollen and Whaley 2004). Stochastic volatility increases the kurtosis of multi-period returns, while any negative correlation between volatility and prices shows up in negative skewness as noted in Section 11.9. Negative correlation is a feature of stock dynamics and explains why stocks have a different smile shape to foreign exchange. A mathematical discussion of smile shapes follows in Sections 14.5 and 14.6.

Figure 14.6 first appeared in Taylor and Xu (1994a) and shows the result of regressing a ratio of implieds for DM/\$ calls, $\sigma_{\text{implied}}(X)/\sigma_{\text{implied}}(F)$, against the moneyness variable defined by $\log(F/X)$. The symbols show fitted values for various T. The U-shapes are clear and they flatten as T increases. Further U-shapes can be seen in Campa, Chang, and Reider (1998).

Figure 14.4 shows the typical equity shape for a single day of FTSE 100 options. The general decline in equity implieds as X increases is emphasized by Rubinstein (1994). His Figure 2 for a typical day has an S&P 500 index implied of 24% when the ratio X/S equals 0.84, but the implied is only 14% when the ratio is 1.08. Within this range there are a further twelve exercise prices and the implied volatility is a monotonic decreasing function of X. Further equity pictures can be seen in Dumas, Fleming, and Whaley (1998), Duffie et al. (2000), Aït-Sahalia (2002), and Pan (2002).

14.4.6 Implied Surfaces

A three-dimensional picture of all the implieds plotted against T and X provides a surface plot. Models for the dynamic behavior of the surface and illustrative examples can be found in Skiadopoulos, Hodges, and Clewlow (1999), Tompkins (2001), Cont and da Fonseca (2002), and Panigirtzoglou and Skiadopoulos (2004).

14.4.7 Implied Indices

There are several ways to combine implieds into a single representative number. An important example is the VIX index of Fleming, Ostdiek, and Whaley (1995), which represents a hypothetical American option on the S&P 100 index that is at-the-money and thirty calendar days from expiry. Four call and four put implieds are weighted to define the index, using pairs of exercise prices that bracket the asset level combined with the nearby and next expiry dates. A new VIX index is based upon a model-free variance expectation, given later by equation (14.44).

14.5 Option Prices when Volatility Is Stochastic

Option prices can be calculated for continuous-time stochastic volatility models, providing we make some assumptions. We now suppose there are no jumps in the price and volatility processes, show how option prices can be calculated, and then consider the interpretation of implied volatility when volatility is stochastic.

14.5.1 Theoretical Framework

The theory of stochastic volatility option pricing was developed by Hull and White (1987), Johnson and Shanno (1987), Scott (1987), and Wiggins (1987). The mathematics and economic theory are presented in detail in books on this subject by Fouque, Papanicolaou, and Sircar (2000) and Lewis (2000). We follow the analysis in the two books and in Hull and White (1987, 1988).

The two state variables, defined by the asset price S_t and variance $V_t = \sigma_t^2$, are supposed to have real-world dynamics defined by a pair of diffusion equations

$$dS = \mu S \, dt + \sigma S \, dW \qquad (14.28)$$

and

$$dV = \alpha \, dt + \eta \, dZ \qquad (14.29)$$

with correlation ρ between the Wiener processes $\{W_t\}$ and $\{Z_t\}$, often referred to as the correlation between dW and dZ. We assume the correlation is strictly between -1 and 1. The terms μ, α, and η are typically general functions of V and a parameter vector θ. For the real-world volatility process we can then write

$$dV = \alpha(V, \theta_P)\, dt + \eta(V, \theta_P)\, dZ. \tag{14.30}$$

An important example is the *square-root volatility model*, defined for real-world volatility by

$$dV = (a_P - b_P V)\, dt + \xi_P \sqrt{V}\, dZ \tag{14.31}$$

with three positive parameters a_P, b_P, and ξ_P.

The market is not complete because there are two state variables and only one of them is traded. Consequently, risk-neutral pricing methods alone cannot be used to obtain a unique option price. Instead there are an infinite number of equivalent probability measures Q, each reflecting a different risk-premium function for volatility, for which discounted prices, $\exp(-(r - q)t)S_t$, are a martingale. It is standard to assume the price dynamics for measures P and Q are provided by the same family of diffusion processes. The risk-neutral process is then

$$dS = (r - q)S\, dt + \sigma S\, d\tilde{W} \tag{14.32}$$

and

$$dV = \alpha(V, \theta_Q)\, dt + \eta(V, \theta_P)\, d\tilde{Z}, \tag{14.33}$$

with the same correlation ρ between the Wiener processes $\{\tilde{W}_t\}$ and $\{\tilde{Z}_t\}$ as for the real-world process. Note that only the drift rates have changed, from $\mu(V, \theta_P)S$ to $(r - q)S$ and from $\alpha(V, \theta_P)$ to $\alpha(V, \theta_Q)$. For the square-root example the risk-neutral volatility dynamics simply become

$$dV = (a_Q - b_Q V)\, dt + \xi_P \sqrt{V}\, d\tilde{Z}. \tag{14.34}$$

European option prices are the discounted expected payoffs at expiry, using the density function for S_T defined by measure Q and denoted by f_Q. Thus the fair price for a call is

$$c = e^{-rT} E^Q[\max(S_T - X, 0)] = e^{-rT} \int_X^\infty (x - X) f_Q(x)\, dx. \tag{14.35}$$

This equation is identical to (14.15), but now the density f_Q is not lognormal.

14.5.2 Volatility Risk

We discuss the market price of volatility risk before explaining how option prices can be calculated. The change in the volatility drift from the real-world dynamics to the risk-neutral dynamics is, in theory, determined by the pricing of the risk accepted when holding an asset whose value will change if volatility changes. This risk premium can be time-varying and the assumption that it has a form that allows us to retain the function $\alpha(V)$ in (14.33) is merely pragmatic.

There are three common ways to deal with the risk premium issue. The first assumes $\theta_P = \theta_Q$ and hence the premium is zero. This is often stated as an assumption that volatility is uncorrelated with aggregate consumption (Hull and White 1987, p. 283). The parameters θ_Q can then be estimated from historical data, i.e. from a times series of underlying asset prices. The second way assumes that we can retain the function $\alpha(V)$. Some parameters can then be obtained from historical data (e.g. ξ_P in (14.34)), but others (e.g. a_Q, b_Q) must be inferred from option prices. The third way commences option pricing with the risk-neutral dynamics, without taking any position about the volatility risk premium. All the parameters θ_Q are then inferred from a panel of option prices.

14.5.3 Calculations

Stochastic volatility option prices can sometimes be calculated from "closed-form" equations. This can be done for the square-root volatility model and some more complicated specifications, as discussed in the next section. Other specifications, such as the continuous-time version of the standard SV model mentioned in Section 13.4, have no known "closed-form" and option prices must be obtained by Monte Carlo methods. In the most general situation, when $\rho \neq 0$, equations (14.32) and (14.33) must then be rewritten in discrete time and simulated. We could obtain asset prices $S_{i,T}$ at time T from simulations labeled by $i = 1, 2, \ldots, N$. The integral in (14.35) would then be estimated by

$$\hat{c}_N = \frac{e^{-rT}}{N} \sum_{i=1}^{N} \max(S_{i,T} - X, 0). \tag{14.36}$$

However, the same accuracy can be obtained much faster by using variance reduction methods, such as the antithetic and control variate methods (Hull and White 1987; Boyle, Broadie, and Glasserman 1997).

14.5.4 The Zero Correlation Special Case

The fair price of a European call option has a simpler representation when the two Wiener processes $\{W_t\}$ and $\{Z_t\}$ are independent and any risk premium function is also independent of $\{W_t\}$. These are reasonable assumptions for some assets, particularly foreign exchange. Hull and White (1987) show the fair price is an expectation across Black–Scholes prices. Let

$$\bar{V} = \frac{1}{T} \int_0^T V_t \, dt \tag{14.37}$$

be the average variance during the life of the option, with $g(v)$ its density function for the risk-neutral dynamics conditional on the initial value V_0. Also let $c_{BS}(\sqrt{v})$ now denote the Black–Scholes price when the volatility rate is $\sqrt{v}$. Then the

Hull–White price is

$$c = E^Q[c_{BS}(\sqrt{\bar{V}}) \mid V_0] = \int_0^\infty c_{BS}(\sqrt{v})g(v)\,dv. \qquad (14.38)$$

This integral can be evaluated by Monte Carlo methods but only V_t then needs to be simulated.

14.5.5 Implied Volatilities for the Special Case

Option prices from a stochastic volatility model define implied volatilities in exactly the same way as do observed market prices. These SV implieds help us to see how SV option prices differ from Black–Scholes prices and can partially explain the general smile shapes observed in empirical implieds.

The simplest case is when $\rho = 0$ and (14.38) applies. The simplest approximation then notes that at-the-money BS option prices are almost proportional to volatility, when $\sigma\sqrt{T}$ is not large (equation (14.21)), so that c_{BS} and E^Q can be interchanged in (14.38) to give

$$c \cong c_{BS}(E^Q[\sqrt{\bar{V}} \mid V_0]). \qquad (14.39)$$

This result indicates that implieds are approximately the risk-neutral expected value of $\sqrt{\bar{V}}$. We may therefore say that an implied volatility is approximately the market's expectation of volatility during the lifetime of the option if these three conditions all apply:

(i) there is no volatility risk premium;

(ii) there is no correlation between price and volatility shocks;

(iii) the option is approximately at-the-money.

More accurate approximations when $\rho = 0$ are obtained by series expansions. Let μ_* and σ_* be the mean and standard deviation of the risk-neutral random variable $\bar{V}$, for a fixed value of T and conditional on a specific value for V_0. Taylor and Xu (1994a) and Ball and Roma (1994) both show that the approximate square of the implied volatility is

$$\sigma^2_{\text{implied}}(X) \cong \mu_* + \frac{\sigma_*^2}{4T\mu_*^2}\left[\log\left(\frac{X}{F}\right)^2 - T\mu_* - \tfrac{1}{4}T^2\mu_*^2\right]. \qquad (14.40)$$

The quadratic function of $\log(X/F)$ obviously generates a U-shaped smile as X varies. The exact minimum of the smile occurs when the exercise price X equals the forward price F (Renault and Touzi 1996) and then the implied is less than the square root of the conditional expectation of $\bar{V}$ (Hull and White 1987).

Taylor and Xu (1994a) also provide an approximation for the ratio of two implieds,

$$\frac{\sigma_{\text{implied}}(X)}{\sigma_{\text{implied}}(F)} \cong 1 + \frac{\sigma_*^2}{8T\mu_*^3}\left(\log\left(\frac{X}{F}\right)\right)^2. \qquad (14.41)$$

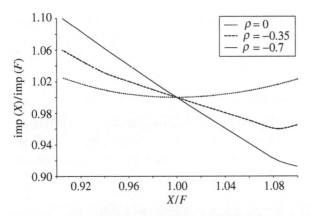

Figure 14.7.   Theoretical ratios of implieds for a square-root process.

The ratio depends on T, V_0, and the process defining V_t. It decreases towards 1 as T increases, when either V_t or its logarithm follows a mean-reverting Ornstein–Uhlenbeck (OU) process. Empirical analysis of several years of FX implieds finds smiles whose magnitudes are very approximately double the size predicted by (14.41). Figure 14.6 shows the fitted relationship between the ratios and $M = \log(F/X)$, from a regression of ratios on $M/\sqrt{T}$, $M^2/\sqrt{T}$, M/T, M^2/T, and other variables.

14.5.6 *Implied Volatilities for the Square-Root Process*

It is much more difficult to find general results about implieds when the correlation ρ is not restricted. The only well-known results are for the square-root volatility process given by (14.34). Hull and White (1988) present option prices as infinite series in the "volatility of volatility" parameter ξ, previously called ξ_P. Then

$$c = c_{BS}(\sqrt{E^Q[\bar{V}]}) + f_1\xi + f_2\xi^2 + \cdots \qquad (14.42)$$

for functions f_i of the variables $a_Q, b_Q, \rho, V_0, r, q, T$, and X. The first three terms of the series shown above provide an accurate approximation to the exact solution for realistic parameter values. Taylor and Xu (1994b) use Hull and White's approximate formula for c to derive approximations for implied volatilities, including the following ratio:

$$\frac{\sigma_{\text{implied}}(X)}{\sigma_{\text{implied}}(F)} \cong 1 + \rho\xi A_1 \log(X/F) + (A_2 + A_3\rho^2)\xi^2(\log(X/F))^2 \quad (14.43)$$

with each of A_1, A_2, and A_3 being positive functions of the variables a_Q, b_Q, V_0, and T. This formula shows implieds are approximately a quadratic function of X, but now the minimum implied will not occur at the forward price when $\rho \neq 0$.

The minimum implied is in fact far from F, for realistic negative values of ρ, when the exact implieds are calculated from the exact option pricing formula of Heston (1993). Figure 14.7 shows typical exact ratios of implieds for 30-day options, based upon parameter values estimated by Taylor and Xu (1994b) from the prices of S&P 500 futures. When ρ is either -0.35 or -0.7 the ratio is approximately a linear function of ρ over the range shown in Figure 14.7.

14.5.7 *Variance Expectations*

Carr and Madan (1998) and Britten-Jones and Neuberger (2000) show that a complete set of call option prices $c(X)$ can be used to infer the risk-neutral expectation of the integrated variance until time T when the risk-neutral price and volatility dynamics are defined by the diffusion equations (14.32) and (14.33). From Itô's lemma,

$$dS/S - d(\log S) = \tfrac{1}{2} V \, dt$$

and thus

$$E^Q \left[\int_0^T V_t \, dt \right] = 2(r - q)T - 2E^Q[\log(S_T/S)] = -2E^Q[\log(S_T/F)].$$

The payoff $\log(S_T)$ can be replicated by investing in a static portfolio that takes positions in option contracts. Consequently, it can be shown that

$$E^Q \left[\int_0^T V_t \, dt \right] = 2e^{rT} \left[\int_0^F \frac{p(X)}{X^2} \, dX + \int_F^\infty \frac{c(X)}{X^2} \, dX \right], \tag{14.44}$$

with $p(X) = c(X) + e^{-rT}(X - F)$ defining the prices of put options. This equation can provide informative volatility forecasts (Jiang and Tian 2004), which are discussed in Section 15.7. The equation also underpins futures trading on volatility at the Chicago Board Options Exchange (CBOE).

14.6 Closed-Form Stochastic Volatility Option Prices

Let $P_1 = N(d_1)$ and $P_2 = N(d_2)$ be the two probabilities that appear in the Black–Scholes call formula, so that

$$c_{BS} = Se^{-qT} P_1 - Xe^{-rT} P_2. \tag{14.45}$$

A call option expires *in-the-money* when $S_T > X$. This event has probability P_2 for the risk-neutral measure Q, when prices follow a GBM process. The event occurs with the higher probability P_1 for another measure Q^*, for which the drift rate of the GBM process is increased from $r - q$ to $r - q + \sigma^2$. Expressions like (14.45) can be derived when the price dynamics are more complicated than GBM and, in some cases, the two probabilities can be calculated very rapidly by numerical methods. The resulting "closed-form" solutions can be useful for pricing options and hence for interpreting implied volatilities. They also provide a methodology for extracting implied risk-neutral densities from observed option prices, to be discussed at the end of Section 16.5.

14.6.1 Square-Root Volatility Processes

Heston (1993) provides the first rigorous SV option pricing formula that can be evaluated rapidly. The risk-neutral dynamics, for measure Q, are given by

$$Y_t = \log(S_t), \qquad V_t = \sigma_t^2,$$

$$dY = (r - q - \tfrac{1}{2}V)\,dt + \sqrt{V}\,d\tilde{W}, \tag{14.46}$$

$$dV = (a - bV)\,dt + \xi\sqrt{V}\,d\tilde{Z}, \tag{14.47}$$

and correlation ρ between $d\tilde{W}$ and $d\tilde{Z}$. Heston proves that the fair price of a call option is

$$c = Se^{-qT}P_1 - Xe^{-rT}P_2 \tag{14.48}$$

for probabilities that are given by integrals that incorporate complex-valued functions. The term P_2 is derived from the characteristic function (c.f.) of Y_T for measure Q, while P_1 is derived from the c.f. of Y_T for a measure Q^* that is applicable after changing the drift rates in both (14.46) and (14.47). The equations for P_1 and P_2 are given in the appendix to this chapter. Heston (1993) provides numerical examples and illustrates the separate influences of the parameters ξ and ρ on the theoretical price c. Further examples and a discussion of return distributions are included in Das and Sundaram (1999).

Several people have described the characteristic function of Y_T for more general risk-neutral dynamics than the square-root stochastic volatility (SRSV) specification given by (14.46) and (14.47). They then derive probabilities and hence more general option prices. Bates (1996) modifies SRSV by adding a jump component to the right-hand side of (14.46) to define SRSVJ dynamics. He shows this can explain exchange rate smiles, when there are occasional large jumps.

Bakshi, Cao, and Chen (1997) and Scott (1997) extend the SRSVJ dynamics to incorporate a stochastic short-term interest rate. Bakshi et al. obtain the characteristic function of Y_T when r also follows a square-root diffusion process, as in Cox et al. (1985). Bakshi et al. assess the relative usefulness of stochastic volatility, price jump, and stochastic interest-rate features when pricing and hedging options. They find that stochastic volatility is the most important feature and that price jumps are also useful when pricing short-term options. Subsequently, Bakshi, Cao, and Chen (2000) give further results for long-term equity options. Das and Sundaram (1999) also argue that both stochastic volatility and jump components are required to explain observed implied volatilities.

Duffie, Pan, and Singleton (2000) provide an impressive general analytic treatment of valuation problems that use transformations such as characteristic functions. Their results are for so-called affine jump-diffusions, which include the SRSV dynamics as a special case. These affine models have coefficients that are linear functions of the state variables. For example, in (14.46) and (14.47) the terms that multiply dt and the squares of the terms that multiply dW and dZ are all linear functions of the state vector $(Y_t, V_t)'$. Their framework permits jumps in volatility (which can be contemporaneous with jumps in the price) and multiple factors in the volatility process, in addition to all of the other features already mentioned. Applications include the pricing of exotic options. They illustrate the match between theoretical and observed option prices when volatility is stochastic, for various jump specifications.

14.6.2 Other Processes

Zhu (2000) also provides a detailed analysis of closed-form option pricing formulae derived from characteristic functions. Results are given for a variety of price dynamics, including an Ornstein–Uhlenbeck (OU) diffusion process for volatility. The OU analysis supplements option pricing studies for this process by Stein and Stein (1991), Ball and Roma (1994), and Schöbel and Zhu (1999). Closed-form solutions are also available when the OU process for volatility has increments defined by a jump process, as shown by Barndorff-Nielsen and Shephard (2001). Further pricing results for their jump process are given by Barndorff-Nielsen, Nicolato, and Shephard (2002) and by Nicolato and Venardos (2003).

A general theoretical framework for "closed-form" option prices is presented by Carr and Wu (2004). They obtain option prices for time-changed Lévy processes using characteristic functions, and describe several examples for asset price dynamics that include stochastic volatility and/or jumps. Empirical comparisons of some of their option pricing formulae are provided by Huang and Wu (2004).

14.6.3 Empirical Comparisons between Real-World and Risk-Neutral Dynamics

Various model parameters are theoretically identical for the real-world measure P and the risk-neutral measure Q, as explained in Section 14.5. For the Heston (1993) model, the theoretically identical parameters are the "volatility of volatility" ξ and the correlation ρ between the price and volatility differentials. Some researchers have shown that time series (P) and option price (Q) parameter estimates are inconsistent, which implies the asset price dynamics are mis-specified, while others have attempted to use time series and options data to jointly estimate parameters. Bates (2003) reviews and discusses this literature.

Bates (1996, 2000) finds that the Heston dynamics are mis-specified for the DM/\$ exchange rate and for S&P 500 futures prices, because the parameter ξ implied by option prices is much more than the time series estimate. Consequently, he investigates more complicated price dynamics that includes jumps. Bakshi et al. (1997) use S&P 500 spot and options prices to obtain the same conclusion about ξ. Their estimates of the correlation ρ obtained from panels of option prices are substantial and negative (below -0.55), which contrast with less negative values (around -0.25) obtained from time series of asset returns and changes in implieds.

Joint estimation of real-world and risk-neutral dynamics has been accomplished for the Heston dynamics and various extensions using S&P index data, usually for the 500-share index, commencing with Chernov and Ghysels (2000). They find that time series information does not enhance option pricing. Pan (2002) uses joint data to estimate the risk premium for price jumps and finds that it is correlated with volatility. Jones (2003) generalizes the volatility dynamics in two ways: first the volatility differential $d\tilde{Z}$ is multiplied by ξV^{γ} instead of $\xi \sqrt{V}$ and second the correlation ρ is made a function of V. Eraker (2004) obtains a more satisfactory description of spot and options data by including volatility jumps in the price dynamics.

14.7 Option Prices for ARCH Processes

Less attention has been given to option pricing for discrete-time ARCH processes, in comparison with research for continuous-time stochastic volatility processes. An attraction of ARCH methods is that observed prices for the underlying asset can be used to select the price dynamics. However, the discrete-time context of ARCH methods complicates theoretical analysis and excludes an independent volatility risk premium from the option pricing solutions.

14.7.1 Theoretical Framework

To obtain fair option prices in an ARCH framework, using a risk-neutral measure Q, it is necessary to make additional assumptions. Duan (1995) and Bollerslev and Mikkelsen (1999) provide sufficient conditions to apply a risk-neutral valuation methodology. For example, it is sufficient that a representative agent has constant relative risk aversion and that returns and aggregate growth rates in consumption have conditional normal distributions. Kallsen and Taqqu (1998) derive the same option pricing solution as Duan (1995) without making assumptions about utility functions and consumption. Instead, they assume that intraday prices are determined by a GBM with volatility determined once a day from a discrete-time ARCH model.

The discrete timescale is now defined by trading periods, labeled by t. At time 0 we wish to price European options that expire at time n and we make use of returns $r_t = \log(S_t) - \log(S_{t-1})$ that define information sets $I_t = \{r_{t-j}, j \geqslant 0\}$. Following the general framework of Section 9.5, returns have conditional distributions for the real-world measure P of the form

$$r_t \mid I_{t-1} \stackrel{P}{\sim} N(\mu_t, h_t),$$

with

$$z_t = \frac{r_t - \mu_t}{\sqrt{h_t}} \stackrel{P}{\sim} \text{i.i.d. } N(0, 1). \tag{14.49}$$

Duan (1995) shows that the conditional distributions change for the risk-neutral measure Q to

$$r_t \mid I_{t-1} \overset{Q}{\sim} N(\rho - \delta - \tfrac{1}{2}h_t, h_t),$$

with

$$\tilde{z}_t = \frac{r_t - (\rho - \delta - \tfrac{1}{2}h_t)}{\sqrt{h_t}} \overset{Q}{\sim} \text{ i.i.d. } N(0, 1). \tag{14.50}$$

The parameters ρ and δ now denote the one-period risk-free and dividend rates, such that one dollar and one share respectively grow to $\exp(n\rho)$ dollars and $\exp(n\delta)$ shares after n trading periods.

As in Section 14.5 for SV processes, the change in the expected return as the measure changes reflects the risk premium for the asset. Unlike the SV case, there is not an independent change in the drift rate of the volatility equation; the same functions h_t appear in (14.49) and (14.50).

The theoretical fair price of a call option is once more given by the present value of its expected terminal price; thus,

$$c = \mathrm{e}^{-\rho n} E^Q[c_n \mid I_0] = \mathrm{e}^{-\rho n} E^Q[\max(S_n - X) \mid I_0]. \tag{14.51}$$

This expectation can be evaluated by Monte Carlo methods after specifying the functions μ_t and h_t. A closed-form expression for the expectation is only known for a contrived ARCH specification given by Heston and Nandi (2000). Price and volatility shocks are perfectly correlated for the diffusion limit of their discrete-time specification, unlike the general correlation permitted in the related SV closed-form formula of Heston (1993).

The conditional market price of risk for the underlying asset is

$$\lambda_t = \frac{\mu_t - (\rho - \delta - \tfrac{1}{2}h_t)}{\sqrt{h_t}}. \tag{14.52}$$

Following most implementations of ARCH option pricing, we now assume that this quantity is some constant λ. From (14.49) and (14.50), the standardized returns for the two measures are then related by

$$z_t = \tilde{z}_t - \lambda. \tag{14.53}$$

14.7.2 GARCH(1, 1)

The functions μ_t and h_t are as follows for the popular GARCH(1, 1) model, when we assume a constant market price of risk:

$$\mu_t = \rho - \delta - \tfrac{1}{2}h_t + \lambda\sqrt{h_t}$$

and

$$h_t = \omega + \alpha(r_{t-1} - \mu_{t-1})^2 + \beta h_{t-1} = \omega + (\alpha z_{t-1}^2 + \beta)h_{t-1}. \tag{14.54}$$

Monte Carlo simulation of returns, using measure Q, is achieved by knowing h_1 and then evaluating

$$\tilde{z}_t \sim N(0, 1),$$
$$r_t = \rho - \delta - \tfrac{1}{2}h_t + \sqrt{h_t}\,\tilde{z}_t, \tag{14.55}$$
$$h_{t+1} = \omega + (\alpha(\tilde{z}_t - \lambda)^2 + \beta)h_t,$$

for $1 \leqslant t \leqslant n$. The asset price at expiry is $S_n = S_0 \exp(r_1 + \cdots + r_n)$. For N simulations that deliver terminal asset prices $\{S_{i,n}, 1 \leqslant i \leqslant N\}$, the fair option price can be estimated by

$$\hat{c} = \frac{e^{-\rho n}}{N} \sum_{i=1}^{N} \max(S_{i,n} - X, 0). \tag{14.56}$$

The efficiency of the estimate can be improved by standard antithetic and control variate methods (Duan 1995; Taylor 2002). Alternative computational methodologies are provided by the series approximation of Duan, Gauthier, and Simonato (1999) and the efficient lattice algorithm of Ritchken and Trevor (1999). Duan (1995) discusses numerical examples in his paper that can be used to check implementations of his option pricing formula.

14.7.3 Long Memory ARCH

The evidence for long memory effects in volatility, noted in Sections 10.3, 11.10, and 12.9, motivates incorporating these effects into option pricing methods. Bollerslev and Mikkelsen (1996, 1999) apply the theoretical framework for ARCH option pricing to the FIEGARCH$(1, d, 1)$ specification. This specification is defined by equation (10.17) and option prices are obtained by using (10.19) and (14.53) to define the risk-neutral dynamics. Bollerslev and Mikkelsen's methodology is followed in Taylor (2002), from which we obtain the illustrative results for S&P 100 index options shown in Figures 14.8–14.10. These figures summarize features of the ten sets of implied volatilities when ARCH option prices are calculated on the final trading days of the ten years from 1989 to 1998 inclusive.

The first two figures are for the EGARCH(1) special case when $d = \psi = 0$, with persistence parameter $\Delta = 0.982$, and asymmetry parameter

$$A = \frac{\gamma - \vartheta}{\gamma + \vartheta} = 3.9$$

estimated from daily returns. This special case is a short memory specification and all the relevant information in the history I_0 is provided by the conditional variance h_1. Figure 14.8 shows the volatility term structures for ATM options with lives up to two years. The shapes are monotonic and commence at values given by h_1. Figure 14.9 shows the corresponding "smiles" for three-month options when

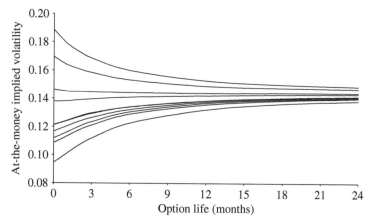

Figure 14.8.   Ten volatility term structures for a short memory process.

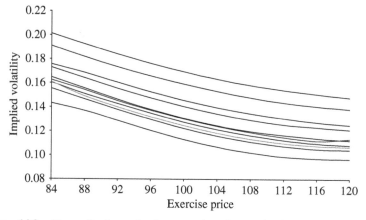

Figure 14.9.   Ten smile shapes for three-month options and a short memory process.

the index series is rescaled so that $S_0 = 100$ when the options are priced. These skewed shapes are a consequence of the strong asymmetry in the volatility process. Figure 14.10 shows the corresponding term structures for the long memory case when $d = 0.4$. These shapes depend on the entire history I_0, which has been shortened to the previous 1000 daily returns. Some of the long memory shapes are not monotonic, there are some intersections, and the convergence to a limiting value is extremely slow. The "smile" shapes for the short and long memory cases are very similar and these functions of the exercise price X are almost parallel to each other.

14.8   Summary

Rational option prices depend on the stochastic process followed by the price of the underlying asset. Option prices can be derived by a risk-neutral valuation

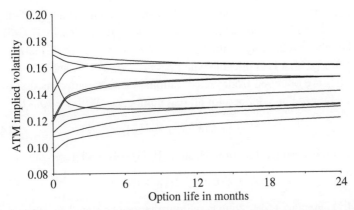

Figure 14.10. Ten volatility term structures for a long memory process with $d = 0.4$.

methodology for many stochastic processes, including the interesting cases when volatility is itself stochastic. Stochastic volatility explains why the Black–Scholes formula can only approximate observed option prices. It also explains the general forms of the patterns seen in empirical implied volatilities when they are viewed as functions of either the exercise price or the remaining time until an option expires.

Further Reading

Bates, D. S. 2003. Empirical option pricing: a retrospection. *Journal of Econometrics* 116:387–404.

Duan, J.-C. 1995. The GARCH option pricing model. *Mathematical Finance* 5:13–32.

Heston, S. L. 1993. A closed-form solution for options with stochastic volatility with applications to bond and currency options. *Review of Financial Studies* 6:327–343.

Hull, J. 2000. *Options, futures and other derivative securities*, 4th edn. Englewood Cliffs, NJ: Prentice-Hall.

Hull, J. and A. White. 1987. The pricing of options on assets with stochastic volatilities. *Journal of Finance* 42:281–300.

Xu, X. and S. J. Taylor. 1994. The term structure of volatility implied by foreign exchange options. *Journal of Financial and Quantitative Analysis* 29:57–74.

14.9 Appendix: Heston's Option Pricing Formula

The option pricing formula of Heston (1993) requires two calculations of the probability that $Y_T = \log(S_T)$ exceeds $\log(X)$ when the state vector $(Y_t, V_t)'$ has initial value $(Y_0, V_0)'$ and dynamics

$$dY = (R + uV)\,dt + \sqrt{V}\,dW, \qquad (14.57)$$

$$dV = (a - cV)\,dt + \xi\sqrt{V}\,dZ. \qquad (14.58)$$

The terms a, c, R, u, ξ are parameters, as is the correlation ρ between the Wiener processes $\{W_t\}$ and $\{Z_t\}$.

The first probability is P_2, obtained for the risk-neutral measure Q when $R = r - q$, $u = -\frac{1}{2}$, and $c = b$, which gives the price dynamics in (14.46) and (14.47). The other probability in the option pricing formula (14.48) is P_1 given by the measure Q^* that is applicable when $R = r - q$, $u = \frac{1}{2}$, and $c = b - \rho\xi$.

Probabilities are obtained from the conditional characteristic function of Y_T, here denoted by $g(\phi)$ and defined for all real numbers ϕ. With $i = \sqrt{-1}$,

$$g(\phi) = E[e^{i\phi Y_T} \mid Y_0, V_0], \tag{14.59}$$

which is a complex-valued function. Heston (1993) solves PDEs to obtain

$$g(\phi) = \exp(C + DV_0 + i\phi Y_0) \tag{14.60}$$

with C and D calculated from long equations that can be stated as

$$C = RT\phi i + a\xi^{-2}\left[hT - 2\log\left(\frac{1 - k\exp(dT)}{1 - k}\right)\right],$$

$$D = \frac{h(1 - \exp(dT))}{\xi^2(1 - k\exp(dT))},$$

with

$$d = [(\rho\xi\phi i - c)^2 - \xi^2(2u\phi i - \phi^2)]^{1/2},$$
$$h = c - \rho\xi\phi i + d, \tag{14.61}$$
$$k = \frac{h}{h - 2d}.$$

The conditional probability that Y_T exceeds $\log(X)$ is given by a standard inversion formula:

$$P(Y_T \geqslant \log(X) \mid Y_0, V_0) = \frac{1}{2} + \frac{1}{\pi}\int_0^\infty \text{Re}\left[\frac{\exp(-i\phi\log(X))g(\phi)}{i\phi}\right]d\phi \tag{14.62}$$

with $\text{Re}[\cdot]$ representing the real part of a complex number (Kendall, Stuart, and Ord 1987). The integral can be evaluated rapidly and accurately by numerical methods. Option prices for a set of X-values can be calculated together, as the same values of $g(\phi)$ are required for all X.

Equation (14.62) provides the conditional cumulative distribution function of S_T; thus,

$$F(x) = P(S_T \leqslant x \mid Y_0, V_0) = 1 - P(Y_T \geqslant \log(x) \mid Y_0, V_0).$$

The conditional density of S_T is consequently

$$f(x) = \frac{dF}{dx} = \frac{1}{\pi x}\int_0^\infty \text{Re}[\exp(-i\phi\log(x))g(\phi)]\,d\phi. \tag{14.63}$$

15

Forecasting Volatility

Several methods for forecasting volatility are reviewed in this chapter. Forecasts derived from option prices and intraday asset prices are of particular interest— they incorporate more volatility information than the history of daily asset prices and they provide superior predictions.

15.1 Introduction

Forecasts of volatility are important when assessing and managing the risks of portfolios that may include derivative securities. A remarkable variety of methods have been used and the conclusions obtained often appear to be contradictory. This variety reflects the fact that volatility is inherently unobservable, so that forecasts must be made of related observable quantities. It also reflects the increasing difficulty of the forecasting task as the forecast horizon increases.

These issues have led some people to question the possibility of making useful volatility forecasts, particularly more than two weeks into the future, despite the descriptive success of ARCH and stochastic volatility models. However, much of the evidence that forecasts are inaccurate is attributable to the use of a very noisy proxy for volatility, such as squared daily returns (Andersen and Bollerslev 1998b). Useful forecasts of both equity and exchange rate volatility *can* be made, at least one month into the future, when realized volatility is measured accurately using high-frequency prices (e.g. Blair et al. 2001b; Li 2002; Martens and Zein 2004; Pong et al. 2004).

Option prices are a source of valuable information when forecasting volatility. Option traders incorporate historical price information, and further information about future events which influences volatility, into option prices. These prices have the potential to provide the best forecasts when option markets are efficient and future volatility is the only relevant unknown variable. Consequently, this chapter concentrates on forecasts that make use of implied volatilities. The superior out-of-sample accuracy of such forecasts, compared with predictions given by the history of daily asset prices, is now well documented (e.g. Xu and Taylor 1995; Blair et al. 2001b; Ederington and Guan 2002b). This conclusion does not generally hold, however, when the asset price history is expanded to include intraday asset prices.

Poon and Granger (2003) provide a comprehensive survey of recent volatility forecasting studies. Most studies only predict the volatility of one asset or portfolio. Alexander (2001) covers the more general problem of predicting variances and covariances, within a multivariate context.

Sections 15.2 and 15.3 cover forecasting methodology. Of major importance are definitions of the volatility target that is to be predicted and measures of how well the predictions agree with subsequent outcomes. Methods that only use the history of asset prices are defined and reviewed in Section 15.4. The more interesting methods that also use option prices are covered in Sections 15.5–15.7. The construction of a forecast from the many available implied volatilities is first discussed, followed by low-frequency applications of regression and ARCH methods. These are followed by comparisons of historical and option forecasts of volatility, when high-frequency data are used to both forecast and measure volatility.

15.2   Forecasting Methodology

Forecasting tasks that are repeated through time use information I_t known at time t to produce a forecast f_{t+H} of some target quantity y_{t+H} that is observed at the later time $t + H$. Most volatility forecasting exercises use a daily timescale, so that t counts trading days. This will be assumed in this methodological section. Initially, it is also supposed that the forecast horizon H is simply one day. To simplify the discussion it is also assumed that expected returns are zero. It is easy to adapt the following methods when expected returns are either constant or some function of the information I_t.

15.2.1   The Volatility Target

Some proxy for volatility must be forecast, because volatility cannot be observed. Measures of realized volatility are often employed. One popular choice is the squared return, so $y_{t+1} = r_{t+1}^2$. This has the theoretical advantage, explained later in this section, that optimal forecasts of squared returns can also be optimal forecasts of the unobserved squared volatility, σ_{t+1}^2. However, return outliers are amplified when they are squared and then forecast errors are typically very large compared with other times. Consequently, another popular proxy is the absolute return, so that $y_{t+1} = |r_{t+1}|$. Forecasts of y_{t+1} can then be scaled to deliver unbiased forecasts of σ_{t+1}.

Any realized volatility measure calculated from one daily return will be a noisy estimate of that day's volatility. Less noisy estimates can be obtained from intraday prices. The daily range,

$$y_{t+1} = \log(p_{t+1}^+) - \log(p_{t+1}^-), \tag{15.1}$$

calculated from daily high and low prices, p_{t+1}^+ and p_{t+1}^-, is one possibility that has been used in forecasting studies (e.g. Taylor 1987). Another is the scaled squared range of Parkinson (1980), which is defined by equation (12.44).

High-frequency datasets are very useful for defining and evaluating volatility forecasts. Andersen and Bollerslev (1998b) explain the advantages of a volatility target defined by the realized volatility measure of Sections 12.8 and 12.9, namely

$$y_{t+1} = \hat{\sigma}_{t+1}^2 = \sum_{k=1}^{N} r_{t+1,k}^2 \qquad (15.2)$$

with N the number of intraday returns $r_{t+1,k}$, whose sum is r_{t+1}. Forecasts of this target have been evaluated in several recent research papers, for example, Taylor and Xu (1997), Blair et al. (2001b), and Andersen et al. [ABDL] (2003).

Implied volatility (IV) may be a suitable volatility target if forecasting is intended to enhance option hedging strategies. However, it is only possible to use the best forecast of IV to infer the best forecast of a latent volatility variable if several assumptions are made; these include a correctly specified option pricing formula.

15.2.2 Information and Forecasts

The information set I_t is selected by the forecaster. The set might only contain a history of asset prices. Typical forecasts are then conditional variances defined by ARCH models. These and other time series forecasts are reviewed in Section 15.4. Alternatively, the set might only contain implied volatilities. Indeed, one option price at time t might suffice to identify the optimal volatility forecast, assuming an efficient options market. The most interesting research studies use both an asset price history and implied volatilities to compare the predictive accuracy of these sources of volatility information. Several examples are reviewed in Sections 15.5–15.7.

15.2.3 Loss Functions

The accuracy of forecasts is evaluated by some loss function, $L(y_{t+1}, f_{t+1})$, that represents the penalty or cost when we predict f_{t+1} but the outcome is y_{t+1}. The forecaster's objective is then to minimize the expected loss. Loss functions are often some simple function of the forecast error, $e_{t+1} = y_{t+1} - f_{t+1}$, that is motivated by statistical convenience. Two examples are the squared error, e_{t+1}^2, and the absolute error $|e_{t+1}|$. The assumed symmetry between positive and negative forecast errors could be inappropriate. When it is more costly to underpredict volatility than to overpredict it, the LINEX function can be used,

$$L(y_{t+1}, f_{t+1}) = \exp(\lambda e_{t+1}) - 1 - \lambda e_{t+1}, \qquad (15.3)$$

for some positive parameter λ (Granger 1999; Hwang, Knight, and Satchell 2001). Another statistical loss measure is the squared proportional error,

$$L(y_{t+1}, f_{t+1}) = \left(\frac{y_{t+1} - f_{t+1}}{f_{t+1}}\right)^2, \tag{15.4}$$

which is robust against heteroskedasticity in the forecast errors.

Economic loss functions, which measure the impact of forecasting mistakes upon financial decisions, may be more relevant. For example, West, Edison, and Cho (1993) make use of utility functions, Fleming, Kirby, and Ostdiek (2001) relate volatility forecasts to portfolio weights, and Engle and Rosenberg (1995) emphasize hedging errors.

One forecasting method is more accurate than another if its average loss is less. Tests of the null hypothesis that methods have identical expected losses are reviewed by Diebold and Mariano (1995).

15.2.4   In- and Out-of-Sample

Many forecasts depend on parameters. There are several, for example, in ARCH specifications for the next day's variance. These parameters are sometimes estimated from data spanning several years and then applied to the calculation of forecasts during the same time period. This is called *in-sample* forecasting. It may not deliver realistic results about forecast accuracy (e.g. Dimson and Marsh 1990). Likewise, future information should not be used to guide the selection of a parametric specification. The preferred methodology is to use only data until time t to obtain the parameters and functional form of a forecast f_{t+1}. The forecasts are then *out-of-sample*. The parameters may then be re-estimated once a day from a sample of fixed size, thus defining *rolling* parameter values.

15.2.5   General Forecast Horizons

The target quantity y_{t+H}, for a general horizon of H days, could simply measure volatility at the future time, e.g. r_{t+H}^2 or $|r_{t+H}|$. It is much more usual, however, to predict some measure of the total volatility from times $t+1$ to $t+H$ inclusive. This is particularly appropriate if we use the forecast to price an option that expires after H days.

Typical targets are the sum of H realized volatilities. Low- and high-frequency examples are

$$y_{t+H} = \sum_{j=1}^{H} r_{t+j}^2 \quad \text{and} \quad y_{t+H} = \sum_{j=1}^{H}\sum_{k=1}^{N} r_{t+j,k}^2. \tag{15.5}$$

Realized standard deviations are also predicted, defined perhaps by

$$y_{t+H} = \sqrt{\frac{1}{H}\sum_{j=1}^{H} r_{t+j}^2}. \tag{15.6}$$

These are biased estimates of the theoretical quantity defined by replacing r_{t+j} by σ_{t+j}. The bias can be substantial when H is small but it can perhaps be ignored when H is at least ten (Fleming 1998, p. 324); equation (15.12) quantifies the bias when the horizon H is a single day.

It is theoretically incorrect to define H day forecasts of the targets in (15.5) by the simple scaling rule

$$f_{t+H} = Hf_{t+1}, \tag{15.7}$$

when volatility is a mean-reverting process. Instead, f_{t+H} should be nearer than Hf_{t+1} to the long-run average level of y_{t+H}, illustrated later by equation (15.23), if we disregard the possibility of future changes in this level.

Daily observations of the H-day forecast errors, $e_{t+H} = y_{t+H} - f_{t+H}$, will be autocorrelated, up to lag $H - 1$. There are $H - 1$ shared days in the forecast horizons commencing at times t and $t + 1$, and surprises during these days will have a similar impact upon the errors e_{t+H} and e_{t+H+1}. This dependence reduces the power of forecast comparisons. The standard errors of regression coefficients need to be adjusted, as in Jorion (1995) and many other studies, for example, by using the techniques of Hansen (1982) and Newey and West (1987).

15.3 Two Measures of Forecast Accuracy

15.3.1 *Minimizing Mean Squared Errors*

The mean squared error (MSE) criterion is often preferred when forecasts are evaluated, because the conditional mean of the target is then the optimal forecast.

For forecasts $f_{t+1}^{(j)}$ made at times $t_1 \leqslant t \leqslant t_2$, by methods indexed by j, the empirical MSEs are

$$\text{MSE}(j) = \frac{1}{t_2 - t_1 + 1} \sum_{t=t_1}^{t_2} (y_{t+1} - f_{t+1}^{(j)})^2. \tag{15.8}$$

A useful measure of forecast accuracy is the proportion of the variability of the outcomes y_{t+1} explained by the forecasts, which is the linear function of MSE defined by

$$P(j) = 1 - \frac{\sum(y_{t+1} - f_{t+1}^{(j)})^2}{\sum(y_{t+1} - \bar{y})^2} \tag{15.9}$$

with $\bar{y}$ the average outcome. The best method for observed data has the minimum value of $\text{MSE}(j)$ and the maximum value of $P(j)$. Ideally, this will also happen to be the method that has the minimum value of

$$E[(y_{t+1} - f_{t+1}^{(j)})^2 \mid I_t]$$

for all possible information in the sets I_t.

The theoretical problem of using I_t to find the number f_{t+1} that minimizes $E[(y_{t+1} - f_{t+1})^2 \mid I_t]$ is solved by $f_{t+1} = E[y_{t+1} \mid I_t]$, whenever the conditional variance of y_{t+1} is finite. The optimality of the conditional mean allows us to relate optimal forecasts of realized volatility y_{t+1} to optimal forecasts of a volatility variable, such as σ_{t+1}^2.

Chapters 9–11 contain several return processes that have the factorization

$$r_t = \sigma_t u_t \tag{15.10}$$

in conjunction with the assumption that u_{t+1} has zero mean, unit variance, and is independent of $\{\sigma_{t+1}, \sigma_t, \sigma_{t-1}, \ldots, u_t, u_{t-1}, \ldots\}$. For these processes,

$$E[r_{t+1}^2 \mid I_t] = E[\sigma_{t+1}^2 \mid I_t]E[u_{t+1}^2 \mid I_t] = E[\sigma_{t+1}^2 \mid I_t] \tag{15.11}$$

when I_t is any history of returns. Equation (15.11) remains true for daily returns when the history includes intraday returns that have a similar factorization. It is also true when I_t contains options prices, providing we make the reasonable assumption that these prices contain no information about u_{t+1}. The optimal forecasts of $y_{t+1} = r_{t+1}^2$ and σ_{t+1}^2 are then identical. Seeking the best forecast of r_{t+1}^2 is therefore a constructive way to seek the best forecast of σ_{t+1}^2.

Likewise, when $y_{t+1} = |r_{t+1}|$, there is the result

$$E[y_{t+1} \mid I_t] = E[|u_{t+1}|]E[\sigma_{t+1} \mid I_t] \tag{15.12}$$

so the optimal forecasts of $|r_{t+1}|$ and σ_{t+1} are proportional to each other; the term $E[|u_{t+1}|]$ equals $\sqrt{2/\pi}$ when u_{t+1} has a normal distribution. Forecasting σ_{t+1} has the advantage that a finite unconditional MSE is obtained when the process for returns has a finite variance. In contrast, the unconditional MSE is infinite for forecasts of σ_{t+1}^2 when the returns process has infinite kurtosis.

A proportional relationship also exists between optimal forecasts of the price range (see (15.1)) and σ_{t+1}, which is described and exploited in Taylor (1987). There are similar results when the forecast target is the intraday realized volatility $\hat{\sigma}_t^2$.

15.3.2 Correlation Measures

Many volatility forecasting studies report the correlation R between a set of forecasts f_{t+1} and a set of realized volatilities y_{t+1}. Ranking forecasting methods by their values of R^2 is unsatisfactory, however, because the R^2 criterion incorporates a lookback bias. This can be seen by remembering that the empirical R^2 is the proportion of variance explained by the best linear combination, $\alpha + \beta f_{t+1}$, i.e.

$$R^2 = \max_{\alpha,\beta} 1 - \frac{\sum(y_{t+1} - \alpha - \beta f_{t+1})^2}{\sum(y_{t+1} - \bar{y})^2}. \tag{15.13}$$

Thus R^2 provides a biased measure of forecast accuracy, because the best α and β for a forecasting method are only known after all the forecasts have been evaluated. The *ex post* optimization of α and β ensures that $R^2 \geqslant P$, with P the preferred proportion defined by (15.9). The criteria R^2 and P may well produce different ranks for a set of forecasting methods.

One interpretation of R^2 is that it measures information content; higher values indicate more association between the volatility forecast and the volatility outcome. Nevertheless, a relatively high association may arise from a biased forecast that would lead to relatively bad decisions if it was used *ex ante*. Tests of the joint null hypothesis $\alpha = 0$ and $\beta = 1$ are often appropriate, although rejection of the null may say nothing about the efficiency of markets. For example, the null could be rejected for an implied volatility forecast when option prices include a volatility risk premium, as will be discussed further in Section 15.5.

Empirical values of R^2 are small when realized volatility is calculated from one daily return. Suppose $r_{t+1} = \sigma_{t+1} u_{t+1}$, with σ_{t+1} independent of u_{t+1}, and that u_{t+1} has zero mean, unit variance, and finite fourth moment, $k_u = E[u_{t+1}^4]$. Then the squared correlation for predictions of r_{t+1}^2 is bounded as follows:

$$R^2 = [\mathrm{cor}(r_{t+1}^2, f_{t+1})]^2 \leqslant [\mathrm{cor}(r_{t+1}^2, \sigma_{t+1}^2)]^2 = \frac{\mathrm{var}(\sigma_{t+1}^2)}{\mathrm{var}(r_{t+1}^2)} \leqslant \frac{1}{k_u}. \quad (15.14)$$

The upper bound is one-third when u_{t+1} has a normal distribution. Low values of R^2 are a consequence of $r_{t+1}^2 = \sigma_{t+1}^2 u_{t+1}^2$ being a very noisy estimate of σ_{t+1}^2. Much of this noise can be eliminated by instead using the intraday realized volatility $\hat{\sigma}_t^2$, given in (15.2), and then much higher values of R^2 can be obtained (Andersen and Bollerslev 1998b).

When returns are generated by an ARCH process, the conditional variance h_{t+1} equals σ_{t+1}^2 and it defines the optimal forecast made at time t. Andersen and Bollerslev (1998b) derive R^2 for the GARCH(1, 1) model when the forecast is the conditional variance. With α and β now referring to the GARCH parameters used in Sections 9.3 and 9.6, and providing the returns have finite kurtosis, which requires $(\alpha + \beta)^2 + \alpha^2(k_u - 1) < 1$, the optimal R^2 is

$$R^2 = \frac{\alpha^2}{1 - 2\alpha\beta - \beta^2}. \quad (15.15)$$

As α and β approach the boundary that defines infinite kurtosis for returns, R^2 approaches the upper bound $1/k_u$.

15.4 Historical Volatility Forecasts

15.4.1 *Methods*

Historical forecasts and volatility targets are obtained from information sets I_t that only contain asset prices known at time t. Simple benchmark forecasts of the next volatility outcome y_{t+1} are

$$f_{t+1} = y_t, \tag{15.16}$$

$$f_{t+1} = \frac{1}{M} \sum_{i=0}^{M-1} y_{t-i}. \tag{15.17}$$

The previous value forecast, (15.16), is sometimes called a random walk forecast because it is optimal when changes in the target are unpredictable. The moving average of previous values, (15.17), depends on the single parameter M and common values are between 20 and 100 inclusive. The average becomes the historical mean when $M = t$, which defines another benchmark forecast. Many volatility forecasting studies first attempt to demonstrate that there are forecasts that are more accurate than one of these naive benchmarks.

Exponentially weighted moving averages (EWMAs) have a long history in forecasting literature. They are defined recursively by

$$f_{t+1} = \gamma y_t + (1 - \gamma)f_t = \sum_{i=0}^{t-1} \gamma(1 - \gamma)^i y_{t-i} + (1 - (1 - \gamma)^t)f_1. \tag{15.18}$$

EWMAs depend on the smoothing parameter γ and the initial prediction f_1, with $0 < \gamma < 1$. Such forecasts have two advantages. First, they give more weight to the most recent observations. Second, they are robust against changes in the unconditional mean level of volatility that occur over very long periods of time (Pagan and Schwert 1990). EWMAs are used to predict volatility in Taylor (1986) and in the RiskMetrics methodology developed by JPMorgan.

The EWMA forecast is optimal when the outcomes y_{t+1} are generated by an ARIMA(0, 1, 1) process and the loss function is the squared forecast error. As there is plenty of evidence against a unit-root in volatility during recent years, forecasts have been derived from ARMA(p, q) processes (e.g. Schwert 1989; West and Cho 1995) and, more recently, ARFIMA(p, d, q) processes with $0 < d < 1$ (e.g. ABDL 2003; Pong et al. 2004). These forecasts are particularly appropriate when the target y_{t+1} is a high-frequency measure of realized volatility.

ARCH models provide a vast variety of volatility forecasts. Assuming expected returns are a constant μ, the natural volatility target is the next squared excess return, $y_{t+1} = (r_{t+1} - \mu)^2$. This is predicted by the conditional variance $h_{t+1} = \text{var}(r_{t+1} \mid I_t)$. An advantage of the ARCH approach is that maximum likelihood methods can be used to select a specification for h_{t+1} and to estimate the model parameters. Probably the most popular specification for forecasting purposes is GARCH(1, 1). Then

$$h_{t+1} = \omega + \alpha(r_t - \mu)^2 + \beta h_t, \tag{15.19}$$

as has been discussed at length in Sections 9.3 and 9.4. Asymmetric specifications are, however, appropriate for equity markets. The GJR(1, 1) specification, of Sections 9.7 and 9.8, is the convenient extension of GARCH(1, 1) defined by

$$h_{t+1} = \omega + (\alpha + \alpha^- S_t)(r_t - \mu)^2 + \beta h_t \qquad (15.20)$$

with $S_t = 1$ if $r_t < \mu$, otherwise $S_t = 0$.

So far we have only described predictions one period into the future. Now let $H > 1$ be a general horizon for more distant forecasts and suppose the target y_{t+H} is the sum of H one-period realized volatilities, as illustrated in (15.5). The H-period forecast is then the one-period forecast multiplied by H for the benchmark and EWMA methods. This scaling rule does not apply to forecasts obtained from stationary ARMA or ARCH models. For a general ARCH model, that has a constant conditional expected return, the theoretically optimal forecast of

$$\sum_{j=1}^{H}(r_{t+j} - \mu)^2 \quad \text{is} \quad h_{t+1} + \sum_{j=2}^{H} E[h_{t+j} \mid I_t]. \qquad (15.21)$$

For the GJR(1, 1) model, with symmetric conditional distributions, the average value of S_{t+1} is one-half and hence the above conditional expectations have

$$E[h_{t+j} \mid I_t] = \omega + (\alpha + \tfrac{1}{2}\alpha^- + \beta)E[h_{t+j-1} \mid I_t], \quad j = 2, 3, 4, \ldots . \qquad (15.22)$$

The optimal forecast in (15.21) then simplifies to

$$f_{t+H} = H\sigma^2 + \frac{1 - \phi^H}{1 - \phi}(h_{t+1} - \sigma^2) \qquad (15.23)$$

with $\phi = \alpha + \tfrac{1}{2}\alpha^- + \beta$ and $\sigma^2 = \omega/(1 - \phi)$ respectively equal to the persistence parameter and the unconditional variance of returns. This is identical to formula (9.22) for the GARCH(1, 1) model, as then $\alpha^- = 0$.

15.4.2 Comparisons of Historical Forecasts

Numerous comparisons of the accuracy of naive, EWMA, ARCH, and other historical volatility forecasts are discussed in Poon and Granger (2003). Of particular interest are comparisons between multi-parameter methods (such as GARCH) and single-parameter methods (such as EWMA). These comparisons should avoid insample parameter optimization, because different conclusions can arise for out-of-sample forecasts (see, for example, Dimson and Marsh 1990; Ederington and Guan 2002c).

The early study of Taylor (1986, Chapter 4) makes several comparisons between EWMA and GARCH(1, 1) predictions of the next daily absolute return for forty assets, including stocks, commodities, and currencies. Out-of-sample comparisons of mean squared errors marginally favor the EWMA approach when averages are taken across all the series. The recommended values of the smoothing parameter γ are 0.04 for equities and 0.1 for other assets. Both the EWMA and GARCH predictors are more accurate than the prior sample mean for every series. In contrast, Akgiray (1989) finds GARCH(1, 1) is a more accurate predictor than EWMA for monthly realized variances calculated from daily CRSP index returns between 1963 and 1986.

There is no consensus about the relative accuracy of historical volatility forecasts for equity markets. Tse (1991) and Tse and Tung (1992) prefer EWMA forecasts, respectively for Japan and Singapore. Brailsford and Faff (1996), however, find EWMA is poor for the Australian market and they favor forecasts from the GJR(1, 1) specification. Franses and van Dijk (1996) disagree. They recommend the QGARCH specification (equation (10.7)) for five European markets and find that GJR is much less accurate. Heynen and Kat (1994) evaluate but do not recommend asymmetric specifications; instead they prefer stochastic volatility forecasts to GARCH(1, 1) and EGARCH(1, 1) forecasts for seven major equity markets. Balaban, Bayar, and Faff (2003) is the most comprehensive study and it covers fourteen countries. Their most accurate forecasts of weekly and monthly volatility, obtained from daily index returns, are given by exponentially weighted averages. The variety of conclusions must be a consequence of using a variety of markets, data frequencies, and loss functions. Many of the apparent differences in accuracy across methods may not be statistically significant, as there are often a small number of independent out-of-sample forecast errors.

Exchange rate volatility may be easier to predict. Forecasts from the GARCH(1, 1) specification are recommended in the study of five currencies by Heynen and Kat (1994). They consider horizons ranging from 2 to 100 days, with an out-of-sample period from 1988 to 1992. West and Cho (1995), however, find that a constant is more accurate than GARCH and related forecasts, when making out-of-sample forecasts of the squares of weekly returns from five exchange rates between 1981 and 1989. This negative result may be a consequence of using weekly observations. Taylor (1987) instead uses daily high, low, and close prices, which are used to define a variety of DM/$ volatility forecasts that are more accurate than a constant during a short out-of-sample period from 1982 to 1983.

Several historical forecasts are compared by Ederington and Guan (2002c) for long daily time series of returns from US equities, the S&P 500 index, the DM/$ exchange rate, and US interest-rate securities. The clear winner from their comparisons is a linear function of the EWMA calculated from daily absolute returns. With f_{t+1} defined by (15.18), and with $y_{t+1} = |r_{t+1}|$, their preferred forecast is essentially $\tilde{f}_{t+1} = \alpha + \beta f_{t+1}$. The three parameters α, β, and γ are estimated from data that precedes time $t + 1$. This forecast outperforms a similar construction from squared returns and a variety of forecasts defined by ARCH models.

Intraday volatility forecasting is complicated by the intraday patterns discussed in Section 12.5. Martens et al. (2002) compare several methods that incorporate these patterns into forecasts of realized thirty-minute volatility for exchange rates.

15.5 Forecasts from Implied Volatilities

15.5.1 Which Implieds?

Following publication of the Black–Scholes formula, it was soon known that implied volatility (IV) covaries with realized volatility (Latane and Rendleman 1976; Chiras and Manaster 1978). To produce a volatility forecast from options prices we must select one or more of the available prices. These prices and their corresponding IVs depend on the time to expiry T, the exercise price X, and whether the option is a call or a put. As the call and put IVs are very similar, when the two options have the same T and X, it is usual to average the two numbers. Averaging across call and put implieds reduces any measurement error from nonsynchronous asset and option prices, because the typical call error is then negatively correlated with the put error.

The expiry time T should be matched with the horizon H of the volatility forecast. Many evaluations of IV forecasts first select T and then define $H = T$.

Other evaluations focus on a specific short horizon, usually between one day and one month. Then IVs are often calculated from the options that are nearest to expiry. The nearest IV is, however, particularly noisy when T is only a few days. It is therefore common to select the nearest IV when T is at least one or two weeks, and otherwise the second-nearest IV is selected. Differences between T and H might be expected to handicap IVs in forecasting competitions that also involve historical forecasts. The horizon mismatch can be avoided by estimating a term structure model for the IVs, but this involves extrapolation when H is less than the least value of T. Xu and Taylor (1995) obtain similar results from a term structure IV forecast and the nearest or second-nearest IV.

Smile effects in the IV matrix provide a variety of IV numbers once T has been chosen. This variety is often ignored by only using one value of X. The natural choice is then the X that is nearest to either the asset price S or the forward price F. These choices tend to focus on the most heavily traded options. Alternatively, some combination of IVs can be calculated, with the intention of reducing measurement error and thereby improving forecast accuracy. Most proposals give most weight to nearest-the-money options. Ederington and Guan (2002a) compare several weighting schemes for IVs calculated from S&P 500 futures options. They find that the choice is unimportant, providing bias is removed from the IV forecasts. In a related paper they average the IVs for the two nearest-the-money options (Ederington and Guan 2002b). The VIX index of Fleming et al. (1995) is a similar measure of the at-the-money IV.

Model-free volatility expectations are an important and recent alternative to implied volatilities (Jiang and Tian 2004). For a selected value of T, option prices for all available exercise prices X are used to approximate the variance expectation defined by equation (14.44).

15.5.2 Scaling

Implied volatilities are annualized standard deviations. The equivalent standard deviation over H days is given by the formula

$$IV_{scaled} = \sqrt{\frac{H}{N}} IV \qquad (15.24)$$

with N the number of days in one year. The standard convention is to count only trading days, since volatility is much lower when markets are closed. For a typical one-month forecast, H and N respectively equal 21 and 252.

15.5.3 Interpretation of Implieds as Forecasts

It is tempting to identify an IV forecast of volatility with the market's expectation of average volatility during the forecast horizon. The variation within IVs, from smile effects, shows that this identification cannot be correct for all exercise prices. Theoretical analysis of at-the-money IVs shows that they are candidates for market expectations when volatility is stochastic and additional assumptions are made. From Hull and White (1987), an essential assumption is that volatility has no risk premium, as discussed in Section 14.5. This is not an innocuous assumption. Bakshi and Kapadia (2003) show that some equity option prices are higher than would occur if there was no premium, which can be interpreted as reflecting a negative premium. This is consistent with observed biases in IV forecasts (e.g. Ederington and Guan 2002a,b). There is also evidence of a time-varying premium in currency option prices (Guo 1998).

A more pragmatic interpretation of an IV is that it contains all the information necessary to derive the market's expectation of average volatility during the forecast horizon. In particular, we might hope that some linear combination $\alpha_t + \beta_t IV_t$ is an appropriate forecast, with α_t and β_t estimated from observations of IV and the volatility target up to time t. This approach is followed in Blair et al. (2001b) and Ederington and Guan (2002a). The same idea, with α_t and β_t constant through time, is implicit in many studies that rank forecasting methods using the correlation between volatility outcomes and forecasts.

15.5.4 Comparisons of Implied and Historical Predictors

Several econometric methods and data frequencies have been used to compare the predictive accuracy of volatility forecasts obtained from options prices with those obtained from the history of the asset price. We now discuss several comparative studies. Low-frequency studies that use daily or less frequent price information are discussed under two headings. Initially, we concentrate on regression and related methods, followed in Section 15.6 by a detailed description of studies that are strongly influenced by ARCH methodology. These low-frequency studies lead to the conclusion that the best forecasts can usually be obtained from options prices. High-frequency studies are more recent and are reviewed in Section 15.7. There is much relevant additional information in intraday prices. Indeed, the general conclusion that forecasts from options prices are always best cannot be sustained in a high-frequency context.

15.5.5 Regression Analysis

Regression studies are based upon the encompassing methodology introduced in Fair and Shiller (1989). The model to be estimated in our context is

$$y_{t,t+H} = \alpha + \beta_1 f_{\mathrm{IV},t,t+H} + \beta_2 f_{\mathrm{TS},t,t+H} + e_{t,t+H} \tag{15.25}$$

with y the target to be predicted, f_{IV} a forecast from options prices, f_{TS} a forecast from a time series of returns, and e the forecast error. The forecasts are made at time t. Often the horizon H is the remaining life of a selected option and y is the realized standard deviation of returns from times $t + 1$ to $t + H$ inclusive. Then $t + H$ is the same for several times t and there is substantial autocorrelation among the overlapping errors e. This necessitates correction of standard errors, as explained by Jorion (1995), who applies the method of Hansen (1982). The options market contains all the relevant information about future volatility when $\beta_2 = 0$. At the other extreme, options prices are redundant when forecasting volatility if $\beta_1 = 0$. Estimates of β_1 and β_2 that are obtained by the ordinary least squares method are generally biased because of measurement errors in the IV forecasts. This bias is explained by Christensen and Prabhala (1998). They recommend an instrumental variable regression methodology that reduces the bias.

Ederington and Guan (2002b) provide regression results for S&P 500 futures options from 1983 to 1995. They also summarize and discuss regression results included in Day and Lewis (1992, 1993), Canina and Figlewski (1993), Lamoureux and Lastrapes (1993), Jorion (1995), Guo (1996), and Christensen and Prabhala (1998). Overall, the estimates of β_1 are nearly always positive and reject the null hypothesis $\beta_1 = 0$, while many estimates of β_2 are near zero and accept the possibility $\beta_2 = 0$. IV forecasts are, however, generally biased; univariate regressions of y against f_{IV} usually estimate β_1 to be below one and reject the joint hypothesis that $\alpha = 0$ and $\beta_1 = 1$. These are all tests about information content, rather than out-of-sample accuracy, as emphasized after equation (15.13).

Jorion (1995) investigates forecasts of exchange rate volatility, for DM/\$, SF/\$, and yen/\$ rates from 1985 to 1992. He first regresses daily absolute returns against

implieds, a historical moving average, and a GARCH(1, 1) predictor. The values
of R^2 and hypothesis tests lead to the conclusion that implieds contain all the
relevant information. The DM/\$ estimates are $\hat{\beta}_1 = 0.785$ and $\hat{\beta}_2 = 0.085$ for
the GARCH forecasts, with $R^2 = 0.052$. He then regresses the realized stan-
dard deviation during the remaining lifetimes of the options against the same
explanatory variables and obtains the same conclusions.

The empirical evidence for US equity indices mostly favors implied predictors. Canina and Figlewski (1993) assert that there was virtually no correlation
between implied volatility and subsequent realized volatility for the S&P 100
index, from March 1983 to March 1987. This conclusion does not hold after the
1987 crash, so it might just refer to an unusual period. Errors in the measurement
of implied volatilities and problems that stem from overlapping regressions are
the preferred explanations of Christensen and Prabhala (1998). Their analysis of
S&P 100 data from 1983 to 1995 finds implieds outperform historical forecasts
and often contain all relevant information, particularly after the crash. Similar
conclusions are given by Ederington and Guan (2002b) for the same years, but
for S&P 500 futures options. For predictions of the realized volatility during the
period from seven to ninety days before expiry they estimate $\hat{\beta}_1 = 0.515$ and
$\hat{\beta}_2 = 0.034$, after excluding three months around the 1987 crash. Fleming (1998)
uses the generalized method-of-moments methodology to lend further support to
the superior information content of implied forecasts of S&P 100 index volatility.
He finds implieds are biased predictors during his sample period from 1985 to
1992 that excludes the months around the crash. The forecast errors from implieds
are almost uncorrelated with historical predictors over horizons equal to one day,
one month, and the lifetimes of options. This contrasts with significant correlation
between implieds and the forecast errors made by historical predictors.

15.6 ARCH Forecasts that Incorporate Implied Volatilities

Volatility forecasts can be obtained by estimating ARCH models from the information provided by asset returns and implied volatilities. A forecast for the next
period is defined by the conditional variance of the next return and forecasts further ahead can also be derived. At time t the relevant information set is defined
as $I_t = \{r_{t-i}, v_{t-i}, i \geqslant 0\}$, with v_t a variable obtained from one or more implied
volatilities. Often v_t is the scaled implied for an option that is approximately
at-the-money and near to expiry. The scale factor defined in (15.24) ensures v_t is
a volatility measure for one trading period, rather than for one year. Following
Day and Lewis (1992), we now show how to include implied volatilities in ARCH
models, then we assess the volatility information content of option prices, and
finally we describe the relative accuracy of various forecasts derived from ARCH
specifications.

15.6.1 Variance Specifications

The general ARCH model described in Sections 9.5 and 9.6 is defined by conditional distributions:

$$r_t \mid I_{t-1} \sim D(\mu_t, h_t). \qquad (15.26)$$

The distribution D has conditional mean μ_t and conditional variance h_t. The distribution may be normal, or it may be fat-tailed and a function of a shape parameter. To simplify our presentation of some specifications for h_t we suppose μ_t is constant and henceforth denoted by μ.

The popular GARCH(1, 1) specification can be modified to incorporate the additional implied volatility variable v_t as follows:

$$h_t = \omega + \alpha(r_{t-1} - \mu)^2 + \beta h_{t-1} + \delta v_{t-1}^2. \qquad (15.27)$$

The parameter vector θ of the above specification contains $\mu, \alpha, \beta, \delta, \omega$ plus any shape parameter. With L the lag operator introduced in Section 3.5,

$$(1 - \beta L)h_t = \omega + \alpha(r_{t-1} - \mu)^2 + \delta v_{t-1}^2$$

and hence

$$h_t = \sum_{i=0}^{\infty} \beta^i L^i (\omega + \alpha(r_{t-1} - \mu)^2 + \delta v_{t-1}^2)$$

$$= \frac{\omega}{1 - \beta} + \sum_{i=0}^{\infty} \beta^i (\alpha(r_{t-1-i} - \mu)^2 + \delta v_{t-1-i}^2).$$

Consequently, the weights for the lagged options terms decay at the same rate as those for the lagged squared excess returns. This is an unnecessarily restrictive assumption. A more flexible specification is

$$h_t = \frac{\omega + \alpha(r_{t-1} - \mu)^2}{1 - \beta L} + \frac{\delta v_{t-1}^2}{1 - \beta_v L}, \qquad (15.28)$$

which requires an additional parameter, β_v. To evaluate (15.28), note that expressions of the form $y_t = x_t/(1 - \beta L)$ can be evaluated as $y_t = \beta y_{t-1} + x_t$ after assuming an initial value y_1.

Asymmetric specifications, such as the GJR-GARCH and the EGARCH models in Sections 9.7 and 10.2, can also be modified to include implied volatilities by adding an additional term to the definition of h_t. For example, Day and Lewis (1992) extend EGARCH(1) by changing equation (10.1) to

$$\log(h_t) = \mu_{\log(h)} + \Delta(\log(h_{t-1}) - \mu_{\log(h)}) + g(z_{t-1}) + \delta \log(v_{t-1}^2). \qquad (15.29)$$

15.6.2   Information Content: Theory

Parameter estimates, standard errors, and hypothesis test results are obtained by using the likelihood methods for ARCH models described in Sections 9.5, 9.6, and 10.4.

Tests for information content are of particular interest. There is no *incremental* volatility information in the options prices when a suitable constraint on the parameter vector defines the best model. For example, the options information is ignored when $\delta = 0$ in any one of equations (15.27)–(15.29). This null hypothesis can be assessed by estimating δ and an appropriate standard error, followed by calculating $t = \hat{\delta}/\text{s.e.}(\hat{\delta})$. Rejection of the null is equivalent to statistically significant incremental information.

The other extreme, as regards information content, is when all the relevant volatility information is to be found in option prices. This could be stated as $\alpha = 0$ for the modified GARCH(1, 1) model, which allows h_t to depend on $v_{t-2}, v_{t-3}, \ldots$ as well as on the latest implied v_{t-1}. At an efficient options market, v_{t-1} will contain all the relevant information when measurement errors are negligible, so the null hypothesis is often stated as $\alpha = \beta = 0$. There is then no incremental information in asset returns when the null hypothesis is true. These and similar hypotheses can be decided by likelihood-ratio tests.

Note that the tests do not assess forecast accuracy, because they are "in-sample." Parameter estimates obtained by maximizing the likelihood function, for data at times $1 \leqslant t \leqslant n$, are only known at time n when the data end. The estimated parameters will define *ex ante* forecasts if they are used to predict volatility for times $t > n$.

15.6.3   Information Content: Results

We now review the results of five empirical studies published between 1992 and 1996, which provide results for equities, commodities, and currencies using daily and weekly data. These studies indicate that implied volatilities are generally rich in relevant information. More recent studies also use high-frequency data and are reviewed in Section 15.7.

Day and Lewis (1992) estimate specifications that are similar to the modified GARCH(1, 1) and EGARCH(1) models, (15.27) and (15.29), with conditional normal distributions. Their data are weekly returns (in excess of the risk-free rate) and implied volatilities for the S&P 100 index, for the six years from November 1983 to December 1989. Their GARCH estimates of α and δ for Wednesday to Wednesday returns are respectively 0.27 and 0.32, with robust t-ratios equal to 1.17 and 3.00. However, Friday to Friday returns give t-ratios equal to 1.33 and 0.96. Likelihood-ratio tests indicate that each of the constraints $\alpha = \beta = 0$ and $\delta = 0$ should be rejected for the Wednesday data. Similar results are obtained from the EGARCH estimates. Day and Lewis conclude that both returns and implied volatilities contain incremental information. They suggest that the differences between the results for the Wednesday and the Friday returns may be explained by expiration day effects. Lamoureux and Lastrapes (1993) study two years of daily data for ten US stocks. Their log-likelihoods are higher for GARCH(1, 1) models than for conditional variances that are functions of implieds alone. This indicates that the historical information was the more informative source, but it is difficult to draw conclusions from such short data series.

Kroner, Kneafsey, and Claessens (1995) estimate the modified GARCH(1, 1) model, (15.27), for seven commodities during the four-year period from 1987 to 1990. They find incremental information in both implied volatilities and the history of returns.

Xu and Taylor (1995) also estimate the modified GARCH(1, 1) model, but with conditional generalized error distributions as defined in Section 9.6. Daily returns for four dollar exchange rates from 1985 to 1989 are used for the tests about information content. The implied volatilities come from spot FX options traded in Philadelphia. The null hypothesis that the options information is irrelevant is rejected at low significance levels by t-ratios and by likelihood-ratio test statistics. For example, if L_0 is the maximum log-likelihood when $\delta = 0$ and L_1 is the unconstrained maximum, then LR $= 2(L_1 - L_0)$ should be compared with χ_1^2. The LR values equal 36 for sterling, 45 for the Deutsche mark, 35 for the Swiss franc, and 10 for the yen (their Table 3). All these values exceed 6.63 and hence reject the null hypothesis at the 1% level. The respective estimates of δ are 1.02, 0.93, 0.82, and 0.39. In contrast, the null hypothesis of no incremental information in the returns can only be rejected for the yen. With L_0 now defined as the maximum log-likelihood when $\alpha = \beta = 0$, LR should be compared with χ_2^2. The null hypothesis is rejected at the 5% level when LR exceeds 5.99. The test values are less than 1 for all three European currencies, while LR equals 10.5 for the yen. As the in-sample estimates of α are essentially zero for the European currencies, the Philadelphia options contained all the relevant in-sample information about one-day ahead conditional variances for these currencies. The same conclusion is obtained by Guo (1996), who uses the same GARCH specification and similar exchange rate data for two currencies.

15.6.4 Forecasting Accuracy

Out-of-sample comparisons of forecasts are included in all the studies of information content that have just been reviewed. These comparisons are of more practical relevance than the in-sample tests of hypotheses about information content. Although it is easy to identify the most accurate out-of-sample forecast, it can be difficult to say if a forecast is significantly more accurate than some alternative. In the studies that we discuss, it is found that the in-sample and out-of-sample methodologies support the same conclusions about the sources of incremental information.

Day and Lewis (1992) evaluate R^2 for one-step ahead predictions of squared weekly returns, during the same period as their in-sample tests. The parameters in their ARCH forecasts are, however, obtained from earlier periods. All the values of R^2 from univariate regressions are low. Multivariate regressions do not succeed in identifying the source(s) of relevant information for making predictions. Lamoureux and Lastrapes (1993) innovate by predicting the sum of squared returns during the lifetimes of options. The least mean squared errors for ten stocks, over a two-year period, come from sample averages, followed by GARCH forecasts, with implieds the least accurate. Encompassing regressions provide a different ranking of the information in the forecasts, but these regressions have a lookback bias and are for few independent volatility outcomes.

Kroner et al. (1995) attempt the ambitious task of forecasting commodity price volatility over 225 calendar days. They assess several combinations of historical and implied forecasts and offer evidence that combinations provide the most accurate forecasts.

Xu and Taylor (1995) use daily time series to predict the realized volatility of exchange rates over four-week periods. Forecasts are made for thirty nonoverlapping periods, from October 1989 to February 1992. Their option forecasts are given by either a term structure model for implieds or by the option whose expiry time is nearest to four weeks. Rolling samples of 250 weeks of daily data are used to estimate ARCH parameters. The univariate comparison of forecasts finds that implied volatilities have smaller mean square errors than either GARCH(1, 1) forecasts or the previous realized volatility, for all four currencies considered. The RMSE values for the £/$ forecasts are typical and equal 0.033 for options forecasts, 0.036 for GARCH forecasts, and 0.041 for the previous realized volatility. No significant incremental information is found in the GARCH forecasts when bivariate regressions are estimated. Guo (1996) reports the same out-of-sample conclusion for similar data; implieds are efficient but biased predictors of sixty-day realized volatility and there is no incremental information in sixty-day moving averages and in GARCH forecasts.

15.7   High-Frequency Forecasting Results

Intraday prices provide more accurate measurements of realized volatility than daily prices. They also define more accurate volatility forecasts. Daily high and low prices suffice to obtain significant gains in forecast accuracy (Taylor 1987). In general, low-frequency predictors are outperformed by time series forecasts derived from sums of squared intraday returns (Andersen et al. [ABDL] 2003) and from sums of absolute intraday returns (Ghysels, Santa-Clara, and Valkanov 2004b).

We now discuss some high-frequency studies that compare the accuracy of historical and implied predictors. All the studies measure realized volatility by sums of squared intraday returns. Most use time series of daily sums to predict sums over horizons that range from one day to six months.

15.7.1 ARFIMA Forecasts versus Implied Predictors

Historical forecasts of realized volatility have been obtained from ARFIMA models, motivated by the evidence for long memory effects presented in Section 12.9. A typical model is defined for the logarithms of daily realized volatility $\hat{\sigma}_t^2$ and includes a mean level μ and autoregressive, fractional, and moving-average filters. A filtered sequence of i.i.d. variables ε_t defines the model:

$$\log(\hat{\sigma}_t^2) = \mu + \phi(L)^{-1}(1 - L)^{-d}\theta(L)\varepsilon_t. \tag{15.30}$$

Li (2002) compares out-of-sample ARFIMA forecasts with implied volatilities for three dollar exchange rates from 1995 to 1999. Forecasts are made of sums of squared five-minute returns over time intervals up to six months. The accuracy of the historical and implied forecasts is comparable for the one-month horizon, using the R^2 criterion. The values of R^2 for Deutsche mark, yen, and sterling series are respectively 47%, 51%, and 39% for the implied predictor, compared with 44%, 47%, and 42% for the historical predictor. The values of R^2 are much lower for the six-month horizon. They equal 12%, 14%, and 7% for the historical predictor, and only 2%, 7%, and 0% for the implied predictor. Martens and Zein (2004) note that the values of R^2 are inflated, because overlapping forecasts are used in the regressions.

Pong, Shackleton, Taylor, and Xu (2004) also analyze forecasts for the same three exchange rates, and present out-of-sample comparisons for the period from 1994 to 1998. They obtain ARMA(2, 1) and ARFIMA(1, d, 1) forecasts for realized volatility and compare them with GARCH forecasts and linear functions of at-the-money implied volatilities. They find that the AR(FI)MA forecasts are the most accurate for one-day and one-week forecast horizons; these forecasts then contain significant incremental information beyond the implied volatility information. For the longer horizons of one month and three months, the implied volatilities are at least as accurate as the historical forecasts and they incorporate almost all of the relevant information. The forecasting performances of the short (ARMA) and long (ARFIMA) memory specifications are very similar.

Martens and Zein (2004) study futures markets for the S&P 500 index, the yen/$ rate, and crude oil, from the mid 1990s to the end of 2000. They use both floor and electronic trading records to measure volatility over 24-hour periods. They provide strong evidence for incremental predictive information in the high-frequency returns, for all three assets. ARFIMA forecasts, implied volatility forecasts, and the averages of the two forecasts are compared for the three assets over six horizons, which vary from one to forty days. The average has the lowest values of a mean square error criterion for fifteen of the eighteen comparisons. It also has the highest value of R^2 for fourteen comparisons.

15.7.2 Historical versus Model-Free Option Forecasts

Jiang and Tian (2004) innovate by investigating the in-sample information content of the model-free variance expectation obtained from all option exercise prices, based upon equation (14.44). They evaluate forecasts of S&P 500 realized volatility, defined as the sum of squared five-minute returns, for the period from 1988 to 1994. Their historical forecast for a selected horizon is simply the latest observation of the realized volatility over the same horizon. Their regression results for nonoverlapping, thirty-day horizons provide strong evidence that the model-free forecast subsumes all information in the at-the-money implied volatility and the lagged realized volatility. When the forecasts and the target are specified as standard deviation measures, the regression coefficients are 0.84 for the model-free forecast, −0.05 for the at-the-money implied, and −0.01 for the lagged target, with R^2 equal to 74%. Similar conclusions and estimates are obtained for forecast horizons up to 180 days.

15.7.3 Forecasting Using ARCH Specifications

The ARCH methodology of Section 15.6 has been applied to high-frequency returns in at least two studies. Taylor and Xu (1997) apply the methodology to a year of one-hour conditional variances for DM/$ returns. Their variances are calculated from five-minute returns, hourly returns, and daily implied volatilities v_t; their specification for $h_{t,n}$ modifies equation (12.12) by adding a term $\delta\lambda_n^* v_{t-1}^2$ for hour n on day t. The five-minute returns are found to contain more information than the other variables. For the most general model, there is incremental in-sample information in both the five-minute returns and the implied volatilities, but none in the hourly returns. Forecasts of the realized DM/$ volatility during the next hour are evaluated. These forecasts are compared over a three-month period, with all parameters estimated from data for the previous nine months. Accuracy is measured by both the mean absolute error and the mean squared error. The forecasts that use both five-minute returns and options information are found to be more accurate than the forecasts that only make use of one of these two sources of information.

To conclude our review of empirical evidence, we now present a detailed summary of the study of S&P 100 index volatility by Blair, Poon, and Taylor (2001b). They supplement the GJR(1, 1) model for daily returns r_t by including (i) scaled implied volatilities v_t, (ii) dummy variables d_t that are one for the crash day of 19 October 1987 and are otherwise zero, and (iii) intraday realized volatilities $\hat\sigma_t^2$.

Table 15.1. Parameter estimates for an ARCH model
augmented by realized and implied volatilities.

(Results for the S&P 100 index, obtained using daily time series from January 1987 to December 1992. The conditional variance of the GJR(1, 1) model, augmented to include daily realized and implied volatilities, is defined by equation (15.31). The conditional mean is a constant plus a dummy variable on the crash day of 19 October 1987. The parameters are estimated by maximizing the quasi-log-likelihood function, defined by conditional normal densities. Robust t-ratios are shown in parentheses. The excess log-likelihoods are relative to model 1.)

Parameter	1	2	3	Model 4	5	6	7
$\omega \times 10^6$	2.6891	44.797	0.7298	9.6881	12.5372	6.3594	0.3110
	(1.53)	(3.85)	(1.48)	(0.74)	(0.72)	(0.55)	(0.70)
α	0.0136		0.0085		0.0741		0.0029
	(1.53)		(1.56)		(1.34)		(0.47)
α^-	0.0280		−0.0078		−0.0485		−0.0029
	(1.19)		(−0.79)		(−1.20)		(−0.47)
β	0.9417	0.9793	0.9773	0.5209	−0.3039	0.5954	0.9695
	(33.67)	(118.7)	(130.8)	(1.53)	(−1.93)	(3.58)	(95.89)
$\psi \times 10^3$	1.563	0.590	0.432	2.104	0.800	1.618	0.259
	(2.13)	(1.67)	(1.26)	(1.40)	(0.81)	(0.68)	(0.67)
γ		0.6396	0.5661			0.3718	0.3742
		(3.64)	(3.32)			(1.86)	(1.86)
β_{RV}		0.2523	0.2350			0.0360	0.0539
		(1.51)	(1.53)			(0.23)	(0.39)
δ				0.4313	0.4101	0.3283	0.2816
				(6.31)	(6.06)	(4.47)	(3.27)
β_v				0.1509	0.1553	0.1943	0.1778
				(2.73)	(2.59)	(3.40)	(3.49)
$\log L$	4833.66	4845.80	4848.35	4851.97	4858.48	4859.70	4860.79
Excess $\log L$		12.14	14.69	18.31	24.82	26.04	27.13

Tables 15.1–15.3 are reprinted from a paper in the *Journal of Econometrics*, volume 105, B. J. Blair, S.-H. Poon, and S. J. Taylor, Forecasting S&P 100 volatility: the incremental information content of implied volatilities and high frequency index returns, pp. 5–26, Copyright © (2001), with permission from Elsevier.

Their equation for the conditional variance is

$$h_t = \frac{\omega + (\alpha + \alpha^- S_{t-1})(r_{t-1} - \mu)^2 + \psi d_{t-1}}{1 - \beta L} + \frac{\gamma \hat{\sigma}_t^2}{1 - \beta_{RV} L} + \frac{\delta v_{t-1}^2}{1 - \beta_v L} \quad (15.31)$$

with $S_{t-1} = 1$ when $r_{t-1} < \mu$, otherwise $S_{t-1} = 0$.

The in-sample information content of daily returns, realized volatilities, and daily implied volatilities is assessed from six years of daily conditional variances, from 1987 to 1992. Five-minute and overnight returns are used to calculate $\hat{\sigma}_t^2$, while the VIX index of implied volatilities defines v_t. VIX is defined near the end of Section 14.4 and is intended to contain minimal measurement error. Table 15.1

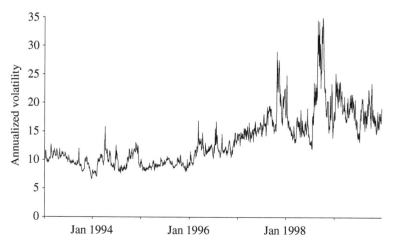

Figure 15.1.   Forecasts of index volatility.

shows the parameter estimates, robust t-ratios, and maximum log-likelihoods for seven models when conditional normal distributions are assumed. Models 1–6 are special cases of the general model 7 defined by (15.31). The columns of Table 15.1 are arranged in the order of ascending likelihood.

The second model only uses the information in realized volatilities and it has a substantially higher log-likelihood than the first model, which only uses daily returns. Combining the historical information sources into the third model leads to acceptance of the null hypothesis (at the 5% level) that all the relevant historical information is in the realized volatilities. The filter $1/(1 - \beta_{RV} L)$ is applied to the intraday variable. As the estimate of β_{RV} is only 0.25 for the second model, most of the information in intraday returns about future volatility comes from the most recent day.

The fourth model only uses the VIX information. As the log-likelihood is 6.17 more than for the second model, which has the same number of parameters, VIX was more informative than the intraday returns. The estimate of the parameter β_v in the filter $1/(1 - \beta_v L)$ is only 0.15, but it has a robust t-ratio equal to 2.73. Models 5–7 are compared with model 4 to decide if VIX contains all the relevant information about the next day's volatility. The key comparison is between model 4 and model 6, which uses both VIX and intraday returns. There are two additional parameters in model 6 and its log-likelihood is 7.73 more than for model 4. The likelihood-ratio test conclusively favors model 6, but it is not robust when the conditional distributions are not normal. The robust t-ratio for the intraday parameter γ equals 1.86 and the one-tail p-value for the test is 3%. It is concluded that there was probably some incremental in-sample information in the intraday returns. Note that comparing γ with δ does not give the correct interpretation of the relative importance of $\hat{\sigma}_{t-1}^2$ and v_{t-1}^2 when calculating h_t. As

Table 15.2. The relative accuracy of S&P 100 index volatility forecasts from January 1993 to December 1999. Values of P for forecasts of sums of (a) squared excess returns, and (b) squared five-minute and overnight returns.

(The tabulated numbers are proportions, P, of the variability of two realized volatility measures explained by four forecasts. The proportion P is defined by equation (15.9). It is a linear function of the mean square forecast error. HV is a simple historic volatility forecast. The GJR, INTRA, and VIX forecasts are obtained from special cases of the ARCH equation (15.31). Forecasts are made once a day. The values of P are calculated from $1769 - N$ forecasts.)

	Forecast	$N = 1$	$N = 5$	$N = 10$	$N = 20$
(a)	HV	0.037	0.089	0.112	0.128
	GJR	0.106	0.085	0.016	0.013
	INTRA	0.099	0.204	0.214	0.250
	VIX	0.115	0.239	0.297	0.348
(b)	HV	0.167	0.243	0.255	0.255
	GJR	0.375	0.289	0.169	0.181
	INTRA	0.383	0.494	0.455	0.465
	VIX	0.401	0.533	0.534	0.545

the average level of v_{t-1}^2 is 2.6 times that of $\hat{\sigma}_{t-1}^2$, for reasons explained by Blair et al., the calculation of h_t for model 6 is dominated by the information in VIX.

Blair et al. evaluate out-of-sample forecasts of the volatility of the S&P 100 index from 1993 to 1999. They predict realized volatility over one, five, ten, and twenty trading days and they calculate it in two ways, firstly from daily returns and secondly from five-minute and overnight returns. The forecasts are obtained from historical volatility (HV), based upon the variance of the previous 100 daily returns, and from three special cases of the ARCH model (15.31). Each special case uses only one source of information, thus the GJR forecasts use r_t, the INTRA forecasts use $\hat{\sigma}_t^2$, and the VIX forecasts use v_t. The parameters of (15.31) are estimated from rolling samples of length 1000 days and they are used to construct one-day-ahead forecasts h_t of the next squared daily excess return. Forecasts further ahead and for the intraday realized volatility are given by appropriate linear combinations of h_t. Figure 15.1 shows the volatility forecasts obtained from the VIX series, stated as annualized standard deviations.

Table 15.2 shows the proportions P of the variability of realized volatility that are explained by each of the four forecasts; P is a linear function of the mean square forecast error and is defined by (15.9). The VIX forecasts have the highest value of P, for both measures of realized volatility and for all four forecast horizons. The INTRA forecasts are the most accurate of those that use index returns, as should be expected. The values of P are much higher when intraday returns are used to calculate the realized volatility target, consistent with the predictions of Andersen and Bollerslev (1998b). The effect is seen most clearly

Table 15.3. Correlations and multiple correlations for S&P 100 index volatility forecasts from January 1993 to December 1999. Values of R^2 for forecasts of sums of (a) squared excess returns, and (b) squared five-minute and overnight returns.

(The tabulated numbers are the squared correlation R^2 from regressions of realized volatility on one or more forecasts. HV is a simple historic volatility forecast. The GJR, INTRA, and VIX forecasts are obtained from special cases of the ARCH equation (15.31). Forecasts are made once a day. The values of R^2 are calculated from $1769 - N$ forecasts.)

	Explanatory variables	$N = 1$	$N = 5$	$N = 10$	$N = 20$
(a)	HV	0.043	0.111	0.151	0.197
	GJR	0.118	0.181	0.189	0.223
	INTRA	0.099	0.212	0.238	0.285
	GJR and INTRA	0.119	0.217	0.240	0.287
	VIX	0.129	0.249	0.304	0.356
	VIX and INTRA	0.129	0.250	0.304	0.356
	VIX and GJR	0.139	0.253	0.304	0.356
	VIX, GJR, and INTRA	0.144	0.253	0.304	0.356
(b)	HV	0.185	0.282	0.309	0.335
	GJR	0.423	0.449	0.395	0.403
	INTRA	0.385	0.506	0.482	0.499
	GJR and INTRA	0.443	0.525	0.490	0.504
	VIX	0.445	0.567	0.559	0.569
	VIX and INTRA	0.448	0.575	0.563	0.576
	VIX and GJR	0.491	0.586	0.564	0.576
	VIX, GJR, and INTRA	0.495	0.586	0.565	0.577

for one-day-ahead forecasts, when P is approximately multiplied by four if the target is intraday realized volatility rather than the squared excess return.

Table 15.3 shows selected values of R^2 when the realized volatility measures are regressed against one or more of the four forecasts. For univariate regressions, VIX again has the highest values. Multivariate regressions that employ VIX only increase R^2 by small amounts that are negligible for the longer forecast horizons.

15.8 Concluding Remarks

The empirical evidence shows that the most accurate forecasts of volatility are often provided by functions of implied volatilities obtained from option prices. Implieds nearly always contain useful information. They usually need to be scaled to remove bias. This may arise because the Black–Scholes formula ignores the stochastic behavior of volatility and any volatility risk premium. Historical information about daily asset prices is also informative, particularly for short-term predictions up to a week ahead, but much (if not all) of this information is incorporated into option prices. Intraday asset prices contain further volatility information that is not reflected by option prices at some markets.

In assessing the evidence it is notable that genuine out-of-sample evaluations of forecasts are relatively rare. In-sample optimization of parameters, either explicitly or by the use of correlations to assess accuracy, unfortunately hinders the interpretation of many forecast comparisons.

Further Reading

Blair, B. J., S.-H. Poon, and S. J. Taylor. 2001. Forecasting S&P 100 volatility: the incremental information content of implied volatilities and high frequency index returns. *Journal of Econometrics* 105:5–26.

Day, T. E. and C. M. Lewis. 1992. Stock market volatility and the information content of stock index options. *Journal of Econometrics* 52:267–287.

Martens, M. and J. Zein. 2004. Predicting financial volatility: high-frequency time-series forecasts vis-à-vis implied volatility. *Journal of Futures Markets* 24:1005–1028.

Xu, X. and S. J. Taylor. 1995. Conditional volatility and informational efficiency of the PHLX currency options market. *Journal of Banking and Finance* 19:803–821.

16

Density Prediction for Asset Prices

Probability densities for future asset prices can often be obtained from previous asset prices and/or the prices of options. This chapter describes many of the methods that have been proposed and provides numerical examples of one-month-ahead predictive densities.

16.1 Introduction

A volatility forecast is a number that provides some information about the distribution of an asset price in the future. A far more challenging forecasting problem is to use market information to produce a predictive density for the future asset price. A realistic density will have a shape that is more general than provided by the lognormal family. In particular, a satisfactory density forecasting method will not constrain the levels of skewness and kurtosis for the logarithm of the predicted price.

It is quite easy to obtain a predictive density by using a history of asset prices to estimate and simulate an ARCH model. The density is then called a *real-world density*, as it reflects the dynamics of real prices. The letter P is used to indicate that a density applies to real prices. Predictive densities can also be obtained from a set of option prices, based upon a theoretical result for complete markets derived by Breeden and Litzenberger (1978). Many empirical methods estimate the *risk-neutral density* for the asset price at the time when the options expire. The letter Q is then used. One major distinction between a P-density and a Q-density is that the expectation of the former reflects the asset's risk while the expectation of the latter does not. There are other distinctions; for example, risk-neutral densities for equity indices are more negatively skewed than real-world densities.

Most of this chapter is about methods for estimating densities from option prices, covering first Q-densities and then transformations that provide P-densities. These estimation methods are reviewed by Jackwerth (1999). They deserve attention because option prices may be anticipated to be more informative than the history of asset prices, following our discussion of volatility forecasts in the previous chapter.

Density estimates have many applications. They can be used to assess market beliefs about political and economic events, to manage risk, to price exotic derivatives, to estimate risk preferences, and to evaluate the rationality of market prices.

Section 16.2 describes and illustrates estimation of a real-world density using a history of asset prices alone. Sections 16.3 and 16.4 then cover risk-neutral density (RND) concepts and estimation in general terms. They are followed by a description of several parametric methods in Sections 16.5 and 16.6 and by nonparametric methods in Section 16.7. Some advice about selecting from among the many RND methods is offered in Section 16.8.

Two types of transformations from Q- to P-densities are described in Section 16.9; one is based on stochastic discount factors and a representative agent model, while the other uses a recalibration function. Both transformations include parameters that can be estimated from a set of density predictions and the actual values of the prices that are predicted. The usefulness of these methods is related to the rationality of the inputs provided by option prices, which is discussed in Section 16.11.

Numerical examples are provided throughout the chapter for one-month-ahead prediction of the FTSE 100 index. An Excel spreadsheet is described in Section 16.10 for a method that is easy to implement, based upon fitting a curve to the implied volatility "smile." Prediction of the probabilities of extreme events is particularly difficult and some guidance is offered in Section 16.12.

16.2 Simulated Real-World Densities

A time-series model for prices, together with a price history, can be used to find a *real-world density* function for a later price by simulating the model. Different models and/or different histories will define different densities. ARCH models are ideal for simulations, because there is only one random term per unit time. These models are discussed here. A feasible but more complicated alternative is simulation of one of the stochastic volatility (SV) models defined in Chapter 11. General SV models are defined using two random terms per unit time, with the additional complication that the two stochastic processes may not be independent of each other.

16.2.1 ARCH Methodology

Simulation methods that provide option prices are discussed in Section 14.7. Similar methods are applicable when estimating real-world densities. Suppose that t counts trading days and that there is a history of m observed daily changes in price logarithms, $I_m = \{r_t, 1 \leqslant t \leqslant m\}$, with $r_t = \log(p_t) - \log(p_{t-1})$. Any dividends are excluded from the "returns" r_t as our intention is to simulate prices and not a measure of total wealth that incorporates dividend payments.

The history I_m is to be used to find the density of the price p_{m+n} after another n days of trading. The current and later prices are also denoted by $S = p_m$ and $S_T = p_{m+n}$ in this chapter, with T measuring the forecast horizon in years.

We suppose that an ARCH model for prices is estimated from the history I_m and that this model is also applicable into the future. For the general structure outlined in Sections 9.5 and 9.6,

$$r_t = \mu_t + e_t = \mu_t + h_t^{1/2} z_t, \tag{16.1}$$

with μ_t the conditional mean and h_t the conditional variance; these conditional moment functions are determined by the information I_{t-1} and a parameter vector θ. The first m standardized residuals z_t are assumed to be independent observations from a common distribution. This distribution has zero mean, unit variance and is denoted by $D(0, 1)$. The final n standardized residuals are random variables.

One simulation involves giving values to $z_{m+1}, \ldots, z_{m+n}$. These can be obtained either by making independent random draws from $D(0, 1)$ or by the bootstrap method that makes independent random selections from the set $\{z_1, \ldots, z_m\}$. The first method is used here, while Rosenberg and Engle (2002) use the bootstrap method to construct densities for the S&P 500 index. The history I_m provides μ_{m+1} and h_{m+1}. From a simulated z_{m+1} we obtain a simulated value for r_{m+1} using (16.1). This value is added to I_m to define I_{m+1} and hence μ_{m+2} and h_{m+2}. Then r_{m+2} follows from the value of z_{m+2} and (16.1) again. Repeating this process, one set of simulated values $z_{m+1}, \ldots, z_{m+n}$ defines one simulated price, $p_{m+n} = p_m \exp(r_{m+1} + r_{m+2} + \cdots + r_{m+n})$. This numerical method can be repeated as often as desired. A very large number of simulations are required to obtain an accurate estimate of the density; 200 000 replications are used by Rosenberg and Engle (2002).

16.2.2 An Example

We illustrate density estimation methods for the FTSE 100 index on one date throughout this chapter. We suppose that on Friday, 18 February 2000, we are interested in finding a density for the index four weeks later, when March futures and options conclude trading at 10:30 local time on 17 March. There are no holidays during these four weeks and thus $n = 20$. The index level was 6165 when the market closed on 18 February 2000. Figure 16.1 shows the index levels during the three months up to the day on which density estimates are sought.

Ten years of daily index levels are used to estimate an asymmetric volatility model. The simplest model of Glosten et al. (1993), defined in Section 9.7, is extended to the GJR(1, 1)-MA(1)-M specification, whose calculations are illustrated in Section 9.8. This specification has

$$\mu_t = \mu + \lambda h_t^{1/2} + \Theta e_{t-1} \tag{16.2}$$

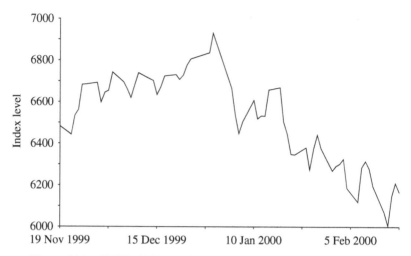

Figure 16.1.   FTSE 100 history for three months until 18 February 2000.

and

$$h_t = \omega + \alpha e_{t-1}^2 + \alpha^- S_{t-1} e_{t-1}^2 + \beta h_{t-1} \qquad (16.3)$$

with

$$S_{t-1} = \begin{cases} 1 & \text{if } e_{t-1} \leqslant 0, \\ 0 & \text{if } e_{t-1} > 0. \end{cases}$$

The ARCH-M parameter λ is insignificant for this dataset; consequently it is set to zero. The distribution of the standardized residuals is assumed to be the standardized t-distribution with ν degrees of freedom, for which the maximum log-likelihood is 21.2 more than for conditional normal distributions. The maximum likelihood estimates of the parameters are $\mu = 3.39 \times 10^{-4}$, $\Theta = 0.052$, $\omega = 5.14 \times 10^{-7}$, $\alpha = 0.0112$, $\alpha^- = 0.0497$, $\beta = 0.9583$, and $\nu = 12.8$. These values can be compared with the S&P 100 estimates in Table 9.3, for a similar ten-year period. It is notable that the persistence parameter of the FTSE data is close to one, as $\alpha + 0.5\alpha^- + \beta = 0.9944$. The magnitude of the asymmetric volatility effect is summarized by the ratio $A = (\alpha + \alpha^-)/\alpha$, which is discussed in Section 10.2. The estimated ratio is high at 5.4, indicating a substantial level of asymmetry, which creates negative skewness in multi-period returns. The first one-day conditional variance, h_{m+1}, equals 1.86×10^{-4}, which is equivalent to an annualized conditional standard deviation equal to 22%. This high level was only exceeded on 5% of the days in the ten-year estimation period. Thus the illustrative densities in this chapter have relatively high levels of dispersion.

A total of $N = 100\,000$ prices are simulated for the index level on 17 March. The parameter values are those already stated, except that ν is increased from 12.8 to 13. Half of the simulated prices are given by an antithetic variable method; if one price is given by $z_{m+1}, \ldots, z_{m+n}$, then the other follows from the values

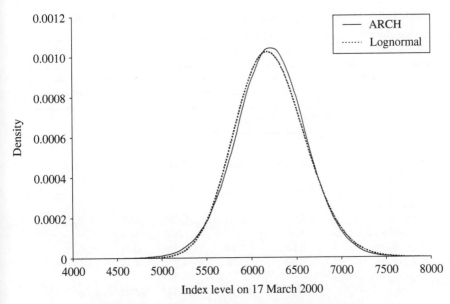

Figure 16.2. A real-world density from an ARCH model.

$-z_{m+1}, \ldots, -z_{m+n}$. The expected value on 17 March from the simulations is 6217, representing an expected rise of 0.84% over four weeks equivalent to 11% per annum. The estimated standard deviation of the change in the index level is $\hat{\sigma} = 389$ during this period of time. The actual value of the index on 17 March was 6558, which is 0.88 standard deviations higher than expected. Approximately 81.5% of the simulated index levels are below the actual outcome.

The N simulated values of p_{m+n}, denoted by $p^{(i)}$, are smoothed to provide the kernel estimate

$$f_P(x) = \frac{1}{Nb} \sum_{i=1}^{N} \phi\left(\frac{x - p^{(i)}}{b}\right) \tag{16.4}$$

with $\phi(\cdot)$ the standard normal density. The bandwidth b is set equal to 40, which approximately equals $\hat{\sigma}/N^{0.2}$. Figure 16.2 shows both the above density and the lognormal density that matches the mean and the variance of the simulated log prices. The simulated distribution of $\log(S_T)$ is slightly skewed to the left and has a small amount of excess kurtosis. The skewness equals -0.25 and the negative value occurs because the asymmetry parameter α^- is positive. The solid curve in Figure 16.2 represents the kernel estimate that can be compared with the dotted curve for the lognormal density; the kernel estimate is higher in the left tail because the ARCH density is skewed. Table 16.1 shows the mean, standard deviation, skewness, and kurtosis for the ARCH simulations and the matching lognormal density.

Table 16.1. Moments for a selection of real-world density estimation methods.
(Results are given for the density of the FTSE 100 index on 17 March 2000, estimated from
index levels and option prices known four weeks earlier. The ARCH specification is defined
in Section 16.2. The generalized beta distribution is defined in Section 16.5. The three GB2
columns are for the risk-neutral density estimated using option prices and two real-world
densities defined in Section 16.9, which are motivated by utility and calibration theory.)

| | ARCH | | GB2 | | |
| | Density P | Lognormal match P | RND Q | Utility P | Calib. P |
Type					
Index statistics					
Mean	6217	6217	6229	6295	6303
Standard deviation	389	391	463	434	394
Skewness	-0.04	0.19	-0.80	-0.71	-0.67
Kurtosis	3.23	3.06	4.37	4.26	4.16
Log(index) statistics					
Mean	8.733	8.733	8.734	8.745	8.747
Standard deviation	0.0629	0.0629	0.0774	0.0714	0.0644
Skewness	-0.25	0	-1.16	-1.04	-0.96
Kurtosis	3.39	3	5.82	5.45	5.14

16.3 Risk-Neutral Density Concepts and Definitions

16.3.1 Preliminary Remarks

The theoretical price of a European option is often written as the discounted
expectation of the final payoff. This is valid when an appropriate probability distribution for the final price of the underlying asset is used. One textbook example
is the binomial set-up where the asset price is now S and will be either $S_T = uS$
or $S_T = dS$ when the option expires. The theoretical price of a call option with
exercise price X is then given by a no-arbitrage argument as

$$c(X) = e^{-rT}[p \max(uS - X, 0) + (1 - p) \max(dS - X, 0)], \qquad (16.5)$$

where p is a risk-neutral probability that prevents arbitrage profits and r is the
risk-free rate (Hull 2000, Chapter 9). The probability p does *not* equal the real-
world chance of the outcome $S_T = uS$ when investors demand a risk premium
for holding the asset. A second textbook example occurs when prices follow
geometric Brownian motion and option prices are given by the Black–Scholes
formula. There is then a lognormal risk-neutral density for S_T, say $\psi(x)$, for
which

$$c(X) = e^{-rT} \int_X^\infty (x - X)\psi(x)\,dx. \qquad (16.6)$$

See, for example, Section 14.3 or Hull (2000, Appendix 11A). This risk-neutral density is not the real-world density of S_T when investors are risk averse.

Theoreticians develop and traders apply pricing formulae that are more complicated than the above examples. The concept of a *risk-neutral density* (RND) then continues to be applicable. Our interest is in using observed market prices for options to infer an *implied* risk-neutral density. Once we have an implied RND we can hope that a simple transformation will give us a useful real-world density. This section continues with notation, definitions, and some key theoretical results. It is followed in Section 16.4 by general principles for finding implied RNDs and then by concrete examples of methods and results in Sections 16.5–16.7. The choice of a best method is discussed in Section 16.8. Transformations that provide real-world densities are covered in Section 16.9, leading to Excel examples in Section 16.10.

Bliss and Panigirtzoglou (2002) list several studies that use implied RNDs to evaluate market expectations concerning economic and political events, as well as asset prices (e.g. Malz 1996; Coutant, Jondeau, and Rockinger 2001; Gemmill and Saflekos 2000). Central banks, in particular, are extremely interested in market perceptions of price distributions (e.g. Söderlind and Svensson 1997), although much of their research has not been published.

16.3.2 Notation and Assumptions

We follow the notation of Chapter 14. The price of an underlying asset now is S and options expire after T years when the asset price is S_T. Prices are assumed to have continuous distributions. The risk-free rate is constant and equals r and the asset pays dividends at a constant rate q, as discussed in Section 14.2. The forward price now to buy the asset at time T, which excludes arbitrage profits, is

$$F = Se^{(r-q)T}. \qquad (16.7)$$

This is also referred to as the futures price and it is a relevant theoretical quantity even if there is no trade in forward or futures contracts. When the asset is a futures contract, $q = r$ and $S = F$.

Only European options are considered in the theoretical analysis. We only discuss call options because the prices of calls and puts are connected by the parity equation (14.2). The exercise price of a general option is X and the call price is then denoted by $c(X)$; it is implicit that c also depends on other variables, such as S and T. Any value $X \geqslant 0$ is permitted, regardless of the finite number of exercise prices that are traded at real markets.

The functions $\phi(\cdot)$ and $N(\cdot)$ continue to respectively represent the density function and the cumulative distribution function of the standard normal distribution.

16.3.3   A Definition of the RND

The letter Q indicates that expectations and probabilities are those that apply in a risk-neutral context. A theoretical risk-neutral density f_Q for S_T is defined here as the density for which theoretical European option prices are the discounted expectations of final payoffs; thus,

$$c(X) = e^{-rT} E^Q[(S_T - X)^+] \tag{16.8}$$

$$= e^{-rT} \int_0^\infty \max(x - X, 0) f_Q(x)\, dx$$

$$= e^{-rT} \int_X^\infty (x - X) f_Q(x)\, dx, \tag{16.9}$$

for a *complete* set of exercise prices, i.e. for all $X \geqslant 0$.

RNDs are defined for all $x \geqslant 0$. Of course $f_Q(x) \geqslant 0$ and

$$\int_0^\infty f_Q(x)\, dx = 1,$$

although some empirical estimates violate one or both of these constraints! A call option that has exercise price zero is almost identical to a forward contract, except the former requires payment now while the latter involves settlement at time T. A payment of either $c(0)$ now or $F = e^{rT} c(0)$ at time T will obtain the asset at time T. Thus we deduce an important constraint on the RND:

$$F = E^Q[S_T] = \int_0^\infty x f_Q(x)\, dx. \tag{16.10}$$

Any European contingent claim whose payoff at time T is solely a function of S_T can be valued using the RND, which provides further motivation for empirical work. The fair price, to be paid now, for the payoff $g(S_T)$ is

$$e^{-rT} E^Q[g(S_T)] = e^{-rT} \int_0^\infty g(x) f_Q(x)\, dx. \tag{16.11}$$

The existence and uniqueness of the RND follows from an equation of Breeden and Litzenberger (1978), assuming $c(X)$ has been defined for all $X \geqslant 0$ and hence the market is complete. Any RND then gives the following results, by differentiating (16.9):

$$\frac{\partial c}{\partial X} = -e^{-rT} \int_X^\infty f_Q(x)\, dx \tag{16.12}$$

and

$$\frac{\partial^2 c}{\partial X^2} = e^{-rT} f_Q(X). \tag{16.13}$$

Thus if any RND exists it must be unique. To demonstrate its existence, begin with (16.13) and substitute this expression into the integral on the right-hand side of (16.9). Providing $c(X)$ satisfies weak conditions that prevent arbitrage profits, f_Q is a density function and the integral simplifies to $e^{rT} c(X)$ as required.

16.3.4 Lognormal Example

We have already discussed risk-neutral pricing for the Black–Scholes framework in Section 14.3, and we now summarize the main results. When real-world prices follow a geometric Brownian motion process,

$$dS/S = \mu \, dt + \sigma \, dW,$$

and real-world probabilities are obtained from the measure denoted by P, then

$$\log(S_T) \stackrel{P}{\sim} N(\log(S) + \mu T - \tfrac{1}{2}\sigma^2 T, \sigma^2 T). \tag{16.14}$$

Replacing μ by $r - q$, and using (16.7), gives the risk-neutral distribution

$$\log(S_T) \stackrel{Q}{\sim} N(\log(F) - \tfrac{1}{2}\sigma^2 T, \sigma^2 T) \tag{16.15}$$

and hence the lognormal RND:

$$\psi(x \mid F, \sigma, T) = \frac{1}{x\sigma\sqrt{2\pi T}} \exp\left[-\frac{1}{2} \left\{ \frac{\log(x) - [\log(F) - \tfrac{1}{2}\sigma^2 T]}{\sigma\sqrt{T}} \right\}^2 \right]$$

$$= \frac{1}{x\sigma\sqrt{T}} \phi(d_2(x)). \tag{16.16}$$

Here $d_2(x)$ is a familiar term from the Black–Scholes formula, (14.8). We use the above parametrization of the lognormal density in this chapter. Inserting the density into (16.9) leads to the Black–Scholes formula,

$$c_{BS}(S, T, X, r, q, \sigma) = c_{BS}(F, T, X, r, r, \sigma)$$

$$= e^{-rT} \int_X^\infty (x - X)\psi(x \mid F, \sigma, T) \, dx. \tag{16.17}$$

This conclusion can be checked by using (14.18).

16.4 Estimation of Implied Risk-Neutral Densities

An implied volatility provides information about the future dispersion of the asset price from one observed option price. An implied risk-neutral density is a far more ambitious object—it provides information about the entire distribution of a later asset price from several observed option prices. Theory provides few insights into an appropriate specification for the RND $f_Q(x)$. Many types of density functions provide reasonable fits to observed option prices, so there is plenty of scope for individual preferences. These are apparent in a variety of methods, that are surveyed in Jackwerth (1999) and, to a lesser degree, in Bahra (1997), Cont (1999), Jondeau and Rockinger (2000), and Bliss and Panigirtzoglou (2002). We first describe the estimation problem and then introduce some illustrative data.

16.4.1   Three Equivalent Problems

The following three problems are essentially identical.

(i) Specify the RND $f_Q(x)$ for all $x \geqslant 0$.

(ii) Specify call prices $c(X)$ for all $X \geqslant 0$.

(iii) Specify implied volatilities $\sigma_{\text{implied}}(X)$ for all $X > 0$.

To see this, note that f_Q gives c from (16.9), while c gives f_Q from (16.13). Also, any price c within the rational bounds ((14.3) and (14.4)) defines an implied volatility (and vice versa) by solving

$$c(X) = c_{\text{BS}}(S, T, X, r, q, \sigma_{\text{implied}}(X)). \qquad (16.18)$$

These are equivalent problems providing it is impossible to make arbitrage profits; for example, $\sigma_{\text{implied}}(X)$ must not be a function that has $\partial^2 c / \partial x^2 < 0$ and hence $f_Q(x) < 0$ for some values of x.

Data Issues

Implied RNDs are extracted from a dataset of N contemporaneous European call prices, all of which expire after T years. Call i has exercise price X_i, option price $c_{\text{m}}(X_i)$, and implied volatility $\sigma_{\text{m,implied}}(X_i)$. The additional subscript "m" is employed in this notation to emphasize that the values are given by market prices.

The original data may be rather different. American option prices can be converted to approximately equivalent European prices by inserting American implied volatilities into a Black–Scholes formula; approximate American implieds can be obtained from the formulae of Barone-Adesi and Whaley (1987). Any available European put prices should be converted to call prices, using the put–call parity equation (14.2).

After making as many of the above conversions as necessary, we may now have pairs of option and asset prices, $c'_{\text{m}}(X'_i)$ and S_i, for similar but varying times T_i until expiry. Approximately contemporaneous prices $c_{\text{m}}(X_i)$ are given by inserting the implieds for the noncontemporaneous data into the Black–Scholes call formula for suitable fixed values of S and T. If we assume that the implied volatility is only a function of the exercise price divided by the underlying asset price, then X_i and $c_{\text{m}}(X_i)$ can be defined by

$$\frac{X_i}{S} = \frac{X'_i}{S_i},$$

$$c'_{\text{m}}(X'_i) = c_{\text{BS}}(S_i, T_i, X'_i, r, q, \sigma'_i),$$

$$c_{\text{m}}(X_i) = c_{\text{BS}}(S, T, X_i, r, q, \sigma'_i). \qquad (16.19)$$

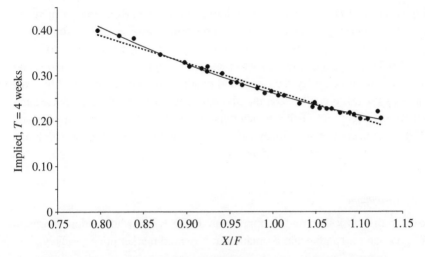

Figure 16.3. Implied volatilities for FTSE options on 18 February 2000.

Some exercise prices may occur more than once in a dataset. It may be appropriate to retain repeated values. Alternatively, they can be eliminated by only keeping the observations that are closest to a particular time. The standard rule for any choices between calls and puts that have the same exercise prices is to prefer out-of-the-money options. Outliers occur in some option datasets, that can be detected by checking for violations of boundary conditions and for implied volatilities that are incompatible with the other observations.

Illustrative Data

Densities are estimated on 18 February 2000 for the level of the FTSE 100 index when the March 2000 options expire at 10:30 on 17 March. Only the prices of European options are used here because they were traded more often than American options. These options can be valued as options on March futures because the options expire when the futures are finally settled. Each option price can be matched with an almost contemporaneous futures transaction.

The European option price data provided by LIFFE contains 80 March trades on 18 February and 96 matched pairs of bid and ask quotations. After deleting 2 trades and 2 quote pairs that are obviously misrecorded, the data have 26 different exercise prices for trades and 30 for quotations. There is less noise in the mid-quote implied volatilities, when they are plotted against the exercise prices. This is a good reason to prefer the mid-quote option prices and they also have a slightly wider range of exercise prices. Only one trade observation is retained, corresponding to an exercise price that has no quotes. The 31 exercise prices range from 4975 to 7025 with steps of size 50 between many of them. When an exercise price X_i' had more than one quote during the day we only retain the quote nearest to 12:00.

Equation (16.19) was then used to define contemporaneous option prices at 12:00 on 18 February, when the March futures price was $F = 6229$, after replacing S by F and q by r. The adjusted exercise prices range from 4966 to 7013. Figure 16.3 displays the implied volatilities, plotted against X/F. The dotted and solid lines are respectively the linear and quadratic functions provided by least squares estimates. It can be seen that the implieds vary considerably, decreasing from 40% for deep out-of-the-money puts to 26% for at-the-money options and to 20% for some out-of-the-money calls. The implied volatility function is almost linear over $0.80 \leqslant X/F \leqslant 1.05$ but decreases less rapidly to the right of this range.

16.4.2 Estimation

The estimation task is to find an appropriate RND $f_Q(x)$ whose pricing formula $c(X)$ gives an acceptable approximation to observed market prices, thus

$$c_{\mathrm{m}}(X_i) \cong c(X_i) = \mathrm{e}^{-rT} \int_{X_i}^{\infty} (x - X_i) f_Q(x)\, \mathrm{d}x, \quad 1 \leqslant i \leqslant N. \qquad (16.20)$$

Equivalently, the density $f_Q(x)$ should correspond to an implied volatility function $\sigma_{\mathrm{implied}}(X)$ that has

$$\sigma_{\mathrm{m,implied}}(X_i) \cong \sigma_{\mathrm{implied}}(X_i), \quad 1 \leqslant i \leqslant N. \qquad (16.21)$$

Assuming the X_i are sorted from low to high values, we may be able to obtain an implied RND that fits well throughout the range from X_1 to X_N. However, *all* estimation methods implicitly use extrapolation to estimate $f_Q(x)$ in the tail regions, $x < X_1$ and $x > X_N$. Ideally, the estimated risk-neutral probability of the outcome $X_1 \leqslant S_T \leqslant X_N$ will almost equal one. All methods also use interpolation between pairs of exercise prices, but this rarely leads to unreasonable estimates between X_1 and X_N.

The RND is often a parametric function $f_Q(x \mid \theta)$ of M parameters, $\theta = (\theta_1, \ldots, \theta_M)$. It is then common to estimate the parameters by minimizing a sum of squared errors. One criterion is

$$G(\theta) = \sum_{i=1}^{N} (c_{\mathrm{m}}(X_i) - c(X_i \mid \theta))^2,$$

with

$$c(X_i \mid \theta) = \mathrm{e}^{-rT} \int_{X_i}^{\infty} (x - X_i) f_Q(x \mid \theta)\, \mathrm{d}x. \qquad (16.22)$$

Another plausible possibility is

$$G(\theta) = \sum_{i=1}^{N} (\sigma_{\mathrm{m,implied}}(X_i) - \sigma_{\mathrm{implied}}(X_i \mid \theta))^2. \qquad (16.23)$$

These criteria must be modified when the number of parameters is large relative to the number of observations, particularly when $M \geqslant N$. This can be done by adding a penalty function to G that is higher when the density is less smooth. Jackwerth and Rubinstein (1996) use a penalty function similar to

$$\lambda \int_0^\infty \left(\frac{\partial^2 f_Q(x \mid \theta)}{\partial x^2} \right)^2 dx \tag{16.24}$$

for some positive constant λ. General weighted least squares criteria and penalty functions are discussed by Bliss and Panigirtzoglou (2002).

16.5 Parametric Risk-Neutral Densities

The discussion of RND specifications is separated into three parts. Parametric specifications of the RND and the implied volatility function are respectively covered in this section and the next section. Nonparametric specifications are then reviewed in Section 16.7.

The lognormal density function $\psi(x \mid F, \sigma, T)$ is an example of a parametric RND. As F is the market's forward price for a specific time T, the only free parameter is σ. One free parameter cannot, however, generate densities that are sufficiently flexible to explain observed option prices. We cover four parametric density specifications for the price S_T, all of which provide "closed-form" option pricing formulae. These specifications have between three and five free parameters. We also note some of their advantages and disadvantages.

16.5.1 Lognormal Mixtures

A mixture of two lognormal densities is probably the most popular parametric RND specification and it was first proposed by Ritchey (1990). The mixture density is a weighted combination of lognormal densities,

$$f_Q(x) = p\psi(x \mid F_1, \sigma_1, T) + (1 - p)\psi(x \mid F_2, \sigma_2, T). \tag{16.25}$$

This is a density function if $0 \leqslant p \leqslant 1$ and it is an RND if

$$F = pF_1 + (1 - p)F_2.$$

The standard deviation, skewness and kurtosis of S_T can be derived from

$$E[S_T^n] = pF_1^n \exp(\tfrac{1}{2}(n^2 - n)\sigma_1^2 T) + (1 - p)F_2^n \exp(\tfrac{1}{2}(n^2 - n)\sigma_2^2 T). \tag{16.26}$$

There are five parameters in the vector $\theta = (F_1, F_2, \sigma_1, \sigma_2, p)$. The risk-neutrality constraint reduces the number of free parameters to four, which is sufficient to obtain a variety of flexible shapes. Figures 16.4 and 16.5 show examples for one-month densities when $F = 6000$, $F_2 = F_1 + 600$, and $\sigma_1 = 2\sigma_2$. On the first of these figures, $p = 0.25$ and $\sigma_1 = 0.2$, 0.3, or 0.4. On the second, $p = 0.1$,

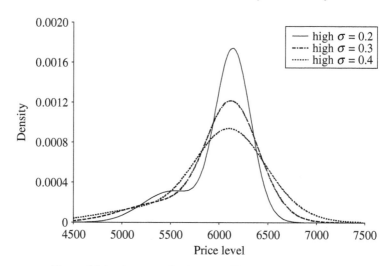

Figure 16.4. Lognormal mixtures, different volatility levels.

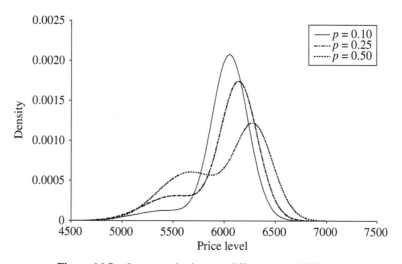

Figure 16.5. Lognormal mixtures, different probabilities p.

0.25, or 0.5 and $\sigma_1 = 0.2$. These illustrative densities are skewed to the left, as occurs in many empirical examples; some are also bimodal.

A mixture distribution is particularly appropriate for asset prices when the density of S_T depends on one of two future states that will be determined before time T. For example, p might be the probability that a government is re-elected, with $\psi(x \mid F_1, \sigma_1, T)$ the density conditional on this event and $\psi(x \mid F_2, \sigma_2, T)$ the density conditional on the event not occurring (Gemmill and Saflekos 2000). However, mixture densities are generally used as RNDs when there is no obvious motivation from a set of future states.

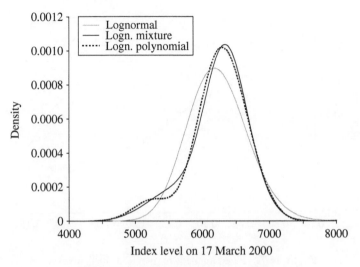

Figure 16.6. Three risk-neutral densities.

Mixing lognormal densities is the recipe that makes option prices a mixture of Black–Scholes prices. As

$$c_{\mathrm{BS}}(F, T, X, r, r, \sigma) = e^{-rT} \int_X^\infty (x - X)\psi(x \mid F, \sigma, T)\,dx, \qquad (16.27)$$

the theoretical option prices are

$$c(X \mid \theta, r, T)$$

$$= e^{-rT} \int_X^\infty (x - X)[p\psi(x \mid F_1, \sigma_1, T) + (1 - p)\psi(x \mid F_2, \sigma_2, T)]\,dx$$

$$= pc_{\mathrm{BS}}(F_1, T, X, r, r, \sigma_1) + (1 - p)c_{\mathrm{BS}}(F_2, T, X, r, r, \sigma_2). \qquad (16.28)$$

It is usually fairly easy to estimate the RND parameters, by minimizing one of the functions defined in Section 16.4, although difficulties locating the global minimum have been reported (Jondeau and Rockinger 2000; Coutant et al. 2001; Bliss and Panigirtzoglou 2002). It is therefore advisable to compare the optimization results obtained from several initial values. The constraint that the variables F_1, F_2, σ_1, σ_2 are all positive can usually be omitted from the optimization problem. Note, though, that there are two solutions to the estimation problem because the numerical values of (F_1, σ_1, p) and $(F_2, \sigma_2, 1 - p)$ can always be interchanged.

The parameter estimates for the illustrative FTSE 100 March options on 18 February 2000 are $p = 23.8\%$, $F_1 = 5735$, $\sigma_1 = 31.1\%$, $F_2 = 6383$, and $\sigma_2 = 18.1\%$. They are obtained by minimizing the sum of squared errors for 31 call prices, giving a minimum value of 175 for the function G defined by (16.22). The estimated standard deviation of the price errors equals 2.5, which is less than the average bid–ask spread. Figure 16.6 shows the estimated RND as a solid

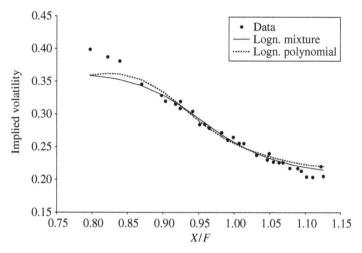

Figure 16.7. Fitted implieds for two RND methods.

curve. The density is skewed to the left because the higher standard deviation is associated with the lower of the two lognormal means. Figure 16.6 also shows the density estimate when the RND is lognormal, with $\sigma = 25.9\%$, represented by a light line. Compared with the lognormal, the mixture density is seen to have more density in the left tail and less in the right tail. Figure 16.7 shows the estimated implied volatility function, again as a solid curve. The fit is satisfactory except for the exercise prices furthest from the futures price. Table 16.2 includes the mean, standard deviation, skewness, and kurtosis for both S_T and $\log(S_T)$. The estimated probabilities beyond the minimum and maximum exercise prices are also tabulated. They equal 1.2% and 2.4%, so that more than 96% of the estimated probability is for index values within the range of the traded exercise prices.

Lognormal mixtures have been estimated for interest rates (Bahra 1997; Söderlind and Svensson 1997; Coutant et al. 2001), exchange rates (Campa et al. 1998; Jondeau and Rockinger 2000), and equity indices (Gemmill and Saflekos 2000; Bliss and Panigirtzoglou 2002; Anagnou, Bedendo, Hodges, and Tompkins 2002; Liu, Shackleton, Taylor, and Xu 2004). A mixture of three lognormals has seven free parameters. It is estimated by Melick and Thomas (1997) for the prices of crude oil futures during the Gulf War in 1990 and 1991. They motivate the mixture by uncertainty about the future supply of Kuwaiti oil.

The mixture method is fairly easy to apply, it guarantees a nonnegative estimated density and it is intuitive when p can be identified with the probability of a relevant future event. The estimation of four free parameters may, however, be excessive, leading to estimates that are sensitive to the discreteness of option prices (Bliss and Panigirtzoglou 2002). Another potential shortcoming is that estimated RNDs may be bimodal and hence may be counterintuitive.

Table 16.2. Moments for a selection of risk-neutral density estimation methods. (Results are given for the density of the FTSE 100 index on 17 March 2000, estimated from option prices four weeks earlier. G is the minimum of the sum of squared option pricing errors, across 31 exercise prices that range from 4975 to 7025. The six methods are the lognormal, a mixture of two lognormals, the generalized beta, the lognormal-polynomial, and linear and quadratic implied volatility functions.)

	Logn.	Logn. mixture	GB2	Logn. poly.	IVF linear	IVF quad.
Minimum value of G	5740	175	118	241	171	115
Index statistics						
Mean	6229	6229	6229	6229	6229	6229
Standard deviation	447	460	463	463	460	467
Skewness	0.22	−0.66	−0.80	−0.63	−0.79	−0.98
Kurtosis	3.08	3.71	4.37	4.02	4.02	5.66
Probability below lowest X	0.1%	1.2%	1.4%	1.5%	1.3%	1.5%
Probability above highest X	4.6%	2.4%	2.1%	2.3%	1.3%	1.8%
Log(index) statistics						
Mean	8.734	8.734	8.734	8.734	8.734	8.734
Standard deviation	0.0717	0.0764	0.0774	0.0769	0.0767	0.0790
Skewness	0	−0.93	−1.16	−0.93	−1.11	−1.58
Kurtosis	3	4.30	5.82	4.50	5.26	10.48

16.5.2 The GB2 Distribution

Four parameters are required to obtain general combinations of the mean, variance, skewness, and kurtosis of future asset prices. Bookstaber and McDonald (1987) and McDonald and Bookstaber (1991) propose and apply the generalized beta distribution of the second kind, called GB2, that has four positive parameters, a, b, p, and q. The density function for S_T is

$$f_{\text{GB2}}(x \mid a, b, p, q) = \frac{a}{b^{ap} B(p, q)} \frac{x^{ap-1}}{[1 + (x/b)^a]^{p+q}}, \quad x > 0. \quad (16.29)$$

The B function is defined in terms of the gamma function by

$$B(p, q) = \Gamma(p)\Gamma(q)/\Gamma(p + q). \quad (16.30)$$

Bookstaber and McDonald (1987) describe several special cases, including a lognormal limit when $a \to 0$ and $q \to \infty$ in a particular way.

Multiplication of the GB2 density by x^n defines a function that is proportional to another GB2 density, in which p is replaced by $p + (n/a)$ and q is replaced by $q - (n/a)$:

$$x^n f_{\text{GB2}}(x \mid a, b, p, q)$$
$$= \frac{b^n B(p + n/a, q - n/a)}{B(p, q)} f_{\text{GB2}}(x \mid a, b, p + n/a, q - n/a), \quad (16.31)$$

providing $n < aq$. This is a very useful property. It permits a simple and economically meaningful transformation of a GB2 Q-density into a GB2 P-density, as we will see in Section 16.9. It also leads to the following expression for the moments of the distribution:

$$E[S_T^n] = \frac{b^n B(p + n/a, q - n/a)}{B(p, q)} \quad \text{when } n < aq. \tag{16.32}$$

Substituting $n = 1$ gives the constraint that ensures the density is risk-neutral, assuming $aq > 1$:

$$F = \frac{b B(p + 1/a, q - 1/a)}{B(p, q)}. \tag{16.33}$$

This result shows that b is a scale parameter. We may regard a, p, and q as the free parameters and then derive b from F and the above constraint. It is difficult to interpret the free parameters. Note that moments do not exist when $n \geqslant aq$. The kurtosis of S_T is therefore infinite when $aq \leqslant 4$.

Option prices now depend on the cumulative distribution function (c.d.f.) of the GB2 distribution, denoted by F_{GB2}. This function can be evaluated using the c.d.f. of the beta distribution, denoted by F_β, which is the incomplete beta function:

$$F_\beta(u \mid p, q) = \frac{1}{B(p, q)} \int_0^u t^{p-1} (1 - t)^{q-1} \, dt. \tag{16.34}$$

A change of variable inside an integral shows that

$$F_{\text{GB2}}(x \mid a, b, p, q) = F_{\text{GB2}}((x/b)^a \mid 1, 1, p, q) = F_\beta(u(x, a, b) \mid p, q) \tag{16.35}$$

with the function u defined by

$$u(x, a, b) = \frac{(x/b)^a}{1 + (x/b)^a}. \tag{16.36}$$

Call prices are then as follows, assuming the four parameters are constrained by (16.33):

$$\begin{aligned}
c(X) &= e^{-rT} \int_X^\infty (x - X) f_{\text{GB2}}(x \mid a, b, p, q) \, dx \\
&= F e^{-rT} [1 - F_{\text{GB2}}(X \mid a, b, p + a^{-1}, q - a^{-1})] \\
&\quad - X e^{-rT} [1 - F_{\text{GB2}}(X \mid a, b, p, q)] \\
&= F e^{-rT} [1 - F_\beta(u(X, a, b) \mid p + a^{-1}, q - a^{-1})] \\
&\quad - X e^{-rT} [1 - F_\beta(u(X, a, b) \mid p, q)]. \tag{16.37}
\end{aligned}$$

Estimation of the parameter vector, $\theta = (a, b, p, q)$, by minimizing one of the functions defined in Section 16.4, is again fairly straightforward. One method is to minimize over a, p, and q, with $a > 0$, $p > 0$, $aq > 1$, and b given

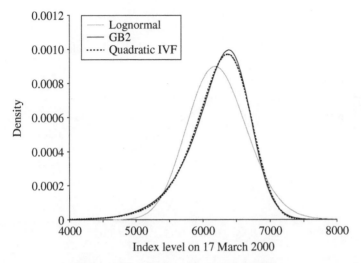

Figure 16.8. Further risk-neutral densities.

by (16.33). In Excel, the B function can be evaluated using three values of GAMMALN(z) which calculates $\log(\Gamma(z))$, while the function $F_\beta(u \mid p, q)$ equals BETADIST(u, p, q). The only technical problem is selecting the initial values when performing the parameter estimation.

The parameter estimates for the illustrative FTSE 100 dataset are $a = 27$, $b = 6750$, $p = 0.59$, and $q = 2.37$. The minimum sum of squared errors is included in Table 16.2. It remains less than the minimum for the lognormal mixture even when either p or q is constrained to be one. Figures 16.8 and 16.9 show the estimated GB2 risk-neutral density and implied volatility functions, using solid curves. The GB2 and mixture densities are similar but the GB2 provides a much better fit to the observed implied volatilities.

The RND for the general GB2 distribution has been estimated for the S&P 500 and the sterling/dollar rate by Anagnou et al. (2002). It has also been estimated for S&P 500 futures (Aparicio and Hodges 1998) and the spot FTSE 100 index (Liu et al. 2004). The special case when $q = 1$ is the Burr-3 distribution, which has been estimated for soybean futures by Sherrick, Garcia, and Tirupattur (1996).

The GB2 density is easy to estimate, a nonnegative density is guaranteed, and we will later see a convenient transformation from an RND to a real-world density. The major obstacle to its use is the interpretation of the parameters a, p, and q.

16.5.3 Lognormal-Polynomial Density Functions

Standardized returns have standard normal distributions when prices have lognormal distributions. Madan and Milne (1994) develop an elegant theory of contingent claims valuation that assumes the density of standardized returns is the standard normal density multiplied by a general function. This function can be

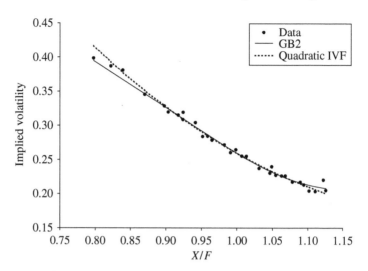

Figure 16.9. Fitted implieds for two more RND methods.

approximated by a polynomial. The density of prices is then a lognormal density multiplied by a polynomial function of $\log(x)$.

This method involves more mathematics than the others. All the following distributions are for the risk-neutral measure Q. We begin by supposing the change in the logarithm of the futures price, $\log(F_T) - \log(F)$, has finite variance $\sigma^2 T$ and mean equal to $\mu T - \frac{1}{2}\sigma^2 T$. This defines two parameters μ and σ. Then we define the standardized "futures return" Z by

$$Z = \frac{\log(F_T/F) - (\mu T - \frac{1}{2}\sigma^2 T)}{\sigma\sqrt{T}} \tag{16.38}$$

so that Z has mean 0 and variance 1. The densities of Z and $S_T = F_T$ are related by

$$f_{S_T}(x) = \frac{1}{x\sigma\sqrt{T}} f_Z(z), \tag{16.39}$$

with

$$z = \frac{\log(x) - \log(F) - \mu T + \frac{1}{2}\sigma^2 T}{\sigma\sqrt{T}}.$$

Of course $Z \sim N(0, 1)$ and $\mu = 0$ when the distribution of F_T is lognormal.

The general form of the density for Z is

$$f_Z(z) = \phi(z) \sum_{j=0}^{\infty} b_j H_j(z), \tag{16.40}$$

for constants b_j and normalized Hermite polynomials H_j, commencing with

$$H_0(z) = 1, \qquad H_1(z) = z, \qquad H_2(z) = \frac{1}{\sqrt{2!}}(z^2 - 1),$$

$$H_3(z) = \frac{1}{\sqrt{3!}}(z^3 - 3z), \qquad H_4(z) = \frac{1}{\sqrt{4!}}(z^4 - 6z^2 + 3), \qquad \cdots . \tag{16.41}$$

These polynomials are "orthogonal," a property here defined by integrals as

$$\int_{-\infty}^{\infty} H_i(z) H_j(z) \phi(z) \, dz = \begin{cases} 1 & \text{if } i = j, \\ 0 & \text{if } i \neq j. \end{cases} \tag{16.42}$$

It follows that

$$\int_{-\infty}^{\infty} H_j(z) f_Z(z) \, dz = b_j. \tag{16.43}$$

Since $f_Z(z)$ is the density of a standardized random variable,

$$b_0 = 1, \qquad b_1 = 0, \qquad b_2 = 0,$$

$$\text{skewness}(Z) = E[Z^3] = \sqrt{6} b_3,$$

$$\text{kurtosis}(Z) = E[Z^4] = 3 + \sqrt{24} b_4. \tag{16.44}$$

The coefficients b_j, $j \geqslant 3$, are constrained because the density of F_T is risk-neutral, as is shown later in equations (16.47) and (16.51).

Most implementations of the method assume the ratio $f_Z(z)/\phi(z)$ is a polynomial of order four. Then $b_j = 0$ for $j \geqslant 5$ and the parameter vector becomes $\theta = (\mu, \sigma, b_3, b_4)$. The risk-neutrality constraint reduces the number of free parameters to three. It is important to appreciate that b_3 and b_4 must then be constrained to ensure the density is never negative. Jondeau and Rockinger (2001) show the kurtosis of Z is between three and seven when the distribution is symmetric and that the maximum kurtosis is less for skewed distributions. The permissible range of skewness values for Z depends on the kurtosis, with all feasible values within ± 1.05.

The payoff from a call option is a function of Z, which can be represented as an infinite-order polynomial by

$$(F_T - X)^+ = \sum_{k=0}^{\infty} a_k(X) H_k(Z). \tag{16.45}$$

The functions $a_k(X)$ do not depend on Z. Therefore, by applying the orthogonality property (16.42), we can obtain

$$c(X) = e^{-rT} E[(F_T - X)^+] = e^{-rT} \sum_{j=0}^{\infty} a_j(X) b_j. \tag{16.46}$$

Likewise, the futures price is given by

$$F = E[F_T] = \sum_{j=0}^{\infty} a_j(0)b_j. \tag{16.47}$$

Implementation requires $f_Z(z)/\phi(z)$ to be a polynomial of finite order J, so that $b_j = 0$ for $j > J$. The usual choice is $J = 4$. The required functions $a_j(X)$ are then

$$a_0(0) = Fe^{\mu T}, \qquad a_3(0) = \frac{\beta^3}{\sqrt{6}}Fe^{\mu T}, \qquad a_4(0) = \frac{\beta^4}{\sqrt{24}}Fe^{\mu T}, \tag{16.48}$$

and, for $X > 0$,

$$a_0(X) = Fe^{\mu T}N(D_1) - XN(D_1 - \sigma\sqrt{T}),$$

$$a_3(X) = \frac{\beta}{\sqrt{6}}Fe^{\mu T}[\beta^2 N(D_1) + (2\beta - D_1)\phi(D_1)],$$

$$a_4(X) = \frac{\beta}{\sqrt{24}}Fe^{\mu T}[\beta^3 N(D_1) + (3\beta^2 - 3\beta D_1 + D_1^2 - 1)\phi(D_1)] \tag{16.49}$$

with

$$\beta = \sigma\sqrt{T} \quad \text{and} \quad D_1(X) = \frac{\log(F/X) + (\mu + \frac{1}{2}\sigma^2)T}{\sigma\sqrt{T}}. \tag{16.50}$$

These formulae can be derived from equations in Madan and Milne (1994).

Assuming $J = 4$, the parameter vector $\theta = (\mu, \sigma, b_3, b_4)$ is estimated by minimizing one of the functions suggested in Section 16.4, with the risk-neutrality constraint

$$1 + \frac{\beta^3 b_3}{\sqrt{6}} + \frac{\beta^4 b_4}{\sqrt{24}} = e^{-\mu T}. \tag{16.51}$$

Further constraints may also be required to exclude negative density estimates, as discussed by Jondeau and Rockinger (2001).

The parameter estimates for the illustrative FTSE 100 dataset include $b_3 = -0.397$ and $b_4 = 0.217$ when b_3 and b_4 are not constrained. The density of Z is then negative for $2.4 \leqslant z \leqslant 4.0$ corresponding to a narrow range of asset price levels beyond the highest exercise price, between 7600 and 7700. Adding constraints that ensure the density of Z is not negative on a suitable grid leads to the estimates $\mu = 8.88 \times 10^{-4}$, $\sigma = 0.278$, $b_3 = -0.379$, and $b_4 = 0.308$. The sum of squared errors, G, then equals 241 compared with 161 for the unconstrained optimization. Figures 16.6 and 16.7 show the estimated lognormal-polynomial risk-neutral density and implied volatility functions, using dotted curves. The curves are similar for the lognormal-polynomial and the lognormal mixture specifications, although the density of the polynomial variety is less smooth for index levels around 5500.

Lognormal-polynomial density functions are estimated by Madan and Milne (1994) and Ané (1999) for the S&P 500 index, Jondeau and Rockinger (2000, 2001) for the French franc rate against the Deutsche mark, and Coutant et al. (2001) for French interest rates. The method has strong theoretical foundations and is fairly easy to implement. However, negative densities can often only be avoided by restricting the levels of skewness and kurtosis permitted in the density functions.

Similar but more complicated functions of lognormal and polynomial terms are given by the Edgeworth expansion method of Jarrow and Rudd (1982). Details and examples can be found in Corrado and Su (1996, 1997), Jondeau and Rockinger (2000), and Brown and Robinson (2002).

16.5.4 Densities from Stochastic Volatility Processes

Any risk-neutral specification of the process followed by asset prices has the potential to yield estimates of RNDs. A realistic specification will incorporate stochastic volatility. Quick density estimates will follow if the formula for option prices has a "closed form." A plausible asset price process is therefore the stochastic volatility diffusion process of Heston (1993), discussed in Section 14.6. The risk-neutral dynamics for the asset price S_t and the variance V_t are then

$$d(\log S) = (r - q - \tfrac{1}{2}V)\,dt + \sqrt{V}\,dW,$$
$$dV = (a - bV)\,dt + \xi\sqrt{V}\,dZ, \tag{16.52}$$

with correlation ρ between dW and dZ. Numerical integration provides both the option pricing formula $c(X)$ and the risk-neutral density $f_Q(x)$, as functions of the parameter vector $\theta = (a, b, \xi, \rho, V_0)$ and the observable quantities S, r, q. The pricing formula is

$$c(X) = Se^{-qT}P_1(X) - Xe^{-rT}P_2(X), \tag{16.53}$$

with the probabilities $P_1(X)$, $P_2(X)$, and the density $f_Q(x)$ given by integrals stated in the appendix to Chapter 14.

There are five free parameters in the pricing formula and the density function. This may be an excessive number if the parameters are estimated from option prices for one expiry time T. As the parameters are the same for all T, it is logical to estimate them from a matrix of option prices that combines several values of X with several values of T. This cannot be done for most of the other methods for estimating RNDs. Jondeau and Rockinger (2000) tabulate parameter estimates for the FF/DM exchange rate on two days. The estimates from single values of T are similar for a and ρ, but are rather variable for b, ξ, and particularly V_0. The joint estimates when T is one, three, six, and twelve months are more plausible.

16.6   Risk-Neutral Densities from Implied Volatility Functions

Implied volatilities deviate from a constant function when the RND deviates from a lognormal density. Thus it may be easier to specify an implied volatility function (IVF) than an RND. Also, implied volatilities are directly observable which makes IVF estimation attractive.

16.6.1   Theory

The simpler notation $\sigma(X \mid \theta)$ is now used for the IVF, $\sigma_{\text{implied}}(X)$, with θ a set of parameters. Then the call price formula is

$$c(X \mid \theta) = c_{\text{BS}}(S, T, X, r, q, \sigma(X \mid \theta)). \qquad (16.54)$$

The function $\sigma(X \mid \theta)$ is often assumed to be a polynomial. Shimko (1993) was the first to suggest a quadratic,

$$\sigma(X \mid \theta) = a + bX + cX^2, \qquad (16.55)$$

so that $\theta = (a, b, c)$.

When the call price formula does not permit arbitrage profits, the RND follows from (16.13) as

$$f_Q(X) = e^{rT} \frac{\partial^2 c}{\partial X^2}. \qquad (16.56)$$

An analytic RND expression follows by differentiating (16.54), to give

$$e^{rT} \frac{\partial c}{\partial X} = -N(d_2) + (X\sqrt{T}\phi(d_2)) \frac{\partial \sigma}{\partial X} \qquad (16.57)$$

and

$$e^{rT} \frac{\partial^2 c}{\partial X^2}$$

$$= \phi(d_2) \left\{ \frac{1}{\sigma X \sqrt{T}} + \left(\frac{2d_1}{\sigma} \right) \frac{\partial \sigma}{\partial X} + \left(\frac{d_1 d_2 X \sqrt{T}}{\sigma} \right) \left(\frac{\partial \sigma}{\partial X} \right)^2 + (X\sqrt{T}) \frac{\partial^2 \sigma}{\partial X^2} \right\}, \qquad (16.58)$$

with d_1 and d_2 the Black–Scholes functions of X defined by

$$d_1(X) = \frac{\log(F/X) + \frac{1}{2}\sigma(X)^2 T}{\sigma(X)\sqrt{T}}, \qquad (16.59)$$

$$d_2(X) = d_1(X) - \sigma(X)\sqrt{T}.$$

The partial derivatives are zero and the density is lognormal (see (16.16)) when the IVF is a constant. The calculation of the density can always be checked against the numerical approximation

$$f_Q(X) \cong e^{rT} \frac{c(X + \delta) - 2c(X) + c(X - \delta)}{\delta^2} \qquad (16.60)$$

with δ a small fraction of X.

The density obtained from (16.56) is automatically risk-neutral, if weak constraints apply to $\sigma(X \mid \theta)$. This can be checked using integration by parts:

$$\int_0^\infty x \frac{\partial}{\partial x}\left(\frac{\partial c}{\partial x}\right) dx = \left[x \frac{\partial c}{\partial x}\right]_0^\infty - \int_0^\infty \left(\frac{\partial c}{\partial x}\right) dx$$

$$= [0 - 0] - [c]_0^\infty$$

$$= -[0 - Fe^{-rT}] = Fe^{-rT}. \qquad (16.61)$$

16.6.2 Implementation

The original strategy for implementing the IVF method is to select a parametric function $\sigma(X \mid \theta)$, guided by inspection of observed implieds, that has a few parameters (Shimko 1993). Plausible functions, including quadratics, are not guaranteed to give nonnegative densities and implieds for all positive X. These conditions usually have to be checked. In some cases it is sufficient that they apply for a range of values over which the integrals of $f_Q(x)$ and $x f_Q(x)$ are respectively very near to one and the forward price. Lee (2004) offers advice about extrapolation of the IVF.

A linear IV function provides a good fit to the illustrative option prices, with $a = 0.870$ and $b = -0.977 \times 10^{-4}$. To prevent negative values, this function cannot be extrapolated beyond $X = 8900$; this is unimportant because the linear IVF defines an adequate density function over the interval from 0 to 8000. The minimized sum of squared price errors equals 171 for this two-parameter specification, which compares well with the 175 for a lognormal mixture that has four free parameters. A quadratic IV function reduces G to 115, which is similar to the 118 obtained by the GB2 method. The parameter estimates are then $a = 1.78$, $b = -3.93 \times 10^{-4}$, and $c = 2.40 \times 10^{-8}$, for which the IVF and the RND are always positive; the minimum value of the quadratic is 0.168 at $X = 8200$. Figures 16.8 and 16.9 show the estimated risk-neutral density and quadratic implied volatility functions, using dotted curves. For our data, these functions are very similar to those for the GB2 distribution within the range of traded exercise prices. The quadratic IVF density has a long left tail and the most negative skewness of all the methods. Table 16.2 includes summary statistics for the IVF method and the three parametric methods described in the previous section. Section 16.10 illustrates the quadratic IVF calculations using an Excel spreadsheet.

A second strategy has been developed by Malz (1997a) and guarantees that the tails of the RND are well behaved. The original market data, made up of pairs of exercise and option prices, $(X_i, c_m(X_i))$, is converted into pairs of deltas and implied volatilities, (δ_i, σ_i), with

$$\delta_i = \frac{\partial}{\partial S} c_{BS}(S, T, X_i, r, q, \sigma_i) = e^{-qT} N(d_1(X_i, \sigma_i)) \qquad (16.62)$$

and the function d_1 given by (16.59). A parametric relationship $\sigma = g(\delta \mid \theta)$ is then estimated. From this the IVF is given by numerically solving the equation

$$\sigma(X) = g(e^{-qT} N(d_1(X, \sigma(X)))).\qquad(16.63)$$

The RND is then obtained from the numerical second differences of the theoretical call prices, using (16.54) and (16.60). Each tail of the RND is approximately lognormal as $\sigma(X)$ is approximately constant for small X ($\delta \cong 0$) and large X ($\delta \cong e^{-qT}$). Malz (1997b) uses a quadratic function $\sigma = a + b\delta + c\delta^2$ to estimate the RND from only three FX option prices.

A third strategy uses many more parameters by fitting a cubic spline to the observed implieds, either as a function of X (Campa et al. 1998) or as a function of delta (Bliss and Panigirtzoglou 2002, 2004). These splines are more flexible than simple polynomials. They are general cubics between the observations and they are constrained so that the functions and their first two derivatives are continuous. Either a perfect fit can be guaranteed (Campa et al.) or the quality of the fit can be traded off against the smoothness of the fitted function after subjectively selecting a trade-off parameter (Bliss and Panigirtzoglou). Splines are also used by Bates (1991, 2000), but to fit the call pricing formula instead of the implied volatility function.

16.7 Nonparametric RND Methods

Parametric methods restrict the shapes that can be estimated for RNDs. The extra generality of nonparametric alternatives introduces new problems, however, including subjective choices, assumptions of stability through time, and inappropriate shapes.

16.7.1 Flexible Discrete Distributions

Flexible shapes are obtained by adopting a minimal set of constraints in conjunction with a large number of degrees of freedom. Rubinstein (1994) achieves this by estimating discrete probability distributions that have $n + 1$ possible values S_j. Then $p = (p_0, p_1, \ldots, p_n)$ is an RND if

$$p_0, p_1, \ldots, p_n \geqslant 0, \quad \sum_{j=0}^{n} p_j = 1, \quad \text{and} \quad \sum_{j=0}^{n} p_j S_j = F.\qquad(16.64)$$

A large value of n is preferable, typically in excess of 100. The option pricing formula is now

$$c(X) = e^{-rT} \sum_{j=0}^{n} p_j \max(S_j - X, 0).\qquad(16.65)$$

Also, the probabilities are proportional to the prices of butterfly spreads when the differences $S_{j+1} - S_j$ are all equal to a common, positive value Δ:

$$p_i = e^{rT} \frac{c(S_{i+1}) - 2c(S_i) + c(S_{i-1})}{\Delta}, \quad 0 \leqslant i \leqslant n. \tag{16.66}$$

The vector p can be estimated by minimizing a variety of functions. Jackwerth and Rubinstein (1996) seek low values of $g(p) + \omega G(p)$ with G measuring the match between observed and fitted option prices (as in (16.22)) and with g measuring the smoothness of the RND by

$$g(p) = \sum_{j=0}^{n} (p_{j-1} - 2p_j + p_{j+1})^2. \tag{16.67}$$

The positive trade-off parameter ω is chosen subjectively and $p_{-1} = p_{n+1} = 0$. They describe an efficient optimization algorithm and illustrate its results for S&P 500 index options from 1986 to 1993. This algorithm does not guarantee nonnegative probabilities, although it seems they can be avoided by a careful choice of the range of possible prices, S_0 to S_n. Jackwerth (2000) describes a related estimation methodology that seeks low values for the curvature of the implied volatility function rather than for the curvature of the RND as in (16.67). He finds all the estimated probabilities are nonnegative for stated values of ω and $S_n - S_0$.

16.7.2 Kernel Regression Methods

Nonparametric regression estimates can avoid making assumptions about the shape of a regression function. Aït-Sahalia and Lo (1998, 2000) consider estimation of either the call price formula or the implied volatility function (IVF) using option price datasets across several days; each dataset contains prices for several expiry times. Estimation is easier when the number of explanatory variables is reduced as much as possible. The simplest way to implement the method estimates the IVF as a function of $Z = X/F_T$ and T, with F_T the futures price now for a transaction at time T, as in Aït-Sahalia and Lo (2000) and Aït-Sahalia, Wang, and Yared (2001). This method relies on the IVF being stable during the estimation period. This is a strong assumption. It is empirically dubious for a whole year of option prices, as used by Aït-Sahalia and Lo (1998, 2000) in their research into S&P 500 data for 1993. Aït-Sahalia and Duarte (2003) describe an alternative nonparametric method that enforces the constraint that the RND is nonnegative. Fewer data are then required to estimate densities.

16.7.3 Convolution Approximation

The positive convolution approximation method of Bondarenko (2003) has similarities with both nonparametric smoothing methods and parametric mixture methods. His RNDs are mixtures of normal densities that have equispaced means and identical standard deviations. The weights of the component normal densities are obtained by solving a quadratic programming problem.

16.7.4 Entropy Methods

The entropy of a general RND is defined by

$$I(f_Q) = -\int_0^\infty f_Q(x)\log(f_Q(x))\,dx = -E^Q[\log(S_T)]. \qquad (16.68)$$

Buchen and Kelly (1996) suggest estimating the RND by maximizing the entropy subject to the constraint that a set of observed option prices are perfectly matched by the theoretical call price formula. Entropy maximization may appear to make few assumptions. However, the RND has a special form when N option price constraints are included. The solution then depends on $N+1$ Lagrange multipliers λ_i:

$$f_Q(x) = h(x) \Big/ \int_0^\infty h(y)\,dy \quad \text{with } h(x) = \exp\left(\lambda_0 x + \sum_{i=1}^N \lambda_i (x - X_i)^+\right).$$
$$(16.69)$$

This continuous density has $N+1$ segments, each of which is an exponential function. The first multiplier ensures the distribution is risk-neutral. The multipliers must be estimated by numerical solution of a system of nonlinear equations. Coutant et al. (2001) include numerical examples of the estimated RNDs for interest-rate futures. Stutzer (1996) also applies the principle of maximizing entropy. Two criticisms of the method are that it is inappropriate to exactly match observed option prices (that are necessarily discrete) and that maximization of $-E^Q[\log S_T]$ is an ad hoc objective.

16.8 Towards Recommendations

No one can say which method for estimating implied RNDs is best. Several methods are likely to be satisfactory when enough exercise prices are traded and their range captures most of the risk-neutral probability. A satisfactory method will score highly on the following eight criteria.

(i) Estimated densities are never negative.

(ii) General levels of skewness and kurtosis are allowed.

(iii) The shapes of the tails are fat relative to lognormal distributions.

(iv) There are analytic formulae for the density and the call price formula.

(v) Estimates are not sensitive to the discreteness of option prices.

(vi) Solutions to the parameter estimation problem are easy to obtain.

(vii) Estimation does not involve any subjective choices.

(viii) Risk-neutral densities can be transformed easily to real-world densities.

Often it will also be appropriate to expect methods to deliver unimodal densities.

Nearly all methods are known to be unsatisfactory for at least one of the above criteria, including the following: lognormal mixtures, criteria (iii), (v), (vi); lognormal-polynomials, (i), (ii), (viii); stochastic volatility, (ii), (iv), (vi); parametric implied volatility functions, (i), (viii); spline IVFs, (iii), (iv), (viii); flexible discrete distributions, (vi), (vii); kernel regressions (iv), (vi), (viii). Only the GB2 method of Section 16.5 appears to satisfy all the above criteria but it has not yet received much critical scrutiny.

There are few recommendations in the research literature because most RND studies only evaluate one method. Bahra (1997) prefers lognormal mixtures to parametric IVFs. Campa et al. (1998) prefer flexible discrete distributions to lognormal mixtures and cubic splines for IVFs, although all three methods give comparable densities. Jondeau and Rockinger (2000) compare lognormal mixtures, lognormal-polynomials and Edgeworth expansions, jump-diffusions, and stochastic volatility specifications. They prefer lognormal mixtures for short-lived options and otherwise jump-diffusions. Coutant et al. (2001), however, prefer lognormal-polynomials to lognormal mixtures and entropy maximization. Bliss and Panigirtzoglou (2002) prefer implied volatility functions, made up from splines, to lognormal mixtures.

16.9 From Risk-Neutral to Real-World Densities

The relationship between the real-world density $f_P(x)$ and the risk-neutral density $f_Q(x)$ can be estimated from time series of asset and option prices in at least two ways. We first consider a method that specifies a transformation from f_Q to f_P using economic theory and then present an econometric method that avoids such theory; examples of appropriate formulae for f_P are given by equations (16.76) and (16.91). Both methods are illustrated for FTSE densities at the end of this section.

16.9.1 Transformations from Stochastic Discount Factors

The theory of asset pricing relates current prices to expectations of discounted future prices. When the market has a formula for pricing call options across all exercise prices,

$$c(X) = e^{-rT} E^Q[(S_T - X)^+]$$

$$= e^{-rT} \int_0^\infty (x - X)^+ f_Q(x) \, dx$$

$$= e^{-rT} \int_0^\infty (x - X)^+ \frac{f_Q(x)}{f_P(x)} f_P(x)\, dx$$

$$= E^P[m(S_T)c_T(S_T, X)]. \tag{16.70}$$

Here $c_T(S_T, X) = (S_T - X)^+$ is the price of the option at time T and the *stochastic discount factor* for all options is the random variable $m(S_T)$ defined as

$$m(S_T) = e^{-rT} \frac{f_Q(S_T)}{f_P(S_T)}. \tag{16.71}$$

Another name for the stochastic discount factor is the *pricing kernel*. Equation (16.70) is the foundation of asset pricing theory based upon present and future consumption. Cochrane (2001) provides a comprehensive discussion of the theory for many areas of finance. Its application to option prices is also covered by Aït-Sahalia and Lo (2000) and Rosenberg and Engle (2002).

Theory relates the stochastic discount factor to the utility function of a representative agent when some assumptions are made, thereby providing insight into a suitable formulation for the ratio $f_Q(x)/f_P(x)$. Various theoretical assumptions are employed by Jackwerth (2000) and Aït-Sahalia and Lo (2000), who cite earlier contributions by Lucas (1978), Constantinides (1982), and Merton (1992) among others. With sufficient assumptions, the stochastic discount factor is simply proportional to the representative agent's marginal utility of terminal consumption, which can be equated to the terminal asset price. Then

$$m(x) = \lambda \frac{du}{dx} \tag{16.72}$$

for some utility function $u(x)$, with λ an irrelevant positive constant.

The power utility function is used to obtain real-world densities from risk-neutral densities by Bakshi, Kapadia, and Madan (2003), Bliss and Panigirtzoglou (2004), and Liu et al. (2004). With

$$u(x) = \begin{cases} \dfrac{x^{1-\gamma}}{1 - \gamma}, & \gamma \neq 1, \\ \log(x), & \gamma = 1, \end{cases} \tag{16.73}$$

the marginal utility is

$$u'(x) = \frac{du}{dx} = x^{-\gamma} \tag{16.74}$$

and the relative risk aversion is constant and equal to the CRRA parameter γ:

$$\text{RRA}(x) = -\frac{xu''(x)}{u'(x)} = \gamma. \tag{16.75}$$

The parameter γ is positive when the agent is risk averse and it equals zero for the special case of a risk-neutral agent. From equations (16.71), (16.72), and (16.74), the real-world density is then proportional to the risk-neutral density multiplied by x^γ, hence

$$f_P(x) = x^\gamma f_Q(x) \bigg/ \int_0^\infty y^\gamma f_Q(y)\, dy. \qquad (16.76)$$

The above integral has to be evaluated numerically for many RND methods.

There are at least three important analytic formulae for $f_P(x)$ based upon power utility functions. First, geometric Brownian motion for asset prices makes $f_Q(x)$ lognormal as in (16.16). Multiplication of f_Q by $x^\gamma = \exp(\gamma \log(x))$, followed by simplifying the exponent of the exponential function, leads to the conclusion that f_P is also lognormal. We obtain

$$f_P(x) = x^\gamma \psi(x \mid F, \sigma, T) \bigg/ \int_0^\infty y^\gamma \psi(y \mid F, \sigma, T)\, dy$$
$$= \psi(x \mid Fe^{\gamma\sigma^2 T}, \sigma, T). \qquad (16.77)$$

The densities f_P and f_Q have the same volatility parameter σ, with different expectations given by

$$E^P[S_T] = Se^{(r-q+\gamma\sigma^2)T} \quad \text{and} \quad E^Q[S_T] = Se^{(r-q)T}. \qquad (16.78)$$

The annualized risk premium, when expected returns are continuously compounded, is given by

$$T^{-1} \log(e^{qT} E^P[S_T]/S) - T^{-1} \log(e^{qT} E^Q[S_T]/S) = \gamma\sigma^2. \qquad (16.79)$$

Thus the CRRA parameter γ then equals the annualized risk premium for the underlying asset divided by σ^2. For a typical equity index premium of 6% per annum and a volatility of 15% per annum we obtain $\gamma = 2.67$. Conversely, within the Black–Scholes pricing framework both f_P and f_Q are lognormal; if the assumptions of the representative agent model also apply, then the agent must have a power utility function.

Second, suppose f_Q is the mixture of two lognormal distributions defined in Section 16.5, i.e.

$$f_Q(x) = p\psi(x \mid F_1, \sigma_1, T) + (1-p)\psi(x \mid F_2, \sigma_2, T). \qquad (16.80)$$

From the formula for the moments of the mixture distribution (equation (16.26)),

$$f_P(x) = x^\gamma f_Q(x)/k(\theta)$$

with

$$k(\theta) = pF_1^\gamma \exp(\tfrac{1}{2}(\gamma^2 - \gamma)\sigma_1^2 T) + (1-p)F_2^\gamma \exp(\tfrac{1}{2}(\gamma^2 - \gamma)\sigma_2^2 T). \qquad (16.81)$$

This density is also a mixture of lognormal densities. From (16.77) it can be shown that

$$f_P(x) = p^*\psi(x \mid F_1^*, \sigma_1, T) + (1-p^*)\psi(x \mid F_2^*, \sigma_2, T)$$

with

$$F_i^* = F_i \exp(\gamma \sigma_i^2 T), \quad i = 1, 2,$$

$$\frac{1}{p^*} = 1 + \frac{1-p}{p} \left(\frac{F_2}{F_1} \right)^\gamma \exp(\tfrac{1}{2}(\gamma^2 - \gamma)(\sigma_2^2 - \sigma_1^2)T). \tag{16.82}$$

Third, suppose f_Q is the GB2 density defined by equation (16.29), with four parameters a, b, p, and q. Then (16.31) shows that f_P is also a GB2 density, with parameters $a, b, p + (\gamma/a)$, and $q - (\gamma/a)$, providing $\gamma < aq$.

16.9.2   Estimates of the CRRA Parameter γ

Estimation of γ in the context of the representative agent model is known to be a difficult problem, because analysis of consumption data leads to implausible high estimates that are necessary to explain the "puzzling" high level of the equity premium (e.g. Mehra and Prescott 1985). As our particular interest in γ is to use it to move from risk-neutral to real-world densities, it is logical to select γ to obtain a good match between observed asset prices and real-world densities. We could simply note that γ and f_Q together determine the risk premium for the asset, as illustrated by (16.79), so an estimate of γ can be inferred from an estimate of the premium. More sophisticated alternatives to matching the mean of observed asset prices are either maximizing the likelihood of the observations or minimizing test criteria that detect mis-specification of the real-world densities. These alternatives may, however, in effect be an indirect way to obtain satisfactory means for P-densities.

Bliss and Panigirtzoglou (2004) use spline methods to fit their Q-densities for both S&P 500 options (1983–2001) and FTSE 100 options (1992–2001). They then select γ to make the P-densities conform as closely as possible with the calibration criteria introduced after the next paragraph. This requires minimization of a likelihood-ratio test statistic proposed by Berkowitz (2001). Their estimates of γ vary with the option horizon T. They equal 3.9 (FTSE) and 4.0 (S&P) for a horizon of four weeks. The similarity of the estimates for the US and UK markets occurs for all horizons up to four weeks and is interesting. They also report similar measures of risk aversion when the utility function is assumed to be an exponential function.

Liu, Shackleton, Taylor, and Xu (2004) fit risk-neutral densities to high-frequency, FTSE 100 option prices from 1993 to 2000. They use nonoverlapping P-densities to define the likelihood of a set of 83 four-week returns. Maximizing the likelihood as a function of γ gives estimates equal to 3.8 and 4.0, respectively for lognormal mixture and GB2 densities. Likelihood comparisons are made between densities obtained from option prices and the utility transformation, densities obtained by simulating an asymmetric ARCH model estimated from daily index returns, and encompassing densities that combine the option and historical densities. Significant incremental density information is found in the option densities, at the 2% significance level, but it is not found in the historical densities at the 5% level.

16.9.3 Calibration Conditions

Any method that produces a time series of real-world densities f_P can be appraised by checking if the densities are properly calibrated. Let F_P and F_P^{-1} respectively denote the cumulative distribution function (c.d.f.) and its inverse function (not its reciprocal), so

$$F_P(x) = \int_0^x f_P(y)\,dy \quad \text{and} \quad u = \int_0^{F_P^{-1}(u)} f_P(y)\,dy \qquad (16.83)$$

for $0 \leqslant u \leqslant 1$, here assuming the density is defined for $x \geqslant 0$ and that it is a positive and continuous function. Also let F_{correct} be the actual real-world c.d.f., which is unknown. Observe that the c.d.f. of the random variable $U = F_P(S_T)$ is

$$P(U \leqslant u) = P(S_T \leqslant F_P^{-1}(u)) = F_{\text{correct}}(F_P^{-1}(u)), \quad \text{for } 0 \leqslant u \leqslant 1. \quad (16.84)$$

The two c.d.f.s F_P and F_{correct} are identical when the density of S_T is correctly specified. When this happens,

$$P(U \leqslant u) = F_P(F_P^{-1}(u)) = u. \qquad (16.85)$$

Thus U is uniformly distributed, between 0 and 1 inclusive, if and only if the density of S_T is correctly specified.

Furthermore, suppose density $f_{P,i}$ is produced at time t_i for the asset price at time $t_i + T_i$ and these densities do not overlap, i.e. $t_i + T_i \leqslant t_{i+1}$. Then the stochastic process $\{U_i\}$ is i.i.d., with the above uniform distribution, when all the densities are correctly specified. The two assumptions of uniformity and independence can be checked either separately (Diebold, Gunther, and Tay 1998) or jointly by using tests described in Berkowitz (2001). The data for these tests, when there are n densities, are given by the observed cumulative probabilities,

$$u_i = F_{P,i}(S_{t_i+T_i}), \quad 1 \leqslant i \leqslant n. \qquad (16.86)$$

16.9.4 Recalibration Transformations

The cumulative probabilities u_i should be compared with the uniform distribution whenever densities are produced for several nonoverlapping periods. Summary statistics, such as the minimum, maximum, and the three quartiles, may then indicate that the densities are not correctly calibrated. For example, if few of the u_i are less than one-quarter, this is evidence that the densities overestimate the probability of a moderate to large fall in the asset price.

Fackler and King (1990) describe recalibration methods that improve a set of densities when they are judged against the assumption that their c.d.f.s are uniformly distributed. Their method can be applied to any set of estimated densities and can be used to directly transform risk-neutral densities into real-world densities. The key assumption is that the u_i are all observations from a common probability distribution.

Now let $f(x)$ and $F(x)$ denote the uncalibrated density and cumulative distribution function of S_T obtained from some method. The definition of f is not important; for example, it might be an RND or it might be a utility adjusted RND given by (16.76). Define the random variable U and its c.d.f., the calibration function $C(u)$, by

$$U = F(S_T) \quad \text{and} \quad C(u) = P(U \leqslant u). \tag{16.87}$$

The random variable $C(U)$ is uniformly distributed, because

$$P(C(U) \leqslant u) = P(U \leqslant C^{-1}(u)) = C(C^{-1}(u)) = u. \tag{16.88}$$

Now define the calibrated cumulative distribution function F_P and a random variable U_P by

$$F_P(x) = C(F(x)) \quad \text{and} \quad U_P = F_P(S_T) = C(F(S_T)) = C(U). \tag{16.89}$$

Then U_P is uniformly distributed and hence F_P is correctly specified.

The only catch is that we need to know the function C. This could be estimated from a set of observations u_i. A simpler approach is to assume a parametric specification. Fackler and King (1990) use the cumulative function of the beta distribution, which is the incomplete beta function defined by (16.34). This is now written as

$$C(u) = \frac{1}{B(\alpha, \beta)} \int_0^u t^{\alpha-1}(1-t)^{\beta-1} \, \mathrm{d}t. \tag{16.90}$$

The calibrated density is then

$$\begin{aligned}
f_P(x) &= \frac{\mathrm{d}F_P(x)}{\mathrm{d}x} = \frac{\mathrm{d}C(F(x))}{\mathrm{d}x} = \frac{\mathrm{d}C}{\mathrm{d}F}\frac{\mathrm{d}F}{\mathrm{d}x} \\
&= \frac{F(x)^{\alpha-1}(1-F(x))^{\beta-1}}{B(\alpha, \beta)} f(x).
\end{aligned} \tag{16.91}$$

The special case $\alpha = \beta = 1$ corresponds to the original densities f being correctly specified.

When f is a risk-neutral density f_Q, equation (16.91) converts f_Q to a real-world density f_P. Fackler and King (1990) use the equation to convert risk-neutral lognormal densities into properly calibrated real-world densities for the prices of corn, soybeans, live cattle, and hogs.

Liu et al. (2004) recalibrate risk-neutral mixture and GB2 densities for the FTSE 100 index, by maximizing the likelihood of a set of observed values for S_T. Their

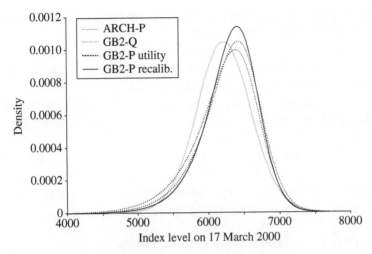

Figure 16.10.   Real-world densities.

estimates of the two positive parameters are $\hat{\alpha} = 1.4$ and $\hat{\beta} = 1.1$. They show that a necessary and sufficient condition for the utility function $u(x)$ implicit in (16.91) to have the risk-aversion property $u''(x) < 0$ is $\beta \leqslant 1 \leqslant \alpha$, with $\alpha \neq \beta$. The likelihood estimates become $\hat{\alpha} = 1.3$ and $\hat{\beta} = 1$ when the risk-aversion constraint is applied. All their sets of densities are satisfactorily calibrated, according to a Kolmogorov–Smirnov test. However, the least value of the Kolmogorov–Smirnov statistic is obtained for historical densities provided by ARCH simulations.

16.9.5   FTSE Example

Four densities for the index level on 17 March 2000 are plotted in Figure 16.10. The ARCH density of Section 16.2 is shown by a light continuous curve. Its mode is to the left of the other three modes, all of which are derived from option prices and GB2 densities. The risk-neutral GB2 density, defined and discussed in Section 16.5, is represented by the light dotted curve. It is transformed into a real-world GB2 density, with CRRA parameter $\gamma = 2$, using equation (16.76) and the parameters defined in the paragraph after equation (16.82). This real-world density is shown by the dark dotted curve. The risk-neutral density is also adjusted using the calibration equation (16.91), with $\alpha = 1.3$ and $\beta = 1.1$, to give the values on the dark, continuous curve; this real-world density is not a GB2 density. The selected values of the parameters γ, α, and β give annualized risk premia equal to 14% and 15% for the utility and recalibration methods. The premia are high because volatility was at a high level on 18 February 2000.

From Figure 16.10, the ARCH density is seen to have a lower mean than the GB2 real-world densities. This occurs because the ARCH density is estimated at the close of spot trading on 18 February while the option-based densities are obtained from prices at midday on the 18th; the index futures contract fell by 87 points from midday until the spot market closed.

Table 16.1 includes the first four moments of S_T and $\log(S_T)$ for each of the four plotted densities. All the densities obtained from option prices are much more negatively skewed than the ARCH density. The option densities also have much more excess kurtosis. The transformations from Q- to P-densities reduce the standard deviation, skewness, and kurtosis statistics, but the reductions are not substantial.

The skewness statistics for four-week-ahead FTSE 100 densities, from 1993 to 2000, are similar to those for the example given here. They average -0.7 for Q-densities and -0.6 to -0.5 for P-densities obtained by utility or recalibration transformations, but only -0.1 for ARCH densities (Liu et al. 2004).

16.10   An Excel Spreadsheet for Density Estimation

This section only illustrates the calculation of risk-neutral and real-world densities. Excel calculations are shown in Exhibit 16.1 for the method that assumes the implied volatility function is a quadratic. This is a straightforward method that is generally satisfactory within the range of traded exercise prices. The spreadsheet formulae are shown in Table 16.3. The calculations could certainly be simplified by writing a few Visual Basic functions.

The data used for the calculations are similar to one-third of the data used to obtain the previous illustrative results in this chapter. Cells B2–B5 contain the present spot rate S, the time until expiry of the option contracts T, the risk-free rate r, and the dividend yield q. These are used to obtain the present futures price F for a contract having the same lifetime as the options. As we know F for the FTSE data, the values of S and q have been replaced by the values of F and r. Cells A11–A21, B11–B21, and D11–D21 contain the option data, which comprise exercise prices, market implied volatilities, and European option prices. One way to obtain the implied volatilities is by repeated use of the Solver tool. If necessary, this can be done using the subsidiary spreadsheet Exhibit 16.2, whose formulae for cells E11, G11, and H11 are identical to those in Exhibit 16.1.

The implied volatility function is assumed to be defined by

$$\sigma(X) = a + b(X/d) + c(X/d)^2 \tag{16.92}$$

with a, b, and c parameters and with d a user-chosen scaling factor that is placed in cell G2. The implied volatility function defines the implieds in cells C11–C21, that depend on the parameter values in cells E2–E4. From these implieds we obtain the call prices in cells E11–E21 and the squared pricing errors shown in F11–F21. The sum of the squared pricing errors, shown in cell E6, is minimized using Solver by varying the contents of cells E2–E4. It is advisable to try a few

	A	B	C	D	E	F	G	H	I	J	K	L
1	Market variables			Parameter	Value		Divisor					
2	S	6229		a	1.3993		10000					
3	T	0.0767		b	-2.6721							
4	r	0.059		c	1.3559							
5	q	0.059		Sum of squared errors	38.25							
6	F	6229		G								
7	exp(-rT)	0.9955										
8												
9		implied market	quadratic	call price market	from IVF	sqd. error	sigma*(T^.5)	d1				
10	X											
11	4975	0.3984	0.4056	1253.03	1253.6	0.32	0.1123	2.0575				
12	5225	0.3808	0.3733	1011.33	1010.2	1.29	0.1034	1.7516				
13	5425	0.3455	0.3488	818.77	819.5	0.54	0.0966	1.4790				
14	5625	0.3194	0.3253	633.42	635.4	4.01	0.0901	1.1772				
15	5875	0.3039	0.2975	425.39	422.0	11.23	0.0824	0.7514				
16	6025	0.2785	0.2816	306.36	308.3	3.71	0.0780	0.4660				
17	6225	0.2646	0.2614	183.16	181.0	4.76	0.0724	0.0451				
18	6425	0.2373	0.2422	85.54	88.6	9.56	0.0671	-0.4283				
19	6625	0.2260	0.2242	34.31	33.5	0.61	0.0621	-0.9617				
20	6825	0.2129	0.2072	10.01	8.8	1.42	0.0574	-1.5636				
21	7025	0.2049	0.1913	2.29	1.4	0.80	0.0530	-2.2430				
22												
23						Utility parameter			Recalibration values			
24		Q-density	P via utility	P via calib.		Gamma	2		Alpha	1.3		Integral
25	Integral	0.999997	1.000000	1.000000					Beta	1.1		1.00558
26	Mean	6228.99	6295.75	6304.07					Constant B	0.6874		
27												
28					To find Q-density …					For Q mean		Q-density
29	x	Q-density			sigma	d/dx	d1	d2	X*sqrt(T)		Q-cdf	*(x^gamma)
30	2000	1.308E-08	1.341E-09	4.345E-10	0.9191	-0.0002130	4.590	4.336	553.9	2.617E-05	3.375E-06	1.349E-06
31	2020	1.395E-08	1.459E-09	4.743E-10	0.9149	-0.0002124	4.571	4.318	559.4	2.819E-05	3.645E-06	1.467E-09
32	2040	1.487E-08	1.586E-09	5.171E-10	0.9107	-0.0002119	4.552	4.300	565.0	3.034E-05	3.934E-06	1.595E-09
33	2060	1.584E-08	1.722E-09	5.633E-10	0.9064	-0.0002113	4.533	4.282	570.5	3.262E-05	4.241E-06	1.732E-09

Exhibit 16.1. An example of density calculations using option prices.

Table 16.3. Formulae used in the density estimation spreadsheet.

Cell	Formula
B6	=B2*EXP(B3*(B4-B5))
B7	=EXP(-B3*B4)
E6	=SUM(F11:F21)
C11	=$E$2+($E$3*A11/$G$2)+($E$4*A11*A11/($G$2*$G$2))
E11	=$B$7*($B$6*NORMSDIST(H11)-A11*NORMSDIST(H11-G11))
F11	=(E11-D11)^2
G11	=C11*SQRT($B$3)
H11	=0.5*G11+(LN($B$6/A11)/G11)
B30	=EXP(-0.5*H30*H30)*((1/(E30*I30))+(2*G30*F30/E30) +(G30*H30*I30*F30*F30/E30) +(I30*2*$E$4/($G$2*$G$2)))/SQRT(2*PI())
C30	=L30/$L$26
D30	=B30*(K30^($J$24-1))*((1-K30)^($J$25-1))/$J$26
E30	=$E$2+($E$3*A30/$G$2)+($E$4*A30*A30/($G$2*$G$2))
F30	=($E$3/$G$2)+2*$E$4*A30/($G$2*$G$2)
G30	=(LN($B$6/A30)+0.5*E30*E30*$B$3)/(E30*SQRT($B$3))
H30	=G30-E30*SQRT($B$3)
I30	=A30*SQRT($B$3)
J30	=A30*B30
K30	=1-NORMSDIST(H30) +I30*F30*EXP(-0.5*H30*H30)/SQRT(2*PI())
L30	=B30*((A30/$B$6)^$G$24)
M30	=A30*C30
N30	=A30*D30
B26	=K330-K30
B27	=($A$31-$A$30)*SUM(J30:J330)
C26	=($A$31-$A$30)*SUM(C30:C330)
C27	=($A$31-$A$30)*SUM(M30:M330)
D26	=($A$31-$A$30)*SUM(D30:D330)
D27	=($A$31-$A$30)*SUM(N30:N330)
J26	=EXP(GAMMALN(J24)+GAMMALN(J25)-GAMMALN(J24+J25))
L26	=($A$31-$A$30)*SUM(L30:L330)

different initial values for the optimization problem. Exhibit 16.1 shows the best solution obtained.

The risk-neutral and two real-world densities are shown in columns B to D, from row 30 onwards. The range of possible prices S_T when the options expire has to be selected so that there is almost no probability that the outcome for S_T is outside the range. The cumulative risk-neutral probabilities are useful when selecting the range. They are shown in column K and are given by

$$F_Q(x) = 1 + e^{rT}\frac{\partial c}{\partial x} = 1 - N(d_2) + X\sqrt{T}\phi(d_2)\frac{\partial \sigma}{\partial x}, \qquad (16.93)$$

	A	B	C	D	E	F	G	H
1	Market variables			To find the implied volatilities:				
2	S	6229						
3	T	0.0767		Use Solver to obtain cell F11 = 0 by changing cell C11.				
4	r	0.059		Then repeat for row 12, etc.				
5	q	0.059						
6	F	6229						
7	exp(-rT)	0.9955						
8								
9				call price	call price			
10	X		sigma	market	BS model	difference	sigma*(T^.5)	d1
11	4975		0.3984	1253.03	1253.03	0.00	0.1103	2.0923
12	5225		0.2500	1011.33	1000.17	11.17	0.0692	2.5732
13	5425		0.2500	818.77	803.81	14.96	0.0692	2.0306
14	5625		0.2500	633.42	613.98	19.44	0.0692	1.5077
15	5875		0.2500	425.39	398.65	26.74	0.0692	0.8797
16	6025		0.2500	306.36	289.08	17.27	0.0692	0.5156
17	6225		0.2500	183.16	173.19	9.97	0.0692	0.0439
18	6425		0.2500	85.54	93.50	-7.96	0.0692	-0.4128
19	6625		0.2500	34.31	45.26	-10.95	0.0692	-0.8556
20	6825		0.2500	10.01	19.61	-9.60	0.0692	-1.2851
21	7025		0.2500	2.29	7.61	-5.32	0.0692	-1.7023

Exhibit 16.2. Calculation of implied volatilities.

from equations (16.12) and (16.57); for the quadratic IVF,

$$\frac{\partial \sigma}{\partial x} = \frac{b}{d} + \frac{2cx}{d^2}.$$

Densities are obtained for the range from 2000 to 8000 on the spreadsheet, with a step size of 20, and hence the density values are located in rows 30–330.

The risk-neutral density $f_Q(x)$ is in column B and is given by equation (16.58), with $\partial \sigma/\partial x$ as above and with $\partial^2 \sigma/\partial x^2 = 2c/d^2$. The utility transformation to a real-world density uses the CRRA parameter γ in cell G24. Then $f_P(x)$ is proportional to $(x/F)^\gamma f_Q(x)$, which is in column L. The approximate numerical integral of $(x/F)^\gamma f_Q(x)$ is in L26 and is used to calculate the values of $f_P(x)$ in column C. The calibration parameters α and β that appear in equation (16.91) are in cells J24 and J25, with $B(\alpha, \beta)$ in J26. These values and the cumulative probabilities in column K are used to obtain the calibrated real-world density in column D. The integrals of the functions f and xf are shown in the rectangle B26:D27. These are all numerical approximations except for the integral of f_Q. The integrals of xf use the values in columns J, M, and N. Note that the last two columns are not visible on Exhibit 16.1.

16.11 Risk Aversion and Rational RNDs

The usefulness of implied risk-neutral densities f_Q for the estimation of real-world densities f_P may depend on observed option prices being correct within some theoretical framework. Mispriced options will complicate the interpretation of f_Q. A particular possibility is that out-of-the money put options on equity indices are overpriced, relative to other options, reflecting anxiety about market crashes and/or buying pressure (Bates 2000, 2003; Jackwerth 2000; Bollen and Whaley 2004). A transformation from an empirical f_Q to an empirical f_P may then unravel the effects of mispricing and produce a correctly calibrated density, but it may not. It is possible that all transformations that are consistent with economic theory produce real-world densities that are incompatible with observed real-world asset prices. If so, we can say f_Q is irrational. We now consider research that discusses the rationality of risk-neutral density estimates f_Q by making comparisons with real-world density estimates f_P that are independently estimated from the history of asset prices.

Estimates of risk aversion have been used to assess the rationality of RNDs. From the representative agent model, the representative utility function has derivative

$$u'(x) = \frac{e^{-rT} f_Q(x)}{\lambda f_P(x)} \tag{16.94}$$

for some positive constant λ (see equations (16.71) and (16.72)). A rational utility function has a negative second derivative for all values of x. Thus one way to assess the rationality of RNDs is to check if $f_Q(x)/f_P(x)$ decreases as x increases, after using some history of asset prices to estimate f_P as in Section 16.2. An equivalent method is to estimate the risk aversion function implied by the first and second derivatives of the utility function, namely

$$RA(x) = -\frac{u''(x)}{u'(x)} = \frac{f_P'(x)}{f_P(x)} - \frac{f_Q'(x)}{f_Q(x)}$$
$$= \frac{d}{dx} \log\left(\frac{f_P(x)}{f_Q(x)}\right). \tag{16.95}$$

This function must be positive for all x if the utility function is rational. The same condition applies to the relative risk aversion function,

$$RRA(x) = x RA(x). \tag{16.96}$$

Empirical estimates of RRA can be used to assess rationality and the applicability of a power utility function, whose RRA function is constant and equal to the CRRA parameter γ (see equation (16.75)).

An important issue when we check empirical ratio functions $f_Q(x)/f_P(x)$ is that f_Q is given by more information than the history of asset prices used to obtain f_P. We know from Chapter 15 that the extra information is reflected by the standard deviation of f_Q being a more accurate predictor of volatility than the standard deviation of f_P. These standard deviations are not even equal on average when volatility risk is priced, as noted in Section 14.5. It is not known what can be learnt from a single empirical ratio function when different information defines the two densities. We may hope that the noise created by the differences can be reduced by calculating an average across several ratio functions.

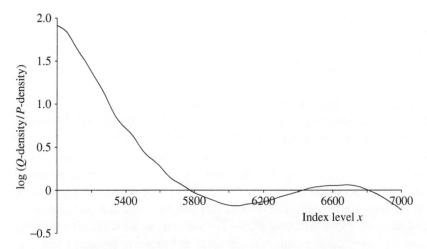

Figure 16.11.   Logarithm of the ratio of Q- and P-densities.

Figure 16.11 shows an estimate of the function $\log(f_Q(x)/f_P(x))$ for the illustrative FTSE data; f_Q is obtained from the GB2 method and adjusted to make it contemporaneous with f_P given by the ARCH density of Section 16.2. It can be seen that $f_Q(x)/f_P(x)$ is estimated to be an increasing function for $6060 \leqslant x \leqslant 6680$, which can be restated as negative risk aversion for $0.97 \leqslant x/F \leqslant 1.07$.

Jackwerth (2000), Aït-Sahalia and Lo (2000), and Rosenberg and Engle (2002) all estimate RA once a month from one-month options on the S&P 500 index; Jackwerth does this for the decade from 1986 to 1995, Aït-Sahalia and Lo only consider 1993 and Rosenberg and Engle cover 1991 to 1995. Their methodologies are quite different. Jackwerth finds that the averages of the RA functions are credible before the crash of October 1987 but appear irrational afterwards. Post-crash, the estimated RA is negative in the range $0.96 \leqslant x/F \leqslant 1.01$. RA also increases for $x/F \geqslant 0.99$, which is incompatible with power and other utility functions. Jackwerth concludes that the most likely explanation of the RA estimates is that the market has consistently mispriced some options. It is possible that his real-world density estimates contribute to the apparent irrationality; his kernel estimates ignore stochastic volatility while his GARCH(1, 1) estimates do not allow for negative skewness in one-month returns (which can be obtained using a GJR(1, 1) model).

Aït-Sahalia and Lo obtain their RND estimates using the kernel regression methods mentioned in Section 16.7, which rely on the implied volatility function being stable through time. The sensitivity of their results to this suspect assumption is unknown. Their RRA estimates are positive, but appear to be inconsistent with a power utility function.

Rosenberg and Engle use the GJR-GARCH model to estimate f_P and then estimate empirical pricing kernels (EPKs) by polynomial functions that best match observed option prices. Thus their methodology separately estimates f_P and f_Q/f_P. Like Jackwerth, they estimate RA to be irrational; it is negative in the range $0.96 \leqslant x/F \leqslant 1.02$. They also show that RA is a time-varying quantity, that is counter cyclical; risk premia are low (high) near business cycle peaks (troughs).

Risk aversion estimates have also been obtained for other assets, including Italian bond futures (Fornari and Mele 2001), the CAC 40 index (Pérignon and Villa 2002), and the FTSE 100 index (Liu et al. 2004).

A different methodology for assessing the rationality of implied risk-neutral densities is used by Aït-Sahalia et al. (2001). Their results are for three-month options on the S&P 500 index from 1986 to 1994. They make no assumptions about the representative investor. Instead they assume index dynamics are determined by a one-factor diffusion process, so volatility is deterministic. The risk-neutral version of these dynamics is estimated and shown to produce RNDs that differ significantly from those implied by option prices. They then show that adding a jump component (that permits rare crashes) can partly reconcile the differences between the two sets of RNDs. Related evidence against deterministic volatility is given in Buraschi and Jackwerth (2001).

16.12   Tail Density Estimates

It is very difficult to estimate the probabilities of extreme price movements. Market implied densities may be useful within the range of traded exercise prices but outside this range they are merely extrapolations. The most practical way to estimate tail probabilities is to make use of the extreme value theory that was noted in Section 12.12.

All densities are now supposed to be real-world densities and we consider shapes for the left tail, that corresponds to an extreme fall in the asset price. Let $f(x)$ and $F(x)$ denote the density and the cumulative function of a future price and let $g(r)$ and $G(r)$ denote these functions for the return defined by $r = \log(x) - \log(S)$.

Then extreme value theory suggests we select

$$G(r) \propto (-r)^{-\alpha}, \quad r \leqslant r_{\mathrm{L}}, \tag{16.97}$$

for some tail index α and some threshold $r_{\mathrm{L}} < 0$. We may suppose that one of the methods presented in this chapter gives us a credible density $f(x)$ over some interval around the current price, from which we can determine the values of $g(r_{\mathrm{L}})$ and $G(r_{\mathrm{L}})$ for plausible threshold levels. We then use the power law (16.97) to specify the left tail density and cumulative functions as

$$g(r) = g(r_{\mathrm{L}})\left(\frac{r}{r_{\mathrm{L}}}\right)^{-(\alpha+1)}, \quad r \leqslant r_{\mathrm{L}}, \tag{16.98}$$

and

$$G(r) = G(r_L)\left(\frac{r}{r_L}\right)^{-\alpha}, \quad r \leqslant r_L. \tag{16.99}$$

As $G(r)$ is the integral of g from minus infinity to r, the tail index is constrained to be

$$\alpha = -\frac{r_L g(r_L)}{G(r_L)} = -\frac{r_L x_L f(x_L)}{F(x_L)} \tag{16.100}$$

with x_L the price level that corresponds to a return r_L.

The above remarks motivate the following empirical strategy: estimate a price density $f(x)$ and then seek an appropriate threshold for which the tail index given by (16.100) is appropriate. Appropriate values of α are between three and five, according to the literature mentioned in Section 12.12. For the illustrative FTSE data and the real-world density defined by recalibrating the risk-neutral GB2 density, $\alpha = 3.02$ when the threshold is a futures return r_L equal to -15%. The estimated probability of a futures price below $x_L = 5340$ is $G(r_L) = F(x_L) = 2.0\%$. The probabilities of even larger price falls during the four-week period under scrutiny can be estimated from (16.99). For example, the estimated probability of the event $S_T < 5040$ is 1 in 130 so an event as extreme as this occurs on average once every ten years. The 25-year event is $S_T < 4670$ for which the futures price must fall by at least 25%.

16.13 Concluding Remarks

Research into density prediction has so far produced many methods but few conclusions. Simulation of ARCH models is a straightforward method, although it requires a substantial amount of numerical calculations. Option-based methods have the advantage of using more information but may be less reliable if option prices are incompatible with a rational theoretical framework. Further research, that compares and combines real-world densities derived from ARCH and option methodologies, is necessary to provide guidance about the most appropriate method for density prediction. The likelihood of observed asset prices, calculated from their predictive densities, is an important statistic for measuring the accuracy of a method. The compatibility of cumulative probabilities with a uniform distribution is also important.

Further Reading

Bliss, R. R. and N. Panigirtzoglou. 2004. Option-implied risk aversion estimates. *Journal of Finance* 59:407–446.

Jackwerth, J. C. 1999. Option implied risk-neutral distributions and implied binomial trees: a literature review. *Journal of Derivatives* 7(4):66–82.

Jackwerth, J. C. 2000. Recovering risk aversion from option prices and realized returns. *Review of Financial Studies* 13:433–451.

466   *16. Density Prediction for Asset Prices*

Jondeau, E. and M. Rockinger. 2000. Reading the smile: the message conveyed by methods which infer risk neutral densities. *Journal of International Money and Finance* 19:885–915.

Melick, W. R. and C. P. Thomas. 1997. Recovering an asset's implied PDF from option prices: an application to crude oil during the Gulf crisis. *Journal of Financial and Quantitative Analysis* 32:91–115.

Symbols

A summary of selected important symbols, functions, and acronyms is provided here. Chapter and section number references to examples and/or definitions are shown in square brackets. Inevitably, several symbols have more than one role.

Roman Letters

A A proportion of the variance of an ARMA(1, 1) model [3.6], or a measure of asymmetry in an ARCH model [10.2]

b An estimate of the variance of an autocorrelation multiplied by the number of observations [5.3]

B A trading rule bandwidth [7.2], or a beta coefficient [16.5]

c A price of a call option [14.2], or a trading cost [7.9]

d A dividend payment [2.5], or a level of fractional differencing [3.8]

d_1 A function used in the BS formulae, likewise d_2 [14.3]

D A general distribution [9.6]

e The number 2.718 28....

e The residual term in an ARCH model [9.5]

f A density function [3.2], or a futures price [2.5], or a forecast [3.5, 15.2]

F A futures or forward price [14.2], or a cumulative distribution function [2.5], or the Fama–French random walk test statistic [6.3]

g The residual term in the log. variance of an EGARCH model [10.2]

h A conditional variance [9.5]

H A forecast horizon [15.2], or a half-life parameter for forecasts [9.4]

i Square root of -1

I An information set [9.5], sometimes the history of prices [5.2, 7.2]

j Counts intraday trading periods [12.5]

J A jump variable [13.5], or the Jegadeesh random walk test statistic [6.3]

k The kurtosis [4.6], or a standardized forecast [7.2]

K The runs test statistic [6.5]

l The logarithm of an absolute excess return [4.10, 11.5], or the likelihood of one observation [9.4, 10.4]

L	The lag operator [3.5], or the likelihood of a set of observations [9.5, 10.4, 11.6], or the parameter of the channel trading rule [7.2]
m	The stochastic discount factor [16.9]
n	A number of observations in a time series [4.2]
N	A number of: time periods over which a multi-period return is calculated [5.3, 11.9], information events [8.3], intraday periods [12.8], or jumps [13.5]; the general normal distribution [3.2], or the c.d.f. of the standard normal distribution [14.3], or the news impact function [10.2]
p	An asset price [2.5], or the price of a put option [14.2], or a probability parameter [16.5], or the number of autoregressive parameters [3.5], or of lagged functions of returns in an ARCH model [9.5]
P	A probability [2.5], or a real-world probability measure [14.3]
q	The number of moving-average parameters [3.5], or of lagged conditional variances in an ARCH model [9.5], or the quantity of an asset [7.2], or the dividend yield rate [14.2]
Q	A risk-neutral probability measure [14.3], or a portmanteau test statistic [4.9]
r	A return on investment [2.5], or a risk-free interest rate [14.2]
R	An annual return [4.3], or an excess return made by a futures trader [7.9], or a correlation [15.3]
R/S	A rescaled range test statistic [6.6]
s	A historical standard deviation [4.2], or a squared excess return [4.11], or a spectral density function [3.3]
S	An asset price in continuous time [13.4], or a sign variable in asymmetric ARCH [9.7] or volatility models [11.9]
t	Time, measured in trading periods [2.5]
T	The time until expiry of a derivative contract [14.2], or the trend test statistic [6.3]
u	A zero-mean, unit-variance random variable [8.4], whose distribution is sometimes normal, or a utility function [16.9], or a cumulative probability [16.9]
v	A forecast error when predicting squared residuals [9.2, 9.3]
V	The variance of a sum of returns [5.3], or the stochastic variance process [13.4]
VR	A ratio of variances [5.3]

W   A Wiener process [3.10, 13.2], or a **BDS** test statistic [6.7]

x A possible outcome of a random variable [3.2],
for example, a later asset price [16.3]

X A random variable [3.2], or the exercise price of an option [14.2]

y A target when forecasting volatility [15.2]

Y A random variable [3.2], for example,
the logarithm of an asset price [14.6]

z A standardized test statistic [4.1, 5.3, 7.3],
or standardized residual [9.5]

Z A Wiener component in a stochastic variance process [13.4]

Greek Letters

α Multiplier of the lagged squared return in an ARCH model [9.3],
or the average log volatility in a SV model [11.5], or the mean of
a continuous-time process [13.3]

α^- An additional multiplier for squares of
lagged negative returns [9.7]

β Multiplier of the lagged conditional variance in
an ARCH model [9.3], or the standard deviation of
log. volatility in a SV model [11.5]

γ Multiplier of the absolute standardized residual in an EGARCH
model [9.2], or the relative risk aversion parameter [16.9]

Γ The gamma function [9.6]

δ A correlation parameter in an asymmetric volatility model [11.9]

Δ An autoregressive parameter in an EGARCH model [10.2],
or a small time increment [13.3]

ε A white noise variable [3.5]

η A white noise variable [3.4, 11.5], or a tail-thickness parameter [9.6]

θ A moving-average parameter [3.5], or a vector of
parameters [9.5, 11.6, 16.4]

ϑ Multiplier of the standardized residual in an EGARCH model [9.2]

Θ A moving-average parameter [9.5]

κ A continuous-time mean-reversion parameter [13.3]

λ An autocovariance of a stochastic process [3.3], or an ARCH-M
parameter [9.5], or a proportion of daily variance [12.5],
or the intensity rate of a Poisson process [13.5]

μ The mean of a random variable [3.2],
sometimes a conditional mean [9.5]

ν The degrees-of-freedom parameter for the t-distribution [9.6],
        or an implied volatility [15.6]

ξ The volatility parameter in a square-root process [13.3],
        which often measures the "volatility of volatility" [14.6]

π The number 3.141 59...

ρ An autocorrelation of a stochastic process [3.3],
        or a correlation between two Wiener processes [13.4]

σ The standard deviation of a random variable [3.2],
        or a measure of volatility [11.2]

τ The difference between two times, often called a lag [3.3]

ϕ An autoregressive [3.5, 11.5] or a persistence [9.7] parameter

Φ The c.d.f. of the standard normal distribution [3.2]

ψ A lognormal density function [16.3]

ω A frequency [3.3], or a constant term in an ARCH model [9.3]

Mathematical Functions and Notation

x^+ The maximum of x and zero
$\exp(x)$ The exponential function (the number e raised to the power x)
$\log(x)$ The natural logarithm of x
$x \cong y$ x is approximately equal to y
$\max(x, y)$ The maximum of x and y

Notation for Random Variables [Section 3.2]

$X \sim \cdots$ The distribution of X is $\cdots$.
$E[X]$ The expectation of a random variable X
$\text{var}(X)$ The variance of a random variable X
$Y \mid X$ A random variable Y conditional on another variable X
$\text{cor}(X, Y)$ The correlation between two random variables
$\text{cov}(X, Y)$ The covariance between two random variables

Acronyms

AR   Autoregressive [3.5]
BS   Black–Scholes [14.3]
c.d.f. Cumulative distribution function [3.2]
CH   Conditionally heteroskedastic [9.1]
EMH   Efficient market hypothesis [5.2]
FI   Fractionally integrated [3.8]
I   Integrated [3.7]

i.i.d.   Independent and identically distributed [3.2]
MA   Moving average [3.5]
MD   Martingale difference [3.4]
RND   Risk-neutral density [16.3]
RWH   Random walk hypothesis [5.2]
SV   Stochastic volatility [11.2]
SWN   Strict white noise [3.4]
WN   White noise [3.4]

Compound Acronyms

ARFIMA   Autoregressive, fractionally integrated,
                 moving average [3.8]
GARCH   Generalized autoregressive conditionally
                 heteroskedastic [9.3]
EGARCH   Exponential, generalized, ... [10.2]
FIEGARCH   Fractionally integrated, exponential,
                 generalized, ... [10.3]

References

Abhyankar, A., L. S. Copeland, and W. Wong. 1995. Nonlinear dynamics in real-time equity market indices: evidence from the U.K. *Economic Journal* 105:864–880.

———. 1997. Uncovering nonlinear structure in real-time stock market indices: the S&P 500, the DAX, the Nikkei 225 and the FTSE-100. *Journal of Business and Economic Statistics* 15:1–14.

Abraham, A. and D. L. Ikenberry. 1994. The individual investor and the weekend effect. *Journal of Financial and Quantitative Analysis* 29:263–277.

Acar, E. 1993. Economic evaluation of financial forecasting. PhD thesis, City University, London.

———. 2002. Expected returns of directional forecasters. In *Advanced trading rules* (ed. E. Acar and S. E. Satchell), 2nd edn, pp. 51–80. Oxford: Butterworth Heinemann.

Acar, E. and P. Lequeux. 1999. Trading rules profits and the underlying time series properties. In *Financial markets tick by tick* (ed. P. Lequeux), pp. 255–301. Chichester: Wiley.

Adler, M. and B. Dumas. 1983. International portfolio choice and corporation finance: a synthesis. *Journal of Finance* 38:925–984.

Ahn, D.-H., J. Boudoukh, M. P. Richardson, and R. F. Whitelaw. 2002. Partial adjustment or stale prices? Implications from stock index and futures return autocorrelations. *Review of Financial Studies* 15:655–689.

Aït-Sahalia, Y. 2002. Telling from discrete data whether the underlying continuous-time model is a diffusion. *Journal of Finance* 57:2075–2112.

Aït-Sahalia, Y. and J. Duarte. 2003. Nonparametric option pricing under shape restrictions. *Journal of Econometrics* 116:9–47.

Aït-Sahalia, Y. and A. W. Lo. 1998. Nonparametric estimation of state-price densities implicit in financial asset prices. *Journal of Finance* 53:499–547.

———. 2000. Nonparametric risk management and implied risk aversion. *Journal of Econometrics* 94:9–51.

Aït-Sahalia, Y., P. A. Mykland, and L. Zhang. 2005. How often to sample a continuous-time process in the presence of market microstructure noise. *Review of Financial Studies* 18:351–416.

Aït-Sahalia, Y., Y. Wang, and F. Yared. 2001. Do option markets correctly price the probabilities of movement of the underlying asset? *Journal of Econometrics* 102:67–110.

Akaike, H. 1974. A new look at statistical model identification. *IEEE Transactions on Automatic Control* 19:716–723.

Akgiray, V. 1989. Conditional heteroscedasticity in time series of stock returns: evidence and forecasts. *Journal of Business* 62:55–80.

Akgiray, V. and C. G. Lamoureux. 1989. On the estimation of the parameters of the stable Paretian distribution. *Journal of Business and Economic Statistics* 7:85–93.

Alexander, C. O. 2001. *Market models*. Chichester: Wiley.

Alexander, S. S. 1961. Price movements in speculative markets: trends or random walks? *Industrial Management Review* 2:7–26.

Alexandré, H., I. Girerd-Potin, and O. Taramasco. 1998. High frequency exchange rate forecasting by the nearest neighbours method. In *Nonlinear modelling of high frequency time series* (ed. C. Dunis and B. Zhou), pp. 279–291. Chichester: Wiley.

Alizadeh, S., M. W. Brandt, and F. X. Diebold. 2002. Range-based estimation of stochastic volatility models. *Journal of Finance* 57:1047–1091.

Allen, F. and R. Karjalainen. 1999. Using genetic algorithms to find technical trading rules. *Journal of Financial Economics* 51:245–271.

Anagnou, I., M. Bedendo, S. D. Hodges, and R. Tompkins. 2002. The relation between implied and realised probability density functions. University of Warwick, UK.

Andersen, T. G. 1994. Stochastic autoregressive volatility: a framework for volatility modeling. *Mathematical Finance* 4:75–102.

———. 1996. Return volatility and trading volume: an information flow interpretation of stochastic volatility. *Journal of Finance* 51:169–204.

Andersen, T. G., L. Benzoni, and J. Lund. 2002. An empirical investigation of continuous-time equity return models. *Journal of Finance* 57:1239–1284.

Andersen, T. G. and T. Bollerslev. 1997a. Heterogeneous information arrivals and return volatility dynamics: uncovering the long-run in high frequency returns. *Journal of Finance* 52:975–1005.

———. 1997b. Intraday periodicity and volatility persistence in financial markets. *Journal of Empirical Finance* 4:115–158.

———. 1998a. DM–dollar volatility: intraday activity patterns, macroeconomic announcements, and longer run dependencies. *Journal of Finance* 53:219–265.

———. 1998b. Answering the skeptics: yes standard volatility models do provide accurate forecasts. *International Economic Review* 39:885–905.

Andersen, T. G., T. Bollerslev, and F. X. Diebold. 2003. Some like it smooth and some like it rough: untangling continuous and jump components in measuring, modeling, and forecasting asset return volatility. University of Pennsylvania, PA.

———. 2005. Parametric and nonparametric volatility measurement. In *Handbook of financial econometrics* (ed. Y. Aït-Sahalia and L. P. Hansen). Amsterdam: North-Holland. In press.

Andersen, T. G., T. Bollerslev, F. X. Diebold, and H. Ebens. 2001. The distribution of realized stock return volatility. *Journal of Financial Economics* 61:43–76.

Andersen, T. G., T. Bollerslev, F. X. Diebold, and P. Labys. 2000. Exchange rates standardized by realized volatility are (nearly) Gaussian. *Multinational Finance Journal* 4:159–179.

———. 2001. The distribution of realized exchange rate volatility. *Journal of the American Statistical Association* 96:42–55.

———. 2003. Modeling and forecasting realized volatility. *Econometrica* 71:579–625.

Andersen, T. G. and B. E. Sørensen. 1996. GMM estimation of a stochastic volatility model: a Monte Carlo study. *Journal of Business and Economic Statistics* 14:328–352.

Anderson, H. M., K. Nam, and F. Vahid. 1999. Asymmetric nonlinear smooth transition GARCH models. In *Nonlinear time series analysis of economic and financial data* (ed. P. Rothman), pp. 191–207. Boston, MA: Kluwer.

Anderson, T. W. and A. M. Walker. 1964. On the asymptotic distribution of the autocorrelations of a sample from a linear stochastic process. *Annals of Mathematical Statistics* 35:1296–1303.

Andreou, E. and E. Ghysels. 2002. Detecting multiple breaks in financial market volatility dynamics. *Journal of Applied Econometrics* 17:579–600.

Ané, T. 1999. Pricing and hedging S&P 500 index options with Hermite polynomial approximation: empirical tests of Madan and Milne's model. *Journal of Futures Markets* 19:735–758.

Ané, T. and H. Geman. 2000. Order flow, transaction clock and normality of asset returns. *Journal of Finance* 55:2259–2284.

Antoniou, A. and P. Holmes. 1994. Systematic risk and returns to stock index futures contracts: international evidence. *Journal of Futures Markets* 7:773–787.

Aparicio, S. D. and S. D. Hodges. 1998. Implied risk-neutral distributions: a comparison of estimation methods. University of Warwick, UK.

ap Gwilym, O., M. Buckle, and S. Thomas. 1999. The intra-day behaviour of key market variables for LIFFE derivatives. In *Financial markets tick by tick* (ed. P. Lequeux), pp. 151–189. Chichester: Wiley.

Areal, N. M. P. C. and S. J. Taylor. 2002. The realized volatility of FTSE-100 futures prices. *Journal of Futures Markets* 22:627–648.

Ariel, R. A. 1987. A monthly effect in stock returns. *Journal of Financial Economics* 18:161–174.

———. 1990. High stock returns before holidays: existence and evidence on possible causes. *Journal of Finance* 45:1611–1626.

Arnott, R. D. and P. L. Bernstein. 2002. What risk premium is 'normal'? *Financial Analysts Journal* 58(March):64–85.

Arteche, J. 2004. Gaussian semiparametric estimation in long memory in stochastic volatility and signal plus noise models. *Journal of Econometrics* 119:131–154.

Avramov, D., T. Chordia, and A. Goyal. 2004. The impact of trades on daily volatility. University of Maryland.

Baba, Y., R. F. Engle, D. F. Kraft, and K. F. Kroner. 1991. Multivariate simultaneous generalized ARCH. University of California, San Diego.

Bachelier, L. 1900. Theory of speculation. Reprinted in *The random character of stock market prices* (ed. P. Cootner), pp. 17–78 (1964). Cambridge, MA: MIT Press.

Bahra, B. 1997. Implied risk-neutral probability density functions from option prices: theory and application. Bank of England, London.

Baillie, R. T. 1996. Long memory processes and fractional integration in econometrics. *Journal of Econometrics* 73:5–59.

Baillie, R. T. and T. Bollerslev. 1989a. Common stochastic trends in a system of exchange rates. *Journal of Finance* 44:167–181.

———. 1989b. The message in daily exchange rates: a conditional-variance tale. *Journal of Business and Economic Statistics* 7:297–305.

———. 1994. Cointegration, fractional cointegration and exchange rate dynamics. *Journal of Finance* 49:737–745.

Baillie, R. T., T. Bollerslev, and H. O. Mikkelsen. 1996. Fractionally integrated generalized autoregressive conditional heteroskedasticity. *Journal of Econometrics* 74:3–30.

Bakshi, G., C. Cao, and Z. Chen. 1997. Empirical performance of alternative option pricing models. *Journal of Finance* 52:2003–2049.

———. 2000. Pricing and hedging long-term options. *Journal of Econometrics* 94:277–318.

Bakshi, G. and N. Kapadia. 2003. Delta-hedged gains and the negative market volatility risk premium. *Review of Financial Studies* 16:527–566.

Bakshi, G., N. Kapadia, and D. B. Madan. 2003. Stock return characteristics, skew laws, and the differential pricing of individual equity options. *Review of Financial Studies* 16:101–143.

Balaban, E., A. Bayar, and R. W. Faff. 2003. Forecasting stock market volatility: evidence from fourteen countries. University of Edinburgh, UK.

Ball, C. A. and A. Roma. 1994. Stochastic volatility option pricing. *Journal of Financial and Quantitative Analysis* 29:589–607.

Ball, C. A. and W. N. Torous. 1983. A simplified jump process for common stock returns. *Journal of Financial and Quantitative Analysis* 18:53–65.

Bams, D., K. Walkowiak, and C. C. P. Wolff. 2004. More evidence on the dollar risk premium in the foreign exchange market. *Journal of International Money and Finance* 23:271–282.

Bandi, F. M. and J. R. Russell. 2004a. Microstructure noise, realized variance, and optimal sampling. University of Chicago.

———. 2004b. Separating market microstructure noise from volatility. *Journal of Financial Economics*. In press.

Bansal, R. and C. Lundblad. 2002. Market efficiency, asset returns, and the size of the risk premium in global equity markets. *Journal of Econometrics* 109:195–237.

Banz, R. W. 1981. The relationship between return and market value of common stocks. *Journal of Financial Economics* 9:3–18.

Barndorff-Nielsen, O. E., E. Nicolato, and N. Shephard. 2002. Some recent developments in stochastic volatility modelling. *Quantitative Finance* 2:11–23.

Barndorff-Nielsen, O. E. and N. Shephard. 2001. Non-Gaussian Ornstein–Uhlenbeck based models and some of their uses in financial economics. *Journal of the Royal Statistical Society* B 63:167–241.

———. 2002a. Estimating quadratic variation using realised variance. *Journal of Applied Econometrics* 17:457–477.

———. 2002b. Econometric analysis of realized volatility and its use in estimating stochastic volatility models. *Journal of the Royal Statistical Society* B 64:253–280.

———. 2004a. Power and bipower variation with stochastic volatility and jumps. *Journal of Financial Econometrics* 2:1–48.

———. 2004b. Econometrics of testing for jumps in financial economics using bipower variation. *Journal of Financial Econometrics*. In press.

———. 2005a. *Continuous time approach to financial volatility*. Cambridge University Press.

———. 2005b. Impact of jumps on returns and realised variances: econometric analysis of time-deformed Lévy processes. *Journal of Econometrics*. In press.

Barone-Adesi, G. and R. E. Whaley. 1987. Efficient analytic approximation of American option values. *Journal of Finance* 42:301–320.

Bates, D. S. 1991. The crash of '87: was it expected? The evidence from options markets. *Journal of Finance* 46:1009–1044.

———. 1996. Jumps and stochastic volatility: exchange rate processes implicit in Deutsche mark options. *Review of Financial Studies* 9:69–107.

———. 2000. Post-'87 crash fears in the S&P 500 futures option market. *Journal of Econometrics* 94:181–238.

———. 2003. Empirical option pricing: a retrospection. *Journal of Econometrics* 116:387–404.

Baumol, W. and J. Benhabib. 1989. Chaos: significance, mechanism, and economic applications. *Journal of Economic Perspectives* 3:77–105.

Bauwens, L. and D. Veredas. 2004. The stochastic conditional duration model: a latent variable model for the analysis of financial durations. *Journal of Econometrics* 119:381–412.

Baxter, M. W. and A. J. O. Rennie. 1996. *Financial calculus*. Cambridge University Press.

Becker, K. G., J. E. Finnerty, and K. J. Kopecky. 1993. Economic news and intraday volatility in international bond markets. *Financial Analysts Journal* 49(May):81–86.

———. 1995. Economic news and equity market linkages between the U.S. and U.K. *Journal of Banking and Finance* 19:1191–1210.

Beckers, S. 1981. A note on estimating the parameters of the diffusion-jump model of stock returns. *Journal of Financial and Quantitative Analysis* 16:127–140.

Beckers, S. 1983. Variance of security price returns based on high, low and closing prices. *Journal of Business* 56:97–112.

Bekaert, G. and G. Wu. 2000. Asymmetric volatility and risk in equity markets. *Review of Financial Studies* 13:1–42.

Berkowitz, J. 2001. Testing density forecasts, with applications to risk management. *Journal of Business and Economic Statistics* 19:465–474.

Berndt, E. R., B. H. Hall, R. E. Hall, and J. A. Hausman. 1974. Estimation and inference in nonlinear statistical models. *Annals of Economic and Social Measurement* 3:653–665.

Berry, D. T. and M. K. Howe. 1994. Public information arrival. *Journal of Finance* 49:1331–1345.

Bessembinder, H. 1993. An empirical analysis of risk premia in futures markets. *Journal of Futures Markets* 13:611–630.

Bessembinder, H. and K. Chan. 1992. Time-varying risk premia and forecastable returns in futures markets. *Journal of Financial Economics* 32:169–193.

——. 1995a. Do the profits from technical trading rules reflect inefficiencies? Arizona State University, Tempe.

——. 1995b. The profitability of technical trading rules in the Asian stock markets. *Pacific-Basin Finance Journal* 3:257–284.

——. 1998. Market efficiency and the returns to technical analysis. *Financial Management* 27:5–17.

Black, F. 1976a. The pricing of commodity contracts. *Journal of Financial Economics* 3:167–179.

——. 1976b. Studies of stock price volatility changes. *Proceedings of the American Statistical Association, Business and Economic Statistics Section*, pp. 177–181.

Black, F. and M. Scholes. 1973. The pricing of options and corporate liabilities. *Journal of Political Economy* 81:637–659.

Blair, B. J., S.-H. Poon, and S. J. Taylor. 2001a. Modelling S&P 100 volatility: the information content of stock returns. *Journal of Banking and Finance* 25:1665–1679.

——. 2001b. Forecasting S&P 100 volatility: the incremental information content of implied volatilities and high frequency index returns. *Journal of Econometrics* 105:5–26.

——. 2002. Asymmetric and crash effects in stock volatility for the S&P 100 index and its constituents. *Applied Financial Economics* 12:319–329.

Blattberg, R. C. and N. J. Gonedes. 1974. A comparison of the stable and Student distributions as models for stock prices. *Journal of Business* 47:244–280.

Bliss, R. R. and N. Panigirtzoglou. 2002. Testing the stability of implied probability density functions. *Journal of Banking and Finance* 26:381–422.

——. 2004. Option-implied risk aversion estimates. *Journal of Finance* 59:407–446.

Board, J. L. G. and C. M. S. Sutcliffe. 1995. The relative volatility of the markets in equities and index futures. *Journal of Business Finance and Accounting* 22:201–223.

Bodie, Z. and V. I. Rosansky. 1980. Risk and return in commodity futures. *Financial Analysts Journal* 36(May):27–39.

Bollen, N. P. B. and R. E. Whaley. 2004. Does net buying pressure affect the shape of implied volatility functions? *Journal of Finance* 59:711–753.

Bollerslev, T. 1986. Generalized autoregressive conditional heteroscedasticity. *Journal of Econometrics* 31:307–327.

——. 1987. A conditionally heteroskedastic time series model for security prices and rates of return data. *Review of Economics and Statistics* 59:542–547.

——. 1988. On the correlation structure for the generalized autoregressive conditional heteroskedastic process. *Journal of Time Series Analysis* 9:121–131.

Bollerslev, T. 1990. Modelling the coherence in short-run nominal exchange rates: a multivariate generalized ARCH approach. *Review of Economics and Statistics* 72:498–505.

Bollerslev, T., R. Y. Chou, and K. F. Kroner. 1992. ARCH modeling in finance: a review of the theory and empirical evidence. *Journal of Econometrics* 52:5–59.

Bollerslev, T., R. F. Engle, and D. B. Nelson. 1994. ARCH models. In *Handbook of econometrics*, pp. 2959–3038, vol. IV. Amsterdam: North-Holland.

Bollerslev, T., R. F. Engle, and J. M. Wooldridge. 1988. A capital asset pricing model with time varying covariances. *Journal of Political Economy* 96:116–131.

Bollerslev, T. and H. O. Mikkelsen. 1996. Modeling and pricing long memory in stock market volatility. *Journal of Econometrics* 73:151–184.

———. 1999. Long-term equity anticipation securities and stock market volatility dynamics. *Journal of Econometrics* 92:75–99.

Bollerslev, T. and J. M. Wooldridge. 1992. Quasi-maximum likelihood estimation and inference in dynamic models with time varying covariances. *Econometric Reviews* 11:143–172.

Bollerslev, T. and J. H. Wright. 2000. Semiparametric estimation of long-memory volatility dependencies: the role of high-frequency data. *Journal of Econometrics* 98:81–106.

Bollerslev, T. and H. Zhou. 2002. Estimating stochastic volatility diffusion using conditional moments of integrated volatility. *Journal of Econometrics* 109:33–65.

Bondarenko, O. 2003. Estimation of risk-neutral densities using positive convolution approximation. *Journal of Econometrics* 116:85–112.

Bookstaber, R. M. and J. B. McDonald. 1987. A general distribution for describing security price returns. *Journal of Business* 60:401–424.

Booth, G. G. and U. G. Gurun. 2004. Financial archaeology: capitalism, financial markets, and price volatility. Michigan State University.

Boudoukh, J., M. P. Richardson, and R. F. Whitelaw. 1994. A tale of three schools: insights on autocorrelations of short-horizon stock returns. *Review of Financial Studies* 7:539–573.

Bouman, S. and B. Jacobsen. 2002. The Halloween indicator, 'Sell in May and go away': another puzzle. *American Economic Review* 92:1618–1635.

Box, G. E. P., G. M. Jenkins, and G. Reinsel. 1994. *Time series analysis, forecasting and control*. Englewood Cliffs, NJ: Prentice-Hall.

Box, G. E. P. and D. A. Pierce. 1970. Distributions of residual autocorrelations in autoregressive integrated moving average models. *Journal of the American Statistical Association* 65:1509–1526.

Boyle, P., M. Broadie, and P. Glasserman. 1997. Monte Carlo methods for security pricing. *Journal of Economic Dynamics and Control* 21:1267–1321.

Brailsford, T. J. and R. W. Faff. 1996. An evaluation of volatility forecasting techniques. *Journal of Banking and Finance* 20:419–438.

Breeden, D. T. and R. H. Litzenberger. 1978. Prices of state-contingent claims implicit in option prices. *Journal of Business* 51:621–651.

Breidt, F. J. and A. L. Carriquiry. 1996. Improved quasi-maximum likelihood estimation for stochastic volatility models. In *Modeling and prediction: honoring Seymour Giesel* (ed. J. Lee, W. Johnson, and A. Zellner), pp. 228–247. New York: Springer.

Breidt, F. J., N. Crato, and P. de Lima. 1998. The detection and estimation of long memory in stochastic volatility. *Journal of Econometrics* 83:325–348.

Britten-Jones, M. and A. Neuberger. 2000. Option prices, implied price processes, and stochastic volatility. *Journal of Finance* 55:839–866.

Brock, W. 1987. Notes on nuisance parameter problems in BDS type tests for IID. University of Wisconsin at Madison.

Brock, W., W. Dechert, and J. Scheinkman. 1987. A test for independence based on the correlation dimension. University of Wisconsin at Madison.

Brock, W., W. Dechert, J. Scheinkman, and B. LeBaron. 1996. A test for independence based on the correlation dimension. *Econometric Reviews* 15:197–235.

Brock, W., J. Lakonishok, and B. LeBaron. 1992. Simple technical trading rules and the stochastic properties of stock returns. *Journal of Finance* 47:1731–1764.

Brock, W. and B. LeBaron. 1996. A dynamic structural model for stock return volatility and trading volume. *Review of Economics and Statistics* 78:94–110.

Brockwell, P. J. and R. A. Davis. 1991. *Time series: theory and methods*, 2nd edn. New York: Springer.

Brown, C. A. and D. M. Robinson. 2002. Skewness and kurtosis implied by option prices: a correction. *Journal of Financial Research* 25:279–282.

Brown, P., D. Keim, A. Kleidon, and T. Marsh. 1983. New evidence on the nature of size-related anomalies in stock prices. *Journal of Financial Economics* 12:33–56.

Brown, S. J. and J. B. Warner. 1985. Using daily stock returns: the case of event studies. *Journal of Financial Economics* 14:3–31.

Buchen, P. W. and M. Kelly. 1996. The maximum entropy distribution of an asset inferred from option prices. *Journal of Financial and Quantitative Analysis* 31:143–159.

Buraschi, A. and J. C. Jackwerth. 2001. The price of a smile: hedging and spanning in option markets. *Review of Financial Studies* 14:495–527.

Byers, J. D. and D. A. Peel. 2001. Volatility persistence in asset markets: long memory in high/low prices. *Applied Financial Economics* 11:253–260.

Byoun, S., C. C. Y. Kwok, and H. Y. Park. 2003. The expectations hypothesis of the term structure of implied volatility: evidence from foreign currency and stock index options. *Journal of Financial Econometrics* 1:126–151.

Cai, J. 1994. A Markov model of switching-regime ARCH. *Journal of Business and Economic Statistics* 12:309–316.

Campa, J. M. and P. H. K. Chang. 1995. Testing the expectations hypothesis on the term structure of volatilities in foreign exchange rate options. *Journal of Finance* 50:529–547.

Campa, J. M., P. H. K. Chang, and R. L. Reider. 1998. Implied exchange rate distributions: evidence from OTC option markets. *Journal of International Money and Finance* 17:117–160.

Campbell, J. Y. and L. Hentschel. 1992. No news is good news: an asymmetric model of changing volatility in stock returns. *Journal of Financial Economics* 31:281–318.

Campbell, J. Y., A. W. Lo, and A. C. MacKinlay. 1997. *The econometrics of financial markets*. Princeton University Press.

Canina, L. and S. Figlewski. 1993. The informational content of implied volatility. *Review of Financial Studies* 6:659–681.

Carr, P., H. Geman, D. B. Madan, and M. Yor. 2002. The fine structure of asset returns: an empirical investigation. *Journal of Business* 75:305–332.

———. 2003. Stochastic volatility for Lévy processes. *Mathematical Finance* 13:345–382.

Carr, P. and D. B. Madan. 1998. Towards a theory of volatility trading. In *Volatility* (ed. R. A. Jarrow), pp. 417–427. London: Risk Books.

Carr, P. and L. Wu. 2004. Time-changed Lévy processes and option pricing. *Journal of Financial Economics* 71:113–141.

Chan, L. K. C. and J. Lakonishok. 1993. Institutional trades and intraday stock price behavior. *Journal of Financial Economics* 33:173–199.

Chang, E. C. 1985. Returns to speculators and the theory of normal backwardation. *Journal of Finance* 40:193–207.

Chang, E. C., J. M. Pinegar, and R. Ravichandran. 1993. International evidence on the robustness of the day-of-the-week effect. *Journal of Financial and Quantitative Analysis* 28:497–513.

Chang, Y. and S. J. Taylor. 1998. Intraday effects of foreign exchange intervention by the Bank of Japan. *Journal of International Money and Finance* 17:191–210.

———. 2003. Information arrivals and intraday exchange rate volatility. *Journal of International Financial Markets, Institutions and Money* 13:85–112.

Chen, H. and V. Singal. 2003. Role of speculative short sales in price formation: the case of the weekend effect. *Journal of Finance* 58:685–705.

Chernov, M., A. R. Gallant, E. Ghysels, and G. E. Tauchen. 2003. Alternative models for stock price dynamics. *Journal of Econometrics* 16:225–257.

Chernov, M. and E. Ghysels. 2000. A study towards a unified approach to the joint estimation of objective and risk neutral measures for the purpose of options valuation. *Journal of Financial Economics* 56:407–458.

Chesney, M. and L. O. Scott. 1989. Pricing European currency options: a comparison of the modified Black–Scholes model and a random variance model. *Journal of Financial and Quantitative Analysis* 24:267–284.

Cheung, Y. W. and L. K. Ng. 1992. Stock price dynamics and firm size: an empirical investigation. *Journal of Finance* 48:1985–1997.

Chib, S. 2001. Markov chain Monte Carlo methods: computation and inference. In *Handbook of econometrics* (ed. J. J. Heckman and E. Leamer), vol. V, pp. 3569–3649. Amsterdam: North-Holland.

Chib, S., F. Nardari, and N. Shephard. 2002. Markov chain Monte Carlo methods for stochastic volatility models. *Journal of Econometrics* 108:281–316.

———. 2005. Analyisis of high dimensional multivariate stochastic volatility models. *Journal of Econometrics*. In press.

Chiras, D. P. and S. Manaster. 1978. The information content of option prices and a test for market efficiency. *Journal of Financial Economics* 50:125–150.

Chopard, B., O. V. Pictet, and M. Tomassini. 2000. Parallel and distributed evolutionary computation for financial applications. *Parallel Algorithms and Applications Journal* 15:15–36.

Chou, R. Y. 1988. Persistent volatility and stock returns—some empirical evidence using GARCH. *Journal of Applied Econometrics* 3:279–294.

———. 2004. Forecasting financial volatilities with extreme values: the conditional autoregressive range model. *Journal of Money, Credit and Banking*. In press.

Chow, K. V. and K. C. Denning. 1993. A simple multiple variance ratio test. *Journal of Econometrics* 58:385–401.

Christensen, B. J. and N. R. Prabhala. 1998. The relation between implied and realized volatility. *Journal of Financial Economics* 50:125–150.

Christie, A. A. 1982. The stochastic behavior of common stock variances: value, leverage and interest rate effects. *Journal of Financial Economics* 10:407–432.

Clark, P. K. 1973. A subordinated stochastic process model with finite variance for speculative prices. *Econometrica* 41:135–155.

Cochrane, J. H. 1988. How big is the random walk in GNP? *Journal of Political Economy* 96:893–920.

———. 2001. *Asset pricing*. Princeton University Press.

Comte, F. and E. Renault. 1998. Long memory in continuous-time stochastic volatility models. *Mathematical Finance* 8:291–323.

Condoyanni, L., J. O'Hanlon, and C. W. R. Ward. 1987. Day-of-the-week effect on stock returns: international evidence. *Journal of Business Finance and Accounting* 14:159–174.

Connolly, R. A. 1989. An examination of the robustness of the weekend effect. *Journal of Financial and Quantitative Analysis* 24:133–169.

———. 1991. A posterior odds analysis of the weekend effect. *Journal of Econometrics* 49:51–104.

Conrad, J. and G. Kaul. 1989. Mean reversion in short-horizon expected returns. *Review of Financial Studies* 2:225–240.

Constantinides, G. M. 1982. Intertemporal asset pricing with heterogenous consumers and without demand aggregation. *Journal of Business* 55:253–268.

Cont, R. 1999. Beyond implied volatility. In *Econophysics* (ed. J. Kertesz and I. Kondor). Dordrecht: Kluwer.

Cont, R. and J. da Fonseca. 2002. Dynamics of implied volatility surfaces. *Quantitative Finance* 2:45–60.

Cont, R. and P. Tankov. 2003. *Financial modelling with jump processes*. Boca Raton, FL: Chapman & Hall.

Corrado, C. J. and T. Su. 1996. Skewness and kurtosis in S&P 500 index returns implied by option prices. *Journal of Financial Research* 19:175–192.

———. 1997. Implied volatility skews and stock index skewness and kurtosis implied by S&P 500 index option prices. *Journal of Derivatives* 4(Summer):8–19.

Coutant, S., E. Jondeau, and M. Rockinger. 2001. Reading PIBOR futures options smiles: the 1997 snap election. *Journal of Banking and Finance* 25:1957–1987.

Cox, J. C., J. E. Ingersoll, and S. A. Ross. 1981. The relationship between forward prices and futures prices. *Journal of Financial Economics* 9:321–346.

———. 1985. A theory of the term structure of interest rates. *Econometrica* 53:385–407.

Cox, J. C. and S. A. Ross. 1976. The valuation of options for alternative stochastic processes. *Journal of Financial Economics* 3:145–166.

Crack, T. F. and O. Ledoit. 1996. Robust structure without predictability: the "compass rose" pattern of the stock market. *Journal of Finance* 51:751–762.

Cross, F. 1973. The behavior of stock prices on Fridays and Mondays. *Financial Analysts Journal* 29(November):67–69.

Dacorogna, M. M., R. Gençay, U. A. Müller, R. B. Olsen, and O. V. Pictet. 2001. *An introduction to high-frequency finance*. San Diego, CA: Academic Press.

Dacorogna, M. M., U. A. Müller, R. J. Nagler, R. B. Olsen, and O. V. Pictet. 1993. A geographical model for the daily and weekly seasonal volatility in the foreign exchange market. *Journal of International Money and Finance* 12:413–438.

Dacorogna, M. M., U. A. Müller, R. B. Olsen, and O. V. Pictet. 1998. Modelling short-term volatility with GARCH and HARCH models. In *Nonlinear modelling of high frequency time series* (ed. C. Dunis and B. Zhou), pp. 161–176. Chichester: Wiley.

Daniel, K. 2001. The power and size of mean reversion tests. *Journal of Empirical Finance* 8:493–535.

Daniel, K. and S. Titman. 1997. Evidence on the characteristics of cross sectional variation in stock returns. *Journal of Finance* 52:1–33.

Daniels, H. 1966. Autocorrelation between first differences of mid-ranges. *Econometrica* 34:215–219.

Danielsson, J. 1994. Stochastic volatility in asset prices: estimation with simulated maximum likelihood. *Journal of Econometrics* 64:375–400.

———. 1997. Multivariate stochastic volatility models: estimation and a comparison with VGARCH models. *Journal of Empirical Finance* 5:155–173.

Danielsson, J. and C. G. de Vries. 1997. Tail index and quantile estimation with very high frequency data. *Journal of Empirical Finance* 4:241–257.

Daníelsson, J. and J. F. Richard. 1993. Accelerated Gaussian importance sampler with application to dynamic latent variable models. *Journal of Applied Econometrics* 3:S153–S174.

Das, S. R. and R. K. Sundaram. 1999. Of smiles and smirks: a term structure perspective. *Journal of Financial and Quantitative Analysis* 34:211–239.

Dawson, E. R. and J. M. Steeley. 2003. On the existence of visual technical patterns in the U.K. stock market. *Journal of Business Finance and Accounting* 30:263–293.

Day, T. E. and C. M. Lewis. 1992. Stock market volatility and the information content of stock index options. *Journal of Econometrics* 52:267–287.

———. 1993. Forecasting futures market volatility. *Journal of Derivatives* 1(Winter):33–50.

Day, T. E. and P. Wang. 2002. Dividends, nonsynchronous prices, and the returns from trading the Dow Jones Industrial Average. *Journal of Empirical Finance* 9:431–454.

DeGennaro, R. P. and R. E. Shrieves. 1997. Public information releases, private information arrival and volatility in the foreign exchange market. *Journal of Empirical Finance* 4:295–315.

De Jong, F. and T. Nijman. 1997. High frequency analysis of lead-lag relationships between financial markets. *Journal of Empirical Finance* 4:259–277.

Dichev, I. D. and T. D. Janes. 2003. Lunar cycle effects in stock returns. *Journal of Private Equity* 6(4):8–29.

Diebold, F. X., T. A. Gunther, and A. S. Tay. 1998. Evaluating density forecasts with applications to financial risk management. *International Economic Review* 39:863–883.

Diebold, F. X. and A. Inoue. 2001. Long memory and regime switching. *Journal of Econometrics* 105:131–159.

Diebold, F. X. and R. S. Mariano. 1995. Comparing predictive accuracy. *Journal of Business and Economic Statistics* 13:252–263.

Dimson, E. and P. Marsh. 1990. Volatility forecasting without data-snooping. *Journal of Banking and Finance* 14:399–421.

———. 1999. Murphy's law and market anomalies. *Journal of Portfolio Management* 25(Winter):53–69.

Dimson, E., P. Marsh, and M. Staunton. 2002. *Triumph of the optimists: 101 years of global investment returns*. Princeton University Press.

Ding, Z. and C. W. J. Granger. 1996. Modeling volatility persistence of speculative returns: a new approach. *Journal of Econometrics* 73:185–215.

Ding, Z., C. W. J. Granger, and R. F. Engle. 1993. A long memory property of stock market returns and a new model. *Journal of Empirical Finance* 1:83–106.

Dominguez, K. M. E. 2003. The market microstructure of central bank intervention. *Journal of International Economics* 59:25–45.

Dooley, M. P. and J. R. Shafer. 1983. Analysis of short-run exchange rate behavior: March 1973 to November 1981. In *Exchange rate and trade instability: causes, consequences and remedies* (ed. D. Bigman and T. Taya), pp. 43–69. Cambridge, MA: Ballinger.

Drost, F. C. and T. E. Nijman. 1993. Temporal aggregation of GARCH processes. *Econometrica* 61:909–927.

Duan, J.-C. 1995. The GARCH option pricing model. *Mathematical Finance* 5:13–32.

———. 1997. Augmented GARCH(p, q) process and its diffusion limit. *Journal of Econometrics* 79:97–127.

Duan, J.-C., G. Gauthier, and J. Simonato. 1999. An analytical approximation for the GARCH option pricing model. *Journal of Computational Finance* 2:75–116.

Dueker, M. J. 1997. Markov switching in GARCH processes and mean-reverting stock market volatility. *Journal of Business and Economic Statistics* 15:26–34.

Duffee, G. R. 1995. Stock returns and volatility: a firm-level analysis. *Journal of Financial Economics* 37:399–420.

Duffie, D., J. Pan, and K. J. Singleton. 2000. Transform analysis and asset pricing for affine jump-diffusions. *Econometrica* 68:1343–1376.

Dufour, A. and R. F. Engle. 2000. Time and the price impact of a trade. *Journal of Finance* 55:2467–2498.

Dumas, B., J. Fleming, and R. E. Whaley. 1998. Implied volatility functions: empirical tests. *Journal of Finance* 53:2059–2106.

Dunis, C. L., M. Gavridis, A. Harris, S. Leong, and P. Nacaskul. 1998. An application of genetic algorithms to high frequency trading models: a case study. In *Nonlinear modelling of high frequency time series* (ed. C. Dunis and B. Zhou), pp. 247–278. Chichester: Wiley.

Durbin, J. and S. J. Koopman. 2000. Time series analysis of non-Gaussian observations based on state space models from both classical and Bayesian perspectives. *Journal of the Royal Statistical Society* B 62:1–28.

Dusak, K. 1973. Futures trading and investor returns: an investigation of commodity market risk premiums. *Journal of Political Economy* 81:1387–1406.

Easley, D. and M. O'Hara. 1992. Time and the process of security price adjustment. *Journal of Finance* 47:905–927.

Ebens, H. 1999. *Realized stock volatility*. Johns Hopkins University.

Ederington, L. H. and W. Guan. 2002a. Measuring implied volatility: is an average better?, which average? *Journal of Futures Markets* 22:811–837.

———. 2002b. Is implied volatility an informationally efficient and effective predictor of future volatility? *Journal of Risk* 4(Spring):29–46.

———. 2002c. Forecasting volatility. University of Oklahoma.

Ederington, L. H. and J. H. Lee. 1993. How markets process information: news releases and volatility. *Journal of Finance* 49:1161–1191.

———. 1995. The short run dynamics of the price adjustment to new information. *Journal of Financial and Quantitative Analysis* 30:117–134.

Elton, E. J., M. J. Gruber, and J. C. Rentzler. 1987. Professionally managed, publicly traded commodity funds. *Journal of Political Economy* 60:175–199.

Embrechts, P., C. Klüppelberg, and T. Mikosch. 1997. *Modelling extremal events for insurance and finance*. Berlin: Springer.

Engle, R. F. 1982. Autoregressive conditional heteroscedasticity with estimates of the variance of United Kingdom inflation. *Econometrica* 50:987–1007.

———. 1990. Discussion: stock market volatility and the crash of 87. *Review of Financial Studies* 3:103–106.

———. 2000. The econometrics of ultra-high-frequency data. *Econometrica* 68:1–22.

———. 2002. Dynamic conditional correlation: a simple class of multivariate generalized autoregressive conditional heteroskedasticity models. *Journal of Business and Economic Statistics* 20:339–350.

Engle, R. F. and T. Bollerslev. 1986. Modelling the persistence of conditional variances. *Econometric Reviews* 5:1–50.

Engle, R. F. and G. González-Rivera. 1991. Semiparametric ARCH models. *Journal of Business and Economic Statistics* 9:345–359.

Engle, R. F. and K. F. Kroner. 1995. Multivariate simultaneous generalized ARCH. *Econometric Theory* 11:122–150.

Engle, R. F. and G. G. J. Lee. 1999. A permanent and transitory component model of stock return volatility. In *Cointegration, causality and forecasting: a Festschrift in honor of C. W. J. Granger* (ed. R. F. Engle and H. White), pp. 475–497. Oxford University Press.

Engle, R. F., D. M. Lilien, and R. P. Robins. 1987. Estimating the time varying risk premia in the term structure: the ARCH-M model. *Econometrica* 55:391–407.

Engle, R. F. and J. Mezrich. 1995. Grappling with GARCH. *Risk* 8(September):112–117.

Engle, R. F. and V. K. Ng. 1993. Measuring and testing the impact of news on volatility. *Journal of Finance* 48:1749–1778.

Engle, R. F., V. K. Ng, and M. Rothschild. 1990. Asset pricing with a factor ARCH covariance structure: empirical estimates for Treasury Bills. *Journal of Econometrics* 45:213–238.

Engle, R. F. and J. V. Rosenberg. 1995. GARCH gamma. *Journal of Derivatives* 2(Winter):47–59.

Engle, R. F. and J. R. Russell. 1997. Forecasting the frequency of changes in quoted foreign exchange prices with the autoregressive conditional duration model. *Journal of Empirical Finance* 4:187–212.

——. 1998. Autoregressive conditional duration: a new model for irregularly spaced transaction data. *Econometrica* 66:1127–1162.

Epps, T. W. and M. L. Epps. 1976. The stochastic dependence of security price changes and transaction volumes: implications for the mixture-of-distributions hypothesis. *Econometrica* 44:305–321.

Eraker, B. 2004. Do stock prices and volatility jump? Reconciling evidence from spot and option prices. *Journal of Finance* 59:1367–1403.

Eraker, B., M. Johannes, and N. G. Polson. 2003. The impact of jumps in volatility and returns. *Journal of Finance* 58:1269–1300.

Etheridge, A. 2002. *A course in financial calculus.* Cambridge University Press.

Fackler, P. L. and R. P. King. 1990. Calibration of option-based probability assessments in agricultural commodity markets. *American Journal of Agricultural Economics* 72:73–83.

Fair, R. C. and R. J. Shiller. 1989. The informational content of *ex ante* forecasts. *Review of Economics and Statistics* 71:325–332.

Fama, E. F. 1965. The behavior of stock market prices. *Journal of Business* 38:34–105.

——. 1976. *Foundations of finance.* Oxford: Basil Blackwell.

——. 1991. Efficient capital markets. II. *Journal of Finance* 46:1575–1617.

Fama, E. F. and K. R. French. 1988. Permanent and temporary components of stock prices. *Journal of Political Economy* 96:246–273.

——. 1992. The cross-section of expected stock returns. *Journal of Finance* 47:427–465.

——. 1995. Size and book-to-market factors in earnings and returns. *Journal of Finance* 50:131–155.

——. 1998. Value versus growth: the international evidence. *Journal of Finance* 53:1975–1999.

——. 2002. The equity premium. *Journal of Finance* 57:637–659.

Fama, E. F. and R. Roll. 1971. Parameter estimates for symmetric stable distributions. *Journal of the American Statistical Association* 66:331–338.

Fang, Y. and D. Xu. 2003. The predictability of asset returns: an approach combining technical analysis and time series forecasts. *International Journal of Forecasting* 19:369–385.

Ferguson, M. F. and R. L. Shockley. 2003. Equilibrium "anomalies". *Journal of Finance* 58:2549–2580.

Fields, M. J. 1931. Stock prices: a problem in verification. *Journal of Business* 4:415–418.

Fink, R. E. and R. B. Feduniak. 1988. *Futures trading: concepts and strategies.* New York Institute of Finance.

Fiorentini, G., G. Calzolari, and L. Panatoni. 1996. Analytic derivatives and the computation of GARCH estimates. *Journal of Applied Econometrics* 11:399–417.

Fisher, L. 1966. Some new stock market indices. *Journal of Business* 39:191–225.

Fleming, J. 1998. The quality of market volatility forecasts implied by S&P 100 index option prices. *Journal of Empirical Finance* 5:317–345.

Fleming, J., C. Kirby, and B. Ostdiek. 2001. The economic value of volatility timing. *Journal of Finance* 56:329–352.

——. 2003. The economic value of volatility timing using "realized" volatility. *Journal of Financial Economics* 67:473–509.

Fleming, J., B. Ostdiek, and R. E. Whaley. 1995. Predicting stock market volatility: a new measure. *Journal of Futures Markets* 15:265–302.

Fleming, M. J. and E. M. Remolona. 1999. Price formation and liquidity in the U.S. Treasury market: the response to public information. *Journal of Finance* 54:1901–1915.

Fornari, F. and A. Mele. 1996. Modeling the changing asymmetry of conditional variances. *Economics Letters* 50:197–203.

——. 2001. Recovering the probability density function of asset prices using GARCH as diffusion approximations. *Journal of Empirical Finance* 8:83–110.

Fouque, J.-P., G. Papanicolaou, and K. R. Sircar. 2000. *Derivatives in financial markets with stochastic volatility*. Cambridge University Press.

Franses, P. H. and D. van Dijk. 1996. Forecasting stock market volatility using non-linear GARCH models. *Journal of Forecasting* 15:229–235.

——. 2000. *Non-linear time series models in empirical finance*. Cambridge University Press.

French, K. R. 1980. Stock returns and the weekend effect. *Journal of Financial Economics* 8:55–70.

French, K. R. and R. Roll. 1986. Stock return variances: the arrival of information and the reaction of traders. *Journal of Financial Economics* 17:5–26.

French, K. R., G. W. Schwert, and R. F. Stambaugh. 1987. Expected stock returns and volatility. *Journal of Financial Economics* 19:3–29.

Frenkel, M., C. Pierdzioch, and G. Stadtmann. 2001. The foreign exchange market interventions of the European central bank. *Banca Nazionale del Lavoro Quarterly Review* 54:249–287.

Fridman, M. and L. Harris. 1998. A maximum likelihood approach for non-Gaussian stochastic volatility models. *Journal of Business and Economic Statistics* 16:284–291.

Friedman, B. M. and D. I. Laibson. 1989. Economic implications of extraordinary movements in stock prices. *Brookings Papers on Economic Activity* 2:137–189.

Gallant, A. R., D. A. Hsieh, and G. E. Tauchen. 1991. On fitting a recalcitrant series: the pound/dollar exchange rate, 1974–83. In *Nonparametric and semiparametric methods in econometrics and statistics* (ed. W. A. Barnett, J. Powell, and G. E. Tauchen), pp. 199–240. Cambridge University Press.

——. 1997. Estimation of stochastic volatility models with diagnostics. *Journal of Econometrics* 81:159–192.

Gallant, A. R., C. T. Hsu, and G. E. Tauchen. 1999. Using daily range data to calibrate volatility diffusions and extract the forward integrated variance. *Review of Economics and Statistics* 81:617–631.

Gallant, A. R., P. E. Rossi, and G. E. Tauchen. 1992. Stock prices and volume. *Review of Financial Studies* 5:199–242.

Garman, M. B. and M. J. Klass. 1980. On the estimation of security price volatilities from historical data. *Journal of Business* 53:67–78.

Gemmill, G. T. and A. Saflekos. 2000. How useful are implied distributions? Evidence from stock index options. *Journal of Derivatives* 7(Spring):1–16.

Gençay, R., G. Ballochi, M. M. Dacorogna, R. B. Olsen, and O. V. Pictet. 2002. Real-time trading models and the statistical properties of foreign exchange rates. *International Economic Review* 43:463–492.

Geweke, J. 1981. The approximate slope of econometric tests. *Econometrica* 49:1427–1442.

Geweke, J. and S. Porter-Hudak. 1983. The estimation and application of long memory time series. *Journal of Time Series Analysis* 4:221–238.

Ghysels, E., C. Gourieroux, and J. Jasiak. 1998. High frequency financial time series data: some stylized facts and models of stochastic volatility. In *Nonlinear modelling of high frequency financial time series* (ed. C. Dunis and B. Zhou), pp. 127–159. Chichester: Wiley.

——. 2004. Stochastic volatility duration models. *Journal of Econometrics* 119:413–433.

Ghysels, E., A. C. Harvey, and E. Renault. 1996. Stochastic volatility. In *Handbook of statistics*, vol. 14, *Statistical methods in finance* (ed. C. R. Rao and G. S. Maddala), pp. 119–191. Amsterdam: North-Holland.

Ghysels, E., P. Santa-Clara, and R. Valkanov. 2004a. There is a risk-return tradeoff after all. *Journal of Financial Economics*. In press.

——. 2004b. Predicting volatility: getting the most out of return data sampled at different frequencies. *Journal of Econometrics*. In press.

Gilmore, C. G. and G. M. McManus. 2001. Random walk and efficiency tests of Central European equity markets. *Managerial Finance* 29(4):42–61.

Gleick, J. 1987. *Chaos: making a new science.* New York: Viking Press.

Glosten, L. R., R. Jagannathan, and D. Runkle. 1993. Relationship between the expected value and the volatility of the nominal excess return on stocks. *Journal of Finance* 48:1779–1801.

Goetzmann, W. N. 1993. Patterns in three centuries of stock market prices. *Journal of Business* 66:249–270.

Goetzmann, W. N., R. G. Ibbotson, and L. Peng. 2001. A new historical database for the NYSE 1815 to 1925: performance and predictability. *Journal of Financial Markets* 4:1–32.

González-Rivera, G. 1998. Smooth transition GARCH models. *Studies in Nonlinear Dynamics and Econometrics* 3:61–78.

Goodhart, C. A. E. and L. Figliuoli. 1991. Every minute counts in financial markets. *Journal of International Money and Finance* 10:23–52.

Goodhart, C. A. E. and M. O'Hara. 1997. High frequency data in financial markets: issues and applications. *Journal of Empirical Finance* 4:73–114.

Gourieroux, C. and J. Jasiak. 2001. *Financial econometrics.* Princeton University Press.

Grammig, J., M. Melvin, and C. Schlag. 2004. Internationally cross-listed stock prices during overlapping trading hours: price discovery and exchange rate effects. *Journal of Empirical Finance*. In press.

Granger, C. W. J. 1980. Long memory relationships and the aggregation of dynamic models. *Journal of Econometrics* 14:227–238.

——. 1999. *Empirical modeling in economics, specification and evaluation.* Cambridge University Press.

Granger, C. W. J. and A. P. Andersen. 1978. *An introduction to bilinear time series models.* Gottingen: Vandenhoeck and Ruprecht.

Granger, C. W. J. and Z. Ding. 1995. Some properties of absolute return: an alternative measure of risk. *Annales d'Economie et de Statistique* 40:67–91.

Granger, C. W. J. and N. Hyung. 2004. Occasional structural breaks and long memory with an application to the S&P 500 absolute stock returns. *Journal of Empirical Finance* 11:399–421.

Granger, C. W. J. and R. Joyeux. 1980. An introduction to long-memory time series models and fractional differencing. *Journal of Time Series Analysis* 1:15–29.

Granger, C. W. J. and O. Morgenstern. 1970. *Predictability of stock market prices.* Lexington, MA: Heath.

Granger, C. W. J. and P. Newbold. 1976. Forecasting transformed series. *Journal of the Royal Statistical Society* B 38:189–203.

——. 1986. *Forecasting economic time series,* 2nd edn. New York: Academic Press.

Grassberger, P. and I. Procaccia. 1983. Measuring the strangeness of strange attractors. *Physica* D 9:189–208.

Greene, M. T. and B. D. Fielitz. 1977. Long-term dependence in common stock returns. *Journal of Financial Economics* 4:339–349.

Greene, W. H. 2000. *Econometric analysis,* 4th edn. Englewood Cliffs, NJ: Prentice-Hall.

Gultekin, M. and B. Gultekin. 1983. Stock market seasonality: international evidence. *Journal of Financial Economics* 12:469–481.

Guo, D. 1996. The predictive power of implied stochastic variance from currency options. *Journal of Futures Markets* 16:915–942.

——. 1998. The risk premium of volatility implicit in currency options. *Journal of Business and Economic Statistics* 16:498–507.

Hagerman, R. L. 1978. More evidence on the distribution of stock returns. *Journal of Finance* 43:1213–1221.

Hagerud, G. E. 1997. A new non-linear GARCH model. PhD thesis, Stockholm School of Economics.

Hamilton, J. D. 1988. Rational-expectations econometric analysis of changes in regime: an investigation of the term structure of interest rates. *Journal of Economic Dynamics and Control* 12:385–423.

——. 1994. *Time series analysis.* Princeton University Press.

Hamilton, J. D. and R. Susmel. 1994. Autoregressive conditional heteroskedasticity and changes in regime. *Journal of Econometrics* 64:307–333.

Hansen, B. E. 1994. Autoregressive conditional density estimation. *International Economic Review* 35:705–730.

Hansen, L. P. 1982. Large sample properties of generalized method of moments estimators. *Econometrica* 50:1029–1054.

Harris, L. E. 1986. A transaction data study of weekly and intradaily patterns in stock returns. *Journal of Financial Economics* 16:99–117.

——. 1987. Transaction data tests of the mixture of distributions hypothesis. *Journal of Financial and Quantitative Analysis* 22:127–141.

Harrison, P. 1998. Similarities in the distribution of stock market price changes between the eighteenth and twentieth centuries. *Journal of Business* 71:55–79.

Harvey, A. C. 1989. *Forecasting, structural time series models and the Kalman filter.* Cambridge University Press.

——. 1998. Long-memory in stochastic volatility. In *Forecasting volatility in financial markets* (ed. J. Knight and S. E. Satchell). London: Butterworth-Heinemann.

Harvey, A. C., E. Ruiz, and N. Shephard. 1994. Multivariate stochastic variance models. *Review of Economic Studies* 61:247–264.

Harvey, A. C. and N. Shephard. 1996. Estimation of an asymmetric stochastic volatility model for asset returns. *Journal of Business and Economic Statistics* 14:429–434.

Harvey, C. R. and R. Huang. 1991. Volatility in the foreign currency futures market. *Review of Financial Studies* 4:543–570.

Harvey, C. R. and A. Siddique. 1999. Autoregressive conditional skewness. *Journal of Financial and Quantitative Analysis* 34:465–487.

Hasbrouck, J. 1991. Measuring the information content of stock trades. *Journal of Finance* 46:179–207.

———. 1995. One security, many markets: determining the contributions to price discovery. *Journal of Finance* 50:1175–1199.

———. 2003. Intraday price formation in U.S. equity index markets. *Journal of Finance* 58:2375–2399.

Hawawini, G. and D. B. Keim. 1995. On the predictability of common stock returns: worldwide evidence. In *Finance* (ed. R. A. Jarrow, V. Maksimovic, and W. T. Ziemba), pp. 497–544. Amsterdam: North-Holland.

———. 2000. The cross section of common stock returns: a review of the evidence and some new findings. In *Security market imperfections in world wide equity markets* (ed. D. B. Keim and W. T. Ziemba), pp. 3–43. Cambridge University Press.

He, C. and T. Teräsvirta. 1999. Properties of moments of a family of GARCH processes. *Journal of Econometrics* 92:173–192.

Hentschel, L. 1995. All in the family: nesting symmetric and asymmetric GARCH models. *Journal of Financial Economics* 39:71–104.

Heston, S. L. 1993. A closed-form solution for options with stochastic volatility with applications to bond and currency options. *Review of Financial Studies* 6:327–343.

Heston, S. L. and S. Nandi. 2000. A closed-form GARCH option valuation model. *Review of Financial Studies* 13:585–625.

Heynen, R. C. and H. M. Kat. 1994. Volatility prediction: a comparison of the stochastic volatility, GARCH(1, 1) and EGARCH(1, 1) models. *Journal of Derivatives* 2(Summer): 50–65.

Heynen, R. C., A. Kemna, and T. Vorst. 1994. Analysis of the term structure of implied volatilities. *Journal of Financial and Quantitative Analysis* 29:31–56.

Hiemstra, C. and J. D. Jones. 1997. Another look at long memory in common stock returns. *Journal of Empirical Finance* 4:373–401.

Hill, B. M. 1975. A simple general approach to inference about the tail of a distribution. *Annals of Statistics* 3:1163–1174.

Hirshleifer, D. and T. Shumway. 2003. Good day sunshine: stock returns and the weather. *Journal of Finance* 58:1009–1032.

Hodrick, R. J. 1987. *The empirical evidence on the efficiency of forward and futures foreign exchange markets.* Chur, Switzerland: Harwood Academic.

Hong, P. Y. 1991. The autocorrelation structure for the GARCH-M process. *Economics Letters* 37:129–132.

Hosking, J. 1981. Fractional differencing. *Biometrika* 68:165–176.

Hsieh, D. A. 1989. Testing for nonlinearity in daily foreign exchange rate changes. *Journal of Business* 62:339–368.

———. 1991. Chaos and nonlinear dynamics: application to financial markets. *Journal of Finance* 46:1839–1877.

Hsu, D.-A. 1980. Further analyses of position errors in navigation. *Journal of Navigation* 33:452–474.

———. 1982. A Bayesian robust detection of shift in the risk structure of stock market returns. *Journal of the American Statistical Association* 77:29–39.

Huang, J.-Z. and L. Wu. 2004. Specification analysis of option pricing models based on time-changed Lévy processes. *Journal of Finance* 59:1405–1439.

Huang, X. and G. E. Tauchen. 2004. The relative contribution of jumps to total price variance. Duke University, NC.

Hudson, R., M. Dempsey, and K. Keasey. 1996. A note on the weak form efficiency of capital markets: The application of simple technical trading rules to U.K. stock prices—1935 to 1964. *Journal of Banking and Finance* 20:1121–1132.

Hull, J. 2000. *Options, futures and other derivative securities*, 4th edn. Englewood Cliffs, NJ: Prentice-Hall.

Hull, J. and A. White. 1987. The pricing of options on assets with stochastic volatilities. *Journal of Finance* 42:281–300.

——. 1988. An analysis of the bias in option pricing caused by a stochastic volatility. *Advances in Futures and Options Research* 3:29–61.

Hupperets, E. C. J. and A. J. Menkveld. 2002. Intraday analysis of market integration: Dutch blue chips traded in Amsterdam and New York. *Journal of Financial Markets* 5:57–82.

Hurst, H. 1951. Long term storage capacity of reservoirs. *Transactions of the American Society of Civil Engineers* 116:770–799.

Hwang, S., J. Knight, and S. E. Satchell. 2001. Forecasting non-linear functions of returns using linex loss functions. *Annals of Economics and Finance* 2:187–213.

Ibbotson, R. G. and P. Chen. 2003. Long-run stock returns: participating in the real economy. *Financial Analysts Journal* 59(January):88–98.

Ito, A. 1999. Profits on technical trading rules and time-varying expected returns: evidence from Pacific-Basin equity markets. *Pacific-Basin Finance Journal* 7:283–330.

Itô, K. 1951. On stochastic differential equations. *Memoirs, American Mathematical Society* 4:1–51.

Ito, T. and V. V. Roley. 1987. News from the U.S. and Japan: which moves the yen/dollar exchange rate? *Journal of Monetary Economics* 19:255–277.

Jackwerth, J. C. 1999. Option implied risk-neutral distributions and implied binomial trees: a literature review. *Journal of Derivatives* 7(Winter):66–82.

——. 2000. Recovering risk aversion from option prices and realized returns. *Review of Financial Studies* 13:433–451.

Jackwerth, J. C. and M. Rubinstein. 1996. Recovering probability distributions from option prices. *Journal of Finance* 51:1611–1631.

Jacquier, E., N. G. Polson, and P. E. Rossi. 1994. Bayesian analysis of stochastic volatility models. *Journal of Business and Economic Statistics* 12:371–417.

——. 2004. Bayesian analysis of stochastic volatility models with fat-tails and correlated errors. *Journal of Econometrics* 122:185–212.

Jaffe, J. and R. Westerfield. 1985. The week-end effect in stock returns: the international evidence. *Journal of Finance* 41:433–454.

——. 1989. Is there a monthly effect in stock market returns? Evidence from foreign countries. *Journal of Banking and Finance* 13:237–244.

Jarrow, R. A. and A. Rudd. 1982. Approximate valuation for arbitrary stochastic processes. *Journal of Financial Economics* 10:347–369.

Jegadeesh, N. 1991. Seasonality in stock price mean reversion: evidence from the U.S. and U.K. *Journal of Finance* 46:1427–1444.

——. 2000. Discussion. *Journal of Finance* 55:1765–1770.

Jensen, M. C. 1978. Some anomalous evidence regarding market efficiency. *Journal of Financial Economics* 6:95–101.

Jiang, G. J. and Y. S. Tian. 2004. The model-free implied volatility and its information content. *Review of Financial Studies*. In press.

Johnson, H. and D. Shanno. 1987. Option pricing when the variance is changing. *Journal of Financial and Quantitative Analysis* 22:143–152.

Johnson, T. C. 2001. Return dynamics when persistence is unobservable. *Mathematical Finance* 11:415–445.

Jondeau, E. and M. Rockinger. 2000. Reading the smile: the message conveyed by methods which infer risk neutral densities. *Journal of International Money and Finance* 19:885–915.

——. 2001. Gram-Charlier densities. *Journal of Economic Dynamics and Control* 25:1457–1483.

——. 2003. Conditional volatility, skewness and kurtosis: existence, persistence, and co-movements. *Journal of Economic Dynamics and Control* 27:1699–1737.

Jones, C. M., G. Kaul, and M. L. Lipson. 1994. Transactions, volume and volatility. *Review of Financial Studies* 7:631–651.

Jones, C. S. 2003. The dynamics of stochastic volatility: evidence from underlying and options markets. *Journal of Econometrics* 116:181–224.

Jones, S. L., W. Lee, and R. Apenbrink. 1991. New evidence on the January effect before personal income taxes. *Journal of Finance* 46:1909–1924.

Jorion, P. 1995. Predicting volatility in the foreign exchange market. *Journal of Finance* 50:507–528.

Jorion, P. and W. N. Goetzmann. 1999. Global stock markets in the twentieth century. *Journal of Finance* 54:953–980.

Jubinski, P. D. and M. Tomljanovich. 2003. An examination of the introduction of options on the volatility of the underlying individual equity securities. Colgate University, Hamilton, NY.

Kallsen, J. and M. S. Taqqu. 1998. Option pricing in ARCH-type models. *Mathematical Finance* 8:13–26.

Kamstra, M., L. Kramer, and M. Levi. 2003. Winter blues: seasonal affective disorder (SAD) and stock market returns. *American Economic Review* 93:324–343.

Kanzler, L. 1998. A study of the efficiency of the foreign exchange market through analysis of ultra-high frequency data. DPhil thesis, University of Oxford.

Kariya, T., Y. Tsukuda, J. Maru, Y. Matsue, and K. Omaki. 1995. An extensive analysis on the Japanese markets via S. Taylor's model. *Financial Engineering and the Japanese Markets* 2:15–86.

Karpoff, J. M. 1987. The relation between price changes and trading volume: a survey. *Journal of Financial and Quantitative Analysis* 22:109–126.

Kawaller, I. G., P. Koch, and T. Koch. 1987. The temporal price relationship between S&P 500 futures prices and the S&P 500 index. *Journal of Finance* 42:1309–1329.

Keim, D. B. 1983. Size-related anomalies and stock market return seasonality: further empirical evidence. *Journal of Financial Economics* 12:12–32.

——. 1989. Trading patterns, bid–ask spreads, and estimated security returns: the case of common stock at calendar turning points. *Journal of Financial Economics* 25:75–97.

Kendall, M. G. 1953. The analysis of economic time series. Part I. Prices. *Journal of the Royal Statistical Society* A 96:11–25.

Kendall, M. G., A. Stuart, and J. K. Ord. 1983. *The advanced theory of statistics*, vol. 3, 4th edn. London: Charles Griffin.

——. 1987. *The advanced theory of statistics*, vol. 1, 5th edn. London: Charles Griffin.

Keynes, J. M. 1930. *A treatise on money*, vol. II. London: Macmillan.

Kho, B.-C. 1996. Time-varying risk premia, volatility, and technical trading rule profits: evidence from foreign currency futures markets. *Journal of Financial Economics* 41:249–290.

Kim, C.-J., C. R. Nelson, and R. Startz. 1998. Testing for mean reversion in heteroskedastic data based on Gibbs-sampling-augmented randomization. *Journal of Empirical Finance* 5:131–154.

Kim, C.-W. and J. Park. 1994. Holiday effects and stock returns: further evidence. *Journal of Financial and Quantitative Analysis* 29:145–157.

Kim, D. and S. J. Kon. 1994. Alternative models for the conditional heteroscedasticity of stock returns. *Journal of Business* 67:563–598.

Kim, M. J., C. R. Nelson, and R. Startz. 1991. Mean reversion in stock prices? A reappraisal of the empirical evidence. *Review of Economic Studies* 58:515–528.

Kim, S., N. Shephard, and S. Chib. 1998. Stochastic volatility: likelihood inference and comparison with ARCH models. *Review of Economic Studies* 65:361–393.

King, M., E. Sentana, and S. Wadhwani. 1994. Volatility and links between national stock markets. *Econometrica* 62:905–933.

Knez, P. J. and M. J. Ready. 1996. Estimating the profits from trading strategies. *Review of Financial Studies* 9:1121–1164.

Kofman, P. and M. Martens. 1997. Interaction between stock markets: an analysis of the common trading hours at the London and New York Stock Exchange. *Journal of International Money and Finance* 16:387–414.

Kolb, R. W. 1992. Is normal backwardation normal? *Journal of Futures Markets* 12:75–91.

———. 1999. *Futures, options and swaps*, 3rd edn. Glenview, IL: Scott, Foresman and Co.

Kon, S. J. 1984. Models of stock returns—a comparison. *Journal of Finance* 39:147–165.

Kristensen, D. and A. Rahbek. 2004. Asymptotics of the QMLE for a class of ARCH(q) models. *Econometric Theory*. In press.

Kroner, K. F. and V. K. Ng. 1998. Modelling asymmetric comovements of asset returns. *Review of Financial Studies* 11:817–844.

Kroner, K. F., K. P. Kneafsey, and C. Claessens. 1995. Forecasting volatility in commodity markets. *Journal of Forecasting* 14:77–95.

Lakonishok, J. and M. Levi. 1982. Weekend effects on stock returns: a note. *Journal of Finance* 37:883–889.

Lakonishok, J. and S. Smidt. 1988. Are seasonal anomalies real? A ninety year perspective. *Review of Financial Studies* 1:435–455.

Lamoureux, C. G. and W. D. Lastrapes. 1990. Heteroskedasticity in stock return data: volume versus GARCH effects. *Journal of Finance* 45:221–229.

———. 1993. Forecasting stock return variance: toward an understanding of stochastic implied volatilities. *Review of Financial Studies* 6:293–326.

———. 1994. Endogenous trading volume and momentum in stock return volatility. *Journal of Business Economics and Statistics* 12:253–260.

Latane, H. A. and R. J. Rendleman. 1976. Standard deviations of stock price ratios implied in option prices. *Journal of Finance* 31:369–381.

Leadbetter, M. R., G. Lindgren, and H. Rootzén. 1983. *Extremes and related properties of random sequences and processes*. Berlin: Springer.

LeBaron, B. 1992. Some relations between volatility and serial correlations in stock market returns. *Journal of Business* 65:199–219.

———. 1999. Technical trading rule profitability and foreign exchange intervention. *Journal of International Economics* 49:125–143.

Lee, C. I., M.-S. Pan, and Y. A. Liu. 2001. On market efficiency of Asian foreign exchange rates: evidence from a joint variance ratio test and technical trading rules. *Journal of International Financial Markets, Institutions and Money* 11:199–214.

Lee, R. W. 2004. The moment formula for implied volatility at extreme strikes. *Mathematical Finance* 14:469–480.

Lee, S.-W. and B. E. Hansen. 1994. Asymptotic theory for the GARCH(1, 1) quasi-maximum likelihood estimator. *Econometric Theory* 10:29–52.

LeRoy, S. F. 1989. Efficient capital markets and martingales. *Journal of Economic Literature* 27:1583–1621.

Levich, R. M. and L. R. Thomas. 1993. The significance of technical trading rule profits in the foreign exchange market: a bootstrap approach. *Journal of International Money and Finance* 12:451–474.

Lewis, A. L. 2000. *Option valuation under stochastic volatility.* Newport Beach, CA: Finance Press.

Li, K. 2002. Long-memory versus option-implied volatility predictions. *Journal of Derivatives* 9(Fall):9–25.

Li, W. K. and T. K. Mak. 1994. On the squared residual autocorrelations in nonlinear time series analysis with conditional heteroskedasticity. *Journal of Time Series Analysis* 15:627–636.

Lin, S.-J., J. Knight, and S. E. Satchell. 1999. Modelling intra-day equity prices and volatility using information arrivals—a comparative study of different choices of information proxies. In *Financial markets tick by tick* (ed. P. Lequeux), pp. 27–64. Chichester: Wiley.

Lindgren, G. 1978. Markov regime models for mixed distributions and switching regressions. *Scandinavian Journal of Statistics* 5:81–91.

Ling, S. and M. McAleer. 2002. Stationarity and the existence of moments of a family of GARCH processes. *Journal of Econometrics* 106:109–117.

——. 2003. Asymptotic theory for a vector ARMA-GARCH model. *Econometric Theory* 19:280–310.

Liu, C. Y. and J. He. 1991. A variance-ratio test of random walks in exchange rates. *Journal of Finance* 46:773–785.

Liu, X., M. B. Shackleton, S. J. Taylor, and X. Xu. 2004. Closed-form transformations from risk-neutral to real-world distributions. Lancaster University, UK.

Lo, A. W. 1991. Long-term memory in stock market prices. *Econometrica* 59:1279–1313.

Lo, A. W. and A. C. MacKinlay. 1988. Stock market prices do not follow random walks: evidence from a simple specification test. *Review of Financial Studies* 1:41–66.

——. 1989. The size and power of the variance ratio test in finite samples: a Monte Carlo investigation. *Journal of Econometrics* 40:203–238.

——. 1990a. When are contrarian profits due to stock market over-reaction? *Review of Financial Studies* 3:175–205.

——. 1990b. An econometric analysis of nonsynchronous trading. *Journal of Econometrics* 45:181–211.

——. 1999. *A non-random walk down Wall Street.* Princeton University Press.

Lo, A. W., H. Mamaysky, and J. Wang. 2000. Foundations of technical analysis: computational algorithms, statistical inference and empirical implementation. *Journal of Finance* 55:1705–1765.

Lomnicki, Z. A. and S. K. Zaremba. 1957. On the estimation of autocorrelation in time series. *Annals of Mathematical Statistics* 28:140–158.

Longin, F. M. 1996. The asymptotic distribution of extreme stock market returns. *Journal of Business* 69:383–408.

Loretan, M. and P. C. B. Phillips. 1994. Testing the covariance stationarity of heavy-tailed time series. *Journal of Empirical Finance* 1:211–248.

Lucas, R. 1978. Asset prices in an exchange economy. *Econometrica* 46:1429–1446.

Luger, R. 2003. Exact non-parametric tests for a random walk with unknown drift under conditional heteroscedasticity. *Journal of Econometrics* 115:259–276.

Lukac, L. P. and B. W. Brorsen. 1990. A comprehensive test of futures market disequilibrium. *Financial Review* 25:593–622.

Lukac, L. P., B. W. Brorsen, and S. H. Irwin. 1988. A test of futures market disequilibrium using twelve different trading systems. *Applied Economics* 20:623–639.

Lumsdaine, R. L. 1995. Finite sample properties of the maximum likelihood estimator in GARCH(1, 1) and IGARCH(1, 1) models: a Monte Carlo investigation. *Journal of Business and Economic Statistics* 13:1–10.

——. 1996. Consistency and asymptotic normality of the quasi-maximum likelihood estimator in IGARCH(1, 1) and covariance stationary GARCH(1, 1) models. *Econometrica* 64:575–596.

Luu, J. C. and M. Martens. 2003. Testing the mixture of distributions hypothesis using "realized" volatility. *Journal of Futures Markets* 23:661–679.

Maberly, E. D. and D. F. Waggoner. 2000. Closing the question on the continuation of the turn-of-the-month effects: evidence from the S&P 500 index futures contract. Federal Reserve Bank of Atlanta.

McDonald, J. B. and R. M. Bookstaber. 1991. Option pricing for generalized distributions. *Communications in Statistics* 20:4053–4068.

MacDonald, R. 1988. *Floating exchange rates: theories and evidence*. London: Unwin Hyman.

McLeod, A. I. and W. K. Li. 1983. Diagnostic checking ARMA time series models using squared-residual autocorrelations. *Journal of Time Series Analysis* 4:269–273.

Madan, D. B. and F. Milne. 1994. Contingent claims valued and hedged by pricing and investing in a basis. *Mathematical Finance* 4:223–245.

Madan, D. B. and E. Seneta. 1990. The variance gamma model for share market returns. *Journal of Business* 63:511–524.

Maheu, J. M. and T. H. McCurdy. 2002. Nonlinear features of realized FX volatility. *Review of Economics and Statistics* 84:668–681.

Mahieu, R. and P. Schotman. 1994. Neglected common factors in exchange rate volatility. *Journal of Empirical Finance* 1:279–311.

Malz, A. M. 1996. Using option prices to estimate realignment probabilities in the European monetary system: the case of sterling–mark. *Journal of International Money and Finance* 15:717–748.

——. 1997a. Estimating the probability distribution of the future exchange rate from option prices. *Journal of Derivatives* 5(Summer):18–36.

——. 1997b. Option-based estimates of the probability distribution of exchange rates and currency excess returns. Federal Reserve Bank of New York.

Mandelbrot, B. 1963. The variation of certain speculative prices. *Journal of Business* 36:394–419.

——. 1972. Statistical methodology for non-periodic cycles from the covariance to R/S analysis. *Annals of Economic and Social Measurement* 1:259–290.

Martens, M. 1998. Price discovery in high and low volatility periods: open outcry versus electronic trading. *Journal of International Financial Markets, Institutions and Money* 8:243–260.

Martens, M., Y. Chang, and S. J. Taylor. 2002. Intraday volatility forecasts using different seasonal adjustment methods. *Journal of Financial Research* 25:283–299.

Martens, M. and O. W. Steenbeek. 2001. Intraday trading halts in the Nikkei futures market. *Pacific-Basin Finance Journal* 9:535–561.

Martens, M. and J. Zein. 2004. Predicting financial volatility: high-frequency time-series forecasts vis-à-vis implied volatility. *Journal of Futures Markets* 24:1005–1028.

Meddahi, N. 2002. A theoretical comparison between integrated and realized volatility. *Journal of Applied Econometrics* 17:479–508.

Meddahi, N. and E. Renault. 2004. Temporal aggregation of volatility models. *Journal of Econometrics* 119:355–379.

Mehra, R. and E. C. Prescott. 1985. The equity premium: a puzzle. *Journal of Monetary Economics* 15:145–161.

Melick, W. R. and C. P. Thomas. 1997. Recovering an asset's implied PDF from option prices: an application to crude oil during the Gulf crisis. *Journal of Financial and Quantitative Analysis* 32:91–115.

Melino, A. and S. M. Turnbull. 1990. Pricing foreign currency options with stochastic volatility. *Journal of Econometrics* 45:239–265.

Melvin, M. and X. Yin. 2000. Public information arrivals, exchange rate volatility and quote frequency. *Economics Journal* 110:644–661.

Merrill, A. A. 1966. *Behavior of prices on Wall Street*. Chappaqua, NY: The Analysis Press.

Merton, R. C. 1973. The theory of rational option pricing. *Bell Journal of Economics and Management Science* 4:141–183.

———. 1976. Option pricing when underlying stock returns are discontinuous. *Journal of Financial Economics* 3:125–144.

———. 1980. On estimating the expected return on the market. *Journal of Financial Economics* 8:323–361.

———. 1992. *Continuous-time finance*. Oxford: Basil Blackwell.

Mikosch, T. 1998. *Elementary stochastic calculus with finance in view*. Singapore: World Scientific.

Mills, T. C. 1999. *The econometric modelling of financial time series*, 2nd edn. Cambridge University Press.

Mitchell, H., R. L. Brown, and S. A. Easton. 2002. Old volatility—ARCH effects in 19th century consol data. *Applied Financial Economics* 12:301–307.

Mitchell, M. L. and J. H. Mulherin. 1994. The impact of public information on the stock market. *Journal of Finance* 49:923–949.

Mood, A. M. 1940. The distribution theory of runs. *Annals of Mathematical Statistics* 11:367–392.

Moran, P. A. P. 1967. Tests for serial correlation with exponentially distributed variates. *Biometrika* 54:395–401.

Müller, U. A., M. M. Dacorogna, R. D. Davé, R. B. Olsen, O. V. Pictet, and J. E. von Weizsäcker. 1997. Volatilities of different time resolutions—analyzing the dynamics of market components. *Journal of Empirical Finance* 4:213–239.

Müller, U. A., M. M. Dacorogna, R. B. Olsen, O. V. Pictet, and M. Schwarz. 1990. Statistical study of forign exchange rates, empirical evidence of a price change scaling law, and intraday analysis. *Journal of Banking and Finance* 14:1189–1208.

Müller, U. A., M. M. Dacorogna, and O. V. Pictet. 1998. Heavy tails in high-frequency financial data. In *A practical guide to heavy tails* (ed. R. J. Adler, R. E. Feldman, and M. S. Taqqu), pp. 55–77. Boston, MA: Birkhäuser.

Neely, C. J. 2002. The temporal pattern of trading rule returns and exchange rate intervention: intervention does not generate technical trading profits. *Journal of International Economics* 58:211–232.

Neely, C. J. and P. A. Weller. 2001. Technical analysis and central bank intervention. *Journal of International Money and Finance* 20:949–970.

———. 2003. Intraday technical trading in the foreign exchange market. *Journal of International Money and Finance* 22:223–237.

Neely, C. J., P. A. Weller, and R. Dittmar. 1997. Is technical analysis in the foreign exchange market profitable?: a genetic programming approach. *Journal of Financial and Quantitative Analysis* 32:405–426.

Nelson, D. B. 1988. Time series behavior of stock market volatility and returns. PhD thesis, Massachusetts Institute of Technology.

———. 1989. Modeling stock market volatility changes. *Proceedings, American Statistical Association, Business and Economic Statistics Section*, pp. 93–98.

———. 1990a. Stationarity and persistence in the GARCH(1, 1) model. *Econometric Theory* 6:318–334.

———. 1990b. ARCH models as diffusion approximations. *Journal of Econometrics* 45:7–38.

———. 1991. Conditional heteroskedasticity in asset returns: a new approach. *Econometrica* 59:347–370.

Nelson, D. B. and C. Q. Cao. 1992. Inequality constraints in the univariate GARCH model. *Journal of Business and Economic Statistics* 10:229–235.

Newey, W. K. and D. Steigerwald. 1997. Asymptotic bias for quasi-maximum-likelihood estimators in conditionally heteroskedasticity models. *Econometrica* 65:587–599.

Newey, W. K. and K. D. West. 1987. A simple positive semi-definite heteroskedasticity and autocorrelation consistent covariance matrix. *Econometrica* 55:703–708.

Ng, V. K., R. F. Engle, and M. Rothschild. 1992. A multi-dynamic factor model for stock returns. *Journal of Econometrics* 52:245–265.

Nicolato, E. and E. Venardos. 2003. Option pricing in stochastic volatility models of the Ornstein–Uhlenbeck type. *Mathematical Finance* 13:445–466.

Officer, R. R. 1973. The variability of the market factor of the New York Stock Exchange. *Journal of Business* 46:434–453.

———. 1975. Seasonality in the Australian capital markets. *Journal of Financial Economics* 2:29–52.

Ogden, J. P. 1990. Turn-of-month evaluations of liquid profits and stock returns: a common explanation for the monthly and January effects. *Journal of Finance* 45:1259–1271.

Ohanissian, A., J. R. Russell, and R. Tsay. 2004. True or spurious long memory? A new test. University of Chicago.

O'Hara, M. 1995. *Market microstructure theory*. Cambridge, MA: Blackwell.

Okunev, J. and D. White. 2003. Do momentum-based strategies still work in foreign currency markets? *Journal of Financial and Quantitative Analysis* 38:425–447.

Olson, D. 2004. Have trading rule profits in the currency markets declined over time? *Journal of Banking and Finance* 28:85–105.

Pagan, A. R. 1996. The econometrics of financial markets. *Journal of Empirical Finance* 3:15–102.

Pagan, A. R. and G. W. Schwert. 1990. Alternative models for conditional stock volatility. *Journal of Econometrics* 45:267–290.

Pagan, A. R. and A. Ullah. 1988. The econometric analysis of models with risk terms. *Journal of Applied Econometrics* 3:87–105.

Pan, J. 2002. The jump-risk premia implicit in options: evidence from an integrated time-series study. *Journal of Financial Economics* 63:3–50.

Panigirtzoglou, N. and G. Skiadopoulos. 2004. A new approach to modeling the dynamics of implied distributions: theory and evidence from the S&P 500 options. *Journal of Banking and Finance* 28:1499–1520.

Parkinson, M. 1980. The extreme value method for estimating the variance of the rate of return. *Journal of Business* 53:61–65.

Peiers, B. 1997. Informed traders, intervention, and price leadership: a deeper view of the microstructure of the foreign exchange market. *Journal of Finance* 52:1589–1614.

Penman, S. H. 1987. The distribution of earnings news over time and seasonalities in aggregate stock returns. *Journal of Financial Economics* 18:199–228.

Pérignon, C. and C. Villa. 2002. Extracting information from options markets: smiles, state-price densities and risk-aversion. *European Financial Management* 8:495–513.

Perry, P. R. 1982. The time-variance relationship of security returns: implications for the return-generating stochastic process. *Journal of Finance* 37:857–870.

———. 1983. More evidence on the nature of the distribution of security returns. *Journal of Financial and Quantitative Analysis* 18:211–221.

Peterson, R. L., C. K. Ma, and R. J. Ritchey. 1992. Dependence in commodity prices. *Journal of Futures Markets* 12:429–446.

Pitt, M. K. and N. Shephard. 1999. Time varying covariances: a factor stochastic volatility approach. In *Bayesian statistics* (ed. J. Bernardo, J. O. Berger, A. P. Dawid, and A. F. M. Smith), vol. 6, pp. 547–570. Oxford University Press.

Pong, S., M. B. Shackleton, S. J. Taylor, and X. Xu. 2004. Forecasting currency volatility: a comparison of implied volatilities and AR(FI)MA models. *Journal of Banking and Finance* 28:2541–2563.

Poon, S.-H. 1996. Persistence and mean reversion in U.K. stock returns. *European Financial Management* 2:169–196.

Poon, S.-H. and C. W. J. Granger. 2003. Forecasting volatility in financial markets. *Journal of Economic Literature* 41:478–539.

Poon, S.-H., M. Rockinger, and J. A. Tawn. 2004. Extreme value dependence in financial markets: diagnostics, models, and financial implications. *Review of Financial Studies* 17:581–610.

Poon, S.-H. and S. J. Taylor. 1992. Stock returns and volatility: an empirical study of the U.K. stock market. *Journal of Banking and Finance* 16:37–59.

Poterba, J. M. and L. H. Summers. 1988. Mean reversion in stock prices: evidence and implications. *Journal of Financial Economics* 22:27–59.

Praetz, P. D. 1972. The distribution of share price changes. *Journal of Business* 45:49–55.

———. 1973. Analysis of Australian share prices. *Australian Economic Papers* 12:70–78.

———. 1979. Testing for a flat spectrum on efficient market price data. *Journal of Finance* 34:645–658.

Press, S. J. 1967. A compound events model for security prices. *Journal of Business* 40:317–335.

Rachev, S. and S. Mittnik. 2000. *Stable Paretian models in finance*. Chichester: Wiley.

Ramsey, J. B. and Z. Zhang. 1997. The analysis of foreign exchange data using waveform dictionaries. *Journal of Empirical Finance* 4:341–372.

Ready, M. J. 2002. Profits from technical trading rules. *Financial Management* 31(3):43–61.

Renault, E. and N. Touzi. 1996. Option hedging and implied volatilities in a stochastic volatility model. *Mathematical Finance* 6:279–302.

Richardson, M. P. 1993. Temporary components of stock prices: a skeptic's view. *Journal of Business and Economic Statistics* 11:199–207.

Richardson, M. P. and T. Smith. 1994a. A direct test of the mixture of distributions hypothesis: measuring the daily flow of information. *Journal of Financial and Quantitative Analysis* 29:101–116.

———. 1994b. A unified approach to testing for serial correlation in stock returns. *Journal of Business* 67:371–399.

Richardson, M. P. and J. Stock. 1989. Drawing inferences from statistics based on multi-year asset returns. *Journal of Financial Economics* 25:323–348.

Ritchey, R. J. 1990. Call option valuation for discrete normal mixtures. *Journal of Financial Research* 13:285–296.

Ritchken, P. and R. Trevor. 1999. Pricing options under generalized GARCH and stochastic volatility processes. *Journal of Finance* 54:377–402.

Ritter, J. R. 1988. The buying and selling behavior of individual investors at the turn of the year. *Journal of Finance* 43:701–717.

Rockinger, M. and E. Jondeau. 2002. Entropy densities with an application to autoregressive conditional skewness and kurtosis. *Journal of Econometrics* 106:119–142.

Rogers, L. C. G. and S. E. Satchell. 1991. Estimating variance from high, low and closing prices. *Annals of Applied Probability* 1:504–512.

Roll, R. 1984. Orange juice and weather. *American Economic Review* 74:861–880.

Rosenberg, B. 1970. The distribution of the mid-range: a comment. *Econometrica* 38:176–177.

———. 1972. The behavior of random variables with nonstationary variance and the distribution of security prices. University of California, Berkeley. (Included in (2005) *Stochastic volatility: selected readings* (ed. N. Shephard). Oxford University Press.)

Rosenberg, J. V. and R. F. Engle. 2002. Empirical pricing kernels. *Journal of Financial Economics* 64:341–372.

Rozeff, M. S. and W. R. Kinney. 1976. Capital market seasonality: the case of stock returns. *Journal of Financial Economics* 3:379–402.

Rubinstein, M. 1994. Implied binomial trees. *Journal of Finance* 49:771–818.

———. 2001. Rational markets: yes or no? The affirmative case. *Financial Analysts Journal* 57(March):15–29.

Ruiz, E. 1994. Quasi-maximum likelihood estimation of stochastic volatility models. *Journal of Econometrics* 63:289–306.

Ryden, T., T. Teräsvirta, and S. Asbrink. 1998. Stylized facts of daily return series and the hidden Markov model. *Journal of Applied Econometrics* 13:217–244.

Saacke, P. 2002. Technical analysis and the effectiveness of central bank intervention. *Journal of International Money and Finance* 21:459–479.

Samuelson, P. A. 1965. Proof that properly anticipated prices fluctuate randomly. *Industrial Management Review* 6:41–49.

———. 1976. Is real world price a tale told by the idiot of chance? *Review of Economics and Statistics* 58:120–123.

Sandmann, G. and S. J. Koopman. 1998. Estimation of stochastic volatility models via Monte Carlo maximum likelihood. *Journal of Econometrics* 87:271–301.

Schöbel, R. and J. Zhu. 1999. Stochastic volatility with an Ornstein–Uhlenbeck process: an extension. *European Finance Review* 3:23–46.

Scholes, M. and J. Williams. 1977. Estimating betas from nonsynchronous data. *Journal of Financial Economics* 5:309–327.

Schultz, P. 1985. Personal income taxes and the January effect: small firm stock returns before the war revenue act of 1917. *Journal of Finance* 40:333–343.

Schwarz, G. 1978. Estimating the dimension of a model. *Annals of Statistics* 6:461–464.

Schwert, G. W. 1989. Why does stock market volatility change over time? *Journal of Finance* 44:1115–1153.

——. 1990a. Stock volatility and the crash of '87. *Review of Financial Studies* 3:77–102.

——. 1990b. Stock market volatility. *Financial Analysts Journal* 46(May):23–34.

——. 2003. Anomalies and market efficiency. In *Handbook of the economics and finance* (ed. G. Constantinides, M. Harris, and R. M. Stulz), pp. 937–972. Amsterdam: North-Holland.

Schwert, G. W. and P. J. Seguin. 1990. Heteroskedasticity in stock returns. *Journal of Finance* 45:1129–1155.

Scott, L. O. 1987. Option pricing when the variance changes randomly: theory, estimation, and an application. *Journal of Financial and Quantitative Analysis* 22:419–438.

——. 1991. Random variance option pricing: empirical tests of the model and delta-sigma hedging. *Advances in Futures and Options Research* 5:113–135.

——. 1997. Pricing stock options in a jump-diffusion model with stochastic volatility and interest rates: applications of Fourier inversion methods. *Mathematical Finance* 7:413–426.

Sentana, E. 1995. Quadratic ARCH models. *Review of Economic Studies* 62:639–661.

Shephard, N. 1996. Statistical aspects of ARCH and stochastic volatility. In *Likelihood, time series with econometric and other applications* (ed. D. R. Cox, D. V. Hinkley, and O. E. Barndorff-Nielsen), pp. 1–67. London: Chapman & Hall.

Shephard, N. (ed.). 2005. *Stochastic volatility: selected readings*. Oxford University Press.

Shephard, N. and M. K. Pitt. 1997. Likelihood analysis of non-Gaussian measurement time seies. *Biometrika* 84:653–667.

Sherrick, B. J., P. Garcia, and V. Tirupattur. 1996. Recovering probabilistic information from option markets: tests of distributional assumptions. *Journal of Futures Markets* 16:545–560.

Shimko, D. 1993. Bounds of probability. *Risk* 6(April):33–37.

Silverman, B. W. 1986. *Density estimation for statistics and data analysis*. London: Chapman & Hall.

Skiadopoulos, G., S. D. Hodges, and L. Clewlow. 1999. The dynamics of the S&P 500 implied volatility surface. *Review of Derivatives Research* 3:263–282.

So, M. K. P., K. Lam, and W. K. Li. 1998. A stochastic volatility model with Markov switching. *Journal of Business and Economic Statistics* 16:244–253.

Söderlind, P. and L. E. O. Svensson. 1997. New techniques to extract market expectations from financial instruments. *Journal of Monetary Economics* 40:383–429.

Solnik, B. 1990. The distribution of daily stock returns and settlement procedures: the Paris Bourse. *Journal of Finance* 45:1601–1609.

Stein, E. M. and J. C. Stein. 1991. Stock price distributions with stochastic volatility: an analytic approach. *Review of Financial Studies* 4:727–752.

Stein, J. C. 1989. Overreactions in the options market. *Journal of Finance* 44:1011–1023.

Stoll, H. R. and R. E. Whaley. 1988. Futures and options on stock indexes: economic purpose, arbitrage and market structure. *Review of Futures Markets* 7:224–248.

——. 1990. The dynamics of stock index and stock index futures returns. *Journal of Financial and Quantitative Analysis* 25:441–468.

St. Pierre, E. F. 1998. The impact of option introduction on the conditional return distribution of underlying securities. *Financial Review* 33:105–118.

Stutzer, M. 1996. A simple nonparametric approach to derivative security valuation. *Journal of Finance* 51:1633–1652.

Sullivan, R., A. Timmermann, and H. White. 1999. Data-mining, technical trading rule performance, and the bootstrap. *Journal of Finance* 54:1647–1691.

Sullivan, R., A. Timmermann, and H. White. 2001. Dangers of data mining: the case of calendar effects in stock returns. *Journal of Econometrics* 105:249–286.

Sweeney, R. J. 1986. Beating the foreign exchange market. *Journal of Finance* 41:163–182.

——. 1988. Some new filter rule tests: methods and results. *Journal of Financial and Quantitative Analysis* 23:285–300.

Szakmary, A. C. and I. Mathur. 1997. Central bank intervention and trading rule profits in foreign exchange markets. *Journal of International Money and Finance* 16:513–535.

Taqqu, M. S. and V. Teverovsky. 1996. Semi-parametric graphical estimation techniques for long-memory data. In *Time series analysis in memory of E. J. Hannan* (ed. P. M. Robinson and M. Rosenblatt), pp. 420–432. New York: Springer.

Tauchen, G. E. and M. Pitts. 1983. The price variability-volume relationship on speculative markets. *Econometrica* 51:485–505.

Taylor, N., D. van Dijk, P. H. Franses, and A. Lucas. 2000. SETS, arbitrage activity, and stock price dynamics. *Journal of Banking and Finance* 24:1289–1306.

Taylor, S. J. 1980. Conjectured models for trends in financial prices, tests and forecasts. *Journal of the Royal Statistical Society* A 143:338–362.

——. 1982a. Tests of the random walk hypothesis against a price-trend hypothesis. *Journal of Financial and Quantitative Analysis* 17:37–61.

——. 1982b. Financial returns modelled by the product of two stochastic processes, a study of daily sugar prices 1961–79. In *Time series analysis: theory and practice 1* (ed. O. D. Anderson), pp. 203–226. Amsterdam: North-Holland. (Reprinted in (2005) *Stochastic volatility: selected readings* (ed. N. Shephard). Oxford University Press.)

——. 1983. Strategies for investors in apparently inefficient futures markets. In *Futures markets—modelling, managing and monitoring futures trading* (ed. M. E. Streit), pp. 165–198. Oxford: Basil Blackwell.

——. 1984. Estimating the variances of autocorrelations calculated from financial time series. *Applied Statistics* 33:300–308.

——. 1985. The behaviour of futures prices over time. *Applied Economics* 17:713–734.

——. 1986. *Modelling financial time series*. Chichester: Wiley.

——. 1987. Forecasting the volatility of currency exchange rates. *International Journal of Forecasting* 3:159–170.

——. 1988. How efficient are the most liquid futures contracts? A study of Treasury bond futures. *The Review of Futures Markets* 7:574–592.

——. 1992. Rewards available to currency futures speculators: compensation for risk or evidence of inefficient pricing? *Economic Record* 68(supplement):105–116.

——. 1994a. Modeling stochastic volatility: a review and comparative study. *Mathematical Finance* 4:183–204.

——. 1994b. Trading futures using a channel rule: a study of the predictive power of technical analysis with currency examples. *Journal of Futures Markets* 14:215–235.

——. 1994c. Predicting the volatility of stock prices using ARCH models, with U.K. examples. *Managerial Finance* 20(2):102–117.

——. 1999. Markov processes and the distribution of volatility: a comparison of discrete and continuous specifications. *Philosophical Transactions of the Royal Society of London* A 357:2059–2070.

——. 2000. Stock index and price dynamics in the U.K. and the U.S.: new evidence from a trading rule and statistical analysis. *European Journal of Finance* 6:39–69.

——. 2002. Consequences for option pricing of a long memory in volatility. Lancaster University, UK.

Taylor, S. J. and B. G. Kingsman. 1979. An analysis of the variance and distribution of commodity price changes. *Australian Journal of Management* 4:135–149.

Taylor, S. J. and X. Xu. 1994a. The magnitude of implied volatility smiles: theory and empirical evidence for exchange rates. *Review of Futures Markets* 13:355–380.

———. 1994b. Implied volatility shapes when price and volatility shocks are correlated. Lancaster University, UK.

———. 1997. The incremental volatility information in one million foreign exchange quotations. *Journal of Empirical Finance* 4:317–340.

Timmermann, A. 2000. Moments of Markov switching models. *Journal of Econometrics* 96:75–111.

———. 2001. Structural breaks, incomplete information and stock prices. *Journal of Business and Economic Statistics* 19:299–314.

Tinic, S. M. and R. R. West. 1984. Risk and return: January versus the rest of the year. *Journal of Financial Economics* 13:561–574.

Tompkins, R. G. 2001. Implied volatility surfaces: uncovering regularities for options on financial futures. *European Journal of Finance* 7:198–230.

Toulson, D. L., S. P. Toulson, and A. Sinclair. 1999. Constructing a managed portfolio of high frequency LIFFE futures positions. In *Financial markets tick by tick* (ed. P. Lequeux), pp. 347–375. Chichester: Wiley.

Tsay, R. 2002. *Analysis of financial time series*. New York: Wiley.

Tse, Y. 1999. Market microstructure of the FT-SE 100 index futures: an intraday empirical analysis. *Journal of Futures Markets* 19:31–58.

Tse, Y. K. 1991. Stock returns volatility in the Tokyo Stock Exchange. *Japan and the World Economy* 3:285–298.

Tse, Y. K. and S. H. Tung. 1992. Forecasting volatility in the Singapore stock market. *Asia Pacific Journal of Management* 9:1–13.

Voth, H.-J. 2003. Political risk and stock price volatility: evidence from 10 countries during the interwar period. University of Pompeu Fabra, Barcelona.

Weiss, A. A. 1984. ARMA models with ARCH errors. *Journal of Time Series Analysis* 5:129–143.

———. 1986. Asymptotic theory for ARCH models: estimation and testing. *Econometric Theory* 2:107–131.

West, K. D. and D. Cho. 1995. The predictive ability of several models of exchange rate volatility. *Journal of Econometrics* 69:367–391.

West, K. D., H. J. Edison, and D. Cho. 1993. A utility based comparison of some models of exchange rate volatility. *Journal of International Economics* 35:23–45.

White, H. 1984. *Asymptotic theory for econometricians*. New York: Academic Press.

Wiggins, J. B. 1987. Option values under stochastic volatility: theory and empirical estimates. *Journal of Financial Economics* 19:351–372.

Wishart, J. 1947. The cumulants of the z and of the logarithmic χ^2 and t distributions. *Biometrika* 34:170–178.

Wood, R. A., T. H. McInish, and J. K. Ord. 1985. An investigation of transactions data for NYSE stocks. *Journal of Finance* 40:723–739.

Working, H. 1934. A random difference series for use in the analysis of time series. *Journal of the American Statistical Association* 29:11–24.

———. 1960. Note on the correlation of first differences of averages in a random chain. *Econometrica* 28:916–918.

Wright, J. H. 2000. Alternative variance-ratio tests using ranks and signs. *Journal of Business and Economic Statistics* 18:1–9.

Wu, G. 2001. The determinants of asymmetric volatility. *Review of Financial Studies* 14:837–859.

Xu, X. and S. J. Taylor. 1994. The term structure of volatility implied by foreign exchange options. *Journal of Financial and Quantitative Analysis* 29:57–74.

———. 1995. Conditional volatility and informational efficiency of the PHLX currency options market. *Journal of Banking and Finance* 19:803–821.

Yadav, P. K. and P. F. Pope. 1990. Stock index futures arbitrage: international evidence. *Journal of Futures Markets* 10:573–604.

Yang, D. and Q. Zhang. 2000. Drift-independent volatility estimation based on high, low, open and close prices. *Journal of Business* 73:477–491.

Yilmaz, K. 2001. Market development and efficiency in emerging stock markets. Koc University, Istanbul.

Yu, J. 2004. On leverage in a stochastic volatility model. *Journal of Econometrics*. In press.

Yuan, K., L. Zheng, and Q. Zhu. 2001. Are investors moonstruck? Lunar phases and stock returns. University of Michigan.

Zakoïan, J.-M. 1994. Threshold heteroskedastic models. *Journal of Economic Dynamics and Control* 18:931–955.

Zhou, B. 1996. High-frequency data and volatility in foreign-exchange rates. *Journal of Business and Economic Statistics* 14:45–52.

Zhu, J. 2000. *Modular pricing of options: an application of Fourier analysis*. Berlin: Springer.

Ziemba, W. T. 1991. Japanese security market regularities: monthly, turn-of-the-month and year, holiday and Golden Week effects. *Japan and the World Economy* 3:119–146.

Author Index

McInish, T. H., 305, 315, 318
MacKinlay, A. C., 79, 80, 99, 101–2,
 104, 110–1, 114, 129, 144
McLeod, A. I., 257
McManus, G. M., 112
Madan, D. B., 74, 363–4, 388, 441,
 444–5, 452
Maheu, J. M., 341–2
Mahieu, R., 299
Mak, T. K., 257
Malz, A. M., 429, 447–8
Mamaysky, H., 157
Manaster, S., 407
Mandelbrot, B., 14, 75, 91, 122, 135
Mariano, R. S., 400
Marsh, P., 55, 59, 400, 405
Marsh, T., 64
Martens, M., 194, 317, 342–3, 397,
 407, 415
Maru, J., 127
Mathur, I., 181, 184
Matsue, Y., 127
Meddahi, N., 301, 331
Mehra, R., 454
Mele, A., 216, 464
Melick, W. R., 438
Melino, A., 284, 294
Melvin, M., 193, 342
Menkveld, A. J., 342
Merrill, A. A., 61
Merton, R. C., 54, 148, 364, 369, 372,
 452
Mezrich, J., 261
Mikkelsen, H. O., 216, 235, 240,
 242–4, 249, 255–7, 260–1, 391,
 393
Mikosch, T., 345, 353
Mills, T. C., 42
Milne, F., 441, 444–5
Mitchell, H., 51
Mitchell, M. L., 193
Mittnik, S., 76
Mood, A. M., 134
Moran, P. A. P., 113
Morgenstern, O., 100
Mulherin, J. H., 193
Müller, U. A., 242, 305, 307, 312–5,
 319, 321, 323–4, 326, 346
Mykland, P. A., 332

Nacaskul, P., 326
Nagler, R. J., 242, 314, 319, 321
Nam, K., 216
Nandi, S., 392
Nardari, F., 293, 299
Neely, C. J., 176, 184, 326
Nelson, C. R., 112
Nelson, D. B., 74, 167, 197–8, 201,
 204, 209, 216–20, 235–7, 240,
 245, 247, 253–6, 258, 261, 263,
 279, 295, 299, 360–1
Neuberger, A., 388
Newbold, P., 35, 42–3, 48, 92, 130,
 282
Newey, W. K., 248, 401
Ng, L. K., 241
Ng, V. K., 220, 239, 241, 258, 263–4
Nicolato, E., 390
Nijman, T. E., 216, 322, 343

Officer, R. R., 64, 192
Ogden, J. P., 63
Ohanissian, A., 341
O'Hanlon, J., 17, 60
O'Hara, M., 307, 344
Okunev, J., 181, 183
Olsen, R. B., 242, 305, 307, 312–5,
 319, 321, 323–4, 326–7, 346
Olson, D., 177, 182–3
Omaki, K., 127
Ord, J. K., 115, 305, 315, 318, 396
Ostdiek, B., 342, 383, 400, 407

Pagan, A. R., 249, 253, 255, 271, 273,
 404
Pan, J., 365–6, 383, 389, 391
Pan, M.-S., 112
Panatoni, L., 247, 249
Panigirtzoglou, N., 383, 429, 431,
 435, 437–8, 448, 451–2, 454
Papanicolaou, G., 383
Park, H. Y., 382
Park, J., 61
Parkinson, M., 12, 346, 399
Peel, D. A., 347
Peiers, B., 309, 325, 342
Peng, L., 240
Penman, S. H., 61, 63
Pérignon, C., 464
Perry, P. R., 57, 69, 76
Peterson, R. L., 112

Subject Index

announcements,
  earnings, 61, 64
  macroeconomic news, 68, 192–3
  and volatility, 315–20
anomalies, *see* calendar effects
ARCH model, xiv, 197, 212–7, 269,
  345
  aggregation, 322
  analytic derivatives, 247, 250, 265
  approximation to a bivariate
    diffusion, 360–1
  ARCH(1), 29, 35, 198–9
  ARCH(∞), 201
  ARCH-M, 101, 215, 222, 252–4,
    425–6
  asymmetric, 216, 220–32, 236–42,
    263
  asymmetry ratio, 229, 240–1, 426
  autocorrelations of squared excess
    returns, 200, 203, 221
  comparisons with SV models,
    299–301
  defined by absolute residuals, 216,
    238
  diagnostic tests, 257–8
  diffusion limit, 360–1
  EGARCH(1), 236–41, 259, 300,
    361, 411–2
  exponential, 216, 236–7, 406
    see also EGARCH(1)
  FIEGARCH(1, d, 1), 243–5, 255,
    261, 393–4
  GARCH(1, 1), 39, 199–212,
    219–20, 254, 259, 300, 322,
    360–1, 392–3
    and stylized facts, 200–3
    DM/$ example, 205–12,
      249–50, 277
    forecasts, 204–5, 403–6, 410–5
    moments, 202
    quadratic, 238, 406
    threshold, 238
  GARCH(p, q), 215, 220, 245

GJR(1, 1), 220–32, 238–41, 255,
  425–7
  forecasts, 405–6, 416–20
  S&P 100 example, 225–32,
    250–1
GJR-GARCH, 191, 220–1, 253,
  411, 463
HARCH, 323–4
IGARCH(1, 1), 115–6, 204, 236
information matrix, 246
integrated, 198, 204, 261
intraday specifications, 322–4
kurtosis of returns, 202, 220–1,
  230
Lagrange multiplier test, 254, 258
likelihood theory, 245–51
likelihood-ratio test, 247, 251–2,
  412–3
log-likelihood function, 208, 214,
  219, 225, 245–6
maximum likelihood estimate,
  214, 246
  covariance matrix, 246, 248
  quasi-, 248
multivariate, 263–4
news impact curve, 238–9
nonnormal conditional
  distributions, 217–20,
  236–7, 248, 255, 259, 265,
  323
  supported by hypothesis tests,
    251–2, 259
nontrading periods, 216, 260
option valuation, 391–4
parameter estimation, 208, 214,
  219, 222–5, 229
persistence, 205, 209, 212, 221,
  322–3, 405, 426
  unit root test, 254–6
residuals, 200, 213, 235
robust standard errors, 249–51
robust t-ratio, 254–5, 412, 418
score vector, 246, 265
  outer product, 246

9 780691 134796